Dictionary of Literary Biography

1 *The American Renaissance in New England*, edited by Joel Myerson (1978)

2 *American Novelists Since World War II*, edited by Jeffrey Helterman and Richard Layman (1978)

3 *Antebellum Writers in New York and the South*, edited by Joel Myerson (1979)

4 *American Writers in Paris, 1920-1939*, edited by Karen Lane Rood (1980)

5 *American Poets Since World War II*, 2 parts, edited by Donald J. Greiner (1980)

6 *American Novelists Since World War II, Second Series*, edited by James E. Kibler Jr. (1980)

7 *Twentieth-Century American Dramatists*, 2 parts, edited by John MacNicholas (1981)

8 *Twentieth-Century American Science-Fiction Writers*, 2 parts, edited by David Cowart and Thomas L. Wymer (1981)

9 *American Novelists, 1910-1945*, 3 parts, edited by James J. Martine (1981)

10 *Modern British Dramatists, 1900-1945*, 2 parts, edited by Stanley Weintraub (1982)

11 *American Humorists, 1800-1950*, 2 parts, edited by Stanley Trachtenberg (1982)

12 *American Realists and Naturalists*, edited by Donald Pizer and Earl N. Harbert (1982)

13 *British Dramatists Since World War II*, 2 parts, edited by Stanley Weintraub (1982)

14 *British Novelists Since 1960*, 2 parts, edited by Jay L. Halio (1983)

15 *British Novelists, 1930-1959*, 2 parts, edited by Bernard Oldsey (1983)

16 *The Beats: Literary Bohemians in Postwar America*, 2 parts, edited by Ann Charters (1983)

17 *Twentieth-Century American Historians*, edited by Clyde N. Wilson (1983)

18 *Victorian Novelists After 1885*, edited by Ira B. Nadel and William E. Fredeman (1983)

19 *British Poets, 1880-1914*, edited by Donald E. Stanford (1983)

20 *British Poets, 1914-1945*, edited by Donald E. Stanford (1983)

21 *Victorian Novelists Before 1885*, edited by Ira B. Nadel and William E. Fredeman (1983)

22 *American Writers for Children, 1900-1960*, edited by John Cech (1983)

23 *American Newspaper Journalists, 1873-1900*, edited by Perry J. Ashley (1983)

24 *American Colonial Writers, 1606-1734*, edited by Emory Elliott (1984)

25 *American Newspaper Journalists, 1901-1925*, edited by Perry J. Ashley (1984)

26 *American Screenwriters*, edited by Robert E. Morsberger, Stephen O. Lesser, and Randall Clark (1984)

27 *Poets of Great Britain and Ireland, 1945-1960*, edited by Vincent B. Sherry Jr. (1984)

28 *Twentieth-Century American-Jewish Fiction Writers*, edited by Daniel Walden (1984)

29 *American Newspaper Journalists, 1926-1950*, edited by Perry J. Ashley (1984)

30 *American Historians, 1607-1865*, edited by Clyde N. Wilson (1984)

31 *American Colonial Writers, 1735-1781*, edited by Emory Elliott (1984)

32 *Victorian Poets Before 1850*, edited by William E. Fredeman and Ira B. Nadel (1984)

33 *Afro-American Fiction Writers After 1955*, edited by Thadious M. Davis and Trudier Harris (1984)

34 *British Novelists, 1890-1929: Traditionalists*, edited by Thomas F. Staley (1985)

35 *Victorian Poets After 1850*, edited by William E. Fredeman and Ira B. Nadel (1985)

36 *British Novelists, 1890-1929: Modernists*, edited by Thomas F. Staley (1985)

37 *American Writers of the Early Republic*, edited by Emory Elliott (1985)

38 *Afro-American Writers After 1955: Dramatists and Prose Writers*, edited by Thadious M. Davis and Trudier Harris (1985)

39 *British Novelists, 1660-1800*, 2 parts, edited by Martin C. Battestin (1985)

40 *Poets of Great Britain and Ireland Since 1960*, 2 parts, edited by Vincent B. Sherry Jr. (1985)

41 *Afro-American Poets Since 1955*, edited by Trudier Harris and Thadious M. Davis (1985)

42 *American Writers for Children Before 1900*, edited by Glenn E. Estes (1985)

43 *American Newspaper Journalists, 1690-1872*, edited by Perry J. Ashley (1986)

44 *American Screenwriters, Second Series*, edited by Randall Clark, Robert E. Morsberger, and Stephen O. Lesser (1986)

45 *American Poets, 1880-1945, First Series*, edited by Peter Quartermain (1986)

46 *American Literary Publishing Houses, 1900-1980: Trade and Paperback*, edited by Peter Dzwonkoski (1986)

47 *American Historians, 1866-1912*, edited by Clyde N. Wilson (1986)

48 *American Poets, 1880-1945, Second Series*, edited by Peter Quartermain (1986)

49 *American Literary Publishing Houses, 1638-1899*, 2 parts, edited by Peter Dzwonkoski (1986)

50 *Afro-American Writers Before the Harlem Renaissance*, edited by Trudier Harris (1986)

51 *Afro-American Writers from the Harlem Renaissance to 1940*, edited by Trudier Harris (1987)

52 *American Writers for Children Since 1960: Fiction*, edited by Glenn E. Estes (1986)

53 *Canadian Writers Since 1960, First Series*, edited by W. H. New (1986)

54 *American Poets, 1880-1945, Third Series*, 2 parts, edited by Peter Quartermain (1987)

55 *Victorian Prose Writers Before 1867,* edited by William B. Thesing (1987)

56 *German Fiction Writers, 1914-1945,* edited by James Hardin (1987)

57 *Victorian Prose Writers After 1867,* edited by William B. Thesing (1987)

58 *Jacobean and Caroline Dramatists,* edited by Fredson Bowers (1987)

59 *American Literary Critics and Scholars, 1800-1850,* edited by John W. Rathbun and Monica M. Grecu (1987)

60 *Canadian Writers Since 1960, Second Series,* edited by W. H. New (1987)

61 *American Writers for Children Since 1960: Poets, Illustrators, and Nonfiction Authors,* edited by Glenn E. Estes (1987)

62 *Elizabethan Dramatists,* edited by Fredson Bowers (1987)

63 *Modern American Critics, 1920-1955,* edited by Gregory S. Jay (1988)

64 *American Literary Critics and Scholars, 1850-1880,* edited by John W. Rathbun and Monica M. Grecu (1988)

65 *French Novelists, 1900-1930,* edited by Catharine Savage Brosman (1988)

66 *German Fiction Writers, 1885-1913,* 2 parts, edited by James Hardin (1988)

67 *Modern American Critics Since 1955,* edited by Gregory S. Jay (1988)

68 *Canadian Writers, 1920-1959, First Series,* edited by W. H. New (1988)

69 *Contemporary German Fiction Writers, First Series,* edited by Wolfgang D. Elfe and James Hardin (1988)

70 *British Mystery Writers, 1860-1919,* edited by Bernard Benstock and Thomas F. Staley (1988)

71 *American Literary Critics and Scholars, 1880-1900,* edited by John W. Rathbun and Monica M. Grecu (1988)

72 *French Novelists, 1930-1960,* edited by Catharine Savage Brosman (1988)

73 *American Magazine Journalists, 1741-1850,* edited by Sam G. Riley (1988)

74 *American Short-Story Writers Before 1880,* edited by Bobby Ellen Kimbel, with the assistance of William E. Grant (1988)

75 *Contemporary German Fiction Writers, Second Series,* edited by Wolfgang D. Elfe and James Hardin (1988)

76 *Afro-American Writers, 1940-1955,* edited by Trudier Harris (1988)

77 *British Mystery Writers, 1920-1939,* edited by Bernard Benstock and Thomas F. Staley (1988)

78 *American Short-Story Writers, 1880-1910,* edited by Bobby Ellen Kimbel, with the assistance of William E. Grant (1988)

79 *American Magazine Journalists, 1850-1900,* edited by Sam G. Riley (1988)

80 *Restoration and Eighteenth-Century Dramatists, First Series,* edited by Paula R. Backscheider (1989)

81 *Austrian Fiction Writers, 1875-1913,* edited by James Hardin and Donald G. Daviau (1989)

82 *Chicano Writers, First Series,* edited by Francisco A. Lomelí and Carl R. Shirley (1989)

83 *French Novelists Since 1960,* edited by Catharine Savage Brosman (1989)

84 *Restoration and Eighteenth-Century Dramatists, Second Series,* edited by Paula R. Backscheider (1989)

85 *Austrian Fiction Writers After 1914,* edited by James Hardin and Donald G. Daviau (1989)

86 *American Short-Story Writers, 1910-1945, First Series,* edited by Bobby Ellen Kimbel (1989)

87 *British Mystery and Thriller Writers Since 1940, First Series,* edited by Bernard Benstock and Thomas F. Staley (1989)

88 *Canadian Writers, 1920-1959, Second Series,* edited by W. H. New (1989)

89 *Restoration and Eighteenth-Century Dramatists, Third Series,* edited by Paula R. Backscheider (1989)

90 *German Writers in the Age of Goethe, 1789-1832,* edited by James Hardin and Christoph E. Schweitzer (1989)

91 *American Magazine Journalists, 1900-1960, First Series,* edited by Sam G. Riley (1990)

92 *Canadian Writers, 1890-1920,* edited by W. H. New (1990)

93 *British Romantic Poets, 1789-1832, First Series,* edited by John R. Greenfield (1990)

94 *German Writers in the Age of Goethe: Sturm und Drang to Classicism,* edited by James Hardin and Christoph E. Schweitzer (1990)

95 *Eighteenth-Century British Poets, First Series,* edited by John Sitter (1990)

96 *British Romantic Poets, 1789-1832, Second Series,* edited by John R. Greenfield (1990)

97 *German Writers from the Enlightenment to Sturm und Drang, 1720-1764,* edited by James Hardin and Christoph E. Schweitzer (1990)

98 *Modern British Essayists, First Series,* edited by Robert Beum (1990)

99 *Canadian Writers Before 1890,* edited by W. H. New (1990)

100 *Modern British Essayists, Second Series,* edited by Robert Beum (1990)

101 *British Prose Writers, 1660-1800, First Series,* edited by Donald T. Siebert (1991)

102 *American Short-Story Writers, 1910-1945, Second Series,* edited by Bobby Ellen Kimbel (1991)

103 *American Literary Biographers, First Series,* edited by Steven Serafin (1991)

104 *British Prose Writers, 1660-1800, Second Series,* edited by Donald T. Siebert (1991)

105 *American Poets Since World War II, Second Series,* edited by R. S. Gwynn (1991)

106 *British Literary Publishing Houses, 1820-1880,* edited by Patricia J. Anderson and Jonathan Rose (1991)

107 *British Romantic Prose Writers, 1789-1832, First Series,* edited by John R. Greenfield (1991)

108 *Twentieth-Century Spanish Poets, First Series,* edited by Michael L. Perna (1991)

109 *Eighteenth-Century British Poets, Second Series,* edited by John Sitter (1991)

110 *British Romantic Prose Writers, 1789-1832, Second Series,* edited by John R. Greenfield (1991)

111 *American Literary Biographers, Second Series,* edited by Steven Serafin (1991)

112 *British Literary Publishing Houses, 1881-1965,* edited by Jonathan Rose and Patricia J. Anderson (1991)

113 *Modern Latin-American Fiction Writers, First Series,* edited by William Luis (1992)

114 *Twentieth-Century Italian Poets, First Series,* edited by Giovanna Wedel De Stasio, Glauco Cambon, and Antonio Illiano (1992)

115 *Medieval Philosophers,* edited by Jeremiah Hackett (1992)

116 *British Romantic Novelists, 1789-1832,* edited by Bradford K. Mudge (1992)

117 *Twentieth-Century Caribbean and Black African Writers, First Series,* edited by Bernth Lindfors and Reinhard Sander (1992)

118 *Twentieth-Century German Dramatists, 1889-1918,* edited by Wolfgang D. Elfe and James Hardin (1992)

119 *Nineteenth-Century French Fiction Writers: Romanticism and Realism, 1800-1860,* edited by Catharine Savage Brosman (1992)

120 *American Poets Since World War II, Third Series,* edited by R. S. Gwynn (1992)

121 *Seventeenth-Century British Nondramatic Poets, First Series,* edited by M. Thomas Hester (1992)

122 *Chicano Writers, Second Series,* edited by Francisco A. Lomelí and Carl R. Shirley (1992)

123 *Nineteenth-Century French Fiction Writers: Naturalism and Beyond, 1860-1900,* edited by Catharine Savage Brosman (1992)

124 *Twentieth-Century German Dramatists, 1919-1992,* edited by Wolfgang D. Elfe and James Hardin (1992)

125 *Twentieth-Century Caribbean and Black African Writers, Second Series,* edited by Bernth Lindfors and Reinhard Sander (1993)

126 *Seventeenth-Century British Nondramatic Poets, Second Series,* edited by M. Thomas Hester (1993)

127 *American Newspaper Publishers, 1950-1990,* edited by Perry J. Ashley (1993)

128 *Twentieth-Century Italian Poets, Second Series,* edited by Giovanna Wedel De Stasio, Glauco Cambon, and Antonio Illiano (1993)

129 *Nineteenth-Century German Writers, 1841-1900,* edited by James Hardin and Siegfried Mews (1993)

130 *American Short-Story Writers Since World War II,* edited by Patrick Meanor (1993)

131 *Seventeenth-Century British Nondramatic Poets, Third Series,* edited by M. Thomas Hester (1993)

132 *Sixteenth-Century British Nondramatic Writers, First Series,* edited by David A. Richardson (1993)

133 *Nineteenth-Century German Writers to 1840,* edited by James Hardin and Siegfried Mews (1993)

134 *Twentieth-Century Spanish Poets, Second Series,* edited by Jerry Phillips Winfield (1994)

135 *British Short-Fiction Writers, 1880-1914: The Realist Tradition,* edited by William B. Thesing (1994)

136 *Sixteenth-Century British Nondramatic Writers, Second Series,* edited by David A. Richardson (1994)

137 *American Magazine Journalists, 1900-1960, Second Series,* edited by Sam G. Riley (1994)

138 *German Writers and Works of the High Middle Ages: 1170-1280,* edited by James Hardin and Will Hasty (1994)

139 *British Short-Fiction Writers, 1945-1980,* edited by Dean Baldwin (1994)

140 *American Book-Collectors and Bibliographers, First Series,* edited by Joseph Rosenblum (1994)

141 *British Children's Writers, 1880-1914,* edited by Laura M. Zaidman (1994)

142 *Eighteenth-Century British Literary Biographers,* edited by Steven Serafin (1994)

143 *American Novelists Since World War II, Third Series,* edited by James R. Giles and Wanda H. Giles (1994)

144 *Nineteenth-Century British Literary Biographers,* edited by Steven Serafin (1994)

145 *Modern Latin-American Fiction Writers, Second Series,* edited by William Luis and Ann González (1994)

146 *Old and Middle English Literature,* edited by Jeffrey Helterman and Jerome Mitchell (1994)

147 *South Slavic Writers Before World War II,* edited by Vasa D. Mihailovich (1994)

148 *German Writers and Works of the Early Middle Ages: 800-1170,* edited by Will Hasty and James Hardin (1994)

149 *Late Nineteenth- and Early Twentieth-Century British Literary Biographers,* edited by Steven Serafin (1995)

150 *Early Modern Russian Writers, Late Seventeenth and Eighteenth Centuries,* edited by Marcus C. Levitt (1995)

151 *British Prose Writers of the Early Seventeenth Century,* edited by Clayton D. Lein (1995)

152 *American Novelists Since World War II, Fourth Series,* edited by James and Wanda Giles (1995)

153 *Late-Victorian and Edwardian British Novelists, First Series,* edited by George M. Johnson (1995)

154 *The British Literary Book Trade, 1700-1820,* edited by James K. Bracken and Joel Silver (1995)

155 *Twentieth-Century British Literary Biographers,* edited by Steven Serafin (1995)

156 *British Short-Fiction Writers, 1880-1914: The Romantic Tradition,* edited by William F. Naufftus (1995)

157 *Twentieth-Century Caribbean and Black African Writers, Third Series,* edited by Bernth Lindfors and Reinhard Sander (1995)

158 *British Reform Writers, 1789-1832,* edited by Gary Kelly and Edd Applegate (1995)

159 *British Short Fiction Writers, 1800-1880,* edited by John R. Greenfield (1996)

160 *British Children's Writers, 1914-1960,* edited by Donald R. Hettinga and Gary D. Schmidt (1996)

161 *British Children's Writers Since 1960, First Series,* edited by Caroline Hunt (1996)

162 *British Short-Fiction Writers, 1915-1945,* edited by John H. Rogers (1996)

163 *British Children's Writers, 1800-1880,* edited by Meena Khorana (1996)

164 *German Baroque Writers, 1580-1660,* edited by James Hardin (1996)

165 *American Poets Since World War II, Fourth Series,* edited by Joseph Conte (1996)

166 *British Travel Writers, 1837-1875,* edited by Barbara Brothers and Julia Gergits (1996)

167 *Sixteenth-Century British Nondramatic Writers, Third Series,* edited by David A. Richardson (1996)

168 *German Baroque Writers, 1661-1730,* edited by James Hardin (1996)

169 *American Poets Since World War II, Fifth Series,* edited by Joseph Conte (1996)

170 *The British Literary Book Trade, 1475-1700,* edited by James K. Bracken and Joel Silver (1996)

171 *Twentieth-Century American Sportswriters,* edited by Richard Orodenker (1996)

172 *Sixteenth-Century British Nondramatic Writers, Fourth Series,* edited by David A. Richardson (1996)

173 *American Novelists Since World War II, Fifth Series,* edited by James R. Giles and Wanda H. Giles (1996)

Documentary Series

1. *Sherwood Anderson, Willa Cather, John Dos Passos, Theodore Dreiser, F. Scott Fitzgerald, Ernest Hemingway, Sinclair Lewis,* edited by Margaret A. Van Antwerp (1982)

2. *James Gould Cozzens, James T. Farrell, William Faulkner, John O'Hara, John Steinbeck, Thomas Wolfe, Richard Wright,* edited by Margaret A. Van Antwerp (1982)

3. *Saul Bellow, Jack Kerouac, Norman Mailer, Vladimir Nabokov, John Updike, Kurt Vonnegut,* edited by Mary Bruccoli (1983)

4. *Tennessee Williams,* edited by Margaret A. Van Antwerp and Sally Johns (1984)

5. *American Transcendentalists,* edited by Joel Myerson (1988)

6. *Hardboiled Mystery Writers: Raymond Chandler, Dashiell Hammett, Ross Macdonald,* edited by Matthew J. Bruccoli and Richard Layman (1989)

7. *Modern American Poets: James Dickey, Robert Frost, Marianne Moore,* edited by Karen L. Rood (1989)

8. *The Black Aesthetic Movement,* edited by Jeffrey Louis Decker (1991)

9. *American Writers of the Vietnam War: W. D. Ehrhart, Larry Heinemann, Tim O'Brien, Walter McDonald, John M. Del Vecchio,* edited by Ronald Baughman (1991)

10. *The Bloomsbury Group,* edited by Edward L. Bishop (1992)

11. *American Proletarian Culture: The Twenties and The Thirties,* edited by Jon Christian Suggs (1993)

12. *Southern Women Writers: Flannery O'Connor, Katherine Anne Porter, Eudora Welty,* edited by Mary Ann Wimsatt and Karen L. Rood (1994)

13. *The House of Scribner, 1846–1904,* edited by John Delaney (1996)

14. *Four Women Writers for Children, 1868–1918,* edited by Caroline C. Hunt (1996)

Yearbooks

1980 edited by Karen L. Rood, Jean W. Ross, and Richard Ziegfeld (1981)

1981 edited by Karen L. Rood, Jean W. Ross, and Richard Ziegfeld (1982)

1982 edited by Richard Ziegfeld; associate editors: Jean W. Ross and Lynne C. Zeigler (1983)

1983 edited by Mary Bruccoli and Jean W. Ross; associate editor: Richard Ziegfeld (1984)

1984 edited by Jean W. Ross (1985)

1985 edited by Jean W. Ross (1986)

1986 edited by J. M. Brook (1987)

1987 edited by J. M. Brook (1988)

1988 edited by J. M. Brook (1989)

1989 edited by J. M. Brook (1990)

1990 edited by James W. Hipp (1991)

1991 edited by James W. Hipp (1992)

1992 edited by James W. Hipp (1993)

1993 edited by James W. Hipp, contributing editor George Garrett (1994)

1994 edited by James W. Hipp, contributing editor George Garrett (1995)

1995 edited by James W. Hipp, contributing editor George Garrett (1996)

Concise Series

Concise Dictionary of American Literary Biography, 6 volumes (1988-1989): *The New Consciousness, 1941-1968; Colonization to the American Renaissance, 1640-1865; Realism, Naturalism, and Local Color, 1865-1917; The Twenties, 1917-1929; The Age of Maturity, 1929-1941; Broadening Views, 1968-1988.*

Concise Dictionary of British Literary Biography, 8 volumes (1991-1992): *Writers of the Middle Ages and Renaissance Before 1660; Writers of the Restoration and Eighteenth Century, 1660-1789; Writers of the Romantic Period, 1789-1832; Victorian Writers, 1832-1890; Late Victorian and Edwardian Writers, 1890-1914; Modern Writers, 1914-1945; Writers After World War II, 1945-1960; Contemporary Writers, 1960 to Present.*

Dictionary of Literary Biography® • Volume One Hundred Seventy-Three

American Novelists Since World War II
Fifth Series

Dictionary of Literary Biography® • Volume One Hundred Seventy-Three

American Novelists Since World War II
Fifth Series

Edited by
James R. Giles
and
Wanda H. Giles
Northern Illinois University

A Bruccoli Clark Layman Book
Gale Research
Detroit, Washington, D.C., London

ST. PHILIP'S COLLEGE LIBRARY

Advisory Board for
DICTIONARY OF LITERARY BIOGRAPHY

John Baker
William Cagle
Patrick O'Connor
George Garrett
Trudier Harris

Matthew J. Bruccoli and Richard Layman, Editorial Directors
C. E. Frazer Clark Jr., Managing Editor
Karen Rood, Senior Editor

Printed in the United States of America

The paper used in this publication meets the minimum requirements of American National Standard for Information Sciences–Permanence Paper for Printed Library Materials, ANSI Z39.48-1984. ∞™

This publication is a creative work fully protected by all applicable copyright laws, as well as by misappropriation, trade secret, unfair competition, and other applicable laws. The authors and editors of this work have added value to the underlying factual material herein through one or more of the following: unique and original selection, coordination, expression, arrangement, and classification of the information.

All rights to this publication will be vigorously defended.

Copyright © 1996 by Gale Research
835 Penobscot Building
Detroit, MI 48226

All rights reserved including the right of reproduction in
whole or in part in any form.

Library of Congress Cataloging-in-Publication Data

American novelists since World War II. Fifth series / edited by James R. Giles and Wanda H. Giles.
    p. cm. – (Dictionary of literary biography; v. 173)
"A Bruccoli Clark Layman book."
Includes bibliographical references and index.
ISBN 0-8103-9936-9 (alk. paper)
1. American fiction – 20th century – Bio-bibliography – Dictionaries. 2. Novelists, American – 20th century – Biography – Dictionaries. 3. American fiction – 20th century – Dictionaries. I. Giles, James Richard, 1937-   . II. Giles, Wanda H. III. Series.
PR411.S584 1996
813'.5409'03 – dc21   96-44319
                                                                                      CIP

---

10 9 8 7 6 5 4 3 2 1

To the people who taught us to read, the greatest gift we have had, for their grace and their passion, and in respect

Matthew J. Bruccoli
Edwin Harrison Cady
Jim Corder
James Melville Cox
Orville Clements
Earley Davis
J. Hubert Dunn
Georges Edelen
Richard Ellmann
Warren G. French
Roger and Eva Walker Giles
Rudolph P. Gottfried
Georgia M. and Knofel P. Hancock
Joseph W. Jones
Lyle Kendall
Gordon Mills
Alene Payton
Wallace Stegner
Clara Stephens
Edna Copeland Teaford
Maxine Turnage
Ruth Farlow Uyesugi
Yvor Winters
Samuel Yellen

And, always in hope, for Morgan

Contents

Plan of the Series ix
Introduction xi

Robert Olen Butler (1945-) 3
Joe Nordgren

Don DeLillo (1936-) 14
Paul Civello

Joan Didion (1934-) 37
Mark Royden Winchell

E. L. Doctorow (1931-) 54
Douglas Fowler

J. P. Donleavy (1926-) 73
William Nelles

Maxine Hong Kingston (1940-) 84
Pin-chia Feng

William Kotzwinkle (1938-) 98
Leon Lewis

Elmore Leonard (1925-) 108
David H. Everson

Bobbie Ann Mason (1940-) 118
John D. Kalb

Peter Matthiessen (1927-) 132
William Dowie

Carson McCullers (1917-1967) 148
Judith L. Everson

Gloria Naylor (1950-) 170
Vashti Crutcher Lewis

Thomas Pynchon (1937-) 177
Bernard Duyfhuizen

John M. Krafft

Philip Roth (1933-) 202
S. Lillian Kremer

J. D. Salinger (1919-) 235
Warren French

Gilbert Sorrentino (1929-) 249
Julian Cowley

Jean Stafford (1915-1979) 260
Jeanette W. Mann

Ronald Sukenick (1932-) 271
Julian Cowley

Amy Tan (1952-) 281
Pin-chia Feng

Rudolph Wurlitzer (1937-) 290
Julian Cowley

Books for Further Reading......................298
Contributors...................................308
Cumulative Index...............................311

Plan of the Series

... Almost the most prodigious asset of a country, and perhaps its most precious possession, is its native literary product — when that product is fine and noble and enduring.

Mark Twain*

The advisory board, the editors, and the publisher of the *Dictionary of Literary Biography* are joined in endorsing Mark Twain's declaration. The literature of a nation provides an inexhaustible resource of permanent worth. We intend to make literature and its creators better understood and more accessible to students and the reading public, while satisfying the standards of teachers and scholars.

To meet these requirements, *literary biography* has been construed in terms of the author's achievement. The most important thing about a writer is his writing. Accordingly, the entries in *DLB* are career biographies, tracing the development of the author's canon and the evolution of his reputation.

The purpose of *DLB* is not only to provide reliable information in a convenient format but also to place the figures in the larger perspective of literary history and to offer appraisals of their accomplishments by qualified scholars.

The publication plan for *DLB* resulted from two years of preparation. The project was proposed to Bruccoli Clark by Frederick C. Ruffner, president of the Gale Research Company, in November 1975. After specimen entries were prepared and typeset, an advisory board was formed to refine the entry format and develop the series rationale. In meetings held during 1976, the publisher, series editors, and advisory board approved the scheme for a comprehensive biographical dictionary of persons who contributed to North American literature. Editorial work on the first volume began in January 1977, and it was published in 1978. In order to make *DLB* more than a reference tool and to compile volumes that individually have claim to status as literary history, it was decided to organize volumes by topic, period, or genre. Each of these freestanding volumes provides a biographical-bibliographical guide and overview for a particular area of literature. We are convinced that this organization — as opposed to a single alphabet method — constitutes a valuable innovation in the presentation of reference material. The volume plan necessarily requires many decisions for the placement and treatment of authors who might properly be included in two or three volumes. In some instances a major figure will be included in separate volumes, but with different entries emphasizing the aspect of his career appropriate to each volume. Ernest Hemingway, for example, is represented in *American Writers in Paris, 1920-1939* by an entry focusing on his expatriate apprenticeship; he is also in *American Novelists, 1910-1945* with an entry surveying his entire career. Each volume includes a cumulative index of the subject authors and articles. Comprehensive indexes to the entire series are planned.

With volume ten in 1982 it was decided to enlarge the scope of *DLB*. By the end of 1986 twenty-one volumes treating British literature had been published, and volumes for Commonwealth and Modern European literature were in progress. The series has been further augmented by the *DLB Yearbooks* (since 1981) which update published entries and add new entries to keep the *DLB* current with contemporary activity. There have also been *DLB Documentary Series* volumes which provide biographical and critical source materials for figures whose work is judged to have particular interest for students. One of these companion volumes is entirely devoted to Tennessee Williams.

We define literature as the *intellectual commerce of a nation*: not merely as belles lettres but as that ample and complex process by which ideas are generated, shaped, and transmitted. *DLB* entries are not limited to "creative writers" but extend to other figures who in their time and in their way influenced the mind of a people. Thus the series encompasses historians, journalists, publishers, and screenwriters. By this means readers of *DLB* may be aided to perceive literature not as cult scripture in the keeping of intellectual high priests but firmly positioned at the center of a nation's life.

*From an unpublished section of Mark Twain's autobiography, copyright by the Mark Twain Company

Plan of the Series

DLB includes the major writers appropriate to each volume and those standing in the ranks immediately behind them. Scholarly and critical counsel has been sought in deciding which minor figures to include and how full their entries should be. Wherever possible, useful references are made to figures who do not warrant separate entries.

Each *DLB* volume has a volume editor responsible for planning the volume, selecting the figures for inclusion, and assigning the entries. Volume editors are also responsible for preparing, where appropriate, appendices surveying the major periodicals and literary and intellectual movements for their volumes, as well as lists of further readings. Work on the series as a whole is coordinated at the Bruccoli Clark Layman editorial center in Columbia, South Carolina, where the editorial staff is responsible for accuracy of the published volumes.

One feature that distinguishes *DLB* is the illustration policy – its concern with the iconography of literature. Just as an author is influenced by his surroundings, so is the reader's understanding of the author enhanced by a knowledge of his environment. Therefore *DLB* volumes include not only drawings, paintings, and photographs of authors, often depicting them at various stages in their careers, but also illustrations of their families and places where they lived. Title pages are regularly reproduced in facsimile along with dust jackets for modern authors. The dust jackets are a special feature of *DLB* because they often document better than anything else the way in which an author's work was perceived in its own time. Specimens of the writers' manuscripts are included when feasible.

Samuel Johnson rightly decreed that "The chief glory of every people arises from its authors." The purpose of the *Dictionary of Literary Biography* is to compile literary history in the surest way available to us – by accurate and comprehensive treatment of the lives and work of those who contributed to it.

The *DLB* Advisory Board

Introduction

The United States just after World War II assumed virtually a new identity, and the writing from the late 1940s sometimes seems to have come out of just about as many viewpoints, theories, memories, and readings as there were people living at the time. Writers dealt with the monumentality of experience: the end of the last "good war," the rise of the United States in international politics and commerce, the opening of the universities to nontraditional classes and ethnic groups, the expansion of the literary canon, the new freedoms and strengths of women and ethnic groups, the horror and power of weaponry, decolonization and the explosion of new nations with special relationships to one of the two great powers, and the Cold War, an undeclared state of hostilities that controlled world events and alliances.

In the postwar period prosperity increased, and large families became fashionable, affordable, and socially favored, as the ideal of home and civic life became a myth that would call to, but baffle and elude, writers for the rest of the century. Crime and violence grew in stunning proportion to prewar experience, the juvenile delinquents of the 1950s leading eventually to the drive-by shooters and carjackers of the 1990s, a far move from the shoot-outs and urban violence of Mark Twain's West or Theodore Dreiser's and Frank Norris's cities and their psychological and economic cruelties.

And maybe at the beginning of all of this "Technicolor" – as Tom Wolfe would call it in the 1960s, when it began to dazzle and burn too brightly – stood one image that opened the time: the nurse and the sailor in Times Square celebrating the end of World War II with a kiss vibrant with youth, hope, optimism, strength, confidence, love, and anonymity. What this couple conveyed in the 1945 black-and-white *Life* photograph was not new to human experience, but the expression of it, the vitality and confidence, came out of victory in this war, with the expansion and importance it handed to the United States. Moreover, photographs themselves became an American icon in a nation of cameras and their images, with family albums continuing their domestic popularity, but with new technological potential: television, forensic imaging, computer enhancement. World wars do not create literature; they destroy nearly everything in their paths. But at the end there is the image of that couple kissing, suggesting the hope of a new age, the fearlessness of conquerors in a world where only two decades earlier they or their families were probably, like most Americans, isolated, rural, onlooking.

The undeniable logic behind the tradition of designating 1945 as the beginning of a new era of the American novel is that it was also the year in which the United States discovered itself one of only two world superpowers. For the generation that had fought the Great War of 1914–1918 it was, in the words of a popular song, "a long way to Tipperary," but there was no question that everyone planned to come right back home. The trip that began with the attack on Pearl Harbor has never ended. Home *is* now the undefinable myth and the political battleground. James Jones tried to identify and mourn it in *Some Came Running* (1957). Other American expatriate fiction writers in Europe after the war included Chester Himes, who had learned before leaving the United States that his home country could not foster his genius; neither was it home to James Baldwin.

Writers who stayed in the United States tried to find homes. E. L. Doctorow depicted the harsh existence of the American pioneer, who was essentially homeless, in *Welcome to Hard Times* (1975) and exposed the realities behind the myths of East Coast society in *The Book of Daniel* (1971) and *Ragtime* (1976). Among the many women who struggled over the concept of home, which had suffocated and defined them, was Carson McCullers; the characters of *The Heart Is a Lonely Hunter* (1940) and *The Member of the Wedding* (1946) exist in a small-town Gothic interior landscape. For the characters of Maxine Hong Kingston's *The Woman Warrior* (1976) home is rooted in Chinese myth and family structure. The conventions of the family and the strength of mothers in Chinese American society are also explored in Amy Tan's *The Joy Luck Club* (1989) and *The Kitchen God's Wife* (1991). Ross Lockridge's *Raintree Country* (1948), one of the big books of the twentieth century, is the search by a man throughout time and place for the place in which he and his family have lived for generations. Two of the major writers of the postwar period, John Updike and Toni Morrison, write often on the nature of identity as it is frustrated and occasionally exalted in home and family.

After World War II Americans became richer and busier than ever before. Consumerism assaulted the soul, a situation Updike derided in *Couples* (1968). And the country no longer had the luxury of ignoring international affairs. It could not continue looking on; it had to make and implement decisions. Under President Harry S Truman, Americans undertook the rebuilding of Europe, formerly the center of the worlds of intellect and style. The plan was to use Yankee technology and American generosity. But even as the most clearly powerful and intact of countries, the United States could not escape the profound insecurity and moral uncertainty that were a part of the war's legacy. The full disclosure of the horrors of the Holocaust forced the West to question as never before the inherent decency of human beings. The American technology that destroyed Hiroshima in 1945 – the atomic blast whose ravages John Hersey described so movingly in 1946 – forced the nation to confront the newly discovered human potential to cause the extinction of all life, made possible by brilliant minds and malleable matter. Americans could hardly ignore the fact that the powerful instruments for human annihilation were the clear result of technology, in which they had for so long placed an almost religious faith.

After rebuilding some of Europe with the Marshall Plan, the United States assumed a responsibility to stop the spread of Communism and thus placed itself in opposition to the Soviet Union, the other great superpower to emerge from the war. The resulting Cold War was rung in by Winston Churchill in his "iron curtain" speeches of 1946 and perhaps ended in the collapse of the Soviet bloc in 1989. Just five years after World War II – earlier believed to be a defining event in international warfare – Communist North Korea invaded South Korea. U.S. troops went to aid the besieged Asian nation as part of a UN police action to force out the invaders. The Korean conflict came to an ambiguous end in 1953, after more than 150,000 Americans were killed or wounded. The conflict was not the last tragically indecisive, brutalizing post–World War II experience for the United States in Asia.

Events in Korea forced Americans to realize that there were real limitations to the power of even the strongest of nations, an idea that contributed significantly to a pervasive sense of instability and uncertainty in the United States, back wherever home was. In 1952 Americans elected as their president Dwight D. Eisenhower, commander in chief of the Allied forces in Europe during World War II. Some of his political strength derived from his common touch, the famous smile that met a national need for reassurance and stability, but he was a general, not a father to the country. The 1950s were haunted by a new kind of nightmare, a Communist witch-hunt whose dominant images were congressional committee rooms and microfilm hidden in pumpkins. Attorney Joseph Welch finally asked the tough, smug interrogator Roy Cohn, "Have you no decency, sir?" Decency had once been considered a given in American manners and morals; its loss, or at least diminution, was one of the grave blows of the postwar years. Sen. Joseph McCarthy, a Republican from Wisconsin, had largely inspired the witch-hunt for Communists in places of influence in the United States, but he was joined readily enough by a still-unsettled American nation. Writers and other creative people soon found themselves favorite targets of McCarthyism, with the blacklists that isolated friend from friend and destroyed the careers of suspected Communists, including writers, in the motion-picture, radio, and television industries, and in academia. Ironically, Irwin Shaw, whose *The Young Lions* (1948) was the most optimistic of the major post–World War II novels because of Shaw's declared "faith in the decency of the American people," was among those blacklisted.

The national insecurity and loss of faith in moral certainty inevitably touched the young American writers who began publishing in the late 1940s and early 1950s. Several of them began their careers with war novels, and a recurrent theme in this early World War II fiction is a warning against the imminent danger of an American fascism. Norman Mailer in *The Naked and the Dead* (1948) and Jones in *From Here to Eternity* (1951) created American generals who openly and unapologetically preach the necessity that strong leaders control the weak and directionless masses. This thematic concern was not limited to the war novelists; Saul Bellow's *Dangling Man* (1944) and William Styron's *Lie Down in Darkness* (1951) express anxiety about the existence of grave internal threats to the preservation of American democracy. Even Shaw, with his abiding faith in the common American, wrote, in short stories and *The Troubled Air* (1951), specific protests against McCarthyism and the repression of the freedom of people whose lifework was words. J. D. Salinger's *The Catcher in the Rye* (1951), not an overtly political novel, presented Holden Caulfield – a youth in rebellion against a corrupt society and the "phonies" who profited from it – as an emblematic figure for his entire decade.

In contrast Herman Wouk violated the fictional logic of his otherwise powerful and honest novel *The Caine Mutiny* (1951) by imposing on it an arbitrary ending that seems to advocate adherence to authority, however incompetent or even corrupt it might be. It is impossible to estimate the cost during the 1950s of self-censorship to American literature and to American culture in general. What is clear, though, is that the spirit of the times – a decade now remembered for its full-blown emphases on idealized family life, consumption of goods, and unquestioning adherence to newly created "traditional" values – caused many serious American writers to retreat from involvement in, or commitment to, the dominant culture of the nation. The clearest example of a literary repudiation of mainstream American society came from the talented group of writers known as the Beat generation. Jack Kerouac, Allen Ginsberg, and Lawrence Ferlinghetti were among the best known of the Beats, writers who sought in Zen Buddhism, jazz, and drugs antidotes to what they perceived as the sterile conformity of American life. Though the movement started in New York, California – specifically San Francisco, and even more specifically Ferlinghetti's City Lights bookstore – became the center of the Beat movement; later the city became home to the passive rebels of the so-called counterculture of the 1960s.

Zen was not the only foreign philosophy to influence American literature and American culture in the years following World War II. French existentialism, with its emphasis on the absence of any ethical system in the external universe and the resulting need for each individual to discover or create individual moral truths, had a strong appeal for postwar writers. A kind of fiction that can be called existential realism began to appear on the American literary scene during the 1950s. The work of most of the important writers to emerge in the United States since 1945 includes at least overtones of existentialism. For one remarkable example, perhaps the main consistency in Mailer's constantly evolving literary career has been his self-definition as an American existentialist.

Despite the considerable importance of the 1950s to American literature, 1961 and 1962 more clearly represented the end of one era of the American novel and the beginning of another. In these two years, at the beginning of what would prove to be one of the most turbulent decades in American history, Ernest Hemingway committed suicide and William Faulkner died. The work of these men constituted the triumph of modernism in American fiction; and they had dominated the national literary scene for more than three decades. Indeed, only the writers of the American Renaissance in the nineteenth century (Nathaniel Hawthorne, Herman Melville, Ralph Waldo Emerson, Henry David Thoreau, and Edgar Allan Poe) were so central and vital to American literature for so long as the Lost Generation. Hemingway and Faulkner, its leading figures, produced a body of writing distinguished by its revolutionary sophistication in narrative technique and characterization. Strongly influenced by the narrative innovations associated with Henry James and James Joyce, their work moved American fiction beyond William Dean Howells's "reality of the commonplace."

By the 1960s, however, the Hemingway-Faulkner literary legacy had begun to have an inhibiting effect on the American novel. It was increasingly difficult to surpass the innovations in technique found in such modernist masterpieces as Faulkner's *The Sound and the Fury* (1929) and *Absalom, Absalom!* (1936) and Hemingway's *The Sun Also Rises* (1926). A result of the brilliance of these works was that, to later American writers, modernism was the only valid mode for the twentieth-century novel, but a few rebelled against the limitations of modernist technique. Saul Bellow, who published two novels during the 1940s that conformed to the narrative and structural conventions of modernism, rediscovered in *The Adventures of Augie March* (1953) the formal freedom inherent in Twain's nineteenth-century legacy of the frontier picaresque novel. American novelists searched for narrative structures that would liberate them from the restraints of modernism throughout the 1960s.

The social and political turbulence of that decade contributed to the intensely felt need of many writers to escape virtually any kind of limitations on their art. Few, if any, periods in American history have begun so hopefully or ended so chaotically as the 1960s. In 1960 John F. Kennedy was elected president, becoming the youngest person ever to hold that office. Kennedy's youth, his search for a New Frontier, and his often-quoted inaugural appeal to "ask not what your country can do for you – ask what you can do for your country" seemed to promise a revival of American idealism. The young, academically brilliant administration perceived no limits: the nation was promised a man on the moon within the decade. And existing technology was there for the using: in the 1950s television had become the primary source of entertainment and information for most Americans; and, despite critical lamentations over its superficiality, Kennedy grasped its potential for forming public opinion through the visual sharing of public experience. He had achieved the presidency in part because his appearance against Vice President Richard Nixon in a series of debates had won him the confidence of the American television audience, and he performed masterfully on television throughout his brief term in office.

This administration was confronted with the civil rights movement, led by Dr. Martin Luther King Jr. and many others whose actions received less notice than his. Not wanting to offend the southern wing of the Democratic Party, the president first offered only verbal support to the cause of civil rights, but when pictures of civil rights protesters under attack in the South by water hoses, clubs, police dogs, and tear gas began to dominate national television news, the civil rights movement quickly became the central beneficiary of the youthful idealism to which Kennedy had appealed. The president and Attorney General Robert Kennedy, his brother, saw the inevitability of a direct federal role in the struggle for American civil rights, which in some ways climaxed on 28 August 1963, when King delivered his "I Have a Dream" speech to a crowd of more than two hundred thousand in Washington, D.C. The mall rang with freedom songs from the Lincoln Memorial to the Washington Monument. Singers included Bernice Johnson Reagon of Sweet Honey in the Rock, a hero of the movement, whose cry for freedom expressed the torment of real experience.

That torment had found passionate voice in such novels as Richard Wright's *Native Son* (1940), William Attaway's *Blood on the Forge* (1941), and Ann Petry's *The Street* (1946), and it was later expressed by Toni Morrison, who in 1993 received the first Nobel Prize for literature awarded to a African American, and by Alice Walker in *The Color Purple* (1982). And in a way Ralph Ellison's *Invisible Man* (1952) ratified or predicted them all. Words came to be the most effective weapons for the people struggling in the civil rights movement of the 1960s. With the witness of these men and women, Washington came to see the necessity of passing federal civil rights legislation aimed at ending the barriers – and the bloodshed – legitimized by racial segregation. The civil rights struggle inspired a new activism among Americans – writers, artists, entertainers, students, housewives, clergy, teachers – and Pete Seeger's song "Wasn't That a Time?" expresses the peculiar combination of innocence, wonder, and corruption that the creative community experienced and expressed. Novels of the 1960s by black authors – preceded in the recent past by the occasional work by Willard Motley (such as *Knock on Any Door*, 1947) or the many popular novels of Frank Yerby – came out of the earlier struggle of such writers as novelist and essayist Baldwin (*Go Tell It on the Mountain*, 1953; *Notes of a Native Son*, 1955) and Ellison.

The nation was in a state of turmoil when on 22 November 1963 President Kennedy was assassinated. Few events have been so devastating to the American spirit as this murder and those that followed it in Dallas in the next three days. By the end of the weekend J. D. Tippitt, a young policeman, had also died by gunfire, and so would the alleged assassin, Lee Harvey Oswald – another young, undefined man. In the young president's death there was no easy comprehension. The nation gathered in living rooms, churches, schools, and even department-store furniture showrooms, watching the ceremony of grief. In an extended television event, the last for this television president, the country found some shared solace in watching the lying in state, the funeral, and the processions leading to his burial.

The two other murders introduced other kinds of shock. Officer Tippitt seemed an American Everyman: young, married, with children; he could have been anyone. And when, on live television, Kennedy's accused assassin was shot to death by a Dallas nightclub owner, the killing was an early example of the power of television to stun its audience through the immediacy of image and the quickness with which chaos emerged. Some people were already wondering whether such a passive medium as the novel could remain viable to an audience trained by television to respond so quickly. Oswald's death, moreover, intensified an already-present element of doubt and uncertainty first expressed by the artistic community. Further, it seemed impossible that so slight and insignificant a figure as Oswald could have a significant or decisive effect on American history, and suspicion of conspiracy in the president's death may always haunt the American mind. In years that followed, several books with assassination-plot motifs appeared, among them Bryan Wooley's *November 22* (1981) and Vance Bourjaily's *The Man Who Knew Kennedy* (1967). In 1988 Don DeLillo responded to the paranoia resulting from the events of 1963 with his tour de force novel *Libra*, a fictionalized life of Oswald depicting him as a pathetic part of a conspiracy organized by disaffected CIA agents and organized crime. Three years later and almost thirty years after the assassination, director Oliver Stone reflected the ongoing fascination with Kennedy's death in his movie *JFK*, which suggested a conspiracy so massive and pervasive as to include virtually every level of the U.S. government and military. Mailer continued his flirtation with journalism in 1995, with *Oswald's Tale*.

The nation seemed briefly to rediscover some stability and moral certainty when Kennedy's successor, Lyndon B. Johnson, a Texan who was expected to sympathize with the segregationist South, brilliantly secured the passage of the 1964 Civil Rights Act in a Congress he knew profoundly. Thus the old-style southern politician provided the legislative centerpiece so long sought. That a new stability had arrived seemed especially certain when Johnson was reelected in 1964 in a landslide victory over conservative Barry Goldwater, a westerner who had voted against the civil rights bill. It was a short triumph, a small domestic peace. Events overseas quickly shattered the national recovery and war on poverty.

Not long after Americans first read Hersey's *Hiroshima*, events had begun in Southeast Asia that eventually involved the United States in a new war, one that devastated the spirit in a way not earlier experienced by Americans. Few people knew or noticed that in the 1950s the United States, in an attempt to halt the spread of Communism in Asia, had committed itself to defending a corrupt and authoritarian regime in South Vietnam. As the political situation deteriorated, President Kennedy sent American military advisers, and after Johnson's election in 1964 the United States became heavily involved in a miserable, confusing war in a country that few Americans had known previously. Throughout the next four years increasing numbers of American resources and troops were poured into a struggle doomed from the first – and with the historic example of the French failure to retain its colonial power there shouting futility to those who would listen.

The horror and hopelessness of the American effort was, again via television, brought home to the nation in 1968. Amid repeated assurances by the U.S. government and military that the war was going well, the North Vietnamese forces launched a devastatingly effective offensive against American and South Vietnamese forces during a negotiated cease-fire. Throughout the war television brought shattering images of horror and destruction into the homes of Americans – the naked, crying Vietnamese girl whose clothing had been burned away by napalm, running toward the cameras of a nation that had supplied it; a South Vietnamese general (thus on the side of the United States) executing a bound prisoner with a pistol pressed to his head, the death shown – though nearly suppressed by nationalistic sentiment – in the documentary *Hearts and Minds* (1974). For the first time in the twentieth century – in a national mood far from the loyalty, cooperation, and sacrifice of World War II – a reaction, and even revulsion, against involvement in a military action took to the streets, the newspapers and journals, even the classrooms of the mid 1960s.

More and more young Americans of draft age refused to accept induction into the armed services, and antiwar demonstrations became almost a ritual of daily life on college campuses across the nation. Young men and women devoted to opposition to the war, experimentation with sex and drugs, and rebellion against everything associated with middle-class tradition ("the establishment") became highly visible throughout urban America. While some banded together in active opposition to the war, others heeded the words of Harvard-researcher-turned-LSD-guru Dr. Timothy Leary and chose to "turn on, tune in, and drop out." The residential section of San Francisco surrounding Haight and Ashbury Streets was soon identified as the center of a hippie drug culture. As the opening number of the musical *Hair* (1967) announced to the world, it was the "Age of Aquarius" as well as the time of a "dirty little war" in Southeast Asia.

The dirtiness of the war, in addition to the massive casualties suffered, had to do with a new kind of racial conflict that ripped apart the fabric of national unity in the last half of the 1960s: African Americans, especially in the urban centers in the North and on the West Coast, were outraged by the disproportionate number of young black men being drafted to serve in Vietnam ground forces, and they came to believe that resources of potential use in American inner cities were being wasted in Southeast Asia. The Watts section of Los Angeles in 1965 and the black neighborhoods of Detroit in 1967 suffered massive outbreaks of rioting and looting, and television images of the late 1960s were often of body bags and coffins coming off planes at the edges of burning cities.

All the tensions that had been building throughout the 1960s seemed to explode in the years between 1968 and 1970. On 4 April 1968 Dr. Martin Luther King Jr. was assassinated in Memphis; and on 5 June of that same year Sen. Robert Kennedy, during a campaign for the Democratic presidential nomination, was shot and killed – on television – in Los Angeles just after winning the California Democratic primary. During the summer, national television audiences saw the spectacle of antiwar demonstrators at the Democratic National Convention in Chicago under assault by armed officers in what the federally appointed Walker Commission later called a "police riot." In 1970 National Guard troops fired on and killed student protesters at two universities, Kent State in Ohio and Jackson State in the Mississippi capital.

In 1969 an American did indeed land on the moon; still, Neil Armstrong's walk there, hard to celebrate as first anticipated in the early 1960s, represented one of the few seemingly unequivocal triumphs for American technology in the decade. Yet for the novelist, and especially for the writer of science fiction, even this revolutionary scientific breakthrough had ominous overtones. What had recently belonged to the world of fantasy had become one more aspect of reality; like so many other major historical events during the 1960s, Armstrong's adventure on the moon was shown on television as it occurred. From then on – indeed, from Alan Shepard's 1961 *Gemini* rocket ride – *astronaut* became a part of the vocabulary of ordinary Americans rather than a concept reserved for science fiction. Space science was always national news, but, until the walk on the moon, television images were limited primarily to takeoffs and landings.

Inevitably the relentless turmoil of the 1960s dramatically affected the American novel, calling into even more serious question than in the previous decade the traditional mimetic role of the novel. American writers and critics began to wonder whether fiction could hope to capture such an elusive reality. Even at the beginning of the decade, Philip Roth expressed genuine doubt on this question:

> The American writer in the middle of the 20th century has his hands full in trying to understand, and then describe, and then make *credible* much of the American reality. It stupefies, it sickens, it infuriates, and finally it is even a kind of embarrassment to one's own meager imagination. The actuality is continually outdoing our talents, and the culture tosses up figures almost daily that are the envy of any novelist.

Throughout the rest of the 1960s echoes of Roth's pessimistic analysis, usually with some variations in emphasis, became commonplace in literary magazines. Mailer, among others, wondered whether the daily barrage of information and news from the mass media effectively buried any objective and potentially verifiable reality that might exist. But the novelists continued. Like DeLillo, Joan Didion, in both her fiction and nonfiction, is a writer formed by the 1960s; the title essay in her *Slouching Towards Bethlehem* (1968) is a probing and inventive investigation into the counterculture that emerged during the 1960s in California. Later – in *Americana* (1971), *Great Jones Street* (1973), and *White Noise* (1985) – DeLillo satirized the corrosive effects of a mass-media culture devoted to a simulated reality, and in *Mao II* (1991) he wrote a novel that suggests the end of the novelist as an important cultural figure. In fact, after the 1960s it became somewhat fashionable to issue pronouncements on the death of the novel.

But a genre that had been so central to Western culture for so long would not pass quickly into oblivion. Already seeking alternatives to modernism and traditional realism, American novelists began to invent ways to revitalize the novel. The most venturesome used the chaos and contradictions of the time creatively. First in short stories and then in a novel, *Snow White* (1967), Donald Barthelme perfected his technique of narrative collage, a device that deliberately appeared to echo the fragmentation and randomness of American culture and society. In his first novel, *V.* (1963), Thomas Pynchon transformed the national obsession with plots and conspiracies into an elaborate historical tour de force; in *Gravity's Rainbow* (1973) he explored an even darker and more complex landscape. Other writers, including Ronald Sukenick, Gilbert Sorrentino, and Rudolph Wurlitzer, employed self-conscious and antirealistic narrative techniques. Two World War II novels, one published at the beginning and the other at the end of the 1960s and based on different modes of narrative experimentation, depicted what almost seemed another war than the one described in the late 1940s and early 1950s by Jones, Mailer, and Shaw. With the title of his first novel, *Catch-22* (1961), Joseph Heller coined a phrase that has since become part of the English language as a term to describe bureaucratic and technological irrationality and insanity. In *Slaughterhouse-Five* (1969) Kurt Vonnegut, who had been a prisoner of war in Dresden, Germany – a city of irreplaceable cultural importance and of no great military significance when the U.S. and British air forces destroyed it with a World War II technique known as firebombing – combined literary realism with science fiction to capture and convey the technological horror he had witnessed. In so doing he went beyond the power of television, smashing together internal and external realities and voices incomprehensible through chronological reportage and images.

In a 1967 essay provocatively titled "The Literature of Exhaustion," John Barth concisely expressed the rationale for the continuous search in the 1960s for innovation in fictional technique. Careless readers saw the essay as simply another pronouncement on the death of the novel; and Barth sometimes seems to encourage this kind of misinterpretation. At one point, for instance, he says that he is "inclined to agree" with those who believe that "the novel, if not narrative literature generally, if not the printed word altogether, has by this hour of the world just about shot its bolt." Yet the essay turns out to be a plea for the revitalization of the novel. Barth asserts that contemporary writers of fiction who ignore the work of such literary innovators as the Argentine writer Jorge Luis Borges, the Irish playwright Samuel Beckett, and the Russian-born novelist Vladimir Nabokov are doomed to create outdated and irrelevant fiction. Self-consciousness in narration is the key to creating the kind of art that Barth believes has validity; people need, he says, "novels which imitate the form of the Novel, by an author who imitates the role of Author."

The self-conscious, experimental fiction that Barth advocated – and that he, Barthelme, Vonnegut, Pynchon, Heller, and others wrote – was given different labels, the most common one probably being *metafiction*. Assuredly their work marked a movement of the American novel away from modernism and toward postmodernism. Where Hemingway and Faulkner had perfected techniques ranging from narrative minimalism to complex variations on the stream of consciousness to prevent any overt intrusion of an authorial presence that would destroy the reader's suspension of disbelief, the 1960s practitioners of metafiction devised elaborate methods to expedite such intrusions. In his 1971 critical study *City of Words*, Tony Tanner provides an analysis of the fascination that such elaborate and often self-reflective alternative "realities" as labyrinths, mirrors, and libraries held for these writers. In its use of ironic mysticism and a mock-academic setting, Barth's novel *Giles Goat-Boy* (1966) epitomizes 1960s metafiction.

Responding to the sense that contemporary reality had become too complex and chaotic to be captured by traditional realistic fiction, other writers attempted to erase the commonly accepted boundaries between fact and fiction. Describing contemporary events, Truman Capote in *In Cold Blood* (1965) and Mailer in *The Armies of the Night* (1968) – and later in *The Executioner's Song* (1979) – combined objective reporting with fictional subjectivity to produce a genre variously called nonfiction fiction, faction, or the New Journalism, the third the province of Wolfe, whose one novel, *Bonfire of the Vanities* (1987), came out of years of observation of the complex realities of New York City life. Other writers – for instance, Styron in *The Confessions of Nat Turner* (1967) – chose instead to fictionalize the historic past. Styron's book is not at all the same thing as the popular historical novel; nor is it a glorious revelation of the mythic past, as was Lockridge's *Raintree County*. It is instead a meditation on the connections between past and present American racial hatred and guilt. Finally, for all the speculation during the 1960s that traditional literary realism could no longer capture external reality, it was that decade that saw the publication of at least two novels, Hubert Selby Jr.'s *Last Exit to Brooklyn* (1964) and Joyce Carol Oates's *them* (1969), that alone revitalized the tradition of American literary naturalism.

One must use care to avoid overgeneralizing the influence of the 1960s on the American novel. The decade was, nevertheless, a climactic and defining one for the novel and for American literature in general. It at least resulted in a recognition of the need to reexamine long-standing assumptions about the viability of literary realism and modernism closely, even if such examination resulted in the reaffirmation of either or both these modes of writing.

For the United States the 1970s, while eventually a calmer decade than the preceding one, still had traumatic moments. In 1970, after bombing and then invading the neighboring nation of Cambodia, where the Viet Cong had bases, President Richard M. Nixon began the process of extricating the United States from military involvement in Vietnam. By August 1972 nearly all American troops were withdrawn from Vietnam, and a peace settlement was signed in January 1973, after Nixon had ordered further heavy bombing of North Vietnam. The men and women who served in Vietnam did not receive the kind of homecoming that had traditionally been the reward for returning American veterans of overseas combat, nor were all of them able to enter the workforce.

Every war has produced disabilities among veterans; additionally, the wars after World War II have produced large numbers of drug-addicted men and women, as veterans continued to use opiates discovered abroad to ease their culture shock on return to a consumerist, unthreatened civilian nation. Drug addiction among veterans is a relatively new phenomenon in the middle class, rarely mentioned before the 1960s. By 1985 the Kentucky teenagers in Bobbie Ann Mason's *In Country* would know more about "dope" in Vietnam than did the mothers of the men and women who went to war there.

Tim O'Brien and Larry Heinemann as well as the prolific and successful Stephen King have written on the addiction of their generation as a result of Vietnam.

The conquering heroes of World War II changed in only eight years to the largely neglected forces returning home from Korea. The Vietnam veterans came home to a place where to be ignored was good fortune. The other option was to be denounced openly for having fought in an immoral war. No clear and easily comprehensible justification of the U.S. involvement in Vietnam was ever articulated. When the war ended after the deaths of more than fifty-six thousand American soldiers, overwhelmingly of the lower class and often people of color, the nation wanted above all to forget the entire experience. (In *Hair* "Three-Five-Zero-Zero," a song about the "dirty little war," suggests a war that has become a dirty little secret.) Yet the war has never been forgotten, though in time acceptance of the experience and its responsibilities has begun to seem possible, and the building of the Vietnam War Memorial in Washington, D.C. – designed by a young Asian American woman, Maya Lin – was one of the rare healing acts in the public art of the United States.

It was U.S. mass media that began a realistic evaluation of the war and its legacy. Between 1978 and 1990 American movies explored the horrific nature of military combat in Vietnam and/or the postwar suffering of those who survived it; among the best are *The Deer Hunter* (1978), *Coming Home* (1978), *Platoon* (1986), and *Born on the Fourth of July* (1989). By the late 1980s even television, especially in the series *China Beach,* was beginning to examine the suffering, and the political and moral ambiguity, of the war. The Vietnam writers are still a small group, most of them Vietnam veterans; they have so far produced a small, distinguished body of war fiction. They have used a variety of literary approaches that echo both the early realistic-naturalistic World War II novels of Mailer, Jones, and Shaw and the later postmodernist works of Heller and Vonnegut. Heinemann's *Close Quarters* (1977) and *Paco's Story* (1986) are written in a predominantly realistic mode, while O'Brien's *Going After Cacciato* (1978) experiments with postmodernist narration. Robert Stone and Robert Olen Butler have produced probing examinations of the home-front legacy of the Vietnam War, and Mason's *In Country* was one of the first novels to observe the domestic war: the returns to individual and civil ignorance of the horrors of modern warfare; the mysterious sicknesses that followed the fighting; and the curious, insensitive, invasive, compassionate, and chaotic responses of the people who stayed at home. The sense of near helplessness felt by women after war has seldom been so uncompromisingly stated as in Mason's descriptions of the pot of geraniums held on Mamaw's lap in the long journey from western Kentucky to the Vietnam War Memorial in Washington, D.C., where she at first experiences the agony of not being able to "see" her son and then, with the help of unknown friends, places her flowers under his name.

Initially the landslide reelection of President Nixon in 1972 and the 1973 Paris treaty that – for the United States at least – ended the war seemed to promise the fulfillment of a national longing for unity and stability. That illusion was shattered when a preelection burglary of the Democratic national headquarters in the Watergate building complex in Washington, D.C. – barely noticed when it happened – mushroomed into a complex scandal that reached finally into the White House and in August 1974 forced Nixon to become the first U.S. president to resign from office. A crucial factor in his downfall was television, which broadcast the U.S. Senate hearings in the investigation of the Watergate burglary and its subsequent cover-up by the president and key advisers. Participants in the Senate hearings were quickly cast as heroes and villains in what at times seemed to be a hybrid of a morality play and a soap opera revealing a bizarre underground of laundered money, Cuban American "superpatriots," and renegade CIA agents. The hearings dramatized a sequence of actual events that were clearly improbable if not "unreal."

The Nixon presidency was followed by the administrations of Gerald Ford and Jimmy Carter, which remained free of scandal but were perceived as unfocused and ineffectual. In 1981 a politician at least as adroit as John F. Kennedy in the use of television to create dramatic and instantaneous images assumed the presidency: Ronald Reagan, a former motion-picture actor called "the great communicator" because of his intuitive mastery of mass media, became the first American president since Eisenhower to complete two terms in office. The Reagan presidency represented a return to political conservatism and a repudiation of much of the liberal Democratic agenda that had dominated national politics since Franklin D. Roosevelt's New Deal of the 1930s. Reagan's election was the direct result of a national movement away from political activism. While it represented something of a new national consensus, it alienated many traditional liberals and much of the old intellectual community.

The alienation of serious American writers was partly, but certainly not entirely, the result of national politics. To a significant degree their alienation was related to an evolving ideology in academic circles that denied the traditional role of the novel as the literary genre of the middle class. The influence of the French thinkers Michel Foucault and Jacques Derrida led to new theories – first structuralism and then deconstruction – that questioned traditional assumptions about the nature and purpose of literature and of writing itself. Most structuralists argued that literary texts were interrelated and were not primarily the creation of individual writers but the product of the structure of society's dominant ideas and values. Deconstructionists held that, because of the uncertainty of language itself, all writing inevitably negates its own apparent meanings. Since these two theories assert that the traditional belief in an individual author of a novel is merely a convention and that the elusiveness of language constantly negates the possibility of any consistent theme or intent in any piece of writing, they challenged and repudiated the traditional view of the novel as a controlled individual work designed to speak to a mass audience.

This new emphasis on the fundamentally arbitrary nature of literature and thus of critical judgments about it led to an extensive reexamination of the accepted canon of American literature. Beginning in the 1970s feminist critics, merging some aspects of structuralist theory with the ideas of the French psychoanalyst Jacques Lacan, argued that the canon had traditionally been established by white males and thus reflected an arbitrary and limited approach to American writing. The feminist critical agenda resulted in more than one kind of benefit for American literary studies. It led to the rediscovery of previously undervalued American women writers of the past, among them Kate Chopin, Tillie Olsen, Zora Neale Hurston, Anzia Yezierska, and Meridel Le Sueur. It also inspired new thinking about the proper subject matter for the novel by asserting that books written by men have tended to undervalue, if not ignore or misperceive, the value of women, even in their customary nurturing roles. Finally it brought a new awareness of the stereotypes that male writers have often imposed on female characters and an awareness of contemporary women writing to counter such stereotypes.

The same impulses that have affected feminist literary thinking have inspired, especially in academia, a view of literature – and the novel in particular – as being most important as a form of cultural study. This approach to literature has resulted in a new interest in writers from traditionally marginalized social groups. Beginning in the 1970s such African American women as Toni Morrison, Alice Walker, and Gayl Jones began to exercise an influence on the American novel comparable to that already exerted by Bellow, Roth, and other Jewish American writers. Bellow and Roth have continued their central and prolific careers. Maxine Hong Kingston, Amy Tan, Gus Lee, and other young Asian American novelists have made their initial contributions to the national literature, as have Sandra Cisneros, Raymond Barrio, Rudolfo A. Anaya, Tomás Rivera, Rolando Hinojosa-Smith, and Ana Castillo, who are among the first Hispanics to celebrate their ethnicity since John Rechy in his *City of Night* (1963). Finally the fiction and poetry – perhaps engendered by the 1930s writings of D'Arcy McNickle – of N. Scott Momaday, whose *House Made of Dawn* (1968) was the first contemporary Indian novel, and of later writers such as Louise Erdrich, Leslie Marmon Silko, Gerald Vizenor, and James Welch have inspired a Native American literary renaissance, with Vizenor functioning also as a major scholar of that renaissance.

The contemporary American novel is so rich in cultural diversity that it is difficult to think that until the postwar period scholars innocently defined the novel as a hidebound masculine work. The considerable benefit of newer, broader, and more precise thinking has inevitably resulted in the questioning of old assumptions about the role of the American novelist as the voice of national consensus. Few today speak of the national mission of the American writer with the confident assurance of Emerson or Howells. Fewer successfully play the part of a national man of letters as Edmund Wilson did. For different reasons and in different ways, postmodernist novelists such as Pynchon and even writers speaking for socially marginalized groups must assume that they are addressing much more restricted and limited audiences than the traditional middle-class readership of fiction. There are, in addition, more-prosaic reasons for the contemporary alienation of the serious American novelist from the middle class.

Television has been the communications medium of choice for America for nearly five decades, and for almost that long writers and others have regretted its shallowness and superficiality. American television has trained its audience to respond more readily to instantaneous visual images than to the printed page. In addition the expense of publishing books has accelerated throughout the postwar period, dramatically increasing the cost of hardcover fiction. One example came in 1992, when the hardcover edition of Mailer's *Harlot's Ghost* was published at a price of more than thirty dollars. Since 1939 paperback reprints have evolved as a means of making the novel accessible to the middle class. In a direct response to the rising costs of hardcover fiction, Saul Bellow published two novellas, *A Theft* (1989) and *The Bellarosa Connection* (1989), as paperback originals. Yet the paperback-publishing industry has itself been adversely affected by inflationary pressures.

Still, in spite of all these pressures, some quite serious and important postwar novelists have tried to speak to, and sometimes on behalf of, middle-class America. Updike owes his centrality to the postwar American novel in no small part to his evocation, in four volumes, of the financial and spiritual troubles of his fictional former high-school basketball star Rabbit Angstrom — *Rabbit, Run* (1960), *Rabbit Redux* (1971), *Rabbit Is Rich* (1981), and *Rabbit at Rest* (1990) — in whose life Updike depicts the morally ambiguous social rise of an ordinary American and thus evokes the fiction of Howells and Sinclair Lewis. (In other works Updike displays his versatility by echoing, usually for satiric purposes, the methodology of literary deconstruction).

Other postwar American novelists of impressive talent have revitalized old fictional genres traditionally associated with popular culture. Larry McMurtry has written some novels — including *Horseman, Pass By* (1961) and *Moving On* (1970) — that can best be described as contemporary westerns, and he won a Pulitzer Prize for *Lonesome Dove* (1985), a novel structured around a trail drive, a familiar plot devise to readers of traditional western fiction. Another important Texas novelist, William Humphrey, writing out of the western and southern Gothic traditions, has produced novels such as *Home from the Hill* (1958) and *The Ordways* (1965). Stephen King has attained enormous popularity by revitalizing Gothic and horror fiction, and Elmore Leonard, among others, has brought new perspectives to the detective novel.

Pronouncements on the demise of the novel to the contrary, American fiction since World War II has been, and continues to be, vital indeed. Even if no contemporary American writers can be said to hold the kind of Olympian prominence enjoyed by the two modernist giants Hemingway and Faulkner, post–World War II American fiction is distinguished by a richer diversity of achievements than at any other time in the nation's history.

The challenge for reference books such as the *Dictionary of Literary Biography* volumes devoted to *American Novelists Since World War II* is to select for inclusion those novelists who best illustrate the wide variety of that diversity. As anyone familiar with the history of shifting literary reputations will recognize, such choices represent a real risk. Still, a few contemporary American novelists are already and legitimately called major figures — Bellow, Updike, Mailer, Pynchon, and Morrison. The achievements of others — such as Oates, Roth, and Vonnegut — may well equal, if not surpass, those of some of the names on the previous list. The postwar American novel is healthy and developing.

— *Wanda H. Giles and James R. Giles*

Acknowledgments

This book was produced by Bruccoli Clark Layman, Inc. Karen Rood, senior editor, was the in-house editor.

Production manager is Samuel W. Bruce. Photography editors are Julie E. Frick and Margaret Meriwether. Photographic copy work was performed by Joseph M. Bruccoli. Layout and graphics supervisor is Emily Ruth Sharpe. Copyediting supervisors are Laurel M. Gladden and Jeff Miller. Typesetting supervisor is Kathleen M. Flanagan. Systems manager is Chris Elmore. Laura Pleicones and L. Kay Webster are editorial associates. The production staff includes Phyllis A. Avant, Ann M. Cheschi, Melody W. Clegg, Patricia Coate, Joyce Fowler, Brenda A. Gillie, Stephanie C. Hatchell, Rebecca Mayo, Kathy Lawler Merlette, Pamela D. Norton, Delores Plastow, William L. Thomas Jr., and Allison Trussell.

Walter W. Ross, Steven Gross, and Mark McEwan did library research. They were assisted by the following librarians at the Thomas Cooper Library of the University of South Carolina: Linda Holderfield and the interlibrary-loan staff; reference-department head Virginia Weathers; reference librarians Marilee Birchfield, Stefanie Buck, Stefanie DuBose, Rebecca Feind, Karen Joseph, Donna Lehman, Charlene Loope, Anthony McKissick, Jean Rhyne, Kwamine Simpson, and Virginia Weathers; circulation-department head Caroline Taylor; and acquisitions-searching supervisor David Haggard.

Dictionary of Literary Biography® • Volume One Hundred Seventy-Three

American Novelists Since World War II
Fifth Series

Dictionary of Literary Biography

Robert Olen Butler
(20 January 1945 -)

Joe Nordgren
Lamar University

BOOKS: *The Alleys of Eden* (New York: Horizon, 1981; London: Minerva, 1995);
Sun Dogs (New York: Horizon, 1982);
Countrymen of Bones (New York: Horizon, 1983);
On Distant Ground (New York: Knopf, 1985; London: Minerva, 1995);
Wabash (New York: Knopf, 1987);
The Deuce (New York: Simon & Schuster, 1989);
A Good Scent from a Strange Mountain (New York: Holt, 1992; London: Minerva, 1993);
They Whisper (New York: Holt, 1994; London: Secker & Warburg, 1994);
Tabloid Dreams (New York: Holt, 1996).

SELECTED PERIODICAL PUBLICATIONS – UNCOLLECTED: "Moving Day," *Redbook,* 143 (October 1974): 92-93;
"Upriver to Dexter," *Redbook,* 145 (June 1975): 92-93;
"At the Sound of the Tone, Charlie," *Cosmopolitan,* 186 (January 1979): 198, 220, 222;
"The Deuce," *Genre,* 21 (Winter 1988): 429-450;
"Salem," *Mississippi Review,* 21 (Spring 1993): 193-201;
"Three Ways to Die from the Fifties," *Harper's,* 287 (October 1993): 31-32;
"Boy Born with Tattoo of Elvis," *Conjunctions* (Spring 1994);
"The Handwriting on the Wall," *Virginia Quarterly Review,* 70 (Winter 1994): 51-58;
"Jealous Husband Returns in Form of Parrot," *New Yorker,* 71 (22 May 1995): 80-82.

As of 1996 Butler's publications include eight novels, a prize-winning collection of short stories, and numerous contributions to respected journals

Robert Olen Butler at the time of On Distant Ground
(photograph by Joshua Butler)

and reviews. His defining themes are the suffering that results from thwarted desire and the intimacy that characterizes fundamental human relationships. His crafting of these topics in his collected stories about Vietnamese expatriates living in southwest Louisiana placed him at the forefront of American letters. *A Good Scent from a Strange Mountain* (1992) earned the Pulitzer Prize, the Richard and Hinda Rosenthal Foundation Award from the American Academy of Arts and Letters, the *Southern Review*/LSU Prize for Short Fiction, a PEN/Faulkner Award nomination, and a Guggenheim Fellowship.

Robert Olen Butler was born on 20 January 1945. An only child, he grew up, as did his parents, in the small steel-mill town of Granite City, Illinois, in the river bottoms across the Mississippi from Saint Louis and a few miles northwest of Cahokia State Park. His father, Robert Olen Sr., is a retired actor and former chairman of the theater department at Saint Louis University. Speaking of their relationship, Butler said in a 1993 interview: "It was second nature for us to talk late into the night about books, movies, and theater." His mother, Lucille Hall Butler, is a retired executive secretary, and her stories about Granite City during the Depression inspired the content for *Wabash* (1987), Butler's fifth novel.

Butler moved only twice during his years with his parents. He entered grade school in Springfield, Missouri, and completed fourth grade in Overland Park, Kansas, but when he was ten, his family returned to Illinois. After junior high he went to Granite City High School, becoming president of the student body, and graduated as class covaledictorian in 1963. In the 1950s and 1960s the local steel mills attracted economic exiles from depressed areas of the Midwest and the South, and this led to a collision of cultures that Butler said shaped his personality. During high school and into college, he worked summers at Granite City Steel. He learned to talk Saint Louis Cardinals baseball with coworkers at the blast furnace operation and to discuss aesthetic theory with his father's colleagues.

Planning to major in theater, Butler enrolled at Northwestern University. As a freshman he was cast in four of the school's six major productions for 1963–1964, but in his sophomore year he turned to oral interpretation and playwriting. In addition to required creative-writing courses, he studied for five months with British author Stephen Spender and graduated summa cum laude in June 1967. That fall Butler attended graduate school at the University of Iowa, and on 10 August 1968 he married Carol Supplee. He earned an M.F.A. in playwriting.

Butler suspected that after graduate school he would be drafted for military duty in Vietnam, so he visited the army recruiter in Granite City and enlisted. He committed to a three-year enlistment to be guaranteed a position in counterintelligence, thinking he would be placed in an American field office doing background checks on U.S. Army personnel applying for security clearances. In February 1969 he started basic training in Fort Lewis, Washington, and was then transferred to Fort Holabird, Maryland. From Fort Holabird Butler went to language school in Washington, D.C., and spent a year learning Vietnamese from a native speaker. Fully trained as a linguist, he was assigned in January 1971 to a counterintelligence unit near Bien Hoa and within six months was chosen to be the administrative assistant and interpreter for the American Foreign Service officer advising the mayor of Saigon. Butler left Vietnam in December 1971, and the following month he was mustered out of the army. He told Joseph Olshan (*People*) about his year of active service: "Vietnam ravished me sensually. I made amazing friends, from my favorite leper beggar to the highest officials. After I came back, there were a hundred flashes of memories, prompted by a smell of overripe fruit, a certain perfume, a glimpse of a woman's ankle. And I was filled with the same sense of nostalgia, loss and even aspiration that the Vietnamese in my stories feel."

After his wife and he divorced, Butler moved to New York City and became a reporter for *Electronic News,* owned by Fairchild Publications. On 1 July 1972 he married Marylin Geller. Although he advanced to editor of the journal, he and his second wife decided in mid 1973 to move to Granite City, and he worked as a high-school substitute teacher and freelance writer for a year. Following the birth of a son, Joshua, he rejoined *Electronic News* in Chicago for eighteen months, at which time Fairchild asked him to return to New York to start a newspaper of his own creating. From 1975 until 1985 he was editor in chief of *Energy User News,* a weekly investigative business newspaper targeted for industrial and commercial consumers and managers of energy.

Butler struggled in the 1970s to think of himself as a writer. He explained to Peter Applebome of *The New York Times* that his early novels were completed "in longhand on legal pads supported by a Masonite lapboard as he commuted on the Long Island Rail Road from his home in Sea Cliff, L.I., to his job in Manhattan." Beginning in 1979 he attended four consecutive semesters of advanced creative-writing courses at the New School for Social Research taught by Anatole Broyard, who encouraged him.

Butler has been tagged a Vietnam novelist even though he finds the label disparaging. He told Jon Anderson (*Chicago Tribune*): "It's like saying Monet was a lily-pad painter; artists get at deeper truths." Three of his first four books, however, loosely form a Vietnam trilogy, each novel focusing on a different member of a common group of characters. Clifford Wilkes in *The Alleys of Eden* (1981), Wilson Hand in *Sun Dogs* (1982), and David Fleming in *On Distant Ground* (1985) served in an army intelligence unit located outside Saigon. For months they established a routing for bringing donations to a nearby Catholic orphanage, and on one of these visits, Vietcong soldiers attacked the compound and took Hand prisoner. After the raid Fleming approached Wilkes to act as his interpreter when questioning a suspected VC military insurgent picked up by the National Police. While they interrogated and tortured the man, he died of a heart attack. Within a few days Fleming discovered where Hand was being detained and set out to rescue him. Wilkes's tour would have elapsed in seven months, but his collusion in the prisoner's death upset him to the point of deserting. One morning he stole a jeep and passed Fleming and Hand returning to base camp as he was on his way toward Saigon and an uncertain future.

The Alleys of Eden begins in an alley apartment of Saigon, which is destined to fall soon to the insurgent North Vietnamese. Cliff Wilkes is in bed with the twenty-eight-year-old bar girl with whom he has been living for the past four years, and while Lanh sleeps, he remembers the people who have either by fate or choice previously forsaken him. His father died when Wilkes was fourteen. When he was at college, his mother remarried and began a new but distant life. A political activist whom he befriended at Northwestern University fled to Canada after they had hitchhiked to an antiwar rally on the West Coast. Francine, his former wife, divorced him during his first leave from the army. She wrote to him about marriage: "It is death. It stops me from really connecting to other people. And I have to connect as myself. Not part of a tandem." Wilkes determines not to abandon Lanh. As a precursor for many of Butler's future characters, he must contend with the unforeseen, including changing identities: He deserts from the army; he and Lanh are separated as they flee in the chaos during the fall of Saigon; they are reunited in Speedway, Illinois.

A pivotal scene unfolds when Lanh and he are invited to dinner by their Speedway neighbors, Quentin and June Forbes. The Forbeses honestly wish for Lanh to feel comfortable in their home, yet everything about them – their politics, their horseradish, their expensive china, their beliefs about death and an afterlife – is alien to her. Excluded from what they know, Lanh watches Cliff sneak out of the hiding his desertion from the army has required and bond with people who have a claim on his past. At their apartment that night, she tells him: "I would have felt more comfortable stripped naked and marched through the streets of Saigon before a VC bayonet." Happiness abandons her until she is embraced by a Vietnamese refugee family in town.

Following a disastrous visit to his former wife, in which he is nearly trapped by the police seeking to arrest him, Wilkes returns to Lanh and is intimate with her for a final time. Butler shows them connecting passionately, sensually as woman and man; afterward Wilkes gets dressed and walks into Speedway's deserted main street. Going to Canada, he remembers a female reporter telling him: "A man's home is where he is innocent." He and Lanh have tried to prevail over their cultural barriers, but are unable to revive the Edenic joy they had shared in Saigon.

Vietnam was not a popular subject when Butler started shopping around his manuscript. *The Alleys of Eden* was turned away by a dozen publishers who "admitted every virtue in the book except its marketability," he said. London-based publisher Methuen finally selected the novel for the company's American trade list; however, two months before the novel was published, Methuen notified Butler that it was forgoing the trade-book business. Butler forwarded the manuscript to nine additional publishers before Ben Raeburn, editor of Horizon Press, accepted it in 1980. The book came out the next year and sold eighty-five-thousand copies in paperback.

Within a year Horizon published Butler's second novel, *Sun Dogs*. Sun dogs are "mock suns" formed by ice crystals in the upper atmosphere, and the narrator points out that in the Arctic these reflections of ice "run with the sun, speak to it of things unseen, things that claim a special knowledge." Butler's title assumes far-reaching implications as he examines the depletion of natural and human resources during the energy debate of the early 1980s.

The plot involves Wilson Hand approximately ten years after he had been a prisoner in Vietnam. A self-employed private investigator who is anxious to get away from New York City, Hand accepts Royal Petroleum's offer to find who has been stealing confidential maps and reports from its headquarters at Moonbase on Alaska's North Slope. After he visits his former wife on the afternoon before he is to leave, she jumps to her death from her fourteenth-floor apartment balcony. A newspaper photograph of her bare legs projecting from a smashed windshield and flashbacks to his week in the VC prison camp are the mock suns that pursue Hand in Alaska when winter temperatures plummet to seventy-five degrees below zero.

Dust jacket for Butler's first novel, which draws on his experiences during military service in Vietnam in 1971

Butler attacks corporate ethics in his account of Royal Petroleum's propaganda war. An advocate for the U.S. president's energy independence campaign, Royal wants foreign and domestic consumers to think America has abundant natural reserves. The stolen maps and reports, however, confirm that Alaska is nearly depleted of resources. The company hopes to bury this information and thus give itself time to develop a strategy for capitalizing on the panic that will result when the news is spread. Without suspecting it, Hand has been retained to assist Royal Petroleum in its scheme.

At Moonbase Hand falls in love with a sensuous but untrustworthy woman named Marta Gregory. Marta and he agree to avoid the "emotional clutter of words" when making love, but on one occasion they break their rule of silence, and she discloses that her father's death has overshadowed her life. A cold and imposing Wall Street broker, he became ill when she was twelve and made her sit at his hospital bedside and listen to his regrets for having been so distant. When he started saying all the right things that he previously lacked the time to say, Marta began to hate him. His example has made her distrustful of everyone's sincerity, thus putting feelings connected to loyalty, as she knows, beyond her emotional grasp.

Bush pilot Clyde Mazer, in contrast, possesses a bold vitality for life. Butler creates in him a maverick who drinks, tells stories, squanders money, and flirts with both women and danger. Appalled by deception, he is the one person upon whom Hand can rely. Hand asks Clyde to fly him from Anchorage to Moonbase so he can verify that the trans-Alaskan pipeline is going dry. After crashing onto a mountain ledge in a seldom-used pass of the Brooks Range, they are without food, heat, and light as they huddle inside their makeshift ice cave. Clyde falls asleep, and while listening to his friend's agonized breathing, Hand begins stripping away his clothing as images of VC guards and of Beth stepping onto her balcony crystallize in his mind. Unafraid of dying, he whispers to Clyde in the darkness: "Eat it is finished." Thus Butler unites self-sacrifice and life-fulfilling peace, which he foreshadows in the book's epigraph from Leviticus 22:7: "And when the sun is down, he shall be clean."

Vietnam and *Energy User News* provided Butler with material for his first two books. In *Countrymen of Bones* (1983) he steps beyond personal experiences to probe dimensions of violence against the backdrop of World War II. In the Jornada del Muerto, a section of New Mexico desert known as "the journey of the dead," an archaeologist and a physicist become rivals during the weeks leading to the first experimental atomic detonation on the morning of 16 July 1945. The book's theme compresses into J. Robert Oppenheimer's pronouncement: "I am become Death, the shatterer of worlds."

The most technically innovative of Butler's early novels, *Countrymen of Bones* alternates between characters and locales, simultaneously developing two stories. Darrell Reeves has been trying for a decade, according to his former wife, to excavate his way to God. Employed by the University of Santa Fe, he is sifting through what he thinks to be a burial mound that happens to be located one thousand yards from the spot Oppenheimer has designated as ground zero. Reeves's antagonist, an army scientist named Lloyd Coulter, divides his time between Los Alamos and Trinity Base Camp, ten miles southwest of the archaeological dig. In the opening scene Reeves clutches a weaponlike trowel while looking down the desert wastes. His funds are virtually exhausted, and he worries that his professional intuition might be betraying him since his digging thus far has yielded nothing. As Reeves drifts into listlessness, Butler cuts to Los Alamos two hundred miles to the north. Having been with Oppenheimer for two years, Coulter knows they are at the brink of failure. The plutonium-gun idea is dead; the Holocaust continues in Europe. Time is running out for the Manhattan Project as scientists debate Seth Neddermeyer's implosion theory. By creating parallel narratives, Butler generates intensity for the important moment when Coulter and Reeves will collide.

Reeves has been ordered to complete his work in fifteen weeks and then evacuate. In this time, he unearths the bones of an ancient Indian death cult, meets a disabled former colleague, falls in love with army private Anna Brown, hears of President Franklin D. Roosevelt's death, and in self-defense kills an indignant rancher. Whereas Butler allows Reeves to have a measure of control over his emotions, anger destroys Lloyd Coulter. The son of an abusive father, Coulter lashes out at his coworkers, Oppenheimer, Reeves, and himself. In his worst moment he rapes Anna, driven by some hidden impulse whose mystery is "locked far tighter than the heart of an atom."

Anatole Broyard (*The New York Times*) praised Butler's depiction of Anna Brown for recognizing "love as a powerful violence too, a sublime one that can distract from other kinds." Her encouraging wide-set Indian eyes entice Reeves and Coulter to talk about themselves. Confused about why men are attracted to her, she tells Coulter when rejecting his marriage proposal: "I'm not the kind of girl I sometimes seem. I guess I just don't understand how I come across sometimes." After being raped, she escapes to be with Reeves on the morning of the atomic test.

Butler places the burden of his message on a found artifact. After the bomb detonation, in which Coulter dies, the narrative jumps ahead in time to a hotel room near Times Square. Anna and Reeves are celebrating their honeymoon and the end of the war. From among the ancient burial remains, Reeves has brought with him an ornamental stone collar shaped like a human face with wide-set eyes from which two jagged lines descend. He interprets the jagged lines to be a symbolic mournful expression of impending death, although Anna is quick to disagree. For her they encompass all of human history, conveying grief "at what men can do."

After *Countrymen of Bones* Butler changed publishing houses and editors when Horizon Press was bought out and Ben Raeburn left the firm. Butler took his manuscripts-in-progress, including half of

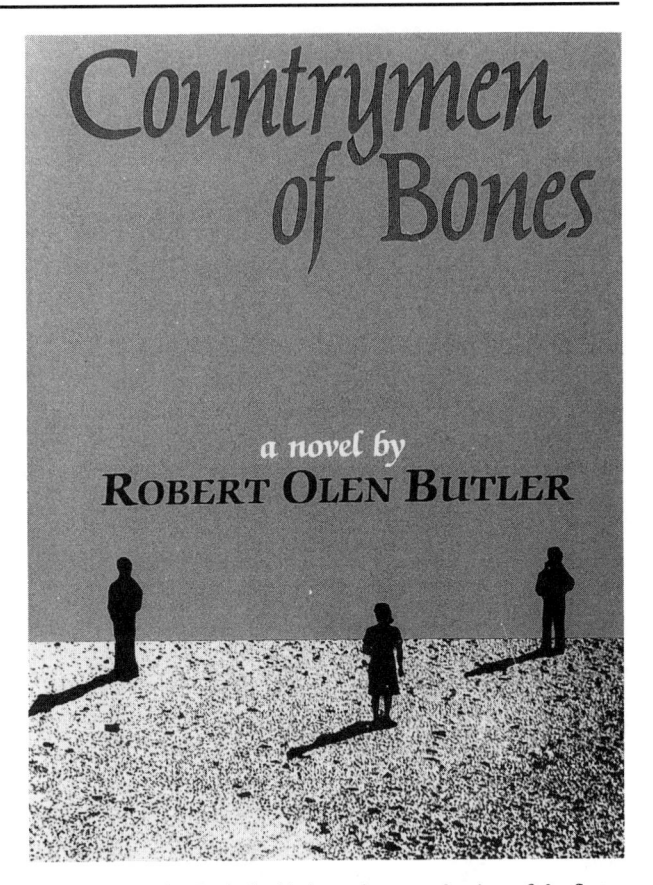

Dust jacket for Butler's third novel, set at the time of the first atomic-bomb test, held at Los Alamos, New Mexico, in 1945

On Distant Ground, the third book in his Vietnam trilogy, to New York agent Candida Donadio. Within two weeks he was a Knopf author and Lee Goerner was his editor.

Whereas *The Alleys of Eden* opens in Vietnam and closes in the United States, *On Distant Ground* begins in the United States and concludes in Vietnam. Dates, settings, and events in the two novels overlap as Capt. David Fleming's ties to Southeast Asia impel him toward surprising decisions. At Fort Holabird in April 1975, Fleming is to go on trial for assisting the enemy during his tour of duty. While awaiting formal court-martial proceedings, he privately arraigns himself for failing as a husband; for losing contact with Nguyen Thi Toyet Suong, a woman with whom he briefly fell in love in Saigon; and for helping a Vietcong prisoner to escape from his captors. Fleming's devotion to truth, in the end, secures his redemption.

Butler structures events from a moment of psychological curiosity. Fleming recalls an episode from his past in which he and his CIA team had seized key Vietcong leaders and were instructed to turn them over to the South Vietnamese. During a visit to these prisoners, he entered a vacant cell and was struck by the phrase *ve-sinh la koe* ("hygiene is healthful") scratched into one of its walls. He knew instantly that he shared a particular "detachment of the mind" that made him fear for the cell's prior occupant as he would for himself. Determined to find the person, he learned he was tracking a man named Pham Van Tuyen (twin), whom he later helped to escape from a South Vietnamese camp. Fleming's recollections thematically elevate human decency to a level above patriotism, and in the present action Butler turns to family issues to underscore Fleming's personal integrity.

Before Fleming's trial concludes, his wife gives birth to their first child. He is allowed to stay at home with Jennifer and David Junior until a verdict is reached, and during a news broadcast one evening, he watches intently as orphans, many of whom have distinctly American features, are being evacuated from Saigon. Their faces stir memories of his affair with Suong, and he is certain he has a four-year-old son whom he must rescue. "He realizes this is madness," says reviewer Joe Klein (*The New York Times*), "but is too self-absorbed to stop himself." Klein adds, "It is a tribute to Mr. Butler's skill as a writer that his story's pyramiding absurdities seem not merely plausible but inevitable." Desire becomes action when Fleming is dishonorably discharged but assigned no prison time.

When Fleming arrives in Vietnam, he is enveloped by the panic of a country on the run. Playing on hunches, he locates Suong's mother, introduces himself to his son Khai, visits the prison where Suong had died, and on two occasions comes face-to-face with Tuyen, currently the director of security in Saigon for the Provisional Revolutionary Government. Their second meeting occurs after Fleming is captured while trying to smuggle Khai out of the city. When the opportunity arises, Tuyen admits that he lacked the bravery ever to have written the words Fleming ascribes to him, but repaying a debt, he arranges for Fleming and Khai to be transported safely to Bangkok. The book's closing asserts that mutual respect is a requisite for reconciliation and peace.

With the success of his fourth novel, Butler's publishing credentials presented him with an opportunity to change careers. In the summer of 1985 he left *Energy User News* and accepted a creative-writing post at McNeese State University, in Lake Charles, Louisiana, where he still teaches. When Joseph Olshan asked about his first visit to Lake Charles, Butler said, "My God, it was [like] the Mekong Delta! The same rice paddies, the same calligraphy of marshland waterways and that subtropical kind of haze. It seemed the most natural place in the world for me to be." Although the setting was natural, he had succumbed to what he called "functional fixedness." Butler had so adapted to writing while riding commuter trains that he told David Streitfeld (*Washington Post*): "I thought I would have to buy a little electric motor and fix it to my chair, hire someone to come in and flap a newspaper. I was having a lot of trouble writing in a quiet room that wasn't moving." Once settled, he began mapping out his fifth novel, *Wabash,* by drawing on his mother's stories about Granite City during the Great Depression.

In 1932 Wabash, Illinois, is mired in corporate intimidation and escalating poverty. Wabash Steel exercises baronial power over the town, and Butler shows it financing community life, regulating local politics, and enforcing strong-arm laws. Deborah and Jeremy Cole are a couple in their early thirties who have yet to recover from the death three years earlier of their only child, Elizabeth. Jeremy carries his misery "like a lump of slag" into the blast furnaces where he works. Since Lizzy's death, physical intimacy has demanded too great an effort from him, so he retreats into his suffering. Deborah is helpless on two fronts. First, she is unable to rescue Jeremy from his pain, and second, she cannot stop the endless bickering between her mother and aunts. Deborah visits her relatives while Jeremy is at the mill, and in bed at night they grieve. When Deborah prevents Jeremy from assassinating John J. Hagemeyer, the company's owner, their passion flares "like a Wabash night, burning them until they are clean."

As in *Countrymen of Bones,* Butler juxtaposes two narratives so that Deborah's battles at home correlate to Jeremy's conflicts at work. Deborah's mother, Miriam, and her aunts, Adah, Berenice, and Della, seem trapped by their sooty lives. Bored, childless, and unmarried, Adah and Della often sit on Miriam's porch swing and fret half-heartedly about their sister Berenice going mad. There is a fifth sister, Effie, about whom the others speak as if she were dead. Deborah now and then visits her eccentric grandmother whose home borders the town dump. Continuing a family tradition, Grandma Birney writes polite but firm warning letters to the river rats clawing around in her house. Deborah hears from her that Effie is alive and residing in Saint Louis, but that she has been ostracized for becoming a Catholic and accepting the Virgin Mary as her true mother. When Grandma Birney dies, Deb-

Dust jacket for the third volume in Butler's loosely connected trilogy of Vietnam War novels

orah persuades Effie to attend her mother's funeral, but the sisters will not be reconciled. Berenice's suicide prompts Deborah to write her own "Dear Rats" letter in which she threatens to poison whoever is taking Jeremy from her.

Jeremy decides to kill Hagemeyer for several reasons. Cronin, an underpaid Hungarian worker, is fired and then hangs himself rather than watch his wife and children go hungry. For taking part in solidarity meetings, Nick Brenner is beaten to a pulp and evicted from his home, one of Hagemeyer's tar-paper shanty houses. A Fourth of July protest march turns into a riot between mounted police and rock-throwing dissidents, with whom Jeremy sides. Following the march, a hired thug tries to kill him. Finally, when his supervisor threatens to harm Deborah, Jeremy borrows a gun from Brenner and plans to shoot Hagemeyer during a political gathering at Lawton where President Herbert Hoover will be endorsing the company owner in his bid for Congress.

Butler invents Nick Brenner and Effie Birney to advance a lesson about losing oneself in either a political or spiritual conversion. Brenner is taken in by Marxist rhetoric and jeopardizes his family's welfare. Discovering that his wife has taken their children and left town, he tells Jeremy: "A family's a corrupt idea anyway. Capitalism in four walls." Effie, similarly, rejects her mother and sisters to join the family of the Roman Catholic Church. Christ and the Virgin Mary sustain her in her masochism as, with a childlike dependency, she clutches to rituals to make her feel clean. Presented as weak, insecure people, Effie and Nick are usurped by organizations that purport to revere their individuality.

Critic Philip Beidler suggests in *Re-Writing America: Vietnam Authors in Their Generation* (1991) that Butler's experimentation leads to "a fiction of brilliant doublings" in which "the renderings of the local and the immediate search out their larger mythic textualizations." In *Wabash* Deborah and Jeremy break from their struggles and picnic on Sun Mound, which is mentioned in *The Alleys of Eden* and which figures more prominently in *Countrymen of Bones*. Describing this and other examples as "mythic-cultural revision," Beidler sees in Butler's

Dust jacket for Butler's fifth novel, based on his mother's stories about life in Granite City, Illinois, during the Depression

work "the archeology of culture at large, writing on the shared ground, the bone palimpsest of American myth itself."

Since 1985 Butler has made Lake Charles his home. In addition to teaching at McNeese, he has obtained funding from the Calcasieu Parish Arts and Humanities Council to initiate creative-writing classes for elementary, junior-high, and high-school students. On a continuing basis he contributes articles and reviews to *The New York Times Book Review,* the *Washington Post,* and the *Chicago Tribune,* and he has participated as a faculty member in well-known programs such as the Iowa Summer Writing Festival, the Port Townsend Writers' Conference, and the Antioch Writers' Workshop. In 1987 he was a charter recipient of the Tu Do Chinh Kien Award given by the Vietnam Veterans of America for "outstanding contributions to American culture by a Vietnam veteran." Butler's second marriage ended in July 1987, and he gained full legal custody of his son. On 21 July 1987 he married Maureen Donlan, his present wife. While working on *The Deuce* (1989) Butler took advantage of his theater training and discovered that he could use a first-person voice to his satisfaction. The experiment "opened realms of my artistic unconscious," he said, "that were previously unaccessible to me."

The Deuce, Butler's sixth novel, is an extended monologue in which he adopts the persona of a seventeen-year-old Amerasian who recounts a lifetime of memories to unravel his identity. Referring to the challenge of writing within a culture other than one's own, Butler told David Streitfeld: "I know the Vietnamese people probably better than I knew most of the people I grew up with. But beyond that, it is an article of faith for the artist — that we can leap in our imaginations into the minds and hearts and souls of people quite different from ourselves."

Butler's narrator states in his opening line: "I wish it was simple just to say who I am, just to say my name is so-and-so and that makes you think of a certain kind of person and that would be me." Names are meaningful to him, and to this point in his life he has been Vo Dinh Thanh, Anthony "Tony" James Hatcher, and "the Deuce," each name representing a different identity. Born in 1968, Vo Dinh Thanh is the six-year-old son of a Saigon bar girl, Vo Xuan Nghi, and an American GI. When his mother brings her clients home to their soiled apartment, Thanh runs outside and blends in with the other "children of dust," for whom war has made life surreal. Nghi is about to collapse from years of selling herself for heroin; thus, when a familiar-looking dark-haired American man named Kenneth appears one afternoon in the spring of 1974, Thanh can feel his life is going to change.

Thanh is also Tony, son of Kenneth Hatcher, a Vietnam veteran and aspiring lawyer who comes to Saigon to reclaim his child. When Kenneth arrives and sees that Nghi is desperate, he buys Thanh from her and brings him to live in Point Pleasant, New Jersey. James Patrick Sloan (*Chicago Tribune*) mentions that instead of soldiers in dirty underwear teaching him English slang, Tony is introduced to "all the appurtenances of suburban life that have about as much meaning as a roomful of rocks from Mars." After Tony's first stepmother seeks a divorce, he and Kenneth try to normalize their relationship by arranging outings to Coney Island, Yankee Stadium, and the Bronx Zoo. One night when his father carelessly refers to Nghi as a "whore and a druggie," Tony steals a few hundred dollars and runs out.

Thanh-Tony is also a sixteen-year-old runaway hiding in New York City. Tony is beaten and robbed within hours of arriving at the Port Authority Bus Terminal. He drifts, as a result, into weeks of panhandling with an alcoholic Vietnam veteran who calls him "the Deuce," the name locals use for Forty-second Street where the wrong people, Joey Cipriani warns him, will "eat you alive." Even though Tony claims to be 100 percent Vietnamese, Joey says, "You can't bullshit me. You're two things. You're Vietnamese and you're an American. A deuce."

Being half-Asian and half-American, the Deuce emerges as Butler's symbol for the collision of cultures that he finds so interesting about the Vietnam War and its aftermath. To make his point, he includes numerous details linking America to Vietnam when Tony runs away from his Jersey Shore home. Tony is sixteen when he sets out to be on his own; his mother was sixteen when she left Vinh Binh province and moved to Saigon. In New York City the Deuce loses his innocence to a sixteen-year-old runaway, Norma, who changes her name to Nicole and begins working the streets. Joey still carries a photograph of the Vietnamese prostitute with whom he fell in love sixteen years ago. On the afternoon the Deuce tracks Mr. Treen, a knife-wielding pederast, to a gay bar, he recoils when he sees a young mother sell her six-year-old boy for sexual favors in exchange for drugs. Forty-second Street, Joey notes, cuts through the city like the Mekong River, drowning the weak and disenfranchised.

Joey Cipriani is perhaps Butler's most tragic character. Claiming to be burdened by the legacies of civilian massacres and Agent Orange, Joey was, in truth, a personnel clerk who left South Vietnam before the Tet offensive of 1968. The war did not divest his life of meaning; Vietnam filled it with purpose. Kenneth tries to make this clear for his son after bringing him home from New York. He explains to Tony that some veterans like Joey have been disoriented after the war because

> What Vietnam really was for them was the only time in their lives when you'd get up in the morning and see the sky really clearly or really appreciate a shower or a dry pair of socks. And not just the little things. It was the only time in their lives when every day you knew for sure that there's something very important at stake on the planet Earth, that issues of life and death and love and even eternity, heaven and hell, are all real, these things exist. You knew that, and you never forgot it for a second, and then you came home and all of that faded away.

Back in Point Pleasant the narrator compares himself to a cicada "burrowed by the root of a tree, waiting his long wait [seventeen years] to emerge one night and play out his life." Butler uses the extended metaphor of the cicada as his vehicle for issues about personal growth and change as Tony "drags himself free" of the identities others have created for him. He leaves again for New York to avenge Joey's murder and to find out what kind of person he is inside. After leading Mr. Treen to his death, he can say with confidence: "I'm a lot of things but I'm one thing, and I have no doubt about that. I'm the Deuce." Loyalty to his past and loyalty to his friend are at the heart of his moral vision as he comes of age in the decade following the Vietnam War.

When Butler was near the end of *The Deuce*, National Public Radio contacted him about contributing to its series, the *Sound of Writing*. He returned to the more than thirty stories he had previously written and found to his interest a Vietnamese folkway about Saigon boys staging fights between insects. He sat down one afternoon, took on the voice of a middle-aged Vietnamese man in Lake Charles trying to come to terms with his Americanized son, and six hours later he had produced "Crickets." Within a few days he had jotted down notes for twenty additional stories, and after contacting Allen Peacock, then his editor at Knopf, about the possibility of doing a collection, he spent the next fourteen months on *A Good Scent from a Strange Mountain*.

Butler's displaced Vietnamese live in places in Louisiana like Gretna, Lake Charles, Versailles, and New Orleans. Some are from North Vietnam and others are from South Vietnam; some are Buddhists, and others are Catholics; some have found America to be a land of plenty, and others eke out a living the best they can. Madison Smartt Bell (*Chicago Tribune*) regards the collection as a "novelistic unit" that maps "a Vietnamese legend onto an American situation," and he believes that "any reader of this book will feel a strange and perhaps salutary sense of exposure and be made to wonder just who are the real Americans." Richard Eber (*Los Angeles Times Book Review*) says about Butler's subject matter and style that he "writes essentially, and in a bewitching translation of voice and sympathy, about what it means to lose a country, to remember it, and to have the memory begin to grow old. He writes as if it were his loss, too."

Having been a midlevel author, Butler told Peter Applebome about winning the Pulitzer Prize for his stories: "It came as a total surprise, something remarkable and wonderful that hit with the

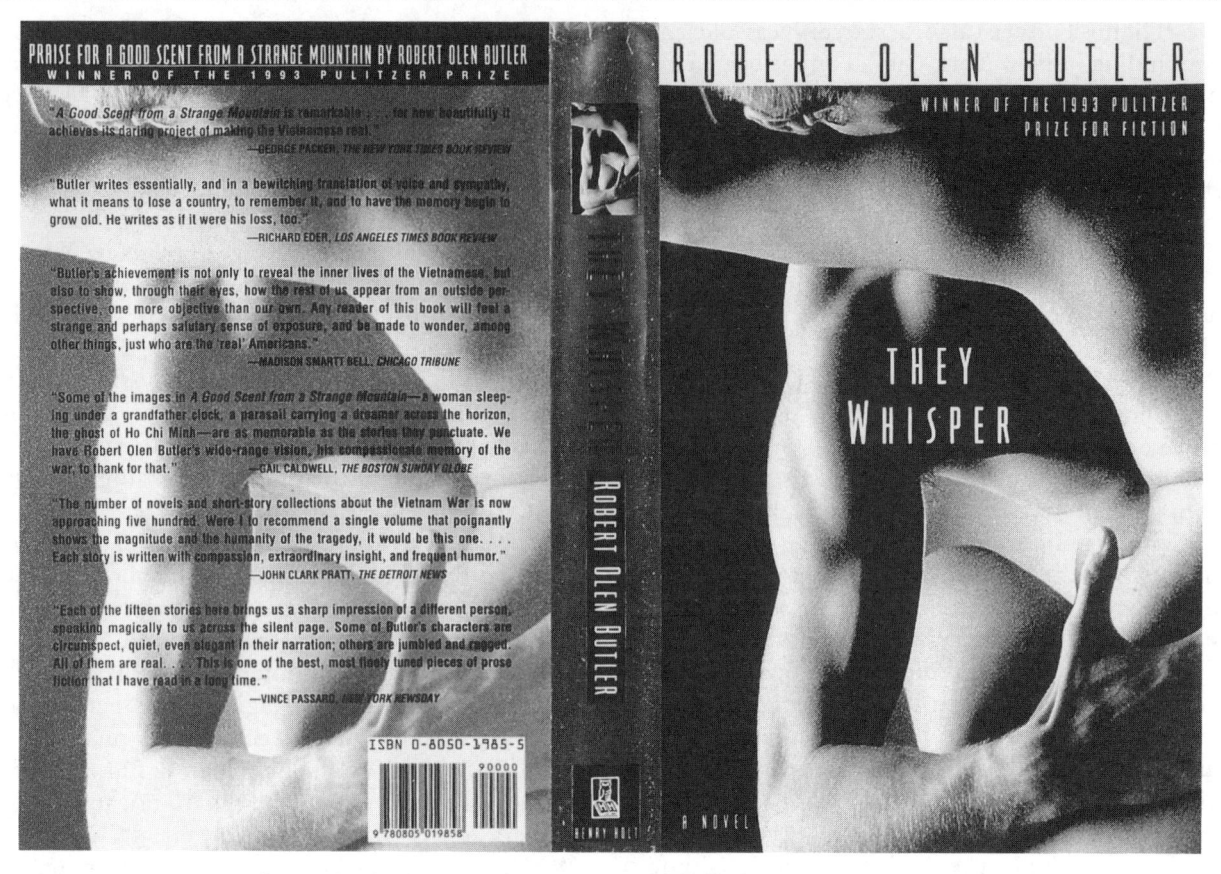

Dust jacket for the novel Butler called "a book full of the truest lies I can tell"

abruptness of a bolt of bayou lightning." The award lifted him considerably, leading to subsequent fellowships from the John Guggenheim Foundation and the National Endowment for the Arts. He was made an honorary doctor of humane letters by McNeese State University in 1993, and in that year he also came under contract to Ixtlan, Oliver Stone's production company, to write a screenplay for *A Good Scent from a Strange Mountain*. As demands for his time increased, Butler replaced his former Masonite lapboard with a notebook computer. Once again he was writing on the go, while flying between reading tours, book signings, and literary festivals.

His reputation secured, in *They Whisper* (1994) Butler set out to write a serious literary work about human sexuality. He had written sexual scenes into his previous novels, but *They Whisper* is devoted entirely to intimacy between women and men. Although confronted by difficulties in language and in what he had to face about himself, he said, "There was no other book I could have possibly written at that moment in my life. It was a book that was absolutely compelling." Like most writers, Butler pulls his subject matter from life experiences, but readers should guard against being lured into the biographical fallacy. He told Sybil Steinberg (*Publishers Weekly*): "[Carlos] Fuentes defines the novel as a pack of lies hounding the truth. This is a book full of the truest lies I can tell."

They Whisper is born of an image of a ten-year-old boy asking a young girl to wiggle her toes under the X-ray machine in his uncle's shoe store in Wabash, Illinois. This private moment of seeing Karen Granger's bones as no other person would ever see them is the first incident that Ira Holloway recalls in his being a lover of women. From this image Butler renders all he has learned about physically and spiritually connecting with life's unspoken sensual mysteries.

The novel is a stream-of-consciousness sojourn that takes place in 1980. Ira Holloway, now thirty-five, stands on a beach watching a parasailor glide over Puerto Vallarta. For the next 333 pages sensory impressions initiate sexual memories that span twenty-five years. In his mental flights to Wabash, New York, Zurich, Bangkok, and Saigon, he projects for each woman along the way a unique inner voice that whispers only to him of her secret desires and joys. Regardless of how intently he listens for their whispers, Ira says, "The answer of each woman does not prevent me from yearning. And it is the yearning I have to understand." From among Ira's many relationships, Butler makes his marriage to Fiona Price the crux of the narrative, demonstrating how love succumbs to obsession.

Soon after returning from Vietnam, Ira meets Fiona Price in New York's East Village. As their relationship evolves, she persuades him to speak about being attracted to other women, unwittingly establishing the groundwork for her ensuing jealousy. Within six months they are married, and while honeymooning in Paris, Ira learns that Fiona was sexually abused by her father, beginning on the night her parents' home caught on fire. Feeling her pain, he laments, "I would give up all my adult touching of Fiona to have held her sexlessly in my arms as a father just that once and cast the man from her life before he could scatter her mind and heart like sparks rising from the burning house." The morning after this secret revelation, Fiona insists that she must return to God if she is to survive.

Following the birth of their son, John, she begins attending Our Lady of Sorrows Catholic Church in Seaview, New York. Fiona wants Ira and John to share in her return to innocence, but the more insistent she becomes, the more they whisper behind her back. When his lawyer informs him that he would never gain legal custody of John should he seek a divorce, Ira decides he can either leave John with Fiona and allow her to create for their son a "terrible self," or he can stay and live two lives, "one to keep Fiona sane and one to whisper to my son all the things that I felt deeply were true." Presented as a sacrifice of his fullest sexual being, Ira forgoes his own happiness to safeguard his son, an attitude which Jane Smiley (*The New York Times*), Diane Johnson (*Vogue*), and Albert Read (*Spectator*), critics of Butler's sexual politics, perceive to be self-aggrandizing.

Fiona also suffers for her choices. Because she can intuit Ira's thoughts about other women, she needs constant reassurances that he yearns sexually only for her. As her doubts intensify, she becomes violent. Though she turns to psychiatry before the Catholic confessional, her religious zeal and escalating mistrust destroy Ira's longing for her, so when they are in bed, he fantasizes about being with other women. If he is too slow in getting an erection, Fiona is lost in envy; if they make love, she is overcome by shame and aches to confess. She wants more than anything for Ira and John to accept the church's sacraments as absolute truths. Should they not side with her, she thinks, then either they are right and she is a fool, or they are wrong and the husband and son she loves are going to hell. Christopher Lehmann-Haupt (*The New York Times*) observes, "The whiteness of burning desire, the compulsion to purify by confessing, the desired purification of death: these themes weave and tangle and knot so intricately in *They Whisper* that against all common-sensical judgments you trace them to the novel's harrowing end."

Butler told Sybil Steinberg that he knew he wanted to become a writer when he was in Saigon. He said of wandering the streets and crouching in doorways at 2 A.M.: "This ravishingly sensual experience illuminated my future as an artist. I understood that what I knew about the world was demanding expression in a fully sensual, moment-to-moment way. I saw that fiction was the medium that would permit me to do this." With seven acclaimed novels in print, he has good reason for saying, "My rich and varied life has been deeply composted in my imagination." Butler intends to write a new book every eighteen months.

Reference:

Philip D. Beidler, *Re-Writing America: Vietnam Authors in Their Generation* (Athens: University of Georgia Press, 1991).

Don DeLillo

(20 November 1936 -)

Paul Civello
University of Minnesota

See also the DeLillo entry in *DLB 6: American Novelists Since World War II, Second Series.*

BOOKS: *Americana* (Boston: Houghton Mifflin, 1971; London: Penguin, 1990);

End Zone (Boston: Houghton Mifflin, 1972; London: Deutsch, 1973);

Great Jones Street (Boston: Houghton Mifflin, 1973; London: Deutsch, 1974);

Ratner's Star (New York: Knopf, 1976; London: Vintage, 1991);

Players (New York: Knopf, 1977; London: Vintage, 1991);

Running Dog (New York: Knopf, 1978; London: Gollancz, 1978);

Amazons, as Cleo Birdwell (New York: Holt, Rinehart & Winston, 1980; London: Granada, 1980);

The Names (New York: Knopf, 1982; Brighton: Harvester, 1983);

White Noise (New York: Viking, 1985; London: Picador/Pan, 1986);

The Day Room (New York: Knopf, 1987);

Libra (New York: Viking, 1988; London: Penguin, 1989);

Mao II (New York: Viking, 1991; London: Cape, 1991).

Don DeLillo at the time of Mao II *(photograph by Joyce Ravid)*

SELECTED PERIODICAL PUBLICATIONS –
UNCOLLECTED: "The River Jordan," *Epoch,* 10 (Winter 1960): 105-120;

"Take the 'A' Train," *Epoch,* 12 (Spring 1962): 9-25;

"Spaghetti and Meatballs," *Epoch,* 14 (Spring 1965): 244-250;

"Coming Sun. Mon. Tues.," *Kenyon Review,* 28 (June 1966): 391-394;

"Baghdad Towers West," *Epoch,* 17 (1968): 195-217;

"The Uniforms," *Carolina Quarterly,* 22 (Winter 1970): 4-11;

"In the Men's Room of the Sixteenth Century," *Esquire* (December 1971): 174-177, 243, 246;

"Total Loss Weekend," *Sports Illustrated* (27 November 1972): 98-120;

"Creation," *Antaeus,* 33 (1979): 32-46;

"The Engineer of Moonlight," *Cornell Review,* 5 (Winter 1979): 21-47;

"Human Moments in World War III," *Esquire* (July 1983): 118-126;

"American Blood: A Journey through the Labyrinth of Dallas and JFK," *Rolling Stone* (8 December 1983): 21-22, 24, 27-28, 74;

"The Runner," *Harper's* (September 1988): 61-63;

"The Ivory Acrobat," *Granta,* 25 (Autumn 1988): 199-212;

"The Rapture of the Athlete Assumed into Heaven," *The Quarterly,* 91 (Fall 1990);

"Pafko at the Wall," *Harper's* (October 1992): 35-70;

"The Angel Esmeralda," *Esquire* (May 1994): 100-109;

"Videotape," *Anteus,* 75/76 (Autumn 1994).

Over the past twenty-five years, Don DeLillo has established himself as one of the most important contemporary American novelists. Prolific and wide-ranging, he has published ten major novels that rework a variety of narrative genres, creating something new out of what had in many cases become stale and hackneyed forms. Yet regardless of the subject matter or genre, DeLillo's central theme is always America. His novels relentlessly probe the postmodern American consciousness in all its neurotic permutations, offering a compelling and disturbing portrait of the contemporary American experience.

Although not as reclusive as J. D. Salinger or Thomas Pynchon, DeLillo nevertheless rigorously maintains his privacy, commenting little on his life or work. He has given few interviews over the years and has avoided participating in the full-fledged book promotions common in the publishing industry, eschewing book signings, talk shows, and lectures. Part of the reason for his silence is his personality. "It's my nature to keep quiet about most things," he told Tom LeClair; "I'm just not a public man," he added in a later interview with Anthony DeCurtis. He would also like to steer interest away from himself and his relationship to his work and focus it upon the novels themselves, novels that, he remarked to Caryn James, have "very little autobiography" in them. To DeLillo, a novel exists in the public sphere, apart from the private life of its author. "I'd rather write my books in private," he told DeCurtis, "and then send them out into the world to discover their own public life."

Despite his reticence, however, some biographical details have entered the public domain. DeLillo was born on 20 November 1936 in New York City, the son of Italian immigrants. He grew up in the predominantly Italian American Fordham section of the Bronx, and he apparently led a typical boyhood centered around family and sports. Reared a Catholic, DeLillo was exposed early on to the mysteries and rituals of the church, and these had a major influence on his work. He has attributed the sense of mystery that permeates his fiction to his Catholic upbringing, as well as his fiction's concern with various forms of discipline, ritual, and spectacle – with anything, as he told LeClair, that like religion "drives people to extreme behavior." Indeed, the relentless focus of his work on the extreme in modern life – particularly on danger and death – is grounded in Catholicism. As he confided to Vince Passaro:

> I think there is a sense of last things in my work that probably comes from a Catholic childhood. For a Catholic, nothing is too important to discuss or think about, because he's raised with the idea that he will die any minute now and that if he doesn't live his life in a certain way this death is simply an introduction to an eternity of pain. This removes a hesitation that a writer might otherwise feel when he's approaching important subjects, eternal subjects. I think for a Catholic these things are part of ordinary life.

DeLillo attended Cardinal Hayes High School in New York, which he despised, and then Fordham University, which he also found less than inspiring. "I slept for four years [at Cardinal Hayes]," he confided to Passaro, and "didn't study much of anything" at Fordham. Nevertheless, while at Fordham he at least attended classes in theology, philosophy, and history and graduated in communication arts in 1958. He has cited his aversion to school as the reason he now refuses to give academic lectures or to teach: "I never liked school," he told DeCurtis, "why go back now?" This antipathy toward formal schooling, however, should not be equated with an indifference to learning, as the massive research projects he undertook in preparation for *Ratner's Star* (1976) and *Libra* (1988) would indicate. It does appear, though, that the greater part of DeLillo's education, especially that which would influence his later work, was obtained outside the classroom, in the cultural milieu of New York. "I think New York itself was an enormous influence," he revealed to Robert R. Harris. "The paintings in the Museum of Modern Art, the music at the Jazz Gallery and the Village Vanguard, the movies of Fellini and Godard and Howard Hawks." Indeed, although he credits writers such as Gertrude Stein, Ezra Pound, and, later, Pynchon and William Gaddis for awakening him to the possibilities of writing, it was the European films, jazz, and Abstract Expressionism to which he was exposed in New York that he acknowledges as primary influences.

After graduating from Fordham, DeLillo began a "short, uninteresting" career at the advertising agency of Ogilvie and Mather. He wrote fiction in his spare time, publishing his first short story, "The River Jordan," in *Epoch* in 1960. Throughout the decade, he would publish a handful of other stories in *Epoch, Kenyon Review,* and *Carolina Quarterly.* It was during this period, too, that the single most important event in DeLillo's development as a writer occurred: the assassination on 22 November 1963 of President John F. Kennedy. DeLillo has suggested that this event was a bigger influence on him than were his literary predecessors. As he told Passaro, the assassination "made me the writer I am — for better or for worse":

> I don't think my books could have been written in the world that existed before the Kennedy assassination.... And I think that some of the darkness in my work is a direct result of the confusion and psychic chaos and the sense of randomness that ensued from that moment in Dallas.

Moreover, the assassination as a media event — a violent public spectacle largely experienced through the visual media of film and television — haunted DeLillo, prompting in large part his continued interest in the power of images in contemporary American society. And his interest in coincidence — in seemingly unimportant events that occur "outside history," as he phrases it, yet manage to hold sway over the imagination — was also fostered by the assassination: he would later learn that Lee Harvey Oswald lived only a few blocks away from him in the Bronx during the early 1950s.

DeLillo quit his job at Ogilvie and Mather in 1964 and began working as a freelance writer in nonfiction. He wrote pieces on such diverse topics as furniture and computers, lived on approximately $2,000 a year, and occupied a small studio apartment in the Murray Hill section of New York that had no stove and had the refrigerator in the bathroom. He began his first novel, *Americana* (1971), in 1966 — "hurling [great chunks of experience] at the page," as he told LeClair. It would take him four years to write because of interruptions in order to make a living and because, as he put it to DeCurtis, "I didn't know what I was doing." Halfway through, however, he realized he was a writer, that his skill had improved from his earlier work in short fiction, and that he would eventually be able to solve the structural problems he perceived in the novel. The first publisher to whom he submitted the manuscript, Houghton Mifflin, accepted it.

Americana is a sprawling, apparently free-form novel, at first glance suggesting that DeLillo had not solved all of its structural problems but ultimately revealing a conscious attempt to flout novelistic conventions. DeLillo told LeClair that "probably the movies of Jean-Luc Godard had a more immediate effect on my early work than anything I'd ever read," and indeed the influence of Godard is manifest in *Americana* in its purposeful disruption of form both to undo convention and to create a new, alternative mode of artistic expression, one capable of exposing and getting beneath the artificiality convention perpetuates. Such a project also possesses an affinity with the Beat aesthetic, and in many ways *Americana* emulates, even satirizes, the "road" novels of writers such as Jack Kerouac. In *Americana*, the Beat quest for the self and for the soul of America becomes a quest for self-purgation — an attempt to rid the self of the media-generated images that constitute it — and the soul of America lies hopelessly buried beneath Americana, beneath, that is, America's images of itself. The power of images and the media's manipulation of them — Godardian themes — are central to *Americana,* and in examining them and their effect on the individual in contemporary America, DeLillo in his first novel introduces concerns he would develop and explore in his subsequent work.

The narrator and protagonist of *Americana*, David Bell, tells his story from the self-imposed exile of a desert island, the consequence of the experiences he will relate. He begins with himself as a twenty-eight-year-old television network executive in New York City, a product of the media now thoroughly enmeshed in its production. His identity is a composite of media images of virility, from the movie icons of Burt Lancaster and Kirk Douglas to the male models of television shaving commercials: "When I began to wonder who I was, I took the simple step of lathering my face and shaving. It all became so clear, so wonderful. I was blue-eyed David Bell. Obviously my life depended on this fact." Yet he is aware of the shallowness of such an identity and of the movie roles and television clichés that he and his network coworkers playact in their daily routines. "There were times when I thought all of us at the network existed only on videotape," he remarks, and this feeling breeds the fear that they are all leading "elapsed" existences that at any time could be "erased forever." He takes the opportunity provided by a proposed television documentary on the Navajo to travel west with three friends: Pike, an old drunkard; Brand, a young Vietnam veteran; and Sullivan, an enigmatic female sculptor.

The second part of the novel consists of various flashbacks to David's childhood and youth, focusing particularly upon his relationships with his

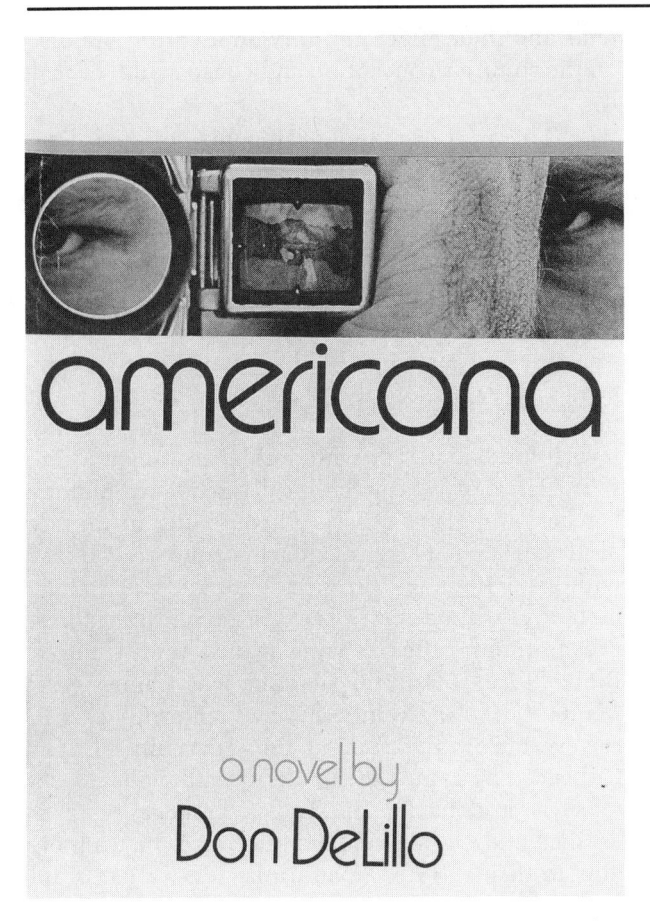

Dust jacket for DeLillo's first novel, which has been compared to the fiction of Jack Kerouac and the motion pictures of Jean-Luc Godard

father, mother, and girlfriends. The flashbacks have the effect of a film montage, creating in their disjunctiveness the portrait of a youth manufactured by the media, an existence that is little more than "an image made in the image and likeness of images." David's father is a television advertising executive who uses his children as test subjects for his commercials, forcing them to watch hour after hour of his commercials in their basement at home. It is media overload, an exaggeration of the media bombardment to which all contemporary American youths are exposed, a "montage of speed, guns, torture, rape, orgy and consumer packaging which constitutes the vision of sex in America." The effect of such a visual assault on everyone is, of course, pernicious. They become what they see on the screen and are ultimately victimized by it. David's father is an insecure, competitive, and rapacious man who views women as objects, prizes for male conquest. David's mother is indirectly a victim of her husband's and the broader culture's attitude and directly a victim of her male gynecologist, who takes this attitude to its extreme and rapes her. The experience renders her psychologically disturbed, and, because she is "not a photograph that could be retouched" or "an advertising campaign," the father can do nothing to help her. David himself, who comments that "all the impulses of the media were fed into the circuitry of my dreams," predictably enough becomes like his father and like the media image of the American male. He uses his girlfriends, unable to escape – even when he wants to – the media clichés and treat them as equals and human beings.

In the third part of the novel, David and his traveling companions stop in a small midwestern town, where David begins to make his own movie, a Godardian experiment in which he uses the camera to try to free himself from the power of the media image, to get beneath its surface. As he says later, his film is an attempt to "unmake meaning" – to unmake, that is, the meaning that the media image has imposed on his life and experience. From the other side of the lens, David hopes to gain a different and insightful perspective on his life, and so he enlists some of the locals and his traveling companions to play the roles of his father, mother, sister, and himself. Perhaps the most revealing insight occurs when his "father" explains the effect of television advertising on the viewer:

> It moves him from first person consciousness to third person. In this country there is a universal third person, the man we all want to be. Advertising has discovered this man. It uses him to express the possibilities open to the consumer. To consume in America is not to buy; it is to dream. Advertising is the suggestion that the dream of entering the third person singular might possibly be fulfilled.

To be an American in the television age, in other words, is indeed to be "an image made in the image and likeness of images." It is to be that third-person singular, a fantasy that effaces the genuine individual and renders him or her indistinguishable from everyone else. David himself embodies this universal third person: a friend tells him that he bears "a strong facial resemblance to a number of Hollywood stars known for their interchangeability."

After David's moviemaking culminates in enacting an Oedipal fantasy – an experience that gives him insight into the difference between the rapacious desire inculcated by the media and human love – he abandons any pretense he ever had about filming the television documentary on the Navajo, leaves his camera and companions behind, and journeys west "to match the shadows of my image and myself." In other words, he goes west to see if he can make his, and America's, image reflect the essential self, not the media creation. Yet all he finds is more Americana, more images of images, more caricatures of the American media culture: a Texan in a Cadillac with an attitude toward women much like his father's, a commune of hippies whose "alternative" lifestyle is itself a media cliché, and a group of men at a test track for automobile and truck tires who carries on a drunken orgy with some Mexican whores. David finally makes what amounts to a pilgrimage, retracing President Kennedy's motorcade route through downtown Dallas – to DeLillo, the scene of America's first great media event in the television age and a symbol of the dark heart lying beneath America's image of itself – and then boards a plane back to New York. He presumably travels from there to his desert island, where he hopes to escape at last the media and its pervasive and pernicious influence.

Americana was not widely reviewed, and those who did review it seemed unsure what to make of this first novel by a relatively unknown writer. Christopher Lehmann-Haupt, in *The New York Times* (6 May 1971), found it structurally flawed, characterizing it as "a loose-jointed, somewhat knobby novel, all of whose parts do not fit together and some of whose parts may not belong at all." He attributed these faults to the fact that *Americana* was "very much a first novel" yet went on to praise DeLillo's fresh and original use of language: "the language soars and dips, and it imparts a great deal." Michael Levin, in *The New York Times Book Review* (30 May 1971), was not as charitable, criticizing DeLillo's characterization and dismissing his language as pointless rhetoric: "There is no real identity to be found in this heaping mass of word-salad. There are thickets of hallucinatory whimsy, an infatuation with rhetoric, but hardly a trace of a man."

After *Americana,* DeLillo devoted himself full-time to writing fiction, abandoning all freelance work. He began his second novel, *End Zone* (1972), within weeks of completing *Americana* and in a burst of creative energy finished it within a year. *End Zone* is a more tautly structured and cohesive novel than *Americana,* perhaps an indication that DeLillo learned quite a bit about the craft of novel writing during the four-year ordeal of *Americana.* DeLillo also shifted his thematic focus with his new novel. Whereas *Americana* was primarily concerned with the influence of the media image on identity in America, *End Zone* explores the more fundamental determinant of language and other ordering systems and their effect not only on identity, but also on the culture's conception and construction of reality.

The narrator and protagonist of *End Zone,* Gary Harkness, is a career college football player who, after being expelled or quitting several prestigious football programs, ends up in athletic exile at tiny Logos College in west Texas. There he encounters an assortment of eccentrics: Emmett Creed, the totalitarian football coach; Major Staley, the nuclear-war-obsessed Air Force ROTC commander on campus; Taft Robinson, the black halfback with a gift for speed and philosophy; Anatole Bloomberg, the Jewish football player who decides to "unjew" himself; Alan Zapalac, the politically active exobiology teacher; and many others. Throughout the largely plotless novel, Gary spends his time conversing with his teammates, his girlfriend, and Zapalac on metaphysical matters; practicing with the team in preparation for the big game against West Centrex Biotechnical Institute; playing war games with Major Staley; and wandering and philosophizing in the west Texas wasteland that surrounds Logos College. The game against Centrex, the novel's climax, is a debacle; the Logos College team is crushed and humiliated, and afterward the team begins to disintegrate. Several players are badly injured; one is killed; Gary and Taft Robinson quit; and Emmett Creed is confined to a wheelchair. The novel ends with Gary on a hunger strike, refusing to eat or drink, being fed through plastic tubes.

But beneath the story line, the main subject is language and the numerous ordering structures contingent upon it. As DeLillo told LeClair, "it may be the case that with *End Zone* I began to suspect that language was a subject as well as an instrument in my work." Language is a tool of thought, a means of apprehending, organizing, and, ultimately, constructing "reality." Yet, to DeLillo, language is an arbitrary system with no claim to a transcendent authority, only one to tradition. In *End Zone* it is the source of all other organizing principles, the primary ordering structure that humanity places on the world. Language establishes the parameters of thought, unifies the paradigms of religion and science, reduces complexities to understandable if inaccurate simplicities, makes possible the analogy between football and war, includes and excludes. The name of the college, Logos, suggests the connection in the Western mind of the word with religious and rational truth, as it also intimates a transcendent authority for it. But the reader finds that Logos College is only the arbitrary construct of its founder, Tom Wade, "a man of reason," who imposed his

DeLillo at the time of Americana *(photograph by Peter Jones)*

"idea" on the nothingness of the west Texas wasteland. Similarly, Emmett Creed, a man "famous for creating order out of chaos," imposes his football "creed" on his team, a creed that eventually leads to its and his destruction. And Major Staley makes the unthinkable, nuclear holocaust, seem rational and comprehensible through the jargon he uses to describe it. Throughout *End Zone* DeLillo shows the reader that arbitrary orders grounded in language but manifest in such things as religion, science, and sports, follow the second law of thermodynamics, moving inevitably toward exhaustion, entropy, chaos. They move, in other words, toward the "end zone."

Yet running counterpoint to the numerous arbitrary orders, or "closed systems," is the suggestion of other possibilities, other ways of conceiving of reality that are "open," regenerative, and therefore less destructive. After the end of the season, the players abandon the closed system of football, with its jargon, gridiron, rule book, time clock, and end zones, and engage in a free-for-all in the snow that suggests to Gary a new harmony between humanity and the planet. It involves abrogating arbitrary grids and rules – "a breaking down of reality," as the player Bing Jackamin had characterized a game. With the illusion of order gone, the mind may be able, in Gary's words, to "remake itself."

Other characters in the novel also begin to see the destructiveness of arbitrarily imposed, closed orders. Myna Corbett, Gary's girlfriend, counters his desire for simplicity and reductiveness, the "snatch," "gash," "pussy" identity imposed on women by the players. Zapalac seeks a new relationship between humanity and the environment, one not solely concerned with exploitation and mastery. Bloomberg realizes the futility of trying to "unjew" himself by "getting rid of the old slang and speech rhythms," by imposing, in other words, a middle-American language and culture on his Jewishness. And, finally, Taft Robinson strives to free himself from the cultural stereotype and "commercial myth" foisted upon the black athlete. He quits the team, remains motionless, and invents a new language through which he may define himself. As DeLillo characterized his own novelistic project to LeClair, these characters all seek to "restructure reality," to invent "a new map of the world." Their success is never assured, and Harkness ends up like David Bell in *Americana,* avoiding impinging structures by withdrawing from the society that perpetuates them.

End Zone reached a wider audience than *Americana,* having been first excerpted in *The New Yorker* (27 November 1971) and then in *Sports Illustrated* (17 April 1972). It was also more widely reviewed and more favorably received. Lehmann-Haupt in *The New York Times* (22 March 1972) called it a "wonderful" novel, the fulfillment of the promise intimated but not achieved by *Americana.* He praised DeLillo's "magnificent verbal talent" and stopped just short of prophesying his ultimate greatness: "The suddenness of his arrival places him among our best young writers. It makes one wonder whether there are any limits at all to his potential growth." Thomas R. Edwards echoed this assessment in *The New York Times Book Review* (9 April 1972). He too found *End Zone* to contain "a more original and efficient vehicle" for DeLillo's vision than *Americana* and asserted that "this richly inventive new talent looks like a major one."

There were, however, some negative reviews. An anonymous reviewer in *Time* (17 April 1972) complained of DeLillo's "overly schematic vision of life," and in the *Antioch Review* (Spring 1972) another anonymous reviewer deprecatingly referred to it as

Dust jacket for DeLillo's third novel, about a rock star who seeks privacy in a hippie commune

"a book for intellectuals": "The jokes are stale, 1960s 'existential' humor . . . and there is something vaguely incongruous about the plethora of profoundly philosophical jocks who inhabit this novel."

DeLillo continued the sports theme of *End Zone* shortly after its publication with another contribution to *Sports Illustrated* (27 November 1972): "Total Loss Weekend," a story about a compulsive gambler who bets on every possible sporting event. But his third novel, *Great Jones Street* (1973), which also appeared within the year, moved into new territory. Having tackled the American pop phenomena of television, film, and football in his first two novels, DeLillo took on a third in *Great Jones Street*: rock and roll. And as in his preceding works, DeLillo chose a protagonist and narrator who is an inside player – in this case Bucky Wunderlick, a rock star – who becomes alienated and attempts to withdraw from society.

The novel begins with Bucky already in exile, having quit his band midtour in Houston. He retreats to a shabby apartment on Great Jones Street in the Bowery of New York City, where he hopes to find solitude and seclusion from the burdens of rock stardom. He soon learns, however, that he cannot escape. First his agent, Globke, appears, having discovered Bucky's hideaway because Transparanoia – the company that produces Bucky's records, manages his finances, and seems to exist solely to promote and exploit Bucky's moneymaking capability – owns the building. Globke is interested in manipulating Bucky's disappearance for profit. Then a member of the Happy Valley Farm Commune – a counterculture community that has moved from the country to the city "to find peace and contentment" and wants to "return the idea of privacy to American life" – deposits a package at Bucky's that contains a new drug developed by the U.S. government that prevents people from forming and uttering words. The action of the novel revolves around this "product" and the various acquaintances of Bucky's who are trying to get their hands on it in order to profit from it: Opel, Bucky's girlfriend, who acts as a bargaining agent for Happy Valley; Azarian, a member of Bucky's band who now represents "certain interests" from the West Coast; Watney, a former British rock star who is now "doing sales, procurements, and operations"; Dr. Pepper, an underground scientist ostensibly assigned to analyze the drug for Happy Valley; Hanes, a messenger for Transparanoia; and Bohack, one of the leaders of Happy Valley. Another product stimulates similar acquisitiveness: Bucky's "mountain tapes," recordings he made while alone at his mountain retreat, which are now highly valuable because of his disappearance. Hanes steals the drug; Globke steals the tapes. Happy Valley forces Hanes to reveal the location of the tapes, which they destroy because the tapes violate what they consider to be Bucky's commitment to "the idea of privacy." They then obtain the drug and force Bucky to take it so that he will not make future transgressions. But the effects of the drug do not last, and Bucky eventually regains his ability to speak.

Bucky is a figure emblematic of the 1960s Zeitgeist, a rock star in the rebellious Mick Jagger and Jim Morrison mold. DeLillo told DeCurtis that Bucky "seems to be at a crossroad between murder and suicide . . . [that] defines the period between 1965 and 1975." The progression of Bucky's music — what DeLillo characterized to LeClair as moving "from political involvement to extreme self-awareness to childlike babbling" — parallels the social movement in America from the political activism of the 1960s to the self-doubt of the 1970s, from anger turned outward to anger directed inward. Bucky's eventual babbling — exhibited on his final album, titled *Pee-Pee-Maw-Maw* — may indicate total dissolution or may be an attempt, like that of Taft Robinson at the end of *End Zone,* to find a new, alternative language, one not co-opted by the mass media and commercial interests. As DeLillo indicated to LeClair, "babbling can be frustrated speech, or it can be a purer form, an alternate speech."

Indeed, Bucky's greatest horror — and a central theme of the novel — involves the commodification of culture in America and the lack of a genuine alternative to it. Bucky himself, like the drug and his mountain tapes, has become a "product," something that can be manipulated and exploited for profit. He no longer presents a rebellious alternative to commercial culture, for he has been co-opted by it. He is a media creation, an image; a representative from ABC tells him that his fans "want images" and that his "power grows" with his actual disappearance — his power, that is, to generate profits.

Such power, however, is not his own. In the postmodern world, power is decentralized, diffuse, underground. Bucky the rock star, much like a fascist dictator, does have the ability to organize social frustrations and energy — the name of Watney's former band, Schicklgruber, is revealing in this regard — and the ability to direct those energies toward himself or to thrust them back on his audience. "What I'd like to do really," he tells an interviewer, "is I'd like to injure people with my sound. Maybe actually kill some of them." But on a deeper level, Bucky in turn is controlled. Toward the end of the novel, Watney tells him that he has no power, that the real power lies with Transparanoia and the "true underground," the money interests. These have the power to sell, and one of the things they sell is Bucky. "Your life," Watney tells him, "consumes itself."

Great Jones Street was considered a disappointment by most reviewers, in large part because it suffered in comparison to *End Zone*. Playing on the football metaphor of that breakthrough success, Lehmann-Haupt in *The New York Times* (16 April 1973) wryly commented that DeLillo in his new novel had run "out of bounds." He called *Great Jones Street* "flat and disappointing," citing a disjunctiveness between the novel's "interesting themes" and its "hurdy-gurdy of a plot." He added that even DeLillo, with all his talent, still needed "the rudiments of novelistic structure to survive." Sara Blackburn, in *The New York Times Book Review* (22 April 1973), likewise found fault with the plot, characterizing the book as a string of "anecdotes that don't accumulate into much of a novel." While admitting that *Great Jones Street* was "full of beautiful writing," she concluded that it was "more of a sour, admirably written lecture than a novel." Walter Clemons, in *Newsweek* (23 April 1973), suggested that *Great Jones Street* be viewed as an "in-between book," an "unsuccessful" interlude between DeLillo's earlier brilliance and what promised to be future excellence. In a dismissive review, Edward Luttwak in the *National Review* (8 June 1973) consigned *Great Jones Street* to the contemporary pack of mediocre "youth-alienation" novels, calling DeLillo's characters and the novel itself "dull" and "boring." *Great Jones Street* was excerpted in the *Atlantic Monthly*.

In contrast to the rapid production of *End Zone* and *Great Jones Street,* DeLillo's fourth novel, *Ratner's Star* (1976), took three years to complete. DeLillo conducted an enormous amount of research in the field of mathematics in preparation, a project he undertook because, as he told LeClair, "I wanted a fresh view of the world." In addition, in 1975 DeLillo married and moved to suburb of New York City.

Ratner's Star is a long, abstruse novel whose primary subject matter is math and logic. In it, DeLillo abandoned the first-person narration he had used in his first three novels but continued his exploration of human ordering structures, their limitations, and their distortions. He also took on yet another literary genre: science fiction. The novel's protagonist, Billy Twillig, is a fourteen-year-old mathematical genius who has won the first Nobel Prize in mathematics for his work on zorgs, a mathematical concept so abstract it cannot be described in words and is understood only by a few people. One of those people is Robert Hopper Softly, Billy's mentor at the Center for the Refinement of Ideational Structures, who recommends Billy to the researchers at a remote research complex known as Field Experiment Number One. The complex's giant computer, Space Brain, has recently received and recorded a transmission consisting of 101 pulses and two gaps in a sequence of fourteen/twenty-eight/fifty-seven from the vicinity of Ratner's Star, a star-planet system in a distant galaxy. Billy is supposed to decipher the message from the "Ratnerians," because the scientists at Field Experiment Number One believe it will "tell us something important about ourselves." A distinguished mathematician, Henrik Endor, had preceded Billy and had apparently failed in the attempt, going mad as a result and retreating to a hole in the ground, where he survives on insect larvae.

Endor is just one of several characters Billy encounters at Field Experiment Number One, most of whom are caricatures of the rational mind and rational attitudes, in the mode of the Menippean satire. Another is Orang Mohole, a physicist whose theory of "Moholean relativity" posits a "value-dark dimension" in which physical laws vary from one frame of reference to another. He discovers that the message was not transmitted from Ratner's Star but reflected from it; the message had its source elsewhere. Billy finally decodes the message, concluding that it is based on notation by sixty (as is our measurement of time) and that the Ratnerians' numbers correspond to our number *52,137,* although he is at a loss to know what this means.

An important subplot that runs throughout the novel involves competition between a large corporation called OmCo Research, which, like Transparanoia in *Great Jones Street,* seems to own everything, and Elux Troxl, the head of a Honduran cartel that will eventually take over OmCo. Troxl and his cartel want to manipulate the world's "money curve" for power and profit, and to this end they use science and the knowledge it can bring to exploit abstraction and exercise control. They lease time on the world's most powerful computers, including Space Brain; try to lease Billy's mathematical mind; and even attempt unsuccessfully to implant something called the Leduc electrode in his brain, which will enable his brain to function like a computer.

In the second part of the novel, Softly takes Billy down to an excavation below the research complex where he and several others are working on a new project called Logicon. They are attempting to develop a universal logical language based on mathematical principles that will enable earthlings to communicate with beings from other galaxies, a language in which all ambiguity and uncertainty have been eliminated. One of the scientists working on this project is Maurice Wu, a Chinese American archaeologist who discovered evidence that a highly developed human culture existed before primitive man – in other words, that human evolutionary history has been one not of linear progression but of an alternating pattern of progression-regression-progression. It is then discovered that Earth lies in a Mohole and that the message reflected from Ratner's Star was originally transmitted from Earth – specifically, from that advanced human culture Maurice Wu had discovered existed before primitive man. The message pinpoints the exact time of an "unscheduled" total solar eclipse, highlighting the insufficiency of science and mathematics, their inability to predict natural phenomena accurately and to be free of uncertainty. As happened with Endor, this failure of the rational drives Softly into Endor's hole, where he digs past the now-dead mathematician. The novel ends with Billy reveling in this cosmic uncertainty, laughing madly while riding away from Field Experiment Number One on a tricycle.

DeLillo told LeClair that *Ratner's Star* was a book of "naked structure," that he wanted it "to be what it was about. Abstract structures and connective patterns. A piece of mathematics." Indeed, as a structure *Ratner's Star,* like mathematics, is itself an example of the human compulsion for order. It is a novel of symmetries, a novel in two mirror-image parts ("Adventures: Field Experiment Number One" and "Reflections: Logicon Project Minus One" – based on the "structural model," as DeLillo informed LeClair, of Lewis Carroll's *Alice's Adventures in Wonderland* and *Through the Looking Glass*). Yet, as in *End Zone,* the symmetries and orders in

Ratner's Star are arbitrary, contrived, and distinctly human constructs that inevitably limit and distort humanity's perception of "reality." They are, as Softly muses, "convenient fictions." "The task," he believes, of the mathematician, the scientist, and, ultimately, the rational human mind "is to work out an abstract scheme which may or may not reflect the composition of the thing itself." Or, as another character says about Moholes: "What we're really doing is imposing our own conceptual limitations on a subject that defies inclusion within the borders of our present knowledge. We're talking *around* it. We're making *sounds* to comfort ourselves. We're trying to peel skin off a *rock*. But this ... is simply what we do to keep from going mad." Indeed, imposing these "conceptual limitations" on phenomena succeeds only in enabling humanity to apprehend those limitations themselves; people get back, in other words, what they project. And so the Ratnerian's message turns out to have been sent from Earth and therefore, in an ironic sense, does in fact "tell us something important about ourselves."

Of course most of the mathematicians and scientists at Field Experiment Number One, including Billy, believe in the purity and efficacy of their ordering structures. To Billy, "mathematics made sense"; it is the opposite of mystery and mysticism. Yet it fails to explain that most alluring of mysteries to Billy, sex, or any other irrational force or entity. One of DeLillo's main points in *Ratner's Star* is the importance of unifying opposites, of uniting the rational and irrational, science and mysticism. Such unification provides the means of going beyond the sterility and limitation of rationalism, or, as in *End Zone,* of avoiding its destructive tendencies – epitomized in *Ratner's Star* by Elux Troxl and his machinations. Thus Pythagoras, the "mathematician-mystic," as DeLillo characterized him to LeClair, is the "guiding spirit" of the novel. And Ratner, the scientist who discovered Ratner's Star and who has since renounced pure science in favor of admitting mysticism, stands at the center of the novel in the chapter pointedly titled "Opposites." "When I go into mystical states," he says, "I pass beyond the opposites of the world and experience only the union of these opposites in a radiant burst of energy." DeLillo has noted, in his interview with DeCurtis, the historical link "between the strictest scientific logic and other mysticism," adding that "modern physicists seem to be moving toward nearly mystical explanations of the ways in which elements in the subatomic world and in the galaxy operate."

Ratner's Star received mixed reviews. Lehmann-Haupt in *The New York Times* (27 May 1976)

Dust jacket for DeLillo's spy thriller about a young stockbroker who becomes involved in international terrorism

called it DeLillo's "most spectacularly inventive novel" and his "best meditation on the excesses of contemporary thought." Once again, Lehmann-Haupt praised DeLillo's brilliant use of language, the "lyric poetry that Mr. DeLillo seems to write as easily as breathing." He did, however, find fault with the novel's "occasional opaqueness." George Stade in *The New York Times Book Review* (20 June 1976) also straddled the fence in assessing what he called "this red giant of a book." He commented that the novel sent "an unambiguous signal that DeLillo has arrived, bearing many gifts," but that "too often ... the razzle-dazzle seems that of a child prodigy, the conspicuous originality somewhat derivative, the dollar unearned, the desperation routine." Peter S. Prescott in *Newsweek* (7 June 1976) likewise found *Ratner's Star* derivative, a novel "running too closely in Pynchon's tracks." While acknowledging DeLillo's ability "to write brilliantly, even movingly," he complained that *Ratner's Star* was also "twice too long," its second half "virtually unbearable."

Ratner's Star was followed by the shorter, more quickly written novel *Players* (1977). Once again, DeLillo grappled with another phenomenon of the contemporary landscape, terrorism, and appropriated another literary genre as his vehicle, the spy thriller. Yet despite the different subject matter and form, DeLillo continued to explore his leitmotivs of the emptiness and alienation of modern life and the effect of the media on it.

The main characters, Pammy and Lyle Wynant, are a young New York City couple who possess the outward trappings of success: Lyle is a trader on the floor of the New York Stock Exchange while Pammy works at the World Trade Center for an organization called the Grief Management Council. The two are terribly bored with their lives, which consist of little beyond their sterile jobs and their reclusive, lonely apartment existence. Things change one day, however, when Lyle's colleague George Sedbauer is shot to death on the floor of the stock exchange. Lyle begins an affair with Rosemary Moore, the new secretary at his firm, and discovers at her home a photograph of her, the dead man, and his assassin. He learns that Sedbauer was involved with a terrorist organization that wants to blow up the stock exchange in order to disrupt what they perceive to be an oppressive system of money and power. Intrigued, Lyle too becomes involved, meeting along the way the true believer Marina Vilar; the uncommitted, duplicitous leader of the group, J. Kinnear; and an FBI agent named Burks. Lyle, like Kinnear, becomes a double agent, relaying information to Burks while still participating in the terrorists' plot.

Pammy, meanwhile, escapes to rural Maine with her coworker Ethan Segal and his homosexual lover Jack Laws. Just as Lyle plays at terrorism, they play at the back-to-nature life. Bored, Pammy and Jack Laws have a sexual encounter, after which Jack, in a grotesque parody of 1960s Vietnamese Buddhist monks, commits suicide by dousing himself with gasoline and igniting it. The novel ends with Pammy back in New York City and Lyle with Rosemary in a nondescript suburban Toronto motel, each as lonely, isolated, and empty as at the beginning.

DeLillo told LeClair that Pammy and Lyle "are more typical of contemporary Americans than people want to believe," that they are "people I recognize." Their malaise is contemporary America's malaise, a product of their insulation, their protection from feeling within the structures of American society. Pammy's job of grief management epitomizes the stultifying effects of a society that organizes emotion and sensation in order to dispose of them. She herself suffers from boredom that she has adopted as a defense against fear, an emotion she later defines as "intense self-awareness." Lyle, too, is cut off from human feeling, for his job is part of an elaborate organization that conceals its own viciousness. "There were rules, standards and customs" in the stock exchange that made it safe. In the abstract symbols of stocks and their values, "aggression was refined away, the instinct to possess.... A picture of the competitive mechanism of the world, of greasy teeth engaging on the rim of a wheel, was nowhere in evidence."

The media facilitate this contemporary dislocation of feeling, substituting sentimentality and illusion for genuine emotion. The movie in the opening chapter — a foreshadowing of the events to come — provides an example of what the narrator calls "the intimacy of distance," the voyeuristic thrill of seeing without being seen, of experiencing without participating. What Lyle says about the stock exchange's teleprinter slips, that they give him "an impression of reality disconnected from the resonance of its own senses," can be said of the television that holds him in its mesh effect for hours each night. And Pammy experiences "a near obliteration of self-awareness" — that is, of genuine fear — by watching a maudlin movie after Jack's self-immolation. Despite her awareness of the movie's artificiality and awfulness, she breaks down in tears, finding it easier to accept and manage grief when it is mediated, distanced, and depersonalized.

The media simultaneously promote the illusion of escape from the banality and boredom of contemporary life by dramatizing popular fantasies. The opening movie depicts "the glamour of revolutionary violence," its appeal to "the most docile soul," foreshadowing Lyle's attraction to the terrorist conspirators. Lyle, by joining the terrorists, acts out his fantasies, becoming a player in a film that is far more interesting than his real life. He tells Kinnear how sexy the life of a conspirator appears to "the true-blue businessman or professor," the "suggestion of a double life" a compelling antidote to a mundane existence. There is even a sense of mystery in a conspiracy that fulfills a human need that the banal organization of contemporary life denies. Marina Vilar sees the established power structure as a great conspiracy, a decentralized system of money that transcends materialism and mortality. Lyle eventually refers to it as "an occult theology of money." Conspiracy, whether of the establishment or the revolutionary, exists because even the most colorless life requires it.

Players received generally favorable reviews. John Leonard in *The New York Times* (11 August 1977) suggested that DeLillo "may be our wittiest writer" and praised his "prose style that amounts to incantation. It is full of stops and magic, an abrupt keening, here and there glissando, crazy syllogisms, rogue puns. It thumps, winks, foreshortens, slides." He further admired DeLillo's acute ear and eye for contemporary life that was evinced in the novel. Diane Johnson in *The New York Times Book Review* (4 September 1977) called *Players* an "elegant, highly finished novel" that succeeded in depicting "the whole state of things" that add up to contemporary experience. She too praised DeLillo's style, commenting that "the wit, elegance and economy of Don DeLillo's art are equal to the bitter clarity of his perceptions." A few reviewers, however, thought the novel's characters too thinly drawn. In *Newsweek* (29 August 1977), Margo Jefferson found them "far less interesting than their surroundings," and Zane Kotker in the *National Review* (28 October 1977) felt that "real people" were missing from the novel. "The players themselves don't compel me." Yet, he added, "DeLillo does compel."

DeLillo's subsequent novel, *Running Dog* (1978), is another spy thriller, the first of his novels to rework the subject matter and genre of one of its predecessors. Like *Players*, it too examines the dynamics and appeal of conspiracy as well as exploring DeLillo's recurrent themes of the power of images, commodification, and human organizing structures.

The novel contains several starkly drawn characters who have or soon come to have complex, often oblique relations with one another. Moll Robbins, a journalist for the radical magazine *Running Dog*, sets out to do a series of articles on "sex as big business." She visits the gallery of an erotic art dealer named Lightborne, where she is introduced to Glen Selvy, a buyer for an unidentified connoisseur of erotica. Selvy, like Kinnear in *Players*, turns out to be a double agent, working for U.S. senator Lloyd Percival as both administrative aide and erotic art buyer, but also for Radial Matrix, a covert branch of a government funding organization that is concerned about the senator's investigation of its practices and therefore uses Selvy to collect dirt on the senator. Radial Matrix, a "systems planning outfit," funds covert operations against foreign governments and political movements unfavorable to U.S. corporate interests. Its leader, the Vietnam veteran Earl Mudger, becomes interested – as does Lightborne, the twenty-two-year-old porn king Richie Armbrister, and the Mafia – in obtaining a film allegedly showing an orgy in Hitler's bunker during the Soviet siege of Berlin. Selvy becomes a target of Radial Matrix and flees west to Marathon Mines, Radial Matrix's former training camp in the Texas desert. He is pursued by two Vietnamese assassins, who eventually kill him. The film, when it is at last viewed in Lightborne's gallery, turns out to be a farce: Hitler as Charlie Chaplin entertaining a few adults and children in the bunker.

DeLillo told LeClair that in *Running Dog* evil acts and attitudes "float in a particular social and cultural medium. A modern American medium." Indeed, in depicting once again the postmodern organization of power, DeLillo presents a world in which good and evil are not fixed values, but negotiable, transferable qualities. Moreover, in this "age of conspiracy," as Moll characterizes the modern moment, power is neither absolute nor localized, but is decentralized, hidden, out-of-control. Radial Matrix, part of an ostensibly benign government agency, has become a breakaway network of conspiracies only tenuously controlled by Mudger. Armbrister and his illicit porn industry lie hidden behind dummy corporations and a self-spun web of paper. The Mafia floats in and out of the competition for the film. And Senator Percival's collection of erotica, which Moll originally feels is "strictly private, isolated from the schemes and intricacies," proves to be inextricable from them.

Yet despite this organization, this "cultural medium," the desire for a reductive, explainable order persists. Selvy, like Gary Harkness and the other football players in *End Zone*, craves limits, preferring life "narrowed down." As DeLillo explained to LeClair, Selvy leaves behind "whatever is difficult about life, whatever is complicated." He becomes a parody of the closed, linear paradigm – a paradigm that the "age of conspiracy" negates – imposing a strict routine upon himself as a means of constructing a self-contained world in which "things fit." But rather than shielding him from the inexplicable, from the greater web of conspiracy in which he becomes embroiled, his reductive yearnings impel him in a "straight line" to his ritual death and decapitation in the west Texas desert. As in *End Zone*, the mind-set of the closed system is shown to be ineffectual, even destructive, in the face of the new reality.

Lightborne tells Moll that "everybody's on camera," and the implications of this modern condition are profound. DeLillo uses the film of Hitler to explore once again the power of images, but also to expose the manipulated image of power. Hitler's parody of Charlie Chaplin reveals the dictator's

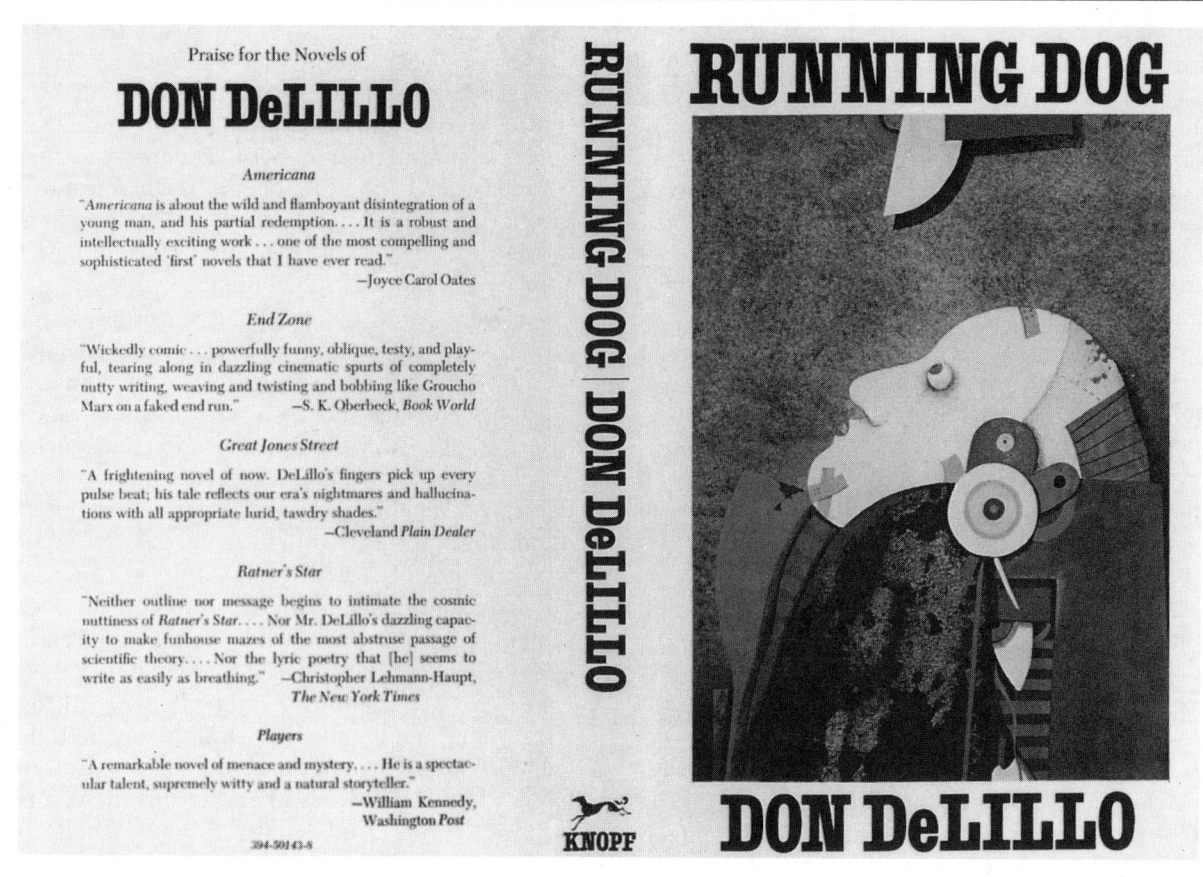

Dust jacket for DeLillo's second spy novel, about a network of conspiracies tied into the illicit pornography business

self-conscious awareness of how the projected image is a charade, a performance. "Film was essential to the Nazi era," declares Lightborne, a propaganda tool that organized "myth, dreams, memory" into a national consciousness. Fascism itself had an erotic appeal – power and sex entwined with all the Nazi paraphernalia of uniforms, leather, jackboots – and this combination of power and sex, captured in the marketable medium of film, turns the movie of an alleged Nazi orgy into a product as desirable as Bucky Wunderlick's "mountain tapes" were in *Great Jones Street*. It is "an object of ultimate desirability, and ultimate dread, simply because it connected to Hitler," DeLillo confided to DeCurtis, a commodity that reveals "the terrible acquisitiveness in which we live." And like Bucky, who had been described as a dictator, Hitler is compared to a "pop hero," a "modern rock 'n' roller," an icon who himself becomes a commodity. When the film is discovered to be merely a self-conscious parody, its marketability is deflated, and Lightborne can only lament: "Who do I sell this to?"

Most reviewers found that *Running Dog* fell short of DeLillo's best efforts, its deliberately austere form, language, and characterization limiting its overall effect. Michael Wood in *The New York Times Book Review* (12 November 1978) thought the novel "a very accurate reflection of a contemporary mood" – namely, the widespread indifference and apathy toward evil – but felt that such a subject proved too narrow and failed to address the complexity of the contemporary American scene. He also faulted the novel for its hackneyed characterizations. Tom LeClair in the *New Republic* (7 October 1978) agreed, calling the characters "as ordinary as dollar movies, prime-time television, and *People* magazine." He, too, considered *Running Dog* limited – "a stimulus-response machine, a transistorized potboiler" – and commented that DeLillo, in striving for starkness, left out "the qualities that make his other fiction so vital *and* lucid." An anonymous reviewer in *The New Yorker* (18 September 1978) praised *Running Dog* lightly, calling it "a romantic novel in the gritty, precisionist, enigmatic modern mode," with DeLillo "in full command of that limited form."

In the years immediately following, DeLillo wrote a two-act play, *The Engineer of Moonlight*

(1979), which has yet to be performed, and lived in Greece for three years researching and writing his seventh major novel, *The Names* (1982). Another examination of the American condition, *The Names* is a postmodern expatriate novel in which DeLillo moves his characters and concerns onto the international scene. It explores American attitudes toward, and interactions with, foreigners and vice versa, focusing on language as the structural underpinning of their divergent conceptions.

Returning to a first-person narrative for the first time since *Great Jones Street,* DeLillo divides the novel into four sections roughly based on four geographical locations: a Greek island, the Peloponnisos, India, and Kansas. James Axton, the narrator and protagonist, is an Athens-based risk analyst for an American company that insures multinational corporations against terrorist acts, a company with connections to the CIA. While visiting his estranged wife and their nine-year-old son, Tap, on a Greek island where his wife is working on an archaeological dig, he learns of a mysterious cult living there that is later suspected of bludgeoning an old man to death in a remote village. James and Owen Brademas, the chief archaeologist, begin a search for other cells of the cult in an attempt to understand their motivations. James and a filmmaker friend, Frank Volterra, pursue the cult on the Peloponnisos, encountering a deserter from The Names – as the cult is called – who confirms James's suspicion that the cult murders those whose initials match the initials of the town where the murder is committed. Owen finds another cell of the cult in the north India desert. Toward the end of the novel, James witnesses the shooting of one of his expatriate friends, an assassination attempt that may have been directed toward James by Greek nationalists. The novel concludes with a scene from Tap's biographical novel based on Owen's childhood in Kansas, a depiction of a revivalist meeting in which Owen, unlike the other revivalists, fails to speak in tongues.

As in *End Zone,* language is the subject as well as the medium in *The Names.* It is the fundamental ordering structure from which different cultures derive their different conceptions of reality. Owen calls language an expression of an "ordering instinct," the human need, perhaps most marked in Western man, to construct a safe, controllable world. The cult takes this instinct to its logical extreme. As Owen surmises, "they fear disorder," desiring a realm "safe from chaos and life." Indeed, the cult functions as the shadow of the Western businessmen and Western archaeologists who have a similar, if less extreme, need for order and control. Owen's comment that "I feel I'm safe from myself as long as there's an accidental pattern to observe in the physical world" – even if that pattern is projected and imposed by himself – points toward the cult's own motivations. In constructing an order, the cultists escape the chaos and madness of the isolated self. Yet the destructiveness of their imposed order, a destructiveness that the reader also witnesses in the dealings of the Western businessmen, does not remain hidden. Owen realizes after his encounter with the cult in northern India that their murders "mock our need to structure and classify, to build a system against the terror in our souls. They make the system equal to the terror."

Throughout the novel, we see Western interests imposing their language and system on foreign cultures in what amounts to postmodern imperialism. One of the expatriates even compares their activities to those of the British Empire of the nineteenth century, complete with "opportunity, adventure, sunsets, dusty death." Isolated in often hostile foreign countries, yet with business interests that give them power over the natives, the expatriates foster in themselves an attitude of arrogance and paranoia. James's "27 Depravities" – a list he composed for his Canadian former wife in which he presumed to identify those qualities of himself that she despised (the last being American) – acts as a metaphor for the expatriate attitude. And since the injurious effects of the Western business interests lie hidden, the expatriates are shielded from any feeling of responsibility. The Greek nationalist Andreas Eliades tells James that "Americans choose strategy over principle every time and yet keep believing in their own innocence."

Beyond the differences in language and power, the Americans stand out from the natives in their spiritual dispossession. As in all of DeLillo's novels, the Americans in *The Names* have lost their sense of spiritual mystery, existing in what Tap will describe in his novel as "the nightmare of real things, the fallen wonder of the world." Science, conspiracy, and decentralized power have replaced religion as sources of wonder, but without religion's transcendent force. Throughout the novel, there are numerous juxtapositions of the Americans who do business and the native populations whose reality is more spiritually centered. Owen, whose business of archaeology involves the scientific appropriation of religious artifacts, is obsessed by the power of religion in the Mideast, its sway over crowds. "Masses of people scare me," he says. "Religion. People driven by the same powerful emotion. All that reverence, awe and dread. I'm a boy from the prairie." Yet from Tap's novel we learn that the prairie of Owen's childhood was no wasteland, but rather bred a profound spiritualism not unlike that of the Middle East, complete with chanting crowds speaking an unintelligible language. As DeLillo told DeCurtis, speaking in tongues is "an alternate reality" – yet an alternative that Americans seem to have lost sight of in the latter twentieth century.

The Names was widely regarded as a departure for DeLillo, a movement away from the fantastic of his previous fiction and toward realism. Most reviewers found the transition a success, though a qualified one. Charles Champlin, in the *Los Angeles Times Book Review* (7 November 1982), was the most enthusiastic, calling the novel "exotic, atmospheric, curiously suspenseful, full of characters at once unusual and fully realized," its theme of contemporary Americans abroad "engrossing." He concluded with the hope that DeLillo "becomes a name for a wider audience to conjure with." Michael Wood in *The New York Times Book Review* (10 October 1982) also praised what he called this "powerful, haunting book, formidably intelligent and agile." Yet Wood also found the novel "a little blurred, its insights scattered rather than collected." Robert Towers, in his review in the *New Republic* (22 November 1982), emphasized the novel's departure from DeLillo's earlier work, citing the "precision and sensuous detail" of its setting. Towers, however, also considered the novel rather fuzzy – "only intermittently compelling as a story" – and condemned the cult as implausible. To him, DeLillo was a writer with "exceptional gifts," but one who had not yet "published a novel whose total impact is equal to the brilliance of its parts." Josh Rubins in the *New York Review of Books* (16 December 1982) likewise found *The Names* more realistic in detail than earlier efforts but similarly felt that the novel's plot was flawed, particularly the "blatantly implausible trail of cult murders." Nevertheless, he concluded by suggesting that DeLillo's new mode evinced in *The Names* intimated that "fantasy's loss could be realism's gain."

After completing *The Names* DeLillo began work on what would become his breakthrough novel, *White Noise* (1985). In 1983, however, he took time off from its composition to research and write an essay on the John Kennedy assassination, "American Blood: A Journey through the Labyrinth of Dallas and JFK," which was published in *Rolling Stone* in December of that year. He received his first major literary award in 1984, the Award in Literature from the American Academy and Institute of Arts and Letters.

But it was *White Noise* that would propel DeLillo into the literary spotlight and widen his audience. A darkly comic novel, *White Noise* focuses on a single American family in another attempt to probe the postmodern American experience. The narrator, Jack Gladney, is a professor of Hitler studies at the College-on-the-Hill in a small midwestern town. He, his wife, Babette, and their children from several different marriages lead an apparently contented life, though a life conditioned by the media and consumer culture that conceals a deeply felt fear of death. When a railroad accident causes toxic gases to be released into the local atmosphere – what the media euphemistically term the "Airborne Toxic Event" – Jack's fear is magnified. The family, along with most of the townspeople, flee the scene in what amounts to a hilarious parody of television-news disasters. After their return home Jack discovers that Babette has been taking a pill called Dylar, which turns out to be an experimental drug designed to assuage one's fear of death. Babette, Jack learns, had prostituted herself to the developer of this drug, Willie Mink, for her fear of death had been too great for her to bear. Jack, whose own fear reaches the breaking point after several traumatic trips to the doctor, seeks out Willie Mink in order to obtain the drug himself and, in another parody of television, to exact revenge on Mink for seducing his wife. He discovers Mink in a tawdry hotel room hopelessly addicted to his own drug, shoots him, and then in an act of human compassion carries him to the hospital. The novel ends with the family once more at peace with itself, however tenuously.

White noise – the sound of all audible radio frequencies heard simultaneously – is the central metaphor of the novel, linking its major themes. As information without meaning, white noise suggests, on one level, the media bombardment designed not to inform the public but to sell commercial products to it. Murray Jay Siskind, Jack's colleague at College-on-the-Hill, calls television "a primal force in the American home," and indeed it constitutes the focal point of the Gladney household. Babette is never more real to her family than when they see her on public-access television, a simulation composed of waves and radiation. In fact, the effect of television, its power to mediate experience, to make the representation replace the represented, manifests itself in nearly every aspect of the Gladneys' lives. Despite seeing the rain with his own eyes, Jack's son Heinrich argues that it cannot be raining because the weather report said it would not rain until that night. During the Airborne Toxic Event, the Gladney children experience symptoms of toxic

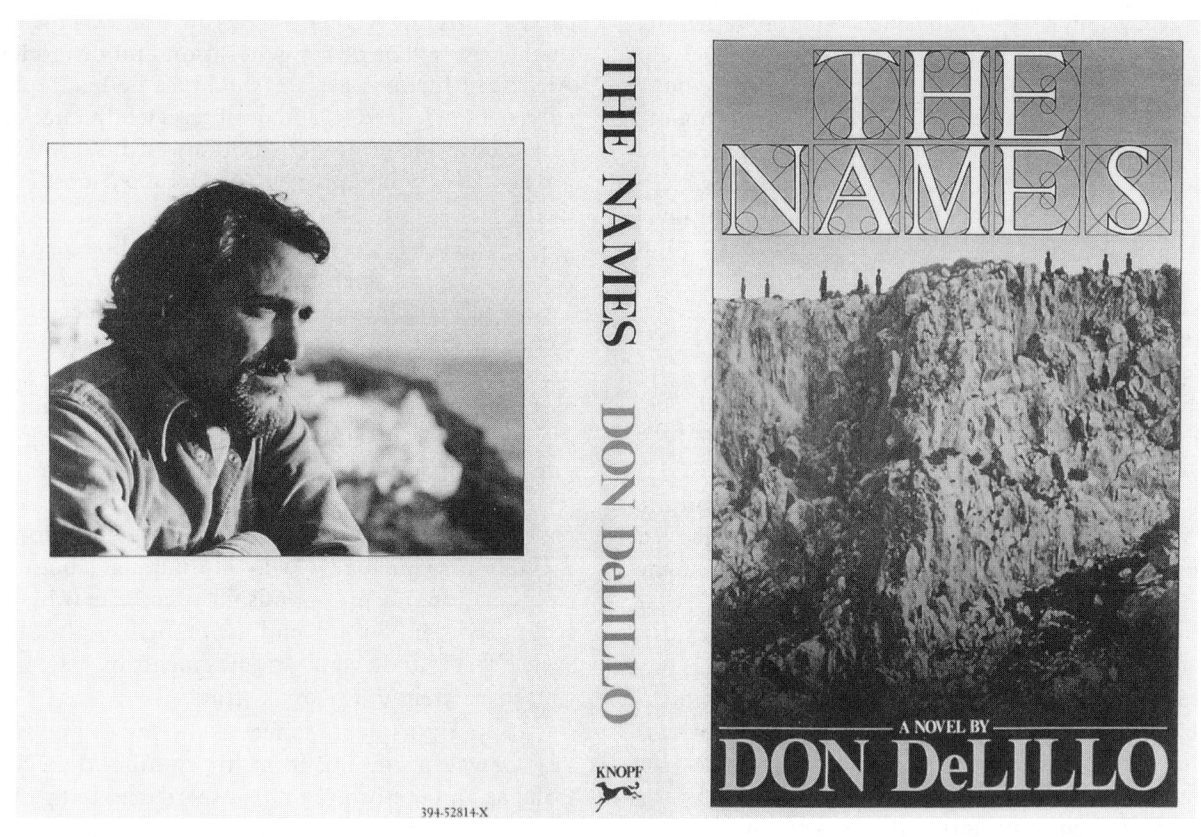

Dust jacket for DeLillo's novel about an American expatriate risk analyst tracking the activities of a murderous cult

exposure only after the media reveal what those symptoms might be. The family's conversations parrot the dialogue of television sitcoms and commercials, the family itself more a representation of television's representations of an American family than vice versa.

The Gladneys, however, are not alone, for the entire contemporary American culture has been removed from the direct apprehension of experience. America has become lost in what Jean Baudrillard has called simulacra, images that in their replication have lost their connection to the represented. A tourist attraction outside town, The Most Photographed Barn in America, draws people to it not for itself, but for the photographed images of it. "We're not here to capture an image," says Murray, but "to maintain one." A quaint American landscape has been replaced in the popular imagination by the image of a quaint American landscape.

One consequence of the mediated existence, of life removed from the direct apprehension of experience, is that life and death become abstractions. The Gladneys are fascinated by "media disaster," the floods, earthquakes, and accidents that make up the television news, but are nonplussed when they find themselves in the midst of one during the Airborne Toxic Event. "I don't see myself fleeing an airborne toxic event," Jack declares. "That's for people who live in mobile homes out in the scrubby parts of the county, where the fish hatcheries are." Death – the real thing as opposed to the media representation of it – elicits profound fear in the Gladneys, Jack describing death as a "white noise" that buzzes below the surface of his apparently placid existence. Murray informs Jack that his attraction to Hitler is a product of his fear. "Hitler is larger than death," he tells him. "You thought he would protect you." Like the German crowds that flocked to Hitler "to form a shield against their own dying," Jack feels, as DeLillo told DeCurtis, that "he can disappear inside ... the vastness, the monstrosity of Hitler himself." And Babette, of course, flees to a smaller-scale cult figure in Willie Mink – representative of so many contemporary charlatans and gurus – to mitigate her own fear.

Yet this highly artificial, mediated American culture is not without its spirituality, however twisted its expression. The Gladneys strive for transcendence through consumerism, experiencing a "fullness of being" after a trip to the supermarket. Murray equates the supermarket, a holy place where shopping has replaced death, with a Tibetan lamasery. Such "spiritualism" is of course ironic, yet DeLillo does not entirely dismiss it. DeLillo told DeCurtis that in *White Noise* he tried to depict a "radiance in dailiness . . . a sense of something extraordinary hovering just beyond our touch and just beyond our vision." It reveals itself in the oracular-sounding names of commercial products ("Toyota Celica," "Panasonic"), in the benediction bestowed by the automatic teller machine when it accepts Jack's request, and in the spectacular sunsets that are a by-product of the Airborne Toxic Event. The sunsets suggest a postmodern sublime, a vision of beauty that evokes awe in the beholder, a spiritual wonder at the power of nature and man.

White Noise was highly acclaimed and won the 1985 American Book Award for fiction. Richard Eder in the *Los Angeles Times Book Review* (13 January 1985) called *White Noise* a "stunning book" that adroitly captured the contemporary American mood. The novel, he declared, was "a moving picture of a disquiet we seem to share more and more." Eder even waxed poetic about DeLillo's talent: "The author is Charon as a master mariner; his flame, like Quevedo's, knows how to swim the icy water. He brings us across the Styx in a lilting maneuver that is so adept that we can't help laughing as we go." Jayne Anne Phillips in *The New York Times Book Review* (13 January 1985) also praised DeLillo's insight into the American psyche, calling *White Noise* "timely and frightening . . . because of its totally American concerns, its rendering of a particularly American numbness." She also found Jack Gladney's narrative voice "one of the most ironic, intelligent, grimly funny voices yet to comment on life in present-day America." Diane Johnson in the *New York Review of Books* (14 March 1985) agreed, citing Jack's "eloquence" as mitigating what might otherwise have been an overly "exacting and despairing view of civilization." Like many reviewers, Walter Clemons in *Newsweek* (21 January 1985) predicted that *White Noise* would gain DeLillo "wide recognition . . . as one of the best American novelists."

DeLillo's two-act play, *The Day Room*, premiered at the American Repertory Theater in April, 1986, then was performed at the Manhattan Theater Club in New York City and published in 1987. During this time, DeLillo was working on his ninth novel, *Libra*, a fictionalized account of the Kennedy assassination that he began in the fall of 1984 before *White Noise* was even published. Perhaps it would be more accurate, however, to say that DeLillo began composing *Libra* from the beginning of his literary career, since the Kennedy assassination was for him the central event of his generation and of modern American history, a watershed that he has repeatedly acknowledged as a major literary influence and to which he had alluded in many of his previous novels. *Libra* would prove to be DeLillo's most artistically successful work to date.

Libra is a historical novel only in the sense that *Ratner's Star* is a science fiction novel or *End Zone* a sports novel. DeLillo uses the historic fact of the Kennedy assassination to construct a new mode of historical fiction, one that undercuts the narrative assumptions and strategies of the genre and of historiography itself. Not interested in offering yet another conspiracy theory or in composing an objective historical re-creation, DeLillo aims, as he claims in his "Author's Note" at the conclusion of *Libra*, to provide a new "way of thinking" about the assassination. He propounds, in effect, a new historical paradigm. To this end, he embellishes and invents "facts" and events and fragments his narrative into three main interwoven strands.

The first strand concerns the life of Lee Harvey Oswald, jumping from his childhood in New Orleans and the Bronx to his experiences in the Marine Corps, his subsequent defection to the Soviet Union, his return to the United States with his Russian bride, their life together with their baby girl, his botched attempt in Dallas on the life of the rightwing Gen. Edwin Walker, his later involvement with and manipulation by Castro sympathizers, anti-Castro conspirators, and government agents, and finally his assassination, or attempted assassination, as DeLillo suggests, of President Kennedy in Dallas.

The second narrative strand involves the conspiracy against the president that is hatched by a group of disaffected former CIA operatives and veterans of the Bay of Pigs debacle. Frustrated with their exile from government espionage and angry at Kennedy for what they consider his failure to support the Bay of Pigs invasion adequately and for his subsequent movement toward rapprochement with Fidel Castro, these former spies plan to counterfeit an attempt on the president's life, leaving a paper trail that would point toward pro-Castro forces, thereby shocking the nation into invading Cuba and overthrowing Castro. The conspiracy, however, spins out of control and becomes a plot to succeed in killing the president, catching him in a crossfire between Cuban exiles on the infamous grassy knoll and Oswald in the sixth-floor window of the Texas School Book Depository.

The final strand focuses on Nicholas Branch, another former CIA man, who has been hired by the agency to write the "secret" history of the assassination. Branch sits alone in his room, surrounded by the accumulated data of the assassination, more of which accrues each day. Branch is at a loss to make sense of it all; he can neither find the original cause or causes of the event, nor reach the end. "Everything is here," he muses, yet it is all white noise, information without meaning. Branch comes to represent the futility of the traditional historiographer, the rationalist who tries to write an objective, chronological narrative of facts. In another twist on his leitmotiv of human ordering structures, DeLillo shows that such linear cohesion is impossible in the postmodern world. DeLillo told DeCurtis that, beginning with the John Kennedy assassination, Americans lost our "sense of a manageable reality," that we are now "much more aware of elements like randomness and ambiguity and chaos." Toward the end of the novel, Branch resigns himself to this new order, concluding that "the conspiracy against the President was a rambling affair that succeeded in the short term due mainly to chance." Given the warren of facts and theories, causes and coincidences that surrounds the assassination, DeLillo implies that only a new paradigm can shed light on it, and he offers *Libra,* as he confided to DeCurtis, as a new historical fiction that may be able "to provide a hint of order in the midst of all the randomness."

DeLillo also revisits his theme of the alienated individual, the outsider in contemporary American society. Branch is not the only character isolated in a "small room"; Oswald's life unfolds in a series of small rooms, as do those of the exiled former CIA operatives. Indeed, the conspiracy against Kennedy and Oswald's role in it seem to emerge from a common desire to escape isolation, to merge with history. DeLillo told DeCurtis that Oswald wanted to "be swept by history right out of the room. Out of the room and out of the *self*. To merge with history is to escape the self." In a letter from Oswald to his brother, which DeLillo uses as the epigraph to *Libra,* Oswald defines happiness as "taking part in the struggle, where there is no borderline between one's own personal world, and the world in general." Oswald, a self-described "zero in the system," tries to transcend his loneliness by giving it "a purpose and a destiny," a grand historic significance. Ultimately, he succeeds.

Libra embodies another of DeLillo's central concerns: the effect of the media, particularly television and film, on the contemporary American consciousness. In his interview with DeCurtis, DeLillo remarked:

> It's strange that the power of television was utilized to its fullest, perhaps for the first time, as it pertained to a violent event.... This has become part of our consciousness. We've developed almost a sense of performance as it applies to televised events. And I think some of the people who are essential to such events are simply carrying their performing selves out of the wings and into the theater. Such young men have a sense of the way in which their acts will be perceived by the rest of us, even as they commit the acts. So there is a deeply self-referential element in our lives that wasn't there before.

Indeed Oswald, whom DeLillo described to DeCurtis as "an actor in real life," is continually watching himself perform, imagining a historical audience for his actions and perceiving everything in relation to himself. Despite his contempt for American consumer culture, he is a product of the images that promote it. He conceives of himself at an early age as a hero in a spy-thriller movie – "Oswald-hero" – and later identifies with Frank Sinatra's character in *Suddenly* and John Garfield's character in *We Were Strangers,* two films about political assassination. His "Historic Diary," which he believes will be read by posterity for clues to himself, reads at times like a play complete with stage and musical directions and, during the scene in which he slashes his wrists, unintentionally parodies a Gillette commercial. Just before the assassination, he sees himself in everything, degenerating into self-referential paranoia in which "everything he heard and saw and read these days was really about him." He becomes, in other words, the hero of his own movie, a movie whose climax – the murder of the president – makes Oswald a star.

Libra became a best-seller and critical success. It won the Irish Times–Aer Lingus International Fiction Prize and was nominated for the American Book Award. In *The New York Times Book Review* (24 July 1988) Anne Tyler called *Libra* a "triumph," a "seamlessly written" novel that was also DeLillo's "richest" and "most complicated." She was especially impressed with DeLillo's rendering of character, his "uncanny perception" and "merciless ear for language" that enabled him to create believable interior voices. Walter Clemons, in *Newsweek* (15 August 1988), describing *Libra* as an "overwhelming" and "ambitious" novel, likewise praised DeLillo's ability in "inventing a convincing interior voice for each" of his characters. Clemons labeled DeLillo "a master of the inarticulate" for his command of the

Dust jacket for DeLillo's novel about a conspiracy to assassinate President John F. Kennedy

colloquial. Richard Eder, in the *Los Angeles Times Book Review* (31 July 1988), was also taken with the characters in this "chilling and penetrating" novel but found their historical basis limiting. In the *New York Review of Books* (18 August 1988) Robert Towers concurred, citing DeLillo's inability "to extricate [Oswald] from his life's record and to launch him as an autonomously functioning and convincing figure in fiction." Nevertheless, Towers lauded *Libra* as an "exceptionally interesting novel," asserting that "one is dazzled by the virtuosity of *Libra*'s construction, by the pungency and ellipses of the dialogue, and by the descriptive brilliance with which the low-life characters materialize before one's eyes." He even went so far as to claim that DeLillo had by now "supplanted both Pynchon and Mailer as chief shamans of the paranoid school of American fiction."

DeLillo began his tenth novel, *Mao II* (1991), in March 1989, shortly after the Ayatollah Khomeini condemned Salman Rushdie to death for blaspheming Islam in *The Satanic Verses* (1989), a threat to artistic freedom that would strongly affect DeLillo and influence his new novel. DeLillo, along with several other writers, read from Rushdie's work at the Columns in New York City in a show of support for Rushdie and freedom of speech that was organized by the Author's Guild, PEN American Center, and Article 19. DeLillo worked on *Mao II* for the next two years, during which time (April 1990) his short play *The Rapture of the Athlete Assumed into Heaven* (1990) was performed by the American Repertory Theater.

Mao II may be DeLillo's most personal novel, for it is his deepest meditation on the position of the writer in contemporary culture. The novel's protagonist, Bill Gray, is a reclusive novelist – not unlike DeLillo – who tries to maintain his individual voice and power within a culture that no longer values individuality or art. Having published two highly regarded novels early in his career, Gray has been struggling ever since with his third, unable to complete it. He lives in a rural hideout in upstate New York with his acolyte Scott Martineau and Scott's girlfriend, the former Moonie Karen Janney. In an effort to free himself from the cult figure he has become since his self-imposed exile, Gray invites Brita Nilsson, a photographer of writers, to his retreat to photograph him. His former editor then enlists him to help free a Swiss poet who has been taken hostage by a terrorist group in Beirut. Gray travels to London to make a public appearance announcing the release of the hostage, but a terrorist bomb prevents the event. He then decides to meet in person with the terrorist leader, Abu Rashid. On the ferry to Beirut, however, he dies from injuries received when he was hit by a car in Athens. The novel ends with Brita in Beirut, having abandoned writers in favor of photographing the new shapers of consciousness, terrorists.

The opening scene of *Mao II* – a mass wedding of thirteen hundred followers of the Reverend Sun Myung Moon in Yankee Stadium – acts as a thematic prologue to the novel. The parents of Karen Janney, one of the brides whose groom was chosen for her by Reverend Moon from a photograph, try to find her in the crowd in order to take her picture. During the ceremony, youths from the slums of the south Bronx race through the upper deck exploding cherry bombs. In this set piece, DeLillo introduces his central themes: the absorption of the individual by the crowd and mass consciousness, the rise of terrorism as a cultural force, and the power of the image.

DeLillo presents an America in which people are bombarded by the media and baffled by experience. As Scott remarks, the news creates "an unremitting mood of catastrophe," turning people inward in fear and breeding the desire to "lose themselves in something larger" – that is, to escape their loneliness and helplessness by surrendering the self to the mass. "They all feel the same," comments the narrator about the participants in the mass wedding, "immunized against the language of self." And emerging to channel and control this pervasive need to transcend the self are a few adept manipulators: religious leaders like Reverend Moon, political leaders like Mao Tse-tung, the Ayatollah Khomeini, and the terrorist Abu Rashid. The media, too, function as manipulators of the masses, foisting pop icons and a common consumer identity on people. "The future," the narrator asserts ominously, "belongs to crowds."

The novelist, DeLillo suggests, resists the push toward conformity and mass consciousness and is therefore dangerous. As DeLillo told Nora Kerr, the novelist tries "to extend the self" rather than subsume it. "It's our way of replying to power and beating back our fear by extending the pitch of consciousness and human possibility." Bill Gray, DeLillo's alter ego in *Mao II*, conceives of himself as "one voice unlike the next" and sees the kidnapping of the Swiss poet as an attempt to silence the artist's uniqueness. Yet even as he raises his voice he knows it is becoming less and less audible, drowned out by media noise and terrorist incursions into the novelist's domain. DeLillo remarked to Kerr that "news of political terror was beginning to move into a narrative that used to be the stronghold of the novelist," and Gray echoes this view when he avers that "novelists and terrorists are playing a zero-sum game. What terrorists gain, novelists lose. The degree to which they influence mass consciousness is the extent of our decline as shapers of sensibility and thought."

The photographic image has always been a concern of DeLillo's, and he continues to explore its power in *Mao II*. Gray tells Brita that "in our world we sleep and eat the image and pray to it and wear it too." Its replication alters people and reality, turning them into "someone's material" that can be exploited. While being photographed, Gray laments that he is becoming a "consumer event." Indeed, like Bucky Wunderlick in *Great Jones Street,* Gray has already become a product, his reclusiveness creating an aura, an anti-image, that boosts sales of his books while reducing their cultural impact. Of course, the epitome of the artist as celebrity and as harmless purveyor of images is Andy Warhol, from whose silk screens of Mao Tse-tung DeLillo appropriated his novel's title. Warhol's work is described as "a maximum statement about the dissolvability of the artist and the exaltation of the public figure" – the artist, in other words, as an apparatus of the consumer culture and the public man as his marketable commodity.

But artists and the media are not the only image mongers. Just as Hitler was depicted as a master manipulator of images in *Running Dog*, so too are the terrorists in *Mao II*. They take the Swiss poet hostage for publicity and stage his release as a media event – an event to which the publishing industry readily assents as a means of selling books. In Beirut, "the streets run with images" of rival terrorist leaders, *Rambo* movies, and American products. The warring factions have taken to shooting the images of their rivals in what has become a war of images. And Abu Rashid succeeds in recruiting young men by giving them an "identity" – namely, his image which they pin to their shirts while they hide their own faces under black hoods.

Mao II won the PEN/Faulkner Award and was generally praised by critics, though many thought DeLillo was a bit too close to his material. Michiko Kakutani, in *The New York Times* (28 May 1991), wrote that "the book succeeds in re-orchestrating all of Mr. DeLillo's favorite themes with new authority and precision." She found the writing "dazzling" and the images "so radioactive that they glow afterward in our minds." Yet she complained of "patches of authorial pontification in the dialogue, and an overly schematic plot." Lorrie Moore, in *The New York Times Book Review* (9 June 1991), echoed that

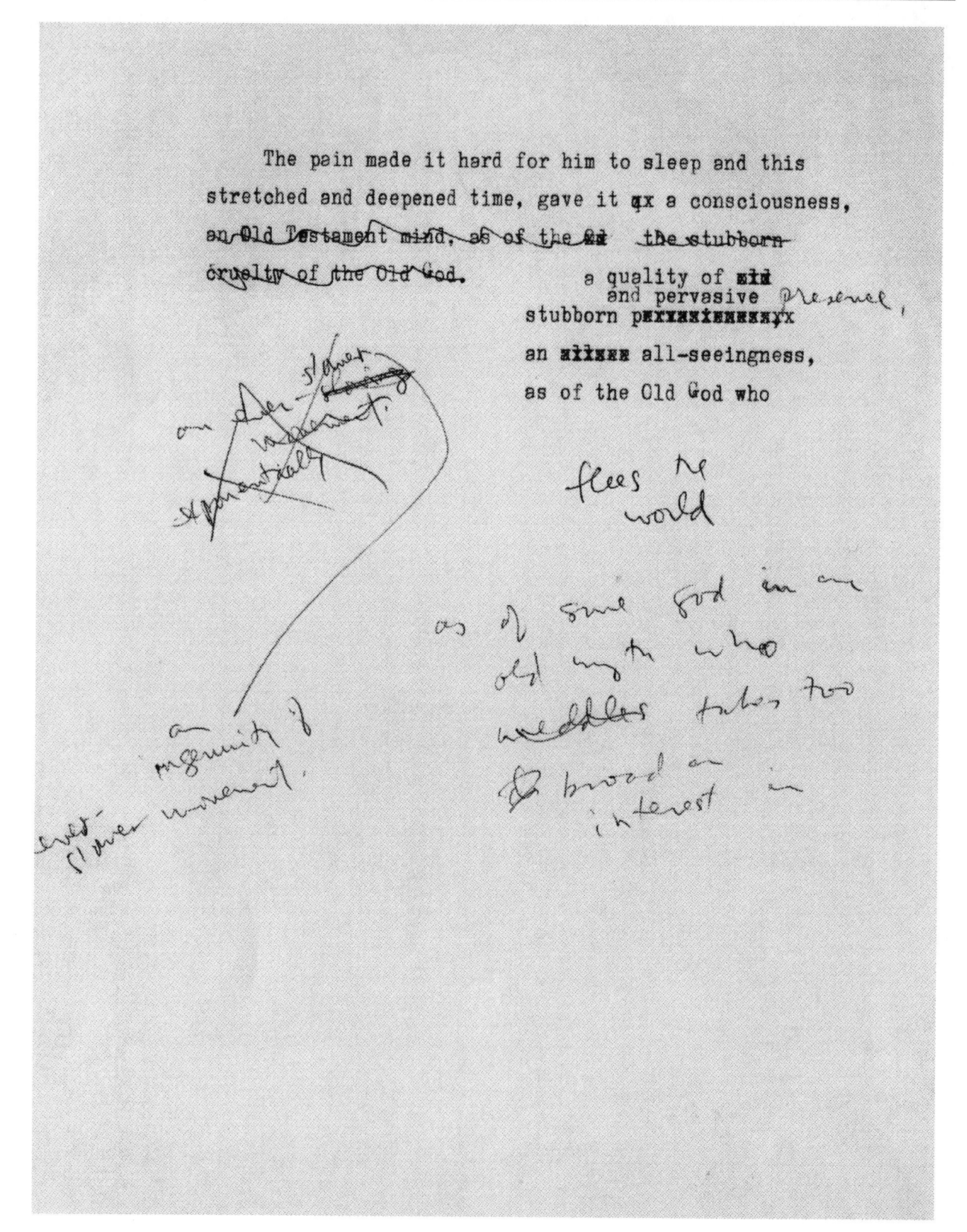

The pain made it hard for him to sleep and this
stretched and deepened time, gave it ~~qx~~ a consciousness,
~~an Old Testament mind, as of the ~~ the stubborn~~
~~cruelty of the Old God.~~   a quality of ~~xxx~~
                              and pervasive presence,
                stubborn ~~pxxxxxxxxxxxx~~
                an ~~xxxxxx~~ all-seeingness,
                as of the Old God who

flees the
world

as of some god in an
old myth who
meddles takes too
broad an
interest in

Pages from the first draft for Mao II *(courtesy of Don DeLillo)*

"I have my hypnotist tonight. It's my last try at giving up the

"I have my yoga tonight.
"Don't leave us alone," Bill said. "We need a referee."
"I have my

"I thought writers have discipline."
"Army ants have discipline.

"I have my hypnotist tonight. It's my last try
     taking
~~im at gettingxdown~~ off some pounds."
"I tell her try not eating," Liz said.
"Well I tried

*I could never do that, sit down day after day after day."
"Army ants have discipline."*

complaint, commenting that at times "Mr. DeLillo makes his characters name and sing all his tunes for him, speaking in dazzling chunks of authorial essay that read as if they had been created by someone who no longer cared — or perhaps no longer knew — how people really spoke." She concluded, however, by asserting that "Mr. DeLillo's new book succeeds as brilliantly as any of his others." Richard Eder, in the *Los Angeles Times Book Review* (9 June 1991), concurred, calling *Mao II* "winged and agile" but perhaps too "confessional." And in *The New Yorker* (24 June 1991), Louis Menand lamented that "it sometimes seems as though his characters have simply become mouthpieces for authorial meditations."

Five years have elapsed since the publication of *Mao II*, the longest hiatus between novels since DeLillo began his career with *Americana* in 1971. But by any standards, DeLillo has been an extraordinarily prolific writer, one whose work has grown in complexity and originality over three decades. He has shown no sign of artistic decline, and there is every reason to expect more work from this provocative and compelling American novelist.

Interviews:

Robert R. Harris, "A Talk with Don DeLillo," *New York Times Book Review*, 10 October 1982, p. 26;

Tom LeClair, "An Interview with Don DeLillo," in *Anything Can Happen: Interviews with Contemporary American Novelists*, edited by LeClair and Larry McCaffery (Urbana: University of Illinois Press, 1983), pp. 79-90;

Charles Champlin, "The Heart Is a Lonely Craftsman," *Los Angeles Times*, 29 July 1984, p. 7;

Caryn James, " 'I Never Set Out to Write an Apocalyptic Novel,' " *New York Times Book Review*, 13 January 1985, p. 31;

William Goldstein, "Don DeLillo," *Publisher's Weekly* (19 August 1988): 55-56;

Anthony DeCurtis, " 'An Outsider in This Society': An Interview with Don DeLillo," *South Atlantic Quarterly*, 89 (Spring 1990): 281-304;

Vince Passaro, "Dangerous Don DeLillo," *New York Times Magazine*, 19 May 1991, pp. 34, 36, 38, 76, 77;

Nora Kerr, " 'I Take the Language Apart,' " *New York Times Book Review*, 9 June 1991, p. 7.

Bibliographies:

James Dean Young, "A Don DeLillo Checklist," *Critique*, 20 (1978): 25-26;

Paula Bryant, "Don DeLillo: An Annotated Biographical and Critical Secondary Bibliography, 1977-1986," *Bulletin of Bibliography*, 45 (September 1988): 208-212.

References:

Paul Civello, *American Literary Naturalism and Its Twentieth-Century Transformations: Frank Norris, Ernest Hemingway, Don DeLillo* (Athens: University of Georgia Press, 1994);

Civello, "Undoing the Naturalistic Novel: Don DeLillo's *Libra*," *Arizona Quarterly*, 48 (Summer 1992): 33-56;

Douglas Keesey, *Don DeLillo* (New York: Twayne, 1993);

Tom LeClair, *In the Loop: Don DeLillo and the Systems Novel* (Urbana: University of Illinois Press, 1987);

Frank Lentricchia, ed., *Introducing Don DeLillo* (Durham: Duke University Press, 1991);

Lentricchia, ed., *New Essays on "White Noise"* (New York: Cambridge University Press, 1991);

Robert Nadeau, *Readings from the New Book on Nature: Physics and Metaphysics in the Modern Novel* (Amherst: University of Massachusetts Press, 1981).

Joan Didion
(5 December 1934 -)

Mark Royden Winchell
Clemson University

See also the Didion entries in *DLB 2: American Novelists Since World War II* [first series]; *DLB Yearbook: 1981;* and *DLB Yearbook: 1986.*

BOOKS: *Run River* (New York: Ivan Obolensky, 1963; London: Cape, 1964);
Slouching Towards Bethlehem (New York: Farrar, Straus & Giroux, 1968; London: Deutsch, 1969);
Play It as It Lays (New York: Farrar, Straus & Giroux, 1970; London: Wiedenfeld & Nicolson, 1971);
A Book of Common Prayer (New York: Simon & Schuster, 1977; London: Wiedenfeld & Nicolson, 1977);
Telling Stories (Berkeley, Cal.: Friends of the Bancroft Library, 1978);
The White Album (New York: Simon & Schuster, 1979);
Salvador (New York: Simon & Schuster, 1983);
Democracy (New York: Simon & Schuster, 1984);
Miami (New York: Simon & Schuster, 1987);
After Henry (New York: Simon & Schuster, 1992);
The Last Thing He Wanted (New York: Knopf, 1996).

MOTION PICTURES: *The Panic in Needle Park,* screenplay by Didion and John Gregory Dunne, Twentieth Century-Fox, 1971;
Play It as It Lays, screenplay by Didion and Dunne, Universal, 1972;
A Star Is Born, screenplay by Didion, Dunne, and Frank Pierson, Warner Bros., 1976;
True Confessions, screenplay by Didion and Dunne, United Artists, 1981;
Hills Like White Elephants, screenplay by Didion and Dunne, HBO, 1991;
Broken Trust, screenplay by Didion and Dunne, Turner, 1995;
Up Close and Personal, screenplay by Didion and Dunne, Touchstone, 1996.

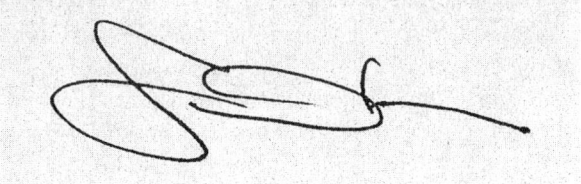

SELECTED PERIODICAL PUBLICATIONS – UNCOLLECTED: "Why I Write," *New York Times Book Review,* 5 December 1976, pp. 2, 98–99;

"Making Up Stories," *Michigan Quarterly Review*, 18 (Fall 1979): 521–534.

Ever since she first appeared on the literary scene in the early 1960s, Joan Didion has been identified as a California writer. Although her heart belongs to the provincial Sacramento of her girlhood, her best-known essays and novels are set in the contemporary Sun Belt. She has been variously described as "a fantastically brilliant writer" and an "entrepreneur of anxiety." Her admirers have compared her to T. S. Eliot and Nathanael West. However, neoconservative critic Joseph Epstein has dismissed her as a purveyor of "freeway existentialism," and one disgruntled feminist has characterized her as "a curious creature, whose sense of literature and life is common, disappointingly conventional, and always problematical." James Dickey has called her "the finest woman prose stylist writing in English today."

Joan Didion was born in Sacramento, California, on 5 December 1934, the daughter of Frank Reese and Eduene Jerrett Didion. As Katherine Usher Henderson points out, neither Didion's parents nor her brother, Jimmy, plays a prominent role in her autobiographical writing. Of much greater importance is the northern California setting itself. Didion's great-great-great-grandmother Nancy Hardin Cornwall came west on a wagon train in 1846, traveling most of the way with the Donner-Reed Party, only to cut north to Oregon before her companions made their way into history by eating their dead. Didion seems to carry the heritage of the frontier in her genes and with it a sense of life's contingency.

After being rejected for admission to Stanford University, Didion enrolled at the University of California at Berkeley in February 1953. In her senior year she published her first short story, "Sunset," in a student literary magazine called *Occident*. That same year, she won *Vogue*'s Prix de Paris Award and, with it, a job on the magazine. She lived for the next eight years in New York writing for *National Review* and *Mademoiselle*, as well as for *Vogue* itself. Also during those years she appeared for three consecutive nights on a television quiz show called *Crosswits*, published her first novel, and married the writer John Gregory Dunne. Curiously these biographical details are either ignored or mentioned only elliptically in "Goodbye to All That," the final selection in Didion's *Slouching Towards Bethlehem* (1968) and her definitive essay on her years in New York. Instead of presenting hard facts, she dredges her emotional memory to describe her complex relationship with this enchanted city of the East.

"Goodbye to All That" (the title apparently borrowed from Robert Graves's autobiography) is divided into four sections, indicated by double-line breaks, which correspond to different stages of the author's life in New York. At first, she is the ingenuous young Sacramento girl who spent her first three days in the big city wrapped in blankets in a hotel room air-conditioned to thirty-five degrees as she "tried to get over a bad cold and a high fever." She did not call a doctor because she knew no doctors in New York; nor did she call anyone to turn down the air conditioner because she did not know how much to tip whoever might come. "Was anyone ever that young?" she asks. "I am here to tell you that someone was." According to Didion, youth is not just a time of life but a state of delusion – the delusion that the emotional costs we incur in life can be indefinitely deferred. When those costs began coming due for her, her youth was over.

The process of disillusionment came only gradually to Didion. During her early years in New York, she was still able to give glib advice to a depressed friend, never realizing that she would eventually suffer his illness. Throughout the second section of her essay (after the initial naiveté has worn off), we see Didion living in New York as if she has been transported into a magic kingdom. In the third section she is simply *living* there – staying up all night (the hint of insomnia is telling), going to work on two or three hours' sleep, moving from one meagerly furnished apartment to another, and breaking ties with old friends. By the fourth section she seems on the verge of a nervous breakdown, disabused of her youthful fantasies and unable to function in the workaday world. Fortunately, she marries a kindly man who does not insist on her cooking dinner.

In June 1964 Didion and Dunne moved from New York to California. Despite a lean first year in which they made $7,000 between them, Didion and Dunne began to establish themselves as accomplished freelance journalists. Their film credits include *The Panic in Needle Park* (1971); the 1976 remake of *A Star Is Born*, on which they made a small fortune although they left the picture before it was completed; and the film versions of two novels – her *Play It as It Lays* (1970) and his *True Confessions* (1981). A third member was added to the Dunne family in 1966, when John and Joan adopted an infant daughter they named Quintana Roo.

During the 1960s Didion devoted much of her literary energy to journalism. In 1968 her collection of magazine pieces titled *Slouching Towards Bethlehem* established her reputation as one of the foremost practitioners of the New Journalism. Another highly regarded volume of essays – *The White Album* – appeared in 1979. By then Didion's second and third novels – *Play It as It Lays* and *A Book of Common Prayer* (1977) – had advanced her to the front rank of contemporary American writers. During the 1980s she produced two full-length nonfiction books – *Salvador* (1983) and *Miami* (1987) – and a fourth novel, *Democracy* (1984). Her third collection of essays, *After Henry*, was published in 1992, and her fifth novel, *The Last Thing He Wanted*, appeared in 1996.

In a lecture delivered at the University of Michigan in 1979, Didion articulated many of her long-standing views on the writing process. She pointed out, for example, that even autobiographical writers edit for coherence. The most obvious example is telling someone a dream. "[W]e interpret the dream as well," she says, "and filter out those details which seem to lead nowhere. We think of our dream as stories, but they are not, at least until we tell them."

What frequently distinguishes professional writers from amateur storytellers is their tendency to "think of their work as a collection of objects." Whether one is dealing with a novel, a story, or an essay, "every piece of work has its own shape, its own texture, its own specific gravity." In order to illustrate the distinctiveness of the writer's perspective, Didion cites an "amiable argument" she had with some members of the Berkeley English department about the merits of F. Scott Fitzgerald's unfinished novel, *The Last Tycoon* (1941). Although she could not disagree with any of the technical objections her academic friends raised to the book, Didion persisted in thinking of *The Last Tycoon* as "a brilliant piece of work." Then she realized what the argument was about:

> They were looking at *The Last Tycoon* not as a fragment of a novel in progress but as the first third of a novel for which we were simply missing the last two-thirds. In other words they saw that first third as completed, frozen, closed – the interrupted execution of a fully articulated plan on Fitzgerald's part – and I saw it as something fluid, something that would change as he discovered where the book was taking him.
> ....
> They saw the writer as someone with a story to tell who writes it down.
> I saw the writer as someone who discovers the story only in the act of making it up.

In an earlier essay on the creative process, "Why I Write," Didion describes writing as "the act of saying *I*, of imposing oneself on other people, of saying *listen to me, see it my way, change your mind.*" Even the essay's title, which she admits to having "stolen" from George Orwell, is verbally suggestive. The vowel sound in all three words of the title, Didion points out, is that of the first-person singular pronoun. It is therefore appropriate that she illustrate her theories about the process of composition by recounting the circumstances that led to her own vocation as a writer.

Because of her failure to take a course in John Milton, Didion had trouble graduating from Berkeley. When the English department finally agreed to give her a degree by the end of the summer if she would come down from Sacramento every Friday to talk about the cosmology of *Paradise Lost*, she sometimes took the Greyhound bus to campus and at other times caught the Southern Pacific's *City of San Francisco* train on the last leg of its transcontinental run. But today she readily admits:

> I can no longer tell you whether Milton put the sun or the earth at the center of his universe in *Paradise Lost*, the central question of at least one century and a topic about which I wrote 10,000 words that summer, but I can recall the exact rancidity of the butter in the City of San Francisco's dining car, and the way the tinted windows on the Greyhound bus cast the oil refineries around Carquinez Straits into a grayed and obscurely sinister light. In short my attention was always on the periphery, on what I could see and taste and touch, on the butter, and the Greyhound bus.

During those undergraduate years, Didion came to realize that she was not meant to be a scholar. Only years later was she able to discover what she was meant to be – "Which was a writer."

Didion's first novel, *Run River* (1963), tells of the twenty-year marriage of Everett and Lily Knight McClellan. Both children of prosperous Sacramento Valley ranchers, Everett and Lily begin their life together by eloping to Reno. Shortly after their wedding and the birth of their two children, they are separated as Everett goes off to the service during World War II. Feeling lonely and betrayed, Lily has an affair with a neighboring rancher and conceives his child. Having been given a hardship discharge because of the death of his father, Everett comes home from the war and is unable to cope with his wife's confession of infidelity. Lily slips away to San Francisco to have an abortion. In the remaining years of their marriage, she and Everett live lives of mutual recrimination.

Dust jacket for Didion's second novel, written as a " 'white' book to which the reader would have to bring his or her own bad dreams"

As the McClellans' marriage disintegrates, the novel's focus widens to include the relationship of Everett's sister, Martha, with a charming social climber named Ryder Channing. After five years of enjoying steady company and frequent sexual intimacies with Martha, Ryder abruptly marries a young socialite. Unable to put her life back together, Martha takes a boat out one stormy night and drowns. At Everett's insistence, she is buried on the ranch. As the years go by, Everett and Lily grow farther apart, and Lily herself takes up with Ryder Channing.

The novel opens as Ryder, who has been awaiting an assignation with Lily on the levee of the McClellan ranch, is shot by Everett. Then time flashes back, providing the reader with a retrospective view of the preceding two decades, 1938–1959. When the action returns to time present, Everett and Lily are anticipating the arrival of the sheriff. Lily remains in the house as Everett returns to the murder scene. A second shot is heard, and Lily realizes that Everett McClellan has taken his own life.

The beginning and end of Didion's novel have the makings of tabloid melodrama ("IRATE HUSBAND SHOOTS RIVAL, SELF"). However, the intervening chapters provide a picture of personal and cultural disintegration of sufficient complexity to raise melodrama to the level of tragedy.

Although *Run River* is not in a narrow and provincial sense *about* California, it belongs to a particular time and place as surely as the writings of William Faulkner and Tennessee Williams do. The novel depicts the social fragmentation of California that results from the dashed dreams of people drawn to the state by its promise of prosperity. Everett and Martha suffer the sort of melodramatic death that creates more problems than it solves for those who are left behind. Lily, however, survives with a stoic resignation and a renewed commitment to the distinctly unpromising role of mother. In a concluding meditation on the westward movement, she comes to see the folly of seeking an El Dorado that will always be just out of reach. What is finally ennobling about Lily's western experience, Didion seems to be saying, is not the dream that gave it birth, but the life force that enables her to survive the failure of that dream.

Didion's abiding fondness for rural Sacramento is evident in much of her autobiographical writing as well as in *Run River*. Upon reading her first collection of essays, Alfred Kazin wrote, "The story between the lines of *Slouching Towards Bethlehem* is surely not so much 'California' as it is her ability to make us share her passionate sense of it." Nevertheless, Didion is no purveyor of facile nostalgia. The prevalent tone in her prose, even at its most elegiac, is one of irony. In a way, Didion is to the upper middle class of the Central Valley what Faulkner was to the Sartorises and Compsons of Mississippi – a chronicler of social change. Nowhere in *Slouching Towards Bethlehem* is this more evident than in her memoir "Notes from a Native Daughter."

After contrasting the region of her childhood and adolescence with what she regards as the suburban wasteland it has become, Didion writes: "All that is constant about the California of my childhood is the rate at which it disappears." The essay concludes with what Didion calls a "Sacramento story." It is about a rancher who once lived outside of town on a spread of six or seven thousand acres. His one daughter went abroad and married a titled foreigner, whom she brought home to live on the ranch. Her father built them a large house that included a music room, a conservatory, and a ballroom. The newlyweds started giving "house par-

"I can't seem to tell what you do get the real points for," Charlotte said. ~~"I mean I seem to miss getting them."~~

~~"So what."~~ "So I guess I'll stick around here a while."

And when his plane was cleared to leave she had walked out to the gate with him and he had said again <u>don't you want to see Marin</u> and she had said <u>I don't have to see Marin because I have Marin in my mind and Marin has me in her mind</u> and they closed the gate and that was the last time Leonard Douglas ever saw Charlotte alive. ~~The last time I ever saw Charlotte was the night two weeks later when she pinned the gardenia on my dress and dabbed the Gres perfume on my wrists like a child helping her mother dress for a party.~~

VICKY: — SPACE BREAK —

¶ The last time I ever saw Charlotte alive was the night two weeks later when I left for New Orleans.

¶ When she pinned her gardenia on my dress.

¶ When she dabbed her Gres perfume on my wrists.

¶ Like a child helping her mother dress for a party.

Page from a draft for A Book of Common Prayer *(courtesy of Joan Didion)* ties that lasted for weeks and involved special trains." These people are now long dead, but an old man – the son of the rancher's daughter and her husband – still lives on the place. That in itself is unremarkable, except that he does not live in the house: it burned over the years, room by room and wing by wing. Now "only the chimneys of the great house are still standing, and its heir lives in their shadow, lives by himself on the charred site, in a house trailer." The last sentence summarizes a dramatic story of the passing of the old order.

Some of Didion's best nonfiction writing is intensely personal even when its ostensible subject is somebody else. By the time she wrote "John Wayne: A Love Song," another essay from *Slouching Towards Bethlehem,* in the early 1960s, John Wayne had become so much a part of our collective national consciousness that Didion was able to move easily between the first-person-singular and the first-person-plural in describing her feelings about him. This "love song" is structured symmetrically; it begins with a discussion of Didion's childhood infatuation with Wayne, proceeds to a camera-eye view of the Duke filming his 165th movie, and concludes by describing a dinner engagement that includes Wayne, an adult Didion, and their respective spouses.

In addition to her gift for the personal essay, Didion is a keen observer of the world around her. For example, she is completely absent from "Some Dreamers of the Golden Dream," one of the best essays in *Slouching Towards Bethlehem*. In this narrative Didion tells the story of Lucille Marie Maxwell Miller, a housewife from San Bernardino County, California, who is tried and convicted of burning her husband to death while he slept in the backseat of their Volkswagen. Didion structures her story thematically rather than chronologically. At the outset she describes the southern California setting and reports the basic circumstances of Lucille's husband's death and her incarceration. Only then does the author provide the details of Lucille Miller's background and the events on the night of her husband's death. Afterward, Didion relates the prosecution's case as the district attorney argues that Lucille drugged her husband and set their car on fire in order to collect his insurance money. He also reveals that Lucille had been having an extramarital affair with one of her neighbors.

By distancing herself from her material, Didion avoids melodrama. Like so many other New Journalists, Didion gives her story the coherence of art by employing what borders on an omniscient point of view. Her omniscience, however, does not take the form of sympathetic identification with her characters (as in John Hersey's *Hiroshima* [1946], Truman Capote's *In Cold Blood* [1965], and Norman Mailer's *The Executioner's Song* [1979]) but is manifest in a series of dogmatic pronouncements that reflects aristocratic disdain for her characters.

The title piece of *Slouching Towards Bethlehem* is one of Joan Didion's most famous journalistic efforts. A vivid and powerful description of life in the Haight-Ashbury section of San Francisco, the essay raises broader questions about the cultural matrix from which Haight-Ashbury was spawned. Didion begins by describing American culture in the mid 1960s in terms resembling William Butler Yeats's prophetic poem "The Second Coming" (from which she derives her title): in this culture, where the center was not holding, "adolescents drifted from city to torn city, sloughing off both the past and the future as snakes shed their skins, children who were never taught and would never now learn the games that had held society together." Most of the rest of *Slouching Towards Bethlehem* consists of a montage of short, fragmented scenes. For the most part, her story is told in short paragraphs, with frequent shifts in scene and little overt narrative transition. Thus, the reading experience itself conveys a sense of fragmentation. However, the general consistency of ambience and mood and Didion's own artistic control are so skillfully managed that these fragments form a larger mosaic.

While Didion was establishing her reputation as a journalist, she was rapidly losing confidence in her ability to write fiction. The year after *Run River* was published, she recalls, "I sat in front of my typewriter and believed that another subject would never present itself. I believed that I would be forever dry. I believed that I would 'forget how.' Accordingly, as a kind of desperate finger exercise, I tried writing stories." She wrote three stories that year and, except for classroom exercises while an undergraduate at Berkeley, none in any other year. By the late 1960s, "Coming Home" had been published in the *Saturday Evening Post* (July 1964), "The Welfare Island Ferry" in *Harper's Bazaar* (June 1965), and "When Did Music Come This Way? Children Dear, Was It Yesterday?" in the *Denver Quarterly* (Winter 1967). In 1978 Didion collected all three stories, along with an introductory essay, in the limited-edition volume *Telling Stories*.

Profiting artistically from her brief foray into short fiction, Didion published her second novel – *Play It as It Lays,* in 1970. Didion has said that her technical intention was to write "a book in which anything that happened would happen off the page, a 'white' book to which the reader would have to bring his or her own bad dreams." She accomplishes this goal by dividing her 214-page book into eighty-seven short chapters (some as short as a single paragraph).

Play It as It Lays tells the story of a young, third-rate film actress named Maria Wyeth. When Maria is introduced, she is in a mental hospital remembering the events of the novel. A native of Silver Wells, Nevada (a former mining community that is now the site of a nuclear test range), Maria is separated from her obnoxiously cruel husband, Carter Lang, and from her brain-damaged daughter, Kate. Although Maria feels genuine maternal love for Kate, the child's condition makes it nearly impossible for that love to be reciprocated. When Maria once again becomes pregnant (probably not by her husband), Carter pressures her into having an abortion by threatening that he will otherwise prevent her from seeing the institutionalized Kate. Following her abortion and lesser traumas, Maria finds herself in bed with Carter's producer, BZ. The purpose, however, is not love but death. BZ, who is a homosexual and thus not erotically interested in Maria, swallows a handful of Seconal and dies in Maria's comforting arms.

Unlike BZ, Maria is averse to examining life, philosophically or otherwise. She tells us that she keeps on living because she hopes someday to get Kate back and go someplace where they can live simply. Maria will do some canning and be a mother to her child. By the end of the novel, however, it is clear that Maria's dream is – in fact – hopeless. Viewed in this light, the closing lines of *Play It as It Lays* seem ironic indeed. Maria says: "*I know what 'nothing' means and keep on playing.* Why, BZ would say. Why not, I say."

Maria may actually believe that she is living for Kate; however, the truth, as Didion's narrative perspective forces the reader to see it, is that Maria continues to live because she does not even share BZ's faith that death produces freedom. Albert Camus said the only truly serious philosophical problem was suicide, deciding whether life is or is not worth living. BZ has answered that question in the negative. Maria, on the other hand, believes that there are *no* serious philosophical problems.

If there is any positive theme in this otherwise nihilistic novel, it is suggested by Didion's title. "*Always when I hear my father's voice*," Maria says, "*it is with a professional rasp, it goes as it lays, don't do it the hard way. My father advised me that life itself was a crap game: it was one of two lessons I learned as a child. The other was that overturning a rock was apt to reveal a rattlesnake. As lessons go those two seem to hold up but not to apply.*" In expecting to find a snake under every rock, Maria is symbolically acknowledging the pervasiveness of evil in an essentially hostile universe. So, how does one live in such an environment? By playing it as it lays, by never taking the hard way in anything. Although Maria has learned this lesson in childhood and continues to live by it, she concedes that such stoic acceptance (if that is what it is) does not really work. It is simply one arbitrary method among many for dealing with the void in which we are doomed to live. It is a lesson that seems to hold up *but not to apply*.

Play It as It Lays was regarded by some critics as too much of a technical tour de force. Didion's third novel, *A Book of Common Prayer* (1977), was almost universally praised, however, for its evocation of contemporary American life and its complex manipulation of style. The present-tense action of this book is set in the imaginary Central American republic of Boca Grande ("Big Mouth"), which is to say that it transpires in a sinister social void. (In the "Letters from Central America" that Didion's protagonist Charlotte tries unsuccessfully to sell to *The New Yorker* she refers to Boca Grande as a "land of contrasts"; however, Didion's narrator, Grace, informs us that this country is, in fact, "relentlessly the same.") Grace Strasser-Mendana, née Tabor, is the reader's guide to Boca Grande as well as a witness to the life and death of Charlotte Douglas, whose story the novel tells. Grace is a sixty-year-old anthropologist who has married into one of the nation's three or four solvent families. Her husband's death has left her "in putative control of fifty-nine-point-eight percent of the arable land and about the same percentage of the decision-making process in Boca Grande." It is in Boca Grande that Grace meets Charlotte Douglas and begins to learn of her confused and pointless life.

Charlotte's story is a deceptively simple one: "she left one man, she left a second man, she traveled again with the first; she let him die alone. She lost one child to 'history' and another to 'complications' . . . ; she imagined herself capable of shedding that baggage and came to Boca Grande, a tourist." Like so many of Didion's characters, Charlotte is a westerner – from Hollister, California. She spends two years at Berkeley, where she meets and marries an untenured English instructor named Warren Bogart. Perversely charming and a bit sadistic, Warren is the first of the men whom Charlotte leaves. He is also the father of the child she loses to history.

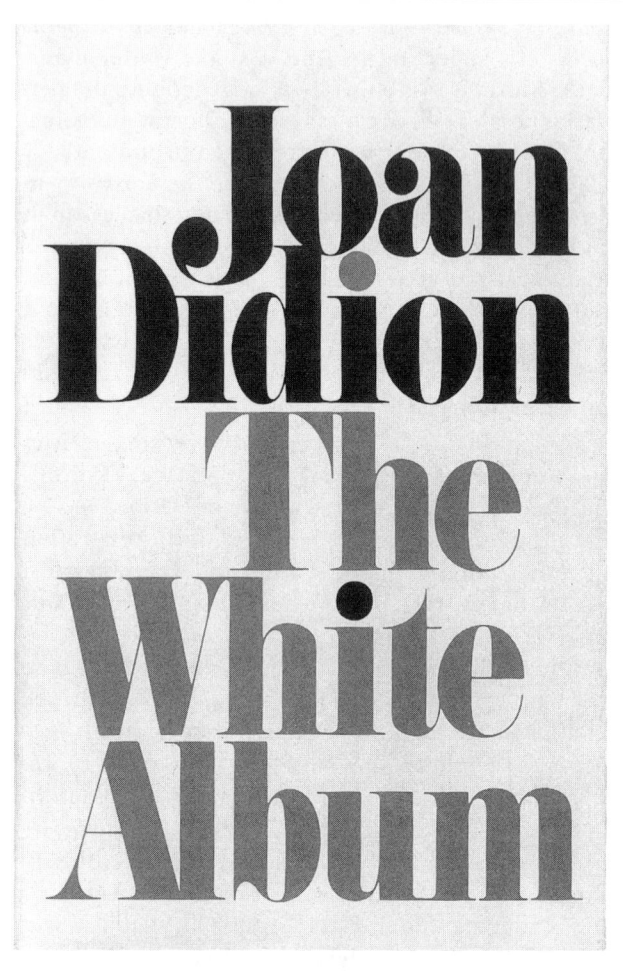

Dust jacket for the collection of essays that includes Didion's observations on the murders of actress Sharon Tate and others by followers of Charles Manson

Although she is only a minor character, that child – Marin Bogart – plays a significant role in her mother's story by deeply affecting Charlotte's psyche. Marin derives much of her credibility from the reader's assumed knowledge of radical youth politics of the late 1960s and early 1970s, particularly of the Patricia Hearst case. Marin (whose name recalls the California county just north of Berkeley, where Hearst was kidnapped by the radical Symbionese Liberation Army) comes from a relatively conventional upper-middle-class background and appears to be a dull, unremarkable adolescent. At sixteen, she "had been photographed with her two best friends wearing the pink-and-white candy-striped pinafores of Children's Hospital volunteers, and had later abandoned her Saturdays at the hospital as 'too sad.'" But at eighteen this same child of the middle class "had been observed with her four best friends detonating a crude pipe bomb in the lobby of the Transamerica Building at 6:30 A.M., hijacking a P.S.A. L-1011 at San Francisco Airport and landing it at Wendover, Utah, where they burned it in time for the story to interrupt the network news and disappeared."

After Marin's disappearance Charlotte conceives another child, this time by her second husband, Leonard Douglas, a prominent San Francisco attorney who specializes in defending radical causes. She then leaves Leonard to return to Warren Bogart, and she and Warren travel through the South, where they stay at a succession of cheap motels after wearing out their welcome with Warren's friends and casual acquaintances. Charlotte finally leaves Warren a second time and returns to New Orleans, where she gives birth prematurely to a hydrocephalic child "devoid of viable liver function." The child dies, and Charlotte flees aimlessly to Boca Grande, hoping someday to be reunited with Marin, for "in a certain dim way Charlotte believed that she had located herself at the very cervix of the world, the place through which a child lost to history must eventually pass."

While in Boca Grande Charlotte tries to live her life oblivious to the random political violence that surrounds her. But finally Charlotte Douglas is herself lost to history. She is shot in one of the periodic shifts in power that constitute the only "history" that Boca Grande has ever known. Grace sees that Charlotte's body is placed in a coffin and flown back to San Francisco. Since she is unable to find a flag with which to drape the coffin, Grace purchases a child's T-shirt printed in an approximation of the American flag. The novel closes with Grace pondering the enigma that was Charlotte Douglas while awaiting her own imminent death by pancreatic cancer.

The final setting of the novel – Boca Grande – more nearly resembles an antisetting. It is not so much a fully realized Central America as it is a touchstone against which Didion can define life among the *norteamericanas*. It makes a certain iconographical sense that Charlotte, whom the local studs call the norteamericana cunt, should spend her final days in Boca Grande, the cervix of the world. After all, Charlotte is a woman who avoids the backward glance, and Boca Grande is a country without history. ("Every time the sun falls on a day in Boca Grande that day appears to vanish from local memory, to be reinvented if necessary but never recalled.") By the end of the novel Charlotte's North American naiveté is nothing short of disastrous in the perverse and cynical environment of Boca Grande. As an ingenuous child of the western United States, she is out of place in a land that lacks a future as well as a past, a land where all time is frozen in a present "relentlessly the same."

A Book of Common Prayer is yet another variation on the theme and characters of *Run River* and *Play It as It Lays*. But it is not at the level of ideas or personalities that *A Book of Common Prayer* distinguishes itself. Like so many modernist novels, this one has been praised more for its form than its content. Specifically, in her use of Grace as narrator, Didion has given her book a coherence lacking in the shifting perspective of her first two novels and an irony that redeems her story from both sentimentality and melodrama.

Grace is what critics Robert Scholes and Robert Kellogg call the "typical Conradian" narrator, a compromise between third-person-omniscient and first-person-protagonist narration. Such a narrator (e.g., Joseph Conrad's Marlow in *The Heart of Darkness* [1902], Fitzgerald's Nick Carraway in *The Great Gatsby* [1925], and even Herman Melville's Ishmael in *Moby-Dick* [1851]) is an eyewitness who tells another person's story and seeks to understand that person "through an imaginative participation in the other's experience." What this leads to, Scholes and Kellogg point out, is the sort of metafiction in which "the factual or empirical aspects of the protagonist's life becomes subordinated to the narrator's understanding of it." Thus, "not what really happened but the meaning of what the narrator believes to have happened becomes the central preoccupation."

But what are we to make of Didion's choice of title? Why call this most secular of stories *A Book of Common Prayer*? Having created a surrogate author in the form of Grace, the real author has greatly limited the ways in which she can speak in her own person. One of the few possibilities left is a suggestive title. The prose of *A Book of Common Prayer* does have a liturgical cadence. The repetition of key phrases and the frequent paragraph divisions give Didion's novel a sound and an appearance not unlike that of the Anglican prayer book. The real significance of Didion's title, however, is probably more thematic than formalistic. She has indicated in her other writings that she considers her background as a white middle-class Episcopalian to have been an important influence on her sensibility. Although Didion scarcely mentions religion in her novel, she concerns herself with the plight of characters from a white, middle-class, Protestant culture. If Marin is sent to an Episcopal day school, it is not because her mother is a devout Episcopalian, but because Charlotte is of a certain cultural heritage.

What Joan Didion has given us in *A Book of Common Prayer* is Grace's attempt to find some sense of order and coherence in the life of Charlotte Douglas. Grace is "witnessing" for Charlotte in much the same way that a believer might witness for her faith. The salient difference, of course, is that Grace has not found order and coherence in Charlotte's life, only chaos and fragmentation; she has not come to rest in a secure faith but remains a confirmed skeptic. The final sentence of the novel is Grace's admission, "I have not been the witness I wanted to be." The indefinite article in Didion's title and the fact that her central intelligence is a cancer victim named Grace only serve as reminders that this novel lacks an objective system of values, along with a reliable mode of narration. Behind Grace's final self-effacement, one senses an author who is no more comfortable with the despair of the religious agnostic than she is with the certitude of the scientific rationalist. This novel is the common prayer of those who, like Grace and Joan Didion herself, have lost only the power, not the will, to believe.

Two years after *A Book of Common Prayer* solidified her reputation as a novelist, Didion published her second collection of essays, *The White Album* (1979). Midway through the title piece of that volume, she writes: "Many people I know in Los Angeles believe that the Sixties ended abruptly on August 9, 1969, ended at the exact moment when word of the murders on Cielo Drive traveled like brushfire through the community, and in a sense this is true. The tension broke that day. The paranoia was fulfilled." The murders are those of Sharon Tate Polanski, Abigail Folger, Jay Sebring, Voytek Frykowski, Steven Parent, and Rosemary and Leno LaBianca; and the passage itself is fairly typical of Didion's "The White Album." The title comes from a record that the Beatles released in 1968. The title of a song from it, "Helter Skelter," was written in blood on the refrigerator at the LaBianca house.

Didion's essay consists of fifteen loosely connected scenes from the late 1960s, scenes that include matters of public concern – such as the activities of Huey Newton and the Black Panthers and the student rebellion at San Francisco State College – and moments of private crisis in the author's own life. Didion is attempting, through the air of physical and psychic violence that pervades these fifteen scenes, to convey a sense of American life at a particular historic moment. We learn, for example, that the author avidly studied the trials of the Ferguson brothers – killers of the silent-screen star Ramon Navarro on Halloween night, 1968 – and that she came to know Charles Manson follower

Linda Kasabian rather well. For Didion these names have a kind of totemic significance. For her they seem to represent American culture as a whole in the late 1960s, an example, one may argue, of the kind of Malibu provincialism that occasionally creeps into Didion's writing.

In addition to narrowness of sensibility, there are also structural problems in "The White Album." Early in the essay Didion says, "We live entirely, especially if we are writers, by the imposition of a narrative line upon disparate images, by the 'ideas' with which we have learned to freeze the shifting phantasmagoria which is our actual experience." What she has given us in "The White Album," however, is not a narrative line but the "disparate images" and "shifting phantasmagoria" themselves. This essay may have been more effective had Didion's focus been less diffuse, had she not left the reader wanting to know so much more about the Fergusons and Linda Kasabian. To begin to appreciate the possibilities that go undeveloped here, one need only consider the author's achievement in "Some Dreamers of the Golden Dream," where she achieves the narrative order that is lacking in "The White Album."

Didion's talent for the personal essay is evident in her elegantly crafted sketch, "In Bed," where she explores the fact that "the physiological error called migraine is central to the given of my life." She describes herself as a "migraine personality," who can spend "most of a week writing and rewriting and not writing a single paragraph." She is able, however, to live with migraine "the way some people live with diabetes" and even to see some usefulness in having to do so. (She speaks of migraine as a "circuit breaker" and talks about the "pleasant convalescent euphoria" that ensues when her headache is over.) We learn from this essay, without ever being explicitly told, that Didion's exquisite literary sensibility has been forged in part by the experience of severe physical pain.

Her ability to describe public personalities is also evident in *The White Album*. A prime example of this is her withering portrayal of the late Episcopal bishop of California in "James Pike, American." Didion sees in Pike "the shadow of a great literary character," comparing him with some of the more ingenuous but morally obtuse characters of Fitzgerald: "One thinks of Gatsby coming up against the East. One also thinks of Tom Buchanan, and his vast carelessness.... One even thinks of Dick Diver, who [like Pike] also started out a winner, and who tried to embrace the essence of the American continent in Nicole as James Albert Pike would now try to embrace it in the Episcopal Church."

Didion's sense of herself as a child of the suburban middle class serves her well in her description of the social architecture of American life. In "On the Mall" she may tell us nothing that is sociologically startling about shopping centers, but she transforms these areas of commerce into mythic landscapes. She conjures up a sense of the postwar boom years, when "for one perishable moment ... the American idea seemed about to achieve itself, via FHA housing and the acquisition of major appliances." Shopping centers were then the enchanted bazaars of democracy.

As befits a fifth-generation Californian, Didion occasionally casts her glance farther west – to the islands of Hawaii. She had done so in *Slouching Towards Bethlehem* with an essay titled "Letter from Paradise, 21° 19' N., 157° 52' W.," and she did again in her novel *Democracy* (1984). In *The White Album* some of her best writing can be found in a series of vignettes entitled "In the Islands." One of these describes with searing clarity the burial of a Vietnam War casualty in an extinct volcano converted into the National Memorial Cemetery of the Pacific. Though not an antiwar polemic, this sketch powerfully evokes the individual human cost of armed conflict.

Didion's acute sense of place and her fascination with the American West serve her well in her long-promised Hawaiian novel, *Democracy*. In "Letter from Paradise" she wrote: "I sat as a child on California beaches and imagined that I saw Hawaii, a certain shimmer in the sunset, a barely perceptible irregularity glimpsed intermittently through squinted eyes." In a column for *New West* magazine written more than a decade later, she revealed that she kept a clock in her bedroom in Los Angeles set to Honolulu time. In *Democracy*, however, Hawaii is less important as a realm of the imagination than as a literal way station between the mainland and America's ultimate western frontier – Southeast Asia. (In "Letter from Paradise," she speaks of sailors who got drunk in Honolulu because "they were no longer in Des Moines and not yet in Da Nang.") As Walt Whitman proclaimed more than a century earlier in his poem "Passage to India" (1871), the roundness of the Earth leads us not to some apocalyptic West but back east from whence we came.

Democracy is the story of Inez Christian Victor, the daughter of a once-prominent island family and the wife of a liberal Democratic senator from New York. Essentially alienated from her husband, Inez

Dust jacket for Didion's political novel set in Hawaii and Southeast Asia at the end of the Vietnam War

maintains a lifelong love affair with a mysterious "information specialist" who operates on the fringes of the CIA and the military-industrial complex. She follows this man, Jack Lovett, to Southeast Asia, where, as South Vietnam is falling to the Communists, he rescues her daughter, Jessica, who had drifted to Saigon because she heard that job opportunities were good there. While in Southeast Asia, Inez sees Jack drown in a hotel pool in Jakarta and brings his body back to Hawaii to be buried under a jacaranda tree at Schofield Barracks (a setting in James Jones's *From Here to Eternity* [1948], a novel Didion writes about admiringly in *Slouching Towards Bethlehem*). She returns to Kuala Lumpur to work with refugees.

Somewhat on the periphery of Inez's story is the public chaos of Indochina and the more private tragedy of the murder of her sister, Janet Christian Ziegler, by their father, Paul Christian. The circumstances of this murder are shrouded in ambiguity. At the time of the shooting Janet was entertaining Wendell Omura, a congressman of Asian descent, and Paul Christian was a genteel racist of the old feudal aristocracy. The suggestions of an interracial affair and of the conflict of cultures seem to be vestiges of the more specifically regional Hawaiian novel Didion says she had tried to write. What she actually produces is a blend of current history and domestic tragedy that starts as a brilliant satire of political manners and blossoms into a strangely compelling romance.

From a purely technical standpoint, the most problematic aspect of *Democracy* is Didion's method of narration. Departing from the more conventional approaches employed in her earlier novels, Didion inserts herself into *Democracy* and claims to have been personally acquainted with her characters. Although this may appear to make Didion's tale a postmodernist novel about novel writing, it also places her in the decidedly premodernist company of such writers as George Eliot and William Makepeace Thackeray, who both inserted themselves into their fiction. By telling us about her problems in writing this book and by treating imaginary characters as if they were as real as the figures in her journalism, Didion may be trying to collapse the distinction between fiction and nonfiction narrative. If the New Journalism brings the techniques of fiction to the writing of fact, this novel brings the illusion of fact to the writing of fiction.

In this imagistic, elliptical novel much is left to conjecture. More than in any of her previous works, Didion has helped fuel this conjecture by an almost compulsive literary allusiveness. Certainly the most significant allusion is to Henry Adams, who published a novel titled *Democracy* in 1880. Although Mary McCarthy, writing in *The New York Times Book Review,* made nothing of the two novels' having the same name, Thomas R. Edwards, writing in the *New York Review of Books,* saw both Didion and Adams as displaced aristocrats who use irony and subtlety to "confront a chaotic new reality that shatters the orderings of simpler, older ways." Perhaps an even more instructive linkage can be drawn between Didion's novel and *The Education of Henry Adams* (1918), particularly its most famous chapter – "The Dynamo and the Virgin."

The thesis of this chapter is that over a period of six hundred years, Western civilization has moved from thirteenth-century unity to nineteenth-century multiplicity, from the age of the Virgin to the age of the dynamo. While this development represents progress to many, those of a traditionalist sensibility (for example, Didion, Adams, T. S. Eliot) realize that there is a dark side to progress, that another name for multiplicity is fragmentation.

That we now live in an age when the ultimate fragmentation is prefigured in nuclear fission and that such an age represents an "advance" even beyond the dynamo occurred to Didion while touring Berkeley's nuclear reactor in Etcheverry Hall in 1979. In a column for *New West* magazine, reprinted in slightly different form in *After Henry* (1992), Didion recalls that experience:

> In my Modern Library copy of *The Education of Henry Adams,* a book I first read and scored at Berkeley in 1954, I see this passage underlined: "... to Adams, the dynamo became a symbol of infinity. As he grew accustomed to the great gallery of machines at the 1900 Paris Exposition – he began to feel the 40-foot dynamos as a moral force, much as the early Christians felt the Cross." After I had left the TRIGA Mark III reactor in the basement of Etcheverry Hall I wondered for a long time what Henry Adams would have made of the intense blue of the Cerenkov radiation around the fuel rods, the blue past all blue, the blue like light itself, the blue that is actually a shock wave in the pool of water and is the exact blue of the glass at Chartres.

It may be significant that *Democracy* ends with Inez observing the light at dawn during nuclear tests in the Pacific. At the end, when Billy Dillon asks Inez for four reasons why she is in Kuala Lumpur, she replies: *"Colors, moisture, heat, enough blue in the air."*

Although Didion has commented frequently on her aversion to politics, the two nonfiction books she published in the 1980s were both highly political. In reading *Salvador* (1982), one gets the eerie sense that life is imitating art. In "Why I Write" Didion noted that her initial inspiration for *A Book of Common Prayer* was the image of the Panama airport at 6:00 A.M. From there it was only a process of extrapolation to make up a country in which to place the airport and a menacing political environment for that country. In *Salvador* Didion takes us back to Boca Grande, even to the point of beginning her account with a description of the El Salvador International Airport. "Most readers will not get very far in this very short book," Gene Lyons wrote in *Newsweek,* "without wondering whether she visited this sad and troubled place less to report than to validate the Didion world view."

Whether or not Lyons's caustic inference is correct, the turmoil in El Salvador was clearly another instance of the center's not holding, of things falling apart. Sooner or later, any writer with a distinctive voice risks falling into self-parody. That Joan Didion should succumb to this pitfall in an extended piece of journalism suggests how predictable her view of the world had become by 1983. Nevertheless, there are places where the writing clearly signals the presence of one of the finest prose stylists in contemporary American letters. Consider, for example, the following description of the Metropolitan Cathedral in San Salvador:

> This is the cathedral that the late Archbishop Oscar Arnulfo Romero refused to finish, on the premise that the work of the Church took precedence over its display, and the high walls of raw concrete bristle with structural rods, rusting now, staining the concrete, sticking out at wrenched and violent angles. The wiring is exposed. Fluorescent tubes hang askew. The great high altar is backed by warped plyboard. The cross on the altar is of bare incandescent bulbs, but the bulbs, that afternoon, were unlit: there was in fact no light at all on the main altar, no light on the cross, no light on the globe of the world that showed the North American continent in gray and the southern in white; no light on the dove above the globe, *Salvador del Mundo.*

John Gregory Dunne has said that as a screenwriter his most instructive experiences have been watching the bad movies of good directors because "in each there is a moment or sequence that stands out in such bold relief from the surrounding debris as to make the reasons for its effectiveness clear." The same is surely true of literature. Although *Salvador* is not really a bad book, it is one of Didion's least effective efforts. She writes her best journalism when she is able to establish a personal connection with a place, as in her elegiac essays about northern California, or when she is discovering the inherent literary qualities of a public phenomenon, as in her rendering of the Lucille Miller story and her deflation of the buffoonish Bishop Pike. In *Salvador* neither is the case.

Because her stay in El Salvador was brief and exclusively professional, Didion had no personal stake in that embattled land. Many of her individual descriptions border on brilliance, but the closest she comes to finding a character who excites her literary interest is in her brief encounters with the American ambassador Deane Hinton. As a cosmopolitan man with western American roots, Hinton seems to be Didion's kind of guy. In his presence she is even able to believe, if only for a moment, that "the American undertaking in El Salvador might turn out to be, from the right angle, in the right light, just another difficult but possible mission in another troubled but possible country."

Although Didion studiously avoids partisan polemics, the political message of her book, beginning with the opening epigraph (from Conrad's *Heart of Darkness*) and running to the final page, is clear: El Salvador is a Third World backwater that cannot be salvaged for U.S. interests, and to take one side or the other there is to fall prey to the sort of self-delusion that afflicted Conrad's Kurtz. Predictably, Ronald Reagan is Didion's Mistah Kurtz. Early in the book, she watched Reagan and Doris Day cavort on Salvadoran television in *The Winning Team,* a 1952 Warner Bros. movie about the baseball pitcher Grover Cleveland Alexander. Then, at the end of the narrative, we see the Great Communicator "certifying" El Salvador's progress toward political stability and human rights, even as the carnage and repression continue.

In *Salvador* we have something like the story of Charlotte Douglas, the norteamericana who lives for a time in a strife-torn Hispanic police state, regards herself as *una turista,* and tries unsuccessfully to sell her vision of reality to *The New Yorker* in a series of "Letters from Central America." *Salvador* is essentially Joan Didion's "Letters from Central America," published originally not in *The New Yorker,* but in the *New York Review of Books.* In reading these letters, one cannot help remembering that at the end of *A Book of Common Prayer,* Grace concedes: "I am less and less certain that this story has been one of delusion. Unless the delusion was mine."

In 1987 Didion once again turned her attention to American policy in Latin America. Her book

Didion at the time of After Henry *(photograph by Colleen Guaitolini)*

Miami (1987) is an extended feature story on the exiled community that fled Castro's reign of terror in the early 1960s and came to dominate the politics and economy of America's most Caribbean city. Didion's real concern, however, is not with immigrant sociology but with the baroque political entanglements of Miami and Washington, D.C. It is a tale of two cities set in what the Cubans would regard as primarily the worst of times. However, the reader who comes to *Miami* looking for specific policy recommendations is likely to be disappointed. Despite her sympathy for the Cuban exiles, Didion is not about to urge Washington to back their counterrevolution and seems to be almost as scornful of the hard-line right-wingers who do so as she is of the cynical pragmatists who simply milk the situation for their partisan advantage.

Of course, one does not read Joan Didion primarily for her sociological or political insight, as acute as those may be at times, but for her amazing facility with language. One opens a book by Didion expecting to find prose that is elegant, precise, witty, and cadenced. Unfortunately, *Miami* disappoints more often than it delivers. Perhaps attempting to write in a manner appropriate to her convoluted subject matter (political intrigue and the like), she sounds too often like a cut-rate Henry James. It is not particularly difficult to navigate her heavily subordinated sentences, but the sound is too often flat.

Fortunately, *Miami* contains enough remnants of Didion at her best to suggest that she has simply misplaced rather than lost her marvelous sense of the absurd. For example, early in the book she writes:

> Inside the autopsy room the hands of the two young men were encased in the brown paper bags which indicated that the police had not yet taken what they needed for laboratory studies. Their flesh had the marbleized yellow look of the recently dead. There were other bodies in the room, in various stages of autopsy, and a young woman in a white coat taking eyes, for the eye bank. "Who are we going to start on next?" one of the assistant medical examiners was saying. "The fat guy? Let's do the fat guy."

The foreign policy endorsed by *Miami* is no different from the one found in *Salvador* – a skeptical isolationism based on the assumption that no good can come from American meddling in the affairs of other countries. Whether it is her own particular version of ethnocentricity or simply hardheaded realism, Didion seems incapable of envisioning Latin American politics devoid of corruption, intrigue, bloodshed, and massive instability.

Over the course of her career Didion has been a frequent contributor to a variety of magazines. In the early 1960s her work appeared most often in *National Review, Mademoiselle,* and *Vogue.* She and Dunne wrote columns for alternating issues of the *Saturday Evening Post* from June 1966 to January 1969 and for *Esquire* from February 1976 to January 1979. Didion also published nine columns of her own in *Life* from December 1969 to April 1970. (Most of the material in *Slouching Towards Bethlehem* and *The White Album* was originally published in these magazines.) Since the late 1970s, she has appeared most frequently in *The New Yorker,* the *New York Review of Books* (which published the original versions of *Salvador* and *Miami*), and a short-lived California publication called *New West* (where she and Dunne shared a column from late 1979 to mid 1980). *After Henry* is a selection of her work from these last three periodicals.

The author of *After Henry* is about as different from the Didion of *Slouching Towards Bethlehem* and *The White Album* as the *New York Review of Books* is from *National Review.* Didion has lost her distaste for politics and her indifferent allegiance to the conservative wing of the Republican Party. The first three selections in *After Henry* ("In the Realm of the Fisher King," "Insider Baseball," and "Shooters Inc.") offer a fashionably contemptuous view of Reagan, George Bush, and the Republican presidential campaign of 1988. One of the essays in the middle section ("Down at City Hall") is a generally unflattering portrait of Los Angeles mayor Thomas Bradley. *After Henry* concludes with a sixty-seven-page story about a young woman who was savagely attacked by several adolescent thugs in New York's Central Park. (Curiously enough, Didion sees the city's outrage over this incident as an exercise in sentimentality.)

Although Didion's shorter political essays are generally no more satisfying than her book-length reports on El Salvador and Miami, she does manage to convey the surrealistic quality of politics in media-made America. In "Insider Baseball," a piece from the *New York Review of Books* that was selected as one of the best magazine essays of 1988, she describes the national conventions of the two major parties: "At the end of prime time, when the skyboxes were dark, the action moved across the skywalks and into the levels, into the lobbies, into one or another Hyatt or Marriott or Hilton or Westin. In the portage from lobby to lobby, level to level, the same people kept materializing, in slightly altered roles. On a level of the Hyatt in Atlanta I saw Ann Lewis in her role as a Jackson adviser. On a level of the Hyatt in New Orleans I saw Ann Lewis in her role as a correspondent for *Ms.*" The paragraph concludes with Didion running into an acquaintance from twenty-five years earlier: "The great thing about those evenings was you could even see Michael Harrington there," she recalls Richard Viguerie saying to her at a party in New Orleans. "[H]ere," she writes, "was the man who managed the action for the American right trying to explain the early 1960s, and evenings we had both spent on Washington Square." One suspects that Didion's essay would have been far more engaging had she written more about those magical evenings of the past and less about the synthetic ones of the present.

Flashes of the old Didion are most apparent in the title essay, an affectionate tribute to her late editor, Henry Robbins, and in "California," a section of six essays that comprise a little less than half of *After Henry*. Perhaps the single most evocative piece is "Pacific Distances," a pastiche of sketches from Didion's column in *New West.* She begins her essay in California when she was a Regents' Lecturer at Berkeley in 1975. (Her observations about her vocation as a writer and the comparisons and contrasts she makes between her present self and the undergraduate self of twenty years earlier are written in a recognizably personal voice.) She then takes us to the nuclear reactor that reminded her of Henry Adams's comments on technology and to the Lawrence Livermore Laboratory. Next, Didion leads us farther west – first to Honolulu (each of her three collections of essays contain selections on Hawaii) and finally to Hong Kong, where she describes a detention camp for Vietnamese refugees. The resonances between this essay and *Democracy* (which Didion had once thought of calling "Pacific Distances") are particularly suggestive.

Perhaps the most effective combination of Didion's regional muse and her more-recent political interests can be found in "Girl of the Golden West," her review of Patty Hearst's autobiography. In a sense, Patricia Campbell Hearst is a classic example of one of the major themes of Didion's writing – the conflict between the new and the old California. Didion recalls that on the same day as Randolph Hearst's badly botched attempt to ransom his daughter with a food giveaway in West Oakland, former California senator William Knowland, "the most prominent member of the family that had run Oakland for half a century [and a childhood hero of Didion], had taken the pistol he was said to carry as protection against terrorists, positioned himself on a bank of the Russian River, and blown off the top of his head." Didion concedes that "there was no actual connection between turkey legs thrown through windows in West Oakland and William Knowland lying face down in the Russian River, but the paradigm was manifest, one California busy being born and another busy dying."

Didion concludes her discussion of Hearst by recalling having read an article on her captors – the Symbionese Liberation Army – in a March 1977 issue of an upscale community paper called the *Bay Guardian*. When she got the paper out to reread that piece, she noticed for the first time a long and favorable report on a San Francisco minister who was said to be a great moral leader and was even compared to César Chavez. This clergyman was responsible for a "a mind-boggling range of social service programs – food distribution, legal aid, drug rehabilitation, nursing homes, free Pap smears – as well as for a 'twenty-seven-thousand-acre agricultural station.'" Once again we have the telling juxtaposition, because "the agricultural station was in Guyana, and the minister . . . was the Reverend Jim Jones."

In 1996 Didion published her fifth novel, *The Last Thing He Wanted*. This book continues the departure from conventional narrative that she had begun with *Play It as It Lays*. It relies less on character development and fully realized action than on repeated image patterns, elliptical transitions, and a prose rhythm so distinctively Didion's own that it opens her once again to charges of self parody. The protagonist, Elena McMahon, has left both her husband, a Hollywood insider of indeterminate profession, and her job as a political reporter for the *Washington Post* to visit her father, a dying arms dealer. Apparently motivated by filial loyalty, she flies to Central America to complete her father's last nefarious transaction. The story gains suspense as Elena falls victim to political intrigues that neither she nor the reader fully understands and that the author never explains. Didion has written a mystery thriller in which all the pieces fail to fall into place in the end. That seems to be her message: the pieces of real-life puzzles don't always fit neatly together.

The Last Thing He Wanted reads less like a novel than like an extended prose poem or, as Laura Shapiro has suggested in *Newsweek*, a film treatment. Didion's characters are similar to those in earlier novels. Elena McMahon is another variation on Charlotte Douglas and Inez Victor. Her husband, Wynn Janklow, is vaguely reminiscent of Leonard Douglas and Harry Victor. The most memorable character, Lena's father, Dick McMahon, seems to be a conflation of Paul Christian and Jack Lovett. The novel's closest approximation of a male protagonist is Treat Morrison, a state department official capable of viewing the world without ideological blinders. He never comes to life as fully as the leading men in any of Didion's previous novels.

What makes *The Last Thing He Wanted* a compelling reading experience is the skill with which Didion constructs her plot. She turned the same trick in *A Book of Common Prayer*. If the story was not quite as absorbing in the earlier novel, it is because that book offered many riches in addition to plot. In *The Last Thing He Wanted* there is precious little but the story – or, perhaps, the failed promise of a story. Didion's one concession to realism is an air of historicity that comes from her recent experience as a political reporter. Even if no names or incidents are recognizably taken from real life, snatches of dialogue and patterns of behavior have the ring of authenticity. All that is needed is a director-auteur and a talented cast to make Didion's narrative shorthand come alive.

In addition to flat characterization and a gratuitously incoherent storyline, Didion's most recent novel falls short of her earlier achievement in at least two other respects – it suffers from relative lack of humor and a blurred narrative focus. Al-

28

MOVEMENT ONE: bring her through the summer to the point when she intervenes, goes to the place. Begin the chapter now in work with her father telling her stories, interwoven with the liquidity, the shedding of her skin.

Without news she was restless, fretful, as if her synapses were shorting out. Events were left incomplete, no overnight polls, no immediate reactions, no spin and counterspin, none of the surge to surround a rumor, a vacuum.

Then a new kind of news began reaching her.

He had always moved without effort around a certain part of the country. He rode along with a fellow he knew, or a fellow he knew was taking a plane over that way.

The American wife of the Chilean painter. Listening to Havana radio driving down the Keys at night. "You start to get it past Key Largo. I drive down by myself a lot at night."

All her life, her whole careful life, had been preparation, an impersonation of another kind of woman. Here she was authentic. Taking off her clothes. She wrapped up the gabardine jacket and the unopened packets of panty hose and left them in the Good Will box at the supermarket.

Open, flat, pale, the whites and pastels absorbing light. Banyan trees on the golf course. White and pink and yellow frangipani, hibiscus, oleander. Palmettos blowing. Drifts of white coral sand, aquamarine water, grey Caribbean sky. Water lapping against the causeway. Bleached light. Construction cranes.

The soft sweet smell of it, the liquidity of it. The ammo stores. Cheap Guns & Ammo Bronson Texas.

The first time Treat Morrison ever saw ~~him~~ Elena
The parfait and bacon.   McMahon
The sense in which they were both outsiders.

Early notes for The Last Thing He Wanted *(courtesy of Joan Didion)* though Didion is rarely thought of as a funny writer, her best work is never lacking in wit. In *Democracy* she is particularly adroit at lampooning the fatuousness of contemporary liberalism. (In his syndicated column, George Will compared *Democracy*'s satire with that of Henry James's *The Bostonians*.) The humorous moments in *The Last Thing He Wanted* are simply not as memorable. Elena's life as a political reporter seems more of an arbitrary plot device than an integral part of the novel. Didion reveals little of Elena's life aboard the campaign plane. The same is true of her earlier role as a Hollywood housewife. Didion knows enough of both worlds to have made more engaging use of her material.

Many of the problems with Didion's fifth novel stem from an inability to find a convincing voice with which to tell the story. As the narrator of *A Book of Common Prayer*, Grace was a convincing and compelling presence. Remove her from that novel and what is left is something very much like *The Last Thing He Wanted*. Most critics are convinced that Didion's introduction of herself as narrator of *Democracy* weakened that book. Too many asides on the difficulty of writing fiction call attention to Didion's artifice. In her most recent novel, she is back at it again. In the second chapter, she identifies herself as "the not quite omniscient author." She says that she had originally intended to write through the persona of a foreign service officer named "Lilianne Owen." She finally abandoned this ruse because of the necessity of constantly saying such things as "She told me later" and "I learned this after the fact." Other writers (Conrad, Fitzgerald, Didion herself) have successfully confronted that problem in the past. The character of the narrator is an integral part of the story he or she tells. The demise of "Lilianne Owen" represents a failure of imagination on Didion's part. The result is a potentially absorbing story that no one, real or imagined, seems capable of telling.

Joan Didion first made her mark in fiction and journalism as an interpreter of the 1960s. If the 1970s and 1980s have not provided her with material nearly so promising, the solution may be for her to move backward in time rather than forward. In one of the most memorable passages in *The White Album*, she writes: "Certain places seem to exist because someone has written about them.... A place belongs forever to whoever claims it hardest, remembers it most obsessively, wrenches it from itself, shapes it, renders it, loves it so radically that he remakes it in his image." If writers own eras as well as places, the time of Didion's life was clearly her youth in postwar Sacramento. She was able to write so well about the social fragmentation of the 1960s precisely because her own values were shaped in a much different world. Unfortunately, her work has become more problematical as she has moved away from her regional roots. If her status as a major contemporary writer seems less certain in the mid 1990s than it did after the appearance of *A Book of Common Prayer* and *The White Album* in the late 1970s, Didion's talent is such that she may yet fulfill the promise of her earlier career. No one is better equipped to be California's Faulkner, or at least its Willa Cather.

Interviews:

Barbaralee Diamonstein, "Joan Didion," in her *Open Secrets: Ninety-four Women in Touch with Our Time* (New York: Viking, 1972), pp. 103–106;

Susan Braudy, "A Day in the Life of Joan Didion," *Ms.*, 5 (February 1977): 65–68, 108–109;

Sara Davidson, "A Visit with Joan Didion," *New York Times Book Review*, 3 April 1977, pp. 1, 35–38.

Bibliography:

Donna Olendorf, "Joan Didion: A Checklist, 1955–1980," *Bulletin of Bibliography*, 32 (January-March 1981): 32–44.

References:

Sharon Felton, ed., *The Critical Response to Joan Didion* (Westport, Conn.: Greenwood Press, 1994);

Ellen G. Friedman, ed., *Joan Didion: Essays and Conversations* (Princeton, N.J.: Ontario Review Press, 1984);

Katherine Usher Henderson, *Joan Didion* (New York: Ungar, 1981);

Mark Royden Winchell, *Joan Didion* (Boston: Twayne, 1980; revised, 1989).

E. L. Doctorow
(6 January 1931 -)

Douglas Fowler
Florida State University

See also the Doctorow entries in *DLB 2: American Novelists Since World War II* [first series]; *DLB 28: Twentieth-Century American-Jewish Fiction Writers;* and *DLB Yearbook: 1980.*

BOOKS: *Welcome to Hard Times* (New York: Simon & Schuster, 1960); republished as *Bad Man from Bodie* (London: Deutsch, 1961);
Big as Life (New York: Simon & Schuster, 1966);
The Book of Daniel (New York: Random House, 1971; London: Macmillan, 1971);
Ragtime (New York: Random House, 1975; London: Macmillan, 1976);
Drinks Before Dinner: A Play (New York: Random House, 1979; London: Macmillan, 1980);
Loon Lake (New York: Random House, 1980; London: Macmillan, 1980);
Lives of the Poets: Six Stories and a Novella (New York: Random House, 1984; London: M. Joseph, 1985);
World's Fair (New York: Random House, 1985; London: M. Joseph, 1986);
Billy Bathgate (New York: Random House, 1989; London: Macmillan 1989);
Jack London, Hemingway, and The Constitution: Selected Essays 1977-1992 (New York: Random House, 1993); republished as *Poets and Presidents* (London: Macmillan, 1994);
The Waterworks (New York: Random House, 1994; London: Macmillan, 1994).

PLAY PRODUCTION: *Drinks Before Dinner,* New York, Estelle R. Newman Theatre, 22 November 1978.

OTHER: Theodore Dreiser, *Sister Carrie,* introduction by Doctorow (New York: Bantam Classics, 1982);
"Art Funding for the Artist's Sake" and "False Documents," in *E. L. Doctorow: Essays and Conversations,* edited by Richard Trenner (Princeton, N.J.: Ontario Review Press, 1983).

SELECTED PERIODICAL PUBLICATIONS –
UNCOLLECTED: "The Bomb Lives!" *Playboy,* 21 (March 1974): 114-116, 208-216;
"After the Nightmare," *Sports Illustrated,* 44 (28 June 1976): 72-82;
"The New Poetry," *Harper's,* 254 (May 1977): 92-95;
"Living in the House of Fiction," *Nation,* 226 (23 April 1978): 459-462;
"Dream Candidate: The Rise of Ronald Reagan," *Nation,* 231 (19-26 July 1980): 65, 82-84.

E. L. Doctorow's narrative art is a distinctive fusion of moral involvement and poetic transformation. Like Philip Roth, he is a fabulist with a lesson to teach his readers about the great century of American ascendancy. Like Norman Mailer and Joseph Heller, he is distrustful of and yet spellbound by the misuses of power. Like William Kennedy, another city boy with a fascination for gangsters, crime and the atonement for crime compel his most sensitive attention. Like Vladimir Nabokov, he believes prose for prose's sake is an art worth a lifetime of devotion. And like Edgar Allan Poe, Herman Melville, Ambrose Bierce, and William Faulkner, he infuses a lurid gleam of the macabre in his created kingdoms, revealing a showy, politically incorrect taste for terror and blood. Leslie Fiedler once pointed out that there is a "disturbing relationship between our highest art and such lowbrow forms of horror pornography as the detective story, the pulp thriller, and the Superman comic book, all of which are . . . the heirs of the gothic." In part Doctorow is a Gothic imagination residing in life-affirming America, and some crucial passages in his work are, indeed, best read as "horror pornography." Yet it is important to notice that the theme of families and what happens to them lies at the marrow of almost all of his fiction, a concern that is rare indeed among male American writers of the late twentieth century.

E. L. Doctorow (photograph © Jerry Bauer)

The son of David Richard and Rose Levine Doctorow, Edgar Lawrence Doctorow was born in New York City to a family with a strong radical bias. He characterizes the milieu as "a lower-middle-class environment of generally enlightened, socialist sensibility." The family resided in the then-middle-class borough of The Bronx. After losing his radio, record, and musical-instrument store in Manhattan during the Depression, Doctorow's father kept his family afloat by working as a salesman of home appliances and later television sets and stereo equipment.

After graduating from the Bronx High School of Science in 1948, Doctorow entered Kenyon College in Ohio. "There were lots of poets on campus, poetry was what we did at Kenyon, the way at Ohio State they played football," Doctorow remarks of his alma mater in *Lives of the Poets* (1984). He had in fact chosen Kenyon because he wanted to study with the poet and essayist John Crowe Ransom. In an essay collected in *Jack London, Hemingway and The Constitution* (1993) Doctorow comments, "To this day I don't understand how I had known about Ransom, how I as a teenager could have made this knowledgeable choice and found my way to central Ohio. Perhaps my high-school guidance counselor saw in my New York folk-singing background the makings of a good Southern Agrarian."

Doctorow ended up majoring in philosophy, not English, and he acted in campus dramatic productions instead of pursuing a literary apprenticeship and an academic career. After earning an A.B. with honors in 1952, he studied English drama and directing at Columbia University (1952–1953) and then served from 1953 to 1955 with the U.S. Army in Germany. He married Helen Setzer on 20 August 1954.

Instead of going back to graduate school under the GI Bill, Doctorow struck out on his own, earning a living as an "expert reader" for film and television production companies in New York. It was exhausting piecework but a wonderful education. He read a book a day, seven days a week, and wrote a twelve-hundred-word synopsis-critique of each book, evaluating its potential for the visual media. An informal evaluation of a novel for Victor Weybright, the editor in chief of the New American Library, led Weybright to hire Doctorow as an associate editor in 1959. By 1964 he was a senior editor, and that same year he was hired as editor in

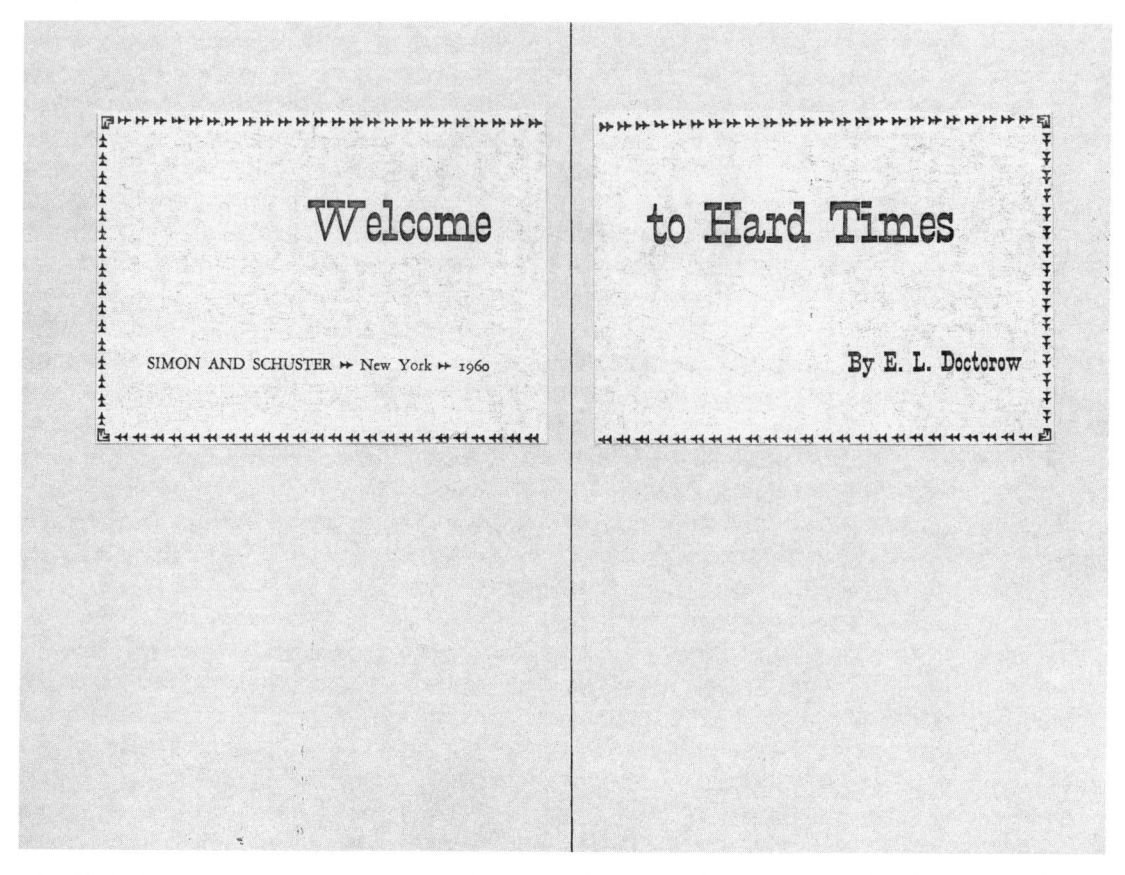

Double-truck title page for Doctorow's first novel, a revisionist western written to "counterpoint" the romantic view of the West created by novelists such as Owen Wister and Louis L'Amour

chief at Dial Press, where he became a vice president and remained until 1969. After leaving Dial Press he became a writer in residence or member of the faculty at the University of California at Irvine (1969–1970), Sarah Lawrence College (1971–1978), the Yale School of Drama (1974–1975), the University of Utah (1975), and Princeton University (1980–1981). Since 1982 he has held the Lewis and Loretta Gluckman Chair of American Literature at New York University.

Critic Stephen Schiff points out that Doctorow uses popular culture and "disreputable" genre materials as the points of departure for stories and novels. The "fantasy materials" in his fiction are "almost touchingly boyish and antiquated: gangsters and cowpokes; broken-spirited poets; tough but frail-looking blondes whisked out of reach by sleekly dangerous hooligans. If Doctorow is indeed the artist as conduit, then what he's channeling is the great American dreamwork: his materials are the stuff of our legends – and our schlock." Indeed, Doctorow once spoke in an interview of purposely choosing to go back to the mind of a young boy in order to lend once more a sense of wonder and what he called "empowerment" to the voice of his narration, "a kind of rhapsodic appreciation of what adults have stopped thinking about." Boys' adventures, he has noted, were the genesis for memorable tales from masters of boys' fiction such as Mark Twain, Charles Dickens, and Robert Louis Stevenson. "At his best," says Schiff, "Doctorow is able to reimagine [these materials] from the ground up, and to reignite the moral and political issues buried in their ashes. Doctorow is like a medium for our dead fictions; as they flow through him, they come out alive and sizzling."

Many of his novels and stories investigate with contagious fascination the archetype of the American criminal genius. "Dedicated criminals live on the extreme edge of civilization, where manners and morals unravel and the underlying impetus of our tribal, primordial origins breaks through," Doctorow has said about his fascination with criminality. "My background, which was safe and conventional, may have made me attentive to life beyond the pale."

The quality of events being "beyond the pale" is certainly intrinsic to much of his fiction, but this criminality and extremism is subject to a powerful countervailing force: the desire to belong to a family. Nearly all Doctorow's central figures come in from the cold, returning to "families" of one sort or another – sometimes homey and loving, sometimes criminal and outcast and ad hoc, or at other times aristocratic and arrogant.

Doctorow's vision of "what the West must really have been like," *Welcome to Hard Times* (1960) not only attracted excellent reviews but was also adapted as a Hollywood movie (1967). The novel is the story of a western massacre, the shaping of a "family" from the survivors of that massacre, and the creation of a tiny parody of a village from the ashes. The opening of the novel is spellbinding: an enormous and sinister Bad Man from Bodie, Clay Turner, fills the bar at the Silver Sun with his leering, wordless menace; he drinks half a bottle of "rot-gut" liquor to clear the prairie dust from his throat and then exposes to the men huddled at the bar the breasts of a red-headed saloon prostitute named Florence. In a few moments Florence is raped and dead; a few paragraphs later four men die, and the town is burned to the ground, setting into motion a bloody revenge plot. The novel is indeed a western, but it is far different from the heroic mode made famous by Owen Wister, Mayne Reid, and Louis L'Amour. Doctorow admitted to an interviewer that he enjoyed taking "disreputable genre materials and doing something serious with them," and the situation in *Welcome to Hard Times* is an example of his taste for packaging the serious within the sensational. Doctorow is a melodramatic writer, and the reader should never ignore the "disreputable" genre energies that animate his work from just below its surface. It is a quality essential to his appeal.

Unlike genre westerns, Doctorow's revisionist western novel is not a simple tale of the triumph of good over evil. Some of the avenging townspeople are transformed into murderers by the end of the book, and the narrator, Blue, a widowed, thoughtful drifter in his late forties, is a gentle and ineffectual wordsmith at first too frightened to fight back. He can only watch, endure, and despise himself for his cowardice in the face of the Bad Man's ferocity. Yet the success of the novel resides more in its forlorn, overcivilized narrative voice than in its dramatic activity. In an interview Doctorow spoke of the myth of the West as a creation of writers "having nothing to do with realities" and said he had written *Welcome to Hard Times* as a conscious "counterpoint to that."

Of all Doctorow's novels to date *Welcome to Hard Times* has excited the longest loyalties and the least dissent. When the novel was published in 1960, Wirt Williams not only praised it as "taut and dramatic and exciting," but he also called attention to Doctorow's imaginative handling of "one of the favorite problems of philosophers: the relationship of man and evil" (*The New York Times Book Review*, 25 September 1960). Williams went on to compare the novel to Joseph Conrad's *Heart of Darkness* (1902): "when the rational controls that order man's existence slacken, destruction comes. Conrad said it best . . . but Mr. Doctorow has said it impressively."

Doctorow's philosophical subtlety gave his book a greater depth and staying power than typical westerns; yet his tale was no less action filled and vivid than those genre novels with their naive triumph of good over evil. Moreover, his presentation of the West-winning epoch of the American adventure as animated more by greed, brutality, and anti-Indian racism than by pioneer heroics has suited the temper of our times. When the novel was republished in 1975, Kevin Starr called it "a superb piece of fiction: lean and mean, and thematically significant" and noted that Doctorow had purposely written nothing less than an "anti-western," taking the "thin, somewhat sordid and incipiently depressing materials of the Great Plains experience and fashioning them into a myth of good and evil" (*The New Republic*, 6 September 1975). Doctorow's dark fable remains one of the best attempts to show that the history beneath American history was worth viewing through the lens of a writer's most sensitive and intelligent skepticism.

Doctorow's next novel, a disappointing attempt at science fiction called *Big as Life,* was not published until 1966. "Unquestionably, it's the worst I've done," Doctorow told one interviewer. "I think about going back and re-doing it some day, but the whole experience was so unhappy, both the writing and the publishing of it, that maybe I never will."

Big as Life begins with a stroke of purest genre science fiction: two humanlike creatures thousands of meters high appear in New York Harbor from a space-time continuum adjacent to our own. Once Doctorow has this magical event in place and has introduced his cast of characters, he falters badly, failing either to frighten or to fascinate the reader. Doctorow does indeed have a story to tell in *Big as Life,* and it is one that most science-fiction and fantasy writers might consider a promising variation on the invasion-from-space motif originated by H. G. Wells in *The War of the Worlds* (1898). But unlike

Dust jacket for Doctorow's fictional examination of the long-term personal, social, and political impact of the spy trial and executions of Julius and Ethel Rosenberg in the early 1950s

a good adaptation of the Wells original, such as John Wyndham's *Day of the Triffids* (1951), Doctorow's book does not effectively exploit the legacy of Wells's great epic. The disappointment of *Big as Life* seems to stem from two sources, one of them mechanical and inherent in Doctorow's choice of story idea, one more subtly bound into his artistic sensibility.

The mechanical problem arises in the attributes he gives his giants and the space-time kingdom from which they have appeared. The giants are helpless – and almost motionless – in this local universe. They have fallen through some sort of cosmic scrim into this world, but the scale of time in which they are still imprisoned is not terrestrial. Although humanlike in almost every respect, the creatures are not only thousands of times larger than living things on earth but thousands of times *slower*. They cannot threaten life on earth because they are immobilized by the glacial timescale in which they are still encased. They are not threats; they are fossils.

This immobilization creates grave difficulties for Doctorow's science-fiction narrative. Wells's *The War of the Worlds* describes an interplanetary battle between species with the stakes being nothing less than survival or extinction, and his novel is filled with heroic action and relentless terror. Doctorow has nothing comparable to offer, and his tale languishes in consequence.

The appearance of the colossi in New York Harbor of course creates a crisis, and America responds with the creation of a sinister superbureau, NYCRAD (New York Command for Research and Defense). NYCRAD is naked authority using the event to justify the insertion of its tentacles into every fiber of American life. The action played out in the balance of the book is largely the story of NYCRAD versus the human beings it has been created to protect – a portrait of America in the grasp of a right-wing insurgency that fails to be a warning, or a prophecy, or a satire, although the book fitfully displays elements of all three modes. Doctorow cannot seem to discover what sort of book he is trying to write, and again and again the reader is alerted for scenes and situations that are promised and then anticlimactically withdrawn.

In writing *Big as Life* Doctorow did not find the formula that could embody his imaginative concerns. That fusion of voice, politics, and point occurred in *The Book of Daniel* (1971). With this novel Doctorow tried yet another narrative form: the historical novel, using the spy trial and executions of Julius and Ethel Rosenberg in the early 1950s as the animating energy at the core of his tale. Doctorow has stated that a device he adapted from commercial television had freed him from a creative block in his writing of the novel: "You remember that television show *Laugh-In?* That was the big hit on television when I was writing *Daniel.* I told people when *Daniel* was published that it was constructed like *Laugh-In*. They thought I was not serious. But the idea of discontinuity and black-outs and running changes on voice and character – it was that kind of nerve energy I was looking for."

The result of Doctorow's experiment with that narrational "nerve energy" is impressive: Daniel Isaacson, the son of parents electrocuted for treason against the United States, is the central consciousness of the tale, but he is by no means the only consciousness, and Doctorow does not commit himself to any spirit of consistency. Sometimes it is 1967, sometimes the early 1950s, sometimes the Depression. The scene shifts from Cold War America to czarist Russia, from a Massachusetts asylum to Disneyland in California to a Bronx schoolyard. With stroboscopic speed the novel takes the reader into the minds of Daniel the graduate student at Columbia University, Daniel the child, Daniel the sexual "tormentor" of his wife, Daniel the social theorist, Daniel the brother grieving for his suicidal sister, and other Daniels as well. The reader is inside the minds of Daniel's parents, alleged spies Paul and Rochelle Isaacson, and briefly even in the mind of their lawyer. There are lectures about the dirty little secrets of American history. There are poems, slogans, and political insights. Doctorow informs the reader of the significance of a society's preferences in capital punishment, and there is a bizarre ground note, part lecture and part magic incantation, that celebrates the deadly power of electricity. The reader is told of Daniel's biblical namesake, of his role as interpreter of dreams and his ability to survive in the lion's den, metaphors for the prophet-seer role of Daniel Isaacson, who sees into the secret nighttime mind of the dangerous kingdom that has destroyed his parents. Nothing exactly like it existed in American prose before *The Book of Daniel*. Doctorow has explained that his decision to speak through Daniel and to have Daniel speak through other sensibilities involved an exhilarating sensation of escape: "I sat down and put a piece of paper in the typewriter and started to write with a certain freedom and irresponsibility, and it turned out Daniel was talking, and he was sitting in the library at Columbia, and I had my book."

Daniel's voice is also the voice of the Vietnam generation, the generation of the Beatles' *Sergeant Pepper's Lonely Hearts Club Band* (1967), the moon landings, the Chicago Seven, Charles Manson, Haight-Ashbury LSD, the Kent State shootings, Malcolm X, flower power, the Watergate scandal, and "Black Is Beautiful" – a generation that seems characterized everywhere by slogans and symbols of upheaval, by its frank, jovial, self-congratulatory rejection of every sort of established authority. *The Book of Daniel* demands that the reader respond to it as a political tract as well as a private description of experience. The novel is unabashedly a work of Left propaganda, as highly charged with moral outrage as George Orwell's *Animal Farm* (1945) and as anxious to reshape the reader's relationship to American historical pretensions as Henry David Thoreau's *Walden* (1854), John Dos Passos's *U.S.A.* trilogy (1930–1936), or Joseph Heller's *Catch-22* (1961).

"I was angry," Doctorow said in an interview. "It seems to me certainly a message of the twentieth century that people have a great deal to fear from their own governments. That's an inescapable world-wide fact. Daniel has a line about every citizen being the enemy of his own country. It is the nature of the governing mind to treat as adversary the people being governed."

Doctorow next published his most famous book, *Ragtime* (1975), delighting and puzzling readers at the same time. *The Book of Daniel* had been obviously modeled on the Rosenberg case, but it was clearly fiction. *Ragtime* took more liberties with history and identity. In this novel Harry Houdini, Henry Ford, J. P. Morgan, Emma Goldman, and a half-dozen other real people speak, think, and interact in ways that cannot be verified historically.

It is one measure of the singularity of *Ragtime* that it can be described as being at the same time a tragicomical novel starring American historical personages and also a sort of prose cartoon strip starring allegorical Everypeople purposely drained of biographical reality. The novel is at once history, cartoon, political fable, and fairy tale. Some of the events in the novel took place historically, and some merely should have. Some of its events are painfully real, while others are charmingly magical. The narrative tone is sardonic and urbane and directed along a privileged wavelength of attitude and allusion; yet the prose itself is intentionally flattened, declarative, chilly. It seems intentionally to parody an eighth-grade American history textbook, but its text would not be included in such histories. If the purpose of *Ragtime* is didactic, the manner is playful, ironic, self-aware, and brushed with the supernatural.

Doctorow's central moral intention seems to be to depict the invasion, from below and within and without, of a smug and secure American WASP (white Anglo-Saxon Protestant) family, circa 1908–1915, a microcosm of American self-conception at about the turn of the twentieth century. The novel is indeed a family and national Bildungsroman: an account of the nature of the American national character and the transformation of its identity. Such an ambitious intention in such a form struck some critics as pretentious.

For example, R. Z. Sheppard spoke irritably of Doctorow's narrative hybrid as an unsatisfactory mix of domestic comedy and cosmic portentousness: "As if Clarence Day had written *Future Shock* into *Life With Father,* Doctorow's images and improvisations foreshadow the 20th century's coming preoccupation with scandal, psychoanalysis, solipsism, race, technology, power and megalomania..." (*Time*, 14 July 1975).

In 1908 America was still a small town three thousand miles wide. Doctorow's crucial point and the moral substance of his novel are based in the masked tensions under that small-town surface. In 1908 America was still pretending. To examine that pretense and what became of it, Doctorow created an Everyfamily, headed by Father. As the story opens he has succeeded in the business of life just as Benjamin Franklin, Abraham Lincoln, and Thomas Edison said a penniless young American male should succeed. In fact, in 1908 Father sounds like a character from one of Horatio Alger's novels. Educated at Groton and Harvard for a leisured but empty life, Father was fortunately forced to become a self-made man when his own father's investments failed after the Civil War. By 1908 he is a manufacturer of fireworks, flags, and patriotic paraphernalia, who has done so well at it that God has rewarded him with a gold watch chain, a good digestion, a substantial income, a fine house in New Rochelle, a "large blond" wife, and a son in a sailor suit – in about that order of importance. He is also a big-game hunter and an amateur explorer of real accomplishment, for the decent American family man in the first decade of the twentieth century wanted to be as much like Theodore Roosevelt as he could manage.

Mother in the Everyfamily learns a great deal about herself in the course of the action. The sailor-suited little boy in the Everyfamily is about nine or ten years old, an artist in embryo (and perhaps an authentic clairvoyant) to whom no one but Doctorow and the reader pay the slightest attention. Also living in the New Rochelle house is Mother's Younger Brother, a moody, rudderless youth of perhaps eighteen pining for the infamous artist's model Evelyn Nesbit, whose husband has murdered the noted architect Stanford White for making her his mistress (an actual event of 1906). Mother's Younger Brother can think only of Evelyn and schemes to have her for himself. (Since Doctorow is writing a fairy tale as well as a history text, the Younger Brother succeeds.)

Nightmare genies are about to penetrate the shell of this smug American microcosm, whose official belief is that "there were no Negroes. There were no immigrants." While Father is gone on an expedition to the North Pole, Mother discovers in the family garden a living baby, who turns out to be the abandoned, illegitimate offspring of a black washerwoman called Sarah and a black ragtime musician, Coalhouse Walker. Doctorow told an interviewer that he heard the true prototype of this story from his wife, and "I found myself using it in *Ragtime*, where I never knew in advance what was going to happen." What happens sets in motion the entire march of events that forms the moral scheme of the novel. It is a tale of race and of property, two enduring American obsessions.

Coalhouse Walker – the musical gentleman "of color" whose refusal to be humiliated racially infuriates a certain sort of white – comes weekly to see his lover and the child he has sired. With each visit to New Rochelle he passes the rowdy Irish crew of the Emerald Isle Engine Company of volunteer firemen. The sight of a black man driving a Ford automobile does not sit well with them. Pretending to be charging him a toll for the use of the road into New Rochelle, the fireman end up defiling and eventually destroying Coalhouse's car. (Here Doctorow is adapting the plot of *Michael Kohlhaas,* an 1808 German novel by Heinrich von Kliest). Coalhouse demands restoration or restitution and is refused. While Sarah is trying to reach the Republican candidate for vice president, Sunny Jim Sherman, to ask him to intervene on her lover's behalf, one of Sherman's military bodyguards strikes her savagely with his rifle butt, badly injuring her chest. When Sarah dies of pneumonia brought on by her chest injuries, Coalhouse sets out to exact a terrible vengeance on white America.

With dynamite and shotgun Coalhouse ambushes and assassinates a half-dozen of the racist

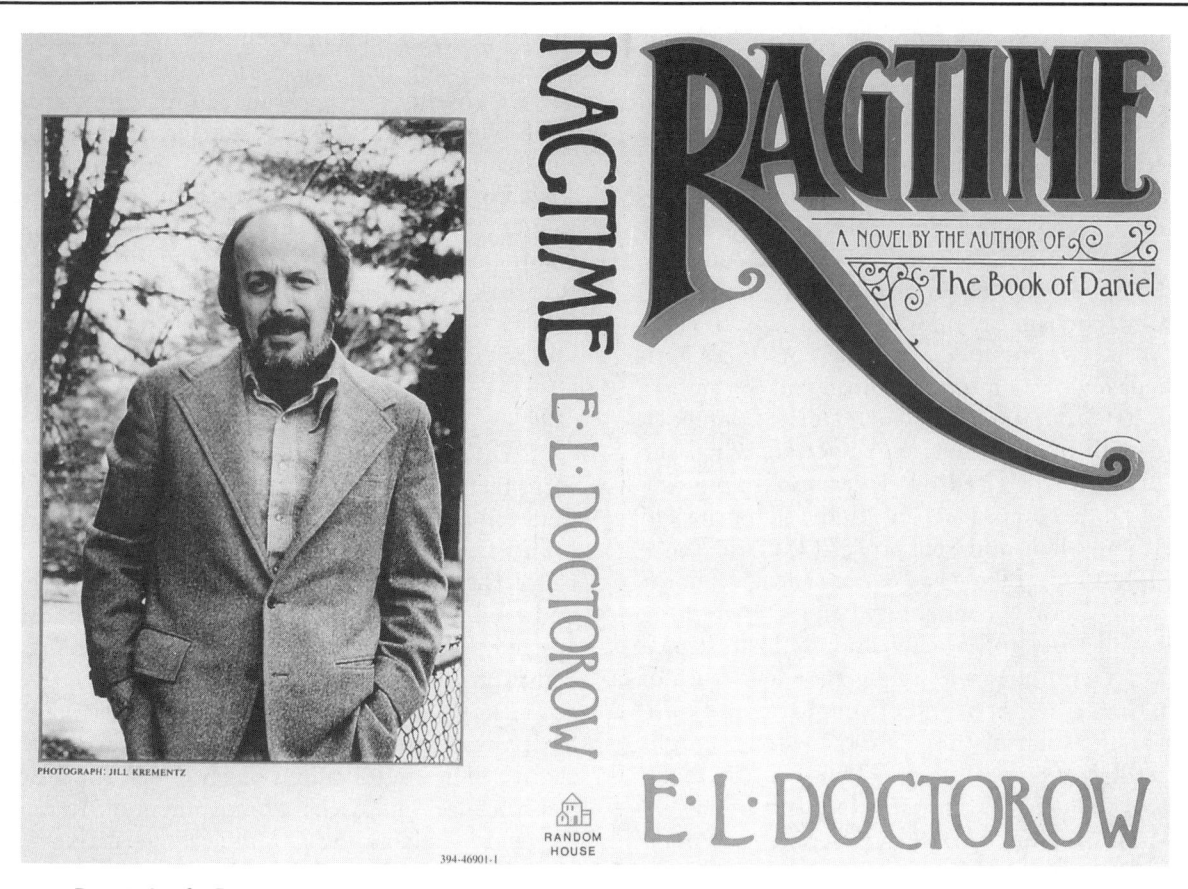

Dust jacket for Doctorow's best-known novel, a mixture of fact and fiction that exposes the social injustice inherent in Americans' complacency about their way of life during the years prior to World War I

firemen. Then the black man the press calls the "killer arsonist" lays siege to New York City, murdering more firemen and taking hostage something far dearer to the white American's heart than mere human life – property. Coalhouse and his rebel band occupy and threaten to dynamite the Pierpont Morgan Library, the recently completed marble building on Thirty-sixth Street that financier John Pierpont Morgan Sr. has built to house the collection of treasures he has accumulated – a vast, representative sampling of what white America values most as artifacts of high culture. Coalhouse's ordnance man is Mother's Younger Brother, lately the chief designer at his brother-in-law's fireworks factory. With this defection compounding Mother's adoption of the black orphan child, Doctorow signals that the smug WASP New Rochelle Everyfamily of 1908, transformed by compassion and outrage, has been changed forever.

Realizing that he will inevitably be destroyed himself for his vigilante presumption, Coalhouse demands that Willie Conklin, the racist fire chief of the Emerald Isle Engine Company, be given over to him for blood justice. This demand is not met, nor does Coalhouse really expect it to be. Then Booker T. Washington, the living embodiment of social humility as the cost of economic advancement for the black race, meets with Coalhouse under a flag of truce and admonishes the revolutionary to see that his intransigent demand for revenge is dragging to their deaths a half-dozen young blacks (and one young white man in blackface, Mother's Younger Brother), solely to satisfy his own vendetta.

To save his men Coalhouse softens his demands, asking only for a simple and symbolic restoration of his automobile; he will not give up his life without transforming its loss into a moral lesson about the rights of black people. Fire Chief Conklin is made to assemble an entire Model T from its disparate parts right at curbside in front of the Morgan Library. Of course Coalhouse and his men realize that the completion of the automobile will signal the musician's destruction, for at that moment he has promised to give himself up to the authorities. The grim climax of the novel occurs as Coalhouse is shot to death in the street by the police.

Behind the geniality of its temperament and the cheerful audacity of its method, *Ragtime* is a dark, violent prophecy from the age of which it is written to the era that comes to read it. For the novel Doctorow invented a style he has called "mock historical-pedantic." By its seeming *negation* of style, it manages to throw into relief the slightest nuance of irony applied to character, episode, or description. It is a fine technical achievement, first-rate writing and incisive teaching. Without seeming effort the novel catches on its radically curved surface a microcosm of America during the first decade of the twentieth century that convinces with the accuracy of its miniaturization and the authority of its dramatic metaphor. Doris Grumbach agreed with many American reviewers when she praised Doctorow's "adroit cleverness" in plotting and the subtle humor just beneath the simplicities of its "Dick-and-Jane-and-Spot prose" (*The New Republic,* 12 July 1975). Like many of her colleagues in the American literary community, she saw nothing wrong with Doctorow's reinvention of historic incident as a technique to highlight the inner truth of the ragtime era, "the world of simplicity and optimism at the turn of the century" when it might have still been possible for America "to make peace between classes and races in this country."

Appearing in 1975, when post-Vietnam America was in a revisionist mood, the novel received high praise in publications such as *The New York Times, The Village Voice, Newsweek, Time, Saturday Review,* and *The New Yorker.* For example, George Stade claimed that Doctorow had achieved an impressive breakthrough in his invention of a technique that could capture "the fictions and the realities of the era of ragtime" (*The New York Times Book Review,* 6 July 1975). Eliot Fremont-Smith said that Doctorow's novel was "simply splendid" on one level and yet also "complicatedly splendid" in its deeper levels of meaning, implication, and irony, "a bag of riches, totally lucid and accessible, full of surprises, epiphanies, little time-bombs that alter one's view of things . . ." (*The Village Voice,* July 1975). Reviewing the novel for the *Washington Post* (13 July 1975), Raymond Sokolov called it "brilliant and graceful" and praised Doctorow's ability to "throw the knowns and unknowns together in a racy plot that uses conventional history as its main premise and spins on outward from there in a zany extrapolation . . . [that turns] history into myth and myth into history." Like many of his colleagues, Walter Clemons of *Newsweek* (14 July 1975) was pleased rather than disturbed by Doctorow's reinventions of episode and encounter, comparing *Ragtime* to F. Scott Fitzgerald's *The Great Gatsby* (1925): "The demarcation between fiction and history is magically dissolved. . . . I found myself looking up details because I *wanted* them to be true. . . . The grace and surface vivacity of *Ragtime* make it enormous fun to read. But beneath its peppy, bracing rhythms sound the neat, sad waltz of *Gatsby* and the tunes of betrayed or disfigured promise that the best American novels play in one key or another." Stanley Kauffmann praised *Ragtime* as "a unique and beautiful work of art about American destiny, built of fact and logical fantasy, governed by music heard and sensed, responsive to cinema both as method and historical datum" (*Saturday Review,* 26 July 1975).

Yet the novelist's meddling with objective historic facts made several reviewers uneasy. They doubted that invented episodes were "truer" than events fixed in historical reality, and – perhaps because Doctorow had sheathed his radical politics and racial pessimism in such a funny, deadpan, "pseudopedantic" style, in the manner of a book for eighth graders – some critics reacted negatively. For example, Hilton Kramer distrusted the message he felt was concealed beneath the novel's surface charm: "The stern realities of Mr. Doctorow's political romance – its sweeping indictment of American life, and its celebration of a radical alternative – are all refracted, as it were, in the quaint, chromatic glow of a Tiffany lamp, and are thus softened and made more decorative in the process" (*Commentary,* October 1975). Martin Green leveled a similar charge, accusing Doctorow of taking "gross liberties with history in the name of art" and of encouraging the reader to indulge himself in a radical chic daydream, "to give ourselves the airs of revolutionaries, in purely fantasy and wish-fulfillment conditions" (*The American Scholar,* Winter 1975–1976). It is likely that critics will continue to be divided on the issue of the political vision of America expressed in *Ragtime* and – as one sort of response to that vision – on the right of an artist to alter and invent a fable "truer" than mere facts.

Doctorow followed *Ragtime* with a play, *Drinks Before Dinner* (1978) and with the novel *Loon Lake* (1980), an audacious book in style and construction. (The reader of *Ragtime* might have suspected that Doctorow would go on to experiment with the deep structures of narrative.) *Loon Lake* is sometimes moving, sometimes funny, and usually interesting, but it is not always successful as drama, social critique, or literary experiment – and not always conscientiously crafted. Yet Anthony Burgess, an innovative novelist himself, said with justice that if Doctorow had not quite brought off his effort he had indeed made "a very honorable attempt at ex-

-50-

I could hear the engine clearly now and knew it was moving at a slow speed. The first I saw of it was a diffuse paling of the darkness along the curve of the embankment. Suddenly I was blinded by a powerful light, as if I had looked into the sun. I dropped to my knees. The beam swung away from me in a transverse arc and a long conical ray of light illuminated the entire rock outcropping, every silvery vein of shist glittering as bright as a mirror, every fern and evergreen flaring for a moment as if torched. I rubbed my eyes and looked for the train behind the glare. It was passing from my left to my right. The locomotive and tender were blacker than the night, a massive movement forward of shadow, but there was a passenger car behind them and it was all lit up inside. I saw a porter in a white jacket serving drinks to three men sitting at a table. I saw dark wood panelling, a lamp with a fringed shade, and shelves of books in leather bindings. Then two women sitting talking at a group of wing arm chairs that looked textured, as if needlepointed. Then a bright bedroom with frost glass wall lamps and a canopied bed and standing naked in front of a mirror was a blonde girl and she was holding up for her examination a white dress on a hangar.

Oh my lords and ladies and then the train had passed through the clearing and I was watching the red light disappear around the bend. I hadn't moved from the moment the light had dazzled my eyes. I'd heard of private

Page from the typescript for Loon Lake *(courtesy of E. L. Doctorow)*

panding the resources of the genre" (*The Saturday Review,* September 1980). *Loon Lake* lacks the emotional focus of *The Book of Daniel* and does not have a source of fascination equivalent to the cast of historical personalities Doctorow commandeered with such bravado for *Ragtime*. Just as with his 1989 crime saga, *Billy Bathgate,* Doctorow seems to get tired of the novel nine-tenths of the way through and concludes his tale with a jarring mixture of exasperation, invention, and fatigue.

Loon Lake is at once three kinds of book: a Depression-era Bildungsroman; a love-triangle thriller in the manner of a hard-boiled detective writer such as James M. Cain (or, more accurately, about half a movie script for a love-triangle thriller); and an ironic critique of that distinctly American symbiosis of capitalism and crime. The elements of the novel include a young man with a taste for adventure, a traveling carnival, decadent old money, management ruthlessly infiltrating a labor strike, and a great deal of sex, some of it well described and erotic and some of it well described and freakishly repulsive. If the structure suggests Vladimir Nabokov, the content summons up Ernest Hemingway, Jack London, Upton Sinclair – and the Warner Bros. B-movie unit of Hollywood, California, circa 1936.

Loon Lake is also something of a science-fiction novel, in structure if not subject. While *Big as Life* derives its shock value from incursion of giants from another space-time continuum breaking through the scrim into a world like this one, it is still recognizably conventional in its narrative structure. *Loon Lake* offers a far more radical dislocation under its surface. Space, time, and event inside it are multiple versions of "our" space, time, and event. Things happen in *Loon Lake*. Then they happen again, but only *almost* the same way that they happened before. Then different things happen altogether, with no final authority as to which event in which space-time continuum "really" takes place. Doctorow's world does not offer us an absolute standard by which to decide.

Doctorow begins his tale in the summer of 1936, in the midst of the Great Depression. A dangerous young street punk known only as Joe goes on the lam from the blue-collar world of Paterson, New Jersey. Protean in personality, Joe is hardly content with shoplifting, alley stabbings with his razor-sharp penknife, robbing the poor box at church, or discovering sex with a Gramercy Park housemaid. He knows he wants to be someone other than himself, but he cannot seem to find the final version of that other.

With each experience Joe feels that "some silent secret presence grew out to the edges of me." The adult world may be hollow and pretending and afraid but merely seeing through it is not enough. Joe will not be tamed by the respectable world, but he also must find out what he is, and so Doctorow sends him out into the vast forests of the northern republic, where invisible energies guide him to his fate – and to himself.

On the open road Joe receives his real political education from hobo socialists in random Hoovervilles, and then he catches on with a carnival on its slow, sordid journey through the lost slag-gray villages of the Adirondacks. Joe has an affair with the owner's wife and then takes off by himself. In the depths of a midnight forest he experiences a vision "of incandescent splendor," a private train car passing only a few yards from him and within it a beautiful naked blond girl trying on a dress. Spellbound, Joe follows the tracks toward the major dramatic locus of the book, the thirty-thousand-acre hideaway of mysterious multimillionaire F. W. Bennett and the rest of the cast that surrounds him, including the kept poet Warren Penfield, the kept woman Clara Lukacs, the kept gangster Tommy Crapo, and, ultimately, the solution to the riddle of Joe's identity.

The critical reception of *Loon Lake* was, on the whole, positive, although nowhere near as enthusiastic as the response to *Ragtime*. In general critics found Doctorow's technical experiments with the novel's interior reality to be distracting. For example, Robert Towers wrote that "there were times when this reader felt trapped in a Barthian funhouse of mirrors and longed for some graspable, salient sense of the whole to emerge" (*The New York Times Book Review,* 28 September 1980), and Clancy Sigal said that "the style – some of it written in a kind of computer-printout blank verse, with side trips to Zen Japan – kept getting in the way. . ." (*New York* 29 September 1980).

Yet most critics also found much to praise behind the technical fireworks. Thus, Towers commented on "the vivid human substance" of Doctorow's tale, and George Stade, reviewing the book for *The Nation* (27 September 1980) called up the musical metaphor that the title for *Ragtime* had made inevitable when he praised *Loon Lake* as "odd and dissonantly beautiful, like a chorus of blues played by Dizzy Gillespie." Stade considered this novel an advance on the politically doctrinaire *Ragtime* in its tone of gentle sympathy and ironic qualification as to Joe's struggle – the essential American struggle – to create one's self from next to nothing:

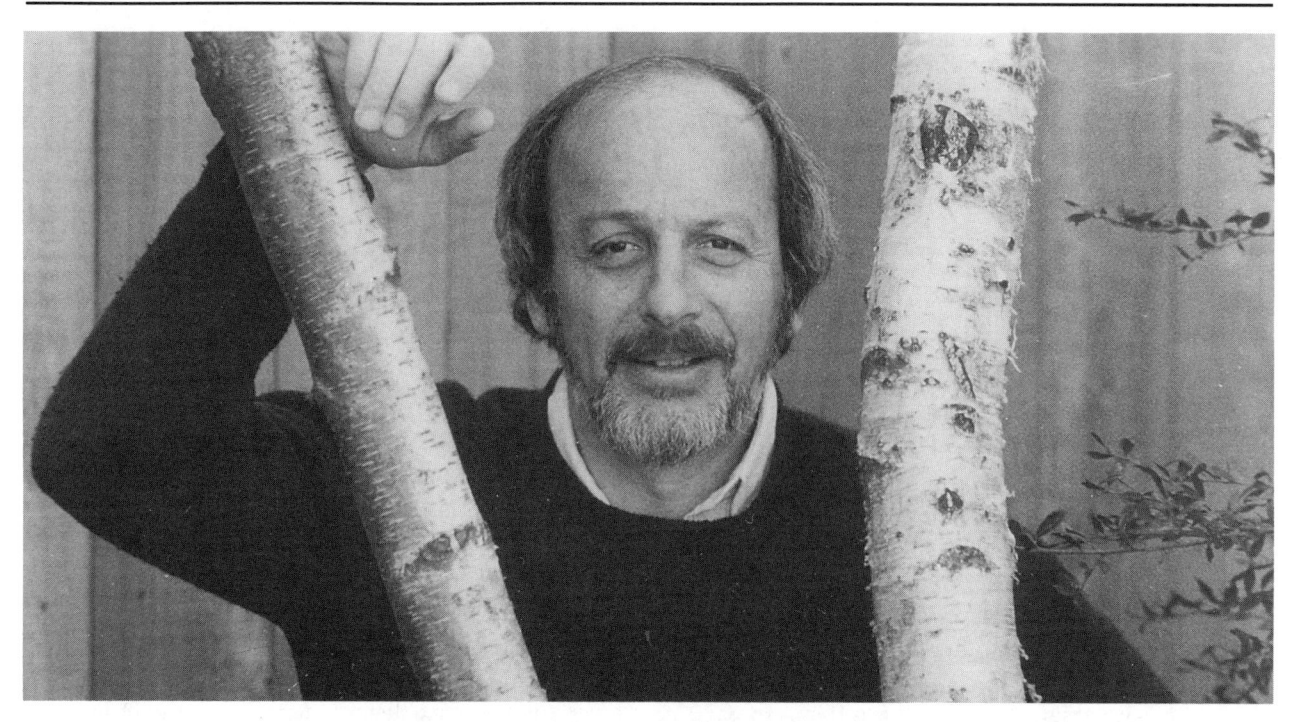

Doctorow at the time of Loon Lake *(photograph by Paul Davis)*

in *Loon Lake* "there is something still more valuable: a tone, a mood, an atmosphere, a texture, a poetry, a felt and meditated vision of how things go with us. It is more useful to a writer of fiction than a social conscience."

Novelist Margaret Atwood complimented the "many brilliant parts" of the novel and found it disappointing only in the hurried, arbitrary transformation of Joe of Paterson into the Master of Loon Lake at the end (*Washington Post Book World*, 28 September 1980). Writing in *The Atlantic Monthly* (September 1980), Benjamin DeMott claimed he liked some aspects of *Loon Lake* much better than he had some dimensions of *Ragtime*: "there are openings toward the human that give the book a freshness – a sweetness, even, that's absent from *Ragtime*."

The truth of two critical dissents, however, cannot be disregarded. In *The New Republic* (20 September 1980), Mark Harris objected to the ending: "In the most indolent fashion Doctorow carries the life of Joe of Paterson 40 years forward with a two-page Who's Who entry concluding this novel. I cannot believe it. A high school creative writing class would never stand for such a thing." An even more vehement attack was came from Dean Flower, writing for *The Hudson Review* (Spring 1981), who loathed Doctorow's "suave new stylistic tricks," and claimed that Joe was a "mechanical pastiche of Gatsby, Willy Stark, and Rojack in Mailer's *An American Dream*. . . . Doctorow's figure remains stuffed, a set of fragments from other books."

Having journeyed so far outward into self-delighting invention and cosmic paradox in the creation of *Loon Lake,* Doctorow returned to more-traditional tones and narrative procedures for his next two books, *Lives of the Poets* and *World's Fair* (1985).

The novella and six short stories in *Lives of the Poets* vary widely in quality as well as in the quotient of autobiography Doctorow put into them. Two of the stories, "The Writer in the Family" and "Willi," are fluently written and cleverly plotted and are informed by Doctorow's constant concerns. Several others, however, seem to be not-quite-successful experiments with voice and incident, and some have elements that seem forced and unconvincing, as if the material or the tone were not really compatible with Doctorow's sensibility.

One of the stories, "The Hunter," is a small masterpiece. Estrangement is the real substance of "The Hunter," a key mood in its haunting and subtle beauty. The tale is set in winter in a dying factory town in upstate New York, and the nameless young woman who is the town's new schoolteacher "has been here just long enough for her immodest wish to transform these children to have turned to awe at what they are." Doctorow gives his flower-child teacher just the sort of imagination, vitality, and narcissism that such a young woman of her generation might be likely to possess. Instead of boring her children with spelling and long division, for example, she leads them all through the big, echoing, near-empty school building, telling them they are a "lost patrol in the caves of a planet far out in space" – and of course, in the deepest sense, they are.

The teacher is not simply a cheery and sympathetic persona who does somersaults along with her students. Doctorow hints at her half-hidden, half-humiliating sexual frustration. She finds herself attracted to a new schoolbus driver, a blond young man, but there is a vexing social and intellectual gulf between them. The driver is just an underemployed, ignorant Joe, and the teacher is put off almost against her will by the fact that he is common. In fact she seems offended that the town is not trying to make itself good enough for her. She performs an act of smug noblesse oblige, reading aloud at the old people's home, and finds herself shocked and repulsed by the vicious egotism of the senior citizens, who mock each other and vie for her attention.

The last passage has a beauty difficult to paraphrase. Avoiding the driver she has rejected when he made a clumsy pass at her, the teacher announces to the children that today is a special day: the town photographer has been summoned to take a picture of the class. "I don't get these school calls till spring," the potbellied man in his string tie complains. "Why, these children ain't fixed up for their picture . . . they ain't got on their ties and their new shoes. You got girls here wearing trousers. . . ." The picture is taken anyway, the teacher holding as many of the children as she can get her arms around, her heart seeming to cry out in secret near hysteria, at least I have these! In its delicacy, accuracy, and grave, disciplined sympathy, "The Hunter" is an impressive achievement.

The title novella, "Lives of the Poets," is altogether different from the other pieces in the collection: funny, intimate, gossipy, unstructured, garrulous, charming, and seemingly autobiographical down to the fine details. While "The Hunter" transforms elements of Doctorow's perceptions into structured art held at arm's length, "Lives of the Poets" seems to anticipate his 1985 novel-memoir, *World's Fair,* in its contagious fascination with that which is *only there.* The reader feels that almost everything here and in *World's Fair* is recovered rather than invented, and the play of intelligence on reality is both the motive and the delight of the piece.

A man alone is in bad company, said Paul Valéry. Doctorow's persona "Jonathan" is not only alone with himself in his new Greenwich Village writer's lair, but he has also just turned fifty, and the dismal occasion of his birthday seems to have forced him into a discussion – if not quite an assessment – of his art and his life, of his successes, his failures, and his feelings. He has left his wife and children in Connecticut and gone to New York, ostensibly to write. Yet his wife has a host of suspicions about the real uses to which the apartment is being put, and the novella confirms the worst of them: Jonathan has a mistress: "I took it for her. I took it for our New York place."

The title of the novella comes from Samuel Johnson's *Lives of the Poets* (1779–1781), but Jonathan's "poets" are the writers and intellectuals, both men and women, who constitute the dramatis personae of his life: wife, lover, friends. Most of them seem to be "couples not entirely together," and Jonathan's own marriage seems to be tottering. Even his success as a writer has something hollow in it: "each book has taken me further and further out so that the occasion itself is extenuated, no more than a weak distant signal from the home station, and even that may be fading." And his social conscience troubles him; he is a guilty success in a Manhattan full of desperate failures.

In depicting the Manhattan of immigrants and aliens Doctorow expresses his "radical Jewish humanism," creating for Jonathan's five-thousand-year-old Jewish conscience the humane, charming, mildly dangerous act that climaxes the novella and lifts his guilt over his success. Brenda, an activist, radical-chic actress, takes Jonathan to an activist church on the Upper West Side, where he sees wretched illegal aliens being cared for by the parish. Jonathan takes a mestizo family into his bohemian writer's digs – complete with diapers, tortilla mix, and dried beans. Though he worries about how long they will stay, he has finally worked out some sort of truce with his social conscience, a way to atone for what the United States is doing in Latin America, "what I have to do to live with myself." Jewish liberal guilt has seldom been so charmingly assuaged.

The importance of lifting such guilt is apparent in Doctorow's experimental play of 1978, *Drinks Before Dinner,* a talky, static attempt to exorcise the demons of guilt, boredom, and surfeit that seem to dwell within American success. At a posh New York dinner party a man called only "Edgar" (Doctorow's first name) holds a gun on Alan, a distinguished and powerful dinner guest from Washington (and a Nobel laureate perhaps modeled on Henry Kissinger). "What a charming and sympathetic man," Edgar exclaims of Alan. "How dangerous. You hear behind his charming and sympa-

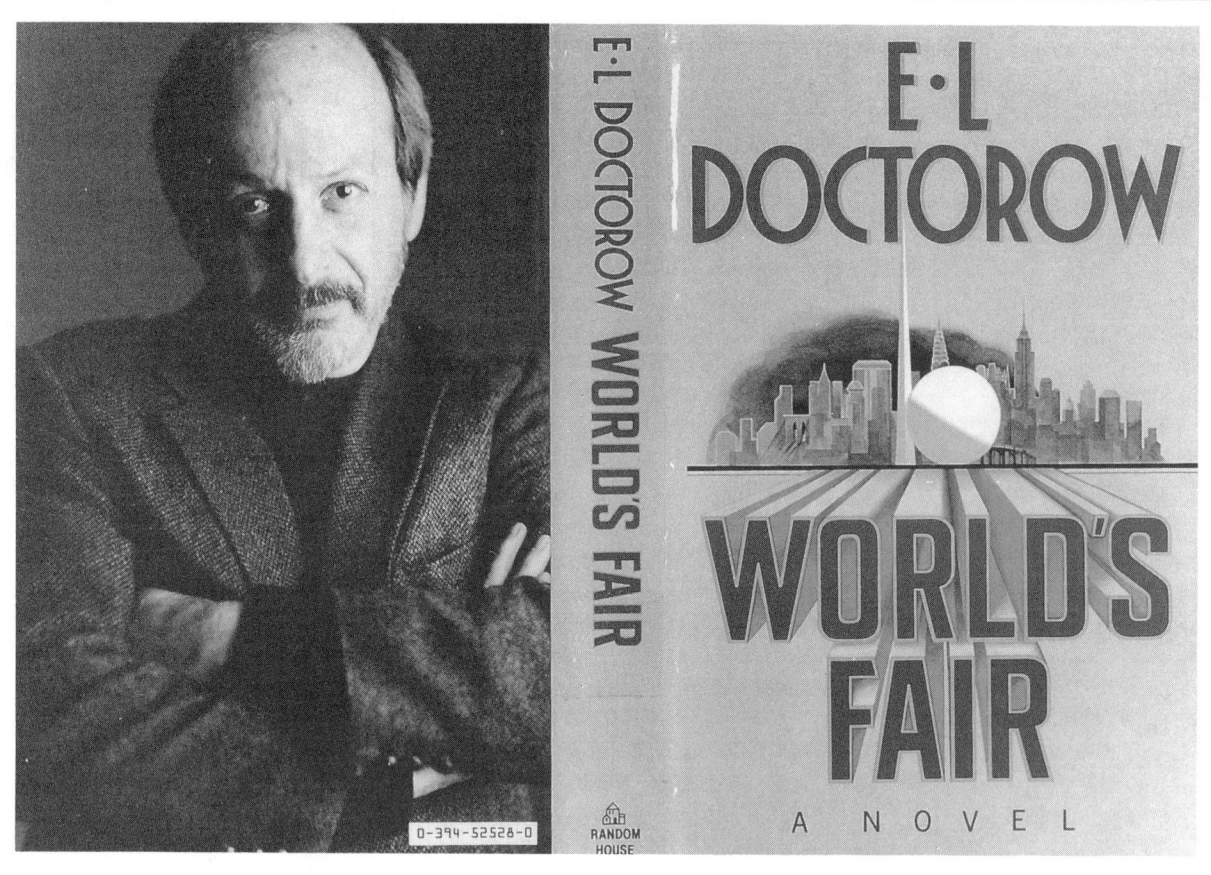

Dust jacket for the autobiographical novel in which Doctorow attempted to "break down the distinction between formal fiction and the actual, palpable sense of life as it is lived"

thetic voice the computer clicks of missiles calculating their trajectory." Nothing comes of Edgar's menace – the gun is not even loaded – and the audience more or less has to agree with Alan's bitter denunciation of Edgar as one of "those hypocrites of privilege who condemns everything but relinquishes nothing . . . one of those spiritual vandals who would like to be a revolutionary but hasn't the balls of a flea."

Reviewing *Lives of the Poets* in *The New Republic* (3 December 1984), James Wolcott observed, "E. L. Doctorow is sneaking open the cupboard doors of his imagination and saying 'Welcome to the clutter.'" Wolcott thoroughly disliked the collection, especially the title novella, which he called "an act of vanity . . . crabbed and pettish, like the book itself." Yet the collection was chosen by *The New York Times* as one of the ten best works of 1984, and Peter S. Prescott gave it a glowing review in *Newsweek* (19 November 1984). "Better than any fiction I know, *Lives of the Poets* illuminates the sources from which fiction springs," Prescott proclaimed.

Doctorow won an American Book Award for *World's Fair,* which he wrote with the intention to "break down the distinction between formal fiction and the actual, palpable sense of life as it is lived." Readers of *The Book of Daniel, Ragtime,* and *Lives of the Poets* were already aware that Doctorow regards facts as only *mere* facts, things that may or may not be true on deeper, poetic levels, and is always willing to substitute a poetic truth for those mere facts. "I have this concept of history as imagery, and therefore as a resource for writing," Doctorow told an interviewer on the publication of *World's Fair.*

The fact that *World's Fair* is most centrally concerned with Doctorow's family relationships is of foremost importance in examining the book as an autobiography. *World's Fair* is his tribute to family life itself, "life as it is lived," a family memoir more than a private memoir, created with neither propaganda nor sentimentality nor condescension.

Literary autobiography offers three primary sorts of fascination. First there is the play of memory on reality itself, for few human acts are so pleasant to experience vicariously as the act of recall, no matter what the object, no matter how trivial the detail. Second, there is the satisfaction of discovering the "original" of things found in the mature fiction.

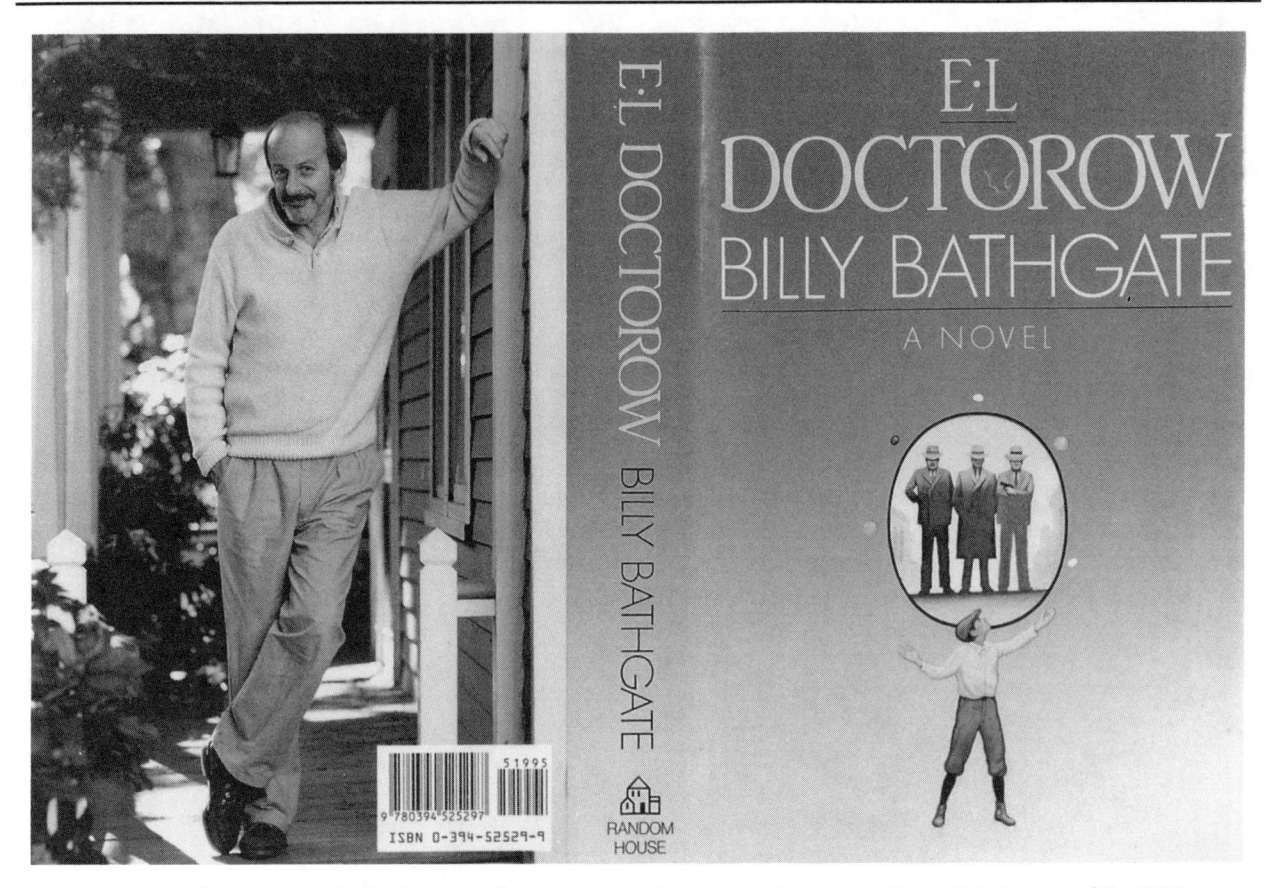

Dust jacket for Doctorow's fictional account of a young man's adventures in the notorious Dutch Schultz gang of the 1930s

World's Fair includes several of these shadow forms, some of them important to the comprehension of Doctorow's stories and novels. Third, there is that delight peculiar to all biography and autobiography: the prophetic awareness that an ordinary childhood conducts toward the extraordinary maturity about which the reader already knows. *World's Fair* is, along with much else, a prophecy, a prophecy magically fulfilled, and the reader takes as much satisfaction in watching things come out as he knows they will as in finding out how destiny turned the trick in the first place.

At school the narrator is a good "citizen" and a good student. There are the movies, of course, and there is that archetypal American-boy discovery, baseball. A brilliant description of Rockaway Beach in 1936 is rendered with vivacious intensity, convincing the reader that the scene conveyed to the young Doctorow a primal sense of nothing less than the world itself: "I learned the enlightening fear of the planet." The year 1936 was a good one for learning about fear, for in Europe "Jewish death was spreading," and Doctorow conveys the way in which a child's mind draws the world's evils in shapes comprehensible to its own size and place.

In *World's Fair* — as in *The Book of Daniel* and *Ragtime* — the accuracy and precision of a microcosm becomes the reader's means of apprehending the energies that are blazing across the surface of history itself. At the real 1939–1940 World's Fair in New York City, a time capsule sponsored by Westinghouse was buried for the edification of people five thousand years later, its contents such signs of our civilization as Margaret Mitchell's best-seller *Gone with the Wind* (1936), a Mickey Mouse plastic cup, a movie of Howard Hughes flying around the world, and the Lord's Prayer in no fewer than three hundred languages. Scores of other children no doubt imitated that time capsule just as Doctorow did, burying his Tom Mix Decoder badge, his Hohner Marine Band harmonica, and his four-page biography of President Franklin D. Roosevelt (with its grade of 100 percent) in a foil-lined mailing tube, but Doctorow's real time capsule for the future is *World's Fair* itself. Time, said poet W. H. Auden, loves words and forgives all those who live by them. Doctorow's memoir is a perfect illustration of the truth of that claim.

Reviewing *World's Fair* for *The New York Times* (24 November 1985), Christopher Lehmann-Haupt indicated that the power of the book lay in its ability to do fine things with ordinary materials: "you shake your head in disbelief and ask yourself how he has managed to do it.... You get lost in *World's Fair* as if it were an exotic adventure. You devour it with the avidity usually provoked by a suspense thriller . . . [the 1930s] are savored in retrospect by a mature intelligence whose memory of childhood is so uncannily vivid, yet who keeps his unsentimental distance with the mock solemn prose that has become Mr. Doctorow's inimitable music." Even though another *New York Times* reviewer, David Leavitt, had mixed feelings about the book because of what he called its "fractured and inconsistent feel," he praised Doctorow's gift for producing "magnificent descriptive passages" (10 November 1985).

The "disreputable genre materials" that inspired *Billy Bathgate* (1989), which won a National Book Critics Circle Award for fiction, may have been the comic book and the Depression-era pulp thriller. Doctorow seems to have tried to give his novel the joyful velocity and preposterousness of what the literary establishment calls "subliterature."

Nothing less than an Horatio Alger miracle allows Billy Bathgate, an underage Bronx nobody, to get himself initiated into the most dangerous, glamorous gang in New York: Billy is juggling near one of Dutch Schultz's illegal-beer barns when he is spotted by the notorious, real-life gangster, who is charmed enough by the lad's discipline and cool to take him on as an amusement and an apprentice. Billy is led by degrees into the inner sanctum of the Schultz gang, with its "purveyed lawless might and military self-sufficiency" and becomes a lad useful to Dutch and his men because, like any captain of industry, the gangster lord needs eyes and ears and a face unknown to the police to run errands, to tail people, to report back: in short, a spy. Thus the novel has a privileged narrator, privy to secrets but distanced enough for his voice to lend a moral and intellectual dimension to the raw action. America is the country of the creation of the self, and the crime novel is one of the truest variants of our national Bildungsroman. From Fitzgerald's *The Great Gatsby* through Mario Puzo's *The Godfather* (1969), William Kennedy's *Legs* (1975), and Ron Hansen's neglected masterpiece *The Assassination of Jesse James by the Coward Robert Ford* (1983), the romance of high crime has engaged some of America's best writers. Of course there is also the sheer escapism of *Billy Bathgate*. As Billy puts it, he risks his life to join the Dutch Schultz gang and live in a "thrilling state of three-dimensional danger." Doctorow has written his novel to do the same for the reader.

Dutch's gang is composed of underworld denizens as colorful as the characters in a comic book. Most successful of all is Otto "Abbadabba" Berman, the dapper hunchbacked mathematical genius who serves as the brains of the gang, a "deviously instructive" presence of perfect reserve and solemn wisdom. Since Billy is fatherless and his laundress mother is eerily disconnected from reality, the gang becomes his new family. (As always Doctorow's fascination with the family asserts itself.)

The gang is a strange family, indeed. Billy watches Dutch kill a greedy fire inspector with his bare hands and stuff his corpse into a garbage can. Right before Billy's eyes troublesome window washers trying to establish their own union are allowed to fall to their deaths from scaffolding fifteen stories above the street, and Dutch himself tells Billy about cutting the throat of a rival numbers-racket boss in a barbershop, a piece of clever professional work with chloroform and razorblade of which the crime boss is extremely proud (and a set piece on which Doctorow has lavished his most craftsmanlike attention). Billy's gift for juggling a few stray objects in the air has led the lad into a dark, thrilling realm just behind the facade of the reasonable world, and he will never submit to commonplace existence again.

Everywhere in *Billy Bathgate* the reader is aware of Doctorow's use of materials from the pulp and celluloid bins of 1930s mass art, such as *Black Mask* and the B-movie offerings of Republic Studios. But just as he was able in *Ragtime* to fill in the outlines of historical personages with vivid lives of his own invention and to reclaim overfamiliar situations from the attic of American popular culture, so in his big crime novel Doctorow transforms the preposterous characters and plots of the comic strip into a creation that rewards the attention of the mature reader.

A collection of fourteen of Doctorow's essays was published in 1993 as *Jack London, Hemingway, and The Constitution*. Like many fiction writers, Doctorow's comprehension of other writers is subtle and accurate; he sees their intentions and technical efforts from the inside and estimates their success from the point of view of craft. In his discussion of Jack London's *Call of the Wild* – often condescendingly dismissed by academic critics as a boy's adventure book – Doctorow discovers a great measure of "complex spiritual life," and he has fascinating things to say about London's technical achievement and his social Darwinism, about the frontier America, and about the moral dimensions of fiction itself. London, Theodore Dreiser, and George Or-

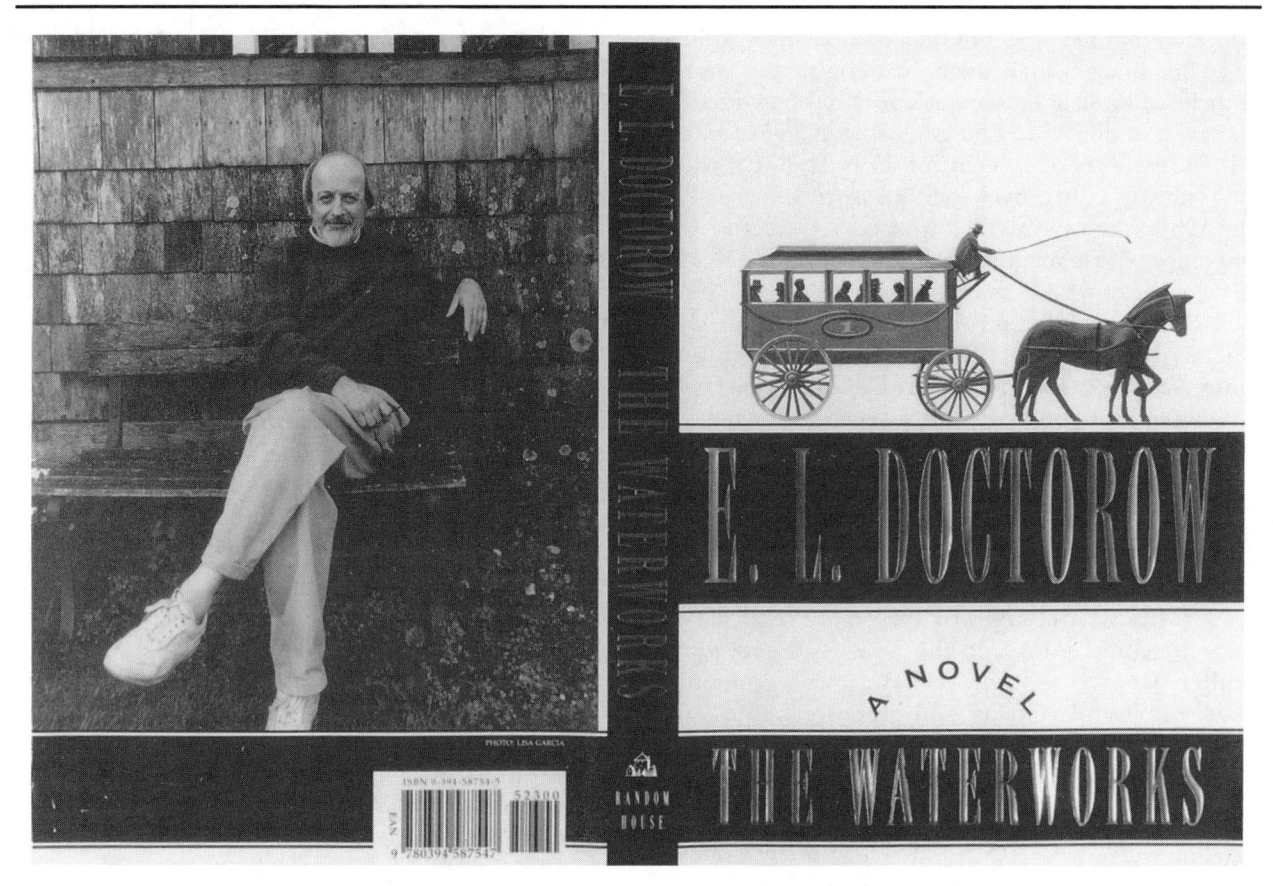

Dust jacket for Doctorow's Gothic tale of a doctor's experiments in prolonging the lives of his millionaire patients with tissues and vital fluids harvested from orphans and street urchins

well were writers animated by urgent moral and political concerns, and Doctorow is perhaps especially perceptive in regard to their work because he shares that interest. "How can any writer-citizen not bless himself for having outlasted the long cold decades of his time?" Doctorow asks rhetorically in his introduction – and it is indeed the half century of the Cold War, "a fifty-year nuclear alert," and its dark moral consequences for the great American experiment in personal liberty that provide the theme for most of his essays.

Reviewing the collection for *The New Republic* (18–25 July 1994), Andrew Delbanco was critical of Doctorow's "mixture of outrage and sentimentality" and noted that, as a political and cultural essayist for the Left, Doctorow tended to sound "callow and even pontifical." Yet the finest of the essays, "James Wright at Kenyon," is focused on neither American cultural misadventure nor Cold War moral deformity. Both James Wright, a classmate of Doctorow who became a distinguished poet, and American collegiate life circa 1948 are depicted with fidelity, affection, and a sort of genial, unillusioned charm both rare and welcome in Doctorow's work.

Inspired by Doctorow's haunting sketch "The Waterworks," originally published in *Lives of the Poets,* Doctorow's 1994 novel, *The Waterworks,* is essentially a Gothic thriller grafted onto a moralist's portrait of the social squalor of New York City in the high decadence of the Gilded Age – a hybrid of Edgar Allan Poe and the muckraking journalist Jacob Riis, perhaps. Doctorow told interviewer Laurel Graeber that he had been named for Poe and that this novel was an effort "to do Poe honor." Once again family feelings form the marrow of Doctorow's concerns.

The tale is narrated by a newspaper editor named McIlvaine, who has a soft spot in his jaded soul for his most talented and least dependable young reporter, Martin Pemberton, the disinherited son of a sinister plutocrat named Augustus Pemberton. The elder Pemberton made his millions by supplying the Union Army with shoddy war material even while continuing to run African slaves to Cuba during a war ostensibly fought to free them. Martin, who wears a military greatcoat to call ironic attention to his father's peculations, refuses to contaminate himself with the family's ill-gotten lucre.

Augustus apparently dies and is apparently buried, but – in a true gothic twist worthy of Poe – Martin accidentally discovers his father is still alive. Augustus and some of his rich, elderly comrades are desperately trying to cheat Time and Death with the aid of a former Civil War battle surgeon called Dr. Sartorius. (The name means "tailor.") Sartorius keeps his clients alive in his catacomb-laboratory under the Croton Holding Reservoir by injecting them with vital fluids and tissues ruthlessly harvested from the vast, anonymous underclass of New York City street urchins. The story of these wizened old millionaires kept alive at the expense of "throwaway children" is nothing if not a strenuous moral parable for the American social project of the 1870s, a time of largely unregulated capitalist expansion fueled by the toil of lower-class men, women, and children.

Harvard historian Simon Schama has praised the "forensic precision" of *The Waterworks* in its portraiture of class exploitation and has confessed that he as a reader was "helplessly and gratefully caught in the current" (*The New York Times Book Review*, 19 June 1994). Yet Rhoda Koenig rightly points out that Doctorow's homage to Poe is so lurid and melodramatic and his homage to the great journalistic muckrakers so obsessive that he ends up failing to engage the reader with either appeal (*Vogue*, June 1994). As with *Big as Life*, Doctorow cannot decide what kind of book he is writing. He has created "metaphors rather than men," Koenig claims, and she holds that his use of "mad-doctor fantasies from B-movies" is a fictive near fiasco. Reviewing the novel for *Maclean's* (25 July 1994), John Bemrose notes that "it is a fable that explores the way the past can control the present."

Judged on its merits as a tale of terror, the book lacks that sense of "less is more" that marks out the best modern efforts to create a Gothic thriller. Doctorow has rightly realized that the spirit of gothicism involves a social backdrop in which the guilty past revenges itself on the pretending present, but in the foreground of his novel his papier-mâché collection of mad-genius resurrectionists, gallant conscience-stricken newshounds, and moonlit graveyard exhumations provokes more comparison to Mel Brooks than to Ira Levin. For all its promise, the novel is an underachieving B-movie melodrama with good social intentions rather than the tale of primal terror and cultural uplift that Doctorow no doubt hoped to create as he stitched it together from fragments of Charles Dickens, Frank Norris, radio serials, urban legends, and comic books.

From the crisp deadpan ironies of *Ragtime* through the purple Faulknerian thunderclouds of *Billy Bathgate* there is no doubt that Doctorow is a writer always pushing at the far edges of his talent in an attempt to achieve work of significance and authority. *The Book of Daniel*, *Ragtime*, and *World's Fair* are perhaps Doctorow's greatest successes, but everything he has published demonstrates not only his talent but his restless search for a new means of expressing what Joseph Conrad considered the treasures that only fiction can bestow: "encouragement, consolation, fear, charm – all you demand – and, perhaps, also that glimpse of truth for which you had forgotten to ask."

Interviews:

Victor Navasky, "E. L. Doctorow: I Saw a Sign," *New York Times Book Review*, 28 September 1980, pp. 44–45;

Richard Trenner, ed., *E. L. Doctorow: Essays and Conversations* (Princeton, N.J.: Ontario Review Press, 1983);

George Plimpton, "The Art of Fiction," *Paris Review*, 101 (Winter 1986): 22–47;

Kay Bonetti, *An Interview with E. L. Doctorow*, American Audio Prose Library, 1990;

Christopher D. Morris, "'Fiction as a System of Knowledge': An Interview with E. L. Doctorow," *Michigan Quarterly Review*, 30 (Summer 1991): 439–456.

Bibliography:

Michelle M. Tokarczyk, *E. L. Doctorow: An Annotated Bibliography* (New York & London: Garland, 1988).

References:

J. Bakker, "The Western; Can It Be Great?" *Dutch Quarterly Review of Anglo-American Letters*, 14, no. 2 (1984): 140–163;

Henry Claridge, "Writing in the Margin: E. L. Doctorow and American History," in *The New American Writing: Essays on American History*, edited by Graham Clarke (New York: St. Martin's Press, 1990), pp. 9–28;

Barbara Cooper, "The Artist as Historian in the Novels of E. L. Doctorow," *Emporia State Research Studies*, 29 (Fall 1980): 5–44;

David Emblidge, "Marching Backward into the Future: Progress as Illusion in Doctorow's Novels," *Southwest Review*, 62 (Autumn 1977): 397–409;

Joseph Epstein, "A Conspiracy of Silence," *Harper's*, 255 (November 1977): 80–92;

Robert Forrey, "Doctorow's *The Book of Daniel:* All in the Family," *Studies in American Jewish Literature,* 2 (1982): 167–173;

Douglas Fowler, *Understanding E. L. Doctorow* (Columbia: University of South Carolina Press, 1992);

Herwig Friedl and Dieter Schulz, eds., *E. L. Doctorow: A Democracy of Perception* (Essen: Die Blau Eule, 1988);

Angela Hague, "*Ragtime* and the Movies," *North Dakota Quarterly,* 50, no. 3 (1983): 101–112;

Geoffrey Galt Harpham, "E. L. Doctorow and the Technology of Narrative," *PMLA,* 100, no. 1 (1985): 81–95;

Carol C. Harter and James R. Thompson, *E. L. Doctorow* (Boston: Twayne, 1990);

Carol Iannone, "E. L. Doctorow's Jewish Radicalism," *Commentary,* 81 (March 1986): 53–56;

Diane Johnson, "The Righteous Artist: E. L. Doctorow," in *Terrorists & Novelists,* edited by Johnson (New York: Knopf, 1982), pp. 141–149;

Paul Levine, *E. L. Doctorow* (London & New York: Methuen, 1985);

Levine, "The Two Cultures of *Ragtime,*" in *High and Low in American Culture,* edited by Charlotte Kretzoi (Budapest: Department of English, Lorand Eotvos University, 1986);

Christopher D. Morris, *Models of Misrepresentation: On the Fiction of E. L. Doctorow* (Jackson: University Press of Mississippi, 1991);

Alan Nadel, "Hero and Other in Doctorow's *Loon Lake,*" *College Literature,* 14, no. 2 (1987): 136–145;

John G. Parks, *E. L. Doctorow* (New York: Continuum, 1991);

Frank W. Shelton, "E. L. Doctorow's *Welcome to Hard Times:* The Western and the American Dream," *Midwest Quarterly,* 25 (Autumn 1983): 7–17;

John Stark, "Alienation and Analysis in E. L. Doctorow's *The Book of Daniel,*" *Critique,* 16, no. 3 (1975): 101–110;

Richard Trenner, ed., *E. L. Doctorow: Essays and Conversations* (Princeton, N.J.: Ontario Review Press, 1983);

Bruce Weber, "The Myth Maker: The Creative Mind of Novelist E. L. Doctorow," *New York Times Magazine,* 21 October 1985, pp. 25–31;

John Williams, *Fiction as False Document: The Reception of E. L. Doctorow in the Postmodern Age* (Columbia, S.C.: Camden House, 1996).

J. P. Donleavy
(23 April 1926 -   )

William Nelles
University of Massachusetts – Dartmouth

See also the Donleavy entry in *DLB 6: American Novelists Since World War II: Second Series.*

BOOKS: *The Ginger Man* [novel] (Paris: Olympia Press, 1955; expurgated editions, London: Spearman, 1956; New York: McDowell, Oblensky, 1958; unexpurgated editions, London: Corgi, 1963; New York: Seymour Lawrence/Delacorte, 1965);

The Ginger Man: A Play (New York: Random House, 1961); republished as *What They Did In Dublin, with The Ginger Man: A Play* (London: MacGibbon & Kee, 1962);

Fairy Tales of New York (New York: Random House, 1961; Harmondsworth, U.K.: Penguin, 1961);

A Singular Man [novel] (Boston & Toronto: Little, Brown, 1963; London: Bodley Head, 1964);

Meet My Maker the Mad Molecule (Boston & Toronto: Little, Brown, 1964; London: Bodley Head, 1965);

A Singular Man: A Play (London: Bodley Head, 1965);

The Saddest Summer of Samuel S (New York: Delacorte/Seymour Lawrence, 1966; London: Eyre & Spottiswoode, 1967);

The Beastly Beatitudes of Balthazar B (New York: Delacorte/Seymour Lawrence, 1968; London: Eyre & Spottiswoode, 1969);

The Onion Eaters (New York: Delacorte/Seymour Lawrence, 1971; London: Eyre & Spottiswoode, 1971);

The Plays of J. P. Donleavy, With a Preface by the Author (New York: Delacorte/Seymour Lawrence, 1972; Harmondsworth, U.K.: Penguin, 1974);

A Fairy Tale of New York (New York: Delacorte/Seymour Lawrence, 1973; London: Eyre Methuen, 1973);

The Unexpurgated Code: A Complete Manual of Survival and Manners (New York: Delacorte/Seymour Lawrence, 1975; London: Wildwood House, 1975);

J. P. Donleavy

The Destinies of Darcy Dancer, Gentleman (New York: Seymour Lawrence/Delacorte, 1977; London: Allen Lane, 1978);

Schultz (New York: Seymour Lawrence/Delacorte, 1979; London: Allen Lane, 1980);

Leila: Further in the Destinies of Darcy Dancer, Gentleman (New York: Delacorte/Seymour Lawrence, 1983); also published as *Leila: Further in the Life and Destinies of Darcy Dancer, Gentleman* (London: Allen Lane, 1983);

De Alfonce Tennis: The Superlative Game of Eccentric Champions, Its History, Accoutrements, Rules, Conduct, and Regimen (New York: Dutton/Seymour Lawrence, 1984; London: Weidenfeld & Nicolson, 1984);

Valerie and J. P. Donleavy on their wedding day (from The History of The Ginger Man, *1994; courtesy of J. P. Donleavy)*

J. P. Donleavy's Ireland: In All Her Sins and in Some of Her Graces (New York: Viking, 1986; London: Michael Joseph, 1986);

Are You Listening Rabbi Löw (London & New York: Viking, 1987; New York: Atlantic Monthly Press, 1988);

That Darcy, That Dancer, That Gentleman (London & New York: Viking, 1990; New York: Atlantic Monthly Press, 1991);

A Singular Country (New York: Norton, 1990; London: Ryan, 1990);

The History of The Ginger Man (Boston: Houghton Mifflin / New York: Seymour Lawrence, 1994);

The Lady Who Liked Clean Rest Rooms (New York: Thornwillow Press, 1996).

PLAY PRODUCTIONS: *The Ginger Man,* London, Fortune Theatre, 15 September 1959; New York, Orpheum Theatre, 21 November 1963;

Fairy Tales of New York, London, Comedy Theatre, 24 January 1961;

A Singular Man, London, Comedy Theatre, 21 October 1964;

The Beastly Beatitudes of Balthazar B, London, 1981; Norfolk, Virginia, Virginia Stage Company, 1986.

RADIO SCRIPT: *Helen,* BBC, August 1956.

SELECTED PERIODICAL PUBLICATIONS – UNCOLLECTED: "An Expatriate Looks at America," *Atlantic,* 238 (December 1976): 37–46;

"The Author and His Image," *Saturday Review,* 6 (20 January 1979): 44–46.

James Patrick Donleavy's long and prolific career as a novelist, playwright, short-story writer, and essayist has made him a well-known contemporary author. Born in the United States, Donleavy has lived in Ireland for most of his adult life, and he became an Irish citizen in 1967. His status as an American writer in exile has often been seen as an important parallel to that of his protagonists, all of whom are, if not technically aliens in their societies, certainly alienated from them. Leading marginal lives as cultural outsiders, his characters are spiritually and often physically threatened by a hostile society and are typically in economic and legal as well as psychological trouble. Despite Donleavy's frequently praised technical virtuosity — and his four decades of continual productivity and popularity — he has had infrequent success with academic critics. In response Donleavy claimed in a 1988 interview with Jean W. Ross that their response to his work "has made me realize that, with rare exceptions, critical opinion was a political stance taken for the benefit of the critic and had little to do with the merit of an author's work."

Donleavy was born in Brooklyn, New York, and raised in The Bronx in a middle-class household in what he recalls as a peaceful neighborhood. His parents, James Patrick and Margaret Donleavy, were both Irish immigrants. After being expelled from Fordham Prep School in his junior year and graduating "narrowly" from Manhattan Prep in June 1944, he joined the U.S. Naval Reserve during World War II. Training as a radar operator for amphibious landing craft, he won an appointment from the fleet to the Naval Academy and attended the Naval Academy Preparatory School, where he met a group of friends and instructors who sparked his interest in writers — especially James Joyce — and in Dublin, Ireland. After the war, "being instantly rejected by every university I applied to in America," Donleavy applied to Trinity College in Dublin, where he studied from 1946 to 1949 on the GI Bill. He married Valerie Heron after leaving Trinity. They had two children before their divorce in 1969. The following year Donleavy married actress Mary Wilson Price, with whom he has two children.

After a brief period in which he considered becoming a professional painter, Donleavy began work on his first novel, *The Ginger Man,* which he completed in 1951, having returned to New York to finish and to seek a publisher for the book. He initially took the manuscript to Scribners, the first, he says, of nearly thirty-five American and British publishing houses to reject the novel for its supposed obscenity. Apart from his difficulty in finding a publisher, he found the national mood of America in the 1950s, then heavily under the influence of McCarthyism, intolerably oppressive, especially for a writer. As he wrote in a letter at the time, "There is a fantastic red scare here, the whole country undergoing a rigorous censorship. I want to go back to Europe where I can regain my dignity."

After Donleavy's return to Ireland, a close friend, the Irish playwright Brendan Behan, knowing that he was unwilling to censor his novel to suit publishers, suggested that he send the manuscript to Olympia Press in Paris, which had a reputation for publishing controversial works. They published an unexpurgated edition of the book in 1955 as part of their pornographic Traveller's Companion series, which features books with titles such as *Tender Was My Flesh* and *The Whip Angels*. The resulting notoriety caused Donleavy some consternation, but it may have helped the book to gain cult status as an underground classic. An American edition, revised to omit some of the sexually explicit passages, was published in 1958 (giving rise to a lengthy series of lawsuits by Olympia against Donleavy). An unexpurgated American edition was published in 1965. The treatment of sex in *The Ginger Man* seems quite tame by 1990s standards, and the book is far more striking for its stylistic innovations than for its sexual explicitness.

The Ginger Man of the title is Donleavy's protagonist, Sebastian Dangerfield, an American attending Trinity College, Dublin, on the GI Bill after service in the U.S. Navy during World War II. While this much of the character might seem autobiographical, Donleavy has identified the model for Dangerfield as another expatriate American in Dublin, Gainor Stephen Crist, in subsequent accounts of his early years as a writer, covering the origins of the book most thoroughly in his *The History of The Ginger Man* (1994). Dangerfield lives with his wife, Marion, and daughter, Felicity, in desperate poverty. Although nominally enrolled as a law student, he spends his time drinking with a variety of colorful and disreputable friends, dodging creditors, and chasing women, and he will clearly never pass his exams.

The exuberantly recounted series of adventures Dangerfield experiences as he lives by his wits from one drink or meal to the next, often involving improbable exaggeration and slapstick comedy, have led to comparisons of Donleavy's book to the picaresque novel and to satirists such as Jonathan Swift. Considered as an example of social or cultural satire, especially in the context of the literary milieu of the 1950s, the depiction of Dangerfield's chaotic life, unprincipled pursuit of pleasure, and intransigence when faced with authority or responsibility led critics to make comparisons to the products of such contemporary literary movements as the Beats in the United States or the Angry Young Men in England, but the book resists such classifications as much as it invites them. The Beat writers saw the exploration of chaos and freedom as part of a spiritual quest, a means to a transcendent, perhaps quasi-religious, end, and the Angry Young Men typically presented their protagonists in rebellion, albeit inarticulately, against an intractable and out-

Opening page from the first formal draft for The Ginger Man *(from* The History of The Ginger Man, *1994; courtesy of J. P. Donleavy)* dated social system. Dangerfield's quest, however, seems to be rather for conventional social respectability and financial security. His nonconformist behavior is not based on a rejection of traditional social distinctions — in fact he is something of a snob — but rather on a refusal to moderate his invariably impulsive behavior and an absurdist's conviction of the futility of all endeavor.

In his *DLB 6* entry on Donleavy, William E. Grant called Dangerfield "a failed conformist rather than a romantic rebel," an assessment that Donleavy has approved. In this essentially nihilistic vision of the world, where class distinctions, however arbitrary, provide one of the few possible centers in the void, the only goal worth seeking is personal physical comfort. As Ihab Hassan remarked early in the history of Donleavy criticism, "Traditional values are not in the process of dying; they have entirely ceased to operate, and their stark absence leaves men to shift for themselves as best they can." The resulting metaphysical situation might be paralleled to that in Samuel Beckett's *Waiting for Godot* (1952), with the stipulation that, while Beckett's tramps seem to be at least implicitly hoping for a meaningful revelation, Donleavy's plot has Dangerfield waiting not for spiritual salvation, but for a long-deferred, and entirely material, inheritance from his father.

Donleavy identifies his characteristic mode as "tragicomedy," and again the parallel with Beckett, an Irishman and expatriate, is inviting: *Waiting for Godot* is subtitled "a tragicomedy in two acts." The novel combines the grim realism suggested by the protagonist's name — the world is a dangerous place for him — with the cartoonish fantasy suggested by the book's title — like the Gingerbread Man, Godot races to stay a step ahead of those who hope to devour him. As bleak as the psychological landscape often appears — and as reprehensible as Dangerfield's behavior can be, especially in his abusive treatment of his wife and daughter, who eventually leave him — *The Ginger Man* is nevertheless as much comic as tragic, with elements of poignancy and sentimentality balancing the elements of lewdness and riotousness and with Dangerfield as much a sympathetic as a repulsive character. Donleavy achieves this balance of identification and condemnation primarily through his complex and highly original handling of point of view, a method that has continued throughout most of his novels and that constitutes one of his stylistic trademarks.

Donleavy adapts the stream-of-consciousness techniques pioneered by James Joyce (yet another expatriate Irish writer, whom Donleavy frequently

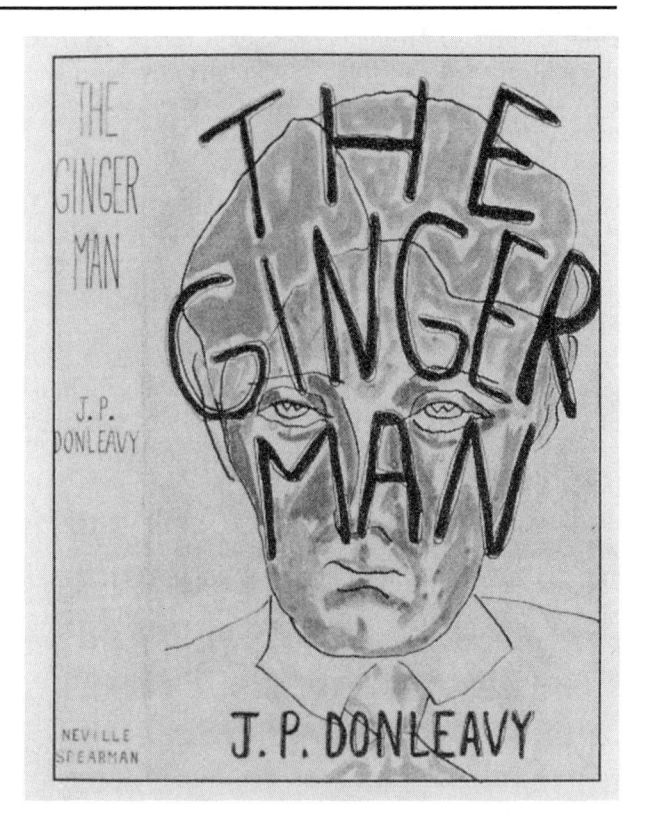

Rejected cover, designed by Donleavy, for the first British edition of his first novel (from The History of The Ginger Man, *1994; courtesy of J. P. Donleavy)*

cites as an inspiration) by freely and rapidly alternating between third-person proper name and pronoun references and first-person pronouns, blurring the boundary between traditional "third-person omniscient" point of view (free focalization) and "first-person subjective" interior monologue (internal focalization), blending past and present tense, external and internal perspectives. As Charles G. Masinton has remarked in his book on Donleavy "this unusual practice gives us the illusion of viewing Dangerfield both from 'within' and 'without,' as it were, at the same time." Donleavy's prose is further marked by his reliance on telegraphic sentence fragments that create at the same time a lyrical, poetic feel and a kaleidoscopic impressionism or perhaps pointillism, giving the reader the impression of "overhearing" the protagonist's thoughts as they form, at a level slightly before or beneath conscious articulation. This lyrical manner is emphasized by the short verses placed at the end of each chapter, which Donleavy modeled after Chinese proverbs.

While Donleavy's distinctive style was generally admired by reviewers of *The Ginger Man,* the continued use of a similar style in later books has sometimes been seen as a weakness. It is one of the chief ironies of Donleavy's critical reception that the widespread early acclaim for his developing a rich and distinctive prose style would quickly give way to attacks for his continuing to use it.

Donleavy next published two plays, a dramatic version of *The Ginger Man* (1961) and *Fairy Tales of New York* (1961); the latter earned him the *Evening Standard* Most Promising Playwright Award, and the two plays were collectively recognized with the Brandeis University Creative Arts Award. He then produced his second novel, *A Singular Man* (1963), in which he explores the situation of George Smith, a rich and reclusive businessman living in New York City. The American setting allows Donleavy to elaborate more fully his vision of the United States, which he also set out in his 1976 *Atlantic* essay, "An Expatriate Looks at America": "It is sad and bitter. Where no man has the opportunity to feel any love. This is a land of lies." Thematically, Donleavy seems to have set himself the task of considering what would happen to Sebastian Dangerfield if his material needs were met, and many critics have seen Smith as a repatriated and wealthy Dangerfield. The approach has the advantage of generalizing the theme of personal alienation from contemporary society by ruling out poverty as the primary obstacle to happiness and concentrating on two other problems less distinctly highlighted in *The Ginger Man*: the impossibility of finding love and of preparing for death, which come to be the major concerns of Donleavy's later work. While poverty is to some extent a solvable problem, Donleavy implies, the necessity of living with the knowledge that we will seldom find love and will certainly find death is less tractable and more universal. Some critics have seen the choice of the generic name "Smith" as a invitation to this sort of allegorical reading. This approach has its drawbacks as well, however, particularly in removing a primary source of the protagonist's motivation for action. Dangerfield's desperate financial straits not only motivated him in the direction of energy, invention, and ceaseless activity but also provided the engine for the plot, however episodic, in his perpetual need to solve his material problems. Smith's wealth, in terms of basic plot, assigns him a role more as passive victim than as active rebel. Where Dangerfield's existence is devoted to the solution of a series of short-term, recurring, and realistically pressing problems, Smith's project is the construction of a monumental mausoleum for his own eventual interment, and the problems fueling his picaresque plot have to be manufactured by plot twists and his own paranoia and melancholy.

Donleavy provides several successfully comical slapstick scenes revolving around Smith's generally hapless sex life, and his considerable gift for witty dialogue produces lively entertainment from page to page, but on the whole reviewers saw Donleavy's writing as in a decline from *The Ginger Man*, a verdict reinforced by the publication the following year of *Meet My Maker the Mad Molecule* (1964), a collection of short stories and sketches that is generally considered to be one of his weakest works.

After publishing a dramatic version of *A Singular Man* (1965), Donleavy produced his only novella, *The Saddest Summer of Samuel S* (1966). The use of a letter as a surname, a device Donleavy repeated in his next book, recalls Joseph K, the protagonist of Franz Kafka's *Der Prozess* (1925; translated as *The Trial*, 1937). Donleavy has frequently cited Kafka as an influence, and the confusing and threatening worlds and victimized characters of Donleavy's novels seem to reflect elements of Kafka's work. Samuel S combines the passivity and melancholy of Smith with the poverty of Dangerfield, and the novella documents his empty life in Vienna, where he devotes his time to seeing a psychiatrist and hoping to find stable romantic love with a woman. That Samuel S conceives of psychoanalysis and love as the two possible cures for his spiritual malaise and his failure to fit into society suggests the transcendent value of love in Donleavy's work, especially when the novella ends with the psychoanalyst giving up on the case. As Masinton has shrewdly observed in his book on Donleavy, "This notion implies that the love between a man and a woman is more than the mutual emotional fulfillment of two mature adults. It suggests that a man's happiness comes not by way of mutual sharing and sacrifice so much as through the reassurance and consolation given by a woman. It partakes more than a little of the child's attitude toward its mother and is very pronounced in Donleavy's works." The frequent use of alliterative titles fits in with this childlike slant, as does Donleavy's observation that he deliberately filters even his adult protagonists' thoughts through the point of view of a small boy; many of them seem to be seeking maternal as much as romantic love, often through relationships with much older women.

Donleavy's next novel, *The Beastly Beatitudes of Balthazar B* (1968), is generally considered one of his most successful. Reviewing the novel for *Saturday Review* (23 November 1968), the widely respected critic Robert Scholes called it "a better book than *The Ginger Man*, richer in its moods and sympathies.

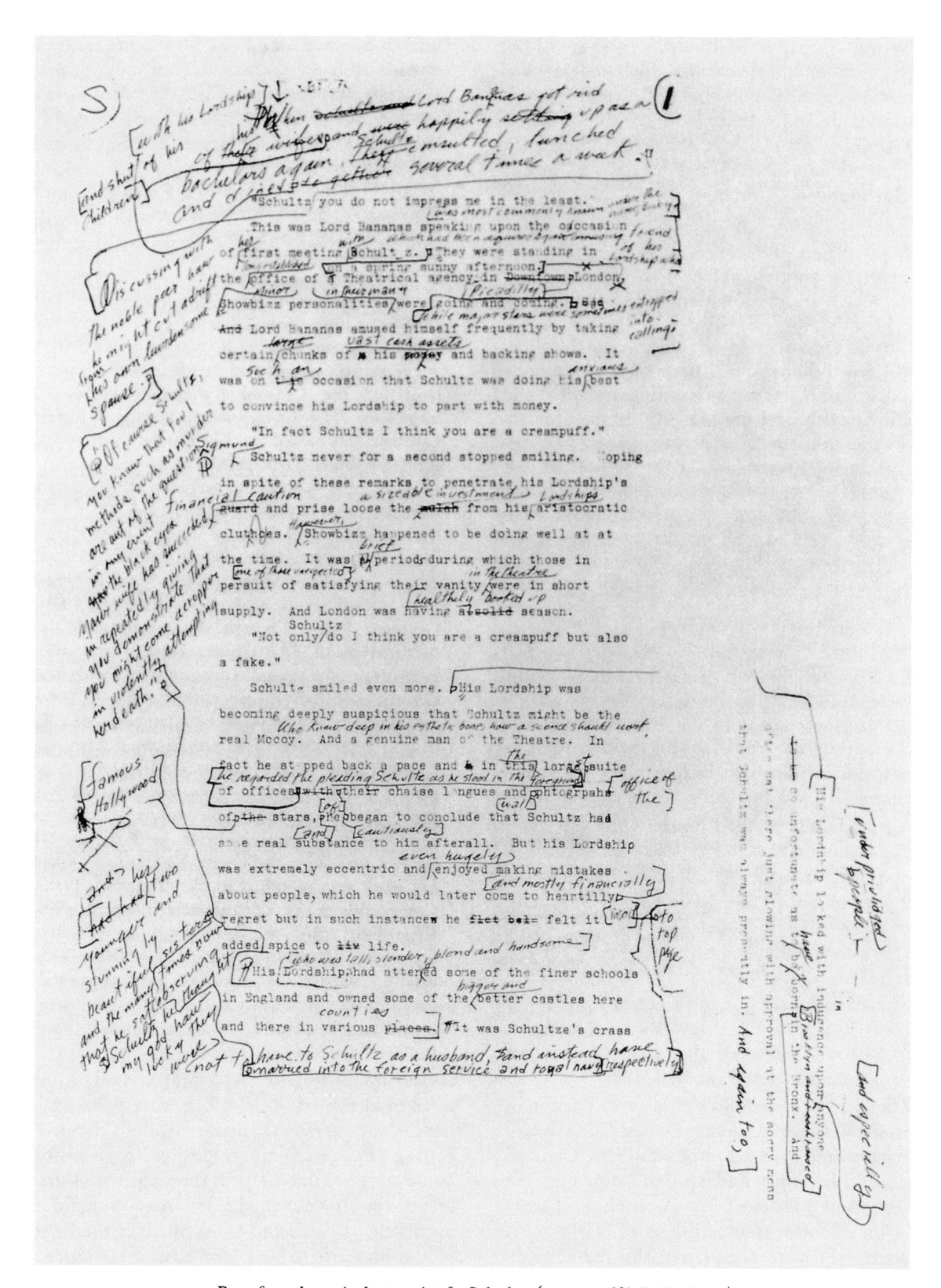

Page from the revised typescript for Schultz *(courtesy of J. P. Donleavy)*

Its prose is honed to a fine edge of humor and tenderness that stops, as it should, just short of poetry." Scholes noted approvingly that Donleavy had also found a more suitable theme: "Not fashionable alienation and disaffection, but plain old loneliness and loss." The novel follows Balthazar B, a wealthy French nobleman of Irish ancestry, on a journey from childhood to middle age, from innocence to experience, through an almost melodramatic series of personal losses – including the early death of his father; exile to public school in England and later to Trinity College in Ireland; separation from his adolescent love, his governess Bella, who seduced him at age twelve; rejection by his adult love, Elizabeth Fitzdare, who, the reader discovers, is dying a lingering death as the result of a riding accident; and finally the death of his mother. Balthazar's melancholy and even pathetic story is relieved, however, by a second chief character, Beefy, whom Balthazar meets at public school and with whom he is reunited at Trinity. Donleavy apparently hit on the strategy of incorporating both of his previously developed types of protagonist into one book by featuring two main characters: Balthazar, embodying the passive and sensitive features of George Smith or Samuel S, and Beefy, embodying the active and bawdy aspects of Sebastian Dangerfield. The ebullient character of Beefy allows the introduction of a range of fast-paced comic scenes that balance well with the pathos of the shy and gentle Balthazar, making for one of Donleavy's most fully developed and rounded works.

Just as Donleavy had disappointed his early critics by following *The Ginger Man* with a series of progressively weaker books, he then followed the widely praised *Beastly Beatitudes of Balthazar B* with *The Onion Eaters* (1971) and *A Fairy Tale of New York* (1973), two works that suggested to several reviewers that he had run out of ideas. *The Onion Eaters* had been discussed as a work in progress since 1964, and *A Fairy Tale of New York* reworked material that had already appeared as a play and as one of the short stories collected in *Meet My Maker*.

The Onion Eaters follows the vicissitudes of Clayton Claw Cleaver Clementine on a downward spiral beginning with his inheritance of Charnel Castle, an Irish manor, and continuing through the introduction of a series of destructive houseguests to the ruin of the manor and loss of his fortune. Most reviewers were not amused by the comedy and were unimpressed by what appeared to be intermittent allegorical or symbolic undertones.

Although critics were not generally enthusiastic about *A Fairy Tale of New York,* several did consider the comic dialogue a return to Donleavy's usual high level, and, as Grant has argued, the novel is also of interest as "the most personal of Donleavy's works since *The Ginger Man.*" As a look at "the violence, greed, and spiritual poverty of the city," the novel, Grant argues, "becomes a kind of gloss on the reasons Donleavy finds America an uninhabitable country," and in his views of city life its protagonist, Cornelius Christian, is closer to Donleavy himself than any of his other fictional characters.

During this period Donleavy also collected his dramatic works in *The Plays of J. P. Donleavy, With a Preface by the Author* (1972), was honored with a citation from the American Academy of Arts and Letters (1975), and published *The Unexpurgated Code: A Complete Manual of Survival and Manners* (1975), a well-reviewed, often funny and inventive, compilation of mock rules of etiquette for social climbers.

Donleavy's next novel, *The Destinies of Darcy Dancer, Gentleman* (1977), returns to the Irish setting and disjointed picaresque structure of his major works, following the adventures of Darcy from youth to adulthood. The influence of the picaresque novel is particularly notable in the abrupt ups and downs of Darcy's fortunes as he switches from country gentleman to servant to confidence man back to wealthy country gentleman. While most critics saw the novel as a return to form for Donleavy, it was viewed as essentially a continuation of the mode of *The Beastly Beatitudes of Balthazar B,* with its upper-class characters and comic subplots. In hindsight, though, Grant was probably correct in calling the book "a new departure for Donleavy." Grant notes, for example, the anachronism of the setting, which – although ostensibly twentieth-century Ireland – invokes a "world of country estates, fox hunting, family retainers, and leisured wealth in which Fielding's characters would have been quite at home." While Donleavy retains, as Grant notes, "the shifting point of view, fragmentary sentences, and flights of lyricism that are the hallmarks of his style," he also made important stylistic modifications to fit this leisurely milieu, particularly in slowing the pace of events and descriptions to mirror the setting. This well-integrated juxtaposition of plot and characters drawn from the tradition of the eighteenth-century novel with Donleavy's distinctively modernist style accounts for much of the freshness of the book, to which Donleavy has written two noteworthy sequels.

Donleavy first published another critical failure, however: the farcical *Schultz* (1979), in which he recounts, in a remarkably straightforward and

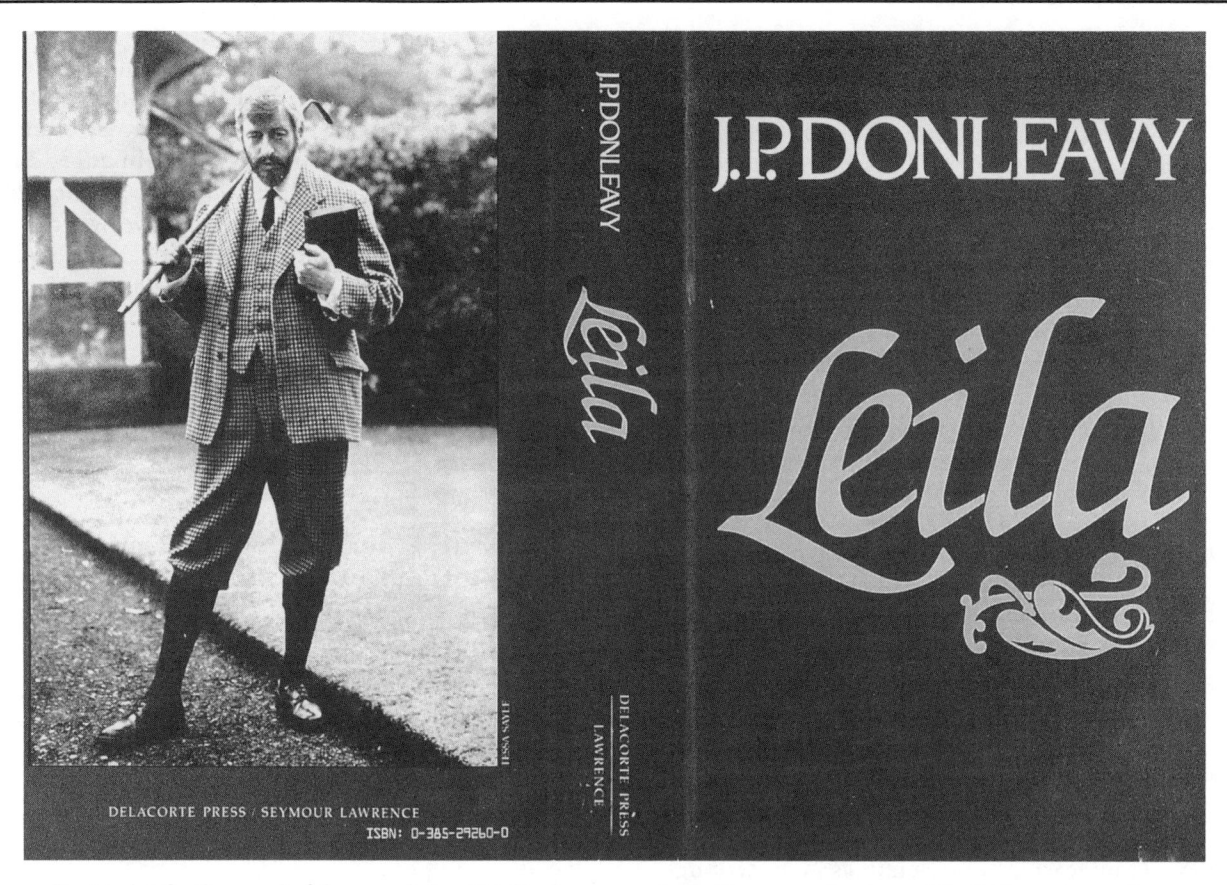

Dust jacket for the second of three novels in which Donleavy recounts the picaresque adventures of the Irish country gentleman Darcy Dancer

entirely uncharacteristic style, the slapstick adventures of Sigmund Schultz, an impecunious Jewish American theatrical producer in London who, despite a long string of failures, has two English aristocrats, Binky Sunningdale and Lord Nectarine, as partners and backers. Despite the predominantly negative verdict from critics, the book was commercially successful enough to justify a sequel, *Are You Listening Rabbi Löw* (1987), which fared little better with the critics and, as usual, little worse with the public. Donleavy has always had a reliable cult following.

Leila: Further in the Destinies of Darcy Dancer, Gentleman (1983) continues the chronicle of Darcy's generally unlucky pursuit of his two major endeavors: his efforts to keep his troubled winter estate, Andromeda Park, intact in the face of a range of physical and economic depredations and his search for love, here centered on the ideal but apparently unattainable Leila, a mysterious orphan recently added to the staff. Many of the characters from the first book reappear: including, among the servants, the polymath gardener Sexton and the tottering butler Crooks; and, among the upper classes, Rashers Ronald, who transforms himself into the earl of Ronald Ronald, and the Mental Marquis, who takes Leila away from Darcy shortly after he has declared his love for her. Critical reaction was mixed, with some critics losing sympathy for the ineffectual character of Darcy, but Donleavy's handling of language was typically cited as a return to his artistic strength after the unusually orthodox prose style of *Schultz*.

After *Leila* Donleavy published three relatively undistinguished books in a row. *De Alfonce Tennis: The Superlative Game of Eccentric Champions, Its History, Accoutrements, Rules, Conduct, and Regimen* (1984) is primarily devoted, after a brief narrative opening, to the elaborate description of an imaginary variation of tennis invented by a club of young bachelors. The parody of conventions, perhaps inspired by the success of *The Unexpurgated Code,* baffled critics, who found the book pointless and unreadable. *J. P. Donleavy's Ireland: In All Her Sins and in Some of Her Graces* (1986) is part autobiographical memoir, part cultural travelogue, covering his life from his childhood in New

York up to the period of *The Ginger Man*. He also wrote *Are You Listening Rabbi Löw* before completing the Darcy Dancer trilogy.

That Darcy, That Dancer, That Gentleman (1990) continues the chronicle of Darcy's efforts to keep Andromeda Park afloat as his resources run out, and much of the book is concerned with his only half-hearted efforts to find a wealthy wife, since the only woman he can imagine truly loving, Leila, is permanently beyond reach as a marchioness in Paris. Among the unsuitable matches he considers are his neighbor Felicity Veronica Durrow-Mountmelton and two American heiresses. The Americans arrive through the matchmaking efforts of Rashers Ronald, who plays a large role in the book as Darcy's virtually permanent houseguest and best, though most unreliable, friend. The climax of the novel is a grand ball at Darcy's estate, at which virtually every character featured in the trilogy makes an appearance. At the end of the book, although chaos and destruction have threatened and largely triumphed throughout, Ronald is engaged to Durrow-Mountmelton, and Darcy is finally reunited with Leila, providing more than usual closure for a Donleavy novel, perhaps by way of winding up the trilogy, and making for one of the happiest and least arbitrary endings in his writings.

Donleavy's next book, *The History of The Ginger Man* (1994), picks up more or less where *J. P. Donleavy's Ireland* leaves off and brings his career full circle with a detailed account, part autobiography and part literary history, of the writing and publication of his first novel, still generally regarded as his masterpiece. The book closes with an irony entirely appropriate for any of his fictional protagonists: Donleavy's twenty-five years of litigation with Olympia Press ended in his becoming the sole owner of the press and its copyrights through a bankruptcy auction, thus placing him in the strange situation of winning a lawsuit against his own company.

While *The Ginger Man* alone, which has sold more than five million copies and has never been out of print, will ensure Donleavy a place in literary history, the question of his critical reputation remains moot. While his Darcy Dancer trilogy arguably represents his greatest sustained achievement as a novelist, the two Schultz books, written during precisely the same period, may be among his greatest critical embarrassments. While some critics have been troubled by the absence of a clear line of development in Donleavy's work and by his artistic swings between good and bad books, it might be stipulated that there is an element of the ungenerous in leveling claims of inconsistency at a writer who has produced twenty books, ten of them long novels, over a forty-year career. It should also be noted that the relative commercial success of most of his books seems seldom to have influenced him to attempt to write down to a larger audience. He appears throughout his career to have written to please himself rather than to gain critical or popular approval. Donleavy's strength as a writer is his highly original and carefully crafted style; he averages between five and twelve complete drafts of each book, and critics agree that, at its best, Donleavy's prose is highly polished and often brilliantly evocative.

Interviews:

Joan Bakewell, "The Novelist J. P. Donleavy Talks to Joan Bakewell," *Listener*, 81 (13 March 1969): 340–341;

Phil Casey, " 'The Ginger Man' Man," *Washington Post*, 28 October 1973, L1, L5;

Molly McKaughan, "The Art of Fiction 53: J. P. Donleavy," *Paris Review*, 63 (Fall 1975): 122–166;

Stella Dong, "J. P. Donleavy Discusses Olympia Press," *Publishers Weekly*, 215 (30 April 1979): 22, 28;

Kurt Jacobson, "An Interview with J. P. Donleavy," *Journal of Irish Literature*, 8 (1979): 38–48;

G. Pascal Zachary, "An Interview with J. P. Donleavy," *San Francisco Review of Books*, 7–8 (December–January 1979–1980): 7;

Jean W. Ross, Interview with Donleavy, *Contemporary Authors*, New Revision Series, volume 24 (Detroit: Gale Research, 1988), pp. 162–164;

Frank Delany, "J. P. Donleavy," *Writers Talk: Ideas of Our Time*, 57, The Anthony Roland Collection of Films on Art (ICA Video, 1989).

Bibliography:

David W. Madden, "A Bibliography of J. P. Donleavy," *Bulletin of Bibliography*, 39, no. 3 (1982): 170–178.

References:

Dean Cohen, "The Evolution of Donleavy's Hero," *Critique: Studies in Modern Fiction*, 12, no. 3 (1973): 95–109;

Donald E. Coonley, "To Cultivate, To Dread: The Concept of Death in *The Ginger Man* and *Herzog*," *New Campus Review*, 22 (Spring 1969): 7–12;

Robert A. Corrigan, "The Artist as Censor: J. P. Donleavy and *The Ginger Man*," *Midcontinent*

American Studies Journal, 8 (Spring 1967): 60-72;

Grace Eckley, "Two Irish-American Novelists: J. P. Donleavy and Jimmy Breslin," *Illinois School Journal,* 55 (1975): 28-33;

Ihab Hassan, "Encounter with Possibility: Three Novels by Gold, Cheever, and Donleavy," in his *Radical Innocence: Studies in the Contemporary American Novel* (Princeton, N.J.: Princeton University Press, 1961), pp. 194-200;

Bruce Janoff, "Black Humor: Beyond Satire," *Ohio Review,* 14, no. 1 (1972): 5-20;

John Johnson, "Tears and Laughter: The Tragic Comic Novels of J. P. Donleavy," *Michigan Academician,* 9 (1976): 15-24;

David L. Kubal, "Our Last Literary Gentleman: The Bourgeois Imagination," *Bucknell Review,* 22, no. 2 (1976): 24-49;

Thomas LeClair, "A Case of Death: The Fiction of J. P. Donleavy," *Contemporary Literature,* 12 (Summer 1971): 329-344;

LeClair, "*The Onion Eaters* and the Rhetoric of Donleavy's Comedy," *Twentieth Century Literature,* 18 (July 1972): 167-174;

Charles G. Masinton, "Etiquette for Ginger Men: A Critical Assessment of Donleavy's *Unexpurgated Code,*" *Midwest Quarterly,* 18 (January 1977): 210-215;

Masinton, *J. P. Donleavy: The Style of His Sadness and Humor* (Bowling Green, Ohio: Bowling Green University Popular Press, 1975);

John R. Moore, "Hard Times and the Noble Savage: J. P. Donleavy's *A Singular Man,*" *Hollins Critic,* 1 (February 1964): 1-4, 6-11; republished in *The Sounder Few: Essays from the Hollins Critic,* edited by R. H. W. Dillard, George Garrett, and John R. Moore (Athens: University of Georgia Press, 1971), pp. 3-17;

John Rees Moore, "J. P. Donleavy's Season of Discontent," *Critique: Studies in Modern Fiction,* 9, no. 2 (1967): 95-99;

Donald E. Morse, "American Readings of J. P. Donleavy's *The Ginger Man,*" *Eire-Ireland: A Journal of Irish Studies,* 26, no. 3 (Fall 1991): 128-138;

Morse, "From Heaven to Hell: Ireland in the Novels of J. P. Donleavy," in *Literary Interrelations: Ireland, England, and the World,* 3 volumes, edited by Wolfgang Zach and Heinz Kosok (Tubingen: Narr, 1987), II: 217-222;

Morse, "The Skull Beneath the Skin: J. P. Donleavy's *The Ginger Man,*" *Michigan Academician,* 6 (1974): 273-280;

Johann A. Norstedt, "Irishmen and Irish-Americans in the Fiction of J. P. Donleavy," in *Irish-American Fiction: Essays in Criticism,* edited by Daniel J. Casey and Robert E. Rhodes (New York: AMS Press, 1979), pp. 115-125;

Norman Podhoretz, "The New Nihilism and the Novel," in his *Doings and Undoings* (New York: Farrar, Straus & Giroux, 1964), pp. 159-178;

Ronald Rollins, "Desire versus Damnation in O'Casey's *Within the Gates* and Donleavy's *The Ginger Man,*" *Sean O'Casey Review,* 1, no. 2 (1975): 41-47;

R. K. Sharma, *Isolation and Protest: A Case Study of J. P. Donleavy's Fiction* (New Delhi: Ajanta, 1983; Atlantic Highlands, N.J.: Humanities Press, 1983);

Patrick W. Shaw, "The Satire of J. P. Donleavy's *Ginger Man,*" *Studies in Contemporary Satire,* 1 (1975): 9-16;

William David Sherman, "J. P. Donleavy: Anarchic Man as Dying Dionysian," *Twentieth Century Literature,* 13 (January 1968): 216-228;

Arland Ussher, Introduction to *The Ginger Man* (New York: McDowell, Oblensky, 1958);

Maurice Vintner, "The Novelist as Clown: The Fiction of J. P. Donleavy," *Meanjin Quarterly,* 29 (Autumn 1970): 108-114;

Gerald C. Weales, "No Face and No Exit: The Fiction of James Purdy and J. P. Donleavy," in *Contemporary American Novelists,* edited by Harry T. Moore (Carbondale: Southern Illinois University Press, 1964), pp. 143-154;

Kingsley Widmer, "Contemporary American Outcasts," in his *The Literary Rebel,* edited by Harry T. Moore (Carbondale: Southern Illinois University Press, 1965), pp. 136-139.

Maxine Hong Kingston

(27 October 1940 -)

Pin-chia Feng
National Chiao-Tung University, Taiwan

See also the Kingston entry in *DLB Yearbook: 1980.*

BOOKS: *The Woman Warrior: Memoirs of a Girlhood Among Ghosts* (New York: Knopf, 1976; London: John Lane, 1977);

China Men (New York: Knopf, 1980);

Hawai'i One Summer: 1978 (San Francisco: Meadow Press, 1987);

Through the Black Curtain (Berkeley: Friends of the Bancroft Library, University of California, 1987);

Tripmaster Monkey: His Fake Book (New York: Knopf, 1989).

OTHER: "Cultural Mis-readings by American Reviewers," in *Asian and Western Writers in Dialogue: New Cultural Identities,* edited by Guy Amirthanayagam (London: Macmillan, 1982), pp. 55-56;

"Personal Statement," in *Approaches to Teaching Kingston's The Woman Warrior,* edited by Shirley Geok-lin Lim (New York: Modern Language Association of America, 1991), pp. 23-25.

SELECTED PERIODICAL PUBLICATIONS –
UNCOLLECTED: "Duck Boy," *New York Times Magazine,* 12 June 1977, pp. 54-58;

"Reservations About China," *Ms.,* 7 (October 1978): 67-68;

"San Francisco Chinatown: A View from the Other Side of Arnold Genthe's Camera," *American Heritage,* 30 (December 1978): 35-47;

"A Writer's Notebook from the Far East," *Ms.,* 11 (January 1983): 85-86;

"An Imagined Life," *Michigan Quarterly Review,* 22 (Fall 1983): 561-570;

"A Chinese Garland," *North American Review,* 273 (September 1988): 38-42;

Maxine Hong Kingston (photograph by Karen Huie)

"Violence and Non-Violence in China, 1989," *Michigan Quarterly Review,* 24 (Winter 1990): 62-67.

One of the most outspoken contemporary feminist writers, Maxine Hong Kingston states in her autobiographical book *The Woman Warrior* (1976), "The swordswoman and I are not so dissimilar.... What we have in common are the words at our backs. The idioms for *revenge* are 'report a crime' and 'report to five families.' The reporting is the vengeance – not the beheading, not the gutting, but the words." With prose that both unsettles Chinese American sexism and American racism, Kingston is a "word warrior" who battles social and racial injustice. It is perhaps surprising that Kingston could not speak English until she started school. Once she had learned it, however, she started to talk stories. Decades later, this once silent and silenced woman is becoming a notable American writer.

Maxine Hong Kingston was born to Chinese immigrant parents, Tom Hong and Chew Ying Lan, in Stockton, California, on 27 October 1940. Her American name, Maxine, was after a blonde who was always lucky in gambling. Ting Ting, her Chinese name, comes from a Chinese poem about self-reliance. The eldest of the six Hong children, Kingston had two older siblings who died in China years before her mother came to the United States. Kingston recalls the early part of her school education as her "silent years" in which she had a terrible time talking. Later Maxine, who flunked kindergarten, became a straight-A student and won a scholarship to the University of California, Berkeley. In 1962 she got her bachelor's degree in English and married Earll Kingston, a Berkeley graduate and an actor. She returned to the university in 1964, earned a teaching certificate in 1965, and taught English and mathematics from 1965 to 1967 in Hayward, California. During their time at Berkeley, the Kingstons were involved in the antiwar movement on campus. In 1967 they decided to leave the country because the movement was getting more and more violent, and their friends were too involved in drugs. On their way to Japan the Kingstons stopped in Hawaii and stayed there for seventeen years.

At first Kingston taught language arts and English as a second language in a private school. In 1977 she became a visiting professor at the University of Hawaii at Honolulu. A few days after she finished the final revisions of *China Men* (1980), a Honolulu Buddhist sect claimed Kingston as a "Living Treasure of Hawaii." Kingston herself, however, was still looking homeward, having always felt like a stranger in the islands. She and her husband moved back to California, while their son, Joseph, stayed in Hawaii and became a musician. In 1992 Kingston became a member of the Academy of Arts and Sciences.

Kingston's writing relies heavily on memory and imagination. "We approach the truth with metaphors," declared Kingston in a 1983 essay, "An Imagined Life." She also told Paula Rabinowitz in a 1987 interview, "The artist's memory winnows out; it edits for what is important and significant. Memory, my own memory, shows me what is unforgettable, and helps me get to an essence that will not die, and that haunts me until I can put it into a form, which is writing." Kingston denies, however, that the use of memory in her writing is simply a form of exorcism, but she insists that it is a way to give substance to the "ghosts," or "visions," in her life. Her writing also denies classification: she is recording the biography of a people's imagination. Her first two books are Kingston's biographies of ancestors whom she has never met and records of things about which she has only heard. Imagination becomes her way to approach these characters and incidents. For instance, she imagines five ways for her father's arrival in America in *China Men*. She is proud of this imaginative feat because by inserting multiple stories into her "biographical" works she is able to transcend generic boundaries and protect the illegal aliens she is writing about at the same time. "To have a right imagination is very powerful," Kingston told Rabinowitz, "because it's a bridge between reality."

The major sources of Kingston's memory and imagination are her mother's stories and her father's silence. Kingston's father, Tom Hong, was a scholar trained in traditional Chinese classics and a teacher in New Society Village before his immigration. In the United States he washed windows until he had saved enough money to start a laundry in New York with three of his friends. Later, Hong was cheated out of his share of the partnership. He moved with his pregnant wife to Stockton and started managing an illegal gambling house for a wealthy Chinese American. A major part of his work, besides taking care of the club, was to be arrested; he was silent about his true name and invented a new name for each arrest. World War II put him out of this cycle of managing and getting arrested because the gambling house was shut down. After a period of unemployment he started his own laundry and a new life for himself and his family in America.

Brave Orchid (or Ying Lan, in Chinese), Kingston's vocal and practical mother, was a doctor who practiced Western medicine and midwifery in China. She did not join her husband in New York until 1940, fifteen years after they had parted. In America, Brave Orchid exchanged her professional status for that of a laundrywoman, cleaning maid, tomato picker, and cannery worker. Undaunted by the difficulties in her life, this "champion talker" educated her children with "talk stories," which included myth, legend, family history, and ghost tales. "Night after night my mother would talk-story until we fell asleep. I could not tell where the stories left off and the dreams began," Kingston recalls in *The Woman Warrior*. Through her talk stories, Brave

Orchid extended Chinese tradition into the lives of her American children and enriched their imagination. Yet Kingston is also aware of the fact that the mother's talking stories were double-edged: "She said I would grow up a wife and slave, but she taught me the song of the woman warrior, Fa Mu Lan," Kingston recollects in *The Woman Warrior*. While Brave Orchid's storytelling was educational, it also reiterated patriarchal and misogynistic messages of traditional Chinese culture. Moreover, as in traditional Chinese education, Brave Orchid did not explain her stories. Kingston needed to interpret her mother's stories and became a storyteller herself.

Her community also played a decisive role in Kingston's writing. Comparing herself to Toni Morrison and Leslie Silko, Kingston argues that what makes their writings vivid and alive is their connection with community and tribe. Yet Kingston refuses to be "representative" of Chinese Americans. "A Stockton Chinese is not the same as a San Francisco Chinese," Kingston stated in an interview with Arturo Islas. Unlike "the Big City" (San Francisco) and "the Second City" (Sacramento), Stockton, a city in the Central Valley of California, has a relatively small Chinese population. At most the Stockton Chinese American community is a minor subculture of Chinese America. Yet Stockton became a "literary microcosm" for Kingston, whose knowledge of China derives from its people. And the language spoken in this community, a Cantonese dialect called Say Yup, supplies Kingston with distinctive sounds and rhythms. What Kingston has done in her writing is to translate the oral tradition of her community into a written one.

Moreover, the physical environment and social class in which Kingston grew up played an important role in her "education" as a writer. Kingston spent her childhood on the south side of Stockton, an area populated by mostly working-class and unemployed people of mixed races. The "Burglar Ghosts," "Hobo Ghosts," and "Wino Ghosts" that crowded young Maxine's childhood memory testify to the importance of street wisdom and survival skills. Kingston insists on the audiotape *Maxine Hong Kingston: Talking Story* (1990) that had she been born in a middle-class suburb, her struggle to be a writer would have been harder.

In contrast Kingston calls her seventeen years in Hawaii an extended vacation. Her time there provided her with the necessary distance and perspective to sort out identity problems and to finish her first two books, *The Woman Warrior* and *China Men*. Kingston was uncertain how her work would be received when she finished *The Woman Warrior*. She was ready to send this collection of fiction to other countries or keep it for posthumous publication if she failed to find a publisher. Luckily, Alfred A. Knopf, Inc. gambled on this unknown writer and published Kingston's book as nonfiction. To the surprise of both publisher and writer *The Woman Warrior* became an immediate best-seller. The book won the National Book Critics Circle Award for nonfiction in 1976 and was rated as one of the top ten nonfiction books of the decade. As late as 1989 it was still on the trade-paperback best-sellers list. Kingston's next book, *China Men,* earned her a National Book Award. Both books are widely taught in literature, women's studies, sociology, ethnic studies, and history classes.

Kingston's success, however, earned her the enmity of some Asian American critics. The most fundamental objection to *The Woman Warrior* is its generic status. Some Asian American critics question whether it is valid to call the book an autobiography when there are so many fictional elements included in her personal experience. Moreover, they fault Kingston for presenting her personal experience as "representative" of the Chinese American community. The real problem, however, seems to rest on those readers who have misconceived the text. In her 1982 essay "Cultural Mis-readings" Kingston herself laments the fact that many critics of the dominant culture have misread her and measured her against the stereotype of the exotic, inscrutable, mysterious Orient. Kingston's first two books belong to the postmodernist mixed-genre tradition. Her books are not autobiography as a specific genre but an "autobiographical form" that combines fiction and nonfiction.

One way to look at Kingston's major works is to regard them as different stories of growth. In *The Woman Warrior* the first-person narrator explores her identity formation in relation to her mother and female relatives. In *China Men* the narrator grows in her understanding of the stories of her male ancestors. Together these two books reveal the development of a Chinese American woman by uncovering the repressed stories of her family and of Chinese American history. *Tripmaster Monkey: His Fake Book* (1989), her true fiction, on the other hand, reports the artistic education of a young Chinese American bohemian, Wittman Ah Sing. Another dominant theme in each of Kingston's major books is finding a mode of articulation for her characters: the silent aunts and the narrator in *The Woman Warrior,* the reticent father and suppressed grandfathers in *China Men,* and the playwright-to-be Wittman in *Tripmas-*

Dust jacket for Kingston's first book, based in part on her mother's "talk stories" about her family's life in China (courtesy of the Lilly Library, Indiana University)

ter Monkey. Evolving along with her writing, Kingston recorded her own growing pains and her struggles to find a distinctive voice.

Kingston's main project in *The Woman Warrior* is to avenge oppression by reporting stories about the women in her family. The book opens with "No Name Woman," a story of her nameless aunt in China. This aunt became a family outcast for getting pregnant out of wedlock and finally drowned herself and her newborn baby in the family well after the villagers raided her house. Brave Orchid reveals this family secret to the young Maxine on the onset of the daughter's menstruation to caution her against sexual indiscretion. At the same time, the mother attempts to suppress this story by forbidding the daughter to repeat it. Kingston, however, purposely reports the story as an act of political resistance to Chinese patriarchy and repression in general. Furthermore she contrives different reasons for her aunt's pregnancy: the aunt could have been a victim of rape and patriarchy; she could also have been a passionate seductress and an individualist. Through active imagination, Kingston gives this aunt life and immortality in her own way.

In "At the Western Palace," the fourth section of *The Woman Warrior*, Kingston tells the story of her other silent Chinese aunt, Moon Orchid. This "thrice-told tale" – told to Kingston by her sister, who in turn heard it from her brother – is the only third-person narrative in the book, and it communicates the hazard of poor adjustment to American reality. Moon Orchid, whose name alludes to her insubstantial presence, has lived comfortably in Hong Kong on the subsidy from her husband. Through the manipulation of Brave Orchid, Moon Orchid is forced to come to America to collect her lost husband and claim her title of first wife. After she discovers her thoroughly Americanized husband, a successful doctor who has remarried, to an English-speaking wife, Moon Orchid's old Chinese life based on an illusion of changeless stability is shattered. Becoming paranoid and morbidly afraid of change, Moon Orchid repeatedly claims she is being followed by foreign "ghosts." She is finally sent to a mental asylum, where she dies.

By telling Moon Orchid's story, however, the narrator creates a voice for this oppressed woman from the East. Brave Orchid diagnoses Moon Orchid's mental disorder as stemming from her misplaced spirit. By recording her aunt's disintegration, Kingston gives Moon Orchid a place in her "mother book" and appeases the aunt's spirit. She even transforms the mental hospital into a quasi-utopian community of women. For the failing Moon Orchid her stay in the mental institution paradoxically brings her needed stability and a temporary place to anchor her spirit. She also finds acceptance from her "daughters," psychiatric patients of different races, and therefore is able to talk "a new story" about perfect communication instead of her old one of persecution.

The second section of *The Woman Warrior*, "White Tigers," is an often anthologized and discussed part of the book because of its fantastic portrayal of a female avenger. This story of the swordswoman is derived from the tale of the legendary Chinese heroine Fa Mu Lan, who substitutes for her aging father in a military conscription. In Kingston's version the swordswoman studies martial arts from a pair of mysterious old couples and leads a peasant uprising against the tyrannous emperor. After she decapitates the misogynist baron who has exploited her village and ruined her childhood, the swordswoman renounces her masculine power and returns to the traditional roles of daughter-in-law, wife, and mother. In "Personal Statement," Kingston calls the story of the swordswoman "a fantasy that inspires the girls' psyches and their politics." By adopting the story of an exemplary woman who has successfully balanced her roles in the public sphere, which is almost always dominated by men, and in the private sphere of home, Kingston is imagining victory over the androcentric Chinese and Chinese American traditions.

While Kingston has been faulted by Asian American critics and sinologists for inaccurate allusions to Chinese stories, the strength of "White Tigers" comes from her rewriting of traditional legends and mythology. In "Personal Statement" Kingston explains that "myths have to change, be useful or forgotten. Like the people who carry them across the oceans, the myths become American. The myths I write are new, American." In "White Tigers," for example, Kingston creatively rewrote traditional myths and appropriates male heroic legends for her woman warrior. Through this creative mythmaking Kingston created a heroine who transgresses traditional gender boundaries. The swordswoman describes how her parents carve their names, vows, and grievances on her back. Although undeniably an act of bodily mutilation, this act represents a coveted family acknowledgment for Chinese and Chinese American women. Furthermore Kingston's description of the script on the swordswoman's back is a deliberate combination of physical and artistic beauty: "If an enemy should flay me, the light would shine through my skin like lace." Through this revision of the chant of Fa Mu Lan, Kingston vicariously satisfied her urgent desire for family recognition.

The mother's story, "Shaman," is situated in the middle of the book. *The Woman Warrior* not only chronicles the development of the daughter Maxine but also the mother's struggle for self-definition. "Shaman" records Brave Orchid's passage from a traditional woman to a respectable woman doctor. After the deaths of her two children born in China, Brave Orchid decided to leave her uneventful life in New Society Village to study medicine in Canton, the capital of the province. In the medical school Brave Orchid earns outstanding grades and summons the courage to challenge the "Sitting Ghost." She volunteers to spend a night in a haunted room in the dormitory, reportedly defeats the ghost as it tries to attack her, and mobilizes the whole student body to participate in her exorcising ritual. In a sense Brave Orchid's struggle with the Sitting Ghost is a symbolic battle with the limits of traditionalism. Back in her village Brave Orchid uses her intelligence to establish herself as a renowned doctor. Not unlike the fantastic swordswoman, Brave Orchid "has gone away ordinary and come back miraculous, like the ancient magicians who came down from the mountains."

Brave Orchid's American daughter must also learn to fight the "ghosts" in her life. *The Woman Warrior* is subtitled *Memoirs of a Girlhood among Ghosts*. "Once upon a time," the narrator recalls, "the world was so thick with ghosts, I could barely breathe; I could hardly walk, limping my way around the White Ghosts and their cars." While some readers may find this use of ghosts jarring, Kingston does not use the term in any pejorative sense. Her world of ghosts is a result of her parents' refusal to acknowledge America and of the shadowy residues of the Chinese past in her childhood and young-adult life. The narrator protests, "whenever my parents said 'home,' they suspended America. They suspend America. They suspended enjoyment, but I did not want to go to China." Significantly, the reconciliation of the mother and the daughter in "Shaman" occurs after the mother finally gives up on the ancestral homeland. "We have no more China to go home to," the aged Brave Orchid laments. The daughter, now released from the "ghost" of China that was imposed on her as a child, can freely acknowledge her matrilineage: "I am really a Dragon, as she is a Dragon, both of us born in the dragon years. I am practically a first daughter of a first daughter."

This reconciliation of mother and daughter precedes "A Song for a Barbarian Reed Pipe," the last section of *The Woman Warrior,* in which Kingston recalls her struggle with a personal voice from kindergarten to the narrative present: "My silence was thickest – total – during the three years that I covered my school paintings with black paint," Kingston writes. The blackness of her paintings is not a sign of mental disturbance, as her American teachers have assumed: "I was making a stage curtain, it was the moment before the curtain parted and rose," the adult Kingston explains. Once the curtain is up, there is "sunlight underneath, mighty operas." This transformation of blackness-inarticulateness into carnivalesque drama provides an excellent metaphor for Kingston's development as a writer. Later, in *Tripmaster Monkey,* a mighty opera unfolds in Wittman's theatrical production.

The psychodrama of young Maxine's linguistic struggle is concretely enacted in an incident that takes place when she is in the sixth grade. One day young Maxine confronts and physically attacks a quiet Chinese American girl, admittedly her double, in a basement bathroom after school. But only "sobs, chokes, noises that were almost words" come out of the girl, never a comprehensible word. "If you don't talk, you can't have a personality," Maxine shouts (to herself as well as to the other girl). Maxine's sadistic cruelty signifies her own inner trauma of inarticulateness. After this underground encounter, Maxine spends eighteen months in bed "with a mysterious illness" and the quiet girl lives under the protection of her family for the rest of her life.

After years of silence the teenager Maxine finds an angry voice in a confrontation with her mother. Before this showdown Maxine has tried unsuccessfully to confess to the two-hundred-odd offenses that she has committed in her young life, such as tormenting the silent girl and stealing from the cash register at the family laundry. "If only I could let my mother know the list," Maxine thought, "she – and the world – would become more like me, and I would never be alone again." Yet the mother puts a stop to Maxine's attempt at communication, and the pain of silence finally drives Maxine to shout out her defiance of Chinese misogynism and her desire to leave home. This triumphant voicing, however, is immediately undercut by the narrator's sorrowful reflection as an older and wiser person: "Be careful what you say. It comes true. It comes true. I had to leave home in order to see the world logically, logic the new way of seeing. I learned to think that mysteries are for explanation. I enjoy the simplicity. Concrete pours out of my mouth to cover the forests with freeways and sidewalks. Give me plastic, periodical tables, t.v. dinner with vegetables no more complex than peas mixed with diced carrots. Shine floodlights into dark corners: no ghost." Her ghost-free new life is based on a rootless sterility represented by the concrete and plastic culture. She has escaped the Chinese interdiction of female speech at the expense of a maternal inheritance of rich imagination. It takes years for Maxine to come to her right artistic voice.

At the end of *The Woman Warrior,* Maxine finishes her story of development with a return to her matrilineage. This reconnection is mediated through that talk story. The daughter continues the story that her mother has started – "The beginning is hers, the ending, mine" – telling about T'sai Yen, a poet who had been abducted by a nomadic tribe, had two children with the barbarian chieftain, and later was ransomed back to China. T'sai Yen brought her song, "Eighteen Stanzas for a Barbarian Reed Pipe," back, and it "translated well." For Kingston, T'sai Yen is an emblem of the artist par excellence, whose poetic power is capable of transforming a weapon, the whistling arrow, into a musical instrument. Like the transformed swordswoman in "White Tigers," T'sai Yen is a word warrior who serves as a model for the author of *The Woman Warrior.* Thus, the interpenetrating stories in *The Woman Warrior* provide a link between Kingston's past and present. The central metaphor of the book is a Chinese knot in which various strands are interwoven into a work of folk art. Kingston, as "an outlaw knot-maker," weaves the past and the present together into an intricate pattern to create her "mother book." By talking stories she successfully builds a matrilineage to counterpoint the traditional Chinese patrilineage and unmuffles a personal yet rooted voice for herself.

Published in 1980, Kingston's second book, *China Men,* is the other part of "Maxine's development." "At one time," Kingston explained, "*The Woman Warrior* and *China Men* were supposed to be one book. I had conceived of one huge book." But she decided to take the men's stories out of her first book because they seemed to interfere with the women's and to collect them in her "father book," a companion piece to her "mother book." Originally, Kingston wanted to call this father book "Gold

Mountain Heroes." Later, however, she changed the title to *China Men* because she feared the original title might confirm a stereotypical concept that the early Chinese immigrants were merely gold diggers. Moreover, *China Men,* a literal translation of the Chinese characters for *Chinese,* overturns the use of the pejorative *Chinamen.* Hence Kingston's neologism at once embattles the historical insult of the Chinese immigrants and proudly acknowledges the ancestral roots of Chinese America.

The foremost political agenda in *China Men* is to claim America for Chinese Americans. Directly influenced by William Carlos Williams's *In the American Grain* (1925), which she calls a biography of America, Kingston purposely starts her story in 1860, where Williams stopped, and carries the American story forward. "In story after story Chinese-American people are claiming America, which goes all the way from one character saying that a Chinese explorer found this place before Leif Ericsson did to another one buying a house here. Buying that house is a way of saying that America – and not China – is his country," declared Kingston in a 1980 interview with Timothy Pfaff. In *China Men* she extends the narrator's personal story to reconstruct a family history, which in turn questions the "official" national history of America. Like the swordswoman in "White Tigers" who substitutes for her father in conscription, the narrator wages a linguistic battle to claim America for four generations of China men. In *The Woman Warrior* Maxine is weaving a strand of matrilineal line into patrilineage; in *China Men* she weaves her own subjectivity into the strands of men's stories. This "appropriation" of the male position also presents a continuation of the word warrior's "revenge by report" project.

Kingston also attempts to "educate" her readers. She compares *China Men* to "a six-layer club sandwich or cake," interlacing six present-day stories of her male relatives with vignettes of myths. She deliberately leaves it up to her readers to figure out the intertextual relationships of the myths and the modern stories. In the prologue, "On Discovery," Kingston revises an episode from a classical Chinese romance: while searching for the Gold Mountain, Tang Ao gets trapped in the Land of Women. He is forced by a group of Amazons to have his ears pierced, to have his feet bound, and to serve at the queen's court. In Tang Ao's story Kingston embeds a double-edged criticism of Chinese sexism and American racism. By highlighting Tang Ao's suffering in his state of effeminization, Kingston created a feminist critique of Chinese sexist practices and an allegory of the "emasculation" of the Chinese immigrants in America. By opening the book with Tan Ao's story Kingston underlines her two main goals in *China Men:* to retrieve the Chinese past and to reexamine American history.

The narrator of *China Men* identifies herself as a family historian with the self-assigned and sometimes disturbing task of safekeeping family histories and memories. In a chance encounter with her newly immigrated aunt from Hong Kong, for example, the narrator first feels reluctant to listen to the aunt's horror stories of the past, but then she recalls her "duty": "I did not want to hear how she suffered, and then I did. I did have a duty to hear it and remember it." In "Personal Statement" Kingston talks about how women play the role of keeper and weaver of stories, whereas men tend to alienate themselves from the past: "The men have trouble keeping Chinese ways in new lands. What good are the old stories? . . . Why not be rid of the mythical, and be a free American?" Claiming an American birthright through storytelling, however, the daughter-storyteller proves the men's desire to forget the past to be mistaken. Kingston's "rememory" of family struggles exposes a history of discrimination and paves the way for personal and communal healing.

As she opens *The Woman Warrior* by retrieving the silenced discourse of a nameless aunt, Kingston prefaces the present-day stories in *China Men* with a story of her father's repressed Chinese past. "You say with the few words and the silence: No stories. No past. No China," the narrator says of her father's denial of the past. She aims specifically to counterpoint his repressive silence: "You fix yourself in the present, but I want to hear the stories about the rest of your life, the Chinese stories. . . . I'll tell you what I suppose from your silences and few words, and you can tell me that I'm mistaken. You'll just have to speak up with the real stories if I've got you wrong." In "The Father from China" the daughter-narrator proceeds to "imagine" her father's development from birth to immigration to New York. Later, Kingston admitted that she found her father's reactions "satisfying" because she has successfully engaged him in a literary dialogue through marginalia that he wrote in a copy of a Chinese translation of *China Men.* Tom Hong wrote his commentary on his daughter's stories in beautiful Chinese calligraphy, giving her the satisfaction of having been treated as an intellectual equal instead of as an object of abusive language in her father's misogynist curses. Moreover, she finally "lured" her father out of his habitual reticence and won his appreciation. Thus, the daughter succeeded in returning the repressed language to the father through her literary creation.

In "The American Father" Kingston describes the father she had known as a child in Stockton. The daughter's most painful memory in this section is perhaps the recollection of how her father became a "disheartened man" after losing his job in the gambling house. His inertia was finally broken when her sister made him so angry that he leaped from his easy chair to chase her (although this sister claims that it was the narrator who was chased). Lured into action the father starts the family laundry business. "The American Father" ends with a description of how the father planted many trees near their house, "trees that take years to fruit," symbolizing the slow yet firm rooting of the Hong family in America.

"The Great Grandfather from the Sandlewood Mountain" and two vignettes on mortality again foreground the importance of speech. As a contract worker on a Hawaiian sugar plantation, Bak Goong (Great Grandfather) is forbidden to talk during work. As a trickster figure, the "talk addict" Bak Goong then invents ways, such as singing and coughing, to circumvent this interdiction: "The deep, long loud coughs, barking and wheezing, were almost as satisfying as shouting. He let out scold disguised as coughs." His final liberating act is to organize a shout party for his fellow Chinese workers. He mobilizes the workers to bury their homesickness and anger in a huge hole: "They had dug an ear into the world, and were telling the earth their secrets." After the party they could talk and sing at work without interference from the white overseers because the workers' unrestrained demonstration of emotion and strength has caused fear among the whites. Moreover, the new ritual of shouting attests to the fact that these Chinese workers in Hawaii are actually Americans because they help to build the land. As Bak Goong proudly exclaims, "We can make up customs because we're the founding ancestors of this place."

"The Grandfathers of the Sierra Nevada Mountains," "The Laws," and "Alaska China Men" highlight the tenacity of the Chinese Americans faced with racial discrimination in the American legal system and in daily life. The narrator places her emphasis on the collective identity of China men – her own grandfather included – in their efforts to conquer natural obstacles and to survive exclusion in America. The American railroad system is physical evidence of China men's contributions. As the narrator states, "After the Civil War, China Men banded the nation North and South, East and West, with crisscrossing steel." Thus, the granddaughter-narrator proudly calls her forefathers "the binding and building ancestors." The narrator provides a vivid description of how Ah Goong and other Chinese workers risked their lives setting off dynamite manually in baskets dangling over ravines. The group spirit of the Chinese workers is most apparent in a railroad-strike episode. After failing to gain equal treatment with white workers in negotiations with the railroad company, the Chinese railroad workers decide to stage a strike and pass on the plan inside the summer solstice cake. Their slogan for the strike is "free men, no coolies, calling for fair working conditions," and their pursuit of freedom resonates with the spirit of American Revolution.

In the middle of *China Men* Kingston includes a catalogue of anti-Chinese exclusion laws from 1868 to 1978. This intrusion of legal documents at first seems incongruous. Yet the juxtaposition of Kingston's personal language and governmental legal language underlies the victimization of Chinese Americans by political manipulation. At the end of "The Grandfather from the Sierra Mountains" the narrator describes how Chinese workers were "driven out," even murdered, after the railroad was completed. Speaking as the daughter of those Chinese American victims, Kingston again illustrates the importance of recovering and remembering the past.

"The Making of More Americans," "The Wild Man of the Green Swamp," and "the Adventure of Lo Bun Sun" include Chinese American and sinocized European adventure stories about where and how Chinese immigrants build their homes. It also registers an ambivalence about where the "home" for Chinese Americans is. Each of the protagonists in the five family stories told in "The Making of More Americans," for instance, needs to decide on their home address. The ghost of Say Goong (Fourth Grandfather) lingers until his brother tells him to go back to China; cousin Mad Sao cannot continue his American life until he escorts the hungry ghost of his mother back to her home village; paranoid Uncle Bun flees America. Kau Goong (Great Maternal Uncle), on the other hand, renounces old China and his old wife and is buried in America; the Hong Kong aunt and uncle immigrate to become the newest addition to the narrator's Chinese American family.

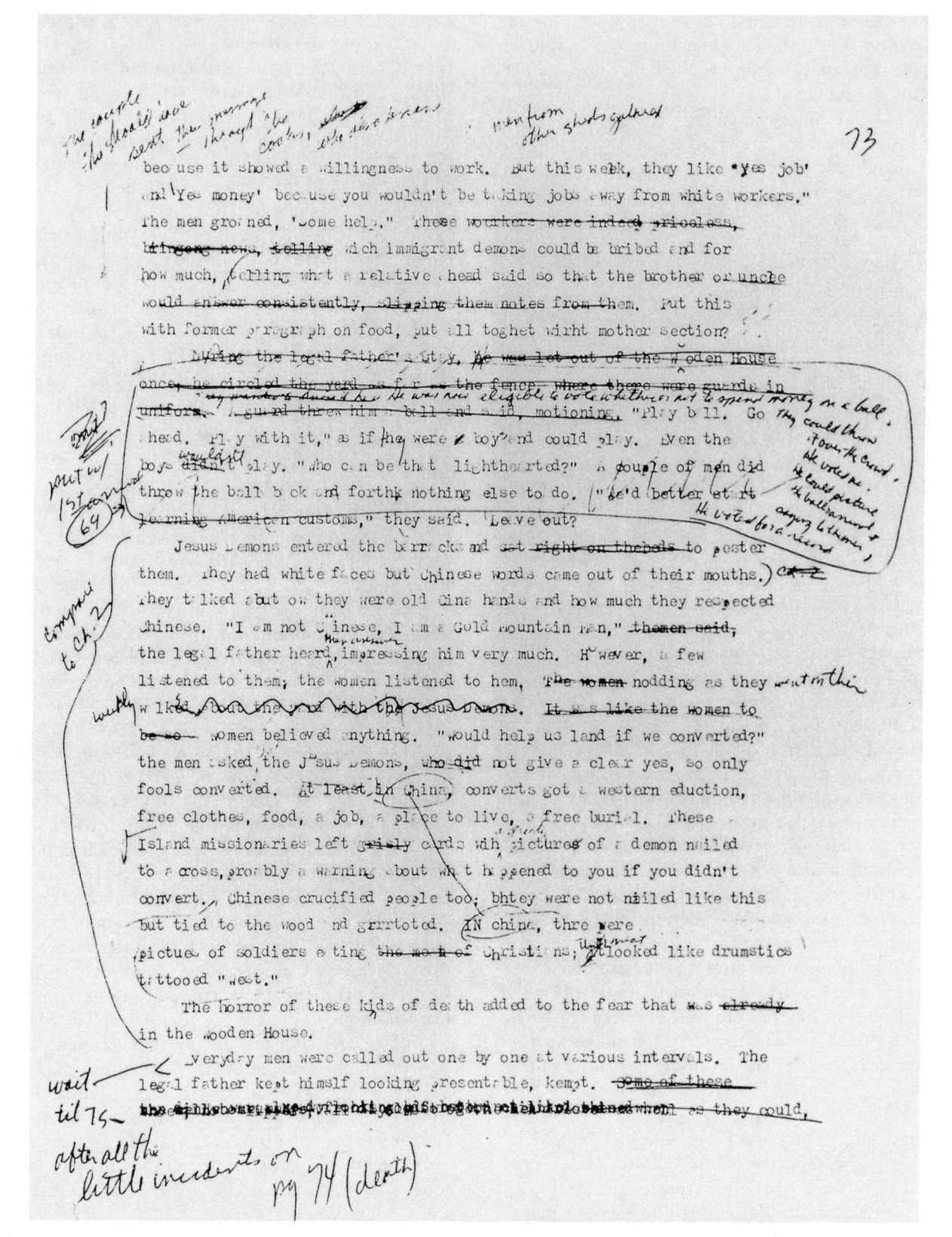

Page from the revised typescript for China Men *(courtesy of Maxine Hong Kingston)*

"The Brother in Vietnam" illustrates another identity problem for Chinese Americans and clearly presents Kingston's pacifist message. Stationed in various Asian countries during the Vietnam War, he feels lost and tries to find a "center" of identity for himself. His anxiety turns into nightmares and muttering in his sleep, which wins him the title of "Champion Complainer." The brother feels ambivalent when he passes the military-security check, which serves as evidence of his Americanness: "The government was clarifying that the family was really American, not precariously American but super-American, extraordinary secure – Q Clearance Americans." Yet he refuses to be trained as a language specialist for fear of being made to interrogate prisoners of wars. His refusal of linguistic exploitation by the military reinforces his kinship with his sister word warrior.

The epilogue, "On Listening," circles back to the prologue, "On Discovery." The narrator recounts a warm discussion among young Filipino Americans about the whereabouts of the real Gold Mountain. Together with "The Brother in Vietnam," this finale extends the text to the next generation of Asian Americans, as the spirit of inquiry and the ability to listen are passed on. Furthermore, Kingston illustrates how the daughter-narrator, in her attentiveness to the heteroglossic "voices" around her, blossoms into an expert storyteller.

For years Kingston was reluctant to visit China for fear that what she discovered there might invalidate everything she was thinking and writing. Her impression of China was also colored by the misogynist Chinese sayings she had heard as a child. In an 1978 essay, "Reservations about China," Kingston also criticized the practice of aborting female fetuses in Communist China. In 1980, after finishing *China Men,* Kingston finally visited China and saw for the first time the China that she has created in her imagination. As she told Rabinowitz, "I think I found that China over there because I wrote it. It was accessible to me before I saw it, because I wrote it. The power of imagination leads us to what's real. We don't imagine fairylands." The warm welcome she received from many Chinese gave Kingston a sense of homecoming, of going back to a place she had never seen but had imagined so well. Having used up her Chinese memory, she could concentrate on her American reality in her next book, *Tripmaster Monkey.*

In a 1980 essay titled "The Coming Book" Kingston envisioned writing a book that "will sound like the Twentieth Century" when read aloud. "The reader will not need a visual imagination, only ears." Nine years later, *Tripmaster Monkey: His Fake Book* was published. In this heteroglossic novel, Kingston continues her project of claiming America and further explores the mentality of Chinese American males. The male protagonist, Wittman Ah Sing, a fifth-generation Californian newly graduated from Berkeley, is a Joycean young artist and a self-appointed playwright of his tribe. Set in the 1960s, *Tripmaster Monkey* recounts Wittman's odyssey through San Francisco, Oakland, Sacramento, and Reno and his efforts to create his own "deep-roots American theater" – "A Pear Garden of the West" – that will perform a continuous play for many nights. Like Kingston's earlier books, *Tripmaster Monkey* is constructed around a web of Chinese intertexts, from the third-person narrator, identified by Kingston as Kwan Yin, the Chinese goddess of mercy, to the Chinese classical romances that serve as sources for Wittman's extended extravaganza. Nevertheless, Kingston skillfully translates these Chinese intertexts into Chinese American idioms with many allusions to Western literature, movies, and bohemian culture.

The title of the novel serves as a metaphor for the mixture of the culture of the bohemians and that of China. Wittman, experiencing drug-induced "trips" in the novel, imitates the mythical Monkey King from a Chinese classic, *Journey to the West.* The Monkey King is a rebellious and mischievous trickster figure who is capable of seventy-two transformations and who, according to legend, is responsible for the introduction of Buddhism into China from the West (India). As Wittman declares to his "would-be girlfriend" Nanci, "I am really the present-day U.S.A. incarnation of the King of the Monkeys." Like the Monkey King, Wittman wants to unsettle established institutions with his outrageous conduct. Significantly, in his one-man show Wittman raves against misleading reviews that describe his play as "East meets West" and "Exotic" by claiming that the play itself is "The Journey *In* the West." Positioning himself *in* the West, the American monkey deploys his play to embody his American "trips." In his rebuttal Wittman also speaks for Kingston, whose works have often been misread. The novel's subtitle, *His Fake Book,* again alludes to *Journey to the West,* in which the Monkey King discovers that the Heart Sutra he has sought is blank and jumps to the conclusion that the scrolls are fake. The scrolls turn out to be authentic after all, but only people with wisdom and insight can decipher them.

Another achievement of *Tripmaster Monkey* is its linguistic innovation. The novel displays an amazing verbal diversity, and, as Kingston predicted, it appeals to the reader's aural sensitivity. It is also a complete American book in that Kingston constantly plays with modern American language: "I already finished writing those Chinese rhythms. So I was trying to write a book with American rhythms," Kingston told interviewer Marilyn Chin. In the "Pig Woman" episode, for instance, Wittman comes across a Chinese American girl, Judy Louis, on the bus to Oakland. Bored by Judy's gibberish, Wittman suddenly visualizes her as a blue boar: "He leaned back in his seat, tried forward, and she remained a blue boar. (You can make a joke about it, you know. 'Boar' and 'bore')." The fantastic metamorphosis reminds the reader of the Circe story, in which men are changed into pigs through magic. It also alludes to the Monkey King's marvelous power of transformation and to his companion, Piggy. In *Tripmaster Monkey* Kingston is a magician with words, transforming linguistic puns into imagined reality. This playfulness with language is also strongly reminiscent of James Joyce's *Ulysses* (1922), another heteroglossic novel.

Wittman's name is another deliberate linguistic game. Wittman Ah Sing is a "man of wit" aspiring to be an heir to the great American poet Walt Whitman, who "sings" about "I" so powerfully in his poetry. In an interview with Shelly Fisher Fishkin, Kingston admitted the strong influence of Whitman on *Tripmaster Monkey*, expressing admiration for the freedom and the wildness of Whitman's language, which to her sounds as though it could have come from modern 1960s slang. She even uses lines from *Leaves of Grass* – such as "Trippers and Askers" – as chapter headings in the novel. Yet her protagonist is not exactly Whitman. While trying to name his son after his favorite poet, Wittman's father, Zeppline Ah Sing, misspelled the name, demonstrating the limitation of imitation and making a transformation that is necessary if Wittman is to be a unique Chinese American poet.

Ah Sing is also an American name that allows Wittman to claim his Chinese American identity. In his solo show Wittman discusses the origin of his American surname: "I'm one of the American Ah Sings. Probably there are no Ah Sings in China. You may laugh behind my family's back, that we keep the Ah and think it means something. I know it's just a sound. A vocative that goes in front of everyone's names. . . . In that Ah, you can hear we had an ancestor who left a country where the language has sounds that don't mean anything – la and ma and wa – like music." The meaningless yet musical vocative in this "new American name" signifies the Ah Sings' link to their Chinese ancestors as well as their new American identity.

In an interview with Phyllis Thompson, Kingston calls Wittman "a prankster," and "a ne'er do well." Wittman is unattractive. He is biased, egocentric, chauvinist, and has other unlikable characteristics. He snubs F.O.B. – fresh off the boat – Chinese immigrants while he himself is sensitive about being discriminated against. The feminist narrator is critical of Wittman's relationship with his "wife," Taña, commenting constantly to the reader that Wittman is going to pay for his androcentric attitude. Yet while Kingston sometimes criticizes him, at other times her treatment of him seems to be almost affectionate, and she always seems to view him with interest.

Kingston's distanced, yet interested, attitude toward this male protagonist indicates a significant breakthrough. After her two successful "memoirs" written mainly from a first-person perspective, Kingston shifted to the third-person point of view for her novel to get away from the shadow of egotism. By writing about a male character, or "The Other," from a distanced perspective, Kingston told Marilyn Chin, she finally found an artistic and psychological solution to her "long struggle with pronouns." Realistically, Kingston pointed out to Fishkin, women did not have such exciting and dramatic lives in the 1960s as men did. By providing a female narrator, furthermore, Kingston dramatizes the tension between male and female perspectives: "He's very macho-spirit. The narrator is the great female, so he struggles with her and fights with her and refuses to accept reality. He has to learn to be one with the female principles of the world." At the end of *Tripmaster Monkey* the narrator allows Wittman to have the spotlight to himself and blesses him in a maternal tone: "Dear American monkey, don't be afraid. Here, let me tweak your ear, and kiss your other ear." This omniscient narrator is also reminiscent of the storyteller in Chinese folk literature and classic romances, who introduces necessary information and guides the reader. Drawing on the Chinese tradition of talk story, Kingston created her female storyteller-narrator to monitor her trickster monkey.

Wittman is a conscientious young artist-to-be struggling to find his own voice. Born backstage to members of a vaudeville troupe, Wittman "really does have show business in his blood." His artistic ambition is to be "the first bad-ass China Man bluesman of America" so that he can create a Chinese American culture that consists of something besides beauty contests and handlaundries. The

Dust jacket for Kingston's novel about a fifth-generation Chinese-American whose chief ambition is to become "the first bad-ass China Man bluesman of America"

most important lesson for Wittman, however, is to learn that military heroism, as represented by the heroes in the Chinese romances, is inadequate. To be a true artist Wittman needs to become a pacifist.

Kingston's own pacifism is readily apparent in *Tripmaster Monkey*. She took part in antiwar marches during her years in Berkeley and worked with a group of resisters in Hawaii to provide sanctuary to deserters. In a 1990 essay titled "Violence and Non-Violence in China, 1989," she praised the Chinese students who attempted to achieve democracy through peaceful means, and she actively supports prodemocracy Chinese student groups. In *Tripmaster Monkey* Kingston's message is unmistakably pacifist: "Our monkey, master of change, staged a fake war, which might very well be displacing some real war," the narrator says in describing the effect of Wittman's three-day play.

Wittman's carnivalesque play is a crystallization of the love of fun. He asserts that instead of digging for gold, his Chinese ancestors came to America to have a good time: "The difference between us and other pioneers, we did not come here for the gold streets. We came here to play. And we'll play again. Yes, John Chinaman means to enjoy himself all the while.... We played for a hundred years plays that went on for five hours a night, continuing the next night, the same long play going on for a week without repeats, like ancient languages with no breaks between words, theater for a century, then dark." Wittman's assertion undermines the stereotype of the money-thirsty Chinese and values fun over materialism. In writing *Tripmaster Monkey* Kingston was finally able to use her abundant sense of humor to the full. She commented to Arturo Islas that her readers often fail to understand the humor in her works, such as the "sitcom" in Moon Orchid's story and the trick Bak Goong plays on the white missionary women: "I guess when people come to ethnic writing," Kingston remarked, "they have such a reverence for it or are so scared that they don't want to laugh." Wittman's outrageous language and behavior, however, force the reader out of this false sense of reverence.

Moreover, Wittman's play is at once universal and culturally specific. His theater is based on the principle of expansion and inclusion: "I'm including everything that is being left out, and everybody who has no place." The content of the play, however, is distinctively Chinese American, mixing Chinese stories and American vaudeville. Bringing back the tradition of the extended theatrical performance, Wittman is able to define a community. As the narrator states, "Community is not built once-for-all; people have to imagine, practice, and re-create it." From a lonely romantic contemplating suicide at the beginning of the novel, Wittman becomes an artist able to shoulder the responsibility of re-creating his community. His play, like Kingston's writing, directly opposes American individualism and embodies the collective spirit of the Chinese American community.

Kingston is now teaching in the English department at the University of California, Berkeley, and writing a book that is tentatively titled "The Fifth Book of Peace," in which she writes about her father's death and the loss of an earlier draft for the book in the 1991 Oakland fire. She links this fire thematically to the Vietnam War, writing about the psychology of conscientious objectors during the war as it is represented by the protagonist of *Tripmaster Monkey* and about her warrior woman's heroic homecoming.

Kingston's works have enchanted and inspired many readers while enraging some others. No matter how her works are received, Kingston succeeds in her "revenge" by reporting the crimes of sexism and racism. Despite her diminutive physical stature, she deserves the title of a word warrior in every sense. Kingston's literary innovations are also significant contributions to American literature. As Kingston herself says, "I am creating part of American literature. . . ." Contemporary American literature has been enriched by the addition of the powerful words of Maxine Hong Kingston.

Interviews:

Timothy Pfaff, "Talk With Mrs. Kingston," *New York Times Book Review,* 19 June 1980, pp. 1, 25-27;

Arturo Islas, "Maxine Hong Kingston," in *Women Writers of the West Coast: Speaking Their Lives and Careers,* edited by Marilyn Yalom (Santa Barbara: Capra Press, 1983), pp. 11-19;

Phyllis Hodge Thompson, "This Is the Story I Heard: A Conversation with Maxine Hong Kingston," *Biography,* 6 (Winter 1983): 1-2;

Paula Rabinowitz, "Eccentric Memories: A Conversation with Maxine Hong Kingston," *Michigan Quarterly Review,* 26 (Winter 1987): 177-187;

Marilyn Chin, "A *MELUS* Interview: Maxine Hong Kingston," *MELUS,* 16 (Winter 1989-1990): 57-74;

Maxine Hong Kingston: Talking Story [audio tape] (NAATA, 1990);

Shelly Fisher Fishkin, "Interview with Maxine Hong Kingston," *American Literary History,* 3 (Winter 1991): 782-791.

References:

King-kok Cheung, *Articulated Silences: Narrative Strategies of Three Asian American Women Writers* (Ithaca, N.Y.: Cornell University Press, 1990);

Cheung, "'Don't Tell': Imposed Silences in *The Color Purple* and *The Woman Warrior*," *PMLA,* 103 (March 1988): 162-174;

Cheung, "Talk Story: Counter-Memory in Maxine Hong Kingston's *China Men*," *Tamkang Review,* 24 (Autumn 1993): 21-37;

Cheung, "The Woman Warrior versus The Chinaman Pacific: Must a Chinese American Critic Choose between Feminism and Heroism?," in *Conflict in Feminism,* edited by Marianne Hirsch and Evelyn Fox Keller (New York: Routledge, 1990), pp. 60-81;

Thomas J. Ferraro, "Changing the Rituals: Courageous Daughtering and the Mystique of *The Woman Warrior*," in *Ethnic Passages: Literary Immigrants in Twentieth-Century America* (Chicago: University of Chicago Press, 1993), pp. 154-190;

Linda Hunt, "'I Could Not Figure Out What Was My Village': Gender vs. Ethnicity in Maxine Hong Kingston's *The Woman Warrior*," *MELUS,* 12 (Fall 1985): 5-12;

Suzanne Juhasz, "Maxine Hong Kingston: Narrative Technique and Female Identity," in *Contemporary American Women Writers,* edited by Catherine Rainwater and William J. Scheik (Lexington: University Press of Kentucky, 1985), pp. 173-189;

Elaine Kim, *Asian American Literature: An Introduction to the Writings and Their Social Context* (Philadelphia: Temple University Press, 1982);

David Leiwei Li, "*China Men*: Maxine Hong Kingston and the American Literary Canon," *American Literary History,* 2 (Fall 1990): 482-502;

Li, "The Naming of a Chinese American 'I': Cross-Cultural Sign/fications in *The Woman Warrior*," *Criticism,* 30 (Fall 1988): 497-515;

Li, "The Production of Chinese American Literary Tradition: Displacing American Orientalist Discourse," in *Redefining the Literatures of Asian-America,* edited by Shirley Lim and Amy Ling

(Philadelphia: Temple University Press, 1992), pp. 319–331;

Shirley Lim, ed., *Approaches to Teaching Kingston's The Woman Warrior* (New York: Modern Language Association of America, 1991);

Amy Ling, *Between Worlds: Women Writers of Chinese Ancestry* (New York: Pergamon Press, 1990);

Ling, "Thematic Threads in Maxine Hong Kingston's *The Woman Warrior*," *Tamkang Review*, 14 (1983–1984): 155–164;

Margaret Miller, "Threads of Identity in Maxine Hong Kingston's *Woman Warrior*," *Biography*, 6 (1983): 13–33;

Carol Neubauer, "Developing Ties to the Past: Photography and Other Sources of Information in Maxine Hong Kingston's *China Men*," *MELUS*, 10 (Winter 1983): 17–36;

Lee Quinby, "The Subject of Memoir: *The Woman Warrior*'s Technology of Idiographic Selfhood," in *De/Colonizing the Subject: The Poetics of Gender in Women's Autobiography*, edited by Sidonie Smith and Julia Watson (Minneapolis: University of Minnesota Press, 1992), pp. 297–320;

Leslie Rabine, "No Lost Paradise: Social Gender and Symbolic Gender in the Writings of Maxine Hong Kingston," *Signs*, 12 (Spring 1987): 471–492;

Roberta Rubenstein, "Bridging Two Cultures: Maxine Hong Kingston," in her *Boundaries of the Self: Gender, Culture, Fiction* (Urbana: University of Illinois Press, 1987), pp. 164–189;

Malini Johar Schueller, "Theorizing Ethnicity and Subjectivity: Maxine Hong Kingston's *Tripmaster Monkey* and Amy Tan's *The Joy Luck Club*," *Genders*, 15 (Winter 1992): 72–85;

Linda Ching Sledge, "Maxine Hong Kingston's *China Men:* The Family Historian as Epic Poet," *MELUS*, 7 (1980): 3–22;

Sidonie Smith, *A Poetics of Women's Autobiography: Marginality and the Fictions of Self-Representation* (Bloomington: Indiana University Press, 1987);

Sau-ling Cynthia Wong, "Autobiography as Guided Chinatown Tour? Maxine Hong Kingston's *The Woman Warrior* and the Chinese-American Autobiographical Controversy," in *Multicultural Autobiography: American Lives*, edited by James Robert Payne (Knoxville: University of Kentucky Press, 1992), pp. 248–275;

Wong, "Necessity and Extravagance in Maxine Hong Kingston's *The Woman Warrior:* Art and the Ethnic Experience," *MELUS*, 15 (1988): 3–26;

Wong, *Reading Asian American Literature: From Necessity to Extravagance* (Princeton, N.J.: Princeton University Press, 1993).

Papers:

A collection of Kingston's papers is at the Bancroft Library, University of California at Berkeley.

William Kotzwinkle

(22 November 1938 -)

Leon Lewis
Appalachian State University

BOOKS: *The Fireman* (New York: Pantheon, 1969);
The Day the Gang Got Rich (New York: Viking, 1970);
Elephant Boy (New York: Farrar, Straus & Giroux, 1970);
The Ship That Came Down the Gutter (New York: Pantheon, 1970);
The Return of Crazy Horse (New York: Farrar, Straus & Giroux, 1971);
The Oldest Man and Other Timeless Stories (New York: Pantheon, 1971);
Elephant Bangs Train (New York: Pantheon, 1971; London: Faber & Faber, 1971);
Hermes 3000 (New York: Pantheon, 1972);
The Supreme, Superb, Exalted and Delightful, One and Only Magic Building (New York: Viking, 1973);
Up the Alley with Jack and Joe (New York: Macmillan, 1974);
The Fan Man (New York: Harmony, 1974; Henley, U.K.: Aidan Ellis, 1974);
Nightbook (New York: Avon/Hearst, 1974);
Swimmer in the Secret Sea (New York: Avon/Hearst, 1975; London: Corgi, 1975);
Doctor Rat (New York: Knopf, 1976; Henley, U.K.: Aidan Ellis, 1976);
The Leopard's Tooth (New York: Seabury, 1976);
Fata Morgana (New York: Knopf, 1977; London: Corgi, 1978);
Herr Nightingale and the Satin Woman (New York: Knopf, 1978; London: Corgi, 1978);
The Ants Who Took Away Time (Garden City, N.Y.: Doubleday, 1978);
Dream of Dark Harbor (Garden City, N.Y.: Doubleday, 1979);
The Nap Master (New York: Harcourt Brace Jovanovich, 1979);
Jack in the Box (New York: Putnam, 1980); republished as *Book of Love* (New York: Houghton Mifflin, 1990);
E.T. The Extra-Terrestrial: A Novel (New York: Putnam, 1982; London: A. Barber, 1982);
Christmas at Fontaine's (New York: Putnam, 1982; London: Deutsch, 1983);

Superman III (New York: Warner, 1983; London: Severn House, 1983);
Great World Circus (New York: Putnam, 1983);
Trouble in Bugland (New York: Godine, 1983);
Queen of Swords (New York: Putnam, 1983; London: Abacus, 1985);
E.T., The Book of the Green Planet: A New Novel (New York: Putnam, 1985);
Seduction in Berlin (New York: Putnam, 1985);
Jewel of the Moon (New York: Putnam, 1985);
The World Is Big and I'm So Small (New York: Crown, 1986);
Hearts of Wood and Other Timeless Tales (Boston: Godine, 1986);
The Exile (New York: Dutton, 1987; London: Bodley Head, 1987);
The Midnight Examiner (New York: Houghton Mifflin, 1989; London: Black Swan, 1990);
The Hot Jazz Trio (New York: Houghton Mifflin, 1989; London: Black Swan, 1991);
The Empty Notebook (Boston: Godine, 1990);
The Million Dollar Bear (New York: Knopf, 1994);
Swimmer in the Secret Sea (San Francisco: Chronicle Books, 1994);
The Game of Thirty (New York: Houghton Mifflin, 1994);
The Bear Went Over the Mountain (New York: Doubleday, 1996).

SELECTED PERIODICAL PUBLICATIONS –
UNCOLLECTED: "Cooking at the Figaro," *New York Times*, 24 June 1972, p. 21;
"Hysterical on 34th Street," *Mademoiselle*, 76 (December 1972): 135, 179–181;
"The Energy Crisis," by Kotzwinkle and Elizabeth Gundy, *Mademoiselle*, 76 (March 1973): 64–65.

While working on a carefully guarded film project in 1982, Steven Spielberg invited the versatile writer William Kotzwinkle to Hollywood. Spielberg had read and enjoyed Kotzwinkle's vivid evocation of the ethos of the late 1960s hippie coun-

William Kotzwinkle at the time of Doctor Rat

terculture in *The Fan Man* (1974) and wanted Kotzwinkle to write a novelization of a movie in production. For Kotzwinkle, the meeting was a "rare moment" leading to the creation of a book about "this rubber geek" – his initial impression of the model for the extraterrestrial in Spielberg's film *E.T.* Acting on the assumption that "I understood Steven's dreams," Kotzwinkle spent five months on his novelization, *E.T. The Extra-Terrestrial* (1982), which eventually sold more than three million copies and briefly drew a reclusive but genial writer into national prominence. Working with Spielberg's original conception and the screenplay by Melissa Mathison, Kotzwinkle captured the essence of the movie's appeal but altered the perspective so that his book uses E.T. himself rather than the boy Elliott as the central narrative consciousness. The combination of an almost childlike innocence linked to a kind of ancient, archetypal source of wisdom is characteristic of a writer who has ranged from lyric expressions of the mysterious wonders of a child's mind in many books for young readers to riveting explorations of the nature of Evil in books tracing the phenomenon of Nazism through the twentieth century. Kotzwinkle has written effectively in a variety of genres and forms so disparate that neither a critical consensus nor a specific audience for his work has taken shape in spite of his accomplishments.

Kotzwinkle was born on 22 November 1938 in Scranton, Pennsylvania, the only child of William John Kotzwinkle, a printing-department manager, and Madolyn Murphy Kotzwinkle, a housewife. In describing the beginnings of his awareness of himself as a writer, Kotzwinkle recalls his father on a hike pointing to the Lackawanna Valley as if presenting the richness of the world to him and his mother taking him to a wading pool where a tadpole in his hand seemed, he said, like an "exquisite jewel." "I became a writer that moment in the valley," Kotzwinkle claims, but he did not actually begin the practice of writing (aside from a poem he wrote at age eight and can still quote) until he found himself "writing poetry from nowhere at college" partly because he found that at Penn State, which he attended after beginning a program in journalism at Rider College in Lawrenceville, New Jersey, the designation "poet" made him more interesting to some women in his classes. Although he was a literature major, he spent much of his time with theater arts students, finding the beginnings of an authentic voice while improvising certain acting exercises. He was dismissed from Penn State when he was caught with a girl in his room during his junior year, and although he was doing poorly in all his courses, John Barth, who was then teaching there, had already noticed some special qualities in his writing.

Kotzwinkle hitchhiked to New York City in 1957 and embraced the beatnik culture of Greenwich Village. A photograph in the *New York Daily News* from 1957 shows Kotzwinkle listening to Jack Kerouac reading poetry that Kotzwinkle said was "like a rocket." Kotzwinkle worked as a short-order cook, department-store Santa Claus, promotions

Dust jacket for Kotzwinkle's novelization of one of Steven Spielberg's most popular movies

copywriter for Prentice-Hall, and a scribe for a scandal tabloid through the 1960s. During this time he wrote regularly but did not publish anything until an old friend from school, Joe Servello, took the manuscript of *The Fireman* to several publishers before Pantheon accepted it in 1969. The story was inspired by his fireman grandfather. He allowed Kotzwinkle to sit at the wheel of a fire truck, and "after such excitement, no ordinary profession could hold me," Kotzwinkle recalls. He felt that *The Fireman* was successful because it was the first piece in which he had connected back to what he called the peak moments of his childhood, and, although the book has remained in print since its publication, initial reactions were mixed. Eleanor Glaser in *School Library Journal* called it "a fair, if unexciting, choice for very young preschoolers," but Sidney D. Long accurately identified one of Kotzwinkle's intentions, observing that the story "reminds the reader how strange and magical to the small child is his everyday world" and noted its success in that

"to read this book is to enter the realm of childhood." Kotzwinkle followed *The Fireman* with several other books for younger readers before completing a volume of short fiction (which he had been working on simultaneously with the juvenile material).

Elephant Bangs Train was published by Pantheon in 1971. Kotzwinkle joined in *Elephant Bangs Train* a sense of the surreal and the fantastic with a contemporary sensibility shaped by the Beat writers he read in college and an impulse to mix experimental forms with lucid, straightforward linear narratives. Kotzwinkle continued to write books for young readers in the early 1970s. In 1974 he published *The Fan Man,* which attracted an underground audience. The distance between the enthusiasm of readers, who discovered the book primarily through a kind of oral network, and the disdain of conventional critics such as Richard Todd, who wrote in *The Atlantic Monthly* that the book was "so cute it could hug itself," established a gulf that re-

Dust jacket for Kotzwinkle's fantasy novel in which animals all over the world rise up against the technological forces that are destroying the environment

mains, separating Kotzwinkle from the critical attention a writer of his capabilities might have expected. Other writers, however, recognized what Kotzwinkle had accomplished. For instance, Kurt Vonnegut wrote a foreword to the twentieth anniversary edition in which he warned even as he declared his delight with the book that "it requires its readers to be skilled performers," and William Kennedy cautioned that it was a "supremely insane novel" but one that "though short and episodic is nevertheless ambitious and cohesive."

The Fan Man is set in the Beat culture of the East Greenwich Village section of Manhattan. The narrative consciousness of the book, Horse Badorties, is an aging beatnik who seeks a spiritual home and unconventional enlightenment. He expresses his thoughts and reactions to the assault of the city on his senses in a Joycean monologue. As Kotzwinkle works with the rhythms, shifts, pauses, and particular vocabulary of Badorties's mind, the narrator's personality emerges through language augmented by imaginative typography, a poetic suspension of syntax, and the manipulation of tenses through punctuation and other inventive structural devices. Still enthusiastic about the great variety of experiences in the city, Badorties fluctuates between manic participation and withdrawal to his pad in a decaying tenement, which he has fashioned into an extension of his inner landscape. His daily routine consists of muddled exercises drawn from inverted axioms of Eastern thought, unorthodox personal rituals like chanting "Dorky" for an entire chapter while oblivious to the entreaties of friends, and sojourns of acquisition wherein he fraudulently obtains useless objects, such as a used school bus with no brakes and a huge propeller, that contribute to the clutter of his life.

While his outlook is primarily comic, Badorties is touched with a sadness. He is involved with an ongoing project, the organization of a kind of concert, but his plans remain in shambles after a year of spasmodic effort. Bogged down in endless inner dialogues about the correct way to proceed, Badorties exhibits a form of comic fanaticism that makes his persistence both admirable and pathetic. The culmination of the book is a final example of misplaced intention as the concert he plans actually takes place while he is miles away in Van Courtland

Park in the northern, almost rural reaches of the city. There he muses about a time in the past when "I used to wander here, man, a spaced-out little Horse Badorties," a return to the magic garden of childhood at the heart of Kotzwinkle's conception of paradise. The last image of Badorties has him under a huge umbrella as rain begins, "ready for the monsoon," comforted by his satchel of worthless objects, apparently out of touch with everything. It is as much a picture of self-sufficiency and serenity as total disengagement. It reflects the author's ambivalent, tender attitude toward Badorties – a mixture of rue, astonishment, and delight. *The Fan Man* is an almost agonizingly sweet lament for a man and for a time, sentimental in its regard for Badorties but sharp-edged enough to avoid the bogus emotion of special pleading.

At the time *The Fan Man* was published, Kotzwinkle was no longer living in New York City. He had married the novelist Elizabeth Gundy ("She had her pieces in place and literature was pouring out of her") in 1970, and the couple settled in an isolated part of New Brunswick, where they lived for years "in a shack without electricity or plumbing" after the farmhouse they bought burned down one Halloween. In the Canadian wilderness, Kotzwinkle claims that he heard in a recurring dream animals who "came to me, night after night, telling me, 'We've got something to say.'" This led specifically to his ecofable *Doctor Rat* (1976), but once he moved to the country Kotzwinkle began a nearly total involvement in the writing life, leading to twenty-five years of steady production of an exceptional variety of books. The same year as *The Fan Man* appeared, *Nightbook*, Kotzwinkle's series of linked short sketches, was published. Kotzwinkle continued to write short fiction while working on longer projects, and in *Nightbook* he developed a double narrative in which Athenian women meeting at the temple of the High Priestess of Demeter tell stories about erotic encounters while accounts of moderately paralleled situations in contemporary America are interwoven – often paragraph by paragraph. The modern author, based loosely on Kotzwinkle in the 1960s, is told to include certain terms on every page, to hold nothing back, and to avoid scenes with animals. Kennedy called the book "high class porn" and "nifty dirt," and Martin Levin noted that it mingles "the scatological and the mythological." Kotzwinkle has purposely tried to undermine the lingering vestiges of a repressive puritan retreat from eros in his work, but here he is also concerned with the struggles of an unpublished writer and has both luxuriated in and parodied the possibilities of pornography in showing the power of the artistic imagination. The stories in *Nightbook* fracture chronology and recorded history; they are antic inventions indicating Kotzwinkle's willingness to push an idea to its limits, while in a larger sense tracing a universal thread of desire through time.

In 1977 *Doctor Rat* won a World Fantasy Award, which brought the author the classification as a "fantasist" among some observers. *Doctor Rat* is an ecofable with a dual-track narrative, "a political book" that confronts "the dangerous split between us and our animal nature." Doctor Rat administers experiments on various species at the behest of unseen human forces, while animals throughout the planet in alternative chapters organize in a rebellion against the technological blight destroying their habitat. Doctor Rat is portrayed as a servant of Nazi ideology, while the animals exhibit traits of spirituality, empathy, and decency representative of the finest qualities of human civilization. There is a lurid fascination to the ingenious rationalizations of Doctor Rat's compulsive, high-energy rantings and frantic explanations to the lab animals, while the noble nature of the free animals functions as an allegorical commentary on social values. The critical response to *Doctor Rat* was unpredictable. Anne Larsen wrote in *The Village Voice*, "it's simply a bad book, a puffed-up book, claiming humility," and Richard Brickner in *The New York Times* agreed that it is "recklessly sentimental in its argument." Yet, while novelist Robert Stone agreed in a probing review that Kotzwinkle had oversentimentalized the animals and demonized human society, he praised the author as "not afraid to take the kind of risks that are necessary for the production of a serious novel" and noted the "fanciful descriptions of animals which are often genuinely poetic and sometimes moving." Kotzwinkle was undeterred by negative notices, but not undisturbed, remarking that "I, of course, am violently in disagreement with my critics. However, we all must do what we think best. I resign myself to being misunderstood and assign my critics a secure place in the arctic, with penguins for company."

Through the latter part of the 1970s, Kotzwinkle continued to examine aspects of evil that were contaminating his interest in what he called "the inner child who wants us to reexperience the world in a spontaneous way." Unable to deflect his discomfort entirely with the antic humor of *The Fan Man*, Kotzwinkle extended his consideration of the darker sides of human experience with a historical novel, *Fata Morgana* (1977), set in the Europe of Louis Napoleon, and an illustrated novella, *Herr*

Dust jacket for the unconventional crime novel Kotzwinkle set in Europe during the reign of Louis Napoleon

Nightingale and the Satin Woman (1978). He maintained an unalloyed optimistic outlook in the young-adult novel *The Leopard's Tooth* (1976), which introduced aspects of evil but dispatched them all in the context of intrepid Victorian virtue. *Fata Morgana* follows Inspector Paul Picard through mysterious labyrinths of conventional crime and mind-clouding magic. His rational procedures are confounded eventually by inexplicable occurrences that drive him back to a child's consciousness of the possibilities of magic and the resonance of the so-called supernatural. Jerome Charyn praised Kotzwinkle for his ability to "move from the mundane to the grotesque, from magic to hard-nosed fact" and, although judging the book's intentions as narrow, felt that it "does entertain all the way through." Hollis Alpert agreed, describing Kotzwinkle as "a fine young writer" who had written "an adult fairy tale" that "sets him well above the more ordinary practitioners." *The Atlantic Monthly*, however, spoke for the more conventional reviewers who seemed troubled by Kotzwinkle's disregard for "rules" of genre, as its critic Phoebe-Lou Adams accused Kotzwinkle of having "done the unforgivable; he has bailed out of a fantasy by turning it all into a dream."

Now living on the coast of Maine, Kotzwinkle responded to the questions about his treatment of fantasy by saying, "My books explore some of the deepest regions of the psyche by combining elements of fantasy with stark reality, humor and horror." His loosely autobiographical recollection of boyhood in central Pennsylvania, *Jack in the Box* (1980), on the other hand, was drawn in almost classically realistic terms conveying the narrowed expectations of small-town life in the 1950s. A kind of working-class version of J. D. Salinger's *Catcher in the Rye* (1951), the novel combines the romantic aura of early childhood with a wry, humorous depiction of the confusing but generally pleasant passage through adolescence of Jack Twiller, an affable, well-meaning, socially insecure young man. Kotzwinkle satirizes many of the staples of coming-of-age fiction while convincingly conveying Jack Twiller's search for a viable identity. *Jack in the Box* was generally overlooked by the more prestigious national magazines and newspapers but received appreciative comments from many local papers.

Kotzwinkle's next book, however, his novelization of *E.T.*, not only projected him into the media spotlight but also established a connection

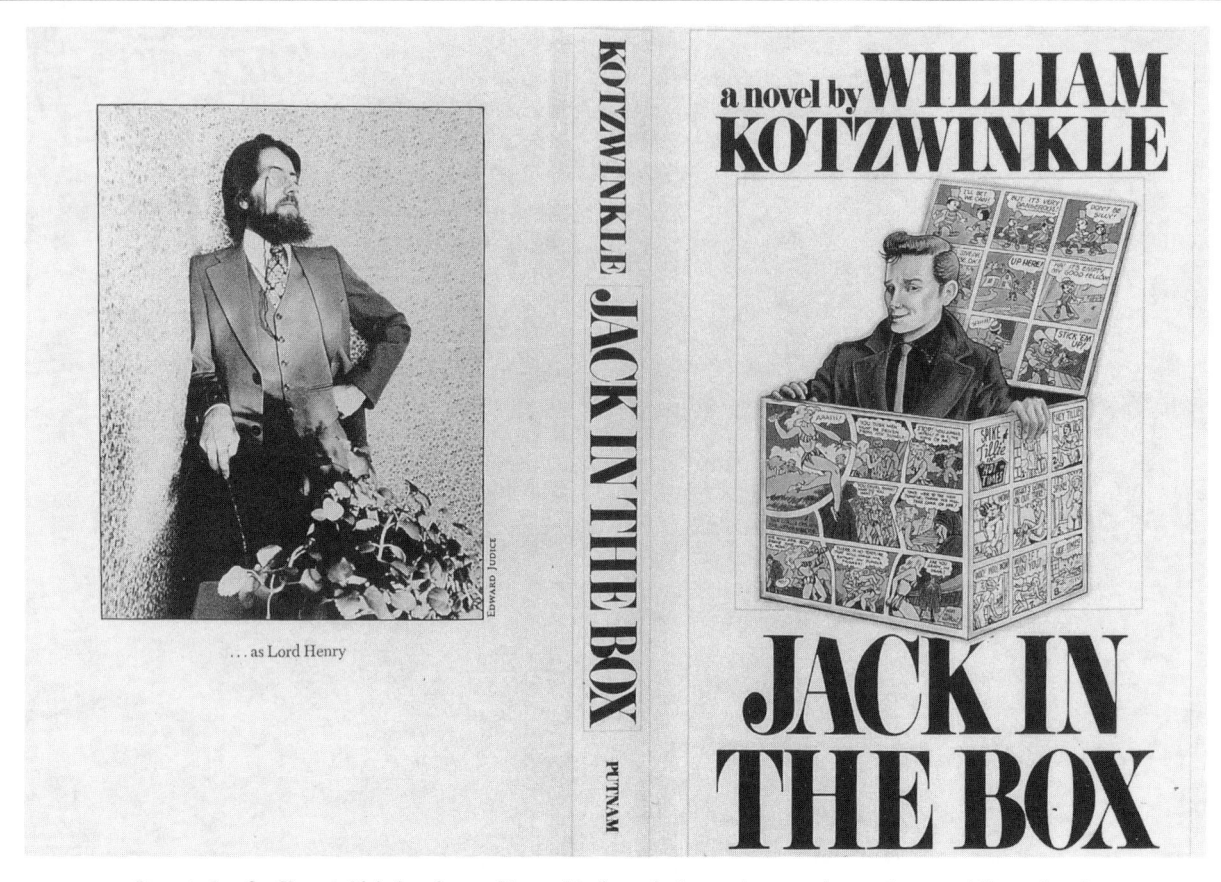

Dust jacket for Kotzwinkle's loosely autobiographical novel about a boy growing up in central Pennsylvania

with the world of film production and at the same time relieved the financial pressures he had faced as a writer. Agreeing with Spielberg that the film's tremendous appeal is centered on E.T.'s "uncanny nature," Kotzwinkle developed his narration from the assumption that E.T. is "definitely not human . . . [he has] a quality of humanity *that is yet to come,* and it has to do with love." Directly challenging what he regarded as the artificial classification of children's books, Kotzwinkle maintained that he wrote *E.T.* "as I've written everything else, making the image glow with as much power as I could put into them," working "to set my lunatic humor loose" and to dramatize "a powerful archetype that is dawning for humanity."

Many critics still regarded Kotzwinkle's novelization as a children's book, but Spielberg saw it as equal to the film, saying the public accepted it as a separate work of art. In a sense, it is the culmination of Kotzwinkle's previous writing for younger readers; he presents E.T. as a manifestation of humanity's undeveloped cosmic consciousness that finds its expression in imagination and fantasy but which can be objectified because it is so much a part of common human desire. E.T. is part of a long tradition of sacred monsters from the fairy-tale world, the wild thing one hopes to find but fears to see, a "scorned Chaplinesque figure who at the same time is some sort of redeemer" enabling people to regain a sense of the spiritual grandeur that modern technology is obliterating. Following his satiric attack on the social tendency to subdue nature in *Doctor Rat,* Kotzwinkle uses E.T. to present the positive side of his environmental concerns through a figure whose strength and appeal comes from his symbiotic bond with every sentient organism in the universe. Without overstressing the religious implications, Kotzwinkle is emphasizing his belief that environment *is* life and that proper care and concern for the planet is essential for the survival of every form of life, as well as a source of nourishment for the soul. The humor that Kotzwinkle finds in Elliott and his family (loosely paralleling Jack Twiller's in *Jack in the Box*) and in E.T. himself ("A walking squash, a strolling watermelon") is balanced by the gradual admiration Kotzwinkle builds for a creature ("venerable star-rover; archaic wanderer; distinguished cosmologist") who is the product of eons of evolutionary advance. Just as Horse Badorties's mind in *The Fan Man* became a site of fascination, E.T.'s daunting mental capabilities are outlined from the perspective of an inner logic that superbly combines the comic hilarity of his incongruous appearance and his awesome cerebral capability. ("He who had once supervised the planet life in the grandest mansion of space was being closeted with a skateboard.") Without Spielberg, the novel would not have existed in its final form, but Kotzwinkle's *E.T.* is an expansion of and commentary on a brilliant film.

Before turning to other projects, Kotzwinkle discussed a sequel with Spielberg ("After several hours we had the rough outline of a story") and spent seven months writing *E.T., The Book of the Green Planet* (1985), an idealistic ecovision of utopia balancing the ecological Hell of *Doctor Rat*. Since E.T., on his home ground, is almost entirely removed from the human world, the book seems set in a fairy-tale realm of fabulous creatures, but even more than *Doctor Rat*, it is a revealing allegory relating human nature to aspects of biodiversity. While there is a story involving E.T.'s attempts to rejoin Elliott, the morphology of the land-life linkage is at the core of the book. During the early 1980s Kotzwinkle concentrated on material of this sort, agreeing to write a novelization of *Superman III* (1983) (which he feels is "artistically done . . . a delight the world has yet to find out about") in which deadpan visual comedy is joined to a meditation on the burdens and obligations of exceptional powers. He also published another collection of short fiction, *Jewel of the Moon* (1985), that includes stories set throughout human history and beyond. Similarly, the long poem *Seduction in Berlin* (1985) blends time, space, dreams, and hallucinations in a mysterious old-world ethos of secrets and spells, while *Queen of Swords* (1983) is a darkened semi-autobiographical reflection in which Kotzwinkle imagines how an unsuccessful writer with something like his background might have fared in the aftermath of the euphoric 1960s. Although it is written in the realistic style of *Jack in the Box*, the protagonist shares Kotzwinkle's interest in alternative modes of self-expression, including various eccentric and idiosyncratic disciplines.

Rarely leaving his home in Maine after the success of E.T. except for trips to Hollywood to work on adaptations of *Jack in the Box* (filmed as *Book of Love* in 1992) and his account of his job as a department-store Santa Claus, *Christmas at Fontaine's* (1982), Kotzwinkle had become identified with a particular kind of fantasy grounded in realism, and his literary production intensified. Increasingly, Kotzwinkle's vision of a childhood world of wonder had been distorted by what he calls "the worst nightmare of history. Nazi Germany had infiltrated the psyche everywhere," and in *The Exile* (1987), he confronted the issue of Evil directly, following David Caspian, an action hero of expensive films, through a dual narrative in which film production in the United States in the late 1980s overlaps with a desperate struggle for survival in Germany during World War II. Caspian's questions about the validity of his acting achievements and his uncertainty about his ability to continue to perform have destabilized his psyche, and he finds himself slowly losing his contemporary identity in incidents of transference where he becomes Felix Falkenhayn in Berlin. Kotzwinkle's mordant satire (which he calls "accurate reporting") of Los Angeles merges with his depiction of the horrors of the Nazi regime – "Past and present collide; fascist Germany and contemporary Lost Angeles interpenetrate," Kotzwinkle says. His sharply realistic style is employed in a narrative that presents shifts in time as a completely plausible aspect of human experience. The capability of the mind to create reality is explored both as a psychic necessity and as a means of examining an artistic performance; Caspian the actor is also an analogue for an artist drawing inspiration from the depths of his psychic structure. Without giving up the humor that distinguishes his best work, Kotzwinkle has invested the setting in Berlin with a feeling of horror and dread. Critical responses to the book were typically mixed. Lawrence Christon in *The Los Angeles Times* complained that Kotzwinkle is "not a careful prose stylist" while acknowledging that he is "a first-rate storyteller," and Herbert Gold called *The Exile* "an ambiguous, entertaining, unsettling performance," observing also that Kotzwinkle's achievement should earn him the rank in American letters that "his quirky talents have long merited."

Returning to the semi-autobiographical mode, Kotzwinkle based *The Midnight Examiner* (1989) on his fifteen-month stint as a writer/editor for a *National Enquirer* type of tabloid. He creates a gallery of eccentric characters whose ambitions to enter the world of respectable publishing have been hilariously sidetracked. Recognizing the seriousness and dignity of their intentions, Kotzwinkle uses comedy warmly here, allowing the writers eventually to become active agents in a story involving a mob tycoon almost as absurd as the stories they have been designing for their readers. The high-spirited parodies of tabloids and the presentation of New York City as a wild carnival of diverting chaos drew almost uniformly appreciative notices. Bill Marx in the *Village Voice* called Kotzwinkle "America's

Dust jacket for three stories Kotzwinkle has set "where the fabric of an ordinary day dissolves, and the other dimension – call it the imagination – bleeds in"

mondo trasho master farceur . . . in a class by himself."

Kotzwinkle's next book, *The Hot Jazz Trio* (1989), continued his pattern of alternating between novels set in a world resembling contemporary America with versions of a place "where the fabric of an ordinary day dissolves, and the other dimension – call it the imagination – bleeds in," as he put it. "Django Rheinhardt Played the Blues," the most ambitious of the three, uses the techniques of surrealism to develop a pastiche wherein "real" figures from history, such as Pablo Picasso and Jean Cocteau, intermingle with magicians in pursuit of a missing woman through "the Plain of Rectangular Configuration." As Diane Manuel observed in *The New York Times,* "some critics find [Kotzwinkle's illusory tales] frustrating to pull apart while others rave about their exquisite hearts. But all agree they're certifiable originals." Nonetheless, her caveat that *The Hot Jazz Trio* "tantalizes but doesn't add up to a full and satisfying meal" summarizes the kind of critical consensus that has kept serious studies of Kotzwinkle's writing out of the academic journals.

The range of Kotzwinkle's writing across the boundaries of traditional genres, the comic-romantic sensibility he brings to his work, and his assertion that "Most of my writing is in some sense an attempt to tap the ancestral or collective memory that dwells in every brick or stone and in our minds" are all factors determining Kotzwinkle's current status. Other factors affecting his contemporary reputation are his work in disparaged areas such as science fiction–fantasy; his successful novelizations of films, another disparaged genre; and his enthusiastic creation of hybrids, such as illustrated poetic sequences that are regarded as subliterary by some traditionalists. His affinity for counterculture aesthetics like that of the Beat artists, his disinterest in promotional tours (with the exception of his work on *The Game of Thirty* [1994], an homage to his editor, Seymour Lawrence), and his occasional observations in the media about the importance of mysticism, Chinese herbal derivatives, and other esoteric phenomena have also contributed to his characterization as an eccentric cult writer.

Books like *The Game of Thirty,* however, may force a revision of this estimation. In this novel

Kotzwinkle has taken the hard-boiled detective novel of Dashiell Hammett and Raymond Chandler and given it a contemporary resonance that connects some of his primary concerns with a gripping suspenseful mystery. Jimmy McShane, his protagonist, has vestiges of the classic Hemingway code hero in his upbringing but is a self-reflective, resilient, flexible postmodern man as well. His "partner" in detection is an actively feminist, brilliantly capable woman. The criminals they must expose and apprehend are monsters of ego-driven selfishness, a contemporary manifestation of evil. The New York City setting functions as a kind of character, and the integration of Egyptology and the game of "30" itself provides a tight structure that enables Kotzwinkle to alternate chapters of riveting tension with his characteristic offbeat humor. The ultimate resolution of the crime involves Kotzwinkle's continuing concern for the unguarded openness of a child's perceptions, a quality he cherishes and which his writing strives to celebrate and preserve. The easy readability of Kotzwinkle's works sometimes is used against him. In a generally enthusiastic review, the British writer Daniel Easterman mentions a "softness at the core of some modern American writing" and complains that in spite of what Kotzwinkle does well, "it's a pity we didn't see more of hell first." Easterman feels that Kotzwinkle's optimistic vision of existence is too narrow to be useful in the late twentieth century. For this reason, Kotzwinkle may be temporarily out of step with some of the dominant critical strictures of his time, but this is unlikely to deter him as he continues to practice his craft with energy and invention. As he predicted in an interview at the height of his public acclaim, "I know I'll end up a little old guy telling stories on a mountain somewhere."

Interviews:

R. E. Nowicki, "An Interview with William Kotzwinkle," *San Francisco Review of Books* (Spring 1985): 7-8;

Walter Gelles, "William Kotzwinkle," *Publishers Weekly,* 236 (10 November 1989): 46-47.

Reference:

L. H. Lewis, "William Kotzwinkle," in *Beacham's Popular Fiction Update* (Washington, D.C.: Beacham Publishing, 1991), pp. 693-704.

Elmore Leonard

(11 October 1925 -)

David H. Everson
University of Illinois at Springfield

BOOKS: *The Bounty Hunters* (Boston: Houghton Mifflin, 1953; London: Hale, 1956);

The Law at Randado (Boston: Houghton Mifflin, 1955; London: Hale, 1957);

Escape from Five Shadows (Boston: Houghton Mifflin, 1956; London: Hale, 1957);

Last Stand at Saber River (New York: Dell, 1959); republished as *Lawless River* (London: Hale, 1959);

Hombre (New York: Ballantine, 1961; London: Hale, 1961);

The Big Bounce (New York: Gold Medal, 1969; London: Hale, 1969);

The Moonshine War (Garden City, N.Y.: Doubleday, 1969; London: Hale, 1970);

Valdez Is Coming (London: Hale, 1969; New York: Gold Medal, 1970);

Forty Lashes Less One (New York: Bantam, 1972);

Mr. Majestyk (New York: Dell, 1974; London: Penguin, 1987);

Fifty-two Pickup (New York: Delacorte, 1974; London: Secker & Warburg, 1974);

Swag (New York: Delacorte, 1976; London: Penguin, 1985); also published as *Ryan's Rules* (New York: Dell, 1978);

The Hunted (New York: Delacorte, 1977; London: Secker & Warburg, 1978);

Unknown Man No. 89 (New York: Delacorte, 1977; London: Secker & Warburg, 1977);

The Switch (New York: Bantam, 1978; London: Secker & Warburg, 1979);

Gunsights (New York: Bantam, 1979);

Gold Coast (New York: Bantam, 1980; London: Allen, 1982);

City Primeval: High Noon in Detroit (New York: Arbor House, 1980; London: Viking, 1987);

Split Images (New York: Arbor House, 1981; London: Allen, 1983);

Cat Chaser (New York: Arbor House, 1982; London: Viking, 1986);

Stick (New York: Arbor House, 1983; London: Lane, 1984);

LaBrava (New York: Arbor House, 1983; London: Viking, 1984);

Glitz (New York: Arbor House, 1985; London: Viking, 1985);

Bandits (New York: Arbor House, 1987; London: Viking, 1987);

Touch (New York: Arbor House, 1987; London: Viking, 1987);

Freaky Deaky (New York: Arbor House, 1988; London: Viking, 1988);

Killshot (New York: Arbor House, 1989; London: Viking, 1989);

Get Shorty (New York: Delacorte, 1990; London: Viking, 1990);

Maximum Bob (New York: Delacorte, 1991; London: Viking, 1991);

Rum Punch (New York: Delacorte, 1992; London: Viking, 1992);

Pronto (New York: Delacorte, 1993; London: Viking, 1993);

Riding the Rap (New York: Delacorte, 1995; London: Viking, 1995);

Out of Sight (New York: Delacorte, 1996).

Collections: *Dutch Treat* (New York: Arbor House, 1985; Harmondsworth, U.K.: Viking, 1987) – comprises *City Primeval*, *The Moonshine War*, and *Gold Coast;*

Double Dutch Treat (New York: Arbor House, 1986) – comprises *The Hunted*, *Swag*, and *Mr. Majestyk*.

MOTION PICTURES: *The Moonshine War*, screenplay by Leonard, M-G-M, 1970;

Joe Kidd, screenplay by Leonard, Universal, 1972;

Mr. Majestyk, screenplay by Leonard, United Artists, 1974;

Stick, screenplay by Leonard and Joseph C. Stinson, Universal, 1985;

52 Pickup, screenplay by Leonard and John Steppling, Cannon, 1986;

The Rosary Murders, screenplay by Leonard and Fred Walton, New Line Cinema, 1987;

Elmore Leonard

Cat Chaser, screenplay by Leonard and Joe Borrelli, Viacom, 1989.

TELEVISION: *High Noon Part II: The Return of Will Kane,* script by Leonard, CBS, 1980;
Desperado, script by Leonard, Universal (NBC), 1988.

Dubbed "The Dickens of Detroit" by *Time* magazine in 1984, Elmore Leonard has written more than thirty novels, as well as many short stories and screenplays. He began his writing career in the early 1950s, turning out short stories for western pulp magazines. Shortly thereafter, he began publishing western novels. The sale of the film rights to some of his westerns led to a long and lucrative association with Hollywood. When the western market dried up in the mid 1960s, he began writing contemporary crime novels; it was not until the early 1980s that he achieved widespread critical acclaim for his crime fiction.

Although one routinely finds Leonard's crime novels shelved in the mystery sections at libraries and bookstores, he rejected the mystery label for his books in a 1990 interview: "They are definitely not mysteries in the classic sense of being puzzles. They're certainly not whodunits. The reader knows everything that's going on – very often more than the main character." Laced with deadpan humor, Leonard's contemporary crime novels explore the underside of American life in the manner of the films noirs of the 1930s and 1940s, undercutting reader expectations by avoiding stereotypical portraits of even the lowest of his low-life characters. His stories depict killers, small-time hoodlums, and reformed criminals who follow codes of conduct that make sense to them, no matter how distorted they may appear to the reader. His chief protagonists are seemingly detached men and women who want to follow the rule of noninvolvement expressed by Jack Ryan, a process server, in *Unknown Man No. 89* (1977): "never get personally involved.... That was rule number one. Don't get too close and start feeling sorry for people. You want to do that, go work for the Salvation Army." Leonard's protagonists, however, are forced by circumstances, and

Dust jacket for Leonard's novel about two small-time Detroit robbers who team up for an increasingly violent crime spree

their own impulses, into the fray. They are seldom without flaws and do not hesitate to fashion their own forms of justice when the law, as it inevitably does, fails. In a play on Raymond Chandler, Michael Wood wrote: "Elmore Leonard's characters are usually tarnished and afraid, but pretty good at surviving."

Many reviewers consider Leonard to be among the best of the hard-boiled crime novelists, a list that includes writers such as Chandler, Dashiell Hammett, James M. Cain, and George V. Higgins. (His work is closer in spirit to the fiction of Cain and Higgins than to that of Chandler and Hammett.) Novelist Walker Percy once said of Leonard: "He is as good as the blurbs say: 'The greatest crime writer of our time, perhaps ever,' " (*The New York Times Book Review,* 4 January 1987), while novelist Martin Amis has called him "a literary genius" and located the essence of that genius in Leonard's ability to "write" jazz (*The New York Times Book Review,* 14 May 1995). Yet another mainstream novelist, Leonard Michaels, has asserted that while reading a book by Leonard "you know every minute who is the boss of this crime novel and why it has been said that he is the best" (*Los Angeles Times Book Review,* 14 May 1995).

No aspect of Leonard's work has been more often singled out for critical praise than his ear for dialogue. He receives high marks for his clean, lean prose. The reader of Leonard's fiction gets the sense that he holds in his considerable imagination a colorful world where all of his characters talk the Leonard talk and walk the Leonard walk. Although Leonard has avoided writing a series with a continuing character, many of his characters appear in more than one novel, as Jack Ryan does in *The Big Bounce* (1969) and *Unknown Man No. 89* and as Ernest "Stick" Stickley does in *Swag* (1976) and *Stick* (1983). (Leonard has said he wrote *Stick* after he noticed on his calendar that Stick was about to get out of prison after seven years and wondered how Stick would react to a changed world.) Sometimes different characters have the same name, such as Majestyk in *The Big Bounce* and *Mr. Majestyk* (1974), and sometimes characters in different novels live in the same location, such as the Della Robbia art deco hotel on

Miami Beach, inhabited by Maurice Zola and Joseph LaBrava in *LaBrava* (1983) and Harry Arno of *Pronto* (1993) and *Riding the Rap* (1995). Leonard's concern with naming his characters stems from his belief that they do not come alive until they have the right names. As he told interviewer Jean Ross: "If I get the name right, the characters will talk." Perhaps parodying his repeated use of the name Lewis, in *Riding the Rap* he names one of the characters Louis Lewis.

Elmore John Leonard Jr. was born on 11 October 1925 in New Orleans, Louisiana, the son of Elmore John Leonard and Flora Amelia Rive Leonard. His father was a scout for General Motors dealerships. After moving around the Southwest, the family settled in Detroit, Michigan. In the fifth grade Leonard was already upsetting reader expectations: influenced by Erich Maria Remarque's World War I novel, *All Quiet on the Western Front* (1929), Leonard wrote a war play in which the coward redeems himself by rescuing the hero. Called "Dutch" by his classmates (after American League pitcher Dutch Leonard), Leonard still goes by that nickname as an adult, and Arbor House has made use of it in titling collections of his novels: *Dutch Treat* (1985) and *Double Dutch Treat* (1986).

After graduating from high school in 1943, Leonard failed a physical for the U.S. Marine Corps and was then drafted into the U.S. Navy, serving in the South Pacific as a Seabee during World War II. (He later used this background in drawing the character of Walter Majestyk in *The Big Bounce*.) On his discharge from the navy Leonard entered the University of Detroit in 1946 as an English and philosophy major. While at the university, he twice entered short-story contests, finishing second once. On 30 July 1949 he married Beverly Cline (with whom he subsequently had five children), and in 1950 he graduated. He took a job as a copywriter for the Campbell-Ewald Advertising Agency in Detroit. Though he soon discovered that writing ads was not the least bit satisfying, he remained with the company until 1961. In the early 1950s he developed the habit of rising at 5 A.M. to get in two hours of fiction writing before going to work to "write zingy copy for Chevrolet trucks." Sometimes he also managed to work on his fiction at the office.

Leonard says he selected the western genre because he liked western films and because there was a market in the pulps for westerns. He narrowed his focus to Arizona Apache country and began a lifetime habit of background research for his fiction by studying histories of the West and photographs of Arizona. (He later hired a research assistant.) His first sale was "Trail of the Apache," a story bought by *Argosy* magazine for $1,000. This success ultimately led to his being represented by the well-known agent H. N. Swanson (whose clients had included, among others, Ernest Hemingway, William Faulkner, and Chandler).

In an interview in *The Armchair Detective* Leonard described how he learned to write westerns by studying Hemingway: "My inspiration came from Ernest Hemingway, his lean style. I saw *For Whom the Bell Tolls* as a western, studied closely how he wrote action sequences as well as dialogue." Yet Leonard has also said that because he sees humor in even the darkest of situations, his books are closer in spirit to Richard Pryor than Hemingway.

In 1953 Leonard published the first of his seven western novels, *The Bounty Hunters*. The most successful of these books is *Hombre* (1961), voted one of the twenty-five best western novels of all time by the Western Writers of America. According to Leonard, he wrote *Hombre* to debunk the hoary "white flag" scene in which the bad guys discuss the situation with the good guys under a flag of truce. The unheroic hero of *Hombre*, John Russell, a prototype for nearly all of Leonard's protagonists, stands aloof from quarrels that do not concern him. Yet, like so many Leonard characters, he is thrust into a life-or-death situation by the actions of others, in this case a botched stagecoach robbery and the greed and cowardice of some of the passengers. Russell manages to get his hands on the loot from the robbery, but then he and some of the passengers become trapped at the top of a hill while the bad guys hold one of the female passengers hostage. After the head villain walks halfway up the hill under a white flag and offers to exchange the woman for the money, Russell says to him: "I have only one question. How are you going to get back down that hill?" – and starts firing. Russell is killed in the final shoot-out. *Hombre* was sold to Twentieth Century-Fox in 1965 for $10,000 and was made into a successful 1967 movie starring Paul Newman and Richard Boone. (In 1957 a Leonard short story, "3:10 to Yuma" – modeled on the classic 1952 western movie *High Noon* – was made into a highly regarded motion picture, starring Glenn Ford.)

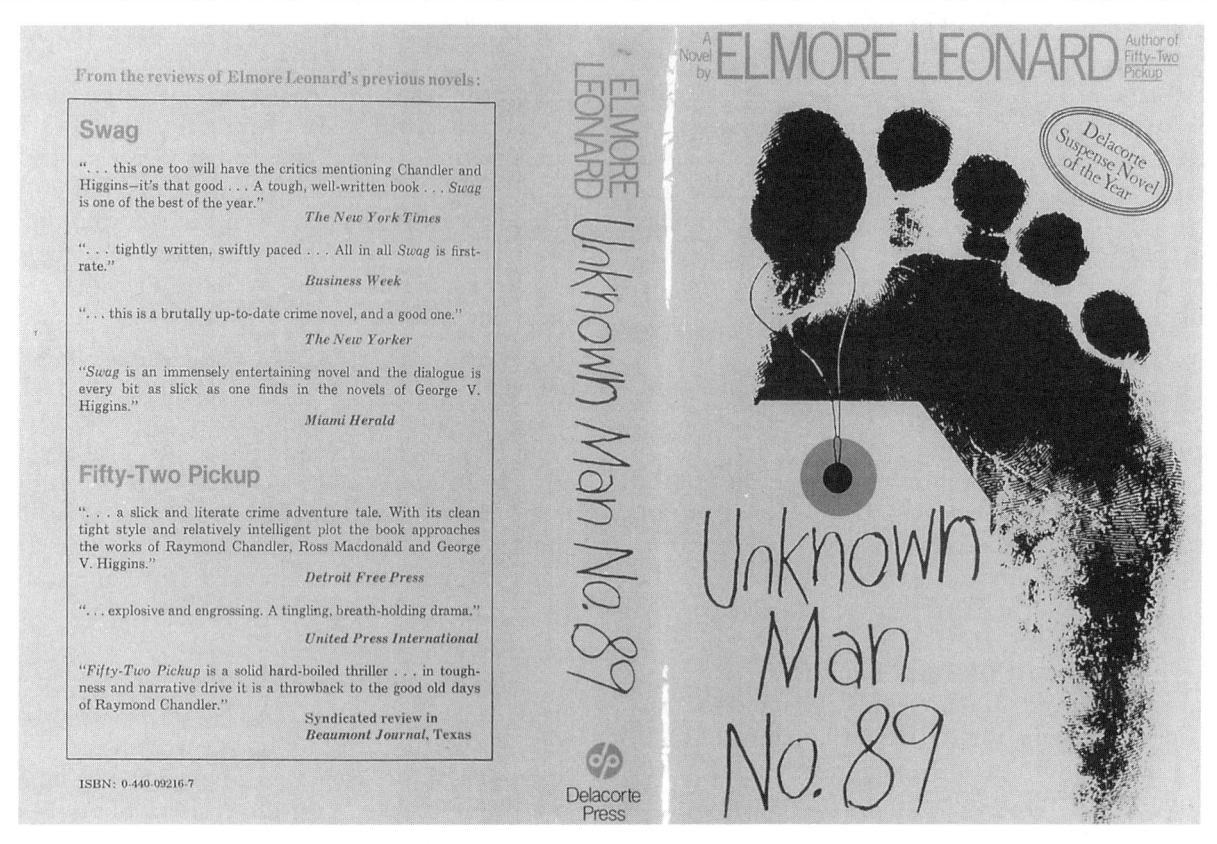

Dust jacket for one of Leonard's novels about process server Jack Ryan

Leonard's westerns include many of the key elements that make his crime novels distinctive, especially the way in which conventional scenes become unconventional. An example is the obligatory showdown between the good guys and the bad guys at the climax of most westerns. In Leonard's second western novel, *The Law at Randado* (1955), the barroom face-off is a "drink-off" rather than a shoot-out, concluding with the youthful deputy, Kirby Frye, easily disarming the lawless, drunken rancher, Phil Sundeen. Leonard has written many variations on the showdown scene in his contemporary crime novels, which he calls "eastern westerns."

In 1961 Leonard left Campbell-Ewald to write industrial films and educational films for Encyclopaedia Britannica Films. Two years later he started the Elmore Leonard Advertising Agency, which he ran until 1966. During that same decade he began writing contemporary crime fiction. Publishers shied away from Leonard's first crime novel, *The Big Bounce,* because it fits easily into no genre category and makes no moral judgments on its amoral protagonists. It was rejected eighty-four times in New York and Hollywood before the film rights were sold for $50,000. Subsequently, the book was sold to Fawcett for publication as a Gold Medal paperback original. The sale of the movie rights allowed Leonard to become a full-time crime fiction and screenplay writer. Set in upper Michigan, *The Big Bounce* bears some resemblance to James M. Cain's crime fiction. Leonard's chief protagonists are Jack Ryan, a failed minor-league baseball player turned burglar, and the psychopathic Nancy Hayes. In a touch characteristic of Leonard's crime fiction, the novel opens as some law enforcement types watch a movie of Ryan using a baseball bat in a fight with the chief of a migrant crew. At the close of the novel Nancy shoots another migrant worker, mistaking him for Ryan. The only remotely sympathetic character in the book is Walter Majestyk, who gives Ryan a second chance with a job. Ironically, Ryan's life is saved because he sits down to watch a few innings of baseball with Majestyk.

In 1973, at the suggestion of his agent, Leonard read the dialogue-driven crime novel *The Friends of Eddie Coyle* (1972), by George V. Higgins, whose technique seems clearly to have influenced Leonard's subsequent works. Yet while many of Higgins's characters deliver rambling monologues, the speech of Leonard's characters tends to be terse, elliptical, and understated.

In 1974 Leonard left his wife of twenty-five years and joined Alcoholics Anonymous. He and Beverly Leonard were divorced in May 1977, and on 15 September 1979 he married Joan Shepard. She died of a sudden illness in 1993. That same year Leonard met and married Christine Kent. Leonard still lives in the Detroit suburb of Bloomfield Village, within one mile of his five children and ten grandchildren, explaining that if he lived in Los Angeles he would spend all his time talking to producers.

During the 1970s and early 1980s Leonard built a modest but solid core readership for his crime novels, often set in Detroit, while he also wrote screenplays such as *Joe Kidd* (1972) for Clint Eastwood and *Mr. Majestyk* (1974) for Charles Bronson. Leonard subsequently turned the Bronson screenplay into a novel. After his old editor at Dell founded Arbor House, he enticed Leonard to sign a contract with the firm, promising less money at first but better promotion of his books. *City Primeval: High Noon in Detroit* (1980) was Leonard's first Arbor House book. The switch paid off. By 1983 Leonard's popularity as a writer had grown to the extent that he was able to sell the screen rights for *Stick* for $350,000 and *LaBrava* for $400,000. About that same time the critics began to weigh in with raves for his work. *LaBrava* was awarded an Edgar for best mystery novel by the Mystery Writers of America. *Glitz* (1985) made the best-seller lists, and Leonard's later novels have appeared there as well. Turning Leonard's crime novels into movies has not worked as well as with the westerns. The film versions of *The Big Bounce* (1969) and *Stick* (1985) were major disappointments to Leonard. His books continue, however, to attract filmmakers. In 1995 director Quentin Tarantino bought the rights to four Leonard novels, and the movie *Get Shorty*, based on Leonard's 1990 novel and starring John Travolta, Danny DeVito, and Gene Hackman, was a hit.

Leonard's crime novels are notable for his trademark "nonstyle": using a third-person, multiple-perspective approach. Despite a minimum of physical description, there is always a strong sense of place in his work. Detroit is the setting for most of his early crime novels, for which Leonard drew on his own deep knowledge of the city and the surrounding area and supplemented with research in the Detroit homicide division. For his later novels Leonard has employed a researcher to scout locations for his novels, including New Orleans, Los Angeles, Miami Beach, Puerto Rico, and Cape Girardeau, Missouri.

Leonard's plots – which he does not outline in advance – veer in unexpected directions that subvert the conventions of the genre. Leonard's black humor usually develops from his characters acting or thinking or expressing themselves in perverse ways that are quite normal for them. It is not surprising – given his screenwriting experience – that Leonard's fiction has a cinematic feel with frequent quick transitions and terse dialogue to move the story.

Swag is notable for its black humor and for the way in which the plot swings in unexpected directions, charging the story with a kind of comic horror. At the outset of the novel Ernest "Stick" Stickley steals a car from the used-car lot where Frank Ryan is a salesman. Ryan identifies Stick in a police lineup, but at the trial Ryan develops sudden "doubts" about his identification and the judge throws the case out. Over drinks in a nearby bar Ryan proposes that he and Stick team up, listing "Ryan's rules for success" in armed robbery on cocktail napkins. Examples include: "be polite," do not get involved with "junkies," and most important, "never tell anyone your business." The two begin what at first is an easy and extraordinarily successful string of small-scale armed robberies of grocery and liquor stores.

In the beginning the pair adhere strictly to the rules. In a bit of typical Leonard lunacy, while the pair are casing a bar, another armed robber makes his move. Ryan and Stick sit back and critique his performance, finding it woefully inadequate, and when the amateur is finished, they pull their guns, disarm the robber, leave him in the hands of the bar patrons in a locked room, and make off with the loot. As Ryan and Stick begin to bicker about small things, they slide into minor violations of the rules for success, usually at Ryan's instigation. Then, after a successful grocery-store robbery, Stick shoots and kills two black muggers who are attempting to relieve him of the contents of his "grocery sack." This act earns high praise from the indignant Ryan, who justifies the murders on the grounds that the muggers are thieves. To which Stick replies: "Frank, we stole it," and Frank responds, "Right, and that makes it ours." Then in a direct violation of his rules,

Dust jacket for one of Leonard's Miami Beach crime novels

Ryan gets the pair involved with three blacks and a punch-drunk former prize-fighter junkie in a daylight robbery of Hudson's department store in downtown Detroit. The caper begins to go bad when the junkie shoots a window washer who has inadvertently witnessed the crime. Then one of the blacks kills the junkie. Later Stick kills the two blacks, who have the swag. Violating the rule never to "tell anyone your business," Stick involves his new girlfriend, who has witnessed the earlier bar robbery and not turned them in to the police. She is to put the loot in her luggage and fly to Florida on the same plane as Frank and Stick, but she flies to Los Angeles instead, leaving behind a key to a locker containing the money. As Ryan and Stick are set to flee Detroit, they are arrested holding the key in an envelope addressed to them.

Of all Leonard's books *Unknown Man No. 89* is the closest to a hard-boiled mystery novel, featuring a main character – process server Jack Ryan – who acts like a private eye in tracking down people and serving them papers. Older and more likable than he was in *The Big Bounce,* Ryan is hired to find a missing person – a killer by the name of Bobby Leary – who soon turns up dead in the Detroit morgue. The rest of the story involves the machinations over who is going to get control of the $150,000 in stock that Leary unwittingly inherited. *Unknown Man No. 89* is Leonard's most personal novel; the subtext is the siren lure of alcohol. Despite the serious subject, however, Leonard is wickedly funny about drunks. Ryan, who is an alcoholic, delivers this account of past drinking tastes to Leary's wife, Denise, who is also an alcoholic: "I used to drink mostly bourbon, over crushed ice, fill up a lowball glass. I also drank beer, wine, gin, vodka, Cuba Libres, Diet-Rite and Scotch, and rye with red pop, but I preferred bourbon. Early Times. I knew a guy who drank only Fresca and chartreuse. . . . A real alcoholic can drink anything, right?" While searching for her after Bobby's murder, he accidentally meets her at an Alcoholics Anonymous meeting, which Leonard describes concisely: "Walk into a room like this anywhere, and if everybody was drinking coffee and smoking cigarettes, it was an A.A. meeting." At the conclusion of the novel Ryan and Denise end up with the money and hope for a new life together.

Virgil asked the career marine, who heard things on the bridge and standing outside the captain's quarters, "How come we *are* here?"

"Making a friendly call on the dons."

"We got here and sat out in the stream till it was good and light so as not to surprise them, coming in."

"Is that a question?"

"When did we become friends with them?"

"Would you understand the situation if I explained it to you?"

"Well, I been to school."

"How far?"

"The sixth grade."

"We're here to protect American citizens and their property," ~~in case of demonstrations and riots.~~

"Protect them from what?"

"You could say ~~How about this,~~" the career marine said, "We're here in case it looks like the insurrectionists are gonna take over their own country before we get a chance to do it ourselves. But don't tell nobody. That's between Captain Sigsbee, the Secretary of the Navy and ~~William~~ Bill McKinley."

Virgil ~~said, "Oh."~~

So he never got to go ashore. One of the midshipmen who did, sent to deliver a message to the consulate, said the city was full of beggars and Spanish soldiers;

Page from the working draft for "Cuba Libra," a novel in progress set in Cuba during the Spanish-American War (courtesy of Elmore Leonard)

As its subtitle suggests, *City Primeval: High Noon in Detroit* is a western in modern-day dress. The book begins in Leonard's typically compelling manner with the ruthless murder of a black Detroit judge and his white girlfriend by Clement Mansell, the "Oklahoma Wildman." The judge, Alvin Guy, has cut Mansell off in traffic while leaving a racetrack, and the initial encounter snowballs into two senseless killings. The reader's reaction to the judge's murder is mixed because it has comic elements and because the judge is presented as a black racist, much resented by the Detroit police for his arbitrary rulings. (Leonard admits that Guy was modeled on a real Detroit judge.) But the murder of the innocent girl warns the reader that Mansell is a bad man possessed of reckless bravado. He has escaped almost certain conviction for an earlier multiple murder in Detroit because of a legal technicality. One of the detectives assigned to the Guy murder is Raymond Cruz, who was on the periphery of the earlier case. Because there are no eyewitnesses, Cruz must link Mansell to the murder weapon, which he took from a dead man in the prior multiple murder. *City Primeval* is suffused with references to western movies. In one telling early scene Cruz – who wears a Wyatt Earp–style mustache – describes to a colleague part of *The Gunfighter* (1950), starring Gregory Peck. In Cruz's retelling a world-weary Peck bluffs a boy who is looking to build a reputation by forcing a fight by asking: "How do you know I don't have a .44 pointed at your belly?" The kid backs down. All Peck has is a paring knife he has been using to trim his nails. Cruz's relationship with Mansell is portrayed as a series of contests escalating from verbal jousts to gunshots, all leading up to a final showdown. The scene plays out as a reversal of *The Gunfighter:* after gunning down Mansell as he is innocently reaching for a bottle opener in his jacket, Cruz picks up the opener and calmly pares his nails while waiting for the other policemen to arrive.

The protagonist of *LaBrava* is Joseph LaBrava, a former secret-service agent who once guarded Bess Truman in Independence, Missouri. Now he works as a photographer in Miami Beach, taking pictures of the quirky residents. He has been described as a watcher, not someone to get involved. Early in the novel, however, he prevents an "ugly drunk" from manhandling a woman employee at a crisis center by blinding the drunk with his camera flash and then disarming him. Part of the plot involves efforts by the drunk, a redneck "rent-a-cop" named Richie Nobles, to get revenge on LaBrava, who later breaks Nobles's arm with a bat (reminding the reader of Jack Ryan). Also as a result of his intervention, LaBrava gets involved with a former film-noir star of the 1940s: Jean Shaw, who is planning her own kidnapping, following the script of one of her movies and using Nobles as a pawn. In contrast to Raymond Cruz, LaBrava has not been able "to be detached, objective enough to take it all the way," that is, to shoot a bad guy in cold blood, in this case a Cuban killer who gets the drop on him. Yet LaBrava is able to distract the man with a typical Leonard ploy: he asks, "how do you know the gun's loaded?" As the villain checks the gun, LaBrava picks up his and shoots him. The novel ends ironically with Jean marrying the older man whom she has tried to bilk by staging her kidnapping. Reviewing *LaBrava* for *The Christian Science Monitor* (4 November 1983), James Kauffman said: "Nobody brings the illogic of crime and criminals to life better," and in *Newsweek* (14 November 1983) Peter S. Prescott called Leonard's novel "a fine story, well-paced and plotted, keenly observed and lightly witty, with a firm sense of character and place."

In *Bandits* (1987), his most overtly political novel, Leonard drew unflattering portraits of the Nicaraguan Contras and the Reagan administration's support for them in the war against the Sandinistas. Leonard assembles a diverse cast of bandits in New Orleans, including a former nun, three ex-cons (one of whom is also a former police officer), and a Miskito Indian gunman. Their chief mission is to rob a ruthless Contra colonel who has raised several million dollars from wealthy Americans for the Contras. The former nun wants to use half the money to help victims of the Contras, and the ex-cons are promised the remainder to pull off the heist. *Bandits* ends with the usual Leonard twist: The Miskito Indian kills the colonel and walks off with half the money, and the former nun gets the other half after she shoots the former policeman, although not fatally, to prevent him from taking the money from her. Reviewing the novel for *The Listener* (9 April 1987), Clancy Sigal said that the enjoyment of reading Leonard's novel "comes not only from his superbly off-the-wall dialogue . . . , tight characterisation and fluid narrative, but from participating in Leonard's experiment with sexual and other politics."

Every so often, critics recognize a genre writer as one who rises "above genre." The publicity accompanying such a reception often engenders increased sales of the writer's work and more critical reviews. Inevitably, some of these reviews express skepticism about the raves the writer has received. Elmore Leonard has been through this cycle. Without question he stands among the elite of contemporary American writers of crime fiction. Whether he deserves to be classed among the best contemporary American authors of mainstream fiction is open to debate. The comparison of Leonard to Charles Dickens seems strained. While Leonard has perfect pitch for a certain kind of jazzlike dialogue, he operates within a narrow range. His protagonists – and his villains – are all the same sort of detached men and women. Yet he is inventive in creating new and bizarre situations that test the mettle of these characters, and he is funny. He is a craftsman with a distinctive voice who writes about one superior crime novel a year. To ask for something more literary from him seems beside the point. As Walker Percy put it in Leonardian understatement: "it will do."

Interviews:

Joel M. Lyczak, "An Interview with Elmore Leonard," *Armchair Detective,* 16 (Summer 1983): 235-240;

Bill Kelley, "This Pen for Hire," *American Film,* 10 (December 1984): 52-56;

Jean W. Ross, Interview with Leonard, in *Contemporary Authors,* New Revision Series, volume 28 (Detroit: Gale Research, 1989), pp. 284-287.

References:

David Geherin, *Elmore Leonard* (New York: Continuum, 1989);

Joseph Hynes, "High Noon in Detroit: Elmore Leonard's Career," *Journal of Popular Culture,* 25 (Winter 1991): 181-187.

Bobbie Ann Mason

(1 May 1940 -   )

John D. Kalb
Salisbury State University

See also the Mason entry in *DLB Yearbook: 1987*.

BOOKS: *Nabokov's Garden: A Guide to Ada* (Ann Arbor, Mich.: Ardis, 1974);
The Girl Sleuth: A Feminist Guide to the Bobbsey Twins, Nancy Drew, and Their Sisters (Old Westbury, N.Y.: Feminist Press, 1975);
Shiloh and Other Stories (New York: Harper & Row, 1982; London: Chatto & Windus, 1982);
In Country (New York: Harper & Row, 1985; London: Chatto & Windus, 1986);
Spence + Lila (New York: Harper & Row, 1988; London: Chatto & Windus, 1989);
Love Life: Stories (New York: Harper & Row, 1989; London: Chatto & Windus, 1989);
Feather Crowns (New York: HarperCollins, 1993; London: Chatto & Windus, 1993).

Bobbie Ann Mason grew "so sick of reading about the alienated hero of superior sensibility" who so frequently dominates twentieth-century American literature that she decided to write fiction about the antithesis. Her characters are ordinary, working-class denizens of rural western Kentucky, often living in Hopewell, her fictional version of her own hometown, Mayfield, or in some unnamed town equally distant from Paducah (which is at least sizable enough to warrant a shopping mall) and nearly a world away from the cities of Louisville and Lexington or Saint Louis, Missouri. Her plain-spoken characters are presented in a direct and unadorned style, which frequently earns her the label of minimalist, "dirty" realist, or – as she recalls John Barth's description – "blue-collar hyper-realist super-minimalist" or "something like that." Mason says her style "comes out of a way of hearing people talk." Typically her characters have arrived at transitional points or impediments in their lives, and while language may fail them in their efforts to articulate their needs and surmount their obstacles, they often find common bonds through popular culture (music, movies, and televi-

Bobbie Ann Mason (photograph © the Estate of Thomas Victor)

sion) and commerce (brand-name products and shopping malls), which invade their formerly remote region. Mason is among the first to use seriously the so-called low art of popular culture as an important underpinning to her literature and the lives of her characters. While she portrays the encroaching impact of urban America on her rural occupants – Wal-Mart replaces the country store, fast food substitutes for traditional home cooking – she usually does so not as a criticism but as a means of providing an accurate and realistic depiction of the people within their changing environments. Her inclusion of these popular elements enhances the sense of meeting real people engaged in their everyday lives.

Bobbie Ann Mason was born on 1 May 1940, in Mayfield, Kentucky, the first of Wilburn Arnett and Christianna Lee Mason's four children, three daughters and one son. The family farm was located just far enough outside Mayfield that she attended a rural elementary school, which she says had "terrible teachers and poor students" and left her wanting to attend the more urban Mayfield schools. She did attend Mayfield High School, and in 1960 she wrote for the local newspaper, the *Mayfield Messenger*. In 1962 she earned her bachelor of arts degree from the University of Kentucky. Following her graduation, she moved to New York City, taking a job as a writer with Ideal Publishing Company, publisher of fan magazines such as *Movie Star*, *Movie Life*, and *T.V. Star Parade*. After about a year in New York she returned to school, receiving an M.A. degree from the State University of New York at Binghamton in 1966 and a Ph.D. in English from the University of Connecticut in 1972. She married writer Roger B. Rawlings on 12 April 1969.

Mason's first published book was her doctoral dissertation, *Nabokov's Garden: A Guide to Ada* (1974), which was followed by another nonfiction work, this time one that paid homage to her childhood heroines, *The Girl Sleuth: A Feminist Guide to the Bobbsey Twins, Nancy Drew, and Their Sisters* (1975). Meanwhile, she taught journalism part-time at Mansfield State College in Mansfield, Pennsylvania, from 1972 to 1979 and began crafting short stories. This return to fiction writing had followed a long, meandering path.

Mason had first tried her hand at writing fiction when she was a child, but "along the way I was stymied quite a lot." She told Lila Havens that she took two creative-writing courses in college and "was committed to writing then, but I didn't get enough encouragement" to continue. She hoped that graduate school would help her learn how to write, but she found the study of literature a distraction from writing fiction. Although she conceded in the same interview that graduate school had some benefits "because I hadn't ever read very much," Mason also complained to Havens that no one told her that graduate school "was a training ground for critics." She told Albert E. Wilhelm, "I'm always embarrassed by references to this Ph.D. because I don't relate back to that and I didn't carry forward any particular knowledge about literature that I studied." Since her childhood was shaped by "isolation and a desire to get out of this isolation," she identifies Nancy Drew and the Bobbsey Twins as her most powerful and lasting "literary" influences: "Those books contain very innocent dreams of quests for clarity, solving a mystery, and wanting to go somewhere, do something, and be somebody. The Bobbsey Twins got to go on a vacation in every single book." When it came to writing on her own, Mason "had to learn how to write from scratch: no amount of studying literature prepared me for knowing how a story is coaxed out of the imagination." Not until she was in her late thirties did she find the encouragement she needed to become a full-time writer when she, in her words, "boldly and arrogantly sent my second finished story to *The New Yorker*."

Although this story and eighteen others that followed it were rejected by *The New Yorker*, the second rejection began a correspondence between Mason and editor Roger Angell. "Roger was the first person in the world who ever said to me, 'You're a writer, you have talent'" – encouragement enough to keep her writing and submitting until her twentieth submission, the short story "Offerings," was accepted and published in the 18 February 1980 issue. After the publication of two further stories in *The New Yorker*, the magazine made a first-reading agreement with her – a long-standing relationship with *The New Yorker* that continues to this day. She not only provides short stories but also frequently contributes to "Talk of the Town" and "Shouts and Murmurs." "Offerings" and fifteen other short stories – works that first appeared in *The New Yorker*, *The Atlantic Monthly*, *Redbook*, and other publications – are collected in her first book of fiction: *Shiloh and Other Stories* (1982), which was nominated for a National Book Critics Circle Award, an American Book Award, and a P.E.N./Faulkner Award and earned her the 1983 Ernest Hemingway Foundation Award for best first fiction. She has also had stories selected for *Best American Short Stories* (1981 and 1983) and *The Pushcart Prize* (1983 and 1996).

All the stories in *Shiloh and Other Stories* feature men and women who have reached some sort of impasse or transitional point in their lives and are searching for catalysts to move them forward, if only just a bit. Most are written in the present tense and arrive at open-ended conclusions. For instance, in "Shiloh" truck driver Leroy Moffitt, at home with his wife, Norma Jean, for the past three months because he has badly injured a leg in an accident, "is not sure what to do next," although he is fairly certain he will not return to making long hauls. When Leroy and Norma Jean married at eighteen, she was

Dust jacket for Mason's first book, based on her doctoral dissertation about a novel by Vladimir Nabokov

pregnant with a child who died in infancy of sudden infant death syndrome. Placed in close quarters for the first time since their marriage sixteen or so years earlier, they begin to notice things about one another that were previously easy to overlook.

After Leroy dabbles with craft kits, he toys with the notion of selling his rig and building a log house, "a real home" for Norma Jean, who wants no part of living in a log cabin. As they sit at the kitchen table, both preoccupied with their singular pursuits – Norma Jean working on an essay for her adult-education class, Leroy working on his building plans with Lincoln logs – "Leroy has the hopeful thought that they are sharing something," but he then realizes his wife is "miles away." Even though he knows their marriage is ending, they take a last trip together to the Civil War battleground at Shiloh, the site of Leroy's mother-in-law's honeymoon and a place she has been pestering them to visit. This trip to Shiloh becomes the setting for the final stage of Leroy and Norma Jean's marriage, not the renewal of their relationship as Leroy might have hoped. Norma Jean finally explains to Leroy that their marriage is over, and he realizes that his dream of building the log house was an empty notion: while he has been trying to repair the dwelling of his marriage, his wife has moved on to other possibilities.

Mason has identified "Residents and Transients," the ninth story in the collection, as the thematic center of *Shiloh and Other Stories:* "there are some people who would just never leave home, because that's where they're meant to be; and others are, well, born to run." Mary, the narrator of "Residents and Transients," came back to rural Kentucky three years before, following an eight-year absence "pursuing higher learning." After she and her husband, Stephen, settle in the farmhouse that her parents have left to move to Florida, she wonders "why I ever went away." When Stephen's job takes him to Louisville, where he is house hunting, Mary begins an affair with her dentist, Larry. The attachment to Larry is most likely superficial and not long-lasting – after all, he finds her every utterance amusing, even the serious ones. Of more importance is her renewed love affair with her parents' farmhouse and cornfields, which came with a family of barn cats that has gradually moved into the house. The issue of residents and transients arises as she explains to Larry that she has been "reading up on cats," which, in the wild, fit into these two broad categories. While scientists first believed that the residents, those who establish home territories, are superior to transients, "the bums, the losers" who "are on the move," new research suggests "that the transients are the superior ones after all, with the greatest curiosity and most intelligence." At the end of the story Mary is as undecided about moving as the scientists are about these cats. As she looks into the odd eyes of a cat named Brenda – one green and the other red – she realizes she is "waiting for the light to change" to determine whether to go or stay. Although the choices Mason's characters frequently face seem easy to define, their possibilities are often narrowly constricted.

In depicting transients Mason uses the phrase "born to run" from Bruce Springsteen's song of that title – a borrowing that seems particularly appropriate in light of her abundant use of popular music, television, brand-name products, and other artifacts of popular culture in most of her writing. The characters in her stories listen to rock and Top 40 radio stations, watch *WKRP in Cincinnati* and Johnny Carson, get their information from *The Today Show* and *Donahue,* drink Coke and Dr. Pepper, eat at McDonald's and Burger King, and work at Kroger and Kmart. It is not surprising then, that Springsteen's "Born in the U.S.A." is the source of the two-line epigraph to Mason's first published novel, *In Country* (1985), a work set in 1984 that explores the still-lingering impact of the Vietnam War on the American psyche: "I'm ten years burning down the road / Nowhere to run ain't got nowhere to go."

Mason did not set out to write about Vietnam. She told Wendy Smith, "I had almost all the characters in my mind, doing things and going through scenes, long before I had any knowledge that any of it had to do with Vietnam," but "I think it came out of my unconscious the same way it's coming out of America's unconscious." A story that Mason says was initially "inspired by some kids I saw on the street corner selling flowers" grew into a potent portrayal of the long-term effects of Vietnam on Samantha Hughes, a recent high-school graduate who never knew her father, Dwayne, because he was killed in the war; on her mother's brother Emmett Smith, who enlisted following the death of his brother-in-law; and on Emmett's veteran buddies who, like him, still have trouble readjusting to everyday life. Moreover, Mason looks deeply into the broad impact of the Vietnam War on the American psychological landscape as a whole.

In the summer of 1984, nearly ten years since the fall of Saigon, Samantha, Emmett, and his friends – denizens of the ironically named Kentucky town of Hopewell – have yet to come to grips with the Vietnam experience. Protagonist Samantha Hughes, known as "Sam," whose consciousness drives the narrative of *In Country,* suffers the same naive innocence about Vietnam that grips much of America. Not certain what Vietnam was all about, only that her father died there, she begins a quest for her father, for some notion of his identity and the ways in which his life filters into her own. As an inquisitive seventeen-year-old, Sam offers an adolescent point of view, sometimes to the point of irritating the reader with her childish notions, other times offering more mature judgments about the behavior of others. For instance, when she tries an affair with Tom, one of the local veterans and a potential conduit to the past that eludes her, their attempt at sex ends abruptly when Tom is unable to maintain an erection. He points out that his impotence is a physical symptom of his psychological problems, that he loses the struggle of "mind over matter," in which his mind "takes me where I don't want to go." When he half-jokingly suggests that what he needs is a $10,000 penis-pump implant, she quickly surmises that indeed that is what he needs, and perhaps – overgeneralizing as a child would – that

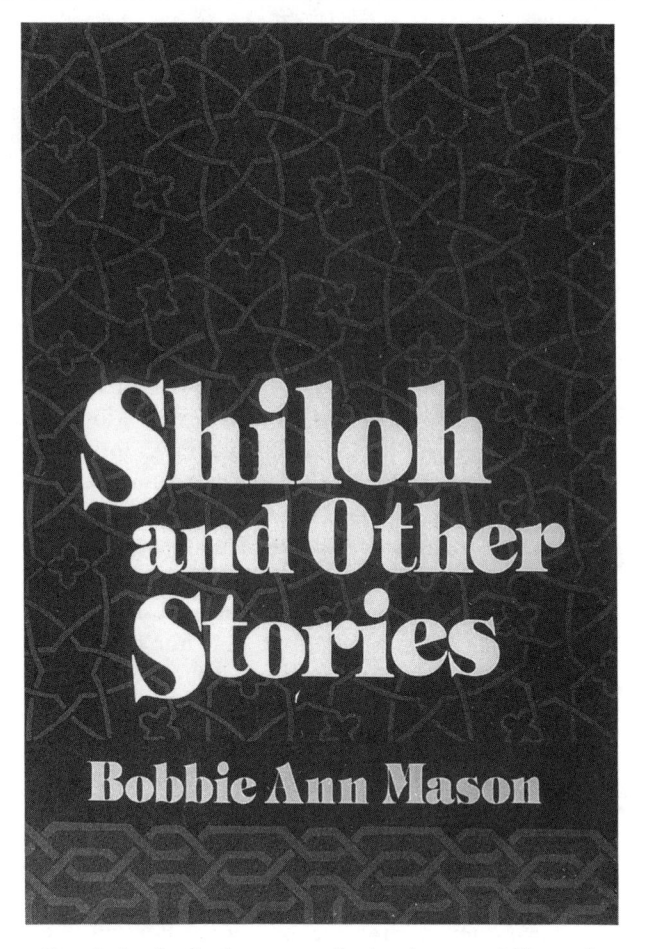

Dust jacket for the short-story collection that earned Mason the 1983 Ernest Hemingway Foundation Award for best first fiction

Emmett's problem with his sometime girlfriend Anita would be similarly and as easily solved. This childish generalization smacks of an American search for simple solutions to complex problems.

On the other hand Sam gains a mature insight into the way in which Emmett's focus on birds – in search of the elusive white egret, his only beautiful memory of Vietnam – is a means of maintaining his sanity: "If he concentrated on something fascinating and thrilling, like birds soaring, the pain of his memories wouldn't come through." Yet such maturity is rare in this young woman, who has spitefully stayed behind in Hopewell, ostensibly to look after her troubled uncle, rather than join her mother, Irene, in Lexington. Irene has recently married Larry Joiner – whom Sam has unaffectionately nicknamed "Lorenzo Jones" – and they have a baby of their own, Heather, who seems to have added to Sam's feelings of displacement. Her jealousy at no longer being the sole beneficiary of her mother's love turns to spiteful anger at her mother's inability to help in the quest for her father. Irene and Dwayne had been married for only a month before he shipped out, and she can barely remember him.

Elements of popular culture – as ubiquitous in this novel as they are in Mason's short stories – provide a means through which Sam makes her efforts to integrate herself with the past and with the people in her present, using songs contemporary to the summer of 1984 – such as "Born in the U.S.A.," which Mason has called "an anthem for Vietnam vets" – as a cultural connection to the war and its disillusioned survivors. Sam's interest in the so-called classic rock of her parents' generation, the music coincident to the war years themselves, serves as a pathway to the past. For much of the narrative she searches the radio airwaves and record stores for a newly released Beatles song, "Leave My Kitten Alone," a sound bite from the past: "She had to find that record.... It was a fresh message from the past, something to go on." She hopes that by sharing this discovery with her mother she will negotiate the differences that separate them. When her mother visits Hopewell, Sam hopes Irene will respond positively to the Kinks album she plays or to the musicians on MTV, but Irene is preoccupied with the present task of tending to her second daughter, Heather. Her mother's seeming disaffection with these cultural artifacts and the realization that her father did not live to hear the Beatles' 1967 album *Sergeant Pepper's Lonely Hearts Club Band* come as immense disappointments to Sam.

Likewise, Emmett is preoccupied with his daily struggle with the memories and losses of his experiences as a soldier in Vietnam. He suffers from sudden throbbing headaches and a spreading case of chloracne, both ostensibly symptoms of his exposure to Agent Orange. While her depictions of her characters illustrate Mason's understanding of the American people's selective amnesia when it comes to the Vietnam War, her portrayals of Agent Orange victims – Buddy Mangrum's intestinal and liver problems and his daughter's birth defects are directly attributable to his exposure to this chemical – and their treatment by the Veterans Administration (VA) indicate a serious indictment of the American government for its failures to deal appropriately with the veterans of this unpopular war. (Emmett's doctor prescribes Tylenol for the headaches and a restrictive diet appropriate for ordinary adolescent acne.) While some veterans, as Sam realizes, "adjusted perfectly well," others need help with their physical, mental, and emotional problems, and the VA, Mason says, has been ineffectual at best.

Emmett has never readjusted to civilian life. He is unemployed and aimless, until he becomes "obsessed" with finding the source of a leak in the basement. His efforts at "Fixing a Hole" (as a song on the Beatles' *Sergeant Pepper* album would have it) keep his mind from wandering and provide a means of concentrating on something outside himself while focusing on what desperately needs repair within. His efforts expose a crack running the length of the foundation of his house, symbolic of the fissures the war has caused in his own personal psyche and that of the nation as a whole. While he jokes, "My basement's flooded and my foundation's weak.... And my house may fall down," his excavation focuses on repairing the real damage to his mental and emotional house and healing the figurative "tipped heart" from which he suffers. As he later reveals to Sam, "I'm damaged. It's like something in the center of my heart is gone and I can't get it back.... I work on staying together, one day at a time.... It takes all my energy." Once he has exposed the foundation, discovered the crack, and felt for dry rot, he realizes that this project, like the process of his self-repair, is only beginning. Despite all his efforts at focusing his attention on foundations or birds, by the time he makes his second plan – a trip to the Vietnam Veterans Memorial in Washington, D.C. – he still "can barely get to the point where I can be a self to get out of."

The trip with Sam and Mamaw (her Grandmother Hughes) to the memorial, which frames the narrative as parts 1 and 3 of the novel, suggests that Emmett is able to continue his newly begun process of self-repair. In the final scene, when he discovers the names of his fallen comrades on the wall, "slowly his face bursts into a smile like flames."

Sam's final state is more ambiguous than Emmett's. Some critics have seen her venturing to Cawood's Pond and pretending to be a soldier "humping the boonies" as demonstrating her maturity and growth. While Sam's relentless search for her father entails a search for the "truth" of the war in Vietnam, she, like many Americans, looks for the easy answers. Emmett and Sam share an infatuation with the popular television series *M*A*S*H*, a program set during the Korean conflict but in its contemporaneity a cultural artifact of the Vietnam War years. Years earlier, when Sam first saw the episode in which the character Colonel Blake is killed, "his death was more real to her than the death of her own father." Now offered nightly in seemingly perpetual syndication, the program frequently portrays simplistic solutions to complex problems. When she was younger, Emmett's stories about Vietnam – before Irene got him to stop telling them – gave Sam the notion of "a pleasant countryside, something like Florida, with beaches and palm trees and watery fields of rice and green mountains." In order to discover her father's experiences, Sam needs to dispense with these postcard and television images.

Early in the book, when Emmett has an "episode" at Cawood's Pond, a "momentary freak-out," or flashback to the war, Sam thinks he needs to talk as the characters on M*A*S*H would talk to the psychiatrist Dr. Freeman, even though she realizes "that on TV, people always had the words to express their feelings, while in real life hardly anyone ever did." In her more mature moments, she recognizes that "sometimes, things were too simple" on M*A*S*H and "how naive the words were" to the Beatles' "All You Need Is Love." Yet her final excursion to Cawood's Pond stems from adolescent pique. She acquires Dwayne's war journal from her grandparents and, oddly yet appropriately, goes to the mall to read it. Within these pages she discovers the soldier-father who has so eluded her. Unlike the letters he wrote to Irene, which cover up and divert attention from the brutality of his environment, Dwayne's journals record the horror and the killing with precision. "Her father hadn't said how he felt about killing the V.C. He just reported it, as though it were something he had to do sooner or later, like taking a test in school." Horrified that her father and Emmett had participated in such activity, she feels that "everything seemed suddenly so real it enveloped her, like something rotten she had fallen into, like a skunk smell." When she arrives home dreading the sight of Emmett, she is furious to find he has gone and has flea-bombed the house. Leaving Emmett the diary and a note asking, "Is that what it was like over there? If it was, then you can just forget about me," she runs away from home and the truth.

While spending a night at Cawood's Pond, she fantasizes that she is "in country," but when Emmett finds her the next morning, he points out the futility of her efforts: "You think you can go through what we went through out in the jungle, but you can't. This place is scary, and things can happen to you, but it's not the same as having snipers and mortar fire and shells and people shooting at you from behind bushes." Her childishly dramatic note and her make-believe "humping the boonies" underscore her immaturity when it comes to dealing with the Vietnam War and veterans. Despite Emmett's warning, Sam – like the nation as a whole – persists in searching for easy solutions. When she and Emmett have an emotional confrontation, she thinks he is "going to come out with some suppressed memories of events as dramatic as the one that caused Hawkeye to crack up in the final episode of M*A*S*H." While Emmett does have a bit of a cathartic episode when he finds her at the pond and he does arrive at the resolve to travel to the Vietnam Veterans Memorial, the process of his healing is only beginning. Similarly, Sam is only beginning to move from adolescence into womanhood. Even on the trip to Washington, she persists in fantasizing about Tom and about Bruce Springsteen pulling her onto the stage for some "Dancing in the Dark." Yet she has decided to join her mother in Lexington, where she will attend the University of Kentucky, instead of staying in Hopewell and enrolling at nearby Murray State, as she had planned earlier. Meanwhile, Emmett will take over Sam's job at the Burger Boy and attend to those repairs to the house in Hopewell. In a text underscored by popular music, television programs, movies, videos, brand names, and shopping malls, Mason rejects the easy, readily available sort of "solutions" offered by popular culture, instead leaving the conclusion of *In Country* appropriately open-ended.

Mason's second novel, *Spence + Lila* (1988), portrays a family in crisis as the aging matriarch, Lila, is in the hospital in Paducah for breast-cancer surgery. The novel is a masterful depiction of the bonds of love between a couple in their sixties as they face their dilemma without the words to express either their fears or their devotion to one another. The novel also looks beyond the changes in this couple's relationship over their many years together to the alterations to their farm and a once-isolated rural South brought about by the invasion of popular culture and the media, the development of shopping malls and connective highways, and the growing economic impossibility of making a living on a small family farm.

Inspired in part by Mason's mother's mastectomy, *Spence + Lila* is dedicated to her parents, siblings, and husband. The title presents the names of Spence and Lila as though they were carved by two young lovers on a tree or a school desk, or as they might appear in a family tree. The novel portrays this couple as facing the real possibility that one may soon be "minus" the other and much less than the "sum" they have become together. The novel is told in present tense by a third-person, limited-omniscient narrator, with the perspective of the chapters alternating between Spence and Lila. (This alternation of controlling consciousnesses follows a consistent pattern for the first half of the novel,

Dust jacket for Mason's first novel, which examines the long-term social effects of the Vietnam War

while in the latter portion two or three consecutive chapters may be from one or the other character's purview.) Mason's younger sister LaNelle illustrated *Spence + Lila*.

Separated for the first time since World War II, the protagonists worry about one another; yet they manage to face their present circumstances with humor and grace despite their justifiable trepidations. After more than forty years of marriage, Spence and Lila Culpepper are both somewhat surprised to be as old as their chronological years indicate, with three adult children – Nancy, Cathy (or "Cat"), and Lee – caught in the challenges and adversities of their own lives. Nancy Culpepper Cleveland and her family made earlier appearances in two of the stories in *Shiloh and Other Stories*: "Nancy Culpepper" and "Lying Doggo." In the former the transient Nancy returns home to her parents' western Kentucky farm to help them move her grandmother into a nursing home; in the latter, one of Mason's rare stories set outside Kentucky (in rural Pennsylvania), Nancy, husband Jack, and son Robert struggle with the necessity of having their aging dog, Grover Cleveland, put to sleep. (The character of Nancy Culpepper is the closest Mason, who has no children, comes to self-portraiture in her fiction.)

Once again Mason's protagonists are rural folk of western Kentucky, who in this case experience culture shock in the modern hospital in Paducah and share a skepticism about language as a means of communicating one's feelings. Spence thinks, "He could say to Lila, 'It's all right. Your breast isn't your life. You can live without it, and I'll accept that.' . . . Words are so inadequate. Phony. Nobody he knows says things like that anyway." Like Sam, he realizes these sorts of words are said by characters who have scriptwriters, not real human beings: "Real love requires something else, something deeper. And sometimes a feeling just goes without saying." *Spence + Lila* is a novel about real love – not saccharine-sweet sentimentality, but the well-aged version of love between two people who have shared a long, sometimes difficult and trying, life together. "Everything he does is for her, even when he goes his own way and she is powerless to stop him," even when he teases her, knowing teasing "rattles her, but it would be out of character for him to behave any other way, and she would respect him less." Uncomfortable as his visits make him, Spence comes every day to see Lila in the hospital. His feeling of impotence, his inability to help Lila, frustrates him. When he suspects that she will need cobalt treatments following her surgery and fears the outcome because he knows of others, such as Lila's friend Reba, who died shortly after beginning such treatments, he realizes he would be unable to object to such a prescription for Lila's health: "There are no significant choices most of the time. You always have to do what has to be done. It's like milking cows. When their bags are full, they have to be milked." Mason expertly conveys the sense that Spence and Lila no longer control their circumstances once they remove themselves from the family farm and enter the domain of doctors and medical science.

Their grown daughters Cat and Nancy are not so easily cowed by the experts. They ask questions of the doctors and challenge their assumptions, something neither parent can do successfully or forcefully enough. When Nancy asks about lumpectomy versus mastectomy, "Lila sees Spence cringe. Nancy has always asked questions and done things differently, just to be contrary." (Yet Spence later admits his pride in his contrary daughter.) When the doctor turns to Lila for questions, she admits, "All the big words make me bumfuzzled. I guess you know your stuff." When the doctor informs Lila that they had indeed removed her breast and told her she "can live without a breast," Lila thinks she may have replied, while still under the influence of the anesthesia, "It would be like living without balls.... You'd find that surprising too, but you could probably get along without them." She is embarrassed by the thought that she might have said such a thing, but she is also "surprised Nancy hasn't said the same thing to the doctor's face."

Lila worries about Spence and how he will manage without her. But because they are human beings, all the characters are equally concerned about their own self-interests as well. Lila considers, "If Spence went first.... She would be afraid to stay on the farm alone, with all the crime spreading out from town into the country these days." She also thinks about the difficulty of finding the words to convey feelings: "Growing into old age toward death is like shifting gears in a car; now she's going into high gear, plowing out into one of those interstates, racing into the future, where all her complicated thoughts that she has never been able to express will be clear and understandable. Her mind cannot grasp these thoughts exactly, but there is something important about movement that she wants to tell."

Moving beyond the changes in the lives of two aging individuals, Mason also considers changes in the rural environment. Their son, Lee, who is always trying to convince Spence to sell some of their land for development, chose not to learn farming and instead "has to work even harder at his factory job." "It makes Spence sick" that Lee "owes almost four hundred dollars a month for a squatty little brick house on a hundred-foot lot in town with no trees." Spence loves his farm: "This is all there is in the world — it contains everything there is to know or possess, yet everywhere people are knocking their brains out trying to find something different, something better." He also realizes, however, that "nowadays" there "wouldn't be a living" in farming a place his size because "a young couple would have to borrow too much to start out."

More important to Spence are the changes of attitudes and values in the modern world that has intruded in his isolated haven. While he seems for the most part to take the changes in stride, when he goes to Wal-Mart, he finds "All the coffee makers and video games and electric ice-cream parlors" he sees there "depressing. People are buying so much junk, thinking it will make them happy. And then when they can't even make a path across the floor through their possessions, they have a yard sale." And without anyplace for folks to go, they "either get drunk or go crazy." Spence "can't imagine what the world is coming to" with the increase in armed robberies and break-ins in his once safe environment. Similarly, Lila thinks that "The world has changed so much: cars, airplanes, television" in the years since she and Spence were wed, and although she "tries to go along with anything new.... It still hurts her to see liquor kept in a house where there are children, to see farmers out spreading manure on their fields on Sundays, to see young people fall away from the church." She undoubtedly shares Spence's distaste for television evangelists and would be as shocked as he if she knew that one of their neighbors grows marijuana plants among his corn, although Spence can understand the economic necessity of this lucrative cash crop. Likewise, she also would concur with Spence's notion that their farm "is the main thing there is — just the way things grow and die, the way the sun comes up and goes down each day. These are the facts of life."

In one of the novel's most humorous scenes the family plays catch with a prosthetic breast after Lila exclaims, "I ain't spending a hundred and fifty dollars for a falsie." As is typically the case with Mason's humor, there is a serious undertone to this playful scene. The woman who brought the prosthesis also offers a packet of "letters to daughters and sons

Dust jacket for Mason's depiction of an aging farm couple facing the wife's grave illness with courage and humor

and husbands" to convey a mastectomy patient's feelings "at this delicate time when you need emotional support." These form letters are another example of simplistic scriptwriting that cannot accurately convey Lila's true feelings. Before leaving the hospital Lila manages to thank her daughters in her own words – "I was always used to doing for y'all, and I never expected you to do for me this way" – but the response she desires from her children is "not words. . . . Holding her child is enough, and Nancy is clinging to her."

By the end of the novel Lila has lost her breast, endured a second operation on her neck to remove the arterial plaque that has caused a series of "tiny strokes," and returned to the "place" they love so well. Although she will still need to undergo chemotherapy for cancer, which has spread into her lymph nodes, and the prognosis is less than certain, her escape from the hospital and return to their home offer their own therapy. Standing in her garden, Lila responds with laughter to Spence's sexually suggestive comment that he has "a cucumber that needs pickling."

The novel ends with a description of Lila's laughter: "The way she laughs is the moment he has been waiting for. . . . Her cough catches her finally and slows her down, but her face is dancing like pond water in the rain, all unsettled and stirring with aroused possibility." Mason ends the story of this couple ambiguously with the return to the family farm and the idyllic garden, this place where the "facts of life" are part of the fabric of their interwoven everyday lives and their love for each other has been indelibly etched.

The various ways in which people handle love (or lack of it) serve as the central issue in Mason's second collection of short fiction, *Love Life: Stories* (1989). This volume comprises fifteen stories that originally appeared in various magazines, including *The New Yorker, The Atlantic Monthly, Mother Jones,* and *Harper's*. In this volume about half the stories are in the present and half in the past, unlike *Shiloh and Other Stories,* in which all but three stories are narrated in the present tense. In her interview with Bonnie Lyons and Bill Oliver, Mason explained another difference between the two collections: "I think the characters' world changed a good bit between the two. I think life was changing so fast that they got more sophisticated, . . . and I'd like to think that the stories have gotten more complex."

Perhaps the alternating narratives for two of the stories are examples of the increased complexity to which Mason refers.

As in *Spence + Lila*, the third-person, present-tense narration of the title story alternates between two perspectives. "Love Life" is narrated from the viewpoints of Opal, a retired Hopewell High School teacher and avid MTV viewer, and her niece Jenny, who has returned to Hopewell from Denver, Colorado. One perceived distinction between Opal and Jenny – beyond their age discrepancy – concerns their love lives: "Opal is not wholly without experience," for there have been men in her life, "though nothing like the casual affairs" in which she supposes Jenny has engaged. Yet Opal and Jenny are similar in their reticence to reveal much of themselves to others. "People confide in Jenny, but Jenny doesn't always tell things back," and Opal is startled by Jenny's tendency to ask personal questions. "Jenny wants to know about her aunt's past love life, but Opal won't reveal her secrets." When Jenny finally begins to explain that she shed tears over the family burial quilt because it reminded her of a former boyfriend who has died, Opal first fears she'll "be required to tell something comparable of her own." (Yet Jenny finds the quilt beautiful and takes it to her apartment, while Opal says it is "ugly as homemade sin" and she is relieved to be rid of it.) Jenny's fascination with other people's lives and loves is her way of not dwelling on her own failures – just as her studied observation of other people's physical handicaps betrays, yet keeps her from focusing on, her own emotional damage. Despite both their fears, Opal is able to comfort Jenny as she reveals her confused emotional state after the death of her former lover, the reason her restlessness brought her back to Hopewell. Opal advises her, "Don't look back, hon" – advice that might apply to most of the protagonists in these stories, as they struggle to understand their own love lives, to recover from lost loves, or to learn to love their own lives.

The narrative technique of "Marita" is less successful. The story alternates between the first-person-present narration of the pregnant title character, who cannot tell her mother what happened at college because "I don't know who he was – it was one of two interchangeable guys, guys I don't know or care to know," and the third-person-past perspective of Marita's mother, Sue Ellen, who figures out Marita's problem and offers the solution of an abortion. The shift in tense and person between these alternating perspectives seems merely complexity for the sake of complexity.

As in Mason's earlier fiction, popular culture lays the groundwork for the stories in *Love Life,* as characters watch reruns of television shows such as *Hogan's Heroes* and *Mary Tyler Moore* (in "Airwaves"), stay up late for *Nightline* and David Letterman (in "Marita"), wake to Rock 95 (in "Airwaves"), listen to radio psychics (in "Sorghum"), and measure their experiences by the topics Phil Donahue covers on his programs (in "Hunktown" and "Airwaves"). Among the best stories in this collection is "Piano Fingers," in which Dean, who is twenty-six years old and feels "suspended somewhere between childhood and old age," is about to lose his job at the downtown drugstore because his boss is going to sell the business. He is also troubled by his marriage, not because there is any lack of love between him and his wife, Nancy, but because everyday "stuff gets in the way." Dean thinks he could write better programs than the "garbage on TV" and often imagines himself as amateur detective Ballinger, "an ordinary guy" who "always manages to turn up the key piece of evidence the authorities have missed." Ever hopeful, Dean buys his daughter Jennifer a practice keyboard he can ill afford because Jennifer's teacher said she has "piano fingers."

One day while sitting in the car, waiting for Jennifer's lesson to end, "The sound of wet leaves against the car on a late-autumn day makes him feel nostalgia for something, he can't remember what," and he realizes something that perhaps describes what most of the stories in *Love Life* are about: "there are such moments, such sensations, that are maybe not memory but just things happening now, things that come into focus suddenly and can be either happy or sad." These potentially happy or sad sudden moments form the crux of much of Mason's writing. And most of her characters face possibilities such as Dean does when he studies the reflection of downtown lights on a bank window: "Some of the lights in the window are reflections of reflections, like a kaleidoscope of possibilities for his life. His trouble, he realizes, is that there are too many choices" and to settle on just one "would mean missing out on almost everything." As Mason told Wilhelm, "the way the South is changing is very dynamic and full of complexity. There's a certain energy there that I don't notice in other parts of the country. It comes out of an innocent hope of possibility. My characters have more opportunities in their lives than their parents did." While the myriad possibilities can make resolving their life and love struggles difficult for her characters, most of Mason's stories, as she told Lyons and Oliver, "tend to end at a moment of illumination." "Piano

Fingers" ends with one of Mason's typically hopeful illuminating images: as Dean and his daughter sit in the car, snow begins to fall, landing on his windshield in "big beautiful splotches – no two alike."

A reluctant transient herself, Mason visited Kentucky regularly, about twice a year, and always thought about returning there to live. Shortly before the death of her father in 1990, she moved to Lexington for an extended stay and dedicated her next novel, *Feather Crowns* (1993), to the memory of her father. In this work she abandoned the dynamic present moment of her hometown, writing instead a historical novel set primarily at the turn of the century. (The earliest time period in any of her previous fiction was the mid twentieth century in "Detroit Skyline, 1949," collected in *Shiloh and Other Stories*.) Despite its historical setting *Feather Crowns*, winner of the Southern Book Award, a finalist for the National Book Critics Circle Award, and the recipient of an enormously positive critical response, treats a phenomenon that continues to exist in the present: the protagonist, Christianna Wilburn Wheeler, comes under the scrutiny of the media of her day, becoming a national celebrity, the equivalent of a present-day pop-culture icon.

During their courtship James Reid Wheeler has told Christianna Wilburn (Mason chose her mother's and father's first names for her heroine), how "he burned" to return to his "daddy's place, where I was raised" once his Uncle Wad "turns loose that section of land I'm supposed to have," where he could "have fields of dark tobaccer and a fruit orchard and a herd of cattle and a stable full of horses, as well as pigs and hens and geese." After their marriage in 1890 and the birth of their third child a few years later, they have moved to this family farm in Hopewell, Kentucky, 150 miles from Christie's home in Dundee. James's description has made the Wheeler farm sound like paradise, but being crammed into the Wheeler homestead with the sizable Wheeler clan for their first year in Hopewell is anything but idyllic: James, Christie, and their three children – Clint, Jewell, and Nannie – are "bunched into one of five small upstairs bedrooms" in a house that is already filled with "Wad and Amanda and their two girls, Lena and Little Bunch; and Wad's sister Alma and her husband, Thomas Hunt, with their five children; as well as Boone, Wad and Alma's sickly brother, and Mammy Dove, their mother."

Christie manages to forge an alliance with Amanda (or Mandy), Wad's young second wife, who early on tells Christie, "We've got to stick together or these Wheelers will be the death of us."

Forced to work in the tobacco fields, Christie grows to hate "the dark-leaf tobacco James loved so much." With the plummeting price of tobacco and their more than $1,000 debt to Wad for their land, Christie and James can ill afford another pregnancy.

In February 1900, when she delivers previously unheard-of quintuplets, Christie and her babies quickly become media darlings. The mayor of Hopewell names her Mother of the Year; the story is picked up by a Saint Louis paper and eventually newspapers nationwide; companies offer the family free merchandise so they can identify themselves in their advertisements as the equivalent of "official sponsors" of the Hopewell Quintuplets; and the railroad adds a stop near the Wheelers' farm so that curious onlookers can come right into Christie's living room to see the natural wonders for themselves. Perhaps the public interprets the birth of the quintuplets as the "cataclysmic upheaval of the earth" that a "noted prognosticator" predicted for the new year of the new millennium, an earthquake to rival the earthquakes of 1811 and 1812 (which had severely altered the western Tennessee landscape).

Mason portrays Christie as a woman on the cusp of the modern age. On the one hand she is frequently influenced by the superstitions and the conventions of her time, while on the other she is a singularly modern woman trapped within those conventions. For instance, Christie enjoys sex, the "unspeakable" pleasures her mother would call "the wifely duty" but that she and James euphemistically refer to as "plowing." Yet, when – despite her exhaustive efforts – she helplessly watches as one by one the five babies who were a result of their parents' "lusty and reckless indulgence" die within a month of their birth, she assumes she is being punished for her sins. Foreshadowing the deaths of the babies, Mason juxtaposes a description of the hungry lust that resulted in the babies' conception with a scene in which elder son Clint tells his brother about the predicted earthquake: "The ground will open into a big ditch and swaller us up." When some of the feathers from the deceased babies' bed are discovered to be in the "bird nest shape" of two feather crowns, Amanda says the appearance of these crowns means "the babies are in Heaven." Christie tries to take comfort in this sign, but she knows that such crowns are traditionally predictors of death. The modern woman in her would like to believe that they are merely coincidental and not particularly meaningful.

The quintuplets' deaths are even more horrible because the 1900 version of the media spotlight

Disc #6/I-chap 6/4

~~Christie's right breast.~~ The tiny last-born ~~was~~ at ~~the~~ Christie's left breast. Christie could barely sit up in the awkward position of holding two babies at once. Alma brought the glass of Sweet-milk to Christie's lips.

"Here, finish this," said Alma.

"I'm hungry," said Christie.

"I don't know if your system's ~~strong~~ stout enough for some bacon and eggs."

"I believe I could even eat butterbeans," said Christie.

Alma hooted. "Well, hold your taters, I'll commence to cooking."

"Everybody's going wild up yonder at the ~~big~~ house," said Esther. "I told 'em they couldn't come yet till I saw how you were. Mandy claims she's going to move ~~in with~~ down here you, so I ~~guess~~ reckon I'll have to lock her up, and your little boys are going around in a spin."

"How's Nannie?"

"Well, Nannie cried. She misses you. and ~~She~~ wouldn't eat her oats."

From the kitchen, Wad said, "Are you finished with them babies yet? I can't stand with my back to you all day."

"Wad, I never saw you at a loss for words," said Christie as Esther shielded the nursing babies from her husband's eyes.

"I ain't never seen anything like this," said Wad. "I ain't never knowed anybody to have FIVE before. Five? It's a goddamn litter."

"I knowed a woman to have three oncet," said Mrs. Willie, suddenly awake and walking the floor in a curious nervous gait, her humped back seeming to follow her with a bounce.

"I ain't never heard of five," said Alma.

"Nobody has five," said Esther, as if the thought had just occurred to her.

*Esther; Amanda
Mandy = Little Bunch
Mrs. Willie = Willy*

Page from the first complete draft for Feather Crowns *(courtesy of Bobbie Ann Mason)* is focused unmercifully on Christianna and her family. Driven by a misguided notion of obtaining some revenge on the curious, she agrees to accompany the preserved bodies of her infants on what the *Hopewell Chronicle* calls "an educational series of lectures and diversions, for the purpose of educating the generally curious and concerned public about the Hopewell Quintuplets and the miraculous event that ended so unfortunately for the Wheelers," but the tour degenerates into a carnival sideshow attraction. Christie's nineteenth-century sentiments would seem to preclude leaving her three children behind and taking a ten-week-long, arduous journey with the preserved bodies of her infants in one glass case and the feather crowns in another.

Amanda, who desires to escape the Wheelers and see the world, is envious when Christie gets the opportunity to travel. Her attraction to Alma's husband, Thomas Hunt, comes primarily from his stories about his excursions as a traveling salesman, which serve as a means through which she can at least vicariously "escape" the confines of the Wheeler household and dream of adventures far removed from her crude tyrant husband, Wad. She eventually has a brief sexual dalliance with Thomas and finds her final escape through suicide.

Ostensibly, Christie and James decide to make the trip for economic reasons – one hundred dollars a week for ten weeks will make short work of their debt to Wad – and because Christie "wasn't ready to let go of her babies. If the world killed her babies and wanted to see them dead to draw some lessons from them, then she would show people more than they bargained for. She'd show them with spite burning in her eyes." Her "urgent purpose" is "to get revenge . . . on people she didn't even know." Yet the modern woman in Christie also feels "a rumble of expectation" in going "to new places," not only to relieve her grief but also to encounter the teeming world that awaits her. This journey, however, exploits the grief of Christie and James, whose trauma is further compounded by the culture shock they experience. The trip nearly destroys the fragile relationship between James and Christie, but they somehow manage to rediscover "the dance they had begun long ago."

While she creates wonderful characters in *Feather Crowns* – particularly the troubled Christie and the Wheeler clan – and successfully delineates the exploitative nature of the family, the general populace, science, and industry, Mason's third, longest, and most ambitious novel is somewhat unsatisfying. Perhaps the focus on the "moment" of the first year of the millennium as it filters into a family's tragedy was insufficient to give a full sense of Christie's life. The novel ends with two coda sections: Christie's 1937 visit to the Dionne quintuplets and a "transcription" of a message to her granddaughter Missy that Christie recorded in 1963, on her ninetieth birthday. The final first-person section is particularly troublesome. While Christie sometimes uses diction appropriate to her region and level of education – in statements such as "I was always busy a-doing something and trying to find out something that nobody else would think to fool with" – she also voices insights in words more appropriate to Mason's third-person narrator, as when Christie says, "I wanted the free and unattached generousness of stranger meeting stranger, where nothing familiar can cast a shadow of obligation on you, or a mirror reflection." This incongruous narrative seems more a device to reach the end of the novel than the sort of satisfying conclusion the novel deserves. While Christie says "I have had quite a life," Mason's novel provides only a defining moment in that life, not the string of moments that give breadth and depth to a life.

For more than a decade, Mason has captured the influence of American popular culture on her once remote region and studied the troublesome impasses and transitional points in the lives of her memorable working-class, plain-speaking characters. Despite the trial that life in the twentieth century brings to these ordinary people, they manage to find hope and possibility rather than despair. Mason is at work on a nonfiction historical work on Kentucky and another short-story collection.

Interviews:

Wendy Smith, "PW Interviews Bobbie Ann Mason," *Publishers Weekly,* 228 (30 August 1985): 424–425;

Lila Havens, "Residents and Transients: An Interview with Bobbie Ann Mason," *Crazy Horse,* 29 (Fall 1985): 87–104;

Enid Shomer, "An Interview with Bobbie Ann Mason," *Black Warrior Review,* 12 (Spring 1986): 87–102;

Michal Smith, "Bobbie Ann Mason: Artist and Rebel," *Kentucky Review,* 8 (Autumn 1988): 56–63;

Albert E. Wilhelm, "An Interview with Bobbie Ann Mason," *Southern Quarterly,* 26 (Winter 1988): 27–38;

Bonnie Lyons and Bill Oliver, "An Interview with Bobbie Ann Mason," *Contemporary Literature,* 32 (Winter 1991): 449–470;

Dorothy Combs Hill, "An Interview with Bobbie Ann Mason," *Southern Quarterly,* 31 (Fall 1992): 85–118.

References:

Edwin T. Arnold, "Falling Apart and Staying Together: Bobbie Ann Mason and Leon Driskell Explore the State of the Modern Family," *Appalachian Journal,* 12 (Winter 1985): 135–141;

Linda Adams Barnes, "The Freak Endures: The Southern Grotesque from Flannery O'Connor to Bobbie Ann Mason," in *Since Flannery O'Connor: Essays on the Contemporary American Short Story,* edited by Loren Logsdon and Charles W. Mayer (Macomb: Western Illinois University, 1987), pp. 133–141;

Ellen A. Blais, "Gender Issues in Bobbie Ann Mason's *In Country,*" *South Atlantic Review,* 56 (May 1991): 107–118;

David Booth, "Sam's Quest, Emmett's Wound: Grail Motifs in Bobbie Ann Mason's Portrait of America After Vietnam," *Southern Literary Journal,* 23 (Spring 1991): 98–109;

Robert H. Brinkmeyer Jr., "Finding One's History: Bobbie Ann Mason and Contemporary Southern Literature," *Southern Literary Journal,* 19 (Spring 1987): 22–33;

Brinkmeyer, "Never Stop Rocking: Bobbie Ann Mason and Rock-and-Roll," *Mississippi Quarterly,* 42 (Winter 1988–1989): 5–17;

Tina Bucher, "Changing Roles and Finding Stability: Women in Bobbie Ann Mason's *Shiloh and Other Stories,*" *Border States,* 8 (1991): 50–55;

Sandra Bonilla Durham, "Women and War: Bobbie Ann Mason's *In Country,*" *Southern Literary Journal,* 22 (Spring 1990): 45–52;

June Dwyer, "New Roles, New History and New Patriotism: Bobbie Ann Mason's *In Country,*" *Modern Language Studies,* 22 (Spring 1992): 72–78;

Richard Giannone, "Bobbie Ann Mason and the Recovery of Mystery," *Studies in Short Fiction,* 27 (Fall 1990): 553–566;

Owen W. Gilman Jr., "In Which Country," in his *Vietnam and the Southern Imagination* (Jackson: University Press of Mississippi, 1992), pp. 45–60;

Barbara Henning, "Minimalism and the American Dream: 'Shiloh' by Bobbie Ann Mason and 'Preservation' by Raymond Carver," *Modern Fiction Studies,* 35 (Winter 1989): 689–698;

Darlene Reimers Hill, "'Use to, the Menfolks Would Eat First': Food and Food Rituals in the Fiction of Bobbie Ann Mason," *Southern Quarterly,* 30 (Winter-Spring 1992): 81–89;

Katherine Kinney, "'Humping the Boonies': Sex, Combat, and the Female in Bobbie Ann Mason's *In Country,*" in *Fourteen Landing Zones: Approaches to Vietnam War Literature,* edited by Philip K. Jason (Iowa City: University of Iowa Press, 1991), pp. 38–48;

G. O. Morphew, "Downhome Feminists in *Shiloh and Other Stories,*" *Southern Literary Journal,* 21 (Spring 1989): 41–49;

Barbara T. Ryan, "Decentered Authority in Bobbie Ann Mason's *In Country,*" *Critique,* 31 (Spring 1990): 199–212;

Matthew C. Stewart, "Realism, Verisimilitude, and the Depiction of Vietnam Veterans in *In Country,*" in *Fourteen Landing Zones: Approaches to Vietnam War Literature,* pp. 166–179;

Leslie White, "The Function of Popular Culture in Bobbie Ann Mason's *Shiloh and Other Stories* and *In Country,*" *Southern Quarterly,* 26 (Summer 1988): 69–79;

Albert E. Wilhelm, "Making Over or Making Off: The Problem of Identity in Bobbie Ann Mason's Short Fiction," *Southern Literary Journal,* 18 (Spring 1986): 76–82;

Wilhelm, "Private Rituals: Coping with Change in the Fiction of Bobbie Ann Mason," *Midwest Quarterly,* 28 (Winter 1987): 271–282;

Marjorie Winther, "*M*A*S*H,* Malls and Meaning: Popular and Corporate Culture in *In Country,*" *Literature Interpretation Theory,* 4 (1993): 195–201.

Peter Matthiessen

(22 May 1927 -)

William Dowie
Southeastern Louisiana University

See also the Matthiessen entry in *DLB 6: American Novelists Since World War II, Second Series.*

BOOKS: *Race Rock* (New York: Harper, 1954; London: Secker & Warburg, 1955); republished as *The Year of the Tempest* (New York: Bantam, 1957);

Partisans (New York: Viking, 1955; London: Secker & Warburg, 1956); republished as *The Passionate Seekers* (New York: Avon, 1955);

Wildlife in America (New York: Viking, 1959; London: Deutsch, 1960; revised edition, New York: Viking, 1987);

Raditzer (New York: Viking, 1961; London: Heinemann, 1962);

The Cloud Forest: A Chronicle of the South American Wilderness (New York: Viking, 1961; London: Deutsch, 1962);

Under the Mountain Wall: A Chronicle of Two Seasons in the Stone Age (New York: Viking, 1962; London: Heinemann, 1963); republished as *Under the Mountain Wall: A Chronicle of Two Seasons in Stone Age New Guinea* (New York: Penguin, 1987; London: Collins Harvill, 1989);

At Play in the Fields of the Lord (New York: Random House, 1965; London: Heinemann, 1966);

Oomingmak: The Expedition to the Musk Ox Island in the Bering Sea (New York: Hastings House, 1967);

The Shorebirds of America, text by Matthiessen, paintings by Robert Verity Clem, and species accounts by Ralph S. Palmer, edited by Gardner D. Stout (New York Viking, 1967); Matthiessen's text republished as *The Wind Birds* (New York: Viking, 1973);

Sal Si Puedes: César Chavez and the New American Revolution (New York: Random House, 1969; revised, 1973);

Blue Meridian: The Search for the Great White Shark (New York: Random House, 1971; London: Harvill Press, 1995);

The Tree Where Man Was Born (New York: Dutton, 1972; London: Collins, 1972);

Peter Matthiessen at the time of Raditzer *(photograph by Mary Gimbel)*

Seal Pool (Garden City, N.Y.: Doubleday, 1972); republished as *The Great Auk Escape* (London: Angus & Robertson, 1974);

Far Tortuga (New York: Random House, 1975; London: Collins Harvill, 1989);

The Snow Leopard (New York: Viking, 1978; London: Chatto & Windus, 1979);

Sand Rivers (New York: Viking, 1981; London: Aurum, 1981);

In the Spirit of Crazy Horse (New York: Viking, 1983; revised, 1991; London: Harvill, 1992);

Indian Country (New York: Viking, 1984; London: Collins Harvill, 1985);

Midnight Turning Gray (Bristol, R.I.: Ampersand, 1984);

Nine-Headed Dragon River: Zen Journals 1969-1982 (Boston: Shambhala, 1986; London: Collins Harvill, 1986);

Men's Lives (New York: Random House, 1986; London: Collins Harvill, 1988);

On the River Styx and Other Stories (New York: Random House, 1989; London: Collins Harvill, 1989);

Killing Mister Watson (New York: Random House, 1990; London: Collins Harvill, 1990);

African Silences (New York: Random House, 1991; London: Harvill, 1991);

Baikal: Sacred Sea of Siberia (San Francisco: Sierra Club, 1992; London: Thames & Hudson, 1992);

East of Lo Monthang: In the Land of Mustang (Boston: Shambhala, 1995).

OTHER: Malcolm Cowley, ed., *Writers at Work: The Paris Review Interviews,* includes an interview with William Styron by Matthiessen and George Plimpton (New York: Viking, 1958);

Paul Brooks, ed., *Everglades,* photographs by Patricia Caulfield, with selections from works by Matthiessen (San Francisco: Sierra Club, 1970);

"The Atlantic Coast," in *The American Heritage Book of Natural Wonders,* edited by Alvin M. Josephy (New York: American Heritage, 1972);

"Search for the White Death," in *Men of Courage,* edited by William Robert Parker (Chicago: Playboy Press, 1972);

"In the Dragon Islands," in *The Audubon Wildlife Treasury,* edited by Les Line (Philadelphia: Lippincott, 1976);

John D. Buksbazen, *To Forget the Self: An Illustrated Guide to Zen Meditation,* foreword by Matthiessen (Los Angeles: Zen Center, 1977);

"Homegoing," in *The Children of Bladensfield,* by Evelyn D. Ward (New York: Viking, 1978);

"Common Miracles," in *Search,* edited by Jean Sulzberger (San Francisco: Harper & Row, 1979);

1000 Adventures: With Tales of Discovery, includes contributions by Matthiessen (New York: Harmony Books, 1983);

Lama Anagarika Govinda, *The Way of the White Clouds: A Buddhist Pilgrim in Tibet,* foreword by Matthiessen (Boston: Shambhala, 1988);

George Catlin, *North American Indians,* edited, with an introduction, by Matthiessen (New York: Viking, 1989).

SELECTED PERIODICAL PUBLICATIONS – UNCOLLECTED:

FICTION

"Martin's Beach," *Botteghe Oscure,* 10 (1952): 310-318;

"The Tower of the Four Winds," *Cornhill,* 166 (Summer 1952): 143-149;

"A Replacement," *Paris Review,* 1 (February 1953): 46-56;

"Lina," *Cornhill,* 169 (Fall 1956): 53-58;

"Speck in the Glades," *Esquire,* 120 (July 1993): 80-83.

NONFICTION

"Annals of Crime," *New Yorker,* 34 (1 November 1958): 119-145;

"A Reporter at Large: Sand and Wind and Waves," *New Yorker,* 41 (3 April 1965): 116-144;

"The Last Great Strand: Corkscrew Swamp Sanctuary," *Audubon,* 69 (March 1967): 64-71;

"A Reporter at Large: To the Miskito Bank," *New Yorker,* 43 (28 October 1967): 120-164;

"The River Eater," *Audubon,* 72 (March 1970): 52;

"Kipahulu: From Cinders to the Sea," *Audubon,* 72 (May 1970): 10-23;

"Lignumvitae – the Last Key," *Audubon,* 74 (January 1972): 20-31;

"In the Dragon Islands," *Audubon,* 75 (September 1973): 4-49;

"Happy Days," *Audubon,* 77 (November 1975): 64-95;

"Stop the GO Road," *Audubon,* 81 (January 1979): 48-65;

"My Turn: The Price of Tellico," *Newsweek,* 94 (17 December 1979): 21;

"How To Kill a Valley," *New York Review of Books,* 27 (7 February 1980): 31-36;

"The Desert Sea," *Geo,* 6 (September 1984): 116;

"Our National Parks: the Case for Burning," *New York Times Magazine,* 11 December 1988, p. 38;

"New York: Old Hometown," *Architectural Digest,* 46 (November 1989): 52;

"Who Really Killed the F.B.I. Men," *Nation,* 252 (13 May 1991): 613;

"Life in Ruins," *Travel Holiday,* 174 (June 1991): 44-51;

"The Trials of Leonard Peltier," *Esquire,* 117 (January 1992): 55-57;

"Journey to the Edge of the World," *Condé Nast Traveler,* 27 (November 1992): 148-159;

"The Last Cranes of Siberia," *New Yorker,* 69 (3 May 1993): 76-86;

"César Chavez," *New Yorker,* 69 (17 May 1993): 82-83;

Matthiessen (right) and fellow fisherman Ted Lester, Amagansett, Long Island, 1955

"Alighting Upon the Daurian Steppe," *Harper's,* 286 (June 1993): 47–55;

"At the End of Tibet," *Audubon,* 96 (March/April 1994): 40–49;

"Survival of the Hunter," *New Yorker,* 71 (24 April 1995): 67–77;

"The Cranes of Hokkaido," *Audubon,* 97 (July/August 1995): 36–47;

"Commentary: Mean Spirit," *Outside,* 20 (October 1995): 41–48, 145.

Peter Matthiessen is among a handful of American authors to be nominated for the National Book Award in both fiction and nonfiction – for the novel *At Play in the Fields of the Lord* (1965) and the travel books *The Tree Where Man Was Born* (1972) and *The Snow Leopard* (1978; for which he won the award). His tour de force novel *Far Tortuga* (1975) stands as a major achievement of technical virtuosity and symbolic resonance, an experimentalist landmark in the modernist tradition of Joseph Conrad, Ernest Hemingway, and William Faulkner. His personal chronicle of Himalayan adventure and discovery, *The Snow Leopard,* has become a classic travel book.

Far Tortuga and *The Snow Leopard,* the pinnacles of Matthiessen's career thus far, rise above a body of work distinguished by its quantity, breadth, commitment, and style. Just below them are the novels *At Play in the Fields of the Lord* and *Killing Mister Watson* (1990), the first volume of an ambitious trilogy, and the chronicles *The Cloud Forest* (1961) and *The Tree Where Man Was Born.* While he has written at least twice as much nonfiction, fiction writing has consumed more energy and time. Typically, Matthiessen can polish the journal of one of his journeys into book form in less than a year. The novels are another story. *Far Tortuga* took eight years to complete, its writing interrupted by trips to California, Africa, the Indian Ocean, Australia, and Nepal; and the Watson trilogy has been more than fifteen years in the making.

During a lifetime filled with activity, Matthiessen has helped to found *The Paris Review,* fished commercially and operated a charter boat, hunted for fossils in the jungles of South America, visited and studied a Stone Age tribe in New Guinea, trekked the mountain paths of Nepal and the plains of Africa, gone diving off the southern coast of Australia to observe the great white shark, and sailed on an old turtling ship out of Grand Cayman Island. He has espoused the causes of Native Americans, commercial fishermen, and migrant workers and has become a master of Zen. Matthiessen's extensive travels and his intensive involvements show him to be a man deeply engaged with the world. Ever since the original publication of his polemic *In the Spirit of Crazy Horse* (1983), which occasioned one of the largest libel suits ever brought against an American author, Matthiessen has been trying to free Leonard Peltier, convicted of the slaying of FBI agents on the Pine Ridge Reservation, and to defend his own authorial integrity. The courts have vindicated Matthiessen, but Peltier remains incarcerated.

Matthiessen has been featured in a PBS documentary on the Florida Everglades, and his *At Play in the Fields of the Lord* has been made into a movie, but he spends no time on publicity appearances. He is a hard worker, and interspersing periods of activity with times for writing suits the paradoxical urges of his nature. His twin instincts are movement and stillness, action and contemplation, search and repose, fierce advocacy and monkish detachment, wildness and calm. His house in Sagaponack, New York, on six acres surrounded by trees and a privet hedge and only a ten-minute walk from the ocean, is quiet. He spends most of his day and even an hour or two in the evening writing in an office detached from the main house. This routine also calls for physical activity – usually in the form of a chore such as cutting logs with a chain saw or perhaps a game of touch football or tennis with neighbors John Irving, James Salter, or E. L. Doctorow – to interrupt the afternoon stillness. On his travels, in the

Dust jacket for the novel in which Matthiessen drew on his experiences in the navy during World War II for a sea story that some reviewers compared to works by Joseph Conrad

midst of his most intense activity, abides a repose, a waiting, a realization that what is important is not what is sought but the finding. Matthiessen practices a contemplation in action. These words in *The Snow Leopard* echo both his American naturalist predecessor Henry David Thoreau and his Zen teachers: "Simplicity is the whole secret of well-being.... I am not here to seek the 'crazy wisdom'; if I am, I shall never find it. I am here to be here."

Each of Matthiessen's books can be seen as a response to what it means "to be here," with the particular "here" ranging from New York and Paris to the remotest outposts of habitation in Africa and New Guinea. Because each work responds to the revelations of the moment, its form and content depend on the nature and contour of the experience. Typically Matthiessen is drawn to the wildest parts of the world by an urge that is at once contemplative and inquisitive. In his fiction and nonfiction his central insight is that oneness with nature's wildness is highly desirable but increasingly difficult. Attaining such unity depends on sensing oneself as a small part of nature and accepting that nature's ferity is part of oneself. Matthiessen's first books were novels, and – though he has since written more nonfiction than fiction – he still sees the latter as the expression of his deepest inspiration and the role of novelist as his highest calling.

The son of Erard A. Matthiessen and the former Elizabeth Carey, Peter Matthiessen was born on 22 May 1927 at Le Roy Hospital in New York City, the second of three children. His father, a prominent architect, later became a trustee of the National Audubon Society and a director of the Nature Conservancy. The Matthiessens were well-off, maintaining a residence on Fifth Avenue overlooking Central Park, a country house with a fine view of the Hudson, and a summer place on Fishers Island, whose coast felt most like home to the young Matthiessen.

He attended St. Bernard's School in Manhattan, which had an all-British faculty and a curriculum that included first-grade Latin, and then Greenwich Country Day School. For prep school he boarded at Hotchkiss in Lakeville, Connecticut, where his early rebelliousness landed him on a corridor for troublemakers when he was a sophomore. A contributor to several school publications, Matthiessen early on decided to become a writer. When he graduated in 1945 with World War II nearing its end, he enlisted in the U.S. Navy and served in Pearl Harbor, assigned not to sea duty as he had hoped, but, because of poor eyesight, to work in the base laundry. He wrote articles for the *Honolulu Advertiser,* managed the navy's golden-glove boxing team, and rose to the rank of ships service laundryman third class before a fight with the shore patrol got him demoted. Returning home from service too late for college enrollment in 1946 and at odds with his parents, he spent a malcontent autumn and winter in New York, staying at a maternal great-aunt's apartment, nursing melancholia with alcohol until one day a concerned and alert elevator man called him down for self-indulgence.

By spring 1946 he was at Yale University, where he deepened his interest in nature with courses in zoology and ornithology and pursued his writing interests as an English major and a columnist for the *Yale Daily News.* In the junior-year-abroad program Matthiessen studied at the Sorbonne in Paris, where he met a strikingly attractive Smith College junior with family connections at least as impressive as his own, Patricia Southgate; they were married two years later, on 8 February 1951. During his senior year at Yale, Matthiessen's writing career was launched when *The Atlantic Monthly* accepted a story, "Sadie," that he had written for creative-writing class. It also won an *Atlantic* best story award of 1951 and helped Matthiessen to garner a job as instructor of creative writing at Yale after he graduated in 1950. When *The Atlantic* took a second story, "The Fifth Day," Matthiessen immediately got an agent and confidently sent her four chapters of a novel, only to be told that his novel had been written more than 150 years earlier by James Fenimore Cooper, who had done it better.

Sobered but undaunted, Matthiessen decided to pursue the writer's life abroad, in Paris. When he and his wife sailed to Europe in the early summer of 1951, several other young Americans with long literary ambitions and short résumés did the same. Irwin Shaw, in his thirties and already a well-known novelist, became the patron of these young arrivistes, calling them collectively "the tall young men" and inviting them to parties and dinners, where they mingled with such Hollywood celebrities as Kirk Douglas, Gene Kelly, Samuel Goldwyn, and John Houston. The Matthiessens' apartment at 14, rue Perceval, a small back street in Montparnasse, became the regular afternoon watering hole for a group that included at one time or another William Styron, George Plimpton, Terry Southern, James Baldwin, Ben Bradlee, Thomas Guinzburg, and Harold "Doc" Humes. With Humes, Matthiessen founded *The Paris Review* and recruited Plimpton to be its editor in chief, a position he still holds. The first issue appeared in 1953, the same year Matthiessen's son Lucas was born.

By August of that year Matthiessen, having finished one novel manuscript and outlined another, sailed back to America and settled in East Hampton, Long Island, with his wife and infant son. He got a job as a commercial fisherman to support his writing. He could write on bad-weather days from spring through fall and full-time during the winter. In 1954 Matthiessen's daughter Sara Carey was born, and his first novel, *Race Rock,* appeared to positive reviews. In *The New York Times Book Review* (4 April 1954) Sylvia Berkman hailed Matthiessen as "a writer of disciplined craft, perception, imaginative vigor and serious temperament." Edward Weeks of *The Atlantic Monthly* (June 1954) praised Matthiessen's writing for its tightness, observation, and power but noted that he was better in scenes of direct action than when depicting his elders at Sunday dinner.

The novel revolves around a troubled young scion of a wealthy family, George McConville, confronting the ghosts of inheritance in the form of two boyhood acquaintances of lesser privilege, one a half-breed Indian raised by the family in second-class status, the other a bastard son of the man who originally owned the McConvilles' coastal land. Balancing the two outsiders are two of George's social equals – his best friend, Sam, and his pregnant lover, Eve. The conflicts among the group are resolved when the four men, now in their twenties, return to the summer place for a weekend that is climaxed by George's divestiture of his heritage as he offers Cady the house: "He drew off the gloved heavy garments one by one, until he was white and naked under the sun. His skin was alive with a clean glory he had not known since a child, a sense of beginnings, of infinite possibilities." Clearly the book raised many of the questions Matthiessen was asking himself about his patrimony, questions that led from "LOST MAN'S RIVER" (the Watson trilogy, Bk. II)

Peter Matthiessen

was a little rough around the edges, but so was Ol' Hickory Andy Jackson, right? First President in the U.S. to hail from the back country! First of great redneck breed that made this country great!"

"Arbie? Why are you so angry?" More quietly, he said, "No, I don't intend a whitewash. But I have to cut away all the myth-making and local spite and gossip, some approximation of the truth." if I hope to arrive at

"Approximation is right!" Arbie grabbed the pages again and shook them. "A damn whitewash, I call it, and for dirty money!" He fell quiet long enough to clean his nails and pare them with his pocket knife. "E. J. Watson was a black-hearted killer," he said then. "I sure don't like to have to tell you that over and over, cause he was your daddy, dammit, and I know you loved him."

"That's right," Lucius said. "I loved him."

****

They spent that evening at a motel camp on the Withlacoochee River. While the old man slept off a long day, Lucius drank his bourbon in the shadow of the porch, face pale in the reflections of the giant cypress in the moon black water, in the shaggy forest silence. The gallinule's eerie whistling, the ancient hootings of barred owls in duet, the horn notes of limpkins and far sandhill cranes from beyond the moss-draped cypress walls, sounds as primordial and perfectly in place as the lichens and shelf fungi fastened minutely to the bark of the great trees, the rich ferns with copper-colored spores springing forth from the old limestone fissures.

Page from the revised typescript for Lost Man's River, *the second novel in Matthiessen's Watson trilogy (courtesy of Peter Matthiessen)*

Dust jacket for Matthiessen's novel about an ill-fated turtle-hunting expedition that becomes a mythic confrontation with death

at first to his refusal to tap parental wealth in supporting himself and his family and later to his embracing Zen. For a first novel, *Race Rock* displays considerable talent and considerable room for improvement. While the style is assured and the plotting intricate, the book is overwritten and lacks distance from the posturing of its principal characters.

Matthiessen followed with *Partisans* (1955). Set in the back streets and alleyways of postwar Paris, with its political intrigues and ideological clashes, this book evokes film noir. As in all three of Matthiessen's early novels, the protagonist is a privileged young American impelled to question what he has been given. Each novel examines a different facet of the question: *Race Rock* deals with personal inheritance and divestiture; *Partisans* focuses on the structure of society and the search for ideals; and *Raditzer* (1961) looks at outsiders and the issue of human brotherhood. In each case the protagonist must choose between competing allegiances: the life of privilege in which he has been raised or the life of struggle that his conscience dictates.

In *Partisans* Barney Sand, the son of a prominent American diplomat (Matthiessen's father-in-law had been one), is a journalist on assignment in Paris when he hears that Jacobi, an important Communist, has been purged from the party. When he was a boy of fourteen, Sand met and was deeply impressed by Jacobi, whom Sand decides to find and interview. Sand's subsequent quest for ideals takes him on a tour of the underside of Paris and engages him in serious discussions of Marxism and capitalism. He is swayed by the Marxist dialectic, but after he finds the fallen Jacobi and realizes how abused he has been by the party, Sand rejects Communism as just another monolith inflexible to the needs of individuals. He comes to see that his father and Jacobi are both idealists who have been treated badly by their respective bureaucracies. Impelled by Jacobi's advice, Sand returns to America to help his father and to try to reform the system from within: "Yet he had to try again, tomorrow in America; he had to keep on trying. And perhaps that trying would come to something in the end, though he might never see the sense in it." Written in the early 1950s, *Partisans* reflects a time given to political and personal idealism, as well as the historical atmosphere of the Cold War and the controversial McCarthy hearings.

Reviewers, usually harder on a second novel than the first, tempered their praise for Matthiessen's control of scene and narrative with reservations about his handling of the characters – who, William Goyen said, "seem only mouthpieces" (*New York Times Book Review,* 2 October 1955). Yet *Partisans* is tighter and more daring than its predecessor. The book shows fine emotional control in presenting a side of the city different from the romantic milieu of expatriate cafés and artists' garrets. Curbing the excesses of his earlier style, Matthiessen learned that less could be more, a lesson he would not forget. The result, marred only by abstract characters and a facile ending, advances Matthiessen's narrative technique with its style, convincing dialogue, and a fine architectonic balance, beginning in light, slipping into the darkness of the Parisian underground, and emerging again into light.

By 1956 Matthiessen's tapestry of fishing, writing, and domesticity had begun to unravel. The fiction was not making any money. The commercial fishermen on the South Fork of Long Island had come on hard times because of scarcity and government regulations, and Matthiessen's marriage was coming to an end. Although the divorce was not formalized until 1958, by the end of 1956 he and his wife had separated. He packed his green Ford convertible with books on wildlife, a shotgun, and a sleeping bag and set off with the intention of visiting all the wildlife refuges in the United States and writing a history of American wildlife. An admitted generalist in the natural sciences, with only a few college courses and a lifetime of interested reading to fall back on, Matthiessen had accumulated what he calls "a lot of slack information" about nature and its creatures. *Wildlife in America* (1959), appearing three years before Rachel Carson's *Silent Spring,* is incisive in its account of vanishing species and has long been one of the central texts of the conservation movement.

During this period of his life, Matthiessen formed a working relationship with *The New Yorker* and its legendary editor William Shawn. When he was still in Paris, Matthiessen and Ben Bradlee had followed the famous murder trial of Yvonne Chevallier, and the magazine featured Matthiessen's account of it as one of its "Annals of Crime" articles (1 November 1958). The following year *The New Yorker* financed Matthiessen's trip to remote areas of Peru and Brazil and published the chronicle of his journey in three installments, which later became *The Cloud Forest.* In the best tradition of travel literature Matthiessen entertained his audience with an account of his five months of exploration up, down, and across South America by boat, plane, train, bus, car, canoe, raft, and foot. About halfway through, however, the narrative enlarges in scope when Matthiessen hears a story about a fossil of a jawbone so huge that its origins would have to be in prehistory. The author becomes a quester, and the tale assumes mythic overtones, dealing with mankind's continual fascination with the mystery of origins. In 1961 that same mystery motivated Matthiessen to join the Harvard-Peabody expedition to New Guinea; the trip resulted in another book of nonfiction, *Under the Mountain Wall* (1962), about a Stone Age tribe never before seen by outsiders.

In the midst of all these travels, Matthiessen brought out his third novel, *Raditzer,* a short, controlled, artistically finished story. The central character, Charlie Stark, is a young American on board a navy troop carrier destined for Honolulu near the close of World War II. Like Matthiessen, Stark is refused sea duty because of a physical defect and is assigned to the base laundry. Another version of the same rich, young author-surrogate of the first two novels, Stark faces the challenge of outsiders: How do I treat those who are radically different? Raditzer is everything Charlie Stark is not: an orphan whose birth certificate calls him "Male Raditzer." Uneducated, unloved, and rodentlike in appearance, he is a drifter, at once cynical and tactless. When the outsider attaches himself to Stark, the child of privilege must decide if he will accept Raditzer's friendship or, like all the others, avoid him. Guilty about his own advantages and impelled toward sympathy for Raditzer as one of society's underprivileged, Stark accepts and tolerates Raditzer "on the grounds that he shares the human condition." This decision, however, draws Stark into deeper involvement than desired and forces him to see in Raditzer his own shadow side, compelling Charlie to face what he "would not face, a secret self, a specter escaped from the dark attic of the mind. He was the bogeyman in childhood cellars . . . but he was also the wretched troll within, the practitioner of dirty adolescent habits, the latent liar, pervert, coward, suddenly incarnate." Throughout the story Raditzer says, "I know you, Charlie," insisting on breaking through Stark's posture of separateness. At the end of the novel Stark acknowledges his ties with Raditzer and his debt of self-knowledge when he steps forward in answer to the officer's question about the missing Raditzer, claiming, "I know him." Matthiessen's larger implication is that there are not two worlds, civilized and savage, but one; and civilization can

Dust jacket for Matthiessen's book about the commercial fishermen on the South Fork of eastern Long Island

only be whole by recognizing and accepting its outcasts.

Shaped into a thoughtful tale with a smaller cast than Matthiessen's previous novels, *Raditzer* reminded more than one reviewer of Conrad. In the *New York Herald Tribune* (29 January 1961) Gene Baro gave three reasons for the comparison: the vividness of the writing about sea and ships, the "confrontation of an imagined exoticism with the real thing," and the "seriousness and subtlety of the moral theme." While there are elements of Conrad and Herman Melville in Matthiessen's novel, it lacks the suspense and color of those earlier authors' sea stories. What is noteworthy about the book is its portrait of the knavish Raditzer, capturing the character's essential innocence as well as his rascality and displaying the author's ability to imagine himself into an alien persona, a quality that came in handy in Matthiessen's subsequent nonfiction explorations. With his trio of novels about a youthful protagonist chagrined by the burden of plenty, Matthiessen established his reputation as a serious writer whose finished style deserved attention. Each of the books displayed distinctive strength as well as obvious flaws, and in each new fictional venture Matthiessen expanded his range, the mark of a writer to be reckoned with.

That reckoning came in Matthiessen's next fictional foray when he abandoned the use of a protagonist cut in his own image and drew on material from his journey to South America. Matthiessen's imagination had been fired by his South American experience, and four years later – with the help of his editor, Joe Fox, who untangled a labyrinth of overlapping plots into chronological sequence – appeared the novel *At Play in the Fields of the Lord*. The story brings together zealous American missionaries, opportunistic soldiers of fortune, corrupt local officials, and a tribe of Indians. Lewis Moon, a halfbred Cheyenne from the United States, becomes the meeting point of civilization and nature when he parachutes into the forest of southeastern Peru during a drug-induced vision. A tribe of Niarunas believes that he is Kisu-man, the Great God of the Rain, and consequently they revere him. Without romanticizing savage life Matthiessen shows in the Niarunas how thoroughly men and women can live as one with nature. By contrasting the missionaries' proselytizing with the adventurers' opportunism – and by casting both of these against Moon's reversion to the primitive – Matthiessen shows that something is always lost in the intrusion of civilization upon the wild, no matter how benign the intention. Matthiessen convinces the reader also that the missionary in his overreaching idealism and the soldier of fortune in his burned-out cynicism are both drawn to the remote corners of the world by a common voice, a call from the depths of nature that appeals to mankind's indelible instinct for exploration. The missionary Martin Quarier and Lewis Moon come together at the end of the novel in their appreciation for the Niarunas, becoming aligned in their determination to protect the tribe against further intrusions by the government.

The sprawling nature of *At Play in the Fields of the Lord* contrasts sharply with Matthiessen's earlier novels. It provides a wealth of detail about the wilderness, and its many plots ask serious questions about ideals, suffering, love-lust, courage, and true morals. The novel shows a path of central humanity that is able to cross the boundary of the civilized and the wild, but it also shows the crossing to be perilous, with no assurances of peace and attainment apart from the drifting and finding of the moment. The book was well received and has come to mark Matthiessen's confirmation as a novelist not only of potential but of accomplishment. Matthiessen's friend William Styron was right to call it "a dense, rich, musical book, filled with tragic and comic resonances."

While in Peru Matthiessen had experimented with the jungle hallucinogen *yage*, or ayahuasca, and the experience convinced him that drugs might lead to a heightened sense of reality. Although he has said that the only passage in his writing directly influenced by drugs is the drug-dream sequence in *At Play in the Fields of the Lord*, Matthiessen continued to use drugs, mostly LSD but also mescaline and psilocybin, for ten years as a way of dealing with the sources of a persistent rage that had affected his life. He credits the drugs for acting as a kind of psychotherapy, putting him in touch with painful childhood memories that had been covered by layers of protective shell. Matthiessen cautions that drugs are not for everyone, and he eventually abjured their use.

In 1960 Matthiessen settled into his present home in Sagaponack, Long Island, then still an area of working potato farms, not the writers' haven it became. Shortly thereafter, while walking on the beach, he met a woman, Deborah Love, whom he married on 16 May 1963. (Love later reminded him that they had first met years before in Paris.) In 1964 the Matthiessen family enlarged with the birth of a son, Alexander, and Peter's adoption of Deborah's daughter, Rue. Marriage and fatherhood did not keep Matthiessen from extensive traveling throughout the 1960s. In 1964 he joined John Teal's expedition to Nunivak Island in the Bering Sea to capture some calves from the only extant herd of musk oxen, an Ice Age animal. The trip resulted in a *New Yorker* article and the book *Oomingmak* (1967). In 1967, again sponsored by the magazine, Matthiessen accompanied commercial fishermen hunting green turtle on an old converted schooner out of Grand Cayman. This trip resulted in another article and provided source material for the novel *Far Tortuga*. The following year he spent time with César Chavez in California and wrote a *New Yorker* profile of him that was later expanded as *Sal Si Puedes* (1969).

Matthiessen's travels continued in the late 1960s, causing considerable strain in his second marriage, but the mark of the wanderer is impressed on his soul. Trips to the Serengeti Plain of East Africa and a voyage organized by well-known diver Peter Gimbel to film the great white shark kept him away from Sagaponack for extended periods. Creatures who navigate long-distance migrations – including the green turtles, wind birds, or great cranes – draw his most rapt commentaries. *Blue Meridian* (1971), the great white shark adventure, describes the pursuit of one such elusive creature. The shark chase begins with practice diving in the Bahamas and ends with the successful filming of the great white off Australia's southern coast. Matthiessen quickly followed this straightforward account with *The Tree Where Man Was Born*, one of his most powerful books of nonfiction, a meditation on the beauty of primitive Africa and its gradual passing.

During his travels around the world, Deborah Matthiessen, who had accompanied him in his drug experimentation, abandoned hallucinogens and discovered Zen. At first Matthiessen was put off by the presence of three Zen monks in his driveway when he returned home from one of his trips, but soon his pique turned to curiosity and then interest. Before long he was joining his wife in her weekend Zen retreats and in practicing meditation. As his involvement with Zen grew, he began to see drugs as an inferior way of intensifying reality and a poor substitute for religious experience, and he stopped using them. Zen became even more important to the couple when Deborah was discovered to have inopera-

Dust jacket for a collection of short stories Matthiessen wrote over a period of four decades

ble cancer. It helped her to face the inevitable with equanimity, and their mutual commitment to Zen deepened their marriage. She died in January 1972.

In 1974 Matthiessen was honored by election to the National Institute of Arts and Letters, and that year he set about completing a novel based on his turtling voyage in the Caribbean. *Far Tortuga* appeared in 1975 to considerable praise from reviewers who uniformly agreed that Matthiessen's construction of the novel was daring. Most used superlatives such as "virtuoso novel" (William Kennedy, *The New Republic*, 7 June 1975), "magnificent performance" (Dave Smith, *Library Journal*, 15 April 1975), and "a work of brilliance" (*Publishers Weekly*, 1 March 1975). The novel is the story of a crusty, old sea captain taking a ragged crew on a doomed turtling expedition to the far-off last domain of the green turtle off the Nicaraguan coast. The boat, the *Lillias Eden*, is barely seaworthy, with an engine in constant need of repair (by an engineer who thinks a thermometer will do as a manifold), a radio that receives but does not transmit, rotting sails, old thatch rope, slack rigging, and masts that are too short. Because of Capt. Raib Avers's hasty outfitting of the *Eden* with twin diesel engines, the deckhouse was elevated, but money ran out before the steering wheel could be relocated. Hence the helmsman has no view of the ship's path. The result serves as a symbol of the modern world, where progress, in terms of engines, is sought at the expense of vision. Ironically it is Captain Raib's voice that is the most stringent in scourging modern times as he laments the killing of all the wildlife that has diminished the days of abundance. His crew, Raib ululates, represents the present generation in their laziness, incompetence, shallowness, and lack of discipline.

This contrast between past and present, the old days and modern times, is just one of the major conflicts revealed in the voices of captain and crew. Matthiessen allows each man to speak without introduction or identification, modeling his dialogue on the screenplay. At first confused by the voices, the reader gradually identifies the nuances of each speaker and senses the startling contrast between the emotional intensity of the crew's desires and the cold matter-of-factness of the impersonal narrator. This conflict between desire and hard reality is another theme of the novel, as captain and crew together must confront the impersonal and unpredictable power of nature in facing "de bleak ocean" and hitting "dat one wild rock."

The journey seems ill-fated from the start. It begins too late in the turtling season. A rival ship, in marvelous condition and piloted by Raib's crass, unprincipled half brother, already has a full load of four hundred turtles by the time the *Eden* has caught seventeen. When Raib decides to steer to Far Tortuga, a distant, legendary island ringed by the remnants of reefs that are rumored to be rife with turtles, he challenges the mysteries of nature. Yet he trusts his superior navigational ability and is confident of success. That he finally fails is attributed to his hubris, both in trusting his own abilities and in failing to compromise in dealing with his crew. His abuse of crewman Brown culminates in his inability to remain quiet when Brown is subduing the hostile Jamaicans with the big knife belonging to Raib's father. He calls Brown a "Goddam thief" and demands that he return the knife. When the leader of the Jamaicans, sensing his opportunity, invites Brown to join them – "Got *pussy,* mahn! Got *rum!*" – Brown waivers, and Raib's final insult – "Go den, and good riddance!" – pushes Brown over the edge. Brown's betrayal shifts the balance of power to the Jamaicans and ultimately precipitates the disastrous night run through the dangerous reefs. Here again, Raib overreaches in his pride. James Grove compares him to Gatsby, Lord Jim, and Ahab, claiming, "he attempts to become more than human, his greatness and tragedy rising out of his striving to capture the immortality he sees symbolized in the gulfweed." When the ship hits the unexpected rock, Raib is thrown from the mast and crashes on the deck just like the flying fish he had used for bait. His words to the fish apply to his own tragic conflict with the elements, "Fly too high, darlin, you fly too high."

Counterpointing Raib as tragic figure is Speedy as comic – Speedy who tried to mitigate Raib's rage and whose utter determination, skill, and good luck allow him to survive the shipwreck. In Matthiessen's Darwinian universe, all humankind must succumb to the blind forces of nature, such as an uncharted rock, but some are more fit to survive. Speedy, whose final gesture of respect for nature is the cutting loose of the green turtle, shows his mettle by acting decisively and refusing to despair. Speedy becomes Matthiessen's figure of hope, his symbol of human potential. At the end he is at harmony with the elements.

The book takes the reader into an elemental world in an elemental way. It is searing. Matthiessen's method, with its liberal use of white space and spare symbols and clusters of words hung in the air, successfully creates a physical object that mirrors the sensations of the trip. His sentences, strung out in careful bareness, rivet the reader's attention to the present experience. Matthiessen tried to eliminate all metaphor from the tale, but the underlying metaphor of a ship at sea with a mission and a variety of dangerous obstacles is clear. The crew is taken on a clearly mythic journey that tosses them together and brings about unexpected growth, rare moments of insight into life, and an archetypal confrontation with death. His technique, at first seemingly quirky and whimsical, proves essential to the book's vision; it is a poetic vision of the starkness and beauty of life lived on the border between the wild sea and man's wild desires.

The four years preceding the appearance of *Far Tortuga* were a time of intense Zen practice for Matthiessen. In the two years following its publication he mitigated his rigorous Zen devotion and turned his energies to polishing a journal he had kept of a November 1973 trip to Nepal with biologist George Shaller. *The Snow Leopard* tells of their 250-mile walk across the Himalayan high country in pilgrimage to one of the most remote Zen shrines, the Crystal Monastery, and in search of the rarely seen snow leopard, which becomes a metaphor for the wonderful elusiveness of nature. At once a spiritual retreat from the business of life and a grieving for Deborah Matthiessen, the book, considered by many to be Matthiessen's best work of nonfiction, won a National Book Award.

Matthiessen's inner journey at this time led him to shift his Zen practice from the more rigorous Rinzai to the Soto sect, which emphasizes "just sitting" and lacks the physical discipline of the warning stick. On 28 November 1980 Tetsugen-sensei, a Soto teacher, officiated at Matthiessen's third marriage, to Tanzania-born Maria Eckhart, a former model and later an editor at *Condé Nast Traveler*. The year after his marriage, Matthiessen was ordained as a Zen priest, and he continues to lead meditation for a congregation that gathers in his old barn, which has been converted into a Zendo. In 1982 Matthiessen traveled with Tetsugen to Japan, visiting the ancient Soto Zen shrines. *Nine-Headed Dragon River* (1986) recounts the pilgrimage and provides a history of Zen, especially in the United States, as well as Matthiessen's personal testimony of his evolving commitment to it, which more recently has led to his receiving Dharma transmission.

Matthiessen continued to write in the 1980s. *Sand Rivers* (1981) resulted from a trip with Maria cation of *On the River Styx and Other Stories* (1989), which collects stories from his earliest in the 1950s to a pair from the late 1980s. The most recent stories in the volume exhibit the fullness of the author's talent. "Lumumba Lives," awarded second prize in the 1990 O. Henry anthology, is a luminous story about recovering the past, man's abuse of nature, and the chasm of race that divides America. It and the title story, "On the River Styx," are Matthiessen's finest stories.

During the latter half of the 1980s, Matthiessen had distracted himself from the harassment of lawsuits by trips to the Everglades of south Florida, gathering material about a mysterious figure whose turn-of-the-century exploits left a legend full of contradictions: loving family man and violent killer, congenial host and tyrant, pioneer and renegade, tax-paying citizen and outlaw. Ever since his childhood vacations in Florida, when Matthiessen heard stories from his father and others about Edgar J. Watson, he was curious. The curiosity became a project, and Matthiessen searched through old newspapers, spoke to everyone he could find who remembered Watson, gathering reams of information, suspicions, rumors, and anecdotes. From these reports and his own imagination came his first novel in sixteen years, *Killing Mister Watson*. Matthiessen claims not historical accuracy but a deeper truth for his large complex novel about a man of mystery and power who was finally set upon and killed by his neighbors and fellow townspeople.

Matthiessen at the time of African Silences *(photograph by Nancy Crampton, 1991)*

and others to the Selous Game Preserve in Tanzania and the East African plains. Two books on Native Americans, *In the Spirit of Crazy Horse* and *Indian Country* (1984), derived from his ongoing research and travel among Indian tribes since 1975. Pulled off the shelves because of the lawsuits against Matthiessen and Viking by an FBI agent and a former governor of South Dakota, *In the Spirit of Crazy Horse* was republished once the courts dismissed the charges in 1990. Matthiessen is more convinced than ever that Leonard Peltier was framed and railroaded into prison for the murders of the two agents. Ever since his book on César Chavez, Matthiessen has championed causes. In *Men's Lives* (1986) he took on the problems of the commercial fishermen of Long Island's South Fork, defending their industry against threatening legislative bans and limning the beauty of their traditional way of life.

Matthiessen returned to Yale in the spring of 1989 to teach a creative-writing seminar. That same year also marked his return to fiction with the publi-

He tells the story through the voices of ten speakers who knew Watson, interspersing their accounts in separate chapters. Since Watson is killed within the first nine pages, the major query is not who did it, but why? Because the answer to that question lies as much in the nature of the region as in the man, the speakers describe the Chokoloskee Bay area, the gateway to Florida's Ten Thousand Islands, a remote place that at the turn of the century was frequented by drifters, renegades, and other outcasts from society. They talk in a relative vacuum, answering the implied question "What do you know about Mister Watson?" and thus reconstructing the events around his coming to the area and finally his death. Matthiessen has always been interested in employing regional voice as a means of capturing reality. In *Killing Mister Watson* he uses the monologue with a nearly infallible ear for distinguishing the nuances of his speakers. He creates narrative flow and gives some centrality to the often conflicting testimonies through the intervention of an aspiring historian's presumably objective recapitulation of events. The device provides continuity

Dust jacket for the first of three novels inspired by Matthiessen's curiosity about a legendary figure who lived in southwest Florida at the turn of the twentieth century

and a way of reconciling conflicting reports, but what prevails is the aura of subjectivity that precedes and colors the telling of all history. Matthiessen's layering of voices, like William Faulkner's before him, questions the degree to which we can get back to an objective description of facts when they are seen so differently from so many different perspectives.

The decision to kill Watson rests finally not on the townspeople's certainty that he committed the murder of which he is accused but on his failure to convince them of his credibility. When he fails to keep his word that he will either return with the alleged killer or bring back his head, the townsmen have had enough and decide to kill Watson, not only because of the murder of which he stands accused but because of the accumulated number of violent events with which Watson has been associated and because of his perceived lack of trustworthiness. Of course, they are also scared of him, and they will sleep peacefully only when he is gone. Behind him Watson has left a trail of bodies so long that the townspeople can attribute his freedom only to the law's impotence and his cleverness.

Matthiessen allows readers to judge for themselves how guilty or innocent Watson is. And the difficulty of the judgment – after hearing from friends, foes, family, and others – suggests that historic events often rest on the sands of subjectivity. It remains to be seen what new insights about Watson's deeds will develop in the subsequent two volumes of the Watson trilogy, which have already been written by Matthiessen. Part two is from the viewpoint of Watson's younger son, Lucius, who protested the family decision not to prosecute his father's murderers and now sets out to write a biography that will exonerate his father. Part three will tell Watson's own version of events.

Matthiessen's fascination with the figure of Watson, the strong man of action and free spirit unbound by society's conventions, has many precedents in his earlier work. The mysterious stranger is Cady of *Race Rock,* Jacobi of *Partisans,* and Moon of *At Play in the Fields of the Lord.* Much of the power of Matthiessen's writing and the ferocity of his imagination stems from his ability to become one with such figures. Born into the patrician privileges of sophisticated society, Matthiessen seems to have grappled with his own shadow side in his sympathetic exploration of the mysterious stranger. And his visits to the wild and remote areas and peoples of the world are another form of this delving into the mystery of otherness, of nature at its extreme unpredictability and intransigence.

Reviewers of *Killing Mister Watson* agreed that the individual voices are captured masterfully by a writer at the height of his powers. Verlyn Klinkenborg, however, observes that "in a sense, he [Matthiessen] has been truer to his voices than to his larger tale," betraying frustration that after reading all this testimony "every question raised by the appearance of this man and by his killing remains unanswered" (*The New Republic,* 5 November 1990). On the other hand the most laudatory reviewer, Ron Hansen, sees Watson's career as quite specifically an indictment of "the heedlessness and hidden criminality that are part and parcel of American devotion to the pursuit of wealth; to its cult of financial success" (*The New York Times Book Review,* 24 June 1990). Reading the story as a kind of *Babbitt,* Hansen claims it is Matthiessen's "most impressive novel." Matthiessen admitted to Malcolm Jones that he was "interested in the redeeming qualities of a man a lot of people would think is some sort of monster" (*Newsweek,* 11 June 1990). Since Matthiessen has always conceived the separate volumes of the Watson saga as one, the appearance of parts two and three should throw considerable light on these issues.

As *Killing Mister Watson* neared publication, Matthiessen expected to concentrate on fiction thereafter, but three more travel books appeared in short order. *African Silences* (1991) draws on visits to western Africa and Zaire in 1978 and to central Africa in 1986, reporting the continued depletion of Africa's wildlife and the diminishment of its unspoiled landscape. *Baikal* (1992) is based on his expedition to the world's deepest and oldest freshwater lake, Baikal in Siberia, at the invitation of musician Paul Winter, who hoped Matthiessen would draw attention to the increasing industrial threats to its ecosystem. *East of Lo Monthang* (1995) records Matthiessen's return to an area not far from the region he visited on the journey described in *The Snow Leopard;* once again remoteness no longer protects a region from the forces of change. During the 1990s Matthiessen has also been to India, Bhutan, Mongolia, eastern Siberia, and Australia to view some of the world's rarest and most beautiful cranes, and to the Faeroe Islands, Iceland, and Greenland, where he observed a whaling harvest by Inuits who still use kayaks and handheld harpoons to stalk their prey. Articles in *Audubon, The New Yorker,* and *Harper's* tell of these expeditions and their author's continued fascination with creatures who grace the most remote places and with societies who still ply primordial trades of survival.

Scott Anderson's detailed and formidable attack on Leonard Peltier's innocence and on Matthiessen's version of events in *In the Spirit of Crazy Horse* appeared in *Outside* magazine in July 1995, occasioning a lengthy, painstaking, and devastating rebuttal from Matthiessen in the October issue of that magazine. The timing of Anderson's piece, Matthiessen explains, could not have been worse for Peltier, who had a petition for executive clemency pending. As much time as distractions such as the *Outside* attack have cost him, Matthiessen has remained staunch in his defense of Peltier, staying in close touch with him during his nineteen years in prison and continuing to lobby for his release.

Amid this flurry of nonfiction since 1990, one story, an excerpt from part two in the Watson trilogy, appeared in the July 1993 issue of *Esquire.* Once all three volumes of this massive and ambitious work have been published, this trilogy will undoubtedly remind the world that Matthiessen's literary legacy is preeminently that of novelist. It remains to be seen, however, whether Matthiessen indeed can devote himself mainly to fiction with so many unchronicled parts of the world still beckoning.

Interviews:

George Plimpton, "The Craft of Fiction in *Far Tortuga,*" *Paris Review,* 15 (Winter 1974): 79–82;

Henry Allen, "Quest for the Snow Leopard's Secret: And Other Journeys Into Meaning with Bestselling Author Peter Matthiessen," *Washington Post,* 13 December 1978: D1, 15;

Wendy Smith, "PW Interviews Peter Matthiessen," *Publishers Weekly,* 229 (9 May 1986): 240–241;

Kay Bonetti, "An Interview with Peter Matthiessen," *Missouri Review,* 12, no. 2 (1989): 109–124;

Paul Rea, "Causes and Creativity: An Interview with Peter Matthiessen," *Re Arts & Letters: A Liberal Arts Forum,* 15 (Fall 1989): 27–40;

Deborah Houy, "A Moment with Peter Matthiessen," *Buzzworm,* 5 (March 1993): 28.

Bibliographies:

D. Nicholas, *Peter Matthiessen: A Bibliography: 1951–1979* (Canoga Park, Cal.: Orirana Press, 1979);

James Dean Young, "A Peter Matthiessen Checklist," *Critique,* 21, no. 2 (1979): 30-38.

Biographies:

Trip Gabriel, "The Nature of Peter Matthiessen," *New York Times Magazine,* 10 June 1990, p. 30;

Nicholas Dawidoff, "Earthbound in the Space Age: Peter Matthiessen Explores the Wild and the Majestic," *Sports Illustrated,* 73 (3 December 1990): 119-124;

Peter Becker, "Zen and the Art of Peter Matthiessen," *M Inc.,* 8 (July 1991): 54;

Michael Shnayerson, "Higher Matthiessen," *Vanity Fair,* 54 (December 1991): 114-132;

Pico Iyer, "Laureate of the Wild," *Time,* 141 (11 January 1993): 42-44.

References:

Bruce Bawer, "Nature Boy: The Novels of Peter Matthiessen," *New Criterion,* 6 (June 1988): 32-40;

Bert Bender, "*Far Tortuga* and American Sea Fiction since *Moby-Dick*," *American Literature,* 56 (May 1984): 227-248;

Bender, *Sea Brothers: The Tradition of American Sea Fiction from Moby-Dick to the Present* (Philadelphia: University of Pennsylvania Press, 1988);

John Cooley, "Matthiessen's Voyages on the River Styx: Deathly Waters, Endangered Peoples," in his *Earthly Words: Essays on Contemporary American Nature and Environmental Writers* (Ann Arbor: University of Michigan Press, 1994);

Marc Dolan, "The 'Wholeness' of the Whale: Melville, Matthiessen, and the Semiotics of Critical Revisionism," *Arizona Quarterly,* 48 (Fall 1992): 27-58;

William Dowie, *Peter Matthiessen* (Boston: Twayne, 1991);

James P. Grove, "Pastoralism and Anti-pastoralism in Peter Matthiessen's *Far Tortuga*," *Critique,* 21, no. 2 (1979): 15-29;

Michael Heim, "The Mystic and the Myth: Thoughts on *The Snow Leopard*," *Studia Mystica,* 4 (Summer 1981): 3-9;

Richard F. Patteson, "*At Play in the Fields of the Lord*: The Imperialist Idea and the Discovery of the Self," *Critique,* 21, no. 2 (1979): 5-14;

Patteson, "Holistic Vision and Fictional Form in Peter Matthiessen's *Far Tortuga*," *Bulletin of the Rocky Mountain Modern Language Association,* 37, no. 1-2 (1983): 70-81;

Rebecca Raglon, "Fact and Fiction: The Development of Ecological Form in Peter Matthiessen's *Far Tortuga*," *Critique,* 35 (Summer 1994): 245-259;

William Styron, *This Quiet Dust and Other Writings* (New York: Random House, 1982), pp. 249-252, 295-298;

W. Ross Winterowd, "Peter Matthiessen's Lyric Trek," in his *The Rhetoric of the 'Other' Literature* (Carbondale: Southern Illinois University Press, 1990), pp. 133-139.

Carson McCullers
(19 February 1917 – 29 September 1967)

Judith L. Everson
University of Illinois at Springfield

See also the McCullers entries in *DLB 2: American Novelists Since World War II* [first series] and *DLB 7: Twentieth-Century American Dramatists.*

BOOKS: *The Heart Is a Lonely Hunter* (Boston: Houghton Mifflin, 1940; London: Cresset, 1943);
Reflections in a Golden Eye (Boston: Houghton Mifflin, 1941; London: Cresset, 1942);
The Member of the Wedding (Boston: Houghton Mifflin, 1946; London: Cresset, 1947);
The Member of the Wedding: A Play (New York: New Directions, 1951);
The Ballad of the Sad Café: The Novels and Stories of Carson McCullers (Boston: Houghton Mifflin, 1951); republished as *The Ballad of the Sad Café: The Shorter Novels and Stories of Carson McCullers* (London: Cresset, 1952);
The Square Root of Wonderful (Boston: Houghton Mifflin, 1958; London: Cresset, 1958);
Clock Without Hands (Boston: Houghton Mifflin, 1961; London: Cresset, 1961);
Collected Short Stories and The Ballad of the Sad Café (Boston: Houghton Mifflin, 1961);
Sweet as a Pickle and Clean as a Pig (Boston: Houghton Mifflin, 1964; London: Cape, 1965);
The Mortgaged Heart, edited by Margarita G. Smith (Boston: Houghton Mifflin, 1971; London: Barrie & Jenkins, 1972);
Collected Stories of Carson McCullers, Including The Member of the Wedding and The Ballad of the Sad Café, edited by Virginia Spencer Carr (Boston: Houghton Mifflin, 1987).

In December 1936 *Story* magazine published "Wunderkind," the first fictional work by teenage author Carson Smith to appear in print. In retrospect her choice of title appears doubly ironic. In the story the term refers to the young protagonist, Frances, an aspiring pianist whose dream of a concert career collapses when she can no longer perform with her usual precision and passion.

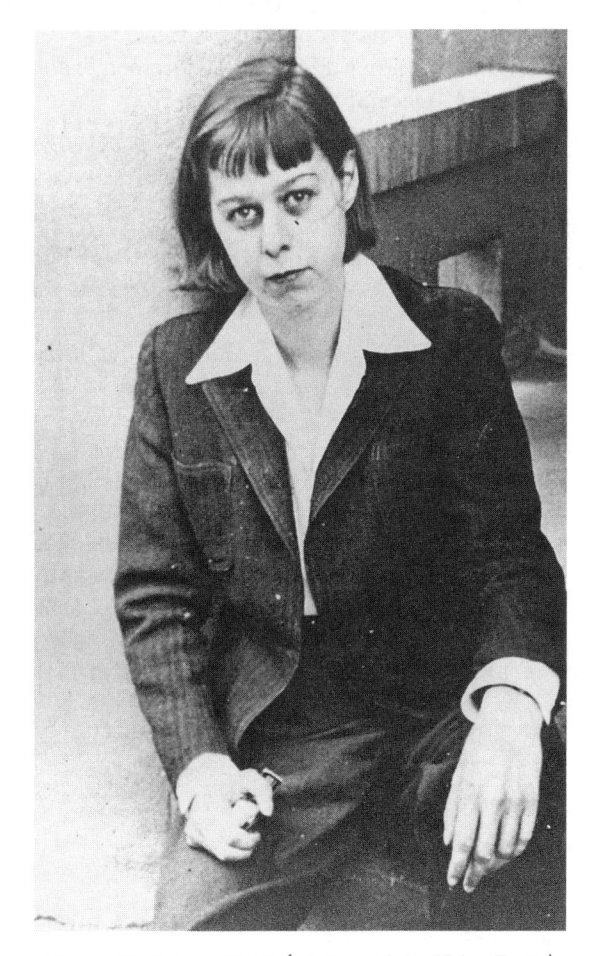

Carson McCullers, 1944 (photograph by Helen Eustis)

"Wunderkind" may also be read as a fictionalized treatment of Carson Smith's own abandoned musical ambition and as a prophetic comment on her destiny as the internationally acclaimed author Carson McCullers.

The firstborn child in her family, Lula Carson Smith was lavished with love but also burdened by maternal expectations of genius. As a girl she – like Frances – trained to be a concert pianist, but her delicate health and the departure of her piano teacher helped to turn her toward a writing career instead.

Lula Carson Smith (right) with her mother, Marguerite Waters Smith, and younger brother, Lamar Smith Jr. (photograph by Jungermann's Studio, Columbus, Georgia)

With her second publication, the commercially and critically successful novel *The Heart Is a Lonely Hunter* (1940), McCullers – then twenty-three – was touted as a literary wunderkind. Over the next decade she produced a body of work that seemed to justify the high hopes raised by such an auspicious debut. After 1950, however, both the quantity and quality of her writing diminished substantially, and following her death in 1967 at age fifty she was increasingly viewed as a fragile talent that had peaked prematurely. Various explanations were offered for the decline of her work and the resulting threat to her reputation, including her painful struggle with personal adversity and her long exile from the South, the region that had stimulated her best-known works. Subsequent interpretations of her career have continued to face the challenge of fairly assessing her eventual achievement in light of her extraordinary initial promise.

The daughter of Lamar and Marguerite Waters Smith, Lula Carson Smith was born on 19 February 1917 in Columbus, Georgia, a mill town of thirty thousand. With its stifling hot summers and snowless winters, as well as its starkly contrasted classes and races, Columbus inspired the literary landscape for McCullers's most memorable fiction. Although she left her hometown for the North in 1934 and never lived permanently in the South after 1940, she is still widely regarded as a Southern writer, even while her best work is recognized for its universal appeal.

Because her canon reflects an abiding identification with underdogs and outcasts, readers sometimes presume that McCullers grew up in poverty. Actually, her father operated his own jewelry store. Lula Carson was never materially deprived, and – more important – her artistic gifts were always nurtured. In elementary school, after she began playing music by ear, she was given a piano and provided lessons. When, as a teenager, she started writing plays and novels, her father bought her a typewriter. The Smiths' support of her artistic endeavors proved to be a mixed blessing, however. It pressured their daughter to cultivate her talent at the expense of a well-rounded development, and it fostered her adult dependence on her mother, especially during periods of poor health.

While in high school Lula Carson learned that qualities rewarded at home as proof of budding genius often brought ridicule or rejection elsewhere. Nevertheless, she asserted her individuality. At thirteen she dropped her feminine first name in favor of her gender-neutral middle name. Although sensitive about her height (5'8"), she accentuated the difference in her appearance by dressing eccentrically. Teachers generally regarded her as an underachiever who pursued her own interests instead of the prescribed curriculum. Unpopular with her peers, she had few friends and seldom dated. Her years as a precocious loner contributed to the compassion for the solitary and the strange that became her literary trademark.

Despite her first serious illness at fifteen – a case of rheumatic fever that was misdiagnosed as pneumonia at the time and did long-term damage to her heart – Carson graduated from Columbus High School in 1933. Her plan to stay at home and focus on her music was disrupted a year later when her piano teacher, Mary Tucker, left the state. Carson felt abandoned by her mentor and uncertain about her vocation.

Nevertheless, that fall she took Tucker's advice that she further her studies at the Juilliard School of Music in New York City. Lamar Smith sold a family heirloom to raise $500 for his daughter's tuition and expenses. Shortly after her arrival in the city, most of the money was lost, or possibly stolen, leaving Carson to support herself. Tennessee Williams, later one of her closest friends, said of this incident, "Perhaps a great musician was lost, but a greater writer was found."

Sporadic daytime employment left Carson free to take night classes in creative writing with Whit Burnett at Columbia University and with Sylvia Chatfield Bates at New York University. During this literary apprenticeship, Carson focused on writing short stories, which she had first attempted in 1933 with "Sucker." The title "Sucker" is a juvenile character's nickname, one that must be painfully shed. Just as Frances in "Wunderkind" goes from child prodigy to teenage has-been, so Richard (the sucker) changes from naïf to cynic when his idolized older cousin cruelly rebuffs him after being rejected by a fickle girlfriend. These early stories display in nascent form concerns that distinguish McCullers's later work, including the portrayal of adolescent anguish and unrequited love.

When Carson returned to Columbus in mid 1935, she met James Reeves McCullers Jr., a soldier stationed nearby at Fort Benning. He shared her literary ambitions and liberal sentiments, and for the next eighteen years their lives were intertwined in an unconventional, bittersweet relationship that profoundly affected her writing. Carson and Reeves married on 20 September 1937 and moved to North Carolina, where they were briefly happy. They had agreed to support one another's artistic aspirations, but Reeves McCullers never wrote anything publishable. Indeed, he never found steady, satisfying work outside the military. As his wife's career accelerated, he grew more reliant on her income and less sure of his own worth.

The couple encountered other difficulties as well. At Carson's initiative, they were often separated after she became successful. Besides periodic stays with her mother, usually when she needed to recuperate, Carson lived intermittently at February House, a Brooklyn salon and boardinghouse run by editor George Davis, and at Yaddo, an artists' colony in Saratoga Springs, New York, where she was stimulated, sometimes to excess, by her association with fellow writers and artists.

Both Carson and Reeves were bisexual. She became infatuated with a succession of women, and at one point she and Reeves were even attracted to the same person, composer David Diamond. The difficulty of negotiating such desires within a marriage, especially when alternative lifestyles were not widely accepted, helps explain why conflicts concerning sexual identity and gender relations recur so forcefully in her fiction.

Carson's chronic poor health also complicated their lives. As a by-product of her rheumatic fever, she suffered several strokes beginning in 1941, and in 1947 she was paralyzed on her left side, unable thereafter to type or play the piano except in a limited way. She had also become an alcoholic. Much as she wanted to be well, she grew accustomed to the attention that came with being ill. Yet the more dependent she became on her husband and her mother for care, the more her ambivalence toward them deepened.

Eventually divorced in 1941, the McCullerses remarried in 1945 following a reconciliation effected largely through correspondence while Reeves served as an army officer in Europe. After the war they bought a house outside Paris, but it did not fulfill their dream of a quiet country life. In 1948, depressed over her increasing invalidism, Carson slashed a wrist. After this suicide attempt, she underwent psychiatric evaluation. She recovered her will to write, leaving Reeves for good in 1953 after he proposed a suicide pact. Later that year he killed

Lula Carson Smith riding a neighbor's pony, 1935

himself with an overdose of drink and drugs. In 1955 she suffered another devastating loss: the death of her mother, with whom she had periodically shared a home in Nyack, New York, after her father died in 1944 and the Columbus ties were severed.

During the last phase of her life McCullers was largely confined to a bed or a wheelchair. She underwent surgery to repair damaged limbs, survived a heart attack, had a cancerous breast removed, and broke a hip and an elbow in a fall. As she told Rex Reed in her final interview, conducted in April 1967, she felt God had confused her with Job. On 15 August she suffered a stroke and remained comatose until her death on 29 September. She was buried in Nyack next to her mother, whose confidence in and devotion to her daughter's genius had never wavered.

Despite the disease and disarray that inexorably dominated her life, McCullers produced what Virginia Spencer Carr calls "an impressive literary legacy": five novels, two plays, twenty short stories, two dozen pieces of nonfiction, and some poetry and verse. Evaluation of this varied body of work has been complicated by its unevenness, especially in relation to the trajectory of McCullers's career. Because *The Heart Is a Lonely Hunter* was such a notable first novel, she set a high standard for herself, one that she equaled or surpassed for a time but could not sustain. Judgment of her later works has proven particularly difficult. Lawrence Graver pronounces them "triumphs of stoicism" but "failures of art." McCullers's reputation remains based on her fiction of the 1940s. There has been little realignment in the relative rank of works from this period of peak productivity, and most of the change registered in recent criticism reflects new approaches to old favorites. Like Flannery O'Connor, Katherine Anne Porter, and Eudora Welty, with whom she is often compared, McCullers has benefited from revisionary readings that dispute her previous marginalization on grounds of gender and region. As scholars redefine what it has meant to be a woman writer from the South, her life and work are attracting renewed interest.

The composition of her first novel illustrates her typical creative process. Her conception of the work jelled slowly, but once it had, she preferred what her imagination had shaped to the possible contradictions of reality. During the winter of 1936–1937 McCullers began mulling over a set of characters who inexplicably kept talking to someone else. Only when she realized that this focal figure was a mute could she turn their stories into a coherent narrative. Near the end of the writing, Reeves McCullers suggested she attend a convention of deaf-mutes to learn more about people with the disability, but Carson declined.

With the encouragement of Bates, she entered part of the manuscript in a fellowship competition sponsored by Houghton Mifflin. Although she did not win, she got a contract on the strength of the first six chapters and an outline. Completed in April 1939, the final draft is generally faithful to the outline. Originally titled "The Mute," the novel was renamed at the suggestion of her editor, Robert Linscott. *The Heart Is a Lonely Hunter* was published in June 1940. Their marriage falling apart, Carson and Reeves then moved to New York City.

The Heart Is a Lonely Hunter impressed most reviewers as a remarkable first novel from so young a writer. Lorine Pruette wondered in *Books* (9 June 1940) "how any young person could know so much" about loneliness. In the *Saturday Review of Literature* (8 June 1940) Ben Ray Redman went further, calling *The Heart Is a Lonely Hunter* "an extraordinary novel in its own right, considerations of authorship apart." Writing for *The New York Times* (16 June 1940), Rose Feld agreed that McCullers had proven herself "a full-fledged novelist whatever her age."

The Heart Is a Lonely Hunter continues to be regarded as one of McCullers's strongest claims to lasting fame, generally ranking in critical estimation just below *The Ballad of the Sad Café* (1951) and *The Member of the Wedding* (1946) among her longer fictions. *The Heart Is a Lonely Hunter* is often cited as an ideal introduction to McCullers's work because it foreshadows nearly everything else she wrote, revealing her literary strengths and limitations. In this first novel she stated at length her master theme: spiritual isolation as the human condition in modern times.

To dramatize this isolation as a universal rather than idiosyncratic state, McCullers interwove the stories of five main characters who struggle to overcome their loneliness and alienation. Her outline reveals her vision of the novel as a fugue in which these characters' voices are developed independently, yet enriched by their interplay. Each chapter centers on one of the five characters, for each of whom she created an individualized third-person style of narration.

Mick Kelly, a teenage tomboy as the story begins, is sometimes seen as the protagonist because her story is given the most space (seven chapters), because she is the most "normal" and thus the easiest character with whom to identify, and because she is the youngest, with the greatest potential for development. Mick's father cannot find steady work; her mother rents rooms in their house to boarders. The three older children still live at home but hold outside jobs. When Mick is not in school, she supervises her younger brothers, George (Bubber) and Ralph. She fantasizes about becoming a conductor or composer, but her family cannot afford a radio, let alone a piano. Her retreats into the "inside room" of imagination provide some relief, as do restless rambles about her small southern hometown.

Mick frequents the New York Café, owned and operated by Biff Brannon and his wife, Alice, who live in the apartment upstairs. They work staggered shifts and are sexually estranged. Biff likes children, but – having become impotent – he contents himself with doting on his niece, Baby Wilson, the daughter of Alice's sister. He is vaguely attracted to Mick, seeing her more as a surrogate child than a love interest, but she misreads his attentions. When Alice dies, ironically of an infant-sized tumor, Biff cultivates the feminine side of his personality, which he had repressed during their marriage. Once constrained by Alice's practicality, Biff's sympathy for the town misfits is now held in check by his general detachment.

Biff's fascination with the freakish causes him to befriend Jake Blount, a rootless radical who drifts into town and finds work with the local carnival. Jake is appalled at the conditions in which the mill hands live and labor, but he lacks the skill to organize them for collective action. His harangues offend the workers instead, driving him to drunken stupors or violent outbursts.

Jake has much in common with Benedict Mady Copeland, physician to the local African Americans, for Dr. Copeland is also thwarted in achieving his goal: justice for his people. Marxism allows him to diagnose their problem, but it also separates him from their culture. While they respect him as a healer, they reject him as a leader. A widower, he is also cut off from his children, only one of whom – Portia, the Kellys' cook – maintains regular contact with him. Reactivation of his tuberculosis sharpens his sense that time is running out for him and his mission.

These characters are individually drawn to John Singer, an engraver who boards at the Kellys' and takes his meals at Biff's. Singer, a deaf-mute who reads lips and uses sign language, is ironically named because he has not spoken in years. He becomes a tabula rasa onto whom the other characters project the wisdom and sympathy they seek. In talking to him, they are really talking to themselves; on the one occasion when they all find themselves in his room, they cannot interact constructively. The narcissism that marks each individual's personal relationship with Singer is revealed in their collective ignorance of his inner life, which centers on a fellow deaf-mute, Spiros Antonapoulos, the most unattractive character in the book: half-witted, obese, and self-absorbed. Even after Antonapoulos becomes unmanageable and must be institutionalized, however, Singer inexplicably attributes the same omniscience and saintliness that the others find in him to Spiros.

As the action unfolds over more than a year, each of the five suffers loss. Bubber accidentally shoots Baby Wilson, whose medical bills sink the Kellys deeper into debt. Mick must drop out of school to work at Woolworth's. According to Linda Huf, Mick typifies female adolescents in American literature of the period, for whom growing up means scaling back expectations. With Alice's death Biff realizes how little he knew her in life. Although he resented her sharpness as a businesswoman, the café suffers in her absence. He explores closer ties with the Wilsons but remains unable or unwilling to risk intimacy. Though he occasionally glimpses things that others miss, he is unable finally to provide an explanation of events that satisfies himself, let alone the reader. Copeland and Blount cannot find common ground in their parallel pursuit of progress for local blacks and working-class whites. The historical division between these groups is reenacted not only in the failed dialogue between the two reformers but also in the race riot that erupts at the carnival. Afterward Jake leaves town no wiser than he came. Dr. Copeland, distraught when his son Willie is crippled in a prison atrocity, retires to await death. The most shocking loss for all, however, comes with Singer's suicide. Shattered by the sudden illness and death of his friend, he returns to his room and shoots himself. His followers now realize how little they know their idol.

Critics disagree about how well the narrative works on different levels in McCullers's first novel and whether it is best approached as a realistic or symbolical book. Leslie Fiedler argues that *The Heart Is a Lonely Hunter* is "the last of the 'proletarian

Reeves and Carson McCullers, late 1930s (photograph by John Vincent Adams)

novels,' a true Depression book." Despite its strong particularization in time and place, however, McCullers's novel has endured while much social protest fiction of the era has faded because McCullers uses the topical to explore the timeless. She puts speeches on the excesses of capitalism and the horrors of racism into the mouths of Blount and Copeland, but — given their limitations — they cannot be considered her spokesmen, and the novel never becomes a tract. *The Heart Is a Lonely Hunter* is stronger at dramatizing than solving social problems partly because these would-be leaders lack followers, but McCullers's stress on the psychological rather than sociological sources of disaffection also precludes the search for collective answers.

Her intriguing reference to *The Heart Is a Lonely Hunter* as a parable on fascism has been interpreted by some to mean that she attacks economic exploitation and racial discrimination as American equivalents of European fascism, which is preparing to envelop the West as the novel ends. Her likelier purpose, though, is to expose the psychology that makes fascism possible – in this case, the mystification of Singer by estranged souls searching for what they lack. This view coincides with Barbara Farrelly's argument that the novel gives literary form to its musical inspiration, Ludwig van Beethoven's Third Symphony, the *Eroica,* which so moves Mick. The composer wrote the *Eroica* to honor of his hero, Napoleon, but withdrew the dedication when Napoleon named himself emperor. Likewise, those who impute superhuman qualities to Singer learn that he too is merely mortal.

To the extent that *The Heart Is a Lonely Hunter* develops along allegorical lines, the significance of its recurrent religious symbolism becomes crucial. Much of this symbolism coalesces in Singer's dream, in which Mick, Biff, Jake, and Benedict kneel at the base of a stairway while Singer kneels halfway up the steps and Antonapoulos kneels at the top. Since Singer has been described in vaguely Christ-like terms (he looks Jewish, is kindly and long-suffering, and dies at thirty-three), some see him as a Christ figure doomed by his God (Antonapoulos) and his followers. Others regard him as, at best, a reluctant messiah because he does not choose his Christ-like role or, at worst, a false messiah since he cannot save anybody, not even himself. The role of Antonapoulos is equally ambiguous. His Greek origins and Buddha-like appearance suggest a pagan or Eastern deity rather than the Judeo-Christian God, yet he prays to Mary and wears a cross around his neck. If he represents God, this role seems consistent with his being more inscrutable than Singer, but not with his being so much less sympathetic. Because of its fuzziness, the religious symbolism is commonly held to be unintentionally muddled (the result of a young writer overreaching herself). On one point there is consensus: in *The Heart Is a Lonely Hunter* man creates God in his own image, not vice versa, with perilous results for both the believer and the object of that belief.

In his introduction to the 1950 edition of McCullers's second book, *Reflections in a Golden Eye* (1941), Tennessee Williams declared it a victim of the critical retrenchment that usually follows high praise for an author's first work. Despite a disappointing initial reception, *Reflections in a Golden Eye* struck him as an advance over *The Heart Is a Lonely Hunter* because McCullers had reined in her "subjective tenderness" and "youthful lyricism," achieving "absolute mastery of design." Whether one agrees with reviewers that she regressed or with Williams that she improved, in neither case can she be accused of having written the same book twice. *Reflections in a Golden Eye* bears only superficial resemblance to its predecessor. Even after efforts to rehabilitate its standing within her canon, it remains her most controversial work.

The germ of the plot came from an incident at Fort Bragg that Reeves reported to Carson while they lived in nearby Fayetteville, North Carolina: a soldier was arrested for spying on residents in the married officers' quarters. In two months during the summer of 1939, McCullers spun out her story about voyeurism at an army post, then set it aside. A year later, while she was living in New York, George Davis found the manuscript and got permission to publish it in *Harper's Bazaar,* where he was fiction editor. After its appearance there in two installments (October and November 1940), *Reflections in a Golden Eye* was published by Houghton Mifflin in February 1941.

Reviews were almost uniformly harsh. In *The Atlantic Monthly* (April 1941) Edward Weeks condemned the book for failing to give a realistic account of army life, which McCullers had never intended. Reviewing the book for *The New Yorker* (15 February 1941), Clifton Fadiman warned the author against her apparent preoccupation with the "strange and startling." Frederick Marsh called the book "vastly inferior" to *The Heart Is a Lonely Hunter* and referred to McCullers as an "*enfant terrible*" (*The New York Times,* 2 March 1941).

One does not have to read far into *Reflections in a Golden Eye* to detect its disturbing qualities. The first paragraph identifies its focus with customary coolness: "There is a fort in the South where a few years ago a murder was committed. The participants in this tragedy were: two officers, a soldier, two women, a Filipino, and a horse." The source of the perverse power of McCullers's novel lies partly in the elements of this situation, but more so in their daring deployment.

None of the six characters (excluding the horse) is totally sympathetic or psychologically whole. Chester Eisinger argues persuasively that three of them live solely by natural instinct: lusty Leonora Penderton; her shallow but satisfying lover, Maj. Morris Langdon; and her secret admirer, Pvt. Elgee Williams. The others represent the equally limited values of a culture cut off from nature: Capt. Weldon Penderton, who is more attracted to his wife's lovers than to her; Alison Langdon, who is depressed over her deformed infant's death and her husband's infidelity; and Anacleto, who is Alison's adoring servant and fellow aesthete. As Arleen Portada has commented, instead of providing a normative frame of reference among the cast, McCullers suggests the desirability of holism by juxtaposing characters who personify its absence.

The static quality of the characters is reinforced by the suffocating scene of the action. The disarming first sentence – "An army post in peacetime is a dull place" – proves paradoxically true and false: the dullness of the post helps to drive its occupants to excess. The fort gains added menace from the rigid military hierarchy and its violent potential. Even the characters' ventures into the surrounding countryside cannot relieve their tension or correct their imbalance. There is no escape from what encloses them, which is as much internal as external. The result is a conclusion that seems at once shocking and inevitable.

In a cast that constitutes a treasure trove of abnormal psychology, the captain is a prime specimen. Repelled by his wife, he is drawn to the men who love her: one in the flesh (Langdon), the other from afar (Williams). Yet he cannot act on his homosexual desires. His friendship with the major is masochistic, while his relationship with the private is sadistic. Penderton has tolerated Leonora's adultery with his superior officer and next-door neighbor out of affection for him, loathing for her, and fear of being left alone. Likewise, the major's wife has not asked for a divorce, although she is so aggrieved by her husband's callousness that she has cut off her nipples because she is unable to support herself and her servant.

In this relational standoff the private becomes the catalytic character. Presented as a Lawrencian primitive, he cares for Leonora's spirited stallion, Firebird, at the base stable. Obsessed with Leonora, he feels compelled to enter her bedroom periodically at night, unnoticed, so he can watch her sleep. In parallel fashion the captain becomes obsessed with Williams, whom he both desires and despises as his opposite. In a haunting scene of nightmarish intensity, Penderton – a poor horseman as well as a cuckold and coward – mounts Firebird and experiences a "frenzied, runaway ride" through the forest. When the exhausted horse stops at last to rest, he beats it savagely, simultaneously punishing the stallion, its keeper, and its owner for their unbridled vitality. His fury is compounded by the fact that Williams witnesses his subsequent collapse. Shortly thereafter, he surprises and kills the private during one of his nocturnal vigils by Leonora's bedside. It is safe to say that none of the surviving characters is changed, let alone redeemed, by this grotesque, yet oddly compelling tragedy.

McCullers at the time of The Heart Is a Lonely Hunter

The sensationalism of the story is heightened by the incongruously flat style in which it is presented. There is also a decided lack of authorial comment on the bizarre events that unfold. Just as the golden eye of the peacock from the title image reflects without seeing, so the storyteller's voice reports without judging. Eisinger calls the unsettling result neither a defense of deviance nor an attack on convention.

In *The Heart Is a Lonely Hunter,* a more diffuse and compassionate book, the reader is invited to care about most of the characters, however misshapen. By contrast, *Reflections in a Golden Eye* is a tightly plotted, relentlessly bleak tour de force in which it is difficult to identify or sympathize with anyone. Although Harold Bloom found that appreciation of the book had increased with time, critics are still sharply divided on its merits. In the fashion of some early reviews they often part company on the issue of its matter versus its manner, recognizing the clinical skill with which McCullers creates the voice and distance to achieve her desired mood but differing over whether the content justifies such stylistic virtuosity. Graver, for example, finds the book disagreeable and pretentious, while Portada calls it the author's most evocative and intriguing work.

Dust jacket for McCullers's first book, which has been called the last of the proletarian protest novels that were popular during the Great Depression of the 1930s

Reflections in a Golden Eye is still not widely considered one of McCullers's best efforts, but it may yet emerge as a minor masterpiece of the macabre.

Unrequited love, a common manifestation of the spiritual isolation that McCullers identified as her master theme, receives its definitive treatment in *The Ballad of the Sad Café*, which Delma Presley has described as "a nearly perfect allegory of loneliness." McCullers's fascination with this important subtheme is foreshadowed in both earlier books, but in *The Ballad of the Sad Café* – most often cited as her finest longer fiction – McCullers refines her exploration of unfulfilled desire while challenging accepted notions about gender and normality. Critics tend to read *The Ballad of the Sad Café* as a revision of *Reflections in a Golden Eye* within the tradition of the Southern Gothic.

The Ballad of the Sad Café was written during a break from the lengthy composition of *The Member of the Wedding* (1946), McCullers's next novel. Dedicated to David Diamond, *The Ballad of the Sad Café* may have been inspired partly by the author's imaginative reflections about the ménage à trois she and Reeves had nearly established with the composer. She completed the work with ease while staying at Yaddo in the summer of 1941, then put it aside as part of projected trilogy of intermediate-length fictions that never materialized. *Harper's Bazaar* published *The Ballad of the Sad Café* in August 1943, and Houghton Mifflin brought it to a wider audience as a part of the important 1951 omnibus edition of McCullers's fiction. It was adapted for the Broadway stage by Edward Albee in the 1963–1964 season and enjoyed only moderate success.

The perfection of *The Ballad of the Sad Café* on the page, impossible to replicate on the stage, begins with McCullers's storytelling technique, which seems simple and natural but is, in fact, quite sophisticated. The narrative has the occasional digressiveness of oral transmission, as is appropriate for the ballad format suggested by the title, and the narrator's tone of voice – along with the retrospective presentation of the action – helps to cushion the impact of content which at first glance seems bizarre even for McCullers. Sounding like a longtime resident of the nameless southern town where the story occurs, the narrator proves knowledgeable without being omniscient, judgmental yet humane, and capable of eliciting the desired response, which is one of sympathy rather than shock.

A short present-tense frame surrounds the extended flashback that recounts the story itself, now long over. As in the opening of *Reflections in a Golden Eye,* the scene is swiftly set, the main characters introduced, the mood established, and the action to come previewed. The locale is familiar to McCullers readers: a humdrum hamlet described as dreary, lonesome, and estranged – terms that equally apply to its inhabitants. The only form of entertainment is listening to the mournful song of the chain gang. But the situation was not always so, the reader is told. The decline of the town has been paralleled by the deterioration of its largest building. Boarded up and listing to the side stands the shell of a café that once thrived there. The decrepit condition of the building, in turn, resembles that of its hermitic occupant, Miss Amelia Evans, formerly the café proprietor. Her sad fate has been determined by two men: one responsible for bringing the café into existence, the other for causing its ruin. She, her business, and the town have all blossomed briefly, then faded forever.

The three principals inhabit the heightened world of folk literature – specifically, the ballad and the legend. The protagonist, Amelia, stands 6'2" tall and has the "bones and muscles" of a man. Another in a long line of virtually motherless McCullers heroines, she was raised by her late father and is a grown-up tomboy, a modern Amazon. Although the name Amelia and the title Miss mark her as female, her appearance and behavior announce her masculinity. She wears overalls and boots, smokes a pipe, and runs a still. At nineteen she further defies expectations of her sex by accepting the proposal of the unlikely suitor Marvin Macy, a local ladies' man and scoundrel, who surprisingly not only selects the unconventional Amelia for his mate but also reforms on her behalf. The marriage ends ten days later, when the bride brutally repulses the bridegroom for daring to attempt consummation of their union. Forced to flee the town in disgrace, he vows vengeance and turns to a life of crime.

While Marvin serves time in the penitentiary, a hunchbacked dwarf arrives in town, claiming to be Amelia's cousin Lymon Willis. Amelia, formerly the beloved and tyrant, now becomes the lover and slave. Like Marvin, she selects the least likely object for her affection and changes her antisocial ways to win his favor. Lymon may represent the child she lacks, and since he is no sexual threat to her, she accepts him despite his selfish and mischievous ways. In his physical repulsiveness and personality defects, Lymon recalls Antonapoulos, and Amelia is just as improbably smitten as Singer, for love is irrational. It is to McCullers's credit, however, that she shifts the reader's attention from the obvious physical ways in which Amelia and Lymon differ from others to the subtler psychological way in which they are all too typical: "most of us would rather love than be loved." In the triangle of *The Ballad of the Sad Café* each person ultimately plays both roles.

Lymon's turn to suffer unrequited love arrives when Marvin comes back to town, intent on punishing Amelia. Lymon instantly adores Marvin, who despises and abuses him but uses his undiminished ardor (whether hero worship or homosexual desire is unspecified) to strike back at Amelia. The café has been born of Lymon's need for social spectacle, and it becomes the scene of the climax. Before an assembled crowd, the former spouses engage in a second showdown that assumes mock-epic proportions and carries strong sexual overtones. Amelia has Marvin pinned to the floor and is poised to best him once again, when Lymon leaps onto her back so his ally can regain the advantage. After Amelia is soundly beaten, the two men leave town; the café falls into disrepair; and she retreats behind its facade, a reminder that to love is to risk betrayal.

Having rendered the ballad of the sad café, the narrator reprises the song of the chain gang in an epilogue subtitled "The Twelve Mortal Men." Like the townspeople, these men are yoked together for a term of hard labor here on earth. Yet out of their personal sorrow they create collective beauty. Their song, though born of adversity, relieves as it expresses their pain and allows them to overcome their individual suffering, if only briefly. The coda clarifies the point of McCullers's parable and places it in a broader context.

McCullers called *The Ballad of the Sad Café* her fairy tale, and with its giantess and dwarf, spells and metamorphoses, it partially supports this claim. Like many of the author's comments about her work, however, this one can be misleading if taken too literally. The figures in the fabulous tale push the limits of realism to extremes not only to fulfill the conventions of this most extravagant genre but also to challenge rigid gender roles and convenient but suspect psychosocial categories such as "normal" and "abnormal."

In *The Heart Is a Lonely Hunter* McCullers expresses through Mick the adolescent's general unease with bodily change and the teenage girl's added resistance to the social restrictions that womanhood entails. By the end of the novel, however, Mick has conformed to the belief that female virtue

Students and staff at the Bread Loaf Writers' Conference, August 1940: (seated) Edna Frederickson, director Theodore Morrison, and McCullers; (standing) Eudora Welty, John Ciardi, Brainard Cheney, Marion Sims, and Louis Untermeyer

means self-sacrifice, especially for one's family. In *The Ballad of the Sad Café* Amelia seems to escape the consequences of her sex well into adulthood, refusing to look or play the powerless part of a woman and defying legal as well as social conventions regarding wifehood. Yet this open rebellion eventually triggers the backlash that ends in her public defeat and the town's capitulation in that outcome, despite its unfairness. Again, McCullers ultimately punishes her heroine's nonconformity, though she clearly shows its causes and consequences.

With equal boldness she pursues a related theme, the vulnerability of popular notions about normality and abnormality. Whereas in *Reflections in a Golden Eye* she portrayed the grotesque for its own sake, developing her cast as a collective case study in psychopathology, in *The Ballad of the Sad Café* she seems intent on showing that the normal and abnormal differ more in degree than in kind. Brilliantly, she attacks the issue at both ends, simultaneously defamiliarizing the commonplace and regularizing the aberrant.

Hugh Massingham, reviewing the omnibus edition that includes *The Ballad of the Sad Café* for the London *Observer* (20 July 1952), suggests how McCullers accomplishes the first of these effects at the outset: "She starts with what . . . appears to be ordinary," describing "a place where nothing happens." Then, "having made everything apparently safe," she exposes the hidden horror beneath the soothing surface. "Her ordinary people are dead right because they are extraordinary," he concludes about the residents, who "have turned in upon themselves so that they are consumed with loneliness."

In parallel fashion McCullers creates freakish characters not solely for their shock value but also to convey their humanity in all its richness, complexity, and, at times, perversity. In so doing, she also undercuts traditional approaches to such characters, whose outer deformities often signify inner deficiencies. While Lymon (and earlier Antonapoulos) may fit the convention of "ugly is as ugly does," this stereotype and its converse seem far less applicable to Amelia and Marvin. Marvin appears normal, even attractive, to the eye, but emerges as a villain, whereas Amelia looks odd, even grotesque, but gains sympathy as his victim. Instead of making the handsome man a hero and the masculine giantess a monster, McCullers nearly reverses their roles. Significantly, in the end all three characters mirror each other and humankind generally in their need to love and their destiny to do so unwisely.

Best known of all McCullers's works because it has reached audiences as a novel, a play, and a motion picture, *The Member of the Wedding* (1951) tested her powers of persistence as no previous project had done. She began drafting it in 1939, and did not complete it until the summer of 1945. As with the composition of *The Heart Is a Lonely Hunter,* part of the delay was aesthetic in nature: McCullers was slow to grasp the dramatic mainspring of her new book. Then, a year into the writing, it came to her with startling speed. Interrupted while finishing Thanksgiving dinner at February House in 1940, she ran outside with fellow resident Gypsy Rose Lee to check on a siren in the street and suddenly realized that her protagonist wanted to unite with her brother and his bride. Anchored by this vision and sustained by a Guggenheim Fellowship in 1942 and a $1,000 grant from the American Academy of Arts and Letters in 1943, she persevered with the book, which remains one of her most respected achievements. Part 1 of the novel appeared in *Harper's Bazaar* in January 1946, and Houghton Mifflin published the book in March.

Though reviews were mixed, subsequent criticism has been more positive. Writing for *The Saturday Review of Literature* (30 March 1946), George Dangerfield praised the "utmost delicacy and balance" McCullers maintained throughout the novel. In *The New York Times* (24 March 1946) Isa Kapp described McCullers's language as having the "freshness, quaintness, and gentleness" of a child's. Diana Trilling, writing for *The Nation* (6 April 1946), accused the author of overidentifying with Frankie. As far as McCullers was concerned, the most insensitive response came in *The New Yorker* (30 March 1946), where Edmund Wilson declared the book "utterly pointless," lacking in drama and structure.

Critics tend to read *The Member of the Wedding* as a revision of *The Heart Is a Lonely Hunter,* much as they see McCullers's two shorter novels as counterpointed. The longer works are often called less stylized, more realistic narratives united by their greater concern with social context and their sensitive treatment of female adolescence. *The Member of the Wedding* is also considered McCullers's most directly autobiographical work. In her introduction to *The Mortgaged Heart* (1971) Margarita Smith, McCullers's younger sister, stated that of all her sister's characters, "vulnerable, exasperating and endearing," Frankie Addams seemed "to her family and friends most like the author herself." McCullers acknowledged that writing the novel had proven therapeutic in one respect. By describing Frankie's desperate desire to join the departing newlyweds, she recalled and worked through the bereavement and dislocation she had felt when the Tuckers, whom she had considered a second family, moved out of her life in 1934. Years later, she confronted her girlhood heartbreak and put it to literary use. Eventually, when she rewrote the novel for the stage, she resumed contact with the Tuckers and healed the breach in their relationship.

The Member of the Wedding differs from several of McCullers's longer fictions in that it has a clearly identifiable protagonist, Frankie Addams, who is often praised as the author's most fully realized character. In spite of her extensive development, critics disagree about how best to interpret Frankie's problem and its resolution. Part of the difficulty arises because she functions on both universal and gender-specific levels, as her names suggest. As Frankie, she is an adolescent "everyman" in her awkward, agonized movement toward maturation. Yet at the same time, as feminist critics remind readers, she bears the special burden of girlhood, which complicates her transition to adult status. As the novel progresses and she decides to call herself first F. Jasmine and then Frances, she experiments with different shades of gender identity.

In part 1, under the sexually ambiguous diminutive of Frankie, she has enjoyed the relative freedom of childhood as a tomboy. But now that she is nearing thirteen and is almost 5'6", she is outgrowing that stage in her life. In part 2 her insistence on the right to take a new name lets Frankie reinvent herself. The persona of F. Jasmine is an attempt to explore and preserve her androgynous options. The initial *F.* mutes without erasing her prior claim to masculine privilege, as Barbara White notes in an essay collected in Bloom. The name *Jasmine* asserts her identification with her brother, Jarvis, and his fiancée, Janice, the couple she regards as "*the we of me.*" In part 3 she finally accepts her formal given name, Frances, and with it her legal and socially prescribed identity as a young woman.

As the instability of her name indicates, Frankie is beset by the question of identity. Cut off from her past and fearful of her future, she is "a difficult girl at a difficult age," in the words of reviewer Sterling North (*Book Week,* 24 March 1946). The Addamses, like most families in McCullers's writings, impede rather than ease her rite of passage: her mother and brother do so by their absence. (Mrs. Addams died when Frankie was born, probably contributing to her daughter's fear of female sexuality, and Jarvis has served with the army in Alaska for the past two years.) Her father does so by his remoteness. (He works long hours at his jewelry store.) In a revelation that likely jars readers in the 1990s more than it did in the 1950s, the narrator — who tells the story from Frankie's perspective — explains that Frankie has slept in the same bed with her father until a few months before the novels opens, when he finally noticed how big she had

Tennessee Williams and Carson McCullers

grown. Frankie interprets this overdue separation as rejection and compensates by inviting her six-year-old cousin, John Henry West, to stay overnight so he can bunk with her. John Henry becomes a substitute brother and the symbol of the childish innocence Frankie must surrender, while Berenice Sadie Brown, the family's black cook, becomes the maternal figure from whom she must separate and the symbol of adult wisdom she must acquire.

Her peers add to Frankie's desperation. Her best friend has moved away. She is pointedly excluded from a local club of teenage girls because of her immaturity; yet the neighborhood children's games bore her. A recent episode of rudimentary sex play with a boy leaves her disturbed, but instead of seeking information about sexuality, she denies or represses the stray facts that come her way.

Frankie not only feels like a secret sinner because of this incident, she also feels like a covert criminal because she has shoplifted – and like an incipient freak because of her height. Furthermore, she is convinced that prisoners in the jail and freaks in the sideshow identify her as one of their own. Despite her histrionics, she is none of the things she fears – pervert, crook, or grotesque. She is only a girl engaged in the natural process of acting out and testing limits that precedes maturation.

On the surface Berenice may seem an odd person to serve as Frankie's guide. She has been married four times, but only once happily – to her first husband, Ludie Freeman, whom she wed at thirteen. After his death, she tried to replicate their relationship with others, but each of her successive mates was more disastrous than the previous one. The second was a drunk, the third crazy, and the fourth so abusive that he gouged out her left eye, now replaced by one made of blue glass. Yet Berenice is the soul of sanity, and without her support Frankie would be desolate.

In an interesting reverse effect, even the genuine grotesques in the novel – the freaks from the carnival – are normalized after a fashion by being linked implicitly to mainstream characters. Frankie, of course, identifies with the eight-foot-tall giant. Berenice working biscuit dough in the kitchen is reminiscent of the fat lady pounding her girth on the midway. The midget seems like John Henry, who appears wise for his years. The "Wild Nigger" from a savage land is like Berenice's foster brother, Honey Brown, who looks Cuban, smokes reefers, and runs "hog wild" before he is jailed.

Frankie's problem reaches crisis proportions on the last weekend in August 1944. She has suffered through a long Georgia summer without the reassuring routine of school, and now the sweltering dog days have made the kitchen an inferno she must escape. The war has also elevated her sense of exclusion from life's drama to a global level. As Susan Gubar argues, the army seems like a fraternity designed to keep her stifled at home while it lets Jarvis travel to cooler, more exotic climes.

On Friday, when Jarvis brings Janice to meet the family, Frankie sees their impending marriage as the answer to her prayers. She will join herself to them after the ceremony on Sunday, fulfilling her fantasies of affiliation and adventure. Unfortunately this dream reveals the full extent of her naïveté about married life and the military. On Saturday Frankie's ignorance of sex and glamorization of soldiering lead to unwelcome advances by a serviceman she meets in a bar; on Sunday her dream drowns out Berenice's warnings and causes Frankie public humiliation when she tries to accompany the newlyweds on their honeymoon, only to be restrained by her father.

After the bride and groom leave she runs away but lets herself be found because she has nowhere else to go. Time, not space, will ease her woes, though it is not so generous with her summer companions. By November, when the action closes, the weather is cool, and school has resumed. Frances has turned thirteen, and she has a new best friend. Since the Addamses are moving, Berenice's services are no longer needed. She will marry a fifth husband, a businessman who is more respectable than exciting. John Henry has died of meningitis, a tragedy that some readers find gratuitous but which Gubar interprets as the symbolic end of Frankie's boyish self. Critics also disagree about how to evaluate Frances's changed condition. Those who have defined her problem as loneliness and its solution as association take hope because with her new friend she seems happy and self-accepting. Yet this adjustment comes at a cost: she is dismissive with Berenice, indifferent to the loss of John Henry, and full of new illusions that differ from the old ones mainly by being more conventional. White notes the irony that in gaining her membership, Frances appears to have lost her self. But, as with Mick, this loss may be the price of negotiating the distance between childhood and womanhood.

As McCullers acknowledged in her preface to *The Square Root of Wonderful* (1958), "It is rare that a writer is equally skilled as a novelist and a playwright." Though she proved more adept at fiction than at drama, her adaptation of *The Member of the Wedding* for the Broadway stage is generally regarded as faithful to the original and effective theater in its own right. It is also the last major achievement of her career, one that helped widen her audience, consolidate her reputation, and secure her financial future.

McCullers's theatrical background was virtually nonexistent when she undertook the task of adapting *The Member of the Wedding*. (She had written plays as a girl and had attended a few professional productions.) Yet she maintained high confidence in her versatility and respected the source of the suggestion that she consider dramatizing *The Member of the Wedding*. Tennessee Williams had read her novel in May 1946 and, sensing that he and McCullers were soul mates, had invited her to summer with him in Nantucket. There, he persuaded her that the book had dramatic possibilities, and they worked each morning – he on *Summer and Smoke* (1947) and she on her adaptation. Both insisted that they were merely friends, not collaborators.

After McCullers finished, her agent, Ann Watkins, reported that no one wanted to produce the play as it stood, but that the Theatre Guild would stage it if McCullers agreed to revise it in conjunction with an experienced playwright. Much to her later regret, McCullers signed a contract with Greer Johnson. After seeing his revision, she was outraged. She dictated a new version and hired a new agent. Johnson sued her for $50,000; the case went to arbitration in November 1948; and the settlement tied up the project for another year.

Finally, veteran director Harold Clurman agreed to take on *The Member of the Wedding* as his fiftieth production, but not without reservations. It was different from any play he had ever done, and its unconventionality made it a risky venture on Broadway. Still, he located its main line of action and felt confident he could dramatize it.

When Ethel Waters read the script in spring 1949, she initially refused the part of Berenice, saying the play was godless. Later, however, the actress met McCullers, who agreed to let Waters interpret the role in her own way. Waters wanted to undercut the mammy stereotype implicit in Berenice's characterization, but she saw her main task as uniting the action without shifting audience attention from Frankie. While Berenice is clearly secondary to Frankie in the novel, the two have a nearly equal number of lines in the play, according to Oliver Evans. Twenty-three-year-old Julie Harris faced her own challenge when chosen to play twelve-year-old Frankie. Novice child star Brandon de Wilde, cast

McCullers and director Harold Clurman going over the script for the dramatic version of The Member of the Wedding, *1949 (photograph by Eileen Darby, Graphic House, Inc.)*

as John Henry, more than managed to hold his own.

When previews of the show opened in Philadelphia on 22 December 1949, its running time was four hours, and cuts had to be made. McCullers insisted on final approval of any changes. She agreed with Clurman and Williams that the barroom scene with the soldier was expendable, allowing the entire action as she had reenvisioned it to take place in the Addams kitchen and yard. With this alteration the play opened on Broadway on 5 January 1950 before an enthusiastic audience. In a run that extended for 501 performances, it grossed more than $1 million. Ineligible for the Pulitzer Prize because it was not an original work, *The Member of the Wedding* won the New York Drama Critics' Circle Award. The three principals reprised their roles in the 1953 Hollywood movie version based on the play.

Reviewers were nearly unanimous in their praise for the players, but they were puzzled by the play. Those connected with the project had recognized its problematic nature from the outset. McCullers knew that dramatizing her novel meant making explicit much that was merely implicit in the original. She also saw that her story lacked a literal antagonist; what Frankie confronted, instead of an opponent, was an abstraction — her need to belong. Clurman agreed that the script was talky and static, with little dramatic movement and no climax. Yet, rather than altering the material to meet the demands of a well-made plot, McCullers and Clurman preserved the qualities that made *The Member of the Wedding* distinctive: its strong central characters, unifying theme, and evocative mood.

The play's formlessness attracted comment from most reviewers. In a largely favorable notice for *The New York Times* (6 January 1950) Brooks Atkinson commented that *The Member of the Wedding* had "practically no dramatic movement" and might not even qualify as a play. Still, he judged it to be art. Unconvinced, Eric Bentley, writing on "The American Drama, 1944-1954" in Alan Downer's *American Drama and Its Critics* (1965), called *The Member of the Wedding* "a little story prolonged by theatrical legerdemain." Even John Van Druten, a champion of the play, confessed in *Playwright at Work* (1953) that it barely moved for the first two acts, and then developed its plot primarily between scenes in the third. In his view, however, this lack of action did not matter because *The Member of the Wedding* was a mood play and a successful one at that. In his *American Drama Since World War II* (1962) Gerald Weales considered the third act flawed by an abrupt, melodramatic shift in tone caused by the offstage deaths of John Henry and Honey Brown in quick succession. (Brown hangs himself in jail — a change from the novel.) Yet Weales insisted that *The Member of the Wedding* represented an innovative advance in dramatic structure.

After the triumphs of the novel and play versions of *The Member of the Wedding*, McCullers's last two major works were disappointing, compromised by circumstances surrounding their creation. They evince her growing obsession with death, occasioned by her own worsening health as well as by the loss of close family members, and also her compulsion to continue writing for her life until its end.

While drafting her play *The Square Root of Wonderful* (1958), McCullers was trying to deal with the suicide of her husband in 1953 and the death of her mother in 1955. She refused to mourn Reeves, but she felt guilty about her role in his self-destruction. She found it easier to grieve for Marguerite, although her mother's constant concern had been smothering at times. In developing the characters and situations in *The Square Root of Wonderful* McCullers drew on her complex, unresolved feelings about these central figures in her life. Evans has commented that McCullers remained too close to her material, never establishing the distance necessary for full artistic control.

The challenge of confronting painful emotions was heightened by the nature of writing for the theater. McCullers knew that the stage play was an inherently plastic medium grounded in the pragmatics of performance. Nevertheless the nature and extent of the collaborative effort involved in producing her own drama differed markedly. When she wrote the script for *The Member of the Wedding* she was a newcomer to playwriting, but she had the advantage of working from her own novel. *The Square Root of Wonderful* represented her first and last attempt as a professional writer to craft a play de novo. In addition she retained less control over the final version of *The Square Root of Wonderful* than she did with *The Member of the Wedding*.

When she completed the first draft of *The Square Root of Wonderful* at Yaddo in mid 1954, McCullers began intensive rewriting of the play with Arnold Saint Subber, the coproducer. For the next few years they worked together almost daily, but the result was a moving target rather than a finished product. The script underwent more than a dozen revisions without ever attaining the final form McCullers sought. Anne Baxter, cast in the lead role, attributed the eventual failure of the play to the fact that no one could handle the necessary rewrites – neither the author nor the three directors nor the various script doctors who came and went, sometimes making changes McCullers did not approve.

Following ominous preview engagements in Princeton and Philadelphia, the play opened on Broadway on 30 October 1957 to disastrous notices. It closed after forty-five performances. Although *The Square Root of Wonderful* did not prove cathartic for its audience, its failure released the author to complete her grieving process – for Reeves, Marguerite, and her latest brainchild. The poor reception of this play was the low point in her career, and she sought help from Dr. Mary Mercer, a psychiatrist who soon dismissed McCullers as a patient but became her close friend.

Because McCullers never finished *The Square Root of Wonderful* to her satisfaction, its text exists only in compromised form. She converted an early version into "Who Has Seen the Wind?," a chilling short story about the destructive effects of terminal writer's block and alcoholism on a marriage somewhat like her own. Published in the September 1956 issue of *Mademoiselle*, this companion piece to the play – and longest of the short stories McCullers published in her lifetime – traces the dying fall of Ken Harris. Taking its title from a children's poem, the story uses wind to symbolize everything Ken must lose: the spirit of creativity, the vitality of love, and the breath of life itself. Ken exhibits some aspects of both Carson and Reeves: like her, he has had a successful first novel and a failed second book; like Reeves, he longs to write but cannot, loves his wife but abuses her, and threatens both their lives.

In 1958 Houghton Mifflin published McCullers's last written version of the play, along with a defensive yet revealing authorial preface. Here she disclosed both the personal sources of its life/death theme and the chaotic conditions that had compromised her original vision. Significantly, McCullers never tried to write another play from scratch, nor did she complete her final collaboration on a musical version of *The Member of the Wedding* with Mary Rodgers.

Despite its title, which is more striking than apt, the mathematical construct on which the action of *The Square Root of Wonderful* rests is the romantic triangle, signaled by the subtitle: "A Love Story." At the apex stands the protagonist, Mollie Lovejoy, torn between suitors who represent opposing values: her two-time former husband, Phillip – a failed writer, problem drinker, and abusive spouse who returns to their upstate New York farm to plead for another reconciliation; and John Tucker, a successful architect and temporary tenant at the farm. Paris, Mollie and Phillip's twelve-year-old son, favors his father's suit, as does Phillip's domineering mother, who is visiting along with her spinster daughter, Loreena. Because Phillip appeals to Mollie's maternal and romantic instincts ("the closest thing to being cared for is to care for someone else," she says in a refrain from *The Ballad of the Sad Café*), her decision is not a foregone conclusion. It comes down to a choice between building a future and embracing life with John or repeating the past and risking self-annihilation with Phillip. When Mollie chooses John, Phillip drives his car into a pond and drowns, having tried to take Paris with him (the better to punish her).

By vindicating her heroine's judgment, McCullers sought to justify her own decision to leave Reeves despite the consequences. Yet – like "Who Has Seen the Wind?" – *The Square Root of Wonderful* represents transmuted rather than literal autobiography, for McCullers endows Mollie as well as Mother Lovejoy with aspects of Marguerite (her resilience and intrusiveness), gives Reeves's military service to John, and supplies Phillip with some of her own experiences. He has been reared by an ambitious mother, known early success and subsequent failure as a writer, and attempted suicide by slashing his wrists. He even speaks lines from one of her poems, "When We Are Lost."

Critical comment on the published version of the play has been no kinder on the whole than reaction to the staged production. Evans is too generous in claiming that the drama reads better than it plays. Weales is closer to the mark when he says its major characters never come to life, especially Phillip, that "dramatically dullest" of souls, the blocked writer. Even the minor characters disappoint: overbearing Mother Lovejoy and her eligible daughter are obviously indebted to Amanda and Laura Wingfield in Tennessee Williams's *The Glass Menagerie* (1944), and Paris, saddled with a nickname that is too young (Lambie) and a vocabulary that is too old, is the last thing one expects from McCullers – an unconvincing adolescent. In *Best Plays of 1957–58* (1968) Louis Kronenberger discerned in the play's competing themes, tones, and tempos "a talent in hopeless disarray." It is not surprising that *The Square Root of Wonderful* has never been revived or adapted to the screen.

Many of McCullers's family, friends, and fans wondered if her final novel, *Clock Without Hands*, would ever be published; after it finally appeared in 1961, some readers and reviewers questioned whether it should have been. McCullers began writing the novel in 1951 and finished it in 1960 after many interruptions, mostly medical. Because her previous novel had appeared a decade and a half earlier and her recent play had been a failure, a great deal was at stake for both author and audience. To her closest companions it seemed miraculous that she had brought the book to closure at all, but this sentiment could not be expected to govern its popular or critical reception.

McCullers corrected galleys in early 1961, assisted by her cousin Jordan Massee and her friend Mary Mercer. During this process Massee called many textual errors to the author's attention, but he found her impatient with editorial suggestions. Advance copies were sent out later that year. When Williams received his, he felt that McCullers needed to revise chapter 4 and redraw the character of Sherman Pew. He urged Massee to persuade the author to postpone publication. Massee understood Williams's concern and admitted that the novel lacked McCullers's usual polish, but he – along with Dr. Mercer – believed that his cousin's psychological well-being depended on the book going to press without further delay. Because McCullers was scheduled for surgery soon, Williams acquiesced, and Houghton Mifflin published the novel in September 1961. Two chapters had appeared previously in periodicals: chapter 1, "The Pestle," in the July 1953 issues of *Botteghe Oscure* (a literary magazine published in Rome) and *Mademoiselle,* and chapter 3, "To Bear the Truth Alone," in the July 1961 issue of *Harper's Bazaar*.

The novel remained on best-seller lists for five months, but it was more of a commercial than a critical success, especially in the United States. Paul Binding, a British critic, called it one of the best Southern novels ever written and unsurpassed on its period. In an essay collected in Bloom, Klaus Lubbers detected in *Clock Without Hands* the culmination of a gradual thematic movement in McCullers's fiction "from the freakish to the wholesome" and "from chaos to order." American critics felt for the most part that she had moved backward rather than forward. Donald Emerson expressed a common complaint, observing that she had been unable to fuse either the realistic and symbolical levels of the story or the private and public roles of characters. *Clock Without Hands* is the only one of McCullers's longer fictions that has not remained in print or been adapted to stage or screen.

Many elements in *Clock Without Hands* are recognizable from her earlier novels: the contemporary small-town setting in the South, the absence of a clear protagonist or central event, the juxtaposition of characters with symbolic overtones, and the concern with barriers to self-knowledge and interpersonal understanding. In its dominant focus, however, *Clock Without Hands* represents a shift in emphasis from her novels, a transition sometimes described as being from eros or personal passion to agape or universal brotherly love.

Written in the closing years of the Depression, *The Heart Is a Lonely Hunter* reflects the politically conscious fiction of the 1930s in its realistic portrayal of capitalistic excess and racial injustice, even as it anticipates the 1940s trend toward fiction about psychological estrangement with its treatment of spiritual isolation. In *The Heart Is a Lonely Hunter* and *The Member of the Wedding* societal concerns generally and race relations specifically contribute to the context without being foregrounded as they are in *Clock Without Hands*. By turning her primary attention from interior experience to the social condition, McCullers may have been registering once again her sensitivity to the changing national mood. During the decade in which the novel was written, civil rights assumed greater urgency for Americans.

Carson and Reeves McCullers in Bachvillers, outside Paris, 1952 (photograph by Louise Dahl-Wolfe)

Although her health never permitted McCullers to be an activist in liberal causes, she had used her pen both as a private citizen and a public figure to protest injustice and promote equality. Therefore, her decision to write an explicitly political novel was not totally unexpected, although in retrospect it was probably unwise because it deflected her from her greatest strength as an author.

In another way, too, *Clock Without Hands* represents a departure for McCullers. *The Heart Is a Lonely Hunter* and *The Member of the Wedding* are both recognized for their sensitive portrayals of troubled female adolescents, with Mick and Frankie's problems overshadowing the struggles of the older characters around them. The four main characters in *Clock Without Hands* – all male – are equally divided between a younger generation facing an uncertain future and an older generation facing a foreshortened one, but the story dwells more heavily on the dread of death that darkens middle and old age. The opening sentence – "Death is always the same, but each man dies in his own way" – rewrites the famous first line of Leo Tolstoy's *Anna Karenina* (1873-1876), while the fate of McCullers's frame character, J. T. Malone, echoes the doomed hero's odyssey toward self-discovery in Tolstoy's *The Death of Ivan Ilych* (1886). When Malone learns in chapter 1 that he has incurable leukemia, he reacts with shock, disbelief, anger, and sorrow – and then searches unsuccessfully for solace in religion, friends, and family. Finally he finds salvation by seizing what is left of his unlived life to assert his better self for the first time. He refuses to carry out a vigilante group's death sentence on Sherman Pew, a black youth who defies white supremacy in the last days of legalized segregation by moving into a restricted area. Time is running out on Malone and on the traditional Southern way of life. McCullers thus links directly the transformation of a diseased individual with that of a sick society.

To make this transition Malone must break with the values embodied by his hero, Fox Clane, a judge and former congressman who is representative of the Old South and – not coincidentally – is mentally as well as physically enfeebled. Despite their long friendship Malone and Clane are more different than alike. Malone, only forty when he becomes ill, is an ordinary man who avoids the limelight until fear for his immortal soul triggers his modest act of heroism. Clane, an older man, is an outsized personality whose public posturing on behalf of doomed ideas is admired by his peers but satirized by the author. In his last scene Clane goes on the radio to attack the Supreme Court desegregation ruling but forgets himself and ironically lapses into the Gettysburg Address, a speech he knows by heart. The contrast between the quiet courage of the dying druggist and the incoherent ravings of the senile judge could not be more complete.

McCullers at her home in Nyack, New York, 1957

A more contrived and confused pairing occurs between Jester Clane, the judge's grandson, and Sherman Pew, the judge's servant. Both are orphans searching for identity, and in finding the truth about their fathers they find themselves — one for better, the other for worse. Jester shares his late father's liberalism, which puts him on a collision course with the judge; Sherman, a foundling, learns that he is the son of a black man and his white lover, a married woman. Just as Sherman discovers the source of his mixed blood and follows in his father's footsteps toward a violent end, so Jester learns the truth about the death of his father, John, a promising lawyer who unsuccessfully defended Sherman's father for murdering his lover's husband. After Judge Clane sentenced his son's client to death, John killed himself. Armed with this information about the father he never knew, Jester tries to save Sherman from certain death, as his father tried to save Sherman's father. He warns Sherman about a plan to bomb his home, but cannot prevent the martyrdom his friend now seeks. After passing up the chance to execute Sherman's killer, Jester decides to study law and complete the work begun by his father.

It is not just the overreliance on coincidence in these converging plotlines that makes the story of the younger generation less compelling. Another serious flaw is that Sherman never comes into clear focus. His values and actions oscillate wildly. At times his intellectual pretensions, materialistic values, and pathological lies make him shallow and pathetic. At other times he engages in acts of cruelty that are villainous and sadistic, such as denying the judge his insulin or hanging Jester's dog. His love/hate relationship with Jester epitomizes the inconsistency of his characterization. Jester is attracted to Sherman but spurned when he acts on his desire. Ostensibly, this rejection is motivated by Sherman's hatred of homosexuality. (He was sexually assaulted as a boy by his foster father.) Yet, in another of McCullers's chains of unrequited love, Sherman seems as obsessed with his landlord, Zippo Mullins, as Jester is with him. Given these contradictions in his portrayal, it is difficult to take Sherman's suicidal gesture as the clearcut heroic statement on racial injustice it seems intended to be.

The last book by McCullers to appear during her lifetime was also her slightest in both size and substance. Confined by ill health to modest projects, she began composing light verse for children. She had long made the vicissitudes of childhood her special literary province, and although she remained childless, she enjoyed the children of friends. She wrote the short and simple nonsense rhymes that largely make up *Sweet as a Pickle and Clean as a Pig* (1964) for the children of her lawyer and the son of her agent. After an editor saw a sampling of the rhymes, they were collected with illustrations by Rolf Gerard. Houghton Mifflin published the slender volume in the fall of 1964, and excerpts appeared in *Redbook* that December. Readers must have agreed with the lukewarm notices because, like McCullers's last novel, it went out of print and was never republished. These lyrics show no sign of McCullers's magic with language and support the conclusion that she was more skillful at writing about children than for them.

More vital to shaping an assessment of her canon is *The Mortgaged Heart,* a posthumously published collection of McCullers's short stories, nonfiction, and poetry selected and introduced by her sister, Margarita Smith, a writer and editor. In this convenient volume Smith assembled much of McCullers's published but uncollected work, along with several early unpublished stories written for Sylvia Bates and included with her perceptive comments. Posthumous release of work considered unpublishable during an author's lifetime often harms rather than helps a reputation, but because McCullers routinely destroyed writing that did not please her, and because Smith generally excluded incomplete or redundant work, the collection minimizes this problem.

This volume contributes to a fuller appreciation of McCullers's canon in several ways. The apprentice stories offer interesting early versions of themes, characters, situations, and techniques that recur in her mature work. Furthermore, the short fiction and the nonfiction provide fascinating evidence of how the author represented her experiences for literary purposes. Carr points out that the self-portraits in the stories were often more covert than those in the longer fiction. As Margaret McDowell observes, critical neglect of McCullers's stories contributes to overgeneralizations about her fiction based mainly on her longer works. McCullers's short fiction is less likely to be set in the South or to feature grotesques, for instance. Finally, by drawing together many of McCullers's occasional poems, es-

Isak Dinesen and Carson McCullers, Nyack, New York, May 1959

says, and articles, the book documents the various forms that she employed over the years.

Despite their availability in *The Mortgaged Heart,* McCullers's poetry and nonfiction continue to be largely ignored. She turned to writing poems later in her career than most authors, and the results were often disappointing to readers accustomed to the poetic quality of her prose. Her most ambitious effort was "The Dual Angel: A Meditation on Origin and Choice," a five-part cycle intended as her Christmas greeting in 1951. As the title suggests, the poem is a metaphysical exploration of the warring aspects of human nature, which McCullers traces to the consummation of God and Lucifer that created humankind. She was proud of this work and dedicated it to her friend and fellow poet Edith Sitwell, who had entertained McCullers in England during its composition in the summer of 1951. Her other published poems are short lyrics, of which "When We Are Lost" is representative. Its two stanzas suggest the writer's admiration for Emily Dickinson, whose manner of dressing in white McCullers imitated late in her own life.

Here McCullers speaks for all who have known existential despair, "transfixed among the self-inflicted ruins," in "agony immobilized."

McCullers's expository prose is interesting mainly for its occasional power to illuminate her creative writing. Like the rest of her work it is uneven. As Smith acknowledged, many of McCullers's essays and articles were done as a change of pace and for ready money. In addition, some – such as her holiday reflections – were probably written under deadline. The most important essays are "The Russian Realists and Southern Literature" (*Decision,* July 1941) and "The Flowering Dream: Notes on Writing" (*Esquire,* December 1959).

In "The Russian Realists and Southern Literature" one can trace some of the influences that shaped her artistic vision. McCullers laments the fact that so much Southern literature since William Faulkner has been termed *Gothic* and prefers to locate the source of its horror and beauty not in the romantic or supernatural but in a "peculiar and intense realism" derived from Fyodor Dostoyevsky. Comparing the modern South to old Russia, she explains the basis for this compatibility in an argument full of what Richard Cook calls "remarkable critical insight." Ironically, although her intention was to correct the mislabeling of modern Southern literature, her very use of the term *Gothic* may have contributed to its heavy-handed application in her own case. "The Flowering Dream: Notes on Writing," which McCullers was still refining until her death, is less a coherently developed argument than a series of distilled insights into the mysteries of the creative process. Full of tantalizing though occasionally misleading comments about her past accomplishments, it also has a prospective air, as if the author were renewing her strength in order to continue her life's work.

Several of the essays are embarrassing if read as art today; yet they have other virtues. The pieces written about World War II are full of patriotic portent that dates badly, yet lends them historical interest as evidence of how McCullers identified with popular attitudes of the time. "A Hospital Christmas Eve" (*Redbook,* December 1967), her last completed work, derives its sole significance from that melancholy fact, and – along with her last play, her last novel, and her last book – suggests the aptness of Louis Rubin's conclusion that when McCullers died few readers believed her best writing remained undone. In the end she was haunted by her reputation as a wunderkind who had failed to "develop or extend her range." Yet in his preface to Carr's indispensable biography, *The Lonely Hunter* (1975), Tennessee Williams reminds the reader, "When physical catastrophes reduce, too early, an artist's power, his/her admirers must not and need not enter a plea nor offer apology. It is not quantity, after all, that the artist is to be judged by. It is quality...." Judged in this light, McCullers left in her fiction of the 1940s a legacy that seems likely to endure.

Bibliographies:

Robert F. Kiernan, *Katherine Anne Porter and Carson McCullers: A Reference Guide* (Boston: G. K. Hall, 1976);

Adrian M. Shapiro, Jackson R. Bryer, and Kathleen Field, *Carson McCullers: A Descriptive Listing and Annotated Bibliography of Criticism* (New York: Garland, 1980);

Virginia Spencer Carr, "Carson McCullers," in *Contemporary Authors Bibliographical Series: American Novelists,* edited by James J. Martine (Detroit: Gale Research, 1986), pp. 293–345;

Carr and Laurie A. Scott, "Carson McCullers," in *Bibliography of American Fiction, 1919–1988,* 2 volumes, edited by Matthew J. Bruccoli and Judith S. Baughman (New York: Facts On File, 1991), II: 338–341.

Biographies:

Oliver Evans, *Carson McCullers: Her Life and Work* (London: Owen, 1965); republished as *The Ballad of Carson McCullers* (New York: Coward-McCann, 1966);

Virginia Spencer Carr, *The Lonely Hunter: A Biography of Carson McCullers* (Garden City, N.Y.: Doubleday, 1975).

References:

Eric Bentley, "The American Drama, 1944–1954," in *American Drama and Its Critics: A Collection of Critical Essays,* edited by Alan Downer (Chicago: University of Chicago Press, 1965), pp. 188–202;

Paul Binding, *Separate Country: A Literary Journey Through the American South* (Jackson: University Press of Mississippi, 1988);

Harold Bloom, ed., *Carson McCullers* (New York: Chelsea House, 1986);

Virginia Spencer Carr, *Understanding Carson McCullers* (Columbia: University of South Carolina Press, 1990);

Richard Cook, *Carson McCullers* (New York: Ungar, 1975);

Chester Eisinger, *Fiction of the Forties* (Chicago: University of Chicago Press, 1963);

Donald Emerson, "The Ambiguities of *Clock Without Hands*," *Wisconsin Studies in Contemporary Literature*, 3 (Fall 1962): 15–28;

Barbara Farrelly, "*The Heart Is a Lonely Hunter*: A Literary Symphony," *Pembroke*, 20 (1988): 16–23;

Leslie Fiedler, *Love and Death in the American Novel*, revised edition (New York: Stein & Day, 1966);

Sandra Gilbert and Susan Gubar, *No Man's Land: The Place of the Woman Writer in the Twentieth Century* (New Haven: Yale University Press, 1990);

Lawrence Graver, *Carson McCullers* (Minneapolis: University of Minnesota Press, 1969);

Linda Huf, *A Portrait of the Artist as a Young Woman: The Writer as Heroine in American Literature* (New York: Ungar, 1983);

Louis Kronenberger, ed., *The Best Plays of 1957–58* (New York: Dodd, Mead, 1968);

Margaret McDowell, *Carson McCullers* (Boston: Twayne, 1980);

Arleen Portada, "Sex-Role Rebellion and the Failure of Marriage in the Fiction of Carson McCullers," *Pembroke*, 20 (1988): 63–71;

Delma Presley, "Carson McCullers and the South," *Georgia Review*, 28 (Spring 1974): 19–32;

Rex Reed, *Do You Sleep in the Nude?* (New York: New American Library, 1968), pp. 48–54;

Louis Rubin, *A Gallery of Southerners* (Baton Rouge: Louisiana State University Press, 1982);

John Van Druten, *Playwright at Work* (New York: Harper, 1953);

Gerald Weales, *American Drama Since World War II* (New York: Harcourt, Brace & World, 1962);

Louise Westling, *Sacred Groves and Ravaged Gardens: The Fiction of Eudora Welty, Carson McCullers, and Flannery O'Connor* (Athens: University of Georgia Press, 1985).

Papers:

The Harry Ransom Humanities Research Center, University of Texas at Austin, acquired a collection of McCullers's papers in 1974–1975 through the writer's literary estate. It includes manuscripts, galley and page proofs, correspondence, photographs, and memorabilia that were in McCullers's possession at the time of her death in 1967. The Robert Flower Collection at Duke University also includes many relevant materials, including letters of Jordan Massee, Mary Tucker, Dr. Mary Mercer, Edward Albee, Edith Sitwell, and Tennessee Williams – with all of whom McCullers corresponded.

Gloria Naylor

(25 January 1950 -)

Vashti Crutcher Lewis
Northern Illinois University

BOOKS: *The Women of Brewster Place* (New York: Viking, 1982; London: Methuen, 1987);
Linden Hills (New York: Ticknor & Fields, 1985; London: Hodder & Stoughton, 1985);
Mama Day (New York: Ticknor & Fields, 1988; London: Hutchinson, 1988);
Bailey's Cafe (New York: Harcourt Brace Jovanovich, 1992; London: Heinemann, 1992).

PLAY PRODUCTION: *Staging a Novel: Bailey's Cafe,* New York City, Mitzi Newhouse Theater, 27 October 1992.

OTHER: *Children of the Night: The Best Short Stories by Black Writers, 1967 to the Present,* edited by Naylor (Boston: Little, Brown, 1995).

SELECTED PERIODICAL PUBLICATIONS – UNCOLLECTED:
FICTION
"A Life on Beekman Place," *Essence,* 9 (March 1979): 84-96;
"When Mama Comes to Call," *Essence,* 13 (August 1982): 78-81.
NONFICTION
"A Message to Winston: To Black Men Who Are Gay," *Essence,* 13 (November 1982): 79-85;
"Love and Sex in the Afro-American Novel," *Yale Review,* 78 (Autumn 1988): 19-31.

The emergence of Gloria Naylor on the American literary scene was sudden – *The Women of Brewster Place* (1982) was her first book – and intense, as Naylor added her voice to those of the few black women who write about real African Americans. Like Paule Marshall, Toni Morrison, and Alice Walker, Naylor writes about characters whose experiences and vernacular more closely resemble those of the majority of black people than those depicted by most earlier black women novelists, both of the nineteenth century and the Harlem Renaissance. Naylor continues the tradition of Zora Neale

Gloria Naylor, 1992 (AP/Wide World)

Hurston, the first African American woman novelist to write without the constrictions of a "double consciousness" to create an art form that explores the richness and complexities of African American life. Naylor's first published fiction, the short stories "A Life on Beekman Place" (March 1979) and "When Mama Comes to Call" (August 1982), appeared in *Essence* magazine. Both stories later became chapters – "The Two" and "Kiswana Browne" – in *The Women of Brewster Place.* In a 1985 conversation with Morrison, Naylor recalled that Marcia Gillespie, the *Essence* editor who read her first short story, gave her the confidence and courage to commit herself to writing. She began crafting *The Women of Brewster Place,* which won the 1983 American Book Award for best first novel, while attending Brooklyn College and working as a switchboard operator. In 1989 Naylor became well known nationwide after the American Broadcasting Company and Harpo Productions produced a highly successful television miniseries based on the novel.

The oldest of three daughters, Gloria Naylor was born to Roosevelt and Alberta McAlpin Naylor in Queens, New York, on 25 January 1950. Her parents had lived in Mississippi, working as sharecroppers; they moved to New York in search of a proper education for their child. In New York Roosevelt Naylor was employed as a subway motorman, and Alberta Naylor worked as a telephone operator. Gloria was a precocious and quiet child who seldom talked, read a book a day, and wrote what her third-grade teacher thought was terrifying science fiction. Recognizing her seven-year-old daughter's creativity, Naylor's mother bought Gloria a small diary in which to write her thoughts. Naylor later began filling spiral notebooks with observations, poems, and short stories. She was a determined and strong-willed teenager who, after graduation from high school in Queens, defied her father by refusing to attend a New York college of his choosing.

After seven years as a Jehovah's Witness missionary in New York and the South, Naylor worked at odd jobs in New York City from 1975 to 1981, finally earning enough to enter Brooklyn College, where she majored in English and earned a B.A. in 1981. A new literary world opened for her in college, where she read fiction by Hurston, Walker, Marshall, and other black women novelists. In a 1993 interview with Allison Gloch, Naylor exclaimed, "I was 27 years old before I knew Black women even wrote books." She went on to Yale University, where she earned an M.A. in African American studies (1983) and wrote her second novel, *Linden Hills* (1985).

After *The Women of Brewster Place* won an American Book Award in 1983, Naylor began receiving other awards and fellowships, including a Guggenheim Fellowship in 1988. By 1992 she had written four critically acclaimed novels.

The critics recognized the brilliance of Naylor's first novel, praising her rich prose, her lyrical portrayals of African Americans, and her illumination of the meaning of being a black woman in America. Reviews and critical essays on Naylor's fiction have often pointed to themes of deferred dreams of love (familial and sexual), marriage, respectability, and economic stability, while observing the recurring messages that poverty breeds violence, that true friendship and affection are not dependent on gender, and that women in the black ghettos of America bear their burdens with grace and courage.

Set mostly in the 1960s with flashbacks to the 1920s, *The Women of Brewster Place* is a tightly focused novel peopled with well-delineated, realistically portrayed African American women. Naylor's use of authentic African American vernacular and precise metaphors are hallmarks of *The Women of Brewster Place*. There are no white characters of significance in the novel, but whites are ever present as unseen modifiers of the lives of the seven women whose stories are told.

These women arrive on Brewster Place, a microcosm of African American urban communities, from the rural South and the urban North. Their characterizations are based on black women Naylor had observed and been fascinated by all her life. Each chapter focuses on one of the women and is capable of standing alone as short fiction.

Mattie Michael, paragon of pride and dignity and the queen mother of Brewster Place, suffered physical and emotional abuse from her father in Tennessee. Though he had doted on Mattie and been understanding about her teenage pregnancy, he could not tolerate her refusal to identify the child's father, and his violent reaction to her silence is explicit testimony that violence is often linked to poverty. Years later, Mattie's son, Basil, whom she has coddled and protected, causes her to lose her home, which she has mortgaged to cover his bond for a criminal offense. In her rented apartment on Brewster Place, Mattie is the touchstone against whom all the other characters are measured. Although she is not always the narrator, her sympathetic voice of reason ultimately becomes the voice of all the Brewster Place women.

The pathos of another resident, Mattie's longtime friend Etta Mae Johnson, lies in her determination to find a husband who will lift her out of poverty and give her social status and acceptability. Her search ends disastrously after she engineers her own seduction by a charismatic preacher. When he treats her no better than a harlot, her chances as a middle-aged woman are dimmed, and her disappointment is wrenching.

Kiswana Browne typifies the upper- and middle-class African American young women who embraced the ideals of black nationalism during the late 1960s. With a lifestyle and values that are in conflict with those of her parents, she leaves their elite black community to live on Brewster Place and help the less fortunate. Her most important contributions there are developing pride in children who

Dust jacket for the novel Naylor set on a mythical sea island located on the border between South Carolina and Georgia

are growing up without direction and organizing the women to withhold rent until the tenements are repaired, thus bringing a sorely needed sense of community to Brewster Place.

Lucielia Louise Turner – granddaughter of Miss Eva, who befriended Mattie when she arrived in Detroit from the South with her baby son – grows up in the same house with Basil. Like Mattie and Etta Mae, Lucielia came to Brewster Place with broken dreams. The physical and emotional abuses of her ne'er-do-well black husband have led to their baby girl's death. In her 1985 conversation with Morrison, Naylor said that she "bent over backward not to have a negative message come through her first novel about Black men." She opens Lucielia's story with a conversation between Lucielia's husband and Ben, the superintendent of the apartment buildings on Brewster Place, showing the reader "that that young man did care about the death of his child, but he had been so beaten down he couldn't come through for his family." As Lucielia lies in bed overcome by grief, Mattie rocks the younger woman in her arms. The scene evokes the blues and Negro spirituals:

> Mattie rocked.... Mattie rocked her out of that bed, out of that room, into a blue vastness just underneath the sun and above time. She rocked her over Aegean seas so clean they shone like crystal, so clear the fresh blood of sacrificed babies torn from their mothers' arms and given to Neptune could be seen like pink froth on the water. She rocked her on and on, past Dachau, where soul-gutted Jewish mothers swept their children's entrails off laboratory floors. They flew past the spilled brains of Senegalese infants whose mothers had dashed them on the wooden sides of slave ships. And she rocked on.
>
> She rocked her into her childhood and let her see murdered dreams. And she rocked her back, back into the womb, to the nadir of her hurt, and they found it....

Mattie helps Lucielia to exorcise this hurt, and though it leaves "a huge hole," Mattie knows that it will heal.

The fourth woman of Brewster Place, Cora Lee, is the only child of a solidly middle-class black family. Neither physically nor mentally abused, she gave birth to her first baby at fifteen. Fascinated by babies but knowing little or nothing about raising children, she keeps on having babies while trying to support them and herself on welfare.

Three of Naylor's four novels, including *The Women of Brewster Place*, examine homosexual relationships. In a 1988 article published in *The Yale Review*, she wrote that early black novelists, male and female, failed to address sexual relationships in the lives of their characters and that none except James Baldwin dared to probe male bonding, although several major black male novelists were homosexual. The chapter titled "The Two" offers poignant glimpses into the complexities of being black and lesbian. On Brewster Place Lorraine and Theresa become pariahs on whom others vent displaced venom. As Lorraine is about to be raped and beaten brutally by a gang of young men, Naylor's narrator comments on the destructive influence of racism on the black male psyche: "So Lorraine found herself, on her knees, surrounded by the most dangerous species in existence – human males with an erection to validate in a world that was only six feet wide." The next morning she regains consciousness in the alley where she was raped, and, crazed by pain, she kills Ben – perhaps mistaking him for one of her attackers when, in fact, he was coming to help her. Ben's death elicits a collective sharing of pain and suffering among the women of Brewster Place, and the community begins to heal.

When *The Women of Brewster Place* was accepted for publication, Naylor treated herself to a trip to southern Spain and Paris, to follow in the footsteps of Ernest Hemingway and James Baldwin. Rather than feeling free and liberated, as a woman traveling alone she experienced isolation and harassment, especially in Spain. Later she "sequestered" herself in a boardinghouse in Cádiz and began writing *Linden Hills*.

It was only after the publication of her second novel that Naylor thought of herself as a writer and knew she would write for the rest of her life. She told Morrison in 1985 "that now after *Linden Hills,* I feel there's a certain validity about what I do, if for nothing than the fact that I can say I write books with an 's.'" In her first novel Naylor had already offered glimpses of the upper-middle-class African American community of Linden Hills. The neighborhood lies in concentric circles as one ascends or descends a hill. At the top of the hill, in an interesting reversal of conventional American urban symbols, is the impoverished community of Putney Swope, which adjoins Brewster Place. The novel suggests that the spiritual and emotional destruction of African Americans lies in their willingness to submerge their African identity for material gain while chasing an American dream of conspicuous consumption.

Linden Hills received extensive critical comment, focusing mostly on structure – Naylor's allegorical use of Dante's *Inferno* and the alternating but independent journeys from naïveté to awareness of two major characters. The reviews were mixed. Most praised Naylor's examination of decadence among the African American middle class, a seldom-treated theme in black fiction, but others commented that Naylor's depictions of relentless degeneracy bordered on didacticism and hindered the reader's willingness to suspend disbelief.

In the 1820s Luther Nedeed I founded Linden Hills as a community for prosperous and successful African Americans. By the late twentieth century the present Luther, the great-great-grandson of the founder, has satanic influence over the Linden Hills residents. Like the other Luthers before him, he leases lots for one thousand years to those who are financially successful and who meet his requirement to repress memories of the historical past so that they may achieve identities that will allow them upward mobility in the white world. He lives at the bottom of the hill, representing consummate black achievement and repression of the past.

Willie, the omniscient observer, works at odd jobs in Linden Hills to earn money to buy Christmas gifts. He relates much of what the reader learns about Linden Hills residents. Willa, wife of the present-day Luther Nedeed, who is exiled in the cellar of the Nedeed home, discovers a horrendous legacy of cruelty and abuse suffered by three generations of Nedeed wives. Both Willie's and Willa's journeys toward new identities and awareness begin on 19 December and end on Christmas Eve. Willie's journey begins at the top of the hill in impoverished Putney Swope, where he finds a former resident of Linden Hills who has forsaken the hypocrisy of Linden Hills for Putney Swope and marriage to a husband who places her well-being over his. As Willie continues down the hill for the next four days, he observes engaging inhabitants of Linden Hills who have become emotionally and morally bankrupt in their rejection of their racial heritage – finally reaching Luther Nedeed, who has figured prominently in each character's spiritual or physical demise.

Willa's psychological journey from naïveté to full awareness of the loss of her identity commences with the death of her infant son from starvation in the dark basement of the Nedeed home. Luther has banished her to the basement because their son's fair skin has led him to believe that the baby is not his child. Willa's painful isolation is reinforced after she finds the photographs and journals of three generations of Nedeed wives who were brutally traumatized by their husbands.

In the confined place where she was "shoved" against her will, Willa discovers her own identity in the history of the other Nedeed wives – as black women before her had discovered their own identities in similar places. In a 1990 interview with Mickey Pearlman, Naylor discussed her use of space as a metaphor for the middle-class woman's existence, explaining that women historically have been "shoved" into closed spaces where they uncover women's history.

On Christmas Eve Willa ascends the stairs, reclaiming her identity as a dutiful Nedeed wife. Naylor has said that she had not wanted Willa to make this choice, which meant that Naylor was compelled to destroy both Willa and Luther. While Willa did not claim her identity as a feminist as Naylor might have wished, Willa does recognize that she can affirm herself in the only role she has known. As Naylor told Morrison in 1985, some of her characters, including Willa and Willie, sometimes seem to act on their own.

Mama Day (1988), Naylor's third novel, is a dense and complex work in which the four major characters seem almost incidental to the pastoral, seemingly Edenic, setting, which is ever changing and seductively real. The only one of Naylor's novels set in the rural South, *Mama Day* has been compared to Morrison's *Beloved* (1987) because Naylor's novel includes spirit possession and a family history that is tragically informed by the death of a child. Reviewing the novel for the *Orlando Sentinel* (14 February 1988), Nancy Pate compared *Mama Day* to William Shakespeare's *The Tempest:* "there is an island.... a terrible storm.... and the myth and magic of a heroine named Miranda."

Critics used the words "*big,*" "*broad,*" "*dense,*" and "*ambitious*" to describe *Mama Day*. Its bigness lies in large part in the author's ability to convey a sense of place. The inhabitants of Willow Springs, a subtropical sea island on the border between South Carolina and Georgia (thus claimed by neither state), have retained a great deal of African culture: some of their traditions, especially religious customs, have remained untouched and untainted by American culture for hundreds of years. The climate is conducive to growing and preserving the medicinal herbs, roots, and vegetation that are still in common use. The inhabitants of this pastoral world include Miranda, known as Mama Day, and her sister, Abigail, who are visited by Abigail's granddaughter, Cocoa, and Cocoa's husband, George, who live in Eurocentric, jaded New York City, which stands in sharp contrast to Willow Springs. Naylor has said that for the pastoral environment of this island she drew on her parents' stories of the rural South and her own experiences as a Jehovah's Witness missionary in that region.

Mama Day is the matriarch of the island, owned by the descendants of former slaves who were given the land by their slave master. Functioning as a traditional African medicine woman, she administers to both the physical and emotional needs of the community. She works her magic through her knowledge of the universe and the local vegetation, but she also seeks modern remedies when she recognizes that her services are insufficient to effect a cure.

Mama Day is a love story – one that Naylor especially enjoyed writing. The arrival of Cocoa (whose real name is Ophelia) and her sophisticated, urbane husband creates a clash of cultures in Willow Springs. Having internalized the nonchalance of the city, Cocoa ignores Mama Day's advice about customs on the island and finds herself "hexed" by an evil woman who fears her husband is smitten with Cocoa. Ironically, while Mama Day's "good" magic works for the rest of the community, it has no curative effect on her beloved Cocoa. Finally she must solicit the aid of Cocoa's husband, who is first tested by the beautiful but foreboding forest. Tragically, he passes the test but loses his own life in the process of saving Cocoa's.

A major theme in Naylor's fiction recurs in *Mama Day:* the loss of African American identity, which must be informed by an African presence. Residents of Willow Springs live a communal life, knowing that their existence is dependent on the well-being of the entire community. They intuitively recognize the African tradition of "We are because I am," and "I am because we are." There are also those in Willow Springs who defy the philosophy that good and evil coexist in the universe, but the good magic of a Mama Day usually triumphs. Another theme in *Mama Day* is the mother/daughter conflict, which leads to the suggestion that a young woman must acknowledge the influence of the mother in her life if she is to understand what it means to be a woman.

In a 1992 interview with Patti Doten, Naylor said that her fourth novel, *Bailey's Cafe* (1992), "is about sexuality." Inspired by Edith Wharton's novel *The House of Mirth* (1905), Naylor wrote a novel focusing on female sexuality and the ways in which women are defined according to society's perceptions. Specifically, she says, *Bailey's Cafe* is about "defusing the Madonna-whore myth," and because Judeo-Christian culture shaped the thinking that created this myth, she moved women from the Bible to the twentieth century, allowing them to tell their stories and show the lives behind the myth. The novel sings the blues of the socially rejected, who arrive at Bailey's struggling to find some measure of solace from a brutal American environment filled with racial and sexual stereotypes. Naylor has explained that the book is "structured ... like a jazz set," with no quotation marks for dialogue, because she wanted her "characters to be singing, not talking." A former navy enlisted man who survived the death and destruction of World War II, Bailey, the owner of the café, evokes a blues lament early in the novel.

Most of the customers who frequent Bailey's Cafe are residents at the boardinghouse next door, which is run by Eve, whose reputation for healing destitute, desperate, but strong-willed women is widespread – reaching as far as Addis Ababa, Ethiopia. The women who come in search

Dust jacket for the novel Naylor has described as her attempt at "defusing the Madonna-whore myth"

of Eve have led tortured lives because their families have chosen to exploit their sexuality. Although outsiders know little of what goes on at Eve's, the community considers her house a bordello, because the men who frequent the boardinghouse must bring flowers or purchase them from Eve's garden to give to the women with whom they will spend the evening. The daughter of a minister, Eve was banished naked from her father's home when he learned that she had discovered her own sexuality. Now she closes the wounds of her female boarders, loving them as she attempts to make them whole again. Sadie, Sweet Esther, Mary, Jesse Bell, and Mariam all tell their stories, which suggest parallels to those of women in the Bible.

Mariam, an Ethiopian Falasha Jew who was expelled from her village because she was pregnant, insists that no man has ever touched her. Her immaculately conceived son is circumcised by Gabe, a Jewish pawnbroker whose never-open shop is next door to the café on the other side from Eve's house. Mariam's baby will bring the blues jams of a new generation to the way stations of the world.

The most fully developed character in the novel is Miss Maples, a male transvestite who arrives at Bailey's Cafe with a Ph.D. from Stanford and a suitcase full of rejection letters from corporations throughout the United States. During a dinner interview with the top executives of a corporation in which he is seeking a marketing job, Miss Maples strips to his waist in an effort to express his hostility toward the unspoken racism of the arrogant and control-obsessed whites who are evaluating him for the position. This scene reminds Miss Maples and the reader of an event that took place years earlier, when he and his aristocratic father had their clothes torn off by members of the Ku Klux Klan and were forced to escape in women's clothes. As Naylor has observed, Miss Maples, who becomes Eve's housekeeper and wears housedresses most of the time, is not concerned about his gender and therefore significantly blurs the meaning of male and female.

Bailey's Cafe was a critical success, with most critics discussing the connections of biblical women to those who come to Bailey's Cafe and praising Naylor for creating another lyrical examination of the lives of African American women.

Notwithstanding an occasional adverse review, critics have generally been effusive in their praise of her works, which have made her readers increasingly sensitive to historical issues of gender, race, and class. Naylor writes at a rolltop desk in her upper Manhattan cooperative apartment facing the Hudson River. She has written a screen version of *Mama Day* and has founded One Way Productions, an independent film company, to produce the movie. In a 1993 interview with Allison Gloch she explained her decision to become a producer: "I don't like to relinquish control. Look at *The Shining*.... They had Jack Nicholson and all that, but King shouldn't have let the book go." She has also considered writing a play about the Clarence Thomas–Anita Hill controversy. Briefly married once, Naylor believes that solitude is too important to her to remarry or have children. As a member of the committee that selects books offered by the Book-of-the-Month Club, she says she is discovering "what literature has been and what it is now." As a writer, she says she intends to write her "wings off."

Interviews:

"Gloria Naylor and Toni Morrison: A Conversation," *Southern Review,* 21 (July 1985): 567–593;

Interview with Gloria Naylor (Columbia, Mo.: American Audio Prose Library, 1988);

Mickey Pearlman, "An Interview with Gloria Naylor," *High Plains Literary Review,* 5 (Spring 1990): 98–107;

An Evening with Gloria Naylor (Minneapolis: Minneapolis Public Library and Information Center, 1991);

Gloria Naylor: A Conversation (San Francisco: California Newsreel, 1992);

Patti Doten, "Naylor in Her Glory," *Boston Globe,* 21 October 1992, p. 77;

Allison Gloch, "A Woman to Be Reckoned With," *Special Report* (January–February 1993): 22–25.

References:

Jacqueline Bobo and Ellen Geiter, "Black Feminism and Media Criticism," *Journal of the Society for Evaluation in Film and Television,* 32 (Autumn 1991): 286–302;

Henry Louis Gates, "Significant Others," *Contemporary Literature,* 28 (Winter 1988): 606–623;

Ellen Gilchrist, "Do You Think of Yourself as a Woman Writer?," *Furman Studies,* 34 (December 1988): 2–13;

Margaret Homans, "The Women in the Cave," *Contemporary Literature,* 29 (Fall 1988): 369–402, 606–623;

K. A. Sandiford, "Gothic and Intertexual Construction in *Linden Hills*," *Journal of American Literature,* 47 (Autumn 1991): 117–139.

Thomas Pynchon
(8 May 1937 -)

Bernard Duyfhuizen
University of Wisconsin – Eau Claire

and

John M. Krafft
Miami University – Hamilton

See also the Pynchon entry in *DLB 2: American Novelists Since World War II* [first series].

BOOKS: *V.* (Philadelphia: Lippincott, 1963; London: Cape, 1963);
The Crying of Lot 49 (Philadelphia: Lippincott, 1966; London: Cape, 1967);
Gravity's Rainbow (New York: Viking, 1973; London: Cape, 1973);
Mortality and Mercy in Vienna (London: Aloes, 1976);
Low-Lands (London: Aloes, 1978);
The Secret Integration (London: Aloes, 1982);
A Journey Into the Mind of Watts (London: Mouldwarp, 1983);
Slow Learner (Boston: Little, Brown, 1984; London: Cape, 1985);
Vineland (Boston: Little, Brown, 1990; London: Secker & Warburg, 1990).

OTHER: Richard Fariña, *Been Down So Long It Looks Like Up to Me,* introduction by Pynchon (New York: Viking, 1983), pp. v-xiv;
Letter to Thomas F. Hirsch (1968), in *The Fictional Labyrinths of Thomas Pynchon,* by David Seed (Iowa City: University of Iowa Press, 1988), pp. 240-243;
Juvenilia (1952-1953), in *Thomas Pynchon: A Bibliography of Primary and Secondary Materials,* by Clifford Mead (Elmwood Park, Ill.: Dalkey Archive, 1989), pp. 155-167;
Donald Barthelme, Introduction to *The Teachings of Don B.: Satires, Parodies, Fables, Illustrated Stories, and Plays,* edited by Kim Herzinger, introduction by Pynchon (New York: Turtle Bay, 1992), pp. xv-xxii;
Liner notes to *Spiked!: The Music of Spike Jones,* Catalyst/BMGMusic, 09026-61982-2, 1994;

Thomas Pynchon (photograph from the 1953 Oysterette, *the Oyster Bay High School yearbook)*

Liner notes to *Nobody's Cool,* by Lotion, Spinart, 9-24643-2, 1995.

SELECTED PERIODICAL PUBLICATIONS – UNCOLLECTED: "Togetherness," *Aerospace Safety,* 16 (December 1960): 6-8;
"Is It O.K. to Be a Luddite?," *New York Times Book Review,* 28 October 1984, pp. 1, 40-41;
"The Heart's Eternal Vow," review of *Love in the Time of Cholera,* by Gabriel García Márquez, *New York Times Book Review,* 10 April 1988, pp. 1, 47, 49;

"The Deadly Sins/Sloth: Nearer, My Couch, to Thee," *New York Times Book Review,* 6 June 1993, pp. 3, 57;

"Lunch with Lotion" [interview], *Esquire,* 125 (June 1996): 84–88, 90.

Thomas Pynchon's ancestral roots go deep into the soil of America – an appropriate genealogy for a writer whose overriding concern in his fictional project is the construction of "America" and the necessary conditions for living within that construction. The first Pynchon in the New World was William Pynchon, who arrived in 1630. As Mathew Winston was among the first to point out, William "was a patentee and treasurer of the Massachusetts Bay Colony and a founder both of Roxbury and of Springfield." Besides being one of the early Puritan settlers of colonial New England, William was the first Pynchon to become an author, writing a tract called *The Meritorious Price of Our Redemption* (1650), which was judged heretical because it challenged the tenets of "Election" (the Puritan belief that the salvation or damnation of each individual was predetermined) that upheld American Puritan theology and social organization. The tract was banned and burned in Boston, and William soon returned to England, presaging the themes of alienation and exile that typify the American experience of so many of Thomas Pynchon's characters. Indeed, as Louis Mackey and others have shown, any complete reading of Pynchon's fiction must consider its American Puritan context.

Many readers of American literature have first encountered the Pynchon name in Nathaniel Hawthorne's *The House of the Seven Gables* (1851) – in which it is spelled "Pyncheon." Two members of the family wrote to Hawthorne to complain about his characterization of their ancestors. One of these disgruntled readers was the Reverend Thomas Ruggles Pynchon, who eventually became the ninth president of Trinity College in Hartford, Connecticut. This nineteenth-century namesake of the present Pynchon is also a worthy literary precursor. In his teaching and scholarship at Trinity, Thomas Ruggles Pynchon examined both science and religion, while another of the twentieth-century Pynchon's thematic preoccupations is the interpenetration of science and scientific theory in late twentieth-century life. Although Thomas Ruggles Pynchon apparently did not concern himself with Thomas Pynchon's favorite nineteenth-century scientific concept, entropy, the Reverend Pynchon's writings do suggest a family predisposition to an interest in science.

A third branch of the family is connected to the once-prosperous stock brokerage firm Pynchon and Company. As Charles Hollander has detailed, Pynchon and Company was active on the New York Stock Exchange during the 1920s, investing in the aviation industry, electric utilities, and Fox Films and General Theaters. In the crash of 1929 and the following economic depression, the firm was hard hit, ultimately suspended from trading on the New York Stock Exchange, and placed into receivership with the Irving Trust Company. A link can be inferred between some key Pynchon and Company investments and some of Thomas Pynchon's interests in rockets (the next generation in aviation), utility and other cartels, and motion pictures. Hollander infers an even deeper conjunction, citing connections, extending back to colonial America, between the Pynchon family and the Morgan family, with Pynchon and Company a "Morgan satrap." Thus, Hollander sees the fall of Pynchon and Company as part of a larger dynastic/historical struggle between older Morgan interests and the emerging Rockefeller interests.

To what degree the sweep of Hollander's inference is valid and to what degree Pynchon's ancestors directly affect his writing are open to debate, but in dealing with a writer whose fictional method thrives on "kute korrespondences," every scrap of biographical detail hints at a deeper story. It is a story Pynchon is reluctant to tell directly. He avoids the contemporary media machine of personality marketing, keeping most of his life relatively secret.

What is known is that Thomas Ruggles Pynchon Jr., was born in Glen Cove, Long Island, New York, on 8 May 1937 and grew up in East Norwich in the town of Oyster Bay. His father was an industrial surveyor and highway engineer and a local Republican politician. It is easy to imagine, given *Gravity's Rainbow* (1973) in particular, how growing up in the atmosphere of World War II, the Korean conflict, and the developing Cold War sensitized Pynchon to the political, social, and cultural issues that shape his writing. In 1953, when he was just sixteen, Pynchon graduated as class salutatorian from Oyster Bay High School, receiving an award for "the senior attaining the highest average in the study of English." The juvenilia published in his high-school paper, *Purple and Gold,* during his senior year already reveal Pynchon's irreverence for authority and his playfulness in naming characters.

In the fall of 1953 Pynchon entered Cornell University as a scholarship student in the recently established engineering physics program. Although Pynchon remained only one year in this program, whose mission was a response to "the expanding technological activities in the country," he maintained his interest in science, particularly the human use and abuse to which science is put. As a sophomore, Pynchon left engineering physics for arts and sciences and then dropped out of Cornell after that year for a two-year tour of duty in the U.S. Navy. He said, in a rare statement about his writing and his life, that his navy experience provided him with one of his favorite characters, Pig Bodine, the archetypal AWOL sailor. Not much more is generally known of Pynchon's navy years (except for some personal information gleaned by David Cowart). His service records were destroyed in a Saint Louis fire; other "official" records – the usual stuff of biographical snoops – have either vanished or been sealed, apparently at Pynchon's request. The story of Pynchon's life becomes increasingly hazy as he undertook his vocation in earnest.

In 1957 he returned to Cornell to complete his degree in English, graduating in June 1959. During those last two years, he became friends with Richard Fariña, to whom he would later dedicate *Gravity's Rainbow*. In memory of Fariña, who died in 1966, Pynchon wrote an introduction to the 1983 edition of Fariña's *Been Down So Long It Looks Like Up to Me* (1966). Pynchon, Fariña, and other friends, including Kirkpatrick Sale, were influenced in these formative years by Beat writers such as Jack Kerouac and Allen Ginsberg, but they were also poised to move beyond their modernist and New Critical education to begin, especially in Pynchon's case, constructing the postmodern. One Cornell professor, Vladimir Nabokov, could obviously have served as a mentor and role model for such a project, but here Pynchon's biography shades into rumor. How much direct contact Pynchon had with Nabokov at Cornell is uncertain. Yet Pynchon's fictional project does have affinities with Nabokov's, not least a love of literary playfulness in naming characters. If Pynchon did attend Nabokov's classes, he received an excellent introduction to classic writers of fiction (see Nabokov's *Lectures on Literature,* 1980) and witnessed Nabokov's meticulous attention to the formal details of narrative construction – lessons that would stand any aspiring writer in good stead.

During his last two years at Cornell Pynchon wrote most of the early stories that – with the exception of "Mortality and Mercy in Vienna" – he later collected in *Slow Learner* (1984): "The Small Rain" (*Cornell Writer,* March 1959), "Mortality and Mercy in Vienna" (*Epoch,* Spring 1959), "Low-Lands" (*New World Writing,* 1960), "Entropy" (*Ken-*

Pynchon (kneeling at center) with fellow members of the Oysterette *staff (photograph from the 1953* Oysterette*)*

yon Review, 1960), and "Under the Rose" (*Noble Savage,* 1961), an early version of chapter 3 of his first novel, *V.* (1963). Pynchon has characterized the stories he wrote at Cornell as "apprentice" fiction; nevertheless, this early work rehearses themes and character types central to his novels. In 1960, having failed to win a Ford Foundation Fellowship to work with an opera company, Pynchon went to work as a technical writer in Seattle, writing about missiles for Boeing. During his two and a half years there he was undoubtedly immersed in the composition of *V.*

"The Small Rain" tells the story of Nathan "Lardass" Levine, a U.S. Army Signal Corpsman sent with his unit to assist in disaster relief after a hurricane in Louisiana. Based on actual events, the story is concerned with "death" and is filled, like the work of many other beginning writers influenced by modernism, with images. As Pynchon has said about this work, "Apparently I felt I had to put on a whole extra overlay of rain images and references to 'The Waste Land' and *A Farewell to Arms.* I was operating on the motto 'Make it literary,' a piece of bad advice I made up all by myself and then took." "The Small Rain" introduces in Levine one of Pynchon's staple protagonists: the schlemiel who seeks minimal involvement with others yet finds himself involved nonetheless; Levine thus prefigures Meatball Mulligan, Benny Profane, Tyrone Slothrop, and Zoyd Wheeler. The story also introduces one of Pynchon's multilevel themes: communication. As in much of Pynchon's other fiction, the characters' failures to communicate effectively drive the plot.

Pynchon appears to have disowned "Mortality and Mercy in Vienna," which was published as a pamphlet in Great Britain in 1976, by neither including nor even mentioning it in *Slow Learner*. The protagonist, Cleanth Siegel, is thrust into the role of host, made responsible for keeping a Washington party going, but he bails out, giddily setting the stage for Irving Loon to open fire on the other party goers with a Browning automatic rifle. The story offers a kind of sketch for the "Whole Sick Crew" in *V.* and uses the party as an objective correlative for communication, including its potential for entropic breakdown – a subject Pynchon returns to in "Entropy."

Published as a pamphlet in London in 1978, "Low-Lands" is the story of the breakup of Dennis Flange's marriage (another failure to communicate). It also introduces the irrepressible Pig Bodine, who looks "like an ape in a naval uniform, squat and leering," and the story includes Pynchon's first fictional manifestation of some sort of world beyond or beneath the surface of everyday life. Flange's marriage to Cindy has reached a breaking point, which the arrival of Bodine and the promise of a long binge of wine drinking exacerbate. Flange and Bodine put up for the night in the center of an enormous garbage dump (Pynchon's play with the "Waste Land" image makes obvious the symbolic depth he invests in the dump), in the night watchman Bolingbroke's shack, which is papered inside with photographs from newspapers stretching back to the 1930s. After more drinking and some "sea stories," Flange is awakened in the middle of the night by one of the gypsies who, Bolingbroke had warned his visitors, wander the dump after dark. When Flange ventures outside, he meets and trustingly follows Nerissa, who is beautiful and "roughly three and a half feet tall." She takes him to her home under the dump, in "a network of tunnels and rooms [built] back in the '30's by a terrorist group called the Sons of the Red Apocalypse, by way of making ready for the revolution. Only the Feds had rounded them all up, and a year or so later the gypsies had moved in." At the close of the story Flange decides to stay with the childlike Nerissa and her childlike rat, Hyacinth, "For a while, at least."

"Low-Lands" shows the first clear signs of the writer to come. The image of the dump with gypsies living beneath it is Pynchon's first evocation of a dispossessed populace outside the "normal" patterns of American life represented by the suburban milieu of Dennis and Cindy. The gypsies' "other world," secret and hidden from everyday view, anticipates Pynchon's use of secret, hidden orders in much of his later fiction. Pynchon's "other" is not always sympathetic like Nerissa, however; both the oppressors and the oppressed can exist hidden from view – although the oppressed are typically the victims of abuses of power by a shadowy "Them." In Pynchon's later fiction paranoia structures how the protagonists become aware of "other orders," and ambiguities in the representation force readers into active engagement with the text to determine the moral and ethical status of these "other orders behind the visible."

Of all Pynchon's stories "Entropy" has received the most critical attention because its theme, reflected in its title, appears so central to understanding Pynchon's fiction as a whole. Looking back at the story in *Slow Learner,* Pynchon was less enthusiastic: "The story is a fine example of a procedural error beginning writers are always being cautioned against. It is simply wrong to begin with a theme, symbol or other abstract unifying agent, and then try to force characters and events to conform to it." Despite Pynchon's retrospective dissatisfaction, "Entropy" provided the testing ground for the contrast between the schlemiel and the introvert, Meatball Mulligan and Callisto, that would later organize *V.* by way of the characters Benny Profane and Herbert Stencil.

"Entropy" foregrounds the theme of entropy in a variety of ways and also schools the reader in applying the metaphor of entropy to representations of breakdown in everyday life. The narrative shifts back and forth between vertically aligned apartments. Mulligan lives downstairs, where he is holding a lease-breaking party. The concept of entropy central to the party scenes comes from communication theory (developed by Bell Telephone engineers), in which the ratio of signal to noise determines the viability of a communication act. For a complex system of disparate conversations and actions like a party to succeed, the ratio must not skew to the point where noise dominates the signal and thus leads to misunderstandings. But of course, precisely this skewing occurs during Mulligan's party, and a fight (the system in disarray) breaks out. Unlike Cleanth Siegel in "Mortality and Mercy in Vienna," however, Mulligan does not walk away from his responsibility, although he considers it: "The way he figured, there were only about two ways he could cope: (a) lock himself in the closet and maybe eventually they would all go away, or (b) try to calm everybody down, one by one." To keep his party "from deteriorating into total chaos," Mulligan works to establish some semblance of order. Although the metaphor of entropy implies an eventual disintegration of order into chaos (and therefore whatever order Mulligan achieves is likely to be short-lived), the effort is ethically laudable because this order arises freely from inside rather than being imposed forcibly or oppressively from outside – by the police, for example.

Upstairs, Callisto lives in a not-quite-hermetic, not-quite-sealed "hothouse" apartment. Here, the thermodynamic concept of entropy is central: through the process of heat transfer, differences in temperature between systems will tend over time toward equilibrium, the hypothetical final equilibrium marking the "heat death" of the universe. Obsessed by the potential for entropy to reduce his life to final equilibrium, Callisto does more to help than to hinder it. He spends much of the story in the futile effort to warm a sick bird back to health (probably transferring heat from, rather than to, the bird), and in dictating a self-indulgent autobiography to his live-in companion, Aubade. Like Henry Adams, to whom he is explicitly compared, Callisto refers to himself in the third person (a trait Pynchon will reuse for Herbert Stencil in *V.*) and tries through the composition of his autobiography to give order to a life he sees slipping inexorably into entropic decline. Where Mulligan's party suffers from the input of too much unregulated energy, Callisto in his self-isolation suffers from too little input and too much regulation – Mulligan's option of locking himself in a closet writ large.

Although the outside temperature's holding steady for three days at thirty-seven degrees has prompted Callisto to fear the imminent heat death of the universe, Aubade may understand that the stifling existence within the apartment, the closed system of their life together, is the real problem. Pynchon's ending is characteristically ambiguous and open:

> Suddenly then, as if seeing the single and unavoidable conclusion to all this [Aubade] moved swiftly to the window before Callisto could speak; tore away the drapes and smashed out the glass with two exquisite hands which came away bleeding and glistening with splinters; and turned to face the man on the bed and wait with him until the moment of equilibrium was reached, when 37 degrees Fahrenheit should prevail both outside and inside, and forever, and the hovering, curious dominant of their separate lives should resolve into a tonic of darkness and the final absence of all motion.

These last lines do figure the motif of entropy as apocalypse, but their point of view, apparently focalized through Callisto's obsession, unwarrantedly presumes that the temperature must remain static and misses the fact that Aubade's smashing the window opens the system, permits exchange. Like the obsessions of characters in Pynchon's other fiction, Callisto's obsession leads to no definitive conclusion, no final answer or resolution. The open, ambiguous ending is a trademark of Pynchon's postmodern fiction.

"Under the Rose," the last of the stories Pynchon wrote at Cornell, clearly signals a direction crucial to his novels. Instead of drawing material directly from his own or his friends' experiences, or from his contemporary world, he sets this story in 1898 in Egypt. As Pynchon acknowledges, "the major 'source' for the story" was Karl Baedeker's 1899 guide to Egypt, which Pynchon found in the Cornell Co-op. He "loot[ed]" Baedekers as well as other guides and sources for details, but the guides also suggested the theme of "tourism" that marks certain characters as outsiders to the cultures through which they move. For "Under the Rose," Pynchon also drew on his interest in "spy fiction, novels of intrigue, notably those of John Buchan," but his deeper concern, displayed in his later fiction as well, focuses on the question of whether "history [is] personal or statistical":

> An alignment like this [leading to a European war, Porpentine] felt, could only have taken place in a Western World where spying was becoming less an individual than a group enterprise, where the events of 1848 and the activities of anarchists and radicals all over the Continent seemed to proclaim that history was being made no longer through the *virtù* of single princes but rather by man in the mass; by trends and tendencies and impersonal curves on a lattice of pale blue lines.

In this story Pynchon moved beyond the issues of personal responsibility that inform the earlier stories to question whether, ultimately, the individual can truly affect history at all. As his later fiction demonstrates, the answer to this question is ambiguous at best, although an ethic of "caring" does emerge as a laudable character trait.

Dust jacket for the first American edition and cover for the advance proof copy of the first British edition of the volume in which Pynchon collected five early short stories

At the center of "Under the Rose" is the personal struggle between two aging spies: Porpentine, a British agent and the central consciousness of the story, and Moldweorp, a German agent. The consummation of their personal battle coincides with the Fashoda crisis, European powers scrambling to consolidate their colonial holdings in Africa. The spy story turns on Porpentine and his colleague Goodfellow's efforts to foil Moldweorp's attempt to assassinate the British consul and thereby propel the European powers into war. (The closing lines mentioning Goodfellow's — in the event, ineffectual — presence in Sarajevo in 1914 to prevent the assassination of Archduke Francis Ferdinand underscore the broader context Pynchon is evoking.)

As Porpentine pursues both his professional duty and his personal mission, however, he loses confidence in his role in the larger historical scheme. In Pynchon's later fiction, this theme is connected to the theme of paranoia and the question of who or what is really responsible for historical events, and to serve what ends. For example, this theme is clear in *V.* in the development of a secondary character from "Under the Rose," Victoria Wren. In the story she is a young woman ostensibly seduced by Goodfellow and drawn by chance into the endgame of the espionage when Porpentine is killed. Her presence at the margin of assassination plots and counterplots and her witnessing Porpentine's murder (in the story at least; in the episode as reworked for chapter 3 of the novel, Victoria may or may not be nearby) cultivate in Victoria a taste for forces of history that have the potential to produce catastrophe; and within the chronological story of *V.*, Victoria's evolution into V. marks the construction of a malevolent "personal" force agitating for Armageddon.

V. (1963) combines many elements of Pynchon's earlier short fiction: characters (Pig Bodine, Rachel), character types (the schlemiel, the introvert, a whole sick crew of party goers), and themes (communication, entropy, the possibility of other realms beyond the visible). Pynchon reworked "Under the Rose," and, more important, he began his postmodern critique of the principles of historical fiction to inform and give significance to the plot. *V.* received unusually extensive attention for a first novel and mainly enthusiastic reviews, not just for its scope, complexity, and erudition, but also for its comic energy. It was awarded the William Faulkner Foundation Award for the best first novel of the year.

Two main narratives make up the novel, the base narrative set in the almost-present, the other ranging over twentieth-century Western history from 1898 on. The base narrative begins on Christmas Eve 1955 and ends in the fall of 1956. It concerns primarily the picaresque adventures of former sailor, former roadworker, sometime night watchman Benny Profane and various members of the Whole Sick Crew. Pynchon draws on the mid 1950s milieu of jazz and the Beat generation, but the major event is the Suez Canal Crisis, which is hinted at throughout the text until it explicitly frames and coincides with events in the sixteenth chapter, set on Malta. Yet the base narrative does not center on the historical movements of 1956, except by highlighting most characters' failure of adequate attention; indeed, "People read what news they wanted to and each accordingly built his own rathouse of history's rags and straws." The seeming avoidance of a direct engagement with the times underscores the shallowness of the Whole Sick Crew and, in many ways, of Profane himself. Yet Pynchon often creates main characters who belie the term *hero* but still earn the reader's sympathies with their failures and their small acts of kindness. The passive Profane fits this role, though reluctantly. Given a choice, he would drop out and yo-yo his way into oblivion. Nevertheless, people keep finding him and relying on him for what feeble aid or solace he can provide.

One of those who eventually turn to Profane is Herbert Stencil, the son of a British spy and the historiographical sleuth of the novel. Stencil, characterized as "He Who Looks for V.," is the filter for much of the historical narrative of the text. At this secondary level Pynchon engages a problematics of narrative transmission. The base narrative is fairly conventional: it has a more or less omniscient third-person narrator, who often uses a character — mostly Profane — as a filter for how the scene is represented. At the second level Stencil becomes an embedded third-person narrator, providing either the direct narrating voice or the indirect narrative filter for the intercalation of four of the six historical chapters about V. The fifth historical chapter (chapter 11) embeds V.'s story in the confessions of Fausto Maijstral, while the sixth, the epilogue, *may* be told by the first-level, base narrator. The historical chapters — 3, 7, 9, 11, 14, and the epilogue — are all analepses from the base narrative, but they are not presented in strict chronological progression. Chapter 3 is set in 1898 in Egypt during the Fashoda crisis; chapter 7 is set in 1899 in Florence; chapter 9 is set in 1922 (with further analepses to 1904) in the South-West Protectorate of Africa; chapter 11 is set during World War II on Malta; chapter 14 is set in 1913 in Paris; and the epilogue is set in 1919 on Malta. As is typical in Pynchon's narrative poetics, these distributed chapters are connected by cross-references and characters (Hugh and Evan Godolphin, for instance), as well as by the narrative object of V. herself. Moreover, the historical episodes are connected to the base narrative through, for example, the plastic surgeon Schoenmaker, who went into medicine because of Evan Godolphin's injuries in World War I and who performs Esther Harvitz's nose job; Father Fairing, who belongs to both the sewer legends of Profane's New York and the Malta of Fausto Maijstral's father; and Fausto and his daughter, Paola. Paola is a would-be dependent of Profane, who also appears as a child in chapter 11 and who is connected as well with the genealogical matrix of V. — possibly as her heir.

Such cross-referencing and plot displacement are routine in narrative poetics, but Pynchon experiments with narrative transmission in three of the historical chapters — 3, 9, and 11 — although the symmetrical distribution with relation to the base narrative, the shifted chronology, and the different narrating situations all destabilize the act of reading by calling attention to the textuality of the narrative. Before turning to the experimental chapters, we will consider some features of the other three.

Chapter 7, Stencil's narration of the 1899 Florence episode, includes a short preface that establishes the relation of the second-level narrating situation to the base narrative. This preface fixes Dudley Eigenvalue as the listener to Stencil's account of his father's encounter with Victoria Wren (V.) and also comments on the nature of Stencil's obsession with V. and with the plot dynamic of conspiracy — although as always in Pynchon, the character's paranoia contributes to the conspiracy structure. As the base narrator states, Stencil

> had discovered, however, what was pertinent to his purpose: that she'd been connected, though perhaps only

tangentially, with one of those grand conspiracies or foretastes of Armageddon which seemed to have captivated all diplomatic sensibilities in the years preceding the Great War. V. and a conspiracy. Its particular shape governed only by the surface accidents of history at the time.

Perhaps history this century, thought Eigenvalue, is rippled with gathers in its fabric such that if we are situated, as Stencil seemed to be, at the bottom of a fold, it's impossible to determine warp, woof or pattern anywhere else. By virtue, however, of existing in one gather it is assumed there are others, compartmented off into sinuous cycles each of which come to assume greater importance than the weave itself and destroy any continuity.

History and V. are continuous here, but upon closer examination, this passage takes away as much "continuity" as it seems to give.

The first part of the passage marks the interpretation Stencil has "discovered" in his researches, but the discovery is overdetermined, "pertinent to his purpose" – so can it really be something "discovered"? The delusions of conspiracy that attend a paranoid's obsession prefigure a shape *not* "governed only by the surface accidents of history at the time"; instead, Stencil's paranoia shapes "history" to fit the demands of his desire, his project. Such a reading becomes more plausible with the second part of the passage, where the shift into Eigenvalue's consciousness marks a different interpretation of Stencil's perspective. Eigenvalue's metaphor of history as a rippled and gathered "fabric" (traced in this image are such historic tapestries as the Bayeux Tapestry and the surreal painting of Remedios Varo that Pynchon mentions in *The Crying of Lot 49*, 1966) suggests that "we are situated" within the fabric. Like Stencil, therefore, the reader can "know" only a small piece of fabric, so to determine any "pattern" or "shape" beyond the self is, if not "impossible," then productive of interpretive uncertainty. Indeed, the delusion of "greater importance" of other "compartmented off" gathers "destroy[s] any continuity." Yet in Stencil's mind continuities exist; however, these may be the products of a narrative impulse to produce a coherent story that doubles, perhaps even replaces, "history this century." This passage underwrites a basic principle: the construction of "story" and the construction of "history" are complementary.

Stencil seems initially to be the narrator in chapter 14, the 1913 Paris episode, telling Profane the story of V.'s voyeuristic-lesbian relationship with the ballerina Mélanie l'Heuremaudit, whose life ends with her savage impalement at the finale of *L'Enlèvement des Vierges Chinoises* (Rape of the Chinese Virgins). The recounting of events becomes problematic, however, when the reader is suddenly told, "If we've not already guessed, 'the woman' is, again, the lady V. of Stencil's mad time-search. No one knew her name in Paris." If Stencil is narrating this story, this comment, as well as much of the subsequent narration of the chapter, seems odd even by his standards. Stencil would appear to offer this story to Profane as part of his effort to persuade Profane to go with him to Malta, but does he tell it this way, or does the base narrator take over the story, either at this moment or for the entire chapter? Stencil's habit of referring to himself in the third person might allow the passage to be read as a simple aside to Profane – but how could Profane (hardly a "we") "guess" the way readers can by this point, or, for Stencil, immersed in his narrating, is such a problem irrelevant?

The epilogue, "1919," articulates a different narrative transmission problem in that Herbert Stencil has no manifest part in narrating this analepsis. It appears to be narrated by the base narrator, but the reader cannot be certain one way or the other, especially since many details of the epilogue are consistent with details of Stencil's V. narratives. Embedded in the epilogue are some snippets from the journals of Herbert's father, Sidney Stencil – which Herbert has read and which thus form yet a third level of narration in the historical chapters 3 and 7. These snippets in the epilogue occasion some of the novel's reflections on the status of the individual in twentieth-century political history; for instance:

"If there is any political moral to be found in this world," [Sidney] Stencil once wrote in his journal, "it is that we carry on the business of this century with an intolerable double vision. Right and Left; the hothouse and the street. The Right can only live and work hermetically, in the hothouse of the past, while outside the Left prosecute their affairs in the streets by manipulated mob violence. And cannot live but in the dreamscape of the future.

"What of the real present, the men-of-no-politics, the once-respectable Golden Mean? Obsolete; in any case, lost sight of. In a West of such extremes we can expect, at the very least, a highly 'alienated' populace within not many more years."

The binary oppositions of Sidney's meditation have often been cited as structuring principles in Pynchon's creation of character – Stencil/Profane: hothouse/street – and for Pynchon's lament over that loss of a middle ground and the resultant alienation. Sidney sees the trap inherent in binary thinking that overgeneralizes the case: "'Short of examining the entire history of each individual participating,' Stencil wrote, 'short of anatomizing each soul, what hope has anyone of understanding a Situation?'" If real history is the accumulation, intersection, and nonintersection of individual histories, then recorded history is woefully incomplete – not to mention that it has been written largely by the victors in support of the dominant ideology. To get beyond those orderly dichotomies and sanctioned texts is for both Stencils to see events falling "into ominous patterns," "ordered into an ominous logic." Narrative logic and pattern inscribe the ultimate moment, death; and Sidney Stencil's death closes the novel at the same time it underwrites the narrative energy that drives Herbert Stencil's quest to fill in the gap he discovered in his father's journal: "There is more behind and inside V. than any of us had suspected. Not who, but what: what is she. God grant that I may never be called upon to write the answer, either here or in any official report."

The story of Sidney Stencil's death in a water spout off Malta would be crucial to Herbert's narrative. As Walter Benjamin has written, "Death is the sanction of everything that the storyteller can tell.... it is natural history to which his stories refer." If Stencil never knows the true circumstances of his father's death, his narratives will lack centralizing authority. Additionally his reluctance to believe Fausto's account of the Bad Priest's (presumably V.'s) death – an account that both validates and threatens the integrity of Stencil's historiographical construct – marks a narrative desire built on the repression of the privileging moment of death. But the base narrator's system of transmission is "authorized" because it includes what Stencil seeks to exclude.

In the preface to chapter 3 Herbert Stencil himself alludes to the power of death in the construction of story: "but if death did come like some last charismatic bestowal, *he'd have no real way of telling. He'd only the veiled references* to Porpentine in [his father's] journals. The rest was *impersonation* and *dream*" (emphasis added). To base the authority of his first narration on the ambiguous ground of "veiled references," "impersonation," and "dream" implies that the "truth" of a narration is always a construct and that Stencil literally has "no real way of telling" the story he sets out to tell – if indeed he "tells" it at all, because to whom he is telling this complex narrative and why are also unclear.

The historical context is the rival espionage activities going on under the surface of the Fashoda incident. Since, to standard history, these activities occurred "under the rose" (to use the title of the short-story version of this chapter), it stands to reason that the story goes yet further "under the rose" to recount, among other things, Victoria Wren's erotic activities. Yet this sordid tale is no mere cliché of the spy-thriller genre. It is prefaced by the observation (the base narrator's or Stencil's) that "'Stencil' appear[s] as only one among a repertoire of identities. 'Forcible dislocation of personality' was what he called the general technique, which is not exactly the same as 'seeing the other fellow's *point of view*'" (emphasis added). Nevertheless, the narrative experiment of the chapter is precisely concerned with "point of view," as the eight sections of the chapter are filtered through seven fully characterized perspectives and a last perspective that approximates the camera eye of a cinematic narration marked by a shift to present tense. Problematic as the chapter is, it is a tour de force of narrative ingenuity.

The "identities" Stencil impersonates are not those of the principle characters, most of whom cover their spying disguised as tourists, but instead the marginalized inhabitants of "Baedeker land," who filter the perspective. Thus, narrative technique merges with a thematic subtext: a critique of the colonialist ideology that assumes "we are civilized" and "jungle law is inadmissible." By foregrounding the perspectives of those oppressed under colonial power, this transmission strategy (Stencil's and/or Pynchon's) challenges cultural histories written by representatives of European imperialism, for whom Fashoda means a struggle for the self-assumed right to exploit Africa. Thus, the Suez Crisis of 1956, the backdrop to the last chapter of the base narrative, joins with the Fashoda incident of 1898 to frame historically the fictional universe of *V*. Once more "story" and "history" come together.

Joseph Conrad's *Heart of Darkness* (1902), another elaborate narrative of colonial abuses, is an analogue and perhaps a model for Pynchon's story of German colonial abuses in South-West Africa in chapter 9 of *V*. Like Conrad, Pynchon uses a frame narrative to distance the reader from the atrocities at the heart of the story; at the same time that technique resituates those atrocities in historical circulation, but a European perspective still obtains. The system of narrative embedding may be formulated as follows: [{(«Firelily's rider–1904» Foppl's Siege Party–1922) Mondaugen tells his experiences at Foppl's to Stencil–1956} Stencil "retells" Mondaugen's story to Eigenvalue–1956].

The reader does not "hear" the story of Mondaugen's "youthful days in South-West Africa" directly from him; instead, it is narrated by Stencil, who had "listened attentively to Mondaugen. The tale proper and the questioning after took no more than thirty minutes. Yet the next Wednesday afternoon at Eigenvalue's office, when Stencil retold it, the yarn had undergone considerable change: had become, as Eigenvalue put it, Stencilized." As rendered, "Mondaugen's Story" is a fifty-page chapter that could not be spoken in "thirty minutes." The process of Stencilization turns a "tale" into a "yarn," which, like chapter 3, also apparently includes the elements of "impersonation and dream." Somewhat like Stencil himself, Mondaugen stands in relation to Foppl's Siege Party as a marginal observer, a voyeur of the decadents who are trying to re-create the era of the previous Herero uprising in 1904 and General von Trotha's genocidal response. Not only is that era evoked through elaborate costuming and the reenactment of atrocities, but it comes to be evoked even in Mondaugen's dreams. However, "if dreams are only waking sensation first stored and later operated on, then the dreams of a voyeur can never be his own." If Foppl is a dark parody of Conrad's Kurtz, the heart of this darkness is the story of "Firelily's rider" that comes increasingly into Mondaugen's dreams in the third section of the chapter by almost seamless transitions that destabilize the text even further.

Firelily's rider is the figure of Europe's (and perhaps, by extension, America's as well) romantic fascination with imperialistic power and domination. The text hints that Foppl is Firelily's rider, but "there was no way to say for certain, later, whether Foppl himself might not have come in to tell tales of when he'd been a trooper, eighteen years ago." In this "later" (whenever that is), uncertainty collapses orderly transmission: each teller transforms the narrative either intentionally to serve a purpose (as Stencil appears to do) or unintentionally in an unknowing surrender to the entropic degradation of communicable information. Hence Eigenvalue interrupts Stencil at one point to ask:

> "They spoke in German? English? Did Mondaugen know English then?" Forestalling a nervous outburst by Stencil: "I only think it strange that he should remember an unremarkable conversation, let alone in that much detail, thirty-four years later. A conversation meaning nothing to Mondaugen but everything to Stencil."

What emerges from this problematic of transmission and authority is a narrative of history's dirty secrets about the colonization of Africa. Chapter 9 explodes the mythology of bringing civilization and progress to the "savages" – a discursive category that always allowed the colonizers distance from the Africans. The beatings, rapes, and killings represented in the story of Firelily's rider demonstrate the corruption of missionary idealism into absolute domination: "you felt like the father colonial policy wanted you to be when it spoke of Väterliche Züchtigung; fatherly chastisement, an inalienable right." Yet beneath this mythology of paternalism, "It had only to do with the destroyer and the destroyed, and the act which united them." Conventional history usually omits this story. Stencil's/Pynchon's displacement of representation through multiple frames and especially through dream draws the horrific history to the surface to compel a revision of historical understanding, not only of this period and place, but of the entire twentieth century.

In a rare published letter, written to Thomas F. Hirsch in 1968, Pynchon says of his use of history:

> When I wrote *V.* I was thinking of the 1904 campaign as a sort of dress rehearsal for what later happened to the Jews in the '30's and '40's.... The problem as I guess you appreciate, with getting the African side of it, is that the Hereros were preliterate and everything available from them is (a) anecdotal and (b) filtered through the literate (McLuhan), Western, Christian biases of European reporters, usually missionaries. But I feel personally that the number done on the Herero head by the Germans is the same number done on the American Indian head by our own colonists and what is now being done on the Buddhist head in Vietnam by the Christianity minority in Saigon and their advisors: the imposition of a culture valuing analysis and differentiation on a culture that valued unity and integration.... I don't like to use the word but I think what went on back in Südwest is archetypical [*sic*] of every clash between the west and non-west, clashes that are still going on right now in South East Asia.

As Pynchon suggests, an unfiltered version of history is unavailable, and the filter usually used has been formulated by Western culture, a culture of "analysis and differentiation," or, in the words of *V.*, "forcible dislocation" of cultures as well as personalities. The forcible dislocation may be subtle or, as in Stencil's case, self-imposed. Paradoxically Stencil's "forcible dislocation of personality" is precisely what enables the demystification – albeit at the risk of remystification – of history.

Chapter 11, "Confessions of Fausto Maijstral," embeds another problematic text in *V.* Fausto writes his confessions in the fourth incarnation of his personal identity – a process of transsubjectivity without a foreseeable end. His memoir-narrative does not simply look back at various stages of the life lived; instead it quotes extensively from the journals written by his previous selves, selves the confessions often displace into the third person. Fausto's explanation of this strategy raises once again the problematic of "story" and "history":

> We can justify any apologia simply by calling life a successive rejection of personalities. No apologia is any more than a romance – half a fiction – in which all the successive identities taken on and rejected by the writer as a function of linear time are treated as separate characters. The writing itself even constitutes another rejection, another "character" added to the past. So we do sell our souls: paying them away to history in little installments. It isn't so much to pay for eyes clear enough to see past the fiction of continuity, the fiction of cause and effect, the fiction of a humanized history endowed with "reason."

But does Fausto get what he pays for in this economy? Is his vision "clear enough to see past" the various fictions that order Western culture? The narrating situation of the confessions is an address to Fausto's daughter, Paola, to explain the circumstances of her birth and to record her childhood participation, during the German bombing of Malta, in the disassembly of the Bad Priest, whose accumulated prostheses presumably identify "her" as V. Readers of *V.* read Fausto's confessions along with Stencil, but they may not share Stencil's response to this text. Readers may experience satisfaction of narrative desire – V.'s death is finally told – but should perhaps beware of "conclusions" arrived at with nearly one-third of the novel remaining. For Stencil (although Fausto's narrative, like the epilogue, would seem to offer independent support for the general shape and theme of his historiographical construct), the certainty of narrative closure is a precursor to his own at least virtual death; once the quest is over, only death remains: "where else would there be to go but back into half-consciousness?"

Stencil's last spoken words in the novel are a question, "Is it really his own extermination he's after?" His last identifiable words inform Profane in a letter that he has a new lead that will keep his quest for V. going. "Story," like "history," is a never-ending process. Readers in the West customarily impose stops to satisfy Western urges for analysis and differentiation, but definitive ends are rare. Even if Stencil's V. did die on Malta in 1943, even if her story has ended, the twentieth-century Western history Stencil constructs around the figure of V. serves his needs, has a certain eccentric validity for readers, and may yet engulf us all. Nevertheless, although the distinction between "story" and "history" may dissolve, the longing for pattern, logic, and shape generates a narrative energy Stencil cannot escape: "V.'s is a country of coincidence, ruled by a ministry of myth. Whose emissaries haunt this century's streets. . . . If the coincidences are real then Stencil has never encountered history at all, but something far more appalling."

Often hailed as an exemplary postmodernist, Pynchon also appears to be a humanist with at least a liberal, if not a more markedly leftward, political leaning. So he, too, seems to find "something [or some things] far more appalling" in the modern world. Writing in the early 1960s, Pynchon must have been affected by the civil rights movement. Although *V.* addresses some racial issues, his last published short story, "The Secret Integration" (*Saturday Evening Post,* 19 December 1964), and his first essay published in the mainstream press, "A Journey into the Mind of Watts" (*New York Times Magazine,* 12 June 1966), more fully articulate an awareness of the conditions of African Americans. The familiar Puritan framework serves as a conceptual model for the social and political constructions underwriting a racist society: African Americans are the "new" Preterite (the passed-over or disinherited) in relation to white America's Elect majority.

In "The Secret Integration," which was also published in pamphlet form in London in 1982, a group of boys in a formerly all-white American small town invents a black friend, Carl Barrington, as the only child of their new black neighbors. They had earlier met a black jazz musician down on his luck, Carl McAfee, whom they were unable to help effectually. The boys may have been too youthfully naive to comprehend all the effects of racism in McAfee's life, but they do understand giving aid and comfort to someone in need. The boys also challenge adult authority, for example, by sabotaging the local paper mill and infiltrating PTA meetings, but their activities may seem like mere harmless pranksterism until the end of the story. Returning home from their hideout, the boys find the Barringtons' lawn littered with garbage they recognize as having come from their own households. They try, sympathetically, to clean up the garbage, but Mrs. Barrington rejects their help and drives them away. At this point the "fiction" of Carl Barrington is finally revealed, and the boys' "integration" shown to be a communal but tenuous desire. Despite their manifest rebelliousness against paren-

Dust jacket for Pynchon's first novel, written for the most part while he was working as a technical writer for the Boeing Corporation

tal authority and narrowness, the boys "banish" Carl, seeming to renounce elusive integration in favor of illusory familial security. The generational rift beginning to manifest itself in the 1960s appears to close again at the end of the story, a loss or betrayal of idealism that is also featured in Pynchon's subsequent novels.

Published as a pamphlet in London (1983), "A Journey into the Mind of Watts" analyzes the social and cultural determinants of what was, until the Los Angeles disturbances of 1992, the most notorious American race riot. Writing in *The New York Times Magazine* nearly a year after the long, hot summer of 1965, Pynchon exposes for white readers, not just the fear and intimidation promoted by the Los Angeles Police Department, which resulted in "Raceriotland," but the systematic dispossession of an entire segment of the American people: blacks. His comparing Watts to the fantasy theme park Disneyland underscores (well before Jean Baudrillard's similar comparison) the pronounced and yet blurred boundaries of these two phenomena in American culture. By using the device of the second person to construct his representation (a device he uses again in *Gravity's Rainbow*), Pynchon brings readers into disquieting proximity to the racism that produces a Watts:

So you groove . . . down the freeway, maybe wondering when some cop is going to stop you because the old piece of a car you're driving, which you bought for $20 or $30 you picked up somehow, makes a lot of noise or burns some oil. Catching you mobile widens The Man's horizons; gives him more things he can get you on. Like "excessive smoking" is a great favorite with him.

If you do get to where you were going without encountering a cop, you may spend your day looking at the white faces of personnel men, their uniform glaze of suspicion, their automatic smiles, and listening to polite putdowns. "I decided once to ask," a kid says, "one time they told me I didn't meet their requirements. So I said: 'Well, what are you looking for? I mean, how can I train, what things do I have to learn so I *can* meet your requirements?' Know what he said? 'We are not obligated to tell you what our requirements are.'"

Yet amid the despair Pynchon finds art "restructuring . . . the riot" in ways that suggest the postmodern is born in the streets, not in the theoretical hothouses of the dominant culture: "In one corner [at a found-art exhibit] was this old, busted hollow TV set with a rabbit-ears antenna on top; inside, where its picture tube should have been, gazing out with scorched wiring threaded like electronic ivy among its crevices and sockets, was a human skull. The name of the piece was 'The Late, Late, Late Show.'" *The Crying of Lot 49*, published the same year as "A Journey into the Mind of Watts," opens with Oedipa Maas standing in the living room being "stared at by the greenish dead eye of the TV tube": for her, the other side of America is about to reveal itself.

In the introduction to *Slow Learner*, Pynchon disparages *The Crying of Lot 49* (1966) as a "story . . . which was marketed as a 'novel,' and in which I seem to have forgotten most of what I thought I'd learned up till then." Many readers disagree with that assessment. *The Crying of Lot 49* won a Richard and Hilda Rosenthal Foundation Award from the National Institute of Arts and Letters, and over the years it has received a disproportionate share of the critical attention lavished on Pynchon. He may well have started *The Crying of Lot 49* as merely a story with which to make some money while working on *Gravity's Rainbow* (perhaps already begun). As the "story" began to exceed the size limit for most periodicals (excerpts did appear in *Esquire* and *Cavalier*), he may have come to see it as a means of fulfilling the standard second-book clause in his contract with J. B. Lippincott so he could negotiate a better deal for *Gravity's Rainbow*. Yet whatever Pynchon's reason for writing *The Crying of Lot 49*, its appearance helped solidify his reputation as a major American novelist.

Short (fewer than two hundred pages) and limited to a single point-of-view character, *The Crying of Lot 49* is often recommended as a good starting point for those interested in reading Pynchon. It tells the story of a mid 1960s suburban California housewife, Oedipa Maas, who, on becoming the executrix of a former lover's will, discovers what appears to be an underground postal system serving those outside the mainstream of American culture. As usual in Pynchon's fiction, the quest, or detective plot, propels the narrative, as Oedipa becomes committed to uncovering the truth about the mysterious Tristero. Moreover, again as usual in Pynchon, the quest for information about Tristero leads Oedipa to raise fundamental questions about herself and about her concept of America. *The Crying of Lot 49* exploits California's reputation for containing a variety of odd and marginal or marginalized subcultures. Published during the early days of the counterculture, the novel marks the mood of much of young America in distrusting the values and institutions of their parents. Pynchon's vision is more problematic, however, as it also suggests that "waiting" as well on society's margins are groups of a decidedly reactionary if not fascist stamp.

Although Pynchon's politics appear to be leftist, he does not indulge in simplistic representations of political struggle. His protagonists, like Oedipa, usually begin as innocent conformers to the status quo and then discover clues to a disturbing reality beyond the appearances manufactured by those in power for easy consumption by the unwary. The politics of Pynchon's fictional universe are based on class rather than party ideology: the wealthy and their multinational corporations are represented as operating ruthlessly above the social contract. Yet the discoveries Pynchon's protagonists make induce paranoia rather than establishing certain truth, and readers are likewise positioned to question the received truths that form cultural identity. As with *V.*, *The Crying of Lot 49* never finally answers either the characters' or the readers' questions: paranoia may be the only way to make some sort of sense of the contemporary American experience.

Thus, at the beginning of *The Crying of Lot 49*, when Oedipa returns home from a Tupperware party (a paradox of a private marketplace institutionalized to maximize corporate profits with minimal overhead) to find herself named executrix of Pierce Inverarity's estate, the stage is set for Oedipa to be shaken out of her middle-class ennui. Her effort to untangle Inverarity's vast corporate holdings leads her away from her husband, Wendell "Mucho" Maas, and toward what might be the recognition of a network of connections operating beneath the surface of America or what might be entrapment in a construct of her own mind. Near the end of the novel, Oedipa frames her dilemma:

> [Inverarity] might himself have discovered The Tristero, and encrypted that in the will, buying into just enough to be sure she'd find it. Or he might even have tried to survive death, as a paranoia; as a pure conspiracy against someone he loved. Would that breed of perversity prove at last too keen to be stunned even by death[?] . . .
> Yet she knew . . . there was still that other chance. That it was all true. That Inverarity had only died, nothing else. Suppose, God, there really was a Tristero then and that she *had* come on it by accident. . . .
> Another mode of meaning behind the obvious, or none. Either Oedipa in the orbiting ecstasy of a true paranoia, or a real Tristero. For there either was some Tristero beyond the appearance of the legacy America, or there was just America and if there was just America then it seemed the only way she could continue, and manage to be at all relevant to it, was as an alien, unfurrowed, assumed full circle into some paranoia.

The reader is left to wonder as well, since the novel ends on the verge of possible revelation, at the auction where the "crying of lot 49" may finally disclose the truth about Tristero.

The ambiguous Tristero, marked in the text by the sign of a muted post horn –

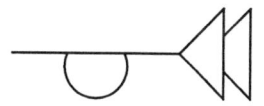

– and the cryptic acronym W.A.S.T.E. ("We Await Silent Tristero's Empire"), is even less tangible than Pynchon's mysterious character V., but possibly more plausible. On the one hand it appears to provide the dispossessed and disenfranchised a means to communicate outside the exploitative, homogenizing, and deadening channels of the official mail system; on the other hand, ironically, it also appears to provide a means to communicate for reactionaries with even more repressive ideologies. Is Tristero a model of democratic freedom or a force serving a sinister power within or beyond our habitual constructions of reality? Either way, the more convinced Oedipa becomes of Tristero's possible existence, the more she begins to doubt everything she had believed before. Rather than finding community in this system, Oedipa finds herself more isolated – whether through her own failure or because of the nature of Tristero is never certain. The theme of alienation runs throughout Pynchon's writing, but it is not simply the modernist/existential condition of being out of step with one's world; instead, alienation is the feeling characters have that their world is only a simulacrum, a construct designed to distract them in the interests of control. In this respect Tristero represents a possible reawakening of those anesthetized by consumerism, mass media, and military-industrial organization. Yet in the end, its gestures appear feeble, and perhaps it too is merely the illusion of a counterforce, constructed to sidetrack safely the impulse to rebel.

Although *The Crying of Lot 49* raises serious political and philosophical issues, it is also a comic novel, with a cast of outrageously named characters, besides Oedipa herself, including Genghis Cohen, Mike Fallopian, Stanley Koteks, Manny di Presso, and Emory Bortz. Some scenes have the quality of slapstick: Oedipa's game of strip Botticelli with the lawyer Metzger, the chase scene at Fangoso Lagoons, the dance at the deaf-mute convention, the mock-Jacobean tragedy that "plays . . . like a Road Runner cartoon in blank verse." The comedy serves as a vehicle for information about Tristero or as a means to interrogate received assumptions about everyday constructions of reality. Even at its most wildly inventive, Pynchon's comedy carries darker implications, and the closer readers look at *The Crying of Lot 49,* the more they are likely to find. Despite the contemporaneity of its plot with the time of its writing, the text is a rich historical tapestry that intensifies the mimetic force of the narrative. The effect is to poise readers at the cusps of a series of either/or propositions: *The Crying of Lot 49* is either comic or serious; it is either totally fictional or closer to reality than one could imagine. Of course it is also possible that the only way out of this conundrum is to reject the either/or construction in favor of a both-and formula, but making such a switch brings the reader no closer to a resolution than before. Like Oedipa, the reader is left to ponder what will come next.

Although *V.* and *The Crying of Lot 49* had been well received critically and Pynchon had already begun to develop a wide readership on American college campuses, *Gravity's Rainbow* (1973) launched him into the first rank of American novelists and made him arguably the preeminent writer of his generation. The novel exploded on the literary scene to immediate acclaim, and even spent a week on *The New York Times* best-seller list. The usually conservative Book-of-the-Month Club made *Gravity's Rainbow* an alternate selection. Yet controversy soon followed. The novel was unanimously nominated by the fiction jury for a Pulitzer Prize, but the Pulitzer advisory board overruled the jury, deeming *Gravity's Rainbow* "'unreadable,' 'turgid,' 'overwritten,' and in parts 'obscene.'" Ironically, the notoriety of this nonaward probably increased the aura surrounding Pynchon's novel. *Gravity's Rainbow* shared a National Book Award with a collection of short stories by Isaac Bashevis Singer. Perhaps out of respect for a fellow writer, Pynchon accepted the National Book Award. (His publisher sent comedian Irwin Corey, an eccentric "professor" of doubletalk, to the award ceremony as a stand-in for Pynchon.) The novel was a runner-up for the annual Nebula Award from the Science Fiction Writers of America. In 1975 Pynchon was awarded the Howells Medal of the American Academy of Arts and Letters and the National Institute of Arts and Letters for the most distinguished work of American fiction of the previous five years; this time he flatly declined the award.

In the 760 pages of *Gravity's Rainbow,* with its numerous intertwined plot lines and more than four hundred characters, Pynchon again creates a vast historical sweep to contextualize the base time of the narrative, its present: from early winter 1944 to early fall 1945, the last months and the aftermath of World War II. Edward Mendelson has called *Gravity's Rainbow* an "encyclopedic" novel, more for the ambition of its cultural project than for the sheer number, range, and complexity of its references. Yet because of its many references, first-time readers often welcome aids such as Khachig Tölölyan and Clay Leighton's *An Index to Gravity's Rainbow* (revised edition, 1989) and Steven Weisenburger's *A Gravity's Rainbow Companion* (1988; second edition forthcoming 1998). It can be argued that *Gravity's Rainbow* is meant to unsettle readers, that its renowned difficulty is part of its intended effect. As in his earlier novels, Pynchon is again concerned with forces operating behind the scenes of perceived reality, but in *Gravity's Rainbow* he more effectively conceives the connection of the historical with the personal.

In Pynchon's first two novels, V. and Tristero are metaphors for clandestine efforts to reorder history. In *Gravity's Rainbow* the V-2 rocket is the central image and organizing principle in the portrayal of the "Rocket State": the ubiquitous, malevolent, world-historical forces, identified as "Them," including multinational military-industrial corporate-governmental-bureaucratic octopuses, producing and deploying rockets as both weapons of mass destruction (ICBM's with nuclear warheads) and vehicles for achieving superpower domination of the next frontier, space. The political ironies of Wernher von Braun's involvement in both the Nazi rocket program and the American race to the moon were not lost on Pynchon, as he was writing *Gravity's Rainbow* in the turbulent late 1960s. Thus, *Gravity's Rainbow* is as much about America in the era of Vietnam and civil rights as it is about Europe at the end of World War II.

"A screaming comes across the sky. It has happened before, but there is nothing to compare it to now": so opens *Gravity's Rainbow*. The "screaming" of an incoming V-2 follows rather than precedes its impact; similarly, images and scenes in *Gravity's Rainbow* often explode on the reader's consciousness before a contextualizing "scream" can organize the reading into some sort of sense. *Gravity's Rainbow* challenges readers to make sense of a text that is, by design, difficult to make sense of. With repeated readings, narratives coalesce; yet, although the reader's interpretive decisions organize the experience of the novel, the text remains unstable and continuously open to diverse interpretations.

For instance, the base narrative of the first part of *Gravity's Rainbow* appears to encompass only nine or ten days, ending on 26 December 1944. However, not all the base incidents plausibly fit into such a short timespan; the narrative also includes many flashbacks, some highly complex; and it begins several plot lines without definitively privileging one. The plot lines centered on Pirate Prentice, Teddy Bloat, Tyrone Slothrop, Tantivy Mucker-Maffick, Ned Pointsman, Roger Mexico and Jessica Swanlake, Katje Borgesius, Captain Blicero and Gottfried, Franz Pökler and his wife and daughter (Leni and Ilse), and Peter Sachsa become, in the first part, the most significant for one level of the storytelling. At the same time the reader has to process Prentice's ability to "manage" other people's fantasies, including one of a giant adenoid besieging London; Slothrop's drug-induced dream of being flushed through the Boston sewer system; Katje's ethnic memory of her ancestor Franz van der Groov's efforts to exterminate the dodoes on Mauritius; and contacts made through mediums such as Peter Sachsa with spirits on the "other side" – most notably Walter Rathenau.

However confusing it is on a first reading, the text subtly connects enough plot threads to form a pattern in which Slothrop, an American lieutenant investigating rocket strikes in London, becomes a reader's prime candidate for protagonist of the novel. Slothrop garners this attention because he is the object of other characters' – especially Pointsman's – scrutiny. He attracts this scrutiny because a map of London hanging in his office, which alleg-

Cover for the unauthorized pamphlet publication of Pynchon's short story about a group of white boys who have an imaginary black playmate

edly marks with colored stars and names the sites of his sexual adventures, coincides with a map of the sites where V-2 rockets have struck (with a mean lag time of 4 1/2 days between Slothrop's pasting up a star and a rocket's striking). Pointsman and Mexico and their colleagues at the White Visitation (a group doing psychological research in support of the war effort) are perhaps understandably spooked by the map. But Bernard Duyfhuizen argues, in his "Starry-Eyed Semiotics" (1981), that the map is an elaborate reader trap that relies on the reader's desire for clear, conventional causality to make sense of the narrative in the early going. Pointsman's reading of the map, based on his obsession with Pavlovian behaviorism and his own equivocal sexuality, convinces some of his colleagues that Slothrop – who was in fact experimentally conditioned in his infancy to have an erection in the presence of a "Mystery Stimulus" – has been conditioned to predict by his erections the location (within a cartographic grid) of rocket strikes.

Readers fall into the trap of Slothrop's map for good reasons. First, focusing on the map gives the reader a target around which to organize many of the disparate elements of the first part of the novel. Second, because Pointsman devises a plot to try to control Slothrop based on the premise of the map, the course of the narrative is directed by Pointsman's misreading. Nevertheless, once the reader learns that the map has been over interpreted, the conception of Slothrop's character needs to be revised. Pynchon's technique of presenting seemingly authoritative detail that can be shown to be a character's misperception requires readers to withhold final judgments and to keep the fiction open to further interpretive possibilities.

On the premise of the map Pointsman has Slothrop assigned to a tour of duty on the French Riviera in an elaborate experiment to expose him to rocket data while monitoring his sexual activity with Katje, who – after quitting her role in Blicero's sadomasochistic game with Gottfried – is recruited by Pointsman to help further his projects. Part of this plan, or of a plan by others also interested in using Slothrop, involves stripping him of his identity papers and his means of returning to London or America. Slothrop and the reader begin to recognize that the plot against Slothrop is even more elaborate than any Pointsman or his allies in Military Intelligence could devise. Moreover, Slothrop appears to be a site at which various political and corporate interests intersect. Yet the reader is never fully apprised of why Slothrop is so important for his watchers to keep under surveillance; nevertheless, the device gives Pynchon many opportunities for comedy and for underwriting both the absurdity and the sinister undercurrent of a military-industrial complex. Becoming increasingly aware that he is being used in ways for which he never volunteered, Slothrop decides to escape and to take his chances tracking information about a mysterious piece of V-2 hardware, the Schwarzgerät, which was used only once, in the equally mysterious Rocket 00000.

Escaping his surveillance, Slothrop enters the "Zone" in the guise of war correspondent Ian Scuffling. If read as a metaphor for American innocence in the face of war, Slothrop is an ironic point of war correspondence, but it is his essential innocence that directs his actions into paths of kindness and benevolence as he wanders through postwar Germany. Although *Gravity's Rainbow* signals the origins of the Cold War mentality of the postwar era and comments obliquely on the American military adventure in Vietnam, the darker images of the text are relieved by a humanism that reiterates Pynchon's persistent theme of the superiority, albeit tenuous, of the Preterite over the Elect in the larger scheme of human affairs. While in the Zone, Slothrop crosses paths with two new characters and their plotlines: Vaslav Tchitcherine, a Russian agent also pursuing rocket information, but only as a means to track his African half brother; and Oberst Enzian, Tchitcherine's half brother and the leader of the Schwarzkommando, African rocket troops now scavenging rocket parts to build Rocket 00001, perhaps to be used to launch Enzian into space.

Slothrop's adventures in the Zone have both a picaresque and a horrific quality, sometimes simultaneously, as he encounters various people needing his "help," including Pig Bodine, Greta Erdmann, Bianca, Gerhardt von Göll, Ludwig, and others. He also takes on a series of further identities: for example, as Rocketman, he infiltrates the Potsdam Conference to liberate six kilos of hashish; and as Plechazunga, an archetypal pig hero, he participates in a north German town's annual festival celebrating a tenth-century rout of Viking invaders. During his adventures, Slothrop continues to seek rocket information, but the information becomes ever less important as he comes to recognize that it is his own understanding of himself he is discovering. Yet his journey to self-discovery is ironic, because his sense of individual identity is also dissipating, and with the failure of his attempt to get discharge papers so he can return to America, the stage is set for his virtual disintegration in the fourth part of the novel.

The adventures and other actions and events of *Gravity's Rainbow* include narrative threads that are clearly fictional on the one hand (such as Blicero's construction and firing of Rocket 00000) and that appear historically plausible on the other. Most significant among the latter is the interpretation some characters and the narrator come to that the political issues of World War II were merely cover for business as usual by multinational corporations, including IG Farben, Shell, and General Electric: "the real business of the War is buying and selling," and the "real war" never ends. Moreover, the scramble for rocket matériel and scientists by both the Americans and the Soviets recounts the birth of the modern "Rocket State." This history reminds the reader that the glories of space exploration, highlighted by the Apollo moon missions undertaken while Pynchon was writing *Gravity's Rainbow*, originated in Nazi weapons of terror and mass destruction and provided a propaganda cover for the refinement of Intercontinental Ballistic Missile technology for the delivery of nuclear warheads. While Slothrop is in the Zone, the first atomic bombs are dropped on Japan; but, as with the Holocaust, Pynchon does not foreground that historic event, concentrating attention instead on issues conventional history routinely obscures. Conventional history, the narrator says, is "at best a conspiracy, not always among gentlemen, to defraud," and, as the spirit-voice of Walter Rathenau puts it, "All talk of cause and effect is secular history, and secular history is a diversionary tactic."

In the fourth part of *Gravity's Rainbow*, "The Counterforce," Mexico, Prentice, Katje, and others attempt to rescue the lost Slothrop. But Pynchon's plots are rarely resolved with neat ties. Slothrop simply diffuses as a character, his fate completely unknowable: Does he die, or make it back to America, or metamorphose into a musical spirit, or a natural being – a tree at the fork in the road not taken? Similarly, many other plotlines fade from the text rather than coming to definitive conclusions. One plotline that is resolved is Tchitcherine's pursuit of Enzian; however, their meeting, during which Tchitcherine does not even recognize his brother, is a simple, humane but anticlimactic exchange by the side of the road rather than the violent confrontation this plot seemed to entail. Another is Gottfried's launch in Rocket 00000. Although in the narrative chronology the launch apparently occurred while Slothrop was still on the Riviera, the narrator recounts it only at the close of the novel (where readers might have expected the launch of Rocket 00001) and in a style that suggests readers are viewing Gottfried's last moments on film. In fact, the novel ends in contemporary Los Angeles, in the Orpheus Theatre, where the movie "we" readers have been watching all along, *Gravity's Rainbow*, has just broken. At the same time, a descending rocket – what was the 00000 going up has become an ICBM coming down – hangs just above the roof of the theater, suggesting that the apocalypse of a nuclear World War III is imminent.

To end in a movie theater is appropriate for *Gravity's Rainbow*. The novel is full of references (some anachronistic) to motion pictures and their power to shape reality. Within the novel, the movie *Alpdrücken* (Nightmare) is the nexus for a series of interconnections. While carrying the identity papers of one of its stars, Max Schlepzig, Slothrop meets its female lead, Greta Erdmann, who forms part of his link to its director, Gerhardt von Göll. Slothrop eventually meets one of the biggest fans of *Alpdrücken*, Franz Pökler, who was so aroused by the concluding rape scene in the movie that he fathered a "shadow-child," Ilse, by projecting Erdmann's image onto his wife, Leni, whom Slothrop eventually also meets. Erdmann was impregnated during the filming of the scene that aroused Pökler and gave birth to her own "shadow-child," Bianca, whom Slothrop also meets. These interconnections suggest the permeability of the boundary between film and reality. As a metaphor for Pynchon's own fictional practice, film demonstrates that alternative constructions of reality can shape everyday life, or at the very least can represent the collective human nightmares of oppression and apocalypse.

In addition to film, politics, and history as nodes in the fictional matrix of *Gravity's Rainbow*, various psychological theories, especially behaviorism, are targets of Pynchon's satiric representation. Behaviorism is one among many suspect systems of control. Like Norbert Wiener's *The Human Use of Human Beings* (1950) – one of the acknowledged sources for Pynchon's fiction – Pynchon's writing implies that the boost war gave to technology outpaced the human ability to maintain control over the future. Behaviorism, as figured by Pointsman and his interest in Slothrop, connects the individual human organism to the forces of technology that appear increasingly to serve the needs of technology itself rather than its human users. In Slothrop the reader witnesses the final loss of self as the technological forces take over.

The "City of the Future," or "Raketen-Stadt," section of part 4 presents a futuristic vision that, as Brian McHale observes in *Constructing Postmodernism* (1992), anticipates the style and themes of much cyberpunk fiction. In Pynchon's novel a set of comic-book superheroes, the Floundering Four, undertakes a mission to save the Radiant Hour. "Tyrone" connects this episode to Slothrop's narrative, but the stylistic shift highlights the tenuousness of the representational matrix of the narrative. Pynchon's postmodernism plays on self-reflexive moments when the narrative suddenly skews, calling attention to how the text is constructed. His style ranges across a broad spectrum from stark realism (such as Katje's encounter as the Domina Nocturna with Brigadier Pudding) to hallucination (such as Slothrop's sewer journey) to the fantastic (such as the City of the Future episode). The line between parts of this spectrum is sometimes blurred, as in the often misread scene in which Pökler imagines "hours of amazing incest" with his daughter. Such stylistic shifts destabilize conventional patterns of reading and lead readers to consider metaphorical constructions of meaning.

One construction of meaning common in Pynchon's novels is the self-reflexive theme of read-

Opening pages of the excerpt from The Crying of Lot 49 *that appeared in the December 1965 issue of* Esquire

ing. Pynchon's protagonists are often on quests to understand their worlds, but their quests mirror readers' experiences in the labyrinths of Pynchon's texts. Although readers may gain knowledge beyond what a character such as Slothrop attains, gaps in available knowledge often frustrate conventional readerly expectations and processes. Readers of and in *Gravity's Rainbow* must either make decisions about textual meaning at the price of repressing alternatives or engage in a practice of both, and reading that acknowledges the undecidability of the text, its essential ambiguity and multiplicity of potential meaning.

A simple case in point occurs soon after Slothrop enters the Zone. He dances with a young girl who emerges "Out of the fire's pale.... He reaches and just manages to find her hand, to grasp her little waist"; but as the scene closes, she seems to "vaporize from his arms." The girl may be "real," or a figment of Slothrop's imagination, or both. She may be a symbol of the dispossessed who populate the Zone. Pynchon's fiction challenges readers, especially critics, to make sense of it, but it simultaneously demonstrates that any attempt to achieve a totalizing understanding that will control the meaning making of the text is doomed to almost certain failure. At best readers produce provisional constructions of the text: thus, the girl of Slothrop's dance can be made to mean in a variety of ways, depending on the particular reading frame the reader applies. For readers, as for Pynchon's characters, the goal of the quest may turn out to be more an understanding of the self than an attainment of the other.

Even before the publication of *Gravity's Rainbow* Pynchon's novels were widely reviewed and frequently mentioned in both the popular press and academic journals. Important as such attention was in establishing Pynchon's reputation, many of the early reviews and essays seem quaint, at best, today. Tony Tanner's extensive treatment of Pynchon in *City of Words* (1971) and Richard Poirier's reviews of Pynchon's first three novels, however, have proven enduringly influential. Joseph W. Slade's *Thomas Pynchon* (1974) was the first book-length overview of Pynchon's fiction and is still the first resort for many Pynchon readers new and old. Reviewing the legacy of Slade's book on the publication of a revised edition in 1990, Brian McHale observed that Slade's "success in 'setting the agenda' has meant that nearly every theme, source and connection he identifies has been fully assimilated into Pynchon criticism by now, and much of what he said first, and perhaps best, passes now for critical commonplace and the consensus view" (*Pynchon Notes,* Spring-Fall 1990). McHale feared Slade's study might have been almost too successful and urged readers not to take Slade's word on Pynchon for the last word. In terms of numbers at least McHale apparently need not fear, given the explosive growth after 1974 of what is sometimes disparaged as the "Pynchon industry."

Surveying Pynchon criticism in 1979, Khachig Tölölyan found some seventy articles, three books, two anthologies of criticism, and many Ph.D. dissertations. (By 1995 the figures stood at more than five hundred articles and chapters, more than thirty books, nine anthologies of criticism, several special issues of journals, a dedicated journal, and perhaps 150 dissertations.) Tölölyan saw the first phase of Pynchon criticism – including, among others, Slade's book and the essays collected by George Levine and David Leverenz in *Mindful Pleasures* (1976) and by Edward Mendelson in *Pynchon: A Collection of Critical Essays* (1978) – as overly concerned with narrow readings of "entropy" and "paranoia" as distinct themes rather than integrated features in a full textual matrix. Tölölyan called for critics to attend to the "*meta-léctures*" in Pynchon's texts, to recognize how "hope" and "possibility" operate in Pynchon's writing as counters to the negative themes focused on by earlier critics and to explore the ideas of "proliferation, power, and control" operating in the texts, ideas that led Tölölyan to see Pynchon as "the most important political novelist of our time."

Thomas Schaub's *Pynchon: The Voice of Ambiguity* (1981) signaled the beginning of the second phase of Pynchon criticism. In a review essay published the same year, Schaub marked his difference from his predecessors while recommending the direction he believed Pynchon criticism should head. Like Tölölyan, Schaub found much wanting in earlier studies, which often failed to recognize how Pynchon's writing "enacts the uncertainties of meaning. Because his books are in many respects about the interpretation of meaning, they resist efforts to impose a consistent pattern upon them. This is especially evident in those efforts which are entirely thematic and which attempt to discern the 'message' of Pynchon's work without attending to its medium." For Pynchon criticism to move beyond such overstatements of reductive meaning, Schaub called for "greater attention to the literary properties of Pynchon's writing." Of particular concern for Schaub were the issues of stylistic instability, genre, literary mode, and characterization. His model for this kind of criticism was Mendelson's essay "Gravity's Encyclopedia" (1976), in which Schaub found "what Pynchon criticism needs: a more thorough sense of Pynchon's literary environment (both contemporary and historical); discussion of underlying sources and demonstration of their use; and further prolonged attention to the processes of Pynchon's writing."

Tölölyan and Schaub both called for the application of literary theory to Pynchon's texts: for Tölölyan through Michel Foucault to new historicism, and for Schaub through structural narratology and poststructuralism to an engagement with Pynchon's text. Tölölyan examined the Pynchon critical enterprise again in a 1983 review of seven recent contributions, including Schaub's *Pynchon: The Voice of Ambiguity* (1981), Tanner's *Thomas Pynchon* (1982), and Richard Pearce's edition of *Critical Essays on Thomas Pynchon* (1981). Synthesizing with Schaub's position, Tölölyan observes that "Pynchon's work is kin both to Foucault's studies of institutional competition [an excellent subsequent example of which is Dale Carter's *The Final Frontier* (1988)] and to Derridean deconstruction, because like them he underscores the struggle for the unequivocal determination and control of meaning-making." This view, particularly as manifested in the formulation of Jacques Derrida, marks the second phase of Pynchon criticism. Of the seven books Tölölyan reviewed, only Schaub's and Tanner's, he said, "address Pynchon's pedagogy of indeterminate meaning as the deconstructive narrative that it is, but as yet we do not have a work that analyzes [what Barbara Johnson calls] 'the specificity of a text's critical difference from itself' – which is to say, one that reads Pynchon's critique of the story-making propensity and the lust for closure."

The deconstructive phase of Pynchon criticism culminated in the early to mid 1980s. Several essays in Charles Clerc's *Approaches to* Gravity's Rainbow (1983) show an awareness of the deconstructive project in Pynchon's texts. Molly Hite's *Ideas of Order in the Novels of Thomas Pynchon* (1983) and number 14 of *Pynchon Notes,* a special issue called *Deconstructing* Gravity's Rainbow (1984), engaged the issue of Pynchon's deconstructionist techniques and themes most fully to that time. Hite explores how epistemologies seeking to order

Dust jacket for the novel Pynchon has described as a "story... in which I seem to have forgotten most of what I thought I'd learned up till then"

Pynchon's fictional worlds – whether characters' inside or readers' outside – result in only a "descriptive residue," while finding no "Holy Center." The contributors to *Pynchon Notes* number 14 focus on issues such as Pynchon's belatedness with relation to the American Dream, the dialectic in *Gravity's Rainbow* between extinction and transformation as tropes for cultural history, and the interdependence of mindless and mindful pleasures in the production of meaning.

Some of the most important work on Pynchon in the 1990s has built on this second phase. Alec McHoul and David Wills's *Writing Pynchon* (1990) is the most thoroughgoing application of poststructuralist theory to Pynchon's writing practice. Hanjo Berressem's *Pynchon's Poetics* (1993) extends beyond Jacques Derrida to the theories of Jacques Lacan and Jean Baudrillard in examining the formation of subjectivity in Pynchon's fiction. Brian McHale's essays collected in *Constructing Postmodernism* (1992) precisely and lucidly demonstrate the theoretical issues readers confront in reading *Gravity's Rainbow* and *Vineland* (1990). For McHale readers of Pynchon are challenged to move from a modernist reading practice grounded in epistemology to a postmodernist practice grounded in ontology – that is, from the question "How do I know this world?" to "What is this world?"

Tölölyan concluded his 1983 review essay by observing "a potentially threatening bifurcation in the criticism of Pynchon's work" between one approach "concerned with the ways in which Pynchon solicits our attention towards the world as represented by his text" and another insisting "that the specifically literary problems of his texts are being ignored." While the second phase of Pynchon criticism concentrated on the latter, more purely literary approach, the third phase – reflected in Kathryn Hume's *Pynchon's Mythography* (1987), Steven Weisenburger's *A Gravity's Rainbow Companion* (1988), Dwight Eddins's *The Gnostic Pynchon* (1990), as well as other works – suggests a reaction against readings that emphasize only Pynchon's deconstructive play of language and his critique of established epistemologies. Weisenburger, for instance, demonstrates Pynchon's crucial reliance on details drawn from the "real" historical world, and also stresses, like several other critics, the thematics of religious and mythic patterns in *Gravity's Rainbow*. Such patterns (Christian, Cabalistic, Jungian, Gnostic, feminist Goddess, and others) coalesce in readings that rescue Pynchon from the darker critical construction of the text as a nihilistic chaos of uncertainty, resituate *Gravity's Rainbow* in a mythographic cosmos, and reclaim the possibility of transcendent certainty. Hume seeks a synthesis with the earlier critical phases at the same time she provides the most compelling model for the humanistic ethos of the third phase. In that phase *Gravity's Rainbow* comes to fulfill "hope" and "possibility" (though perhaps not as Tölölyan formulated them in 1979) in abundance, with critics stressing a humanistic ethos of "kindness," "caring," and "love" as Pynchon's universal "message." Moreover, third-phase critics see Pynchon's attention to messages from the "other side" as evidence of a transcendent vision underscoring a deeply felt – if iconoclastic – spiritualism.

Although the third phase, identified as such by Duyfhuizen in a 1989 review essay (*Novel,* Fall 1989), celebrates the hopeful return of positive vision, by no means has a definitive interpretation of Pynchon been established. The strong books that define this phase suffer from differing degrees of blindness along with their insight and from some return to the criticism by reductive overstatement that Schaub lamented in 1981. In his *Marginal Forces/Cultural Centers* (1992) Michael Bérubé argues that the Pynchon critical cartel has become so vast precisely because Pynchon's texts seem so openly to deny the viability of the critical enterprise. The reader can hardly help identifying with Pynchon's protagonists in their quests for information, and those quests inevitably come up short of their goal. Because Pynchon has so capitalized on uncertainty and ambiguity, critics are drawn into a playful interpretive game with the texts, but often, the more serious the interpretation, the bigger the joke on the critic.

At least two other book-length studies are especially noteworthy: John Dugdale's *Thomas Pynchon: Allusive Parables of Power* (1990) and Deborah L. Madsen's *Postmodernist Allegories of Thomas Pynchon* (1991). Both are rich in political and cultural insight, Dugdale's work being informed by Freudian analysis and Madsen's study exploring the generic fusion of allegory and postmodernist techniques. Useful collections of essays include Patrick O'Donnell's *New Essays on* The Crying of Lot 49 (1991) and Geoffrey Green's *The* Vineland *Papers* (1994). J. Kerry Grant's *A Companion to* The Crying of Lot 49 (1994) may prove most helpful to less experienced readers of Pynchon. Clifford Mead's *Thomas Pynchon: A Bibliography of Primary and Secondary Materials* (1989) is the standard bibliographic source, and it is supplemented by the current bibliography in each issue of *Pynchon Notes*. A special issue of *Pynchon Notes* in 1997 will include indexes to all Pynchon's works. Internet resources include Pomona College's World Wide Web page devoted to Pynchon (http://www.pomona.edu/pynchon/) and Tim Ware's hyperconcordance to Pynchon's fiction (http://www.hyperarts.com).

While the critical industry built on Pynchon milled away, Pynchon himself remained resolutely underground. He surfaced briefly in 1983 with his introduction to the new edition of Richard Fariña's *Been Down So Long It Looks Like Up to Me* and in 1984 with the introduction to *Slow Learner* and the essay "Is It O.K. to Be a Luddite?" in *The New York Times Book Review*. In "Is It O.K. to Be a Luddite?" Pynchon discusses the figure of the "Badass," who is both the product of a technological culture and a Luddite within it, resisting the imposition of technology to control human existence. According to Pynchon the creature constructed in Mary Shelley's *Frankenstein* (1818) is the archetypal Badass, questioning by his existence the misuse of scientific knowledge. In Pynchon's essay the technological specter of the ICBM, metaphorically figured in *Gravity's Rainbow,* merges with the questions surrounding the use and misuse of electronic technology, specifically the computer. As Pynchon demonstrates in *Vineland,* however, the computer can be an information resource and a tool for both the oppressors and the oppressed.

After that modest flurry of activity in 1983–1984, Pynchon again disappeared from public view. He did not emerge even when, in 1988, he was awarded a five-year fellowship by the John D. and Catherine T. MacArthur Foundation, but he did accept the $310,000 grant. That same year he published an admiring review of Gabriel García Márquez's novel *Love in the Time of Cholera* in *The New York Times Book Review* (10 April 1988). A decade and a half after *Gravity's Rainbow,* anticipation of Pynchon's next novel had grown fervent. Rumors of the work in progress had circulated since the 1970s, so when *Vineland* was announced as forthcoming, critics and the popular press alike scurried to celebrate the first Pynchon novel in seventeen years.

Vineland (1990) initially disappointed many readers; yet the fault was not necessarily in the novel. Expectations were high that the new novel would outdo *Gravity's Rainbow,* so some readers could hardly help being let down. Although *Vineland* did receive some favorable reviews, including Salman Rushdie's in *The New York Times Book Re-*

Dust jacket for Pynchon's third novel, the first of his books to become a best-seller

view (14 January 1990), the general response was mixed, and not all the positive reviews did the novel credit. Patient and thoughtful readers (among them N. Katherine Hayles, Madsen, McHale, and Berressem) have begun to see greater depths in *Vineland* than the first wave of reviewers perceived. Nevertheless, some still speculate that *Vineland* could not have been the only novel that consumed Pynchon's time since *Gravity's Rainbow,* and that another big novel is yet to come. In 1994 Pynchon changed publishers, moving from Little, Brown to Henry Holt.

Vineland is set in California in 1984, and its opening line – "Later than usual one summer morning in 1984" – mockingly echoes the "Morning in America" campaign advertisements used in Ronald Reagan's 1984 reelection campaign. *Vineland* is in many ways about Reagan's America and about the erosion of the idealism of the 1960s. While *Gravity's Rainbow* demonstrates some skepticism about the effectiveness of 1960s youth politics, *Vineland* portrays the outright failure of the hippie ideologies of peace and love. Worse, it shows how these ideologies have been co-opted by a commercial culture that tolerates just enough radicalism to keep most people from looking very deeply into what those in power are really up to. Thus, in his fourth novel, Pynchon again focuses on individuals caught on the margins of governmental systems of control.

In the opening scenes of *Vineland,* aging hippie Zoyd Wheeler must fulfill an annual requirement that he publicly demonstrate his insanity so he can continue to receive mental-disability checks – from a government interested, not in ensuring his welfare, but in keeping tabs on his whereabouts. Zoyd's usual stunt is to dress in conspicuous women's clothes and jump through the window of a local bar. By 1984 his annual transfenestration has become a full-scale media event covered by all the local stations, complete with expert analysis. Only this year, Zoyd realizes that the event is no longer under his control at all but is being stage-managed for effectiveness on television. This media exploitation may be the least of his worries. Two old nemeses are closing in on Zoyd: Drug Enforcement Administration field agent and aspiring filmmaker Hector Zuñiga and monomaniacal federal prosecutor Brock Vond, who in the early 1970s enticed away Zoyd's wife, Frenesi Gates, soon after the birth of Zoyd and Frenesi's daughter, Prairie (it is possible that Vond is Prairie's father).

Prairie fills the role of quester familiar from Pynchon's previous novels as she seeks her mother, first through computerized data banks and then through prints of the movies her mother made with the radical collective 24 fps (frames per second) during the late 1960s. What she discovers through these archives and through her mother's friend DL Chastain is that, despite (or perhaps in reaction against) her upbringing by leftist parents blacklisted in Reagan's Hollywood during the McCarthy era of the 1950s, Frenesi became an agent for Vond. Betraying her colleagues and friends and their cause, Frenesi planted the gun used to murder Weed Atman, an initially reluctant leader of a campus uprising at the College of the Surf and thus a founder of the People's Republic of Rock and Roll (PR^3). *Vineland* is neither a nostalgic celebration nor a reactionary renunciation of 1960s counterculture. It does question the simplistic ideology of PR^3, for example, but it also uses Frenesi's filming of Weed's murder to comment on how the images of revolution can be and were used to suppress radicals and to identify them for "Re-Education." Frenesi may not pull the trigger, but she "shoots" on film, and the issue of who controls the image and how it is used is a central theme of *Vineland*.

This theme of the image and its control raises a contentious point in the critical reception of *Vineland:* the role of television. In *Gravity's Rainbow* film provides a densely coded matrix of analogy to the narrative, but in *Vineland* films are often merely trivial television movies (*The Bryant Gumbel Story,* for instance). Worse, to some critics, Pynchon's characters have become addicted to "the Tube." Indeed, DEA agent Hector is so seriously addicted to television that he has to undergo "Tubaldetox" by the National Endowment for Video Education and Rehabilitation (NEVER). The treatment is apparently unsuccessful. The preponderance of references to television, especially to shows such as *The Brady Bunch* and *Gilligan's Island,* underscores a key concern in this novel: the degree to which the response to reality is filtered or always already coded by the overload of television images that have constructed a version of America that suits the economic and social intentions of those in power.

An obvious example is the manipulation of the American political process through control of the images viewers receive, no longer just nightly but twenty-four hours a day. Among the most dedicated television watchers in *Vineland* are the Thanatoids, whose condition is "like death, only different." These undead, hovering in a postmodern purgatory, have lost themselves almost entirely to the video image. They offer an ominous vision of the future as a living death.

Dust jacket for Pynchon's novel about the failure of 1960s idealism in the 1980s

DL and Takeshi Fumimota (teamed up at first as DL's punishment for having put the ninja death touch on Takeshi in a botched attempt to assassinate Vond) make a business of providing karmic adjustment services to the Thanatoids, to ease their passage out of this world. *Vineland* satirizes, not altogether destructively, Californians' penchant for seeking psychological health through Eastern mysticism. Among the satiric vehicles are the Ninjette sisterhood of Kunoichi Attentives and their mountainside retreat, "a sort of Esalen Institute for lady asskickers" that is "notorious ... for having the worst food in the seminar-providing community," where DL, Takeshi, and Prairie find refuge and help. Like *Gravity's Rainbow, Vineland* problematizes rather than dismisses spiritualism and the possibility of powerful forces operating in conjunction with an "other side." And with their ethos of kindness and caring, the Ninjettes – along with DL, Zoyd, and others – represent a counterforce of sorts to the governmental repression represented by Vond.

While Frenesi Gates has some claim to being considered Pynchon's most vicious character ever, Brock Vond is perhaps Pynchon's most distinctly drawn villain. Telegenic, charming, ambitious, and ruthless, he is still ever the mere agent, a hired thug, of those in power. Vond oversteps their bounds, more by his style than in the aims of his program, to pursue his personal agenda of oppression, his flaw emerging in his obsession with Frenesi. He enlists her in the government "snitch system," but he is unable to maintain the total control he desires. One thread of the plot is Vond's attempt to regain control of Frenesi by going after Prairie. His efforts, however, are foiled by the timely defunding of his military operation, halting his plan to snatch Prairie and use her either as bait to trap Frenesi or as a substitute for her mother (a plan about which Prairie herself proves ambivalent).

Dedicated to Pynchon's mother and father, *Vineland* may appear to end with an affirmation of the power of "family" to provide a counterforce to political oppression. It closes during an elaborate, highly ritualized annual family reunion, but this scene of harmony and solidarity (during which the long-awaited reunion of mother and daughter is rendered as a notable anticlimax) is not unmixed with ambiguity and discord, and it cannot counterbalance all the evidence of family dysfunction elsewhere in the novel. At the very end Zoyd and Prairie's dog, Desmond, "*think[s]* he must be *home*" (emphasis added), but that is not to say he is. In this late twentieth-century Vineland, is America being rediscovered, or has "the darkness . . . fallen long stupefied years ago"?

Since the publication of *Vineland*, Pynchon has appeared in print more often than at any other time since the early 1960s. In 1992 he provided the introduction to a posthumously published collection of Donald Barthelme's work, paying homage to an admired contemporary and an old friend. In 1993 he contributed an essay on sloth to a series on the deadly sins published in *The New York Times Book Review*. He also wrote liner notes for *Spiked!: The Music of Spike Jones* (1994) and for the rock band Lotion's album *Nobody's Cool* (1995). Pynchon even interviewed the members of Lotion for *Esquire* magazine in 1996. Some believe that Pynchon is the author of a series of acerbic letters written between the mid 1980s and early 1990 under the pseudonym Wanda Tinasky to the editor of the *Anderson Valley Advertiser* of northern California, but that attribution has not been verified. Pynchon's publisher, Henry Holt, projects that Pynchon's next novel, whose title has not yet been revealed, will appear in spring 1997.

Bibliographies:

Pynchon's Notes, no. 1– (1979–);

Clifford Mead, *Thomas Pynchon: A Bibliography of Primary and Secondary Materials* (Elmwood Park, Ill.: Dalkey Archive, 1989).

References:

Walter Benjamin, "The Storyteller," in his *Illuminations: Essays and Reflections,* edited by Hannah Arendt, translated by Harry Zohn (New York: Harcourt, Brace & World, 1968), pp. 83–109;

Hanjo Berressem, *Pynchon's Poetics: Interfacing Theory and Text* (Urbana: University of Illinois Press, 1993);

Michael Bérubé, *Marginal Forces/Cultural Centers: Tolson, Pynchon and the Politics of the Canon* (Ithaca, N.Y.: Cornell University Press, 1992);

Dale Carter, *The Final Frontier: The Rise and Fall of the American Rocket State* (London: Verso, 1988);

Charles Clerc, ed., *Approaches to* Gravity's Rainbow (Columbus: Ohio State University Press, 1983);

David Cowart, *Thomas Pynchon: The Art of Allusion* (Carbondale: Southern Illinois University Press, 1980);

Deconstructing Gravity's Rainbow, special issue, edited by Bernard Duyfhuizen, *Pynchon Notes,* no. 14 (February 1984);

John Dugdale, *Thomas Pynchon: Allusive Parables of Power* (New York: St. Martin's Press, 1990);

Bernard Duyfhuizen, "Starry-eyed Semiotics: Learning to Read Slothrop's Map and *Gravity's Rainbow,*" *Pynchon Notes,* no. 6 (June 1981): 5–33;

Duyfhuizen, "Taking Stock: 26 Years Since *V.* (Over 26 Books on Pynchon!)," *Novel,* 23 (Fall 1989): 75–88;

Dwight Eddins, *The Gnostic Pynchon* (Bloomington: Indiana University Press, 1990);

J. Kerry Grant, *A Companion to* The Crying of Lot 49 (Athens: University of Georgia Press, 1994);

Geoffrey Green, Donald J. Greiner, and Larry McCaffery, eds., *The* Vineland *Papers: Critical Takes on Pynchon's Novel* (Normal, Ill.: Dalkey Archive, 1994);

N. Katherine Hayles, "'Who Was Saved?': Families, Snitches, and Recuperation in Pynchon's *Vineland,*" in *The* Vineland *Papers,* pp. 14–30;

Molly Hite, *Ideas of Order in the Novels of Thomas Pynchon* (Columbus: Ohio State University Press, 1983);

Charles Hollander, "Pynchon's Inferno," *Cornell Alumni News* (November 1978): 24-30;

Hollander, "Pynchon's Politics: The Presence of an Absence," *Pynchon Notes*, no. 26-27 (Spring-Fall 1990): 5-59;

Kathryn Hume, *Pynchon's Mythography: An Approach to* Gravity's Rainbow (Carbondale: Southern Illinois University Press, 1987);

Douglas Keesey, "*Vineland* in the Mainstream Press: A Reception Study," *Pynchon Notes*, no. 26-27 (Spring-Fall 1990): 107-113;

Peter Kihss, "Pulitzer Jurors Dismayed on Pynchon," *New York Times*, 8 May 1974, p. 38;

George Levine and David Leverenz, eds., *Mindful Pleasures: Essays on Thomas Pynchon* (Boston: Little, Brown, 1976);

Louis Mackey, "*Gravity's Rainbow* and the Economy of Preterition," in *The Meritorious Price of Our Redemption* (1650), by William Pynchon, facsimile edition, edited by Michael W. Vella, Lance Schachterle, and Mackey (New York: Peter Lang, 1993), pp. xxxi-xli;

Mackey, "Paranoia, Pynchon, and Preterition," *SubStance*, 30 (Winter 1981): 16-30;

Deborah L. Madsen, *The Postmodernist Allegories of Thomas Pynchon* (New York: St. Martin's Press, 1991);

Brian McHale, *Constructing Postmodernism* (New York: Routledge, 1992);

McHale, "Slade Revisited, or The End(s) of Pynchon Criticism," *Pynchon Notes*, no. 26-27 (Spring-Fall 1990): 139-152;

Alec McHoul and David Wills, *Writing Pynchon: Strategies in Fictional Analysis* (Urbana: University of Illinois Press, 1990);

Edward Mendelson, "Gravity's Encyclopedia," in *Mindful Pleasures: Essays on Thomas Pynchon*, pp. 161-195;

Mendelson, ed., *Pynchon: A Collection of Critical Essays* (Englewood Cliffs, N.J.: Prentice-Hall, 1978);

Patrick O'Donnell, ed., *New Essays on* The Crying of Lot 49 (New York: Cambridge University Press, 1991);

Richard Pearce, ed., *Critical Essays on Thomas Pynchon* (Boston: G. K. Hall, 1981);

Richard Poirier, "Cook's Tour," *New York Review of Books*, 1, no. 2 (June 1963): 32;

Poirier, "Embattled Underground," *New York Times Book Review*, 1 May 1966, pp. 5, 42-43;

Poirier, "Rocket Power," *Saturday Review of the Arts*, 13 (March 1973): 59-64;

William Pynchon, *The Meritorious Price of Our Redemption* (London, 1650), facsimile, edited by Michael W. Vella, Lance Schachterle, and Louis Mackey (New York: Peter Lang, 1993);

Salman Rushdie, "Still Crazy After All These Years," *New York Times Book Review*, 14 January 1990, pp. 1, 36-37;

Lance Schachterle, "Pynchon and Cornell Engineering Physics, 1953-54," *Pynchon Notes*, no. 26-27 (Spring-Fall 1990): 129-137;

Thomas H. Schaub, *Pynchon: The Voice of Ambiguity* (Urbana: University of Illinois Press, 1981);

Schaub, "Where Have We Been, Where Are We Going?: A Retrospective Review of Pynchon Criticism," *Pynchon Notes*, no. 7 (October 1981): 5-21;

Joseph W. Slade, *Thomas Pynchon* (New York: Warner, 1974; revised edition, New York: Peter Lang, 1990);

Tony Tanner, *City of Words: American Fiction 1950-1970* (New York: Harper & Row, 1971);

Tanner, *Thomas Pynchon* (New York: Methuen, 1982);

Khachig Tölölyan, "Prodigious Pynchon and His Progeny," *Studies in the Novel*, 11 (Summer 1979): 224-234;

Tölölyan, "Seven on Pynchon: The Novelist as Deconstructionist," *Novel*, 16 (Winter 1983): 165-172;

Tölölyan and Clay Leighton, *An Index to Gravity's Rainbow*, revised edition, supplement to *Pynchon Notes* (1989);

Steven Weisenburger, *A* Gravity's Rainbow *Companion: Sources and Contexts for Pynchon's Novel* (Athens: University of Georgia Press, 1988);

Weisenburger, "Thomas Pynchon at Twenty-two: A Recovered Autobiographical Sketch," *American Literature*, 62 (December 1990): 692-697;

Mathew Winston, "The Quest for Pynchon," in *Mindful Pleasures: Essays on Thomas Pynchon*, pp. 251-263.

Philip Roth

(19 March 1933 -)

S. Lillian Kremer
Kansas State University

See also the Roth entries in *DLB 2: American Novelists Since World War II* [first series]; *DLB 28: Twentieth-Century American-Jewish Fiction Writers;* and *DLB Yearbook: 1982.*

BOOKS: *Goodbye, Columbus* (Boston: Houghton Mifflin, 1959; London: Deutsch, 1959);

Letting Go (New York: Random House, 1962; London: Deutsch, 1962);

When She Was Good (New York: Random House, 1967; London: Cape, 1967);

Portnoy's Complaint (New York: Random House, 1969; London: Cape, 1969);

Our Gang (New York: Random House, 1971; London: Cape, 1971);

The Breast (New York: Holt, Rinehart & Winston, 1972; London: Cape, 1973);

The Great American Novel (New York: Holt, Rinehart & Winston, 1973; London: Cape, 1973);

My Life As a Man (New York: Holt, Rinehart & Winston, 1974; London: Cape, 1974);

Reading Myself and Others (New York: Farrar, Straus & Giroux, 1975; London: Cape, 1975).

The Professor of Desire (New York: Farrar, Straus & Giroux, 1977; London: Cape, 1978);

The Ghost Writer (New York: Farrar, Straus & Giroux, 1979; London: Cape, 1979);

Novotny's Pain (Los Angeles: Sylveste & Orphanos, 1980);

Zuckerman Unbound (New York: Farrar, Straus & Giroux, 1981; London: Cape, 1981);

The Anatomy Lesson (New York: Farrar, Straus & Giroux, 1983; London: Cape, 1984);

The Prague Orgy (London: Cape, 1985);

The Counterlife (New York: Farrar, Straus & Giroux, 1987; London: Cape, 1987);

The Facts: A Novelist's Autobiography (New York: Farrar, Straus & Giroux, 1988; London: Cape, 1988);

Deception (New York: Simon & Schuster, 1990; London: Cape, 1990);

Philip Roth at the time of Reading Myself and Others
(photograph by Nancy Crampton)

Patrimony: A True Story (New York: Simon & Schuster, 1991; London: Cape, 1991);

Operation Shylock: A Confession (New York: Simon & Schuster, 1993; London: Cape, 1993);

Sabbath's Theater (Boston: Houghton Mifflin, 1995; London: Cape, 1995).

Collections: *The Philip Roth Reader* (New York: Farrar, Straus & Giroux, 1980; London: Cape, 1980);

Zuckerman Bound (New York: Farrar, Straus & Giroux, 1985) – comprises *The Ghost Writer,*

Zuckerman Unbound, The Anatomy Lesson, and *The Prague Orgy.*

A major writer of twentieth-century American literature, Philip Roth has produced an impressive body of fiction that has attracted widespread critical commentary. His ideas and his wit range widely. Like the great satirists of the past, Roth is concerned with serious public and private subjects – genocide, war, the foibles of modern democracies, family life, the individual's inner turmoil, and the writer's imagination and craft. His prolific career has been marked by dualities of low comedy and high seriousness, contributing to his reception by critics and readers as both enfant terrible and literary elder statesman. Roth addressed this contradiction in *Reading Myself and Others* (1975), admitting that one of his "continuing problems" has been "to find the means to be true to these seemingly inimical realms of experience that I am strongly attached to by temperament and training – the aggressive, the crude, and the obscene, at one extreme, and something a good deal more subtle and, in every sense, refined at the other." He cites Philip Rahv's well-known essay "Paleface and Redskin" (*Kenyon Review,* Summer 1939), which segregated American writers either in the "paleface" mode of Henry James and T. S. Eliot or the "redskin" mode of Walt Whitman and Mark Twain, and notes that in postwar America when "a lot of redskins ... went off to universities and infiltrated the departments of English," they became writers who felt "fundamentally ill-at-ease in, and at odds with both worlds." Roth places himself among these writers, whom he labels "redface," and the result in his work is "a self-conscious and deliberate zigzag," each book "veering sharply away from the one before."

Born to Herman and Besse Finkel Roth in 1933, Philip Roth grew up in a working-class Jewish neighborhood of Newark, New Jersey. In this environment he was educated, he says, to be a good, responsible person, "controlled ... by the social regulations of the self-conscious and orderly lower-middle-class neighborhood ... and by the taboos that had been filtered down ... in attenuated form, from the religious orthodoxy of my immigrant grandparents." After attending Weequahic High School (1946-1950), he spent a year at Newark College of Rutgers University before transferring to Bucknell University in 1951 and graduating magna cum laude and Phi Beta Kappa with a B.A. in English in 1954. He received an M.A. in English at the University of Chicago in 1955, and, after a few months in the U.S. Army, from which he was discharged early because of a back injury, he returned to the University of Chicago in 1956 as a doctoral student in English. By the time he left the program in 1957, several of his stories had been published, and four had won awards. On 22 February 1959 he married Margaret Martinson Williams. They were legally separated in 1963, and she died in an automobile accident five years later. On 29 April 1990 Roth married actress Claire Bloom. They later divorced.

Roth's artistic achievement has been recognized with many awards, honors, and grants, including a Houghton Mifflin Literary Fellowship (1959), a National Institute of Arts and Letters Grant (1959), a Guggenheim Fellowship (1959), a National Book Award and a Jewish Book Council of America Daroff Award in 1960 for *Goodbye, Columbus* (1959), a Ford Foundation Grant in playwriting (1962), a Rockefeller Fellowship (1966), election to the National Institute of Arts and Letters (1970), National Book Critics Circle Awards (1987) for *The Counterlife* (1987) and *Patrimony* (1992), a P.E.N./Faulkner Award (1993) and the *Time* magazine Best American Novel of 1993 award for *Operation Shylock,* and a National Book Award for *Sabbath's Theater* (1995). He has contributed to literary studies as the general editor of the Penguin Writers From the Other Europe series and as a teacher at the University of Chicago (1956-1957), the Iowa Writers' Workshop (1960-1962), Princeton University (1962-1964), the University of Pennsylvania (1965-1977), and Hunter College of the City University of New York (1989-   ).

Roth's literary world is shaped by masters cited in his own fiction – Franz Kafka, Anton Chekhov, Henry James, and Jonathan Swift. While a student, Roth read the great canonical novels whose influence is evident in his subject and style as well as in the literary dialogues of his characters. It was not until he read *The Assistant* (1957), by Bernard Malamud, and *The Victim* (1947), by Saul Bellow, however, that Roth understood the connection between "literature and neighborhood." Citing Malamud's *The Magic Barrel* (1958) and Bellow's *The Adventures of Augie March* (1953) in an interview with Alvin Sanoff, Roth acknowledged that he was moved by Malamud's original manner of giving life to material that he recognized and that he was dazzled by Bellow's "big approach" to arguments, personalities, and language. Among contemporary writers, it is Bellow whom Roth mentions most frequently, identifying him as "the 'other' I have read from the beginning with the deepest pleasure and admiration" in the dedication to *Reading Myself and*

Others. Malamud and Bellow paved the way for Roth's fictional transmission of himself and his Jewish characters.

Although he generally avoids writing about Judaism, Jewishness is an essential condition of Roth's person and fiction. In *The Facts* (1988) he writes, "Not only did growing up Jewish in Newark of the thirties and forties, Hebrew School and all, feel like a perfectly legitimate way of growing up American, but, what's more, growing up Jewish as I did and growing up American seemed to me indistinguishable." Accusations of self-hatred and anti-Semitism began with publication of his early stories "Defender of the Faith" and "Epstein" in *Goodbye, Columbus* and burgeoned with the publication of *Portnoy's Complaint* (1969). Roth has defended himself against these charges in interviews, critical essays, and fictional episodes. In *Reading Myself and Others* he argues, "I have always been far more pleased by my good fortune in being born a Jew than my critics may begin to imagine. It's a complicated, interesting, morally demanding, and very singular experience, and I like that. I find myself in the historic predicament of being Jewish, with all its implications." The hostility of Jewish critics has provided Roth with a major subject for his fiction, the situation of the Jewish American writer.

During a 1984 interview with Hermione Lee, Roth explained that the Jewish quality of his books resides not in their Jewish subjects, but in "the nervousness, the excitability, the arguing, the dramatizing, the indignation, the obsessiveness, the play acting – above all the talking." Since that time his exploration of Jewishness has turned to Jewish subjects, taking a historic, international political turn that includes situating characters in Israeli settings and attributing dialogue to them that is centered on Jewish life and survival. Hillel Halkin is correct in his observation that "a sheer, almost abstract passion for being Jewish seems to grow stronger in Roth's work all the time." Roth's mature, more substantive, and complex treatment of Jewish subjects has garnered wide acclaim.

Roth is a profound comic writer whose characters confront personal and public aspects of modernity. His satiric universe is largely populated by artistic and intellectual second-generation Jews, as well as Israeli and Palestinian nationalists, zany baseball players, mindless media professionals, and corrupt politicians. In this universe, as Murray Baumgarten and Barbara Gottfried observe, "the comic moment reveals the underlying seriousness of contemporary life." Encountering a panorama of fluid social/political/ethnic/cultural late-twentieth-century American experience, his protagonists question the accepted order and challenge conventional behavior and attitudes. They struggle with critical questions of the time – including sexual obsession and the ethics of social, aesthetic, and political choices. Roth's engagement of political subjects has led him to explore the Holocaust, totalitarian repression in eastern Europe, Middle Eastern unrest, the My Lai Massacre, the foibles of American national and international policy, and both overt and genteel manifestations of anti-Semitism. The targets of Roth's satire include bourgeois Jewish parents, academics, novelists and literary critics, politicians, and journalists. With a deft talent for mimicry of accents and speech patterns, Roth moves adroitly from the sociolinguistic matrix of urban and suburban American Jewish life of the 1950s to the double-speak of Nixonian politics, Arab and Israeli nationalist political discourse, the babble of Soviet-bloc bureaucrats, and American media platitudes and clichés.

Starting with *My Life As a Man* (1974) most of Roth's fiction has been highly autobiographical. His protagonists are generally born in the 1930s to middle-class, nonreligious but ethnic Jewish families in Newark, New Jersey. Most have studied and taught literature at the university level and become writers. In the early fiction they generally reject Jewish women of their class and intellectual accomplishments to lust after and then battle with lower-class Gentile women, who are often the products of abusive families. In the later fiction his protagonists graduate to relationships with more intelligent, better educated American and English Gentile women. Although they are detached from the organized Jewish community, they have an abiding interest in exploring their Jewish identities, and in the most recent fiction they have become more immersed in Jewish history in Europe and Israel. Aside from Lucy Nelson in *When She Was Good* (1967), Roth's women are secondary figures, interesting primarily for the way they affect the male protagonist or allow the male to define himself.

Throughout his career Roth has experimented with narrative strategy, producing fiction that has grown increasingly sophisticated and technically interesting. He has mastered the realistic novel, the comedy of manners, and postmodernist fantasy and metafiction. As Roth explained in "Writing American Fiction" (1960), he shifted from the realistic mode to the fantastic because he was convinced that American reality was outdoing the American writer's creative powers. His fictions in the realistic mode – *Goodbye, Columbus* (1959), *Letting Go* (1962),

Dust jacket for Roth's first novel, which draws on his experiences as a graduate student at the University of Chicago during the mid 1950s

and *When She Was Good* (1967) – deal with sensitive individuals breaking down under pressure in the context of American middle-class reality. In an interview with Alan Lelchuk, Roth describes these characters as being "swept away . . . [by] their own righteousness or resentment . . . [and] living beyond their psychological and moral means." *Portnoy's Complaint* (1969), *Our Gang* (1971), *The Breast* (1972), and *The Great American Novel* (1973) depart sharply from the style and tone of his first three novels, relying on fantasy, distortion, bad taste, parody, and caricature to expose the injustices and hypocrisies of society. With *The Ghost Writer* (1979), *The Counterlife* (1987), and *Operation Shylock* (1993) Roth brilliantly juxtaposed social realism with postmodernist fantasy and narrative experiment. A recurrent theme in Roth's fiction has been the subject of fiction and the imagination of the writer. He focuses on the authorial self, the manner in which the novelist draws on his experience to create fictional characters, and the ways in which the writing of fiction is analogous to the processes by which people create and sustain their lives.

Roth arrived on the literary scene in 1959 with *Goodbye, Columbus,* a novella and five stories that introduce his comic, satiric talent to advantage. The title novella, a comedy of manners, underscores the clash between urban and suburban, upper-middle-class and lower-middle-class characters, individual determinism versus social and familial coercion, the Jewish immigrant past and contemporary American values. Its narrator, Neil Klugman, is a lower-middle-class boy from Newark; Brenda Patimkin, the girl he desires, is a Radcliffe student, daughter of an adoring, financially secure, and generous father, who has removed his family from the Jewish immigrant neighborhood of Newark to elegant suburban Short Hills. The mismatched lovers share a summer romance, but the relationship, based primarily on sexual attraction, is too feeble to withstand their social and psychological differences.

Roth presents the increasingly prosperous, upwardly mobile middle class from the vantage point of a young man who does not share their material advantages, but who is educated and feels smugly superior to them. A series of contrasts in their own attitudes and in those of their intimates illuminates the sharp division between the lovers. Neil's cramped space and life as a boarder in the home of an immigrant aunt and uncle contrasts with Brenda's spacious home and posh lifestyle among the nouveau riche. Neil's state-college education and job at a public library pale when they are viewed in the glitter of Brenda's Radcliffe education and summer afternoons spent at the country club. Brenda's bratty, demanding younger sister is similarly juxtaposed with a reserved, polite black schoolboy who frequents the library to look at a book of Gauguin prints. Enticed by the affluence and possibilities of life in Short Hills, Neil is nevertheless wary of the price it exacts and resentful of the Patimkins' vulgar consumerism.

The Patimkins are caught between their ethnic Jewish identity and their desire to be accepted by the upper-class Protestant community of Short Hills. Culturally deracinated, they are in danger of breaking the frayed thread binding them to Jewish communal life. Unlike the protagonist of *The Rise of David Levinsky* (1917), Abraham Cahan's classic tale of Jewish assimilation, who has had a sound Talmudic education, the Patimkins are limited to the outward trappings of Jewish life and essentially lacking in Jewish literacy. Levinsky fully understands the intellectual and cultural price he paid for American assimilation and business success and regrets straying from the values that sustained him as a youth in Russia. The Patimkins fail to comprehend what they lack. Only Mr. Patimkin nostalgically laments his children's inability to understand a word of Yiddish. Although he pleases Mr. Patimkin because he understands Yiddish, Neil is estranged from observant Jewish life. His family is active in the Workman's Circle, signifying a Yiddish-socialist commitment, not an allegiance to religious law. It is not surprising that after the dissolution of the relationship with Brenda on Rosh Hashanah, he goes to work at the library instead of participating in communal prayer in a synagogue.

Roth's detractors interpreted the satire in *Goodbye, Columbus* as an attack on the Jewish community. A closer reading reveals that the butt of his satire is not the Jewish community as a whole but lapsed Jews who have abandoned traditional Jewish values of scholarship and piety to embrace American materialism, Jews so paralyzed by anti-Semitism that they are threatened by the presence of Orthodox Jews. "Eli, The Fanatic," the gem of the collection, exemplifies this theme. The Jewish community of Woodenton – inhabited by assimilated Jews with wooden sensibilities, who practice self-repression as a consequence of the long history of anti-Semitism – is dismayed to learn soon after the Holocaust that a group of displaced Jewish children has been moved into a local mansion, which is to become a yeshiva. The prospect of children and teachers appearing in town in long black caftans and skullcaps is odious to the upwardly mobile middle-class community. Dealing with these Holocaust survivors is at once traumatic and redemptive for Eli Peck, the lawyer retained to evict the yeshiva residents. By the end of the story Eli has succumbed to the greater Talmudic wisdom of the survivor-mentor, has donned the Hasidic suit in metaphoric acceptance of his true identity, and has gone forth to claim the Judaic legacy for his newborn son. Eli's behavior is unintelligible to his neighbors, who assume he has had a nervous breakdown and try ineffectually to tranquilize the "new" Eli. The drug "did not touch [his soul] down where the blackness had reached." Eli – whose Hebrew name means "ascend," "uplift," and "exalted" and whose biblical namesake acted as judge and high priest of the sanctuary at Shiloh – has symbolically become a judge passing sentence on the lapsed Jews of Woodenton.

Three years after achieving critical acclaim for *Goodbye, Columbus,* Roth expanded his treatment of the theme of individual determination versus social and familial coerciveness in his first novel, *Letting Go* (1962), a saga of two young men arriving at different theories about human connections. A long, serious work about the complexities of relationships between parents and children, men and women, and friends, the novel introduces an array of minor choric characters from a broad spectrum of ethnic groups and social classes in scenes drawn from Roth's experiences in Hyde Park and at the University of Chicago while he was a graduate student and part-time instructor. Equally adept at writing a satirical set piece on the social milieu of a pretentious English-department chairman entertaining the faculty or a naturalistic portrait of the downtrodden working poor, the young Roth skillfully captures the accents and intonations of his characters and the nuances of their social worlds.

The novel explores the meaning of self and the impact of involvement with others through the intersecting careers and social lives of two earnest young men who meet as graduate students in English in Iowa. As the title implies, a healthy measure of independence is essential for the survival of the relationship and for each individual's emotional well-being and maturation. Alter egos Gabe Wallach and Paul Herz also struggle with engagement and detachment in their relationships with demanding parents and complicated, troubled women. Each seeks to achieve adult autonomy while maintaining an emotional connection to their fathers. Each confronts ethical dilemmas, is sensitive to moral responsibility, and reaches diametrically opposed conclusions about human connection. Using a contrapuntal structure of foil characters and parallel plots, Roth creates two separate, yet integrated narratives that merge through the interaction of their chief protagonists.

Gabe Wallach, the central consciousness and primary character, is the son of an indulgent and possessive father; he is involved with, but uncommitted to, several women and entangled in the lives of the secondary character, Paul Herz, and his wife, Libby. The death of his mother has left Gabe the primary concern of his lonely father, whom he loves but from whom he strives to maintain a separate life. Despite professional success, Gabe is directionless and troubled, unsure of what his life means. Paul is an earnest composition instructor and struggling novelist suffering under the pressures of social and economic deprivation. He has been estranged from his parents since his marriage to a Gentile, a decision taken to honor his sense of moral obligation but one he regrets as he struggles to live with a neurotic wife.

In the course of the novel Gabe and Paul manipulate one another, their families, and their friends under the guise of love or duty. Drawn to his overworked, poverty-stricken classmate, Gabe initiates their relationship by giving Paul a copy of *Portrait of a Lady* (1881), Henry James's exploration of corrosive, exploitative relationships. Enfolded in the novel is a forgotten letter in which Gabe's mother confesses to manipulating his father under the guise of creating a good life for him. The James novel and the letter are interpretive guides to Gabe's behavior, foreshadowing his obsessive entanglement in the Herzes' marriage. At the heart of Gabe's moral dilemma is his desire to be good to people while remaining sufficiently disengaged from them. Gabe helps Paul to secure a teaching position, visits Paul's parents to effect a reconciliation between father and son, and actively participates in the couple's adoption efforts. Libby Herz perceives Gabe as a rescuer from her husband, whose sexual alienation has frustrated her, and Paul welcomes Gabe for relieving him of responsibility for Libby. The adoption efforts trigger Gabe's emotional crisis and lead to the recognition that he has become excessively embroiled in the affairs of others. As the novel draws to a close, Gabe flees to London to evaluate his past and to make a new beginning.

The novel concludes as it began, with a letter. Paralleling his mother's letter, Gabe's letter admits that he has overstepped the bounds of friendship. Despite his vow to "do no violence to human life, not to another's, and not to my own" – a promise he made in response to his mother's admission – he has interfered in the Herzes' lives, has driven his father to an undesirable marriage, and shares responsibility for his former lover's decision to relinquish her children to her former husband. Yet, unlike Paul, who concludes that connection is undesirable, Gabe understands that freedom does not consist of alienation from those who make claims on the individual.

Roth's next novel, *When She Was Good* (1967), is described by many critics as a self-conscious effort by the author to write a book without Jews, to distance himself from the charges of anti-Semitism and self-hatred that had been leveled against his first two books. Like *Letting Go,* it examines the lives of characters who reached maturity in the 1950s, but unlike its predecessor, which employed an elevated prose style and focused on the psychological stress of urban, college-educated members of that generation, *When She Was Good* turns its sociological gaze on uneducated people from small towns in provincial America who have not had the benefits of higher education, and the language of the novel authentically reflects their mundane existence. Though not a favorite of critics, *When She Was Good* demonstrates that Roth can achieve verisimilitude of character, cultural mores, and language in writing about people outside the familiar Jewish culture of the East Coast. Although the novel seems naturalistic in its accumulation of massive detail, its disruption of simple chronology and its alternating centers of consciousness, as Bernard Rodgers notes, contribute to its technical modernity.

Through delineation of the characters' banal language, Roth forces readers to examine American clichés about morality, family life, law and order, and male/female relationships. A drama of family destructiveness, the novel examines five generations of a midwestern family from the pioneer period of the 1890s through the Cold War era of the 1950s, revealing the deterministic conditions that shape its self-righteous, vindictive antiheroine, Lucy Nelson, and showing how she became a paranoiac shrew and how her life, which began with a desire to be and do good, turned destructive. Lucy Nelson is both victim and villain in a social and family construct that destroys her. She is caught in an environment that is founded on the patriarchal concept of the male as protector and of the female as protected. In her family, however, aside from the strong grandfather who supports several generations, the males are generally unable to perform their pre-

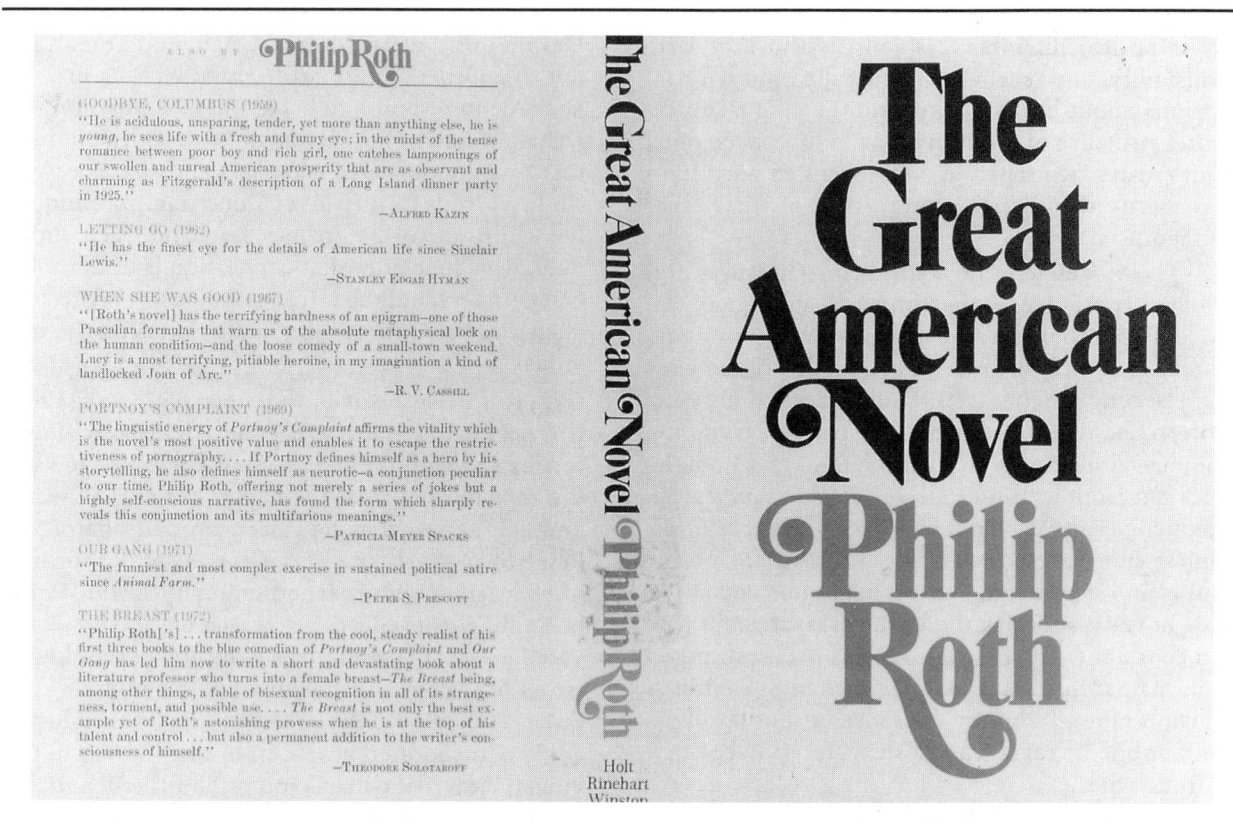

Dust jacket for the satiric novel in which Roth uses baseball as a metaphor "to dramatize the struggle between the benign national myth of itself that a great power prefers to perpetuate, and the relentlessly insidious, very nearly demonic reality ... that will not give an inch in behalf of that idealized mythology"

scribed roles. Lucy grows up resenting her father for abdicating the role of family protector and responsible provider and pitying and resenting her mother for tolerating her husband's weaknesses and remaining a dependent daughter all her life. Abandoning the pretense the other women honor, Lucy rejects the notion of male protection deserving of her submission and strives, instead, for autonomy. She develops a strong self-righteous streak and is determined to replace the family pattern of tolerance for personal weakness with one of confrontation.

The extent to which Lucy is trapped by her social milieu is dramatized in her relationship with and marriage to Roy Bassert, a vapid young man, recently returned from the army and aimlessly waiting to decide what to do with his future. An ordinary boy with a penchant for popular music and Hydrox cookies, Roy courts Lucy with lyrics of popular songs to mask his own inability to think about their relationship. Just as she begins college, her passport away from the family and Roy, Lucy discovers that she is pregnant. She forces Roy to honor his duty to her and the child, and they become trapped in a loveless marriage. Initially Lucy tries to be a submissive and attentive wife, but as Roy's weaknesses become increasingly apparent, she resists. Confident in her own power and moral rectitude, Lucy imposes her will on Roy by shaming him, and to avoid confrontation he generally pretends to be what she wants him to be. Condemned by Roy's family for her dominance and unable to win the moral support of her own people, Lucy becomes hysterical, runs to the local Lover's Lane, where Roy had originally seduced her, and dies, melodramatically, of exposure.

Disparity between ideals and reality constitute the drama of the novel. Having sought to help his family, her grandfather destroyed their ability to function as mature autonomous adults. In the third generation Lucy's reductive self-righteousness and insistence that Roy conform to her values destroys her family. Although readers would be justified in reading this narrative as a limited, sociopsychological exploration of a rigidly moral person, Roth intended a broader interpretation and associated the "moral" rhetoric Lucy used to disguise her vengeful destructiveness with the kind of language the government used about "'saving' the Vietnamese by systematic annihilation." That he had a national fable in mind, with Lucy's attitudes paralleling the national character, is suggested in several of his working titles for the novel: "The American Way," "An American Girl," "Saint Lucy of the Middle West," and "An American Saint."

When She Was Good shares with *Portnoy's Complaint* what Roth sees as the "problematical nature of moral authority and of social restraint and regulation" arising out of conflict between the individual and the family. Addressing the similarities of the books in a response to Diana Trilling's review of *Portnoy's Complaint* in *Harper's* (August 1969) Roth argued that although the novels are "wholly antithetic in cultural and moral orientation," the protagonist in each assumes the position of self-righteous and enraged progeny. The Jewish and Gentile households are different, but the reactions of the unhappy children are the same: "rage as well as a sense of loss and nostalgia."

Portnoy's Complaint integrates two central themes of Roth's work, sexuality and Jewishness. The monologic form of the novel, an analysand speaking to his psychiatrist, is the vehicle for Portnoy's disclosure of childhood memories and adult fixations. Influenced by Franz Kafka, who showed him how to get "hold of guilt ... as a comic idea," Roth created Portnoy as a comic protagonist whose trials and tribulations would elicit sympathy and laughter from readers. Judith Paterson Jones and Guinevera A. Nance observe that Roth takes "the Kafkaesque preoccupation with victimization and guilt to its limits in an exaggeration that resembles burlesque." The teller of his own tragicomic tale, the complaining monologuist characterizes his situation as "living ... in the middle of a Jewish joke." Dr. Spielvogel and the reader are brought into this Jewish joke through the flow of Portnoy's hyperbolic, exclamatory speaking voice.

The psychoanalytic setting provides a realistic justification for Alex Portnoy's fervent soul baring and self-castigation, for his frank sexual language and disclosures. Guilt ridden about the disparity between his public role as humanitarian and his private shame, the "Assistant Commissioner for Human Opportunity" hopes to find a cure for his self-perceived failures and to resolve the conflict that shapes his personality. In the course of his monologue it becomes clear that Portnoy sees himself as the victim of the conflict between the moral principle and the pleasure principle. To illustrate the nature of the conflict Roth presents a humorous account of its genesis, its social consequences, and the comic collision between the forces that shape Portnoy's life.

Dust jacket for Roth's 1977 novel, in which the protagonist hopes to become a "rake among scholars, a scholar among rakes"

Essentially a parodic Bildungsroman, the novel begins with Portnoy's childhood, but Roth departs from conventional lineal development and interjects incidents from various periods in a manner befitting the free-flowing monologue of the psychiatric patient. The unifying element of Portnoy's childhood and adult memories is the tension of his conflict with institutional morality alongside his desire to live responsibly and ethically. At the heart of Portnoy's problems is the mother-child relationship. Sophie Portnoy is not only the dominant figure in her son's infantile and adult sexual fantasies but also the arbiter of morality in the family. A caricature of a stereotypical Jewish mother, Sophie is, according to Sanford Pinsker, "more a Borscht-belt fantasy than an actual person, the easy villain in this self-constructed Rorschach ... the Jewish-Mother joke incarnate, full of sardonic, but ultimately castrating wit." She succeeds in expressing her anxieties about her son's welfare in exaggerated and exasperating interrogations and dire warnings that elicit reader laughter despite Portnoy's despair. Portnoy's father, who suffers from chronic constipation, is a source of sympathetic humor. In Portnoy's view Jake Portnoy is oppressed and powerless, completely dominated by his wife, by WASPS (white Anglo-Saxon Protestants), and by his stubborn sphincter. Although Alex Portnoy recognizes his father's hard work on behalf of the family, he experiences that love and sacrifice as a burden contributing to his guilt.

Rodgers argues persuasively that the influence of Kafka's *Letter to His Father* (written 1919, published 1952), which Roth had been teaching during the time he was writing *Portnoy's Complaint,* may be seen in the construction of Roth's novel as a "filial confession and an indictment, ... which attempts to come to emotional and intellectual terms with the parent its author holds responsible for the neurotic nightmare that is his life." Parallels between Kafka's and Roth's texts include messages acknowledging the domineering parent's influence over the child's imagination, similar childhood memories, and a causal relationship between childhood experiences and adult behavior. Both sons recall their parents as oppressive judges who issued irrational decrees and demanded complete subservience. The comedy of his remorse for transgressing Jewish and family standards, whether it be the dietary prohibitions, masturbation, or lusting after Gentile women, leads Portnoy to discover the depth of guilt in his personality. The "joke on Portnoy," Roth muses in *Reading Myself and Others,* is "that for him breaking the taboo turns out to be as unmanning in the end as honoring it."

Achieving adult masculinity for Portnoy is the capacity to "be bad – and enjoy it"; to desist from being a Jewish mother's well-mannered and well-behaved son. To that end he sets out to rebel against undue parental supervision by claiming autonomy through masturbation and to free himself from the restraints of Jewish law by transgressing dietary laws and pursuing non-Jewish women. Portnoy argues that his pursuit of Gentile women is not merely an effort to break a taboo or an expression of wanting forbidden fruit but an affirmation of assimilation into American society. He wants to ape the brothers of these women, those "engaging, good-natured, confident, clean, swift, and powerful halfbacks for the college football teams." From adolescence on Portnoy is irresistibly attracted to Gentile women. Unlike the Jews of his parents' generation, to whom America meant political asylum and economic opportunity, Portnoy sees America as "a *shikse* nestling under your arm whispering love, love, love, love love!" Sex with "nice" Gentile women, such as Kay Campbell ("The Pumpkin") or Sarah Abbott Maulsby ("The Pilgrim"), is the way to "Conquer America." Having found in Mary Jane Reed ("The Monkey") an attractive and sexually adroit partner who performs feats he had previously only imagined, Alex seeks to educate her, directing her reading in the hope that they can become "The perfect couple: she puts the id back in Yid, I put the oy back in goy." Her hillbilly background and semiliteracy, however, are sources of embarrassment. As Jones and Nance argue, "In recounting his sexual aggression against gentile girls (and their American backgrounds), Portnoy reveals the extent to which women are primarily representational to him. . . . characterized first by being non-Jewish and next by being representative of a particular segment of Americana." Portnoy's ambiguous feelings about discarding ethnicity for assimilation emerge in his ridicule of these women and their society as well as his feelings of superiority.

In the concluding segment of the novel Portnoy seeks normal sexual fulfillment and a meaningful relationship in Israel, but in the land where Jews are the dominant people, he is impotent. Instead of helping him to resolve the warring Jewish and sexual elements of his personality as he hopes, Naomi, a Sabra kibbutznik, gives him a scathing lecture on Jewish self-hatred, denounces his self-deprecating humor, and rebukes him for wasting his life. Naomi's rejection compels Portnoy to face the truth about himself and seek help.

During the 1970s Roth turned his satiric gaze from the individual's psychological plight to the foibles of American public life, introducing burlesque and black comedy to mock political corruption. "On the Air" (1970), *Our Gang* (1971), *The Great American Novel* (1973), and several essays – "Cambodia: A Modest Proposal" (1970), "The President Addresses the Nation" (1973), "Our Castle" (1974), and "Writing and the Powers that Be" (1974) – powerfully denote Roth's moral outrage with contemporary politics. His Juvenalian political satire in *Our Gang,* which he defined as "an exaggerated impersonation, a parody of President Richard M. Nixon's style of discourse and thought," is as caustic as works by Swift or John Dryden. He defends his heavy-handed, broad satire by linking it to the tradition of American political humor represented by James Russell Lowell's *The Biglow Papers* (1848, 1862), David Ross Locke's "Nasby Letters" (1861–1887), H. L. Mencken's parodies written in "Gamalielese," and to the broad comedy of popular culture as seen in Ole Olsen and Chic Johnson, Stan Laurel and Oliver Hardy, Bud Abbott and Lou

Costello, and other slapstick comedians. Two epigraphs, one from Swift's *Gulliver's Travels* (1726) and the other from George Orwell's "Politics and the English Language" (1950), announce Roth's intention to debunk contemporary political jargon. The quotation from *Gulliver's Travels* addresses lying and the resulting confusion in communication, an apt introduction to the character Tricky E. Dixon, who uses language to obfuscate rather than reveal his thoughts. The passage from Orwell goes to the heart of the connection between the debasement of language and unscrupulous politics that is Roth's theme. Through exaggeration and distortion of language and incident, Roth expresses his moral indignation at Nixon's acceptance of the murder of unarmed Vietnamese civilians, highlights the illegal misdeeds of the president's associates, and lampoons media discourse.

The book begins with Dixon's denunciation of "abortion on demand" and promotion of "the sanctity of human life – including the life of the yet unborn." Dixon responds to a troubled citizen who is raising questions about Lt. William Calley's possible abetting of an abortion during the My Lai massacre with sanctimonious double-talk in a manner that reveals his political opportunism and legalistic obfuscation. In a deft parody of the president's style, Roth captures the rhythms of his speech and the warped logic of the Vietnam era through the use of pietistic language and political clichés.

Rodgers points to Roth's "Application of the comic techniques of . . . the nineteenth-century . . . American humorists" in political caricatures that attempt "to expose and deflate" their subjects. The president and his close advisers, dressed in college football uniforms, meet in a "blast-proof underground locker room" to plan strategy against the Boy Scouts of America, who are demonstrating in Washington because they view Dixon's support of the unborn as implicit sanctioning of sexual intercourse. To placate the scouts Dixon considers announcing that his children are adopted and that he is a homosexual, but then one of his advisers informs him that homosexuals also have intercourse. A presidential press conference is the vehicle for Roth's hilarious attack on the mindless prattle of the media. "Mr. Asslick," "Mr. Daring," "Mr. Shrewd," "Miss Charmin," "Mr. Catch-Me-in-a-Contradiction," and "Mr. Fascinated" allow Tricky Dixon to get away with his "San Dementia" promise to bring justice and equality not only to every fetus but to microscopic embryos as well. One absurdity leads to the next as reporters engage Dixon on the voting rights of fetuses. Roth's protest against debased language continues with a crushing caricature of the alliterating Vice President Spiro Agnew in Vice President What's-his-name's comments on the slain President Dixon and a eulogy delivered live on nationwide television by the Reverend Billy Cupcake. The press is chastised again in a burlesque featuring the dean of network commentators, Eric Severehead, who remarks, "A hushed hush pervades the corridors of power. Great men whisper whispers while a stunned capital awaits." The discrepancy between official reverence and ignoble truth surfaces in reports from "Morton Momentous," "Peter Pious," "Ike Ironic," and "Brad Bathos" of the arrival of thousands in Washington to surround the White House – not to grieve but to take credit for the assassination.

Among the scenes that attest to Roth's ingenuity is the final chapter, in which Dixon, now in Hell, makes a speech to the legions of the damned. Campaigning against Satan for the leadership of Hell, he attacks his opponent for being insufficiently aggressive. Basing his campaign on his superlative record of planting "seeds of bitterness and hatred between the races, the generations, and the social classes" in the United States, thus disrupting national harmony for years to come, and on his accomplishments in Southeast Asia, which he turned into "nothing less than Hell on Earth," he claims that he is exceptionally qualified to be the leader of Hell. No longer burdened by "conscience, caution and consideration for one's reputation," as he was when he was president, he views Hell as "a great challenge and a great opportunity." Here he will reach his true potential, and, if elected, he will "see Evil triumph in the end," assuring that "our children, and our children's children, need never know the terrible scourge of Righteousness and Peace."

In *The Great American Novel*, published two years after *Our Gang*, Roth continued to employ fantasy and satire to express his discontent with American public life. Using baseball as a metaphor for a society that has become destructively competitive, Roth exposes deeply revered verities and hypocrisies, satirizing greed, materialism, religious dogma, phony patriotism, racism, and the media. Ben Siegel, one of the most perceptive readers of *The Great American Novel*, astutely observed that the object of Roth's censure is the "disparity in American life between appearance and reality, between professed idealism or good will and an underlying self-seeking grossness or vulgarity."

Roth begins the work by parodying and burlesquing the traditions of the American novel. The first-person narrator, Word Smith, opens his prologue with the line "Call me Smitty," evoking Ishmael's opening line in Herman Melville's *Moby-Dick* (1851) and comparing himself to the narrator who survived the wreck "to tell the tale." Roth defines himself and his work in comparison to Melville, Nathaniel Hawthorne, Mark Twain, and Ernest Hemingway and parodies their work, while ranting against a success-driven literary establishment. In a section titled "My Precursors, My Kinsmen," Word Smith invokes Hawthorne's preface to *The Scarlet Letter* (1850) as the model for his prologue, burlesques Hemingway's statements about "Literatoor," establishes picaresque and oral-tradition links with Twain's *The Adventures of Huckleberry Finn* (1884), and treats *Moby-Dick* as the archetypal allegory of American baseball.

An old sportswriter and a fan of the now-defunct Patriot League, which had previously been on a par with the American and National Leagues, Smith is determined to restore the status and legacy of the suppressed league and the Rupert Mundy team, which became so corrupt that fans and baseball officials conspired to eradicate the team from the national scene and memory. The chronicle of the team's rise and fall is structured as a picaresque, yearlong road journey filled with misadventures and blunders, affording Roth opportunity to create superb short character sketches and fantastic, intricate plot episodes. The novel is set during World War II, when able-bodied players have been called to military service and are replaced by physically and morally handicapped men, social misfits, and psychopaths sporting allegorical or mythological names. Among the grotesques on the team are John Baal, a gambling, drinking, home-run hitting ex-convict; O. K. Ockatur, a midget relief pitcher with "a fierce hatred of all men taller than himself"; Hot Ptah, a fiery catcher with a wooden leg; Bud Parusha, a one-armed outfielder, who uses his mouth to remove the ball from his glove; Frenchy Astarte, whose "specialty" is dropping high infield flies; Roland Agni, an All American forced by his father to join the worst team possible as a lesson in humility; and Ulysses S. Fairsmith, who has been distracted from the business of reality by his determination to find divine providence at work in all events, the morally stern manager and baseball missionary who is driven to his death by the inept Mundys.

The description of the Mundys' game with a group of mental patients is representative of the novel's parodic humor. By taking the game seriously, the Mundys prove themselves to be more deranged than their adversaries. The reader laughs at the neurotic behavior of the players on both sides but also sympathizes with the Mundys' pathetic desire to win. As David Monaghan points out, "the Mundys are able to maintain the illusion that they are involved in a genuine contest only because they have the empty rhetoric of baseball to fall back upon." Addressing the success of Roth's comic style, Monaghan notes, "By subtly exaggerating the absurdities and clichés of sports language, politics, and journalism," Roth simultaneously achieves sufficient association with and distance from pop culture "to make a comment about the ability of the debased American language to effect a radical separation between situation and response."

A prime target of Roth's satire, American economic opportunism is embodied in the owners and managers of the teams in the league, who are motivated by greed and an insatiable lust for power. Frank Mazuma, owner of the Kakoola Reapers, recruited Bob Yamm, the first midget ever to play in the major leagues, reasoning that if the fans wanted to make a hero out of a midget, it was their business – especially if hiring Yamm is good for business. Mazuma encourages the exploitation of Yamm and his wife, aided and abetted by the corrupt media that Roth characterizes as mindless and tasteless exploiters of celebrity. In his criticism of the owners, Roth leaves little doubt of his analogy between the league and the nation: "The fate of the Mundys and of the republic were inextricably bound together." The *R* that once stood for Rupert "must henceforth be considered to stand for nothing less than this great Republic." For Roth, "It was not a matter of demythologizing baseball, . . . but of discovering in baseball a means to dramatize the struggle between the benign national myth of itself that a great power prefers to perpetuate, and the relentlessly insidious, very nearly demonic reality (like the kind we had known in the sixties) that will not give an inch in behalf of that idealized mythology."

The abuse of language is another major target of *The Great American Novel*. Among the most extended and accomplished examples of this aspect of Roth's satire is Fairsmith's appropriation of the rhetoric of religion and patriotism: "For what is a ball park but that place wherein Americans may gather to worship the beauty of God's earth, the skill and strength of His children, and the holiness of His commandment to order and obedience." Other instances include the misappropriation of the rhetoric of the civil rights movement and media exploitation of and by Bob Yamm, who fashions himself as the spokesman for an oppressed group that has been denied the opportunity to play professional baseball. The novel closes with an effective parody of Cold War rhetoric as an owner offers a McCarthyite tirade on the infiltration of American baseball by a Communist Party eager to destroy America and the free-enterprise system. The Patriot League, found to be filled with Communists and fellow travelers, is dissolved; its records obliterated. Although the loftiness of Roth's intent is evident and the satiric baseball metaphor for destructive competition and consuming greed in American life is highly amusing, his farcical approach, as William Gass contends, "compromises the purpose of the novel leaving readers expecting a resolution that they do not get."

While satire shared the stage with fantasy in *The Great American Novel* and *Our Gang,* fantasy dominates Roth's other major book of the early 1970s, *The Breast* (1972). The influence of Kafka is powerfully manifest in this tale of metamorphosis, in which Roth departs from his customary manner of beginning with real people and events and then fantastically exaggerating them for comic effect to convey the nature of their reality. In *The Breast* he reverses that process, beginning with a bizarre and comic transformation of a professor of comparative literature into a 155-pound, six-foot breast, culminating in a five-inch, highly sensitive nipple, and then explores its implications with painstaking realism. Before the change David Kepesh had managed to control his life, surviving a difficult marriage and divorce and developing a sensible relationship with the "even-tempered and predictable" schoolteacher Claire Ovington. Just as he is feeling that his life is comfortable, he undergoes "a massive hormonal influx," "an endocrinopathic catastrophe," and "a hermaphroditic explosion of chromosomes." Kepesh can still speak and hear, but he cannot see, taste, smell, or move. His tactile sensibility, however, the source of his agony and ecstasy, is vastly heightened. Mentally alert, the professor tries to use his intellect to explain his condition, but cannot find a rational explanation for his change. He cannot attribute his condition to the psychological or social causes that account for the plight of other Roth protagonists.

Making the incredible credible, Roth takes great pains to create the impression that Kepesh is a breast and resists the temptation to treat the whole matter comedically. In an interview "On The Breast" with Alan Lelchuk, Roth explained that his approach was to treat this "potentially hilarious situation . . . perfectly seriously" with the goal of convincing the reader "to accept the fantastic situation as taking place in what we call the real world at the same time that [he hoped] to make the reality of the horror one of the issues of the story." Contributing to the aura of realism at the center of the fantasy is Kepesh's tenacious struggle to understand his fate, to confront his new physical reality. By having Kepesh narrate his story, Roth allows the reader to suspend disbelief and participate in the narrator's efforts to find a plausible response to the incredible.

For a time Kepesh believes that he is insane or that all that has transpired is a dream. He contends that he is the victim of an illusion caused by teaching Kafka's *The Metamorphosis* (1915) and Nikolay Gogol's *The Nose* (1836) and theorizes, as Jones and Nance explain, "that he fell so completely under the sway of the 'great imaginations' who created fictions of transformation that he attempted to bridge the gap between art and life and to make the fictions real by actually undergoing metamorphosis." Nonetheless, he is unable to persuade his psychoanalyst that he has "out-Kafkaed Kafka" and become the victim of his own imagination, that whereas Gogol, Kafka, and Swift could only conceive the incredible, he "took the leap. Made the word flesh." The transformation is real, and the way into madness would be to pretend otherwise.

An abandoned effort to create a sequel to *The Breast* led Roth to the realization that the antecedent realistic details of the surreal story were worthy of a novel. Five years after the first book and following publication of *The Great American Novel* and *My Life As a Man,* Roth returned to the cast of *The Breast* for *The Professor of Desire* (1977). He develops the characters more completely and reconsiders Portnoy's theme of the male protagonist struggling with the duality of his persona, his efforts to reconcile the sensual with the moral and serious aspects of his character. Once again the central conflict is between the censorious moralist and the libidinous adventurer torn between conscientious intellectual endeavor and erotic desires.

Secondary characters are paired to objectify the protagonist's psychic conflict. In childhood Kepesh must choose between the influence of his respectable hotelier parents and the vulgar comedian Herbie Bratsky. Kepesh wants to be good, to please his adoring parents, but he is lured by the freedom and exhibitionism of the brash entertainer. His adult psychic dualities are objectified in his professional colleagues: the department head Arthur Schonbrunn, a parody of the proper professor, and the poet Ralph Baumgarten, who ignores the restraints of decorum and decency. Among women Kepesh must choose between the affectionate Eliza-

Dust jacket for Roth's 1981 novel, in which he describes the hazards of literary celebrity

beth and the debauched Birgitta; between the nurturing, loving Claire and the sensual Helen. Although Kepesh is attracted to Baumgarten, Birgitta, and Helen for their guiltless sensuality, he finds it difficult to achieve such freedom in his own life.

To balance the polarities of his character, Kepesh proposes to become, a "rake among scholars, a scholar among rakes" on the model of Thomas Babington Macaulay's description of Richard Steele, and to follow the Byronic dictum of being "studious by day, dissolute by night." While in London on a Fulbright grant to study Arthurian legends and Icelandic sagas, he devotes himself to sexual adventures instead of scholarship, first in the red-light district and then in a ménage à trois with two Swedish women. As with Portnoy, his guilt manifests itself as fear of impotence. Convinced that sexual abandon with Birgitta is inimical to his best interests and that it is not in his nature to be a "shameless carnal force," the rake capitulates to the scholar and he returns to the United States to pursue a Ph.D. free from "temptation." Graduate studies in the United States also fail to command his undivided attention. Kepesh instinctively knows that he should avoid the worldly Helen Baird, but he cannot resist her exotic background, which includes having run off to Hong Kong, at age eighteen, with a married man twice her age. She prefers life to literature and informs the doctoral candidate that she hates books, schools, and libraries, everything to which he is devoted, because they misrepresent life. When their marriage ends in divorce, Kepesh takes refuge in teaching and writing a book on romantic disillusionment in the stories of Anton Chekhov. Like Portnoy, he turns to a psychiatrist to help him gain insight into his conflicted dualities, to understand why love and intimacy are difficult.

The professor's problems with women appear to be resolved when he develops a loving relationship with Claire Ovington, an undemanding, nurturing, intelligent woman, who provides him a refuge from loneliness and impotence. Claire's sane love heals Kepesh psychically and returns him to intellectual productivity. Despite his appreciation of Claire, whom he designates his "rescuer," and his satisfaction with their relationship, by the end of their first year together, memories of his lascivious affair with Birgitta disturb his equilibrium. Counterpoised against an idyllic summer in the country, Kepesh wonders how soon he will tire of Claire's "wholesome innocence." He worries about entrapment and prepares for the demise of the relationship. By the conclusion of the novel, Kepesh believes it is only a matter of time before the man he has become with Claire "will give way to Herbie's pupil, Birgitta's accomplice, Helen's suitor, yes, to Baumgarten's sidekick and defender." Yet unlike Roth's other self-absorbed, conflicted protagonists, Kepesh understands that his failure to reconcile the warring elements of his character is alone responsible for the loss of the relationship.

More penetrating than the love story is the literary theme of the novel. Only the rewards of literature remain a constant satisfaction as a means of gaining perspective on life. In the works of Chekhov and Kafka, Kepesh finds insight on the struggle between liberty and restraint. Through Chekhovian reference, Roth embellishes the reader's understanding of Kepesh, as he finds parallels to his own conflict between compliance and freedom. Kepesh's essay "Man in a Shell," based on a Chekhov story of the same title, examines oppressive conformity in Chekhov's fictional universe and accounts for "Chekhov's pervasive pessimism about the methods – scrupulous, odious, noble, dubious – by which the men and women of his time try in vain to achieve 'that sense of personal freedom' to which Chekhov himself is so devoted." Even when life with Claire is peaceful, Kepesh turns to Chekhov, "Listening for the anguished cry of the trapped and miserable socialized being." Through Kepesh's understanding of the transitory nature of his relationship with Claire, Roth achieves the "feel for the disillusioning moment and for those processes wherein actuality seemingly pounces upon even our most harmless illusions, not to mention the grand dreams of fulfillment and adventure" that he attributes to Chekhov's genius.

Although Chekhov's work assists Kepesh in identifying his problems, it is Kafka who helps him realize that his misery can be borne. In a fictionalized version of Roth's own visit to Kafka's grave in Prague, Kepesh meets a deposed Czech professor of literature who has been deprived of political and professional freedoms during the Soviet seizure of power. This fellow Kafka devotee explains that for him, and others like him, life is made bearable by devotion to literature, that literature offers prototypes of survival. Impotent against an authoritative regime, the Czech professor advises that the bookish should "Sink their teeth into [great prose] . . . . Into the books, instead of the hand that throttles them." Kafka's stories of "thwarted K.'s banging their heads against invisible walls" help Kepesh realize that the enemy is internal. If literature is to save him, it must teach him to make peace between his contending selves.

Before leaving Prague, Kepesh writes a lecture on the theme of erotic desire in the form of Kafka's "Report to an Academy" (1924). The lecture reveals his intention to use literature to confront life, to explain the relevance of his own libidinous history to his teaching of literature. He must acknowledge his erotic life to help his students understand how Gustave Flaubert's *Madame Bovary* (1856) and other great books on erotic desire have referential relationship to their lives. He will teach his students that literature is essentially "referential," that it is located in experience and that it teaches "something of value about life." As Saul Bellow urged symbol hunters to beware, Roth issues a warning to literary critics through the professor's advice to avoid critical jargon and to address the value of fiction beyond structure and symbol. Thus, in a period when influential and trendy authors are positing a theory of meaninglessness, Roth, like Bellow and Cynthia Ozick, insists that life is meaningful and that literature can help us discern its relevance.

Literature as a fictional subject also engages Roth in *My Life As a Man* (1974). One of Roth's best books, this metafiction considers the problem of the artistic mode that best transforms personal experience into art, recounts the story of Peter Tarnopol, who is trying to understand himself as a man and a writer, and introduces Nathan Zuckerman, who becomes the primary vehicle for Roth's portrait of an artist. Through a double layer of indirection – Roth's alter ego, the fictive novelist Tarnopol, who tells the story of his failed marriage through his fictive alter ego, Nathan Zuckerman – Roth raises questions about the ability of fiction and autobiography to present the truth and demonstrates the writer's difficulty in achieving distance from his material.

Tarnopol's effort to exorcise his obsession with a failed marriage, to "demystify" the past by writing about it, illustrates Roth's interest in describing and defining experiential reality through literature and his concern for the uses the writer makes of personal experience. Having previously rebuked readers for identifying him with his protagonists, Roth now teases readers so inclined by ascribing many of the publicly known details of his life to Tarnopol. They share similar childhoods, academic precocity, highly praised first books, Guggenheim Fellowships, teaching positions at large midwestern universities, and unhappy marriages to divorcées who have later died in automobile accidents.

Tarnopol's problem of self-presentation, whether to write from the vantage point of Flaubertian distance or the confessional mode of Henry Miller, remains unresolved and accounts for Roth's structural link of the useful fictions with autobiography. The novel is divided into two parts: "Useful Fictions," which includes two stories featuring Nathan Zuckerman, and Tarnopol's long autobiographical narrative. Hermione Lee argues persuasively that the three narratives present the writer as "victim and analyst, confessor and interpreter of his own sufferings." The first of the two alternative fictions, "Salad Days," is a comic narrative of Nathan Zuckerman's childhood and adolescence in Camden, New Jersey, chronicling his early intellectual and sexual development. In an exuberantly comic tone, it details Zuckerman's protected upbringing by doting parents, his undergraduate rebellion against his working-class Jewish background under the tutelage of an English professor who inspired him to live a life of books, culture, and genteel manners. It also recounts his literary triumphs, his sexual conquest of the local zipper king's daughter, whom Nathan turns from "the perfect little lady" into "the most licentious creature he'd ever known," and an army experience that teaches him that he is no longer master of his own destiny.

The second fiction, "Courting Disaster," which alters some biographical details, is Zuckerman's first-person narrative of his metamorphosis from accomplished son to failed husband. The conflicting desires and allegiances that characterize Tarnopol's real-life surface in the split between Zuckerman's intellectual seriousness and literary high-mindedness and marriage with a woman to whom he is perversely drawn, a woman he wished to be rid of and to whom he "loathed making love." The reader, like Zuckerman himself, is initially perplexed by his decision to marry a neurotic divorcée five years his senior, with a past that includes incest, a violent, degrading marriage, and a proclivity for madness. Reminiscent of Paul Herz, Zuckerman finally attributes his acceptance of this disastrous marriage either to his dependence on literature for his ideas or his insufficient understanding of the wisdom found in literature. For the young man trained in the literature of moral seriousness, Lydia is attractive because he perceives of her as having attained moral stature through suffering and survival. Drawn by the contrast between Lydia's harsh experiences and his own sheltered salad days, he believes she will help him attain manhood when he accepts responsibility for her welfare and that of her child. Enhancing the self-reflexivity of the novel are invented readers and critics of the "Useful Fictions" whose contradictory commentaries echo the judgments of Roth's critics. Tarnopol's sister admonishes the writer to find source material that is distanced from his life. His brother finds literary derivations and influences in the writings of Bellow, Norman Mailer, Miller, and Malamud. Editors profess diametrically opposed views. One approves of "Salad Days" because he reads it as an attack on the "prematurely grave and high-minded author," and he disparages "Courting Disaster" as the work of a "misguided and morbid 'moral' imagination." Another critic views "Salad Days" as "smug, and vicious, and infuriating, all the more so for being so clever and winning" and finds "Courting Disaster" "absolutely heartrending."

In "My True Story," which combines the comic and sober tones of the "Useful Fictions," Tarnopol forsakes the fictitious and the guise of an alter ego to present his version of the life and marriage that has been the subject of his art. His autobiography, like his fictions, endeavors to clarify the writer's obsession with his wife and how he came to marry her "entirely against my inclinations but in accordance with my principles." The "nice civilized Jewish boy" renounced the "nice civilized Jewish girl" because she was "rich, pretty, protected, smart, sexy, adoring, young, vibrant, clever, confident, ambitious" for his ideal Gentile woman, "something taxing . . . something problematical and puzzling," who has lived and suffered and can therefore make him a man. Like Zuckerman, Tarnopol is the victim of his own literary education. He realizes that he sought "intractability," but raised to a high moral level, "somewhere, say, between *The Brothers Karamazov* and *The Wings of the Dove*." He says he wanted the "same sense of the difficult and the deadly earnest that informed the novels I admired most." To his dismay his relationship with Maureen turned out to be the stuff, not of high art, but of melodrama.

Self-presentation remains problematic and unresolved. Tarnopol discovers that his memoir is taking on the nature of fiction, that the self he wants to describe with fidelity is beginning to seem imaginary, that his revelations may be another "useful fiction." He broods over words, worries whether words "born either of imagination or forthrightness" can completely capture the reality they represent, "that words, being words, only approximate the real thing."

In *Zuckerman Bound* (1985), a compilation of three novels – *The Ghost Writer, Zuckerman Unbound* (1981), *The Anatomy Lesson* (1983) – and *The Prague Orgy* (1985), a short epilogue delineating the literary and intellectual pilgrimage of a twentieth-century Jewish American novelist, Roth resurrects Nathan Zuckerman to scrutinize the literary theme more fully than he had in *My Life As a Man*. Zuckerman moves from artistic promise in *The Ghost Writer,* to critical acclaim and public celebrity in *Zuckerman Unbound,* to writer's block and psychosomatic syndrome in *The Anatomy Lesson,* and to artistic and physical regeneration in the *The Prague Orgy.*

The Ghost Writer employs bildungsroman and quest conventions to explore critical questions about art, the relationship of emerging author and literary master, and the writer's moral responsibility to society. This work is cast as a retrospective narrative of a successful novelist, who recalls the early period of his career. After his biological father denounces his work as potentially harmful to the Jewish community, Nathan Zuckerman journeys to the Berkshire home of a famous, reclusive Jewish American writer, E. I. Lonoff, seeking to clarify his identity as a writer and a Jew, as well as to discuss literature and learn from the master. During the course of the brief visit, Nathan is also enlightened by Lonoff's wife, a woman disappointed with her husband's approach to life and art, and by Amy Bellette, a beautiful young woman, a Holocaust survivor whom Lonoff has brought to the United States. One of his best writing students, she is working on his papers for a Harvard collection. Through a series of binary oppositions – bad son/good daughter, martyred wife/sensual mistress, biological father/literary mentor, indulgence/asceticism, Abravanel/Lonoff, stylistic polarities represented by Byron and James – Roth ushers his aspiring writer through a day of encounters presaging personal and professional maturity through dedication to the writer's task.

The first part of *The Ghost Writer,* titled "Maestro," focuses on Zuckerman as Bildungsroman hero, trying to determine whether to follow the model of Lonoff, who resembles Malamud in his restraint and orderly approach to life and art or to fashion his career on the model of the flamboyant, passionate, energetic worldly writer Abravanel, who resembles Bellow. In Lonoff's study Zuckerman reads Henry James's "The Middle Years" (1917), a story about a perfectionist and compulsive reviser. Paralleling James's austere ideal of dedication is Lonoff's asceticism and his stories about "thwarted, secretive, imprisoned souls," which inspire Nathan. Beyond the master's dedication to art, the novice is attracted to Lonoff's fiction for "the feelings of kinship that his stories had revived . . . for our own largely Americanized clan, moneyless immigrant shopkeepers to begin with, who'd carried on a shtetl life ten minutes walk from the pillared banks and gargoyled insurance cathedrals of downtown Newark; . . . for our pious, unknown ancestors, . . . [and] the sense given by such little stories of saying so much." Zuckerman is in awe of the Lonoff hero who, a decade after Hitler, "seemed to say something new and wrenching to Gentiles about Jews, and to Jews about themselves."

Following a Joycean pattern in the "Nathan Dedalus" chapter, Roth portrays a young artist, tracing his relationship to his past, to his family and community. The central conflict is based on the elder Zuckerman's disapproval of Nathan's story about a family inheritance. Echoing the criticism Roth received from Jewish detractors of *Goodbye, Columbus,* father accuses son of writing stories that disparage Jews and promote anti-Semitism. "As far as the Gentiles are concerned," he tells Nathan, "your story . . . is about one thing and one thing only. . . . It is about kikes. Kikes and their love of money." Unsuccessful in his bid to convince Nathan to withdraw "Higher Education," Doc Zuckerman enlists the help of a highly regarded local judge.

Judge Wapter represents the parochial world from which the young writer seeks escape. Although Wapter acknowledges the history of artists' estrangement from community values and claims to be free of intolerance, in his view Nathan has transgressed socially acceptable boundaries. He writes Nathan a hilariously censorious letter posing a series of hostile questions insinuating that Nathan's story would satisfy Julius Streicher or Joseph Goebbels, and he closes by advising the young writer to see the Broadway production of *The Diary of Anne Frank.* Contrary to its intended effect, Wapter's Nazi analogy infuriates Nathan and sustains his defense of freedom of the imagination. Furthermore, the philistine attack convinces him that he is in the tradition of Flaubert, James Joyce, and Thomas Wolfe, all "condemned for disloyalty or treachery or immorality by those who saw themselves slandered in their works."

Nathan's fidelity to family and community is evident both in the affinity he feels for Lonoff's ethnic subjects and his own Anne Frank fantasy. As Roth had earlier metamorphosed Franz Kafka into a Newark Hebrew School teacher in "Looking at Kafka" (1973) so Zuckerman transmogrifies Amy Bellette, Lonoff's refugee-protégée, as Anne Frank, secret Holocaust survivor. The Jewish son who disappoints his parents by "betraying" Jews in his fiction, is enamored of the legendary "sainted" Jewish daughter, whom he imagines sacrificing reunion with her father in order that, through her assumed death, her art and Holocaust witness may live. The Anne that engages Zuckerman's imagination and love is the novice writer, who, like him, desires independence from family and is devoted to free thought and nonconformity. Through his invention of the survivor, Nathan acts out his anxiety about the double burden of the Jewish writer: the need for aesthetic distance from those he writes about and responsibility to their history. Furthermore, his fantasy of marriage to Anne Frank is a means of vindicating himself to his father and assuring eternal invulnerability to charges of anti-Semitism.

To invoke the Anne Frank story for purposes other than Holocaust transmission is fraught with danger. Although Roth's appropriation of a Holocaust victim for Nathan's marriage fantasy and authorial rationalization may seem a lapse of aesthetic judgment, he tempers the lapse with a meditation on anti-Semitism and the response to the Holocaust. Zuckerman argues that the fate of most European Jews during the Holocaust is a subject of indifference to non-Jews, that Anne's story became so popular precisely because "the young girl of her diary was . . . only dimly Jewish . . . the daughter of the father who calmed her fears by reading aloud to her at night not the Bible but Goethe in German and Dickens in English." He understands and makes readers grapple with the realization that "To expect the great callous and indifferent world to care about the child of a pious, bearded father living under the sway of the rabbis and the rituals – that was pure folly. . . . To ordinary people it would probably seem that they had invited disaster by stubbornly repudiating everything modern and European – not to say Christian." The reader is encouraged to escape from the banal Anne of Broadway and Hollywood, to examine the diary from a fresh perspective. Through the artist's reverie, Roth persuasively dislodges Anne from the mythic attic sentimentalist who wrote, "I still believe that people are really good at heart," and introduces a more intellectually and morally astute Anne of the Weterbork transport, Anne of Auschwitz and Belsen, who "had not come to hate the human race for what it was . . . but she did not feel seemly any more singing its praises."

The Ghost Writer ends with an argument between the Lonoffs on the self-absorption of the artist in which Hope refers to her husband's devotion to order and style at the expense of lived experience and human involvement. Nathan recognizes the limitations of Lonoff's isolation; yet he remains sympathetic to the master and values his affirmation. The final lines are a benediction from Lonoff, permission from the spiritual father for the novice to be the writer he wants to be, one who declares artistic independence from family and community whose ethical and ethnic constraints would impede his imagination.

As in *The Ghost Writer,* the most interesting questions in *Zuckerman Unbound* explore the nature of the artist and his connection to his work, his family, his community, and his roots – as well as the separation of writer and subject. At midcareer, thirteen years after the period covered in *The Ghost Writer,* Nathan Zuckerman has lived through three failed marriages, published four novels, and is coping with celebrity. He is acclaimed and denounced for the outrageously and explicitly sexual *Carnovsky,* much as Roth was for *Portnoy's Complaint.* The mail brings an accusation that "it is hardly possible to write of Jews with more bile, contempt, and hatred." For readers incapable of separating the creator from his creative invention, Roth was Zuckerman, just as Zuckerman is Carnovsky. These readers "had mistaken impersonation for confession."

The hazards of fame assault Zuckerman as he rises from obscurity. He is expected to change his lifestyle to accommodate his fortune: to move to a fashionable address, wear designer clothing, spend lavishly, have a financial adviser, and invest so that his money will "make money." Relatively free of his father's censure, since the elder Zuckerman is dying in a Florida nursing home, he is besieged by the public. Most irritating to him are people who presume to comment on his life and work simply because he is a celebrity. Assuming that Carnovsky is autobiographical and that Nathan has breached confidentiality, antagonists condemn the work as anti-Semitic and express sorrow for his parents.

Among the perils of fame is the attention of unwanted admirers and opportunists. Such a figure, presented in the comic mode, is Alvin Pepler, a former marine who accosts Nathan at a Second Avenue delicatessen, flatters him, compares him to other celebrities from the region, and thanks him for putting Newark, their common city of origin, on the literary map. A former celebrity quiz kid and victim of the scandalous rigged shows of the 1950s, Pepler still harbors animosity toward the producers who, he believes, were motivated by anti-Semitic sentiments to engineer his defeat and provided answers for his WASP replacement. Now Pepler claims to be a writer, seeking Nathan's help to publish a book that will set the quiz-show record straight and clear his name. Like the schnorrer who stalks the painter in Malamud's "The Last Mohican" (1958), Pepler persistently turns up to make demands of Nathan. When flattery fails, he succumbs to reproachful spite and threatens to kidnap Nathan's mother if he fails to pay him $50,000. Nathan's refusal to become involved in Pepler's schemes is the catalyst for a farcical attack that includes denigration of Nathan's literary portrayal of Newark and the accusation that the idea for *Carnovsky* was stolen from Pepler.

The last section of the novel, "Look Homeward, Angel," centers on Zuckerman's relations with his family before and after publication of *Carnovsky.* Nathan rushes to the hospital to comfort his father, who has suffered a coronary. Unable to formulate a simple declaration of love, Nathan tries to console his father with a new scientific theory of the endlessly self-renewing life of the universe. The last word Doc Zuckerman utters "into the eyes of the apostate son" is *Bastard*. The father-son antagonism is carried over to the relationship between Zuckerman and his brother, Henry, who confirms that Nathan is the bastard responsible, through writing *Carnovsky,* for their father's decline and death. In his ef-

Dust jacket for the first American edition and cover for an advance proof copy of the first British edition of Roth's 1983 novel, which he later collected with The Ghost Writer *(1979),* Zuckerman Unbound *(1981), and* The Prague Orgy *(1985) as* Zuckerman Bound *(1985)*

fort to force Nathan's recognition he condemns Nathan's lack of literary restraint, his failure to understand that his writing has consequences: "Everything is exposable! Jewish morality, Jewish endurance, Jewish wisdom, Jewish families, – everything is grist for your fun machine."

Nathan discovers, as did Thomas Wolfe, that one cannot go home again. The novel concludes with Nathan's visit to the Newark neighborhood of his childhood, now a black ghetto. Everything has changed. The apartment house where he lived is surrounded by a chain-link fence and inhabited by people to whom he is a nobody. Filled with a sense of loss, Nathan realizes he is "no longer any man's son, . . . no longer some good woman's husband, . . . no longer [his] brother's brother." He is without intimates. He is stripped of the useful past. Zuckerman is truly unbound.

The death of his father and the transformation of Newark at the close of the second book of the trilogy have left Nathan bereft of subject: "No longer a son, no longer a writer. Everything that had galvanized him had been extinguished." At the beginning of *The Anatomy Lesson* Nathan is suffering from back and neck pain, physical discomforts symptomatic of his psychic angst and writer's block. While physicians are unable to diagnose or treat his malady, a psychoanalyst suggests it is self-inflicted punishment; that he is suffering because he is "the atoning penitent, the guilty pariah," the "remorseful son," and "author of *Carnovsky*." Although Zuckerman rejects this theory as well as the view that his unconscious is "suppressing his talent for fear of what it'd do next," he is bereft of inspiration and the physical stamina to write. He turns to painkillers, vodka, and four substitute mothers for comfort. Jenny, a painter, dispenses food and encouragement to change his life and live with her in the mountains of Vermont. Diana, a young college student, does secretarial work for him and makes Nathan feel "as if Temple Drake had hitched up from Memphis to talk about Popeye with Nathaniel Hawthorne." Gloria, his financial adviser's wife, provides food and visits equipped with a nippleless bra, crotchless panties, and a length of braided rope for Nathan's amusement. Jaga, a Polish émigré, treats him for hair loss and entertains him with stories of her mismatched love affairs. Each caters to his sexual desires.

The most entertaining and self-reflexive aspect of *The Anatomy Lesson* is the segment on Nathan's nemesis, Milton Appel, a literary critic, modeled on Irving Howe. Appel's criticism of *Carnovsky* and his "reconsideration" of Zuckerman's fiction in *Inquiry* burlesques Howe's "Philip Roth Reconsidered," published in the December 1972 issue of *Commentary*. Having found Zuckerman's early stories "fresh, authoritative, exact," Appel now describes them as "tendentious junk," and he unleashes an attack that makes "Macduff's assault upon Macbeth look almost lackadaisical." Mirroring Roth's dismay over Howe's review, Nathan is devastated by Appel's hostile review because the critic was one of his literary heroes. As Roth and his colleagues admired Howe's writing, so Zuckerman revered Appel's essays in *The Partisan Review* and the critic's battle to distance himself from his Jewish lower-class background. Admiring Appel's writing about the "the gulf between the coarse-grained Jewish fathers whose values had developed in an embattled American immigrant milieu and their bookish, nervous American sons," Zuckerman has modeled his own style on the Jewish self-consciousness that he discovered in the writing of Appel and other Jewish intellectuals of the period, those characterized as having "The disputatious stance, the aggressively marginal sensibility, the disavowal of communal ties, the taste for scrutinizing a social event as though it were a dream or a work of art." Associating the best of intellectual freedom with the postimmigrant Jewish sons of Appel's generation, Zuckerman bitterly resents Appel's revised assessment precisely because it legitimates Nathan's middlebrow detractors, middle-class and suburbanite Jews whose taste Appel has despised. Unable to puncture the dignity of the critic when he refuses Appel's request for an Op-Ed piece for *The New York Times* on behalf of Israel, Nathan resorts to comical acts of revenge. He impersonates Appel as an infamous pornographer, proprietor of Milton's Millennia and publisher of *Lickety Split*. In an uproarious monologue, he tells a stranger that *Lickety Split* differs from *Playboy* only in its sacrifice of the intellectual articles that make *Playboy* socially acceptable. Zuckerman continues to dissemble in this outrageous style, implicating both Appel and Mortimer Horowitz, a figure resembling Norman Podhoretz, the editor of *Commentary*, in his grotesque inventions.

Recalling Mrs. Lonoff's complaint about her husband in *The Ghost Writer*, Zuckerman discovers that he, too, is guilty of rejecting life for art. Like expatriate writers, fleeing their homelands to "spend the rest of their lives thinking about nothing else," Zuckerman has fled Newark for Chicago and New York; yet he has repeatedly mined Jewish Newark for his fiction. Now that he has lost his subject, he is desperate and claims, "I'm sick of raiding my memory and feeding on the past, . . . I want an active connection to myself. I'm sick of channeling everything into writing. I want the real thing, the thing in the raw, and not for the writing but for itself." This realization prompts Zuckerman to abandon literature for a medical career. Before he is able to execute his plan, however, the novel concludes with an incapacitating accident, his fall against a tombstone in a Jewish cemetery. This emblematic fall results in a fractured jaw, which necessitates wiring his mouth shut. The novel begins and ends with silence. First, the author bereft of subject, cannot write; then, the nonstop talker cannot speak.

The Anatomy Lesson may be read as a simultaneous illustration and critique of the excessive self-reflexivity of contemporary fiction. Unlike the writers Roth's literary men admire – Kafka, James, Chekhov – Zuckerman's imagination has become detached from the world and constrained by the circumscribed universe of the text. He realizes that he has become too self-absorbed to write good fiction. As Jonathan Brent observes, "in Zuckerman we find not the portrait of the artist brought up to date since Stephen Dedalus, but the portrait of the imagination severed from any world except that contained in the artist's mind. While it acts to purify and dramatize its own self-creating conflicts, Zuckerman's imagination is not chastened by any moral, social, political, religious, or even artistic objectives, aside from the requirements of the well-made story." His imagination has not freed him intellectually, emotionally, or spiritually. It has simply detached him from ordinary experience and society; hence, his wish to "unchain himself from a future as a man apart and escape the corpus that was his." The writer who envisioned many possibilities in *The Ghost Writer* is brought in *The Anatomy Lesson* to full comprehension of his limitations. In an interview with Asher Z. Milbauer and Donald G. Watson, Roth explained, "Coming to terms with the profane realities of what [Zuckerman] had assumed to be one of the world's leading sacred professions is for him a terrific ordeal – his superseriousness is what the comedy's about." Contrary to the first volume of the trilogy, which concludes with a validation of Zuckerman's literary voice, the second and third books close with metaphors of loss and silence. In the second, loss of family and neighborhood signify diminished literary subject; in the third, physical pain and loss of voice parallel a blocked writing career and an abandoned vocation. It remains for the epilogue to restore Nathan Zuckerman to literature.

In that epilogue, *The Prague Orgy,* the escape that Zuckerman sought from his profession at the close of *The Anatomy Lesson* is reversed. Now readers encounter the regenerated novelist, the reformed man, and the returned Jew. Zuckerman is re-bound to the heritage that sustains Roth's literary protagonists, to Jewish history and culture. Derived from Zuckerman's notebook entries, the first-person narrative depicts Zuckerman as a respected writer with an international following. In Prague he meets a writer and an actress who have suffered for their art. Sisovsky's work is banned because of a satiric book he wrote at age twenty-five, and Kalinova has been persecuted for playing the role of Anne Frank and abandoning her husband for a Jew. In Soviet-occupied Czechoslovakia there is no aesthetic distance between the self and the roles one plays. Consequently the actress who plays Anne Frank convincingly is branded as a Jew lover in a nation that is officially anti-Zionist, and Anne Frank herself is viewed not as a writer who told the truth about totalitarianism but as a "curse and a stigma." The persecuted couple seek the American's aid in recovering the Yiddish stories of Sisovsky's father, a Holocaust victim characterized as the "Jewish Flaubert." Zuckerman undertakes the mission, which parallels Roth's rescue of East European fiction as general editor of Writers from the Other Europe. In a scene echoing David Kepesh's dream meeting with Kafka's whore, Zuckerman meets with Sisovsky's estranged wife to plead for the elder Sisovsky's manuscripts. He secures the manuscripts, only to have the police confiscate them and expel him from Czechoslovakia on trumped-up charges that he is a "Zionist agent." In Kafka's city Zuckerman, like Joseph K, is arrested without having committed a crime.

The unifying theme of the trilogy is the tension between connection and separation of the writer's artistic and communal responsibilities. The epilogue brings the theme to resolution, affecting a reconciliation of the two loyalties in portraits of writers struggling to survive and be creative under a repressive regime. In the totalitarian context, Zuckerman learns, "stories aren't simply stories; it's what the Czechs have instead of life. Here they have become their stories in lieu of being permitted to be anything else." Storytelling is a form of political resistance. As he wanders around Prague, he recognizes it as a repository of the Eastern European Jewish past and recalls a World War II era childhood fantasy of Jews buying Prague "when they had accumulated enough money for a homeland." Instead of architectural restoration, he imagined the redemption of Prague through Jewish literature, all the stories to be told there, "all the telling and listening to be done, their infinite interest in their own existence, the fascination with their alarming plight, the mining and refining of tons of these stories — the national industry of the Jewish homeland . . . the construction of narrative out of the exertions of survival." Just as storytelling served as a spiritual form of resistance in the long history of oppression of the Jews, so, too, it is an effective form of defiance of Soviet oppression in contemporary Czech society.

Joseph Cohen reads Zuckerman's effort to restore Sisovsky to his rightful literary reputation as the reformed character's enactment of the Jewish charitable principle of *Tsedakah*, and his resistance to sexual temptations as illustrative of acceptance of *Menschlechkeit*, the assumption of adult responsibility. This dignified, compassionate Zuckerman is freed of the pain and obsessions that ruled him in *The Anatomy Lesson;* free of his previous feelings of resentment when others expected solidarity with Jewish causes; free to explore Jewish subjects unencumbered by the derision of Appel and like-minded critics that constitutes much of the interest in *The Counterlife* (1987). Unlike the Zuckerman of the earlier books, who championed self and a psychoanalytic interest in self-definition, the redeemed Zuckerman in *The Prague Orgy* is rooted in history. Retrieving the fiction of a persecuted Jewish writer is a fitting objective for the redeemed author cognizant of his link to Jewish history and literary precursors, cognizant of his responsibility to community. In his dedication to the Sisovsky mission, Zuckerman advances beyond his father's dying characterization of him as a bastard, understands the central place of the Holocaust in Jewish sensibility that was his mother's deathbed legacy, and reestablishes his honor as a Jewish son. *Zuckerman Bound* is thus framed by literary-cultural pilgrimages to spiritual fathers: first to the contemporary fictional master who "seemed to say something new and wrenching to the Gentiles about Jews, and to the Jews about themselves," and finally to the real progenitor, Kafka, who sought and found satisfaction in his Yiddish precursors. In privileging these spiritual fathers who are simultaneously literary perfectionists and writers responsive to Jewish civilization, Zuckerman attains his artistic maturity. In an insightful 1983 review of Roth's fiction through *The Anatomy Lesson,* Hana Wirth-Nesher argues convincingly that "Philip Roth's long odyssey from Newark to Prague is also a turning point in the American Jewish literary tradition, for it marks the passage from a literature of immigration and assimilation into a literature of retrieval, of the desire to be part of a Jewish literary legacy alongside the European and American literary traditions." Having made a pilgrimage to Prague, his spiritual Jerusalem, city of his literary father, to pay his final respects and reclaim his artistic integrity, Zuckerman is ready for a trip to the actual Jerusalem in *The Counterlife,* in which he redefines and comes to terms with his Jewish identity.

The Counterlife is a magnificent metafictional tour de force exhibiting its own configuration as fictional artifice and coincidentally leading readers to contemplate the relationship of fiction to reality. Progressing from the examination of the sources of fiction and the relationship between fiction and autobiography in the trilogy, *The Counterlife* and *Operation Shylock* (1993) are self-reflexive acts, metanarrations that require readers to know the previous fiction. Like *My Life As a Man,* the *Zuckerman Bound* trilogy, and *Operation Shylock, The Counterlife* poses questions about the writer's art, the conflict between the writer's personal and artistic commitments, the conflict between the writer's responsibilities to himself and others. But unlike the earlier works, in which Roth scrupulously adhered to the conventions of realism, he violates them in *The Counterlife* to challenge the realistic view of fiction in an exploration of the purposes of storytelling. He also departs from his earlier references to other writers, designed only to illuminate his texts, themes, and structures, to deconstruct his own text. Yet Roth is not among the postmodernists who substitute theoretical reflection about the resources of narrative for narrative itself. No matter how fragmented the self and how disintegrated the narrative, theory does not assert dominance over story and felt life. He does, however, share with the postmodernists the privileging of the artist as a new type of hero, and he often projects the inner life of the self as the field of action. As Debra Shostak has observed of *The Counterlife:* "In textualizing the self, in seeing the self as narrative, as a discursive invention, Roth recovers metafiction from the implicit nihilism and anxiety of the postmodern decentered or indeterminate self."

Roth's preoccupation in this work is the creation of new identities through the imagination. Characters indulge in self-invention and reinvent each other by telling the same tale differently. Early in the novel Zuckerman declares reality artificial and fiction genuine. He asserts that imagination is "everybody's maker"; that everybody is "a conjuration conjuring up everyone else. We are all each other's authors." In his variation on Luigi Pirandello's theme in *Six Characters in Search of an Author*

(1921), Roth suggests that we are not characters in search of an author, but authors ourselves, creating our realities, shaping our lives. In place of the given single self, Zuckerman posits "a variety of impersonations . . . a troupe of players that I can call on when a self is required." In an interview published in the *London Review of Books* (5 March 1987), Roth distinguished his method in *The Counterlife* from his conventional narrative strategy, noting, "Normally there is a contract between the author and the reader that only gets torn up at the end of the book. In this book the contract gets torn up at the end of each chapter. . . . Because one's original reading is always being challenged and the book progressively undermines its own fictional assumptions, the reader is constantly cannibalizing his own reactions."

The Counterlife may be read in the context of Roth's continuing commentary on the truth of fiction. The issue is examined within a self-contradicting literary form dramatizing life's unpredictable transforming patterns. Five sections of the novel juxtapose alternative lives and interpretations of the characters. Each first-person narrative presents interlocking personal and public histories from disparate points of view and is countered by a connected or opposed account in which Nathan Zuckerman and his younger brother, Henry, live out alternative destinies, live a life counter to the other's and counter to his own, comment on each other's lives, offer corrections and counter interpretations, ultimately transferring the hermeneutic responsibility to readers.

As Roth shatters realistic narrative conventions and offers the brothers multiple contradictory stories (each suffers from heart trouble, experiences impotence, dies, is eulogized, and is revived in a continuous appropriation of one another's stories), he frames questions about the structure of fiction and equations between art and life. The choices involve not only counterlives, but counterinterpretations. Characters and readers must choose between differing readings of situations. Nathan's revisions of the eulogy for Henry illustrate this method. Following his undelivered three-thousand-word eulogy addressing Henry's libidinous motivation for undergoing life-threatening surgery, Nathan twice reinvents the speech. In the "officially authorized version," authorized by the text in chapter one and by Henry's widow, the mourners hear of the husband's loyalty and self-sacrifice, hear that Henry "died to recover the fullness and richness of married love." Displeased with this version, Nathan invents an undramatized scene in which his sister-in-law admits her knowledge of Henry's infidelity.

The novel is most rigorously self-conscious in the "Gloucestershire" section excerpting, revising, and commenting upon the text and the act and art of interpretation. Here the fiction is a meditation on its own composition; the narrative provides its own criticism, anticipates the final section, and includes commentary by Henry and Maria on their own fictional status in voices unmediated by Nathan. After Nathan's demise, Henry searches his brother's papers and discovers all but the "Gloucestershire" chapter of the novel we are reading, that is the transcriptions of his confessions of infidelities with Maria. The objectified Henry is distraught by authorial control and rages against Nathan's deforming fictional transformation of him in "Basel" and "Judea." He suddenly realizes that brothers understand and experience each other as deformations of each other." Henry rants against "his version, his interpretation, his picture refuting and impugning everyone else's and swarming over everything! . . . In his words was our fate – in our mouths were his words." Roth's Barthian playfulness assumes an ever more self-reflexive spin as Henry progresses from the sections the readers have seen already to the final section of the novel, entailing Nathan's hiatus in England. Henry now imagines a counterbook redeeming lives from Nathan's distortions and introduces Maria's repudiation of Nathan's writing. Maria, Nathan's English wife, contributes to the metafictional dazzle by rebelling against the author and charging that the anti-Semitism attributed to the English in the final chapter is really an inversion of Nathan's feelings about Christian women. Her letter to Nathan in the "Christendom" chapter expresses her intention to flee from the text because she cannot abide being mishandled any longer. She even urges Nathan to defy Philip Roth, "to rise in exuberant rebellion against your author and remake your life."

Unlike postmodernists who dazzle the reader with pyrotechnics suggesting the meaninglessness of their universes, Roth's self-reflexive novels project endless possibilities for meaningful experience and suggest that truth is composed not only of the objective reality we perceive but also of the subjective reality we imagine, thereby enlarging our sense of reality by including elements ordinarily not attributed to realism. Complementing the postmodernist self-reflexivity of *The Counterlife* is a return to Jewish history and identity, sharp polemical exchanges by advocates of disparate Jewish ideologies and perspec-

Dust jacket for Roth's 1986 novel, which he has described as a book that "progressively undermines its own fictional assumptions"

tives, and a long ideological debate about Arab-Israeli relations. Bakhtinian dialogic prevails in the "Judea" and "Aloft" debates, yielding a full spectrum of contradictory discourses and possibilities for Jewish and Israeli self-definition and political positions. Contending voices include the brothers Zuckerman; Shuki Elchanan, a liberal Israeli journalist and advocate of compromise with the Arabs; and his antagonist, Mordechai Lippman, proponent of a Jewish Israel to counter omnipresent anti-Semitism, Zionist control of the West Bank and negotiation with Arab neighbors from a position of strength. The brothers take predictably polar positions on assimilation and Jewish nationalism, each arguing his case convincingly. Eager to purge himself of American middle-class materialism, to become a religious Jew in the Jewish state, Henry changes his name to Hanoch, joins a fundamentalist settlement in Judea, and loyally embraces Lippman's militant Zionism. In contrast to Nathan's life of artistic and psychological narcissism, Henry seeks "a larger world, a world of ideology, of politics, of history – . . . a world defined by action, by power, ... a world outside the Oedipal swamp." Conversely, at this stage Nathan champions Jewish survival through Diasporism complementing Zionism and through individual achievement rather than the collective accomplishments of the nation.

Elchanan challenges the writer's professed personal detachment in light of his professional engagement with Jewish history and identity: "In the books all you seem to be worrying about is what on earth a Jew is, while in life you pretend that you're content to be the last link in the Jewish chain of being." Elchanan is the voice of reason, the critical Israeli attuned to the intricacies of Middle East politics and the irony of American Diasporan security and Israeli insecurity. Confounding the Zionist vision, Israelis have become "the excitable, ghettoized jittery little Jews of the Diaspora," and American Jews enjoy "the confidence and cultivation that comes of feeling at home where you are." Despite Nathan's sympathy with Elchanan's position, he confesses that Lippman's "tirades have an eerie reality"; that he has been "outclassed" in debate. In Lippman's presence Nathan feels a "terrifying imagination richer with reality than his own." In a discerning reading of *The Counterlife* Naomi Sokoloff justly concludes that Roth's "multiplications of alternatives . . . puts into question the absoluteness of any one version of Jewishness. As these plural inventions of the Jew put into doubt the authenticity of any one definition, they also imply that any monolithic understanding of Jewishness must be counterfeit."

The theme of Jewish moral conscience is pursued through the voices of Jimmy Ben-Joseph, a demented Jewish American, and an Israeli security guard, who subdues him when he threatens to blow up an El Al plane. During his aborted hijacking of the airliner, Ben-Joseph argues that Jews must "Forget Remembering," that only by abandoning memories of the Holocaust and its concurrent reminder to the Gentiles of their sins can Israel enjoy international support. Jews, he asserts, must lose their suffering, or the world "will annihilate the State of Israel *in order to annihilate its Jewish conscience.*" Whereas the subject of Holocaust remembrance is left undeveloped here in favor of the security agent's Portnoian argument that it is not the Jewish superego that is despised, but the Jewish id, the theory of obliterating Holocaust memory is manifestly disreputable in its attribution to a mentally deranged fanatic. The moral imperative of Holocaust remembrance – briefly evoked in "Eli, the Fanatic," and *The Ghost Writer* and reintroduced in *The Counterlife* – is articulated directly with more thought and detail by two Holocaust survivors – and indirectly by the authorial voice – in *Operation Shylock*.

Ironically, it remains for "Christendom," the final chapter of *The Counterlife,* to exhibit Nathan's amended thinking about Jewish identity and his commitment to Jewish community, a revision and obligation developed in direct reaction to post-Holocaust anti-Semitism and in anticipated fatherhood. Married to his fourth Christian wife, Nathan is now living in England, where he has come to seek refuge in a counterlife as "Maria's husband." His enjoyment of the serenity of English pastoral life is shattered by many enactments of genteel British anti-Semitism. Nathan reinvents his Jewish identity in the social environs of Christian society. The concluding image of the novel, Zuckerman's erect circumcised penis, suggests not the sexual virility of the trilogy but the reestablishment of Nathan's bond to the Jewish past through insistence on circumcision for his son. Choosing Jewish history and engagement over the British pastoral idyll, Nathan affirms the fundamental Jewishness of his being. As he revises language, he edits his vision to embrace the most elemental sign of the covenant. Presumably, in the counterlife to come, Nathan will no longer be the vacuous Jew he has been because he now acknowledges, "Circumcision confirms that there is an us." Through the unconventional and masterful integration of postmodernist self-reflexive imagination and through acknowledgment of the significance of the world external to the text, Roth has achieved the most aesthetically pleasing and intellectually relevant work of his career, a book that far eclipses the authorized postmodernist galaxy.

In the next self-reflexive work, *Deception* (1990), Roth abandons Zuckerman and identifies his central character as Philip, a Jewish American novelist to whom he attributes his own biography and publications. The fictional Philip, like Roth, writes about a character named Zuckerman; is the author of *When She Was Good, Portnoy's Complaint, My Life As a Man,* and *The Ghost Writer;* complains that he writes fiction that is called autobiography and writes autobiography that is interpreted as fiction; lives in England; has an English lover; and occasionally visits Czechoslovakia. In a quarrel with his wife, who discovers his notebook recording conversations with his mistress, Philip insists that the notes are invention and charges her with the weakness of readers who fail to distinguish the real from the imaginary.

In a narrative that eschews exposition and is composed almost entirely of dialogue between Philip and his English lover, whom he later identifies as a model for Maria in *The Counterlife,* Roth challenges readers and critics as he "impersonates" and "ventriloquizes" himself. Juxtaposed with the dialogues of Philip and the English woman are Philip's dialogues with expatriate Czechs, former lovers, and a Polish woman on the topics of sex, infidelity, family, work, psychotherapy, politics, and English anti-Semitism. In one episode of the lovers' game called "reality shift" Philip persuades his mistress to play the part of E. I. Lonoff's biographer, a man who wants to earn quick cash by writing a brief work on the recently deceased Zuckerman. A scene in which Philip responds to the interviewer's questions about Zuckerman and Lonoff illustrates the self-reflexive hermeneutics and comedy of the novel. In an ironic twist Roth uses the occasion of his first fully developed female character since Lucy Nelson to defend himself against the misogynist charge of feminists. Playing prosecutor, his lover asks: "Why did you portray Mrs. Portnoy as a hysteric? Why did you portray Lucy Nelson as a psychopath? Why did you portray Maureen Tarnopol as a liar and a cheat? Does this not defame and denigrate women? Why do you depict women as shrews, if not to malign them?"

Deception also revisits English anti-Semitism, much in the manner of the final chapter of *The Counterlife*. Again there is no adequate resolution to the contradictory reactions of Jew and Gentile to overt anti-Semitism. When Philip tells his English lover about the offensive comment made by a passerby while Philip, Aharon Appelfeld, and the Israeli novelist's son were walking in Chelsea, she is driven to distraction by what she perceives as Philip's obsession with his Jewish identity. While she accuses Jews of hypersensitivity and making "a fuss about being Jewish," she cavalierly underplays British "distaste" for Jews as mere class "snobbery," asserting that the displeasure does not extend to upper-class Jews who are part of the aristocratic establishment and "part of British culture." In their final conversation, a transatlantic telephone dialogue, Philip explains that by returning to New York he recognized not only what he lacked living in England but what is central to his writing, that is, "Jews with force.... Jews with appetite. Jews without shame. Complaining Jews who get under your skin.... Unaccommodating Jews, full of anger, insult, argument, and impudence." Philip realizes, as has Roth, that Jews and a Jewish cultural-social environment are essential to his literary imagination.

Many of the themes of *Operation Shylock* have appeared in his earlier fiction and continue to dominate the novels that follow it — the coalescence of the real and the fantastic, the writer's relationship to his work, Jewish history and identity. Roth also redirects his self-reflexive mode to new and evermore fascinating paths. In contrast to the American Jews of his early fiction, who generally exhibited their ignorance of Jewish culture and history, the personae of *The Counterlife* and *Operation Shylock* are passionate about the Holocaust and Israeli security and politics. Theodore Solotaroff does not exaggerate when he says of Roth's recent fiction, "Jerusalem and the West Bank have become for him what Newark and Short Hills were in the 1950s: not only where the interesting Jewish material lies but where his early master theme has reemerged like a broken spring in a newly upholstered couch." In *Operation Shylock* the contradictory argumentative voices of Israeli dove and hawk heard in *The Counterlife* are resurrected, refined, and even challenged by Palestinian voices in a morality drama on the virtues and vices of Zionism and Diasporism. In a superb achievement Roth explores the dynamics of the Israel-American-Jewish connection and juxtaposes philosophies of a Diasporist American Jew, an Israeli Mossad agent, a Palestinian nationalist, and the American novelist caught in the center of their conflict. George Ziad, a Palestinian intellectual motivated by guilt over his earlier rejection of his father's nationalism and his own rage engendered by the humiliation his people suffer under Israeli rule, criticizes Israel in alternately apt and insane analyses of recent Jewish history. He delivers his anti-Israel diatribes with fervor, condemning not only the Kahanes and the Sharons, but the Israeli doves, the Yehoshuas and the Ozes, the "beautiful Israelis" who, he charges, want their Zionist gains and their morality intact. Ziad is both the Palestinian counterpart to Zionism's Lippman and connected to Jimmy Lustig by his own variation of obliterating Holocaust remembrance. His ideas are described by the fictional Roth as a "pungent ideological mulch of overstatement and lucidity, of insight and stupidity, of precise historical data and willful historical ignorance ... the intoxication of resistance had rendered [Ziad] incapable of even nibbling at the truth, however intelligent he still happened to be." Although Roth clearly conveys his sympathy for Israel, he raises troubling questions about the discrepancy between Israel's own democratic vision and what that nation has become under the dual pressures of the occupation and Arab terrorism. Supplementing Ziad's realistically based, if illogically conceived, political views, is the zany American Diasporist's fantasy of European repatriation of Israelis culminating in "a historic day for Europe, for Jewry, for all mankind when the cattle cars that transported Jews to death camps are transformed ... into decent, comfortable railway carriages carrying Jews by the tens of thousands back to their native cities and towns." Another fascinating character is the Israeli Mossad officer, Smilesburger, a critic of Jewish self-hatred and a political pragmatist. He controls Roth by using Pipik and his mistress to appeal to the novelist's interest in self-impersonation and Jews while forwarding his intention to direct the revision of the *Operation Shylock* manuscript.

Despite his sympathetic treatment of Palestinian suffering, Roth counters the points against Israel and advocates the necessity for the Jewish homeland through Holocaust remembrance, depiction of contemporary anti-Semitism, and his lampoon of Pipik's agenda to repatriate Jews in their European slaughterhouse. His sensitivity to the Jewish state readily emerges in depiction of Israel in the grips of the Demjanjuk trial, extensive dialogues with Holocaust survivors, the fictional novelist's reverie on the murder of Leon Klinghoffer by Palestinian terrorists aboard the *Achille Lauro,* and his ridicule of the London press for its caricature of Menachem Begin standing over a pyramid of dead Arab bodies, while at the same time the paper downplays Arab murders of Israelis and ennobles the Intifada.

Obsession with the authorial self and the theme of distinguishing fact from fiction takes a fantastical postmodernist turn in *Operation Shylock* as Roth once again devises a series of playful contradictory possibilities. He uses the devices of metafiction to examine fictional systems and the way in which reality is transformed by, and filtered through, narrative conventions. After repeatedly reproving readers for confusing him with his protagonists, Roth now professes to be writing a confession, offers himself as the fictional text, and tells interviewers that the events of the novel are autobiographical. According to Harold Bloom, "The degree of the author's experimentation in shifting the boundaries between his life and his work [is] what fascinates about *Operation Shylock*." Deliberately confounding fact and fiction – while creating multiple paradoxical perspectives, reflexive playfulness, and self-conscious orchestration of reader expectations – Roth directs his readers' attention to the hazards of interpretation. Against the backdrop of the Intifada and the Demjanjuk trial, historic events that lend an aura of authenticity to his fantasy, Roth invents a confrontation between a character named Philip Roth to whom he attributes his own books under their real titles and an impostor calling himself Philip Roth whom the fictional Roth derisively renames Moishe Pipik. Recovering from a Halcion-induced emotional breakdown, the beleaguered novelist departs for Israel to interview Aharon Appelfeld and to confront the man who is usurping his persona and making public pronouncements on the state of Israel in Roth's name. Pipik – who dresses like Roth, copies his mannerisms, and can recite his childhood history – is the founder and moving force of Anti-Semites Anonymous, an organization urging its members to abstain from their addiction, and an avid promoter of repatriation of Israelis of European and American origin and descent. Obsessed by the fear that Zionism is the latest threat to the Jewish people and will induce an Arab-wrought Holocaust, Pipik wants to save Israeli Jews from annihilation by expelling Israelis from their land and redistributing them in Europe and America. Fantasy and humor reign as the double is doubled and double-crossed when Roth impersonates Moishe Pipik and becomes an agent of the Israeli intelligence agency in its "Operation Shylock" to uncover Jewish American financial supporters of the Palestine Liberation Organization.

The authorial character is dramatized in self-conflict over the possibility that the impostor is more convincing than he. In an effort at confidence building, he tells himself, "it would be only natural

Roth at the time of Deception *(AP/Wide World)*

to assume that in the narrative contest (in the realistic mode) . . . the real writer would easily emerge as inventive champion, scoring overwhelming victories in Sophistication of Means, Subtlety of Effects, Cunningness of Structure, Ironic Complexity, Intellectual Interest, Psychological Credibility, Verbal Precision, and Overall Verisimilitude. . . ." Nevertheless, the impostor triumphs by abusing every principle of realism.

The literary persona is of primary interest, especially in light of the character's many references to contemporary writers and his own oeuvre. The fictional Roth offers views on the nature of Jewish American writing, referring to Malamud's *The Assistant,* Bellow's *The Victim,* and Jerzy Kosinski's *The Painted Bird* (1965) in a manner evocative of Philip Roth's critical essays. Roth is exceptionally self-referential in *Operation Shylock,* invoking Zuckerman, Kepesh, Tarnopol, and Portnoy by name and offering direct comments on most of his fiction, referring once to *My Life As a Man* and *The Great American Novel,* twice to *Letting Go* and *The Ghost Writer,* thrice to *Portnoy's Complaint,* and five times to the stories in *Goodbye, Columbus.* Roth's friend Ted Solotaroff, a literary critic, makes a cameo appearance, and another friend, Israeli novelist Aharon Appelfeld, is a major dramatic player. The fictional Roth, like the novelist, interviews Appelfeld, framing questions and answers on the literary influence of Bruno Schulz and Kafka on Applefeld's work. Because so much of this material is authentic autobiography, the aura of belief extends to the invented portion of their discussion that addresses the impostor. In this self-conscious story about storytelling, Roth even includes a synopsis of *Operation Shylock* and analyzes the Pipik plot. One of his Israeli handlers invokes the postmodernist assault on mimetic fiction in his contention that the "novelist's imagination will come up with something far more seductive than whatever may be the ridiculous and trivial truth.... Reality. So banal, so foolish, so incoherent – such a baffling and disappointing nuisance." The entire epilogue is devoted to discussion of the book we are reading, a self-reflective resonance of the internal textual assessment in *The Counterlife* and Roth's exchange with Zuckerman in *The Facts*. Now in *Operation Shylock* Roth debates with the Mossad officer about printing a disclaimer, publishing the book as a novel rather than a confession, and deleting the Athens chapter detailing his work on "Operation Shylock," an account that is indeed conspicuous by its absence. Despite its fashionable self-reflexivity, Roth's fiction is more than a self-contained narrative of signs and codes. It continues to express a far wider concern with public events than is customarily associated with postmodern literature. For all its attention to artifice, the novel is a social-political commentary on the nature of Jewish identity, the Arab-Israeli political climate, and other aspects of the world outside fiction, making it more readable than many other postmodernist works.

Postmodernist play and self-referentiality are absent from Roth's next fiction, *Sabbath's Theater* (1995). Even the literary allusions and discussions that distinguish Roth's fiction recede somewhat in this novel. Although literary discussion is no longer accorded the dominant role it played in earlier works, Roth effectively integrates allusions to Anton Chekhov, Leo Tolstoy, William Shakespeare, and William Butler Yeats, as well as a parody of Bellow's *Mr. Sammler's Planet* (1970). Cast as a would-be suicide's retrospective examination of his erotically obsessive life, *Sabbath's Theater* is a lyrical tour de force chronicling the sexual adventures of Mickey Sabbath, a geriatric Alexander Portnoy. An aging puppeteer down on his luck, Sabbath is mourning the loss of his mistress, unable to practice his craft because of crippling arthritis, and preparing to die. Like Portnoy, Sabbath indulges every sexual whim, appearing to enjoy provoking his contemporaries by outrageous descents into the "slimy, suicidal Dionysian side" of his character; he revels in "acts of exhibitionism, voyeurism, fetishism, auto-eroticism and oral coitus." Like his younger counterpart, Sabbath hears his mother's reprimanding voice, but this time that voice comes from the graveyard and memory; it is not screaming at him from the kitchen or outside the bathroom. Like Portnoy, Sabbath has an older brother against whom he measures himself, but this time the brother, Morty, is a dead war hero, shot down over the Philippines.

Though the similarities between Sabbath and Portnoy are interesting, the differences between the two are significant. At thirty-three Portnoy is exuberant and witty, albeit guilty and complaining; at sixty-four Sabbath is bitter and shrill. While the youthful Portnoy behaves outrageously to assert his independence from parental values, Sabbath is outrageous for sheer pleasure; it is his nature. Through the expository narrative, the reader learns that the younger Mickey Sabbath performed prurient puppet shows in the Indecent Theater, a street theater he created. Following his arrest on obscenity charges Sabbath retires to the country and teaches at a small college until an undergraduate reveals that he had telephone sex with her and he loses his position. Roth fills out his protagonist's sexual history with descriptions of bouts of masturbation, attempted seductions of friends' wives, and sniffing the underpants of a friend's adolescent daughter.

The women in Sabbath's life are an odd assortment of Rothian types: a sexual superstar who wins Sabbath's love and a series of troubled or manipulative females who generally make life difficult for the male protagonist. After the mysterious disappearance of his submissive first wife, he lives in a rural setting with an alcoholic second wife, a creature he detests and betrays with Drenka, a voluptuous, married Croatian immigrant. Just when the reader is ready to give up on Sabbath as a boor and a bore, his capacity for love redeems him. In his relationship with Drenka he is compassionate, devoted, and as selfless as he can be. After her death from ovarian cancer, he laments her loss and dwells on the excitement of their lovemaking, a vehicle through which Roth indulges in lengthy descriptions of their trysts. More moving than their sexual life or Sabbath's grotesque homage to his love is Roth's poignant description of Drenka's battle with cancer and her lover's loneliness.

While Roth's earlier young and middle-aged protagonists enjoy good health, Sabbath's obsession with sex is attended by preoccupations with illness and death. His wife, who supports him, is in recovery from the alcoholism to which he has driven her; his mistress succumbs to cancer; a colleague dies; and Sabbath, with fingers crippled by arthritis, is psychologically haunted by his dead mother and brother and contemplates taking his own life. Death hovers over *Sabbath's Theater* from the Shakespearean epigraph – "Every third thought shall be my grave" – through Mickey's lament for his older brother to Drenka's painful demise and Mickey's meditation on suicide.

Despite the omnipresent sense of life's endings, Sabbath's contrapuntal voice sings of life in all its raucous, ribald rowdiness in a verbal avalanche. He "felt uncontrollable tenderness for his own shit-filled life. And a laughable hunger for more. More defeat! More disappointment! More deceit! More loneliness! More arthritis! . . . More disastrous entanglement in everything." Although Sabbath acknowledges his shortcomings, his part in "the nasty side of existence," he celebrates his life as having been "a real human life!" With death beckoning he still reaches for life, convinced that "Something always [comes] along to make you keep living, goddamnit."

Roth is at his best in this novel when he charts Sabbath's decline and describes his return to his childhood neighborhood on a visit to an elderly uncle and his parents' graves. Here the reader learns of the pivotal trauma in his life: the death of his brother in World War II, which caused his mother's emotional withdrawal and transformed the family's relationships and dynamics. The loss of family security, particularly the mediation of an attentive and adoring mother, prompted the teenage Mickey Sabbath to enlist in the merchant marine and subsequently to search for pleasure in foreign brothels and for a woman who would give him comfort and unqualified maternal love as well as erotic excitement. During his visit to his uncle, Sabbath examines the contents of a bureau that belonged to his brother and finds a box marked "Morty's Things," which contains his yarmulke and the flag commemorating his death in the service of his country. This discovery, his visit to the family graves, and his conversation with his uncle are at the heart of Sabbath's decision to defer suicide and accept life. Readers may not develop affection for Mickey Sabbath, but to read *Sabbath's Theater* is once again to experience the exquisite pleasure of a master's extraordinary, beautifully composed prose.

Roth has written about his personal life in two nonfiction books, *The Facts: A Novelist's Autobiography* (1988) and *Patrimony: A True Story* (1991). In *Patrimony*, a memoir of his father's final illness and death, the tone is that of a loving son who shared his father's struggle and celebrates the impact of his father on his life. *The Facts* was begun as therapy during Roth's recovery from a Halcion-induced depression following minor knee surgery gone wrong – an experience Roth fleshed out in *Operation Shylock*. Cast as a Bildungsroman, *The Facts* is centered on the apprenticeship of the writer. Near the midpoint of writing, Roth composed an apologetic letter to Nathan Zuckerman announcing his intentions. Included in the opening pages of the book, the letter describes Roth's strategy of reversing his customary method, in which he progresses from the facts to fiction, and seeks Zuckerman's advice about publication. Roth views the book as "the bare bones, the structure of a life without the fiction." As he informs Zuckerman, "This manuscript embodies my counterlife, the antidote and answer to all those fictions that culminated in the fiction of you." Covering Roth's secure childhood, his college years, romances, marriage, and the publication of his first three books (his life to age thirty-six), the five chapters of *The Facts* focus on significant moments of connection between fact and fiction. The reader learns how different Roth's relationship with his loving, adoring parents was from the parent-child conflicts of his fiction, and how closely his unhappy life with his first wife resembles Tarnopol's disastrous marriage. "Those scenes," Roth writes of *My Life As a Man*, "represent one of the few occasions when I have not spontaneously set out to improve on actuality in the interest of being more interesting." Roth also discusses the early opposition to his work, recalling Jewish hostility toward "Defender of the Faith," his meeting with representatives from the Anti-Defamation League to discuss his early stories, and the "trial" he endured at Yeshiva University, which changed the course of his writing career by providing him a subject that has since dominated his fiction.

Like much of Roth's fiction, *The Facts* is about writing. Zuckerman's reply to Roth conveys the "self-challenging aspect" that is a central component of Roth's life as a novelist. Zuckerman counsels against publication, arguing, "You are far better off writing about me than 'accurately' reporting your own life." Nathan distrusts the editing of the autobiographer, his opportunity for omission, the material that the conscious, manipulative self deletes: "You can't or you won't talk about yourself, other than in this decorous way. . . . it's just as impossible to be proper and modest and well behaved and be a revealing autobiographer as it is to be all that and a

Dust jacket for the novel that earned Roth his second National Book Award

good novelist.... With autobiography there's always another text, a countertext, ... to the one presented." By omitting the imaginative, Zuckerman contends, Roth has written an inaccurate account, and he concludes that reality cannot compete with fiction for exploring truth in its varied nuances. It is Roth as a nice Jewish son that Zuckerman finds uninteresting, for it is a portrait lacking the tension, pride, and zaniness of the fictional characters. Roth, Nathan argues, is "the least completely rendered of all your protagonists"; Roth's talent lies in personifying his experience in fictional lives. Autobiography, Zuckerman asserts, cannot measure up to the deeper truths revealed in fiction, nor can its prose compete with fiction. Truth is not in the bare facts, it is found in the embellished imagination.

A remarkably prolific writer who produces a book almost every other year, Roth has been a controversial and celebrated author since he published his first book in 1959. Critical reaction to Roth's fiction has been mixed. He is a writer about whom neutrality is difficult. While detractors found his early characters and his views of American society disturbing, supporters heralded an original new voice, applauded his satirical talents, marveled at his facility for reproducing the language he heard around him, and appreciated the moral concerns underlying the comic surface of his fiction. Condemned by some as a self-hater and anti-Semite, Roth has also been hailed as an original, provocative voice, as the true chronicler of secular American Jews. This pattern of social rebuke and literary praise followed Roth through the early period of his career. The critical reception of *Portnoy's Complaint* is representative of the contradictory assessment in early critical responses. Marie Syrkin found that "Roth's stunning verisimilitude in trivia too often disguises a failure in truth. ... for under the cartoon of the Jewish joke leers the anti-Jewish stereotype." Sanford Pinsker praised the comic mode of the confession, relating "Portnoy's self-lacerating wit" to traditional Jewish humor and insisting, "Not since Salinger's *Catcher in the Rye* had a novel been so readable, so 'right' for its time and place." Mark Shechner called *Portnoy's Complaint* "the most spectacular instance of Freudian fiction in postwar American literature."

By Roth's midcareer detractors of his ethnic Jewish characters were replaced by critics of his political and sexual satire, which they regarded as vulgar, and by others who found his focus on Zuckerman obsessive. Negative criticism has been supplanted by near universal praise for the postmodernist subjects and style, technical brilliance, and mature engagement of substantive subjects in Roth's later novels. A rare dissenting voice is that of Josh Rubins, who admires the first half of *The Counterlife* but contends that the novel suffers from "metafictional overkill," its central theme of the counterlife "lost in the postmodernist thicket." Illustrative of the widespread positive reading of the later work are Solotaroff's assessment of *Operation Shylock* as "a brilliant novel of ideas, a distinguished genre that is practiced in the United States today about as widely as the epic poem" and Harold Bloom's assessment of *Zuckerman Bound* as meriting "something reasonably close to the highest level of aesthetic praise for tragicomedy." Bloom praises Roth's morality, his "negative exuberance" not in the service of "negative theology, but [intimating] instead a nostalgia for the morality once engendered by the Jewish normative tradition." Equally glowing is Bloom's commendation of *Operation Shylock,* for confirming "the gifts of comic invention and moral intelligence that [Roth] has brought to American prose fiction since 1959."

Discussions of Roth's work generally consider his place in the American tradition and the Jewish American canon, as well as his literary influences – especially those of Kafka and James. They also analyze his dominant comic-satiric mode, the influence of psychoanalytic theory on the fiction, and Roth's contribution to the postmodernist fixation on metafiction and self-reflexivity. Among the many scholars who acknowledge Roth's place within the American tradition while emphasizing the Jewish contextuality of his fiction are Hermione Lee, Judith Paterson Jones and Guinevera A. Nance, Sanford Pinsker, Jay Halio, Alfred Kazin, Murray Baumgarten and Barbara Gottfried, Glenn Meeter, and Stephen J. Whitfield. Kazin describes Roth as a second-generation Jewish American writer whose concern is "the self-conscious Jew, newly middle-class whose identity is problematic." Pinsker finds "an ambivalent, even troubled response to the Jewishness of his congenial material," while Lee calls the Yiddish American voice of his fiction the most spectacular creation of any contemporary Jewish American writer; and Whitfield discusses Roth in the context of twentieth-century Jewish humorists.

Among Roth's most perceptive readers are Lee, Hana Wirth-Nesher, Mark Shechner, Debra Shostak, and Robert Alter – all of whom deal with the centrality of the conflict between the Jewish writer determined to express himself freely and the self-reflexivity and strong identification with Jewish life in the later fiction. A dissenting voice is Bernard Rodgers, who dismisses the Jewish context in favor of situating the fiction in the American realist tradition with connections to James, Theodore Dreiser, nineteenth-century American humorists, and Roth's non-Jewish contemporaries. While his effort to distance Roth from the Jewish literary tradition is unconvincing, Rodgers's analysis of Roth's comic genius and his relationship to nineteenth-century American humorists is persuasive. Essays focusing on Roth as an accomplished literary artificer and experimental writer are collected in volumes edited by Asher Z. Milbauer and Donald G. Watson, Harold Bloom, and Sanford Pinsker and in Thomas Pughe's *Comic Sense: Reading Robert Coover, Stanley Elkin, Philip Roth* (1994).

Of all Roth's critics, the one most quoted and parodied by Roth himself is Irving Howe, who reversed his initial praise for the young writer of *Goodbye, Columbus* in his "Philip Roth Reconsidered." According to Howe, Roth's fiction after *Goodbye, Columbus* is distorted by personal and ideological self-assertiveness and marred by its overemphasis on the satirical mode and vulgarity. Among the many critics coming to Roth's defense, Shechner offers an enlightening account of Roth's role in the battle of "literary-cultural politics," charging Howe with insensitivity to Roth's real gifts of language, wit, and exact rendition of psychological truths. Writing in a countercurrent to the postmodernist vogue that denies the idea of meaning in life and art – that separates life and art in equally meaningless realms – Roth, like Bellow, Ozick, and Malamud, opposes the view of history as an unintelligible flux of phenomena, rejects the postmodernists' view that efforts of the designing or ordering imagination to discover or impose meaning are absurd or fraudulent, and affirms that truth exists beyond as well as in the text, that texts may be read for enlightenment as well as the pleasure given by their artifice. Roth's best work combines an Hebraic moral conscience with postmodern artifice, fashioning a literary universe in which readers may find relevant meaning for their lives.

Interviews:

"Symposium: Jewishness and the Younger Intellectuals," *Commentary,* 31 (April 1961): 306–359;

"Symposium: Second Dialogue in Israel," *Congress Bi-Weekly,* 30 (16 September 1963): 4–85;

Jerre Mangione, *Philip Roth* (National Educational Television, 1966);

"Philip Roth Talks About His Work," *London Review of Books,* 9 (5 March 1987): 7–9;

Linda Matchan, "Philip Roth Faces 'The Facts,'" *Boston Globe,* 4 October 1988, p. 65;

Asher Z. Milbauer and Donald G. Watson, "An Interview with Philip Roth," in their *Reading Philip Roth* (New York: St. Martin's Press, 1988), pp. 1-12;

George J. Searles, ed., *Conversations With Philip Roth* (Jackson: University Press of Mississippi, 1992).

Bibliographies:

Bernard F. Rodgers Jr., *Philip Roth: A Bibliography* (Metuchen, N.J.: Scarecrow, 1974);

Ann Leavey, "Philip Roth: A Bibliographic Essay (1984-1988)," *Studies in American Jewish Literature,* 8 (Fall 1989): 212-218;

Murray Baumgarten and Barbara Gottfried, "Philip Roth," in *Bibliography of American Fiction, 1919-1988,* 2 volumes, edited by Matthew J. Bruccoli and Judith S. Baughman (New York: Facts on File, 1991), II: 429-431.

References:

Mary Allen, "Philip Roth: When She Was Good She was Horrid," in her *The Necessary Blankness: Women in Major American Fiction of the Sixties* (Urbana: University of Illinois Press, 1976), pp. 70-96;

Robert Alter, "Defenders of the Faith," *Commentary,* 84 (July 1987): 52-55;

Aharon Appelfeld, "The Artist as a Jewish Writer," in *Reading Philip Roth,* edited by Asher Z. Milbauer and Donald G. Watson (New York: St. Martin's Press, 1988), pp. 13-16;

Frank Ardolino, "'Hit Sign, Win Suit': Abraham, Isaac, and the Schwabs Living Over the Scoreboard in Roth's *The Great American Novel,*" *Studies in American Jewish Literature,* 8 (Fall 1989): 219-223;

Julian Barnes, "Philip Roth in Israel: The Counterlife," *London Review of Books,* 9 (5 March 1987): 3-9;

Murray Baumgarten and Barbara Gottfried, *Understanding Philip Roth* (Columbia: University of South Carolina Press, 1990);

Charles Berryman, "Philip Roth: Mirrors of Desire," *Markham Review,* 12 (Winter 1983): 23-31;

Harold Bloom, ed., *Philip Roth* (New York: Chelsea House, 1986);

Jonathan Brent, "The Unspeakable Self: Philip Roth and the Imagination," in *Reading Philip Roth,* pp. 180-200;

Hendley W. Clark, "An Old Form Revitalized: Philip Roth's Ghost Writer and the *Bildungsroman,*" *Studies in the Novel,* 16 (Spring 1984): 87-100;

Joseph Cohen, "Paradise Lost, Paradise Regained: Reflections on Philip Roth's Recent Fiction," *Studies in American Jewish Literature,* 8 (Fall 1989): 196-204;

Alan Cooper, "The Jewish Sit-Down Comedy of Philip Roth," in *Jewish Wry: Essays on Jewish Humor,* edited by Sarah Blacher Cohen (Bloomington: Indiana University Press, 1987), pp. 158-177;

Joseph Epstein, "What Does Philip Roth Want?" *Commentary,* 77 (January 1984): 62-67;

Leslie Fiedler, "The Image of Newark and the Indignities of Love: Notes on Philip Roth," in *Critical Essays on Philip Roth,* edited by Sanford Pinsker (Boston: G. K. Hall, 1982), pp. 23-27;

Melvin J. Friedman, "Texts and Countertexts: Philip Roth Unbound," *Studies in American Jewish Literature,* 8 (Fall 1989): 224-230;

William Gass, "The Sporting News," *New York Review of Books,* 20 (31 May 1973): 7-8;

Sander L. Gilman, "The Dead Child Speaks: Reading *The Diary of Anne Frank,*" *Studies in American Jewish Literature,* 7 (Spring 1988): 9-25;

Sam Girgus, "Between *Goodbye, Columbus* and *Portnoy:* Becoming a Man and Writer in Roth's Feminist Family Romance," *Studies in American Jewish Literature,* 8 (Fall 1989): 143-153;

Girgus, "Portnoy's Prayer: Philip Roth and the American Unconscious," in *Reading Philip Roth,* pp. 126-143;

Sol Gittleman, "The Pecks of Woodenton, Long Island, Thirty Years Later: Another Look at 'Eli, the Fanatic,'" *Studies in American Jewish Literature,* 8 (Fall 1989): 138-142;

Sheldon Grebstein, "The Comic Anatomy of Portnoy's Complaint," in *Comic Relief: Humor in Contemporary American Literature,* edited by Sarah Blacher Cohen (Urbana: University of Illinois Press, 1978), pp. 152-171;

Martin Green, "Half a Lemon, Half an Egg," in *Reading Philip Roth,* pp. 73-81;

Michael Greenstein, "Ozick, Roth and Postmodernism," *Studies in American Jewish Literature,* 10 (Spring 1991): 54-64;

Barry Gross, "American Fiction: Jewish Writers, and Black Characters: The Return of 'The Human Negro' in Philip Roth," *MELUS,* 11 (September 1984): 5-22;

Gross, "Sophie Portnoy and 'The Opossum's Death': American Sexism and Jewish Anti-

Gentilism," *Studies in American Jewish Literature,* 3 (1983): 166-178;

Jay Halio, *Philip Roth Revisited* (New York: Twayne, 1992);

Hillel Halkin, "How To Read Philip Roth," *Commentary,* 97 (February 1994): 43-48;

Irving Howe, "Philip Roth Reconsidered," in *Critical Essays on Philip Roth,* pp. 229-244;

Judith Paterson Jones and Guinevera A. Nance, *Philip Roth* (New York: Ungar, 1981);

Donald Kartiganer, "Fictions of Metamorphosis: From *Goodbye Columbus* to *Portnoy's Complaint,*" in *Reading Philip Roth,* pp. 82-104;

Alfred Kazin, "The Earthly City of the Jews," in his *The Bright Book of Life* (Boston: Little, Brown, 1973), pp. 144-149;

Steven G. Kellman, "Philip Roth's Ghost Writer," *Comparative Literature Studies,* 21 (Summer 1984): 175-185;

Milan Kundera, "Some Notes on Roth's *My Life As a Man* and *The Professor of Desire,*" in *Reading Philip Roth,* pp. 160-167;

Hermione Lee, *Philip Roth* (New York: Methuen, 1982);

Cherie Lewis, "Philip Roth on the Screen," *Studies in American Jewish Literature,* 8 (Fall 1989): 205-211;

Joseph Lowin, "Philip Roth and the Novel of Redemption," *Jewish Book Annual,* 47 (1989-1990): 83-98;

Bonnie Lyons, "Jew on the Brain: in 'Wrathful Philippics,'" *Studies in American Jewish Literature,* 8 (Fall 1989): 186-195;

Norman MacLeod, "A Note on Philip Roth's *Goodbye, Columbus* and F. Scott Fitzgerald's *The Great Gatsby,*" *International Fiction Review,* 12 (Summer 1985): 104-109;

John N. McDaniel, *The Fiction of Philip Roth* (Haddonfield, N.J.: Haddonfield House, 1974);

Glenn Meeter, *Bernard Malamud and Philip Roth: A Critical Essay* (Grand Rapids, Mich.: Eerdmans, 1968);

Asher Z. Milbauer and Donald G. Watson, eds., *Reading Philip Roth* (New York: St. Martin's Press, 1988);

Lawrence Mintz, "Devil and Angel: Philip Roth's Humor," *Studies in American Jewish Literature,* 8 (Fall 1989): 154-167;

David Monaghan, "The Great American Novel and My Life As a Man: An Assessment of Philip Roth's Achievement," in *Critical Essays on Philip Roth,* pp. 68-77;

Norman Nielsen, "On Love and Identity: Neal Klugman's Quest in 'Goodbye, Columbus,'" *English Studies,* 68 (February 1987): 79-88;

Nielsen, "The Protest of a Jewish-American Writer and Son: Philip Roth's Zuckerman Novels," *Dutch Quarterly Review,* 17, no. 1 (1987): 38-52;

Nielsen, "Rebellion Against Jewishness: *Portnoy's Complaint,*" *English Studies,* 68 (February 1987): 79-88;

Rei R. Noguchi, "Talking and the Meaning in Dialogue: The Semantic Significance of Sociolinguistic Codes," *Journal of Literary Semantics,* 13 (August 1984): 109-124;

Estelle Gershgoren Novak, "Strangers in a Strange Land: The Homelessness of Roth's Protagonists," in *Reading Philip Roth,* pp. 50-72;

Patrick O'Donnell, "The Disappearing Text: Philip Roth's *The Ghost Writer,*" *Contemporary Literature,* 24 (Fall 1983): 365-378;

O'Donnell, "'None Other': The Subject of Roth's *My Life As a Man,*" in *Reading Philip Roth,* pp. 144-159;

Sanford Pinsker, *The Comedy That 'Hoits': An Essay on the Fiction of Philip Roth* (Columbia: University of Missouri Press, 1975);

Pinsker, "The Facts, The 'Unvarnished Truth,' and the Fictions of Philip Roth," *Studies in American Jewish Literature,* 11 (Spring 1992): 108-117;

Pinsker, "Imagination on the Ropes," *Georgia Review,* 37 (Winter 1983): 880-888;

Pinsker, "Marrying Anne Frank: Modernist Art, the Holocaust, and Mr. Philip Roth," *Holocaust Studies Annual,* 3 (1985): 43-58;

Pinsker, ed. *Critical Essays on Philip Roth* (Boston: G. K. Hall, 1982);

Thomas Pughe, "Philip Roth's Zuckerman Novels as a Comic '*Kunstler-Roman,*'" in his *Comic Sense: Reading Robert Coover, Stanley Elkin, Philip Roth* (Basel: Birkhauser Verlag, 1994), pp. 83-126;

Barbara Koenig Quart, "The Rapacity of One Nearly Buried Alive," *Massachusetts Review,* 24 (Autumn 1983): 590-608;

Bernard F. Rodgers Jr., *Philip Roth* (Boston: Twayne, 1978);

Derek Rubin, "Philip Roth and Nathan Zuckerman: Offenses of the Imagination," *Dutch Quarterly Review,* 13, no. 1 (1983): 42-54;

Jeffrey Rubin-Dorsky, "Philip Roth's *The Ghost Writer:* Literary Heritage and Jewish Irreverence," *Studies in American Jewish Literature,* 8 (Fall 1989): 168-185;

George Searles, *The Fiction of Philip Roth and John Updike* (Carbondale: Southern Illinois University Press, 1985);

Mark Shechner, "Philip Roth," *Partisan Review*, 41, no. 3 (1974): 410-427;

Shechner, "The Road of Excess: Philip Roth," in his *After the Revolution: Studies in the Contemporary Jewish American Imagination* (Bloomington: Indiana University Press, 1987), pp. 196-242;

Debra Shostak, "'This obsessive reinvention of the real': Speculative Narrative in Philip Roth's *The Counterlife*," *Modern Fiction Studies*, 37 (Summer 1991): 197-216;

Ben Siegel, "The Myths of Summer: Philip Roth's *The Great American Novel*," *Contemporary Literature*, 17 (Spring 1976): 171-190;

Clive Sinclair, "The Son is Father to the Man," in *Reading Philip Roth*, pp. 168-179;

Naomi Sokoloff, "Imagining Israel in American Jewish Fiction: Anne Roiphe's *Lovingkindness* and Philip Roth's *The Counterlife*," *Studies in American Jewish Literature*, 10 (Spring 1991): 65-80;

Sokoloff, "Israel and America – Imagining the Other: Natan Shaham's *The Salt of the Earth* and Philip Roth's *The Counterlife*," in *The Other in Jewish Thought and History: Constructions of Jewish Culture and Identity*, edited by Laurence J. Silberstein and Robert L. Cohn (New York: New York University Press, 1994), pp. 326-351;

Theodore Solotaroff, "The Diasporist," *Nation*, 256 (7 June 1993): 778-784;

Solotaroff, "Philip Roth: A Personal View," in his *The Red-Hot Vacuum* (New York: Atheneum, 1970), pp. 306-328;

Janis Stout, "The Misogyny of Roth's *The Great American Novel*," *Ball State University Forum*, 27 (Winter 1986): 72-75;

Marie Syrkin, "The Fun of Self-Abuse," in her *The State of the Jews* (Washington, D.C.: New Republic Books, 1980), pp. 331-337;

Tony Tanner, "Fictionalized Recall – or 'The Settling of Scores! The Pursuit of Dreams!'" in his *City of Words: American Fiction 1950-1970* (New York: Harper & Row, 1971), pp. 295-321;

Adeline R. Tintner, "*The Prague Orgy:* Roth Still Bound to Henry James," *Midstream*, 31 (December 1985): 49-51;

Tintner, "Roth's 'Pain' and James's 'Obscure Hurt,'" *Midstream*, 31 (December 1985): 58-60;

Martin Tucker, "The Shape of Exile in Philip Roth, or the Part is Always Apart," in *Reading Philip Roth*, pp. 33-49;

Duco van Oostrum, "A Post Holocaust Jewish House of Fiction: Anne Frank's Het Achterhuis (The Diary of a Young Girl) in Philip Roth's *The Ghost Writer*," *Modern Jewish Studies*, 9, nos. 3-4 (1994): 61-75;

Daniel Walden, ed., *The Odyssey of a Writer: Rethinking Philip Roth*, special issue of *Studies in American Jewish Literature*, 8 (Fall 1989);

Donald G. Watson, "Fiction, Show Business, and the Land of Opportunity: Roth in the Early Seventies," in *Reading Philip Roth*, pp. 105-125;

Stephen J. Whitfield, "Laughter in the Dark: Notes on American-Jewish Humor," in *Critical Essays on Philip Roth*, pp. 194-208;

Hana Wirth-Nesher, "The Artist Tales of Philip Roth," *Prooftexts*, 3 (September 1983): 263-272;

Wirth-Nesher, "From Newark to Prague: Roth's Place in the American-Jewish Literary Tradition," in *Reading Philip Roth*, pp. 17-32; and in *What Is Jewish Literature?*, edited by Wirth-Nesher (Philadelphia: Jewish Publication Society, 1994), pp. 216-229.

J. D. Salinger

(1 January 1919 -)

Warren French
University of Wales, Swansea

See also the Salinger entries in *DLB 2: American Novelists Since World War II* [first series] and *DLB 102: American Short-Story Writers, 1910–1945, Second Series.*

BOOKS: *The Catcher in the Rye* (Boston: Little, Brown, 1951; London: Hamilton, 1951);
Nine Stories (Boston: Little, Brown, 1953); republished as *For Esmé – With Love and Squalor and Other Stories* (London: Hamilton, 1953);
Franny and Zooey (Boston: Little, Brown, 1961; London: Heinemann, 1962);
Raise High the Roof Beam, Carpenters and Seymour: An Introduction (Boston: Little, Brown, 1963; London: Heinemann, 1963);
The Complete Uncollected Short Stories of J. D. Salinger [pirated edition], 2 volumes (N.p., 1974).

J. D. Salinger

Confronting another in an apparently unending series of collected essays about J. D. Salinger's *The Catcher in the Rye* (1951), a British reviewer once asked with some asperity why nearly every American critic who wrote about the novel seemed compelled to describe his or her own first reading of the book. The reason is that, for many American readers of Salinger's generation and after, Holden Caulfield's confessions contributed to an understanding of their own adolescent experiences. For them the book marks a moment of self-awareness, when they discovered anew their deeper connections to their culture.

Born in New York City, Jerome David Salinger was the younger of two children and the only son born to Sol and Miriam Jillich Salinger. His father was a prosperous meat and cheese importer. The family lived in the fashionable apartment district of upper Manhattan, moving several times before fall 1932, when they settled in an apartment at the corner of Park Avenue and East Ninety-first Street, near the Metropolitan Museum of Art and Central Park – the area where Holden Caulfield's family also lives. At this time Salinger, who had been attending public schools, was enrolled at the fashionable and respected McBurney School in Manhattan. His grades there were below average, and in September 1934 he was sent to Valley Forge Military Academy in Pennsylvania. There he acted in school plays, edited the 1935–1936 class yearbook, and even wrote the lyrics for a quite conventional class song. He also began writing short stories.

None of the stories Salinger wrote at Valley Forge is known to survive, nor are there any from the three years immediately following his graduation in 1936. During that time he drifted. He spent late 1937 and early 1938 in Europe, mainly in Vienna, learning the importing business. After Germany invaded Austria in March 1938, he returned to the United States and enrolled at Ursinus College in Pennsylvania, where he spent one desultory semester in 1938–1939, writing vignettes and brief movie reviews for campus publications. He did not break into a professional writing career until spring 1939, when he enrolled in an evening class in short-story writing taught by Whit Burnett, the editor of the influential *Story* magazine, at Columbia University.

Burnett, who was responsible for the first commercial publication of stories by many important midcentury American writers, was also the first to sense Salinger's potential, accepting "The Young Folks" for the March–April 1940 issue of *Story*. Before the end of the next year, Salinger had also placed short short stories with two popular slick magazines, *Collier's* and *Esquire,* as well as an academic quarterly, the *University of Kansas City Review*. During the same period *The New Yorker* accepted "Slight Rebellion Off Madison," about a young man named Holden Morrisey Caulfield, but delayed publication of the downbeat story for five years. Salinger was drafted into the army in 1942, landed on Utah Beach on D day, and participated in five European campaigns before being discharged in 1945.

The Catcher in the Rye was the culminating project of the first three decades of Salinger's life. After the publication of the novel in 1951, while he still granted brief interviews, Salinger told a reporter that there was a good deal of himself in Holden Caulfield. Yet the novel is not a thinly fictionalized account of the author's experiences. From the environment in which he grew up, Salinger had absorbed the background for his account of a neurotic, idealistic, upper-middle-class New York teenager living in fashionable apartments, attending unrewarding private schools and summer camps, fighting off "phonies," and trying to keep alive a flickering vision of a "nice" place beyond the threatening streets. Salinger obviously endowed his creation with some of his own prejudices and aspirations, but Holden's family – including a younger sister, Phoebe, an older brother, D. B., and a deceased brother, Allie – was quite different from Salinger's own. He has rarely mentioned his only sibling, an older sister, and she refuses to talk about him. His father was a successful but obscure businessman, not a café society lawyer and unsuccessful angel of Broadway shows, like Holden's father.

An early version of Holden Caulfield, William Jameson Junior in "The Young Folks" is more socially inept, less sensitive, less bedeviled, and less sympathetically presented than Holden. Yet William's language is Holden's. Salinger had already found the distinctive voice that is one of the most compelling reasons for the reputation of *The Catcher in the Rye*. It would take him a while to fashion the character.

Salinger may have named him as early as 1941, when he sold "Slight Rebellion Off Madison" to *The New Yorker*. Yet, since he revised the story before it was published in the 21 December 1946 issue, it is impossible to know when he named his character. In the story, as in the novel, Holden Caulfield takes Sally Hayes to the theater. (Morrisey, Holden's middle name in this story, never appears elsewhere in Salinger's fiction.) About half of the sixteen-hundred-word story appears in the novel but not in consecutive passages.

Before "Slight Rebellion Off Madison" was finally published, another, somewhat older Holden Caulfield had lived in Salinger's published fiction and may have died in World War II. In "Last Day of the Last Furlough" (*Saturday Evening Post,* 15 July 1944) – a story praised by Ernest Hemingway when the admiring Salinger met him in Paris in August 1944 – Vincent Caulfield mentions his younger brother Holden as a twenty-year-old missing in action. Vincent says he used to bump into him at a New York "beer joint for college kids and prep-school kids," where he was "the noisiest, tightest kid in the place." Readers learn little more about him in this story or in "This Sandwich Has No Mayonnaise," probably written during the war and published in the October 1945 issue of *Esquire*. Here it is reported that he was only nineteen when "he came through the war in Europe without a scratch," but he was then shipped out to the Pacific, where he is missing in action. The most important link to *The Catcher in the Rye* is the distraught Vincent's characterization of his brother as a "dope" who "can't reduce a thing to a humor, kill it off with a sarcasm, can't do anything but listen hectically to the maladjusted little apparatus he wears for a heart." Holden is not mentioned in "The Stranger" (*Collier's,* 1 December 1945), which conveys the news of Vincent's death on the battlefield. The only sibling mentioned in the story is a younger brother Kenneth, who died as a child (a probable forerunner of Allie in *The Catcher in the Rye*).

In "I'm Crazy," published in *Collier's* three weeks later (22 December 1945), Holden appears as a troubled adolescent. This Holden attends a school

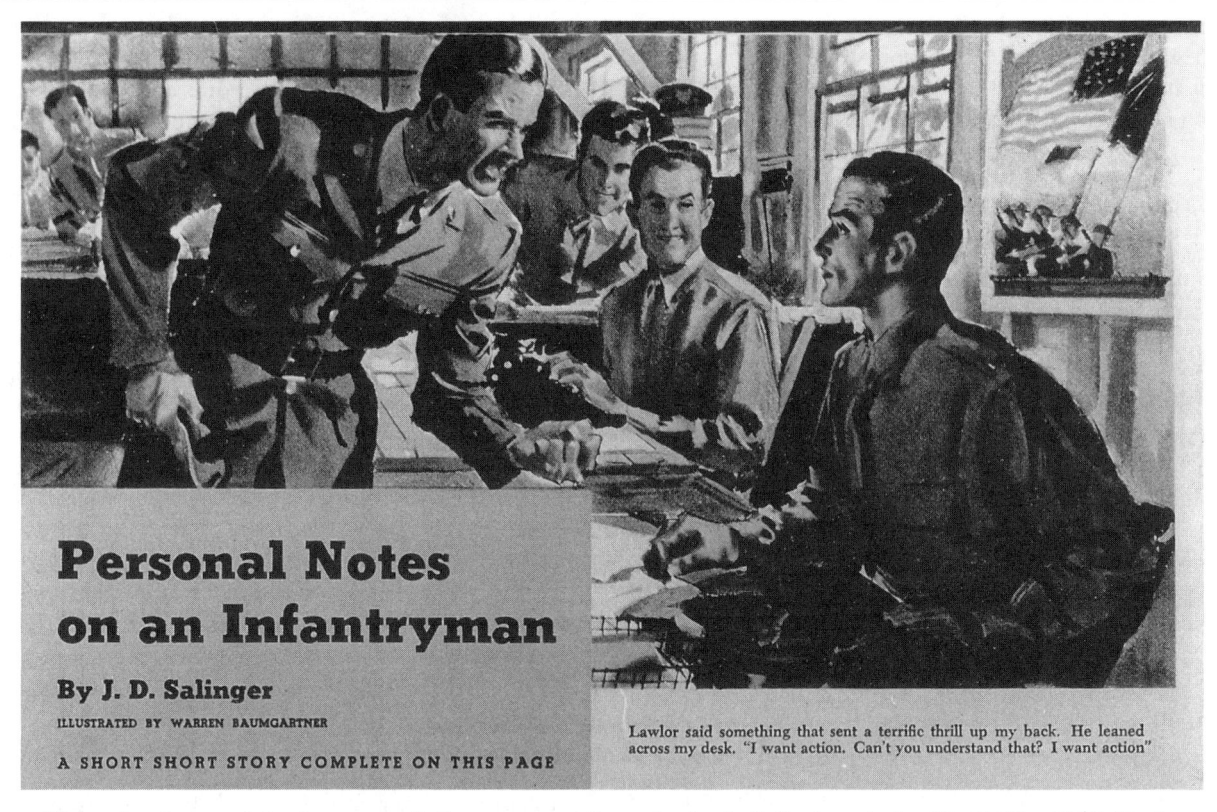

Illustration for one of the short stories Salinger wrote while serving in the U.S. Army during World War II (Collier's, 12 December 1942)

called Pentey Prep. (Holden's school in the novel is Pencey Prep.) Each also has a younger sister, Phoebe, in whom he confides, while the Holden of "I'm Crazy" also has an even younger sister, Viola, who is not mentioned elsewhere in Salinger's fiction. The publication date of this story suggests that it was part of a ninety-page novelette that, according to *New Yorker* staff member William Maxwell, Salinger withdrew from a publishing house that had accepted it.

"I'm Crazy" is the earliest published piece of Salinger's fiction that Holden narrates in the first-person voice used in the novel. The first two episodes of this three-thousand-word story were greatly expanded for use in chapters 1 and 2 of *The Catcher in the Rye*. The third and final episode of the story was entirely rewritten as chapters 21 and 22. Despite the close relationship of episodes in this story and the novel, the Holden of "I'm Crazy" is not the same character who appears in the novel. He is simply drifting from day to day, whereas the Holden in the novel has a vision, however impractical and fanciful. "I'm Crazy" is a strictly traditional story of reconciliation with one's unprepossessing destiny, and its protagonist is not a rebel. He is a nice, polite, confused boy who cannot meet the demands of his fashionable, upwardly mobile parents. His problem is not that he will not conform to a self-seeking, materialistic society, but that he cannot. The Holden Caulfield of *The Catcher in the Rye* is someone else. During the interval between World War II and the Korean War, Salinger reshaped his narrative and transformed Holden from one of the multitude, who accept defeat and become another statistic in the lonely crowd, to an individual who struggles to maintain his integrity even if victory is uncertain.

Although Salinger could have published his novelette in 1945, he decided to revise it, and Holden Caulfield was not seen in Salinger's fiction again until the appearance of *The Catcher in the Rye* five and a half years later. During this period there were many changes in Salinger's life and work that influenced him in reworking and expanding the Holden Caulfield story. Salinger had continued to pursue publication in *The New Yorker* even while he was serving in the military. In October 1944 Louise Bogan, poetry adviser to the magazine, wrote to William Maxwell that a Sergeant Salinger "has been bombarding me with poems for a week or so," by airmail from France. Apparently she was unimpressed, since she asked Salinger's agent for help in stemming the tide. At that time Salinger was in the Hürtgen Forest near Luxembourg preparing to take part in fierce combat as the Germans made a last-ditch stand to turn back the Allies. After that battle Salinger was hospitalized for some time for a nervous condition. It was apparently then that he met his first wife, Sylvia, a French doctor whom he married in September 1945. Little information exists about this marriage, which had ended by July 1946, when Salinger wrote to a friend that his wife had decided to return to France and divorce him. The letter was sent from the Daytona Plaza Hotel in Daytona Beach, Florida, a hostelry that resembles the setting of "A Perfect Day for Bananafish," which seems to draw on Salinger's experiences and feelings at that time. That story, published in the 31 January 1948 issue of *The New Yorker*, was the first of three stories the magazine accepted in 1948. By the time *The Catcher in the Rye* appeared in 1951, Salinger had become known as a "*New Yorker* writer."

William Faulkner once paid Salinger the compliment of calling him the best of "the present generation of writing" because *The Catcher in the Rye* "expresses so completely" what Faulkner himself had tried to say about the tragedy of a youth who found "when he attempted to enter the human race, . . . there was no human race there." Later, however, Faulkner expressed the reservation that there was only enough material in the book for a short story. Faulkner is right in the sense that the first 220 pages provide a background for the fast-moving action of the last 50. The long, episodic buildup in *The Catcher in the Rye,* is essential, however, to create a rapport between Holden and the reader.

Leaving school early, Holden has a series of adventures and misadventures in New York that are akin to the archetypal night journey as rite of passage into maturity. This portion of the novel culminates with Holden's return to his family's apartment, where he finds Phoebe home alone. Holden's problem with growing up is that taking on adult responsibility is fraught with uncertainties. When Phoebe asks him if he would like to be a lawyer like their father, he expresses the fear of the "phoniness" that has haunted him throughout the novel. He says lawyers are "all right if they go around saving innocent guys' lives all the time, . . . but you don't *do* that kind of stuff if you're a lawyer. . . . And besides. Even if you *did* go around saving guys' lives and all, how would you know if you did it because you really *wanted* to save guys' lives, or . . . what you *really* wanted to do was be a terrific lawyer, with everybody slapping you on the back and congratulating you. . . . ?" "How would you know you weren't being a phony?" he asks and answers: "The trouble is, you *wouldn't*." The only prospect that pleases him is the unrealistic one of keeping children from growing up and – in the process of this guardianship – remaining childlike himself. Holden confesses to Phoebe that he wants only to be a "catcher in the rye" protecting little children from falling off "some crazy cliff." Some readers have interpreted this confession as the climactic revelation of the novel, expressing the vision that Holden will cling to for the rest of his life. Yet he changes his mind completely the next day, when his own childhood ends in a loss of innocence, the sort of "fall" he had hoped to prevent as "catcher in the rye."

Even before Holden finishes explaining himself to Phoebe, she jolts his immature self-confidence by informing him schoolmarmishly that he has not gotten the line from Robert Burns's poem right; in it a body *meets* a body "coming through the rye," allowing the other individual to pass by. Holden will not abandon his private version of the line immediately, for it seems the perfect metaphor to express his thoughts.

After he flees the family apartment to avoid confronting his parents, Holden's faith in his ability to spot phonies is put to the test. He seeks refuge and a night's rest at the apartment of Mr. Antolini, whom Holden considers the best and bravest teacher he has ever had. Antolini fears that Holden is headed for a terrible fall and asks him to ponder a statement by Austrian psychoanalyst Wilhelm Stekel (1868-1940): "The mark of the immature man is that he wants to die nobly for a cause while the mark of the mature man is that he wants to live humbly for one." This piece of advice appears irrelevant in Holden's situation, because Holden has shown no inclination to put his life on the line for anything. Antolini is further discredited as a source of help when, later that night, Holden is suddenly wakened by Antolini, who is patting him on the head. Taking this gesture as a sign of homosexual intention, Holden runs out of the apartment. After a hard night on a bench in Grand Central Station (which he advises readers to avoid as depressing), Holden wonders whether he could have been wrong about Antolini, "if maybe he just liked to pat guys on the head when they're asleep. I mean how can you tell about that stuff for sure? You can't." Critics' speculations about Antolini's intentions have tended to distract attention from the importance of this episode to the development of Holden's point of view. Salinger may well be suggesting that the mark of maturity is neither living humbly nor dying nobly for a cause but rather

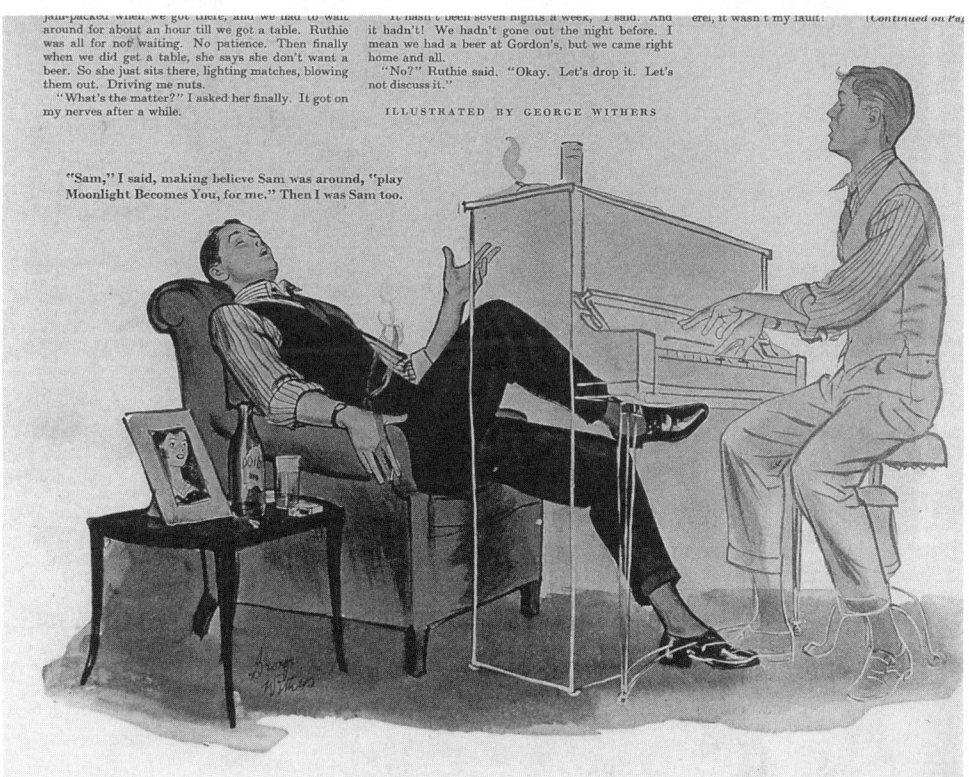

Illustrations for two stories Salinger sold to The Saturday Evening Post *during the 1940s: "The Varioni Brothers," illustrated by Al Moore (17 July 1943) and "Both Parties Concerned," illustrated by George Withers (26 February 1944)*

struggling to develop an open mind instead of fixedly maintaining a closed one.

Shortly after his second thoughts about Antolini, Holden becomes frightened by the idea of disappearing while crossing a street, a fear that goes back to the opening pages of the novel and to "I'm Crazy." The fear becomes a phobia as Holden starts to call desperately for his dead brother, Allie, to save him. This terror is related to Holden's frenzied behavior when Allie died, as well as to another recurrent motif that also appeared first in "I'm Crazy" – Holden's concern about what happens to the ducks when the lake freezes over in Central Park. Having decided never to return to home or school again, Holden is afraid he may disappear with the ducks. He pleads with Allie not because he wants to join him in death, but because he wants Allie to help him make his way in this world.

Holden's concern for the world leads to an episode in which the words "fuck you" appear six times. This episode has resulted in some of the most serious misunderstandings of the novel and has led some to attempts to ban the book and prevent schoolchildren from reading it. Yet Holden never uses these words himself. Indeed each time he sees the words scrawled in a public place he is driven into the same kind of frenzy that he felt after Allie's death, and he tries to remove the obscenity before a young child like Phoebe can see it. At first he succeeds, but when he encounters the words scratched in stone, he realizes his crusade is hopeless.

Shortly after the crushing defeat of his attempt to purify the world to which small children are exposed, Holden experiences the fall that Antolini anticipated. Holden goes into a men's room, having decided in disgust that there is no "nice" place. He passes out and collapses on the floor. Believing he could have killed himself in the fall, he recovers and feels better. He has survived. He has experienced "a fortunate fall" into the understanding that he is responsible only to himself.

This awareness is immediately challenged, however, when he meets Phoebe and is troubled to learn that she wants to run away with him. He can change her mind only by going home with her after she rides the Central Park carousel. The idea of experiencing a fall is stressed as Holden watches the children grabbing for the gold (actually brass) ring, just beyond easy reach. Although he fears that Phoebe may fall off her horse, he says nothing. He has forsaken his vision of being catcher in the rye because he now recognizes that "The thing with kids is, if they want to grab for the gold ring, you have to let them do it, and not say anything. If they fall off, they fall off, but it's bad if you say anything to them." He knows now that people cannot be sheltered from all temptations; they must take responsibility for themselves.

This precept may be more easily perceived than applied, for as the brief last chapter of the novel implies, Holden is still torn between minding his own business and meddling in others' lives. When one psychoanalyst asks him whether he will apply himself when he goes back to school, he cannot tell. He has learned how to live with other people, and in so doing he has begun "missing everybody"; but he has no idea yet of what he is going to do with himself. He has an open mind. Salinger has left Holden in an ambiguous state of maturity, with his future openended.

When *The Catcher in the Rye* was published in July 1951, reviews were generally good. Reviewing the book for *The New York Times* (16 July 1951), Nash K. Burger called it "an unusually brilliant first novel." It was a main selection of the Book-of-the-Month Club and was on the *Times* best-seller list for seven months, reaching fourth place in October. Yet no reviewer foresaw its becoming the classic novel of a generation. It would be five years before academics began writing about the novel and assigning it to their students. By 1968, however, it was listed as one of the top twenty-five American best-sellers since 1895. In the late 1980s it was still selling about a quarter of a million copies per year.

Several times before he completed *The Catcher in the Rye* Salinger himself expressed doubts about ever writing a novel, calling himself essentially a short-story writer; and he has never published a second novel. Yet many critics have treated his stories about the Glass family – including the four long stories collected in *Franny and Zooey* (1961) and *Raise High the Roof Beam, Carpenters and Seymour: An Introduction* (1963) – as parts of a novel. His first published story about a member of the Glass family was the 1948 *New Yorker* story "A Perfect Day for Bananafish." Although he was still working on the final version of Holden Caulfield's story, Salinger's concerns had already begun to turn from the problems of young outsiders growing up in a phony world to the evocation of an idealized "poet-seer."

F. Scott Fitzgerald's *The Great Gatsby* (1925) seems to have influenced Salinger's ideas on this subject. Twice in Salinger's fiction figures closely associated with him speak of schoolboy enthusiasms for *The Great Gatsby*. In *The Catcher in the Rye* Holden confides that he is "crazy" about "old sport" Gatsby. In "Zooey," first published in the 4 May 1957 issue of *The New Yorker*, Salinger's alter ego Buddy

*Illustration by Leon Gregori for Salinger's short story "I'm Crazy" (*Collier's, *22 December 1945), parts of which were later expanded and rewritten for* The Catcher in the Rye

Glass reveals that *The Great Gatsby* was his "Tom Sawyer" when he was twelve and praises narrator Nick Carraway for saying that "everybody suspects himself of having at least one of the cardinal virtues" and that he considers his to be honesty. Nick, who feels "an unaffected scorn" for everything Gatsby represents, nonetheless recognizes "something gorgeous about him, some heightened sensitivity to the promises of life. . . ." It was just such heightened sensitivity that Salinger was trying to capture in his work, especially in the portrayal of Seymour Glass as an "artist-seer" who can transcend squalor but is sacrificed like Gatsby in his pursuit of a false grail.

This new Salinger character type first appeared in "The Inverted Forest" (*Cosmopolitan,* December 1947), published just a month before "A Perfect Day for Bananafish" but probably written earlier than the close proximity of publication dates might imply. Salinger later made particularly vigorous efforts to prevent republication of "The Inverted Forest" and other stories of this period. Certainly his presentations of the two poets – the pathetic Raymond Ford in "The Inverted Forest" and the admirable Seymour Glass in "A Perfect Day for Bananafish" – reveal a remarkable change in the viewpoint underlying his fiction. Salinger biographer Ian Hamilton describes "The Inverted Forest" as "a melodramatic projection of Salinger's own guilt and determinations at this time; indeed, as a defiant apologia addressed to the wife he himself had broken with a year before." Whether "The Inverted Forest" was written a month or years before "A Perfect Day for Bananafish," Salinger's shift in sensibility between the two stories marks a clear advance in his artistic control of his material. The stories can be seen as two disparate attempts to come to terms with the same experience. The most revealing statement in "The Inverted Forest" is Raymond Ford's confession to his wife, "I can't get past half my childhood dogmas." His new mistress exercises absolute control over him, just as his mother did when he was a child, leaving him unable to function independently in adult society. Despite the success of his poetry with a limited coterie, he is still like the Holden Caulfield in "I'm Crazy," who knew that he "wasn't going to be one of those successful guys." Ford knows he will not produce the kind of financially successful popular verse that his mother and his vulgar mistress desire, but as his wife leaves him

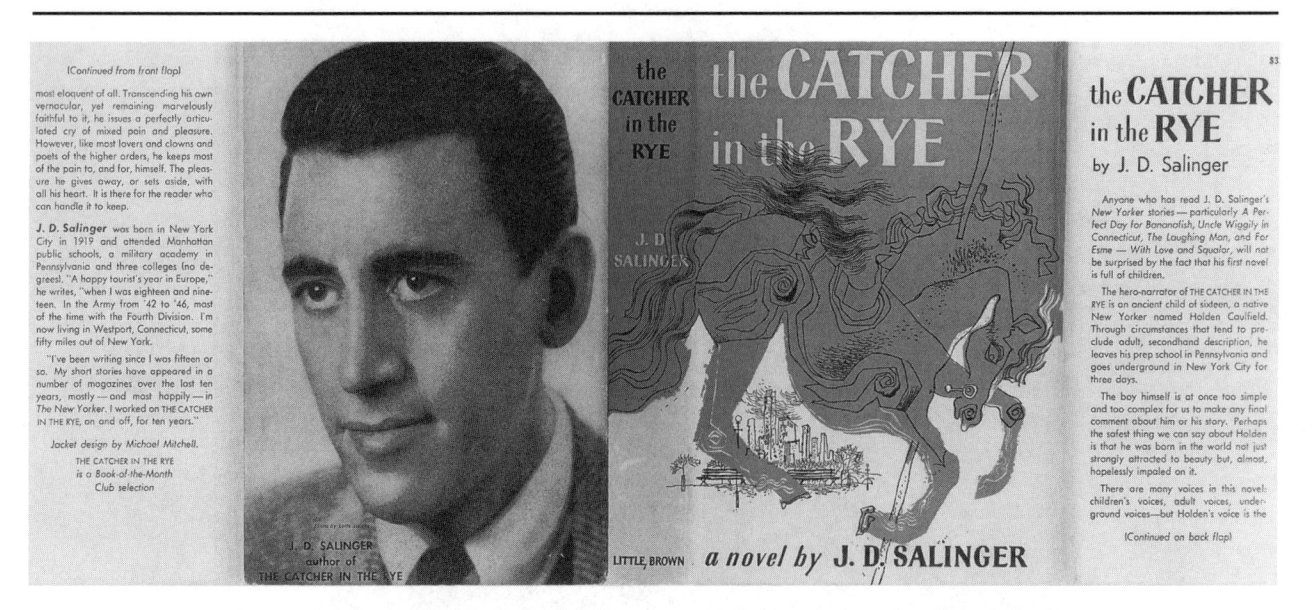

Dust jacket for the novel that earned Salinger a reputation as a major voice of his generation

he is trying to learn to "invent" works for the high-paying popular media.

While the exact basis for the deterioration of the marital relationship between Seymour Glass and Muriel in "A Perfect Day for Bananafish" is never specified, the reader perceives that Seymour retains a kind of childish naiveté and honesty that offends his in-laws, who are trying to make him conform to fashionable New York behavior. (Seymour calls Muriel "Miss Spiritual Tramp of 1948," a perfect description for the mistress in "The Inverted Forest.") Seymour cannot be dominated in the way that Raymond Ford is. Instead, at the climactic moment when he finds that even the child he meets on the beach has succumbed to materialistic temptations, he decides that he would rather be dead.

These two stories of poet-seers throw some light on the episode in *The Catcher in the Rye* where Antolini tells Holden about the immature man wanting "to die nobly for a cause" while the mature man wants "to live humbly for one." Yet in early stories such as "The Inverted Forest" the still-immature man cannot get past childhood dogmas and chooses to live humbly for a cause imposed on him. In contrast Seymour Glass, who will not compromise his vision, chooses death over conformity in a materialistic culture. In *The Catcher in the Rye* Holden fantasizes destroying the "perverty bum" who writes obscenities where small children will see them, but he also knows that he "wouldn't have the guts to do it." Similarly despairing about a degenerate society in "A Perfect Day for Bananafish," Seymour chooses to commit suicide rather than live humbly in it. Not until a decade later would Salinger spell out what drove Seymour to take his life.

After "A Perfect Day for Bananafish" Salinger wrote several stories about the difficulties and possibilities of achieving maturity while maintaining personal integrity in the postwar world of Madison Avenue men in their gray flannel suits. One of them, "Uncle Wiggily in Connecticut," provides the key to the two worlds that influenced Seymour's action. The title characterizes these worlds in its evocation of the innocent fantasy of Howard Garis's children's stories about a whimsical rabbit and the decadent reality of suburban Connecticut. As they converse, two former schoolmates, Eloise and her visitor Mary Jane, become drunker and franker. Eloise evokes the vanished time when she came east from Boise, Idaho, a naive and trusting girl in unfashionable clothes who met a young soldier named Walt (identified in later stories as Seymour Glass's younger brother), who could make her laugh and who called her twisted ankle "poor old Uncle Wiggily." He was killed during the war, not in combat but in a freak explosion as he packed a looted Japanese stove for a colonel much like the man she later married. When he courted her, Eloise's husband told her he loved Jane Austen's novels, but she later found out that he had never read any of them and that his favorite author is L. Manning Vines, who had written a novel about four men starving to death in Alaska. Her life in the suburbs has made her so cynical that her friend feels that she is "getting as hard as nails," but at the end of the story she cries and asks her visitor, "I was a nice girl . . . , wasn't I?" Uncle Wiggily has been trapped.

Another of Seymour Glass's siblings appears in "Down at the Dinghy," set at a lakeside cottage, where the Tannenbaums have remained beyond the end of the usual season to protect their supersensitive four-year-old son, Lionel, from the "perverty bums" that Holden Caulfield rages against. Lionel has already displayed a tendency to run away in the dangerous city when he is upset. As the story opens, Lionel has taken refuge on the family boat and will not tell his mother what distresses him. She is Seymour's sister Beatrice (known as Boo Boo), an extraordinarily resourceful person who finds a technique for wheedling the information out of Lionel. He finally tells her that the maid has told the cleaning lady, "Daddy's a big – sloppy – kike." This revelation makes Boo Boo flinch, "just perceptibly," but she persists in an effort to determine how much damage has been done. It turns out that Lionel thinks *kike* means *kite* and fears that his father, who has been going away to the city to work, may take off for good if Lionel cannot hold onto him.

In letters written to friends before he set off on a trip to Florida and Mexico in March 1952, Salinger hinted that something momentous had happened to him, and on his return he urged his British publisher to bring out a complete text of the thousand-page gospels of Hindu mystic Sri Ramakrishna, a propagator of the Advaita Vedanta system of thought, first propounded by Shankaracharya around the eighth century. Salinger subsequently became associated with the Ramakrishna-Vivekananda Center in New York. Salinger's new interest is alluded to in "De Daumier-Smith's Blue Period," published in the May 1952 issue of the British magazine *World Review*. The title character is a painter about Salinger's age who has an extraordinary experience that strikes him as "having been quite transcendent" and leads to a reversal of his previous lifestyle. No particular system of Eastern thought is emphasized in the story. De Daumier-Smith's experience has been compared to a Zen Buddhist satori (moment of temporary illumination), but Eberhard Alsen argues persuasively that the artist's epiphany ought rather to be compared to the experience of Saint Paul on the road to Damascus in the Acts of the Apostles, where a blinding flash of light leads to his conversion.

Salinger does mention Vedanta in "Teddy" (*The New Yorker*, 31 January 1953). When a young educator asks the ten-year-old title character whether he believes the Vedantic theory of reincarnation, he is politely informed that it is not a theory. Teddy then goes on to explain that in his immediately preceding life he was making a nice spiritual advancement until he met a lady who disrupted his meditations. Salinger commented unfavorably about "Teddy" in "Seymour: An Introduction," where he attributes the tale to his alter ego Buddy Glass and calls it "an exceptionally haunting, memorable, unpleasantly controversial, and thoroughly unsuccessful short story about a 'gifted little boy' aboard a transatlantic liner." When Teddy tries to explain how close he is to final illumination, he admits that in his previous incarnation, even if he had not met the disruptive lady, he was not spiritually advanced enough to go straight to Brahma. "But," he continues, "I wouldn't have had to get incarnated in an *American* body if I hadn't met that lady. I mean it's very hard to meditate and live a spiritual life in America. People think you're a freak if you try to." He also accurately foresees his own death: pushed into an empty swimming pool by his little sister, he dies of a fractured skull. Teddy's dilemma is the same as Seymour's in "A Perfect Day for Bananafish." In a sense Salinger has come back to where he started, failing to break out of the circle. It was time for a fresh start.

On New Year's Day 1953, his thirty-fourth birthday, Salinger moved to the kind of "nice place" that a discouraged Holden Caulfield sought and despaired of finding, the hills of Cornish, New Hampshire, in the upper valley of the Connecticut River. He has lived there ever since. For exactly two years following the appearance of "Teddy," he published no new fiction. *Nine Stories* (1953), which includes the four stories just discussed as well as the widely anthologized "For Esmé – With Love and Squalor," was published in April 1953, with a Zen koan for an epigraph: "We know the sound of two hands clapping / But what is the sound of one hand clapping?" *Nine Stories* went through nine printings before the end of the year, an extraordinary record for a collection of short stories in the United States after World War II.

During his first years in Cornish, Salinger gathered about him a group of high-school students; but their parties began to break up when one of them wrote a short article about him for the *Claremont Daily Eagle*. One day some of the teenagers arrived at his house and found it surrounded by a tall wooden fence. Soon after his arrival in Cornish Salinger had met Claire Douglas, a nineteen-year-old student at Radcliffe College of Harvard University and the daughter of a British art critic who had moved with his family to New York after the outbreak of World War II. Their courtship was interrupted by her brief marriage to a Harvard business major; but on 17 February 1955 she and Salinger were married, and he began to lead an even more secluded life than before.

Just three weeks before the wedding, "Franny," Salinger's first new story in two years, appeared in *The New Yorker* (25 January 1955) and received the kind of reception usually reserved for major news events. It was also seriously misunderstood, widening the already yawning gap between Salinger and academic critics.

Although "Franny" has been assimilated into the Glass family legend, John Updike was one of the first to note that there is no internal evidence in the story itself that it was written to launch a series of stories. Franny's last name is never used in the story, nor is the reader told the names of the two brothers who come down to see her in a college play. She tells her boyfriend, Lane Coutell, that she borrowed *The Way of a Pilgrim* (1943) – based on the *Philokalia*, a collection of mystical writings by fathers of the Eastern Orthodox Church – from the college library, but two years later in "Zooey," one of her brothers says she took it from Seymour's desk.

Read most satisfactorily as a companion piece to "Teddy," "Franny" offers a less spectacular path to spiritual salvation than Teddy's, but one most Americans would still regard as freakish. The two stories reflect the Stekelian dilemma with which Antolini confronted Holden, about dying nobly (in Teddy's case, stoically) or living humbly for a cause. Franny is surely an advocate of humble living as she rails against the egotism of her contemporaries and teachers and pleads lyrically that if one repeats the "Jesus Prayer" she has learned from *The Way of a Pilgrim,* one gets to see God. The self-centered and ambitious Lane dismisses her enthusiasms as "mumbo jumbo." To some mundane minds the symptoms of her spiritual crisis have suggested morning sickness. Franny is pregnant by this insensitive cad, they believe, and she is desperately seeking a way to cope with the situation. Especially in view of Salinger's disparagement of promiscuity and sexual obsessions throughout his writings, this reading seems unlikely. Rather he was trying to depict sympathetically a sensitive girl "so sick of pedants and conceited little tearer-downers" that she is on the verge of nervous collapse. She seeks to make her life an unceasing prayer while the boyfriend who says he loves her can only ask, "You actually believe that stuff or what?"

Salinger sought to set the record straight in "Zooey." In this story he shows how Franny's loving family treats her problem on a higher spiritual plane than her self-centered, superficial boyfriend.

Cover for the 1953 paperback edition of Salinger's popular novel. By 1965 it had become one of the top twenty-five American best-sellers of the past seventy years.

The Glass family provides a framework that interrelates those pieces of Salinger's writing in which, as Elizabeth N. Kurian perceptively demonstrates, his characters – without advocating any one religion – find "their final peace in a spiritual ethic, compounded of Zen thought, Vedanta philosophy, and Christian mysticism."

Salinger's attempt to use a New England academic scene as a backdrop for the struggle between egotism and selflessness was not successful, for he had already become too detached from the arena of intellectual one-upmanship. Seymour Glass provided an ideal focus, for he was long dead; and though he had achieved a kind of saintliness in the eyes of his siblings, there was still a mystery about his suicide. Salinger could thus go back to the New York that he had known in the 1930s, but look at it through the detached eyes of an "outsider" family. The Glass family takes shape in "Raise High the

Roof Beam, Carpenters" (*The New Yorker,* 19 November 1955). The family consisted of Les and Bessie Glass, retired vaudeville performers, and their seven children – Seymour, Buddy, Boo Boo, twins Walt and Waker, Zooey, and Franny – most of whom readers had already met in different contexts. The most useful invention was the second son, Buddy, through whom Salinger created a sense of personal participation in family affairs by attributing some of his own fiction to this alter ego.

This identification also afforded the opportunity to experiment with a new type of storytelling, in which conventional rules are ignored while the author attempts to establish a kind of communion with the "amateur reader," a seemingly oblique recognition and rebuke of an annoying tribe of "professional readers" who, as early as 1959, had established what George Steiner called a "Salinger industry," with an output of critical commentary that dwarfed the body of writing it dissected.

Narrated by Buddy, who is looking back from the vantage point of 1955, "Raise High the Roof Beam, Carpenters" is almost entirely devoted to a minute-by-minute account of the afternoon of 4 June 1942, when Seymour fails to appear for his wedding to Muriel Fedder and Buddy sits in the bathroom reading Seymour's journal. Seymour and Muriel end up eloping, setting in motion the events that lead to his suicide in 1948. (Not all dates relating to this marriage are in complete accord in the various stories.) Seymour never appears in "Raise High the Roof Beam, Carpenters," but his voice dominates it as Buddy reads his brother's journals. Buddy offers the reader an analogy between his adulatory conception of Seymour and the great judge of horses in a Taoist fable that Seymour once told the infant Franny, setting the tone for the rest of the story by observing that since Seymour's departure, "I haven't been able to think of anybody whom I'd care to send out to look for horses in his stead."

"Raise High the Roof Beam, Carpenters" and the few published stories that followed it differ from Salinger's earlier writings in the leisurely manner in which they unfold. Some critics find this meandering technique self-indulgent, but it offers the advantage of clarifying the significance of every detail. The reader is not required to absorb a rapid barrage of subtle details as in many *New Yorker* stories; and it is noteworthy that this story was over others – including the much admired "For Esmé – with Love and Squalor" – for inclusion in *Stories from the New Yorker, 1950–1960* (1960), the last anthology of this kind in which Salinger would permit his work to appear.

This mellow, relaxed style was likely a result of the practice of Vedantic meditation, which Seymour recommends in his journals. The development of this new style may also be related to the Salingers' secluded lifestyle in New Hampshire. Their daughter, Margaret Ann, and son, Matthew, were born in 1955 and 1960 respectively, while Salinger was engrossed in the creation of the Glass family legend. What "Raise High the Roof Beam, Carpenters" leads up to is not the surprise announcement that Seymour and Muriel have eloped because Seymour cannot stand all the fashionable rituals of a society wedding, but rather Seymour's concept of marriage, which Buddy reads in Seymour's journal after the news of his elopement and which Salinger wrote while expecting the birth of his first child. Seymour had written, "I've been reading a miscellany of Vedanta all day. Marriage partners are to serve each other. Elevate, help, teach, strengthen each other, but above all, *serve*. Raise their children honorably, lovingly, and with detachment. A child is a guest in the house, to be loved and respected – never possessed, since he belongs to God."

Readers had to wait another three and a half years before they were more fully introduced to Seymour. In the meantime, "Zooey," the sequel to "Franny," appeared in May 1957. In this story the Glass family, participants in a "prose home movie," rallies around their distraught youngest daughter to solve her dilemma. There is a difference between this story and "Raise High the Roof Beam, Carpenters" that indicates the development of Salinger's conception of his craft and his role in relation to his readers. "Raise High the Roof Beam, Carpenters" is basically confessional, an explanation by Salinger's alter ego for his idolization of their fictional creation. The story does not the attempt to convert readers, even indirectly as Franny tried with Lane Coutell in "Franny." "Zooey," however, is essentially and inescapably didactic, presenting a medley of voices trying to set straight not just poor Franny, but anyone who cares to eavesdrop.

A long letter written from Buddy to Zooey opens the story. It provides much more family history than necessary for understanding what follows, suggesting that Salinger did have some sort of plans for a much longer Glass chronicle than has been published. Buddy's letter talks about how he and Seymour have taken over the education of their younger siblings from their solicitous but down-to-earth parents. The older brothers have taught Zooey and Franny about the people who are really important – "the saints, the arhats, the bodhisattvas, the jivanmuktas" — rather than politicians or secular writers such as Homer and William Shakespeare. Buddy's letter also advises Zooey that if, despite family misgivings, Zooey feels he must pursue an acting career, he should by all means do so: "*Act, Zachary Martin Glass . . . but do it with all your might.*"

A long conversation between Zooey and his mother, Bessie Glass, then acquaints the reader with the adversarial tone of friendly household discourse while leaking the news that Franny has finally gotten home but will not talk to anyone about her problems. Zooey hits on the plan of calling her on the telephone and pretending to be Buddy. Franny realizes she is talking to Zooey, despite his attempts to disguise his voice, but she continues the conversation until she drifts off into the "dreamless sleep" that in Salinger's work is the sign that a troubled person has been tranquilized. The advice that gives Franny a joyous feeling "as if all of what little or much wisdom there is in the world were suddenly hers" is much the same as Buddy's advice to Zooey: if one wants to act, one must not scorn "unskilled" audiences. As Seymour once said, one must "be funny for the Fat Lady," because, Zooey says, "*There isn't anyone out there who isn't Seymour's Fat Lady. . . . It's Christ Himself.*"

When "Franny" and "Zooey" were published as a book in 1961, the stories almost immediately reached first place on *The New York Times* best-seller list and stayed there for six months. Although Salinger wrote for the dust jacket that he loved working on the long-term project of the Glass stories, there were few more to come. The next-to-last, "Seymour: An Introduction," had already appeared in *The New Yorker* (6 June 1959).

Through his alter ego Buddy Glass, Salinger finally tackled the problem of explaining Seymour's motive for suicide, the root cause of which he attributed to Seymour's credo: "I say that the true artist-seer, the heavenly fool who can and does produce beauty, is mainly dazzled to death by his own scruples, the blinding shapes and colors of his own sacred human conscience." It is impossible to know if Salinger had this stunning sentiment in mind when he wrote "A Perfect Day for Bananafish." Moreover, the reader should realize that this explanation comes from Buddy, whom Salinger identifies as the author of certain Salinger stories, including "A Perfect Day for Bananafish." After denying that the young man in *The Catcher in the Rye* (here added to the list of Buddy's writings) owed anything to Seymour, Buddy acknowledges that the Seymour of "A Perfect Day for Bananafish" does have a more striking resemblance to Buddy himself than to his brother, whom he now wishes the world to know as "a God-knower." Much that follows in "Seymour: An Introduction" is devoted to Buddy's explanation that when Seymour's 184 poems are finally published, he will stand with the "only three or four *very* nearly non-expendable poets" the United States has produced. About halfway through the story, Buddy reports that he has stopped work on it for two and one half months. When he resumes, he reports some of the advice about writing he received from Seymour. The most specific piece of advice is that he should ask himself, as a reader, "what piece of writing in all the world Buddy Glass would most want to read if he had his heart's choice" and then "sit down shamelessly and write the thing yourself," as Buddy/Salinger was apparently doing in writing this story. There is some truth to Mary McCarthy's snide criticism that "Salinger's world contains nothing but Salinger," as he advises himself to write that which he most wanted to read (*Harper's*, October 1962).

If Salinger is writing what he wants to read, any criticism would be unwelcome. Salinger evidently was beginning to have serious misgivings about his role as a writer. At the beginning of "Seymour: An Introduction," he looks on "my old fair-weather friend the general reader as my last deeply contemporary confidant," but before the story is finished Buddy asks a question that could well have been on Salinger's own mind, "How well do I know the reader? How much can I tell him without unnecessarily embarrassing either of us?" When one feels as much reticence as Salinger toward publishers and the public, the answer is likely to be less and less, to a vanishing point.

After "Raise High the Roof Beam, Carpenters" and "Seymour: An Introduction" appeared as a book in 1963, Salinger published only one more work of fiction, "Hapworth 16, 1924" (*The New Yorker*, 19 June 1965). Republished only in the pirated edition of *The Complete Uncollected Short Stories of J. D. Salinger* (1974), "Hapworth 16, 1924" is one of Salinger's longest and most daring works. After a brief introduction, he abandoned his Buddy Glass persona and undertook to write an extraordinarily long and precocious letter attributed to seven-year-old Seymour, who is writing home from summer camp. Salinger had written short letters, journal entries, and some dialogue for Seymour before, but this long letter is his only published effort to employ Seymour as an alter ego.

Ian Hamilton summed up general critical reaction to the story when he called it "a weird, exasper-

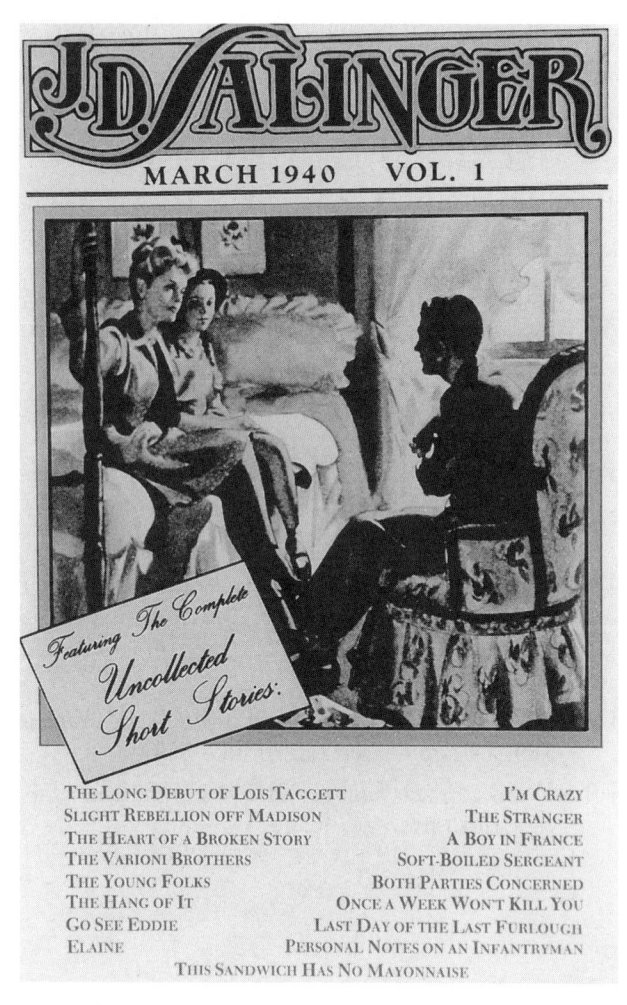

Cover for volume 1 of a two-volume pirated edition of magazine stories Salinger chose not to collect in any of his books. Salinger refused to authorize publication in book form.

ating tour de force." Many commentators have avoided it. Louise Bogan described it as "a disaster," explaining in a letter to anthropologist Ruth Benedict that *New Yorker* staff members " deplored its total cessation of talent." Eberhard Alsen, who has made a conscientious effort to work out the contribution of "Hapworth 16, 1924" to the portrayal of Seymour, has commented that those who share Seymour's "consuming admiration for God should be careful not to let their spiritual quests estrange them from others because this estrangement would ultimately defeat their purpose."

Although young Seymour's precocious style becomes repetitive and tiring, "Hapworth 16, 1924" proceeds enjoyably enough for readers willing to go along with the premise that a seven-year-old boy could so fluently express his extensive worldly experience and his acquaintance with ancient wisdom. Yet just as the letter should be coming to an end, Seymour discovers a fresh pad of paper and begins a preposterously long list of books that turns into a pompous series of recommended readings to improve his parents' (and Salinger's readers') sensibilities.

In 1967 Salinger and Claire Salinger divorced. The children continued to visit Cornish at times. Word occasionally leaked out that Salinger was still writing steadily but had no plans for publication. When two pirated volumes of his uncollected stories appeared in 1974, Salinger denounced the publication as "a terrible invasion of my privacy" (*The New York Times*, 3 November 1974).

In November 1986 Salinger blocked the publication of an unauthorized biography by Ian Hamilton, on the grounds that Hamilton had violated Salinger's copyright by quoting without permission from Salinger letters that their recipients had donated to various libraries. Hamilton then paraphrased the passages he had quoted, but Salinger took him to court anyway, claiming that he had copyrighted the information in the letters as well as the exact words. A federal judge ruled in Hamilton's favor but blocked distribution of the book pending appeal. On 29 January 1987 a U.S. Court of Appeals judge reversed the lower court's decision, stating that Hamilton's paraphrases violated copyright law. In 1988 Hamilton published *In Search of J. D. Salinger*, in which he neither quotes nor paraphrases any of the letters.

After all the publicity surrounding his suit against Hamilton, Salinger continued to guard his privacy. When a serious fire occurred at his Cornish home on 20 October 1992, uninvited visitors were rigorously barred from the property. The most surprising information in *The New York Times* account of the fire was the identification of his spokesperson as his "considerably younger" third wife, Colleen O'Neill. No further information about her or their marriage has been forthcoming.

Salinger may have explained his obsessive desire for privacy in *The Catcher in the Rye*, where Holden describes a short story by his older brother D. B. In "The Secret Goldfish," Holden says, "this little kid . . . wouldn't let anybody look at his goldfish because he'd bought it with his own money." The novel in which this passage appeared put Salinger in a position to pay for his own privacy in Cornish, New Hampshire.

Bibliography:

Jack R. Sublette, *J. D. Salinger: An Annotated Bibliography, 1938–1981* (New York & London: Garland, 1984).

Biography:

Ian Hamilton, *In Search of J. D. Salinger* (New York: Random House, 1988; London: Heinemann, 1988).

References:

Eberhard Alsen, *Salinger's Glass Stories as a Composite Novel* (Troy, N.Y.: Whitston, 1983);

Harold Bloom, ed., *J. D. Salinger: Modern Critical Views* (New York: Chelsea House, 1987);

Betty Eppes, "What I Did Last Summer," *Paris Review,* 80 (24 July 1981): 221–239;

Warren French, *J. D. Salinger* (New York: Twayne, 1963; revised edition, Boston: Twayne, 1976);

French, *J. D. Salinger Revisited* (Boston: Twayne, 1988);

Henry Anatole Grunwald, ed., *Salinger: A Critical and Personal Portrait* (New York: Harper, 1963);

Frederick L. Gwynn and Joseph L. Blotner, *The Fiction of J. D. Salinger* (Pittsburgh: University of Pittsburgh Press, 1958; London: Spearman, 1960);

Elizabeth N. Kurian, *A Religious Response to the Existential Dilemma in the Fiction of J. D. Salinger* (New Delhi, India: Intellectual Publishing House, 1992);

Marvin Laser and Norman Fruman, eds., *Studies in J. D. Salinger* (New York: Odyssey Press, 1963);

William Maxwell, "J. D. Salinger," *Book-of-the-Month Club News,* Midsummer 1951, pp. 5–6;

James E. Miller Jr., *J. D. Salinger* (Minneapolis: University of Minnesota Press, 1965);

Carol and Richard Ohmann, "Reviewers, Critics, and *The Catcher in the Rye*," *Critical Inquiry,* 3 (Autumn 1976): 15–37; (Spring 1977): 599–603; (Summer 1977): 773–777;

Joel Salzberg, *Critical Essays on Salinger's "The Catcher in the Rye"* (Boston: G. K. Hall, 1990);

Jack Salzman, *New Essays on "The Catcher in the Rye"* (New York & London: Cambridge University Press, 1991);

Daniel M. Stashower, "On First Looking into Chapman's Holden: Speculation on a Murder," *American Scholar,* 52 (Summer 1983): 373–377;

George Steiner, "The Salinger Industry," *Nation,* 189 (14 November 1959): 360–363;

John Wenke, *J. D. Salinger: A Study of the Short Fiction* (Boston: Twayne, 1991).

Gilbert Sorrentino

(27 April 1929 -)

Julian Cowley
University of Luton

See also the Sorrentino entries in *DLB 5: American Poets Since World War II, First Series* and *DLB Yearbook: 1980*.

BOOKS: *The Darkness Surrounds Us* (Highlands, N.C.: Jargon Books, 1960);
Black and White (New York: Totem Press/Corinth Books, 1964);
The Sky Changes (New York: Hill & Wang, 1966; revised edition, San Francisco: North Point Press, 1986);
The Perfect Fiction (New York: Norton, 1968);
Steelwork (New York: Pantheon, 1970);
Imaginative Qualities of Actual Things (New York: Pantheon, 1971);
Corrosive Sublimate (Los Angeles: Black Sparrow Press, 1971);
Splendide-Hôtel (New York: New Directions, 1973);
Flawless Play Restored: The Masque of Fungo (Los Angeles: Black Sparrow Press, 1974);
A Dozen Oranges (Santa Barbara, Cal.: Black Sparrow Press, 1976);
White Sail (Santa Barbara, Cal.: Black Sparrow Press, 1977);
The Orangery (Austin & London: University of Texas Press, 1978);
Mulligan Stew (New York: Grove, 1979; London: Marion Boyars, 1980);
Aberration of Starlight (New York: Random House, 1980; London: Marion Boyars, 1981);
Selected Poems 1958-1980 (Santa Barbara, Cal.: Black Sparrow Press, 1981);
Crystal Vision (San Francisco: North Point Press, 1981; London: Marion Boyars, 1982);
Blue Pastoral (San Francisco: North Point Press, 1983; London: Marion Boyars, 1984);
Something Said (San Francisco: North Point Press, 1984);
Odd Number (San Francisco: North Point Press, 1985);
A Beehive Arranged on Humane Principles (New York: Grenfell Press, 1986);

Rose Theatre (Elmwood Park, Ill.: Dalkey Archive Press, 1987);
Misterioso (Elmwood Park, Ill.: Dalkey Archive Press, 1989);
Under the Shadow (Elmwood Park, Ill.: Dalkey Archive Press, 1991);
Red the Fiend (New York: Fromm International, 1995).

TRANSLATION: *Sulpiciæ Elegidia/Elegiacs of Sulpicia* (Mt. Horeb, Wis.: Perishable Press, 1977).

SELECTED PERIODICAL PUBLICATIONS – UNCOLLECTED: "The Moon in Its Flight," *New American Review*, 13 (1971): 153-163;
"Catechism," *Chicago Review*, 25, no. 3 (1973): 19-31.

In *Splendide-Hôtel* (1973) Gilbert Sorrentino writes: "I agree with all those who wish to leave something behind that has the flash of the smallest truth. It is, I admit, sadly, sadly, so much of my life's concern." To confront what he calls in *Something Said* (1984) that "isolate fleck" of truth, he has faced unremittingly the debasement that follows from "manipulation of power through language." In the process he has emerged not only as one of America's finest poets but also as a major novelist of technical resourcefulness and savage dark humor.

William McPheron, in the introduction to his descriptive bibliography of Sorrentino's work, locates him as "a member of that generation which revolted against the dictates of academic verse and consumer fiction by reviving the modernist esthetics of William Carlos Williams and Ezra Pound." What distinguished Sorrentino, McPheron suggests, was his determination to enter into the world of commercial publishing and remain a professional writer without sacrificing his integrity as a literary artist. In an interview with John O'Brien (1981), Sorrentino declared: "I have an absolute belief in

Gilbert Sorrentino (courtesy of Gilbert Sorrentino)

myself." That self-assurance is evident in his unbending dedication, for more than three decades, to the art of prose in the face of unsympathetic market forces. Sorrentino's fiction has grown more opaque and challenging even as publishers have increasingly emphasized commercial considerations.

Born in Brooklyn, New York, Sorrentino was the son of August E. Sorrentino, who was born in Sicily, and Ann Marie Davis Sorrentino, whose ancestry was Irish and Welsh Irish. He was educated at Brooklyn College (now Brooklyn College of the City University of New York), beginning there in 1950. He interrupted his studies to serve from 1951 to 1953 in the U.S. Army Medical Corps. During this time he wrote an "impressionistic" sketch of bordellos in towns on the Mexican border, which he later sent to William Carlos Williams (the two men would be friends until Williams's death in 1963). From 1955 to 1957 he returned to Brooklyn College. With college friends he started the literary magazine *Neon* in 1956, which featured contributions by Williams as well as from younger writers, including Charles Olson, Fielding Dawson, Hubert Selby Jr., LeRoi Jones, and Joel Oppenheimer.

Sorrentino's first book of poetry, *The Darkness Surrounds Us,* was published in 1960 and dedicated to Elsene Wiessner, his first wife. His second collection, *Black and White* (1964), was dedicated to his children Jesse and Delia (He has a third child, Christopher). His marriage to Wiessner ended in divorce, and he subsequently married Vivian Victoria Ortiz, the dedicatee of his first novel, *The Sky Changes* (1966). In the early 1960s Sorrentino also wrote and served as an editor for *Kulchur,* a magazine that assembled an impressive array of writing in opposition to the academic orthodoxy in American literature at the time. Contributors were drawn from the Beats, Black Mountain writers, and the New York School. In 1965 he taught at Columbia University.

McPheron provides the background for the publication of *The Sky Changes* as well as Sorrentino's other work. Sorrentino wrote the novel between 1961 and 1963, writing at night after working during the day, mostly as a proofreader for publishers. By the time of the book's publication, Sorrentino was employed by Grove Press as an assistant editor. Journalist Seymour Krim, who did freelance work for Grove at the time, read the manuscript and praised it in an 8 October 1964 letter to the author: "the writing is so natural and skilled that it can't fail to impress any editor at any bookhouse who cares about the value of language in human intercourse." Krim acted as Sorrentino's agent for the book, placing it with the firm of Hill and Wang.

In this bleak and powerful novel Sorrentino traces the breakup of a marriage during the course of a journey to Mexico on which a couple and their two children are accompanied by a driver. While the episodes in the novel are titled after places on the route, they are not presented in chronological order. The fragmented, stagnant nature of the novel's episodic structure reflects a world without apparent hope. For Sorrentino, the only mode of reply to such a world is literary art. As Eric Mottram puts it in his essay on Sorrentino's fiction, Sorrentino aims to produce "a text which resists being eroded along with its subject by inventing and parodying fictional forms."

The strength of *The Sky Changes* is Sorrentino's refusal to use the conventions (including names) that make reading popular fiction such a comfortable, unchallenging experience. In their place is the recognition that writing grants form and meaning to the raw data of experience. Sorrentino creates a novel of naturalistic power that is also a self-consciously constructed fiction; as Sorrentino told O'Brien: "I'm interested in prose which is absolutely cold, structured and chaste. I think this novel has a numb quality about it." In 1986 North Point Press published a new edition of the novel with two additional chapters that Sorrentino wished to insert.

After teaching at the Aspen Writers Workshop in 1967, Sorrentino in 1968 and 1969 worked on *Steelwork* (1970), his second published novel, while he was working full-time at Grove Press. Developed from an unpublished piece from the mid 1950s, "The Light Fantastic," the novel is set in South Brooklyn during the years 1935 to 1951. Although located in the time and place of Sorrentino's youth and dedicated to a boyhood friend, Donald Walsh, Sorrentino adopted a form that would shield him from what he regarded as the dangers of documentary, historical narrative – primarily the stock emotional responses bound to distort the book's truth, which he described to O'Brien as "the kind of madness that America offers to its citizens." It was the quality of that culture, rather than a specific past, he sought to capture, with the neighborhood as the sole protagonist. There is no story, as such, and even within an individual episode, or a group of episodes that have some evident connection, development occurs not as an end in itself, but as a contribution to the prevailing mood. *The Sky Changes* portrayed local anesthesia; here one finds the generalized emotional and intellectual numbness of what John Martin at Black Sparrow Press, in a 28 December 1970 letter to the author, called "a war-and-profit oriented society with almost nothing to redeem it."

In his third novel, *Imaginative Qualities of Actual Things* (1971), Sorrentino draws on his experience of the New York avant-garde art scene to produce biting satire, puncturing the pretensions of that milieu. Sorrentino spoke to O'Brien of his admiration for the work of Wyndham Lewis, and this novel may be regarded as akin to Lewis's *The Apes of God* (1930) in that Sorrentino seeks "to level the falseness and wretchedness, misery and self-seeking and greed of the artistic world." While the prevailing rage of *Steelwork* is leavened by moments of humor, the anger in *Imaginative Qualities of Actual Things* is directed through incisive comedy and exuberant wordplay, metafictional games and multiple voicing. The material presence of words on the page and the artifice of composition are foregrounded to discourage a facile response by the reader. Sorrentino's combination of technical resourcefulness and relentless savaging of the illusory and the spurious across a range of American experience has characterized his subsequent fiction.

In his interview with O'Brien, Sorrentino spoke critically of writers who were "burning to get a message across to you, burning to tell you the truth of life, the truth of their own lives and experiences, but are totally uninterested in how prose sits on the page in terms of its music, its elegance, and its grace." Dedicated to his old friend Hubert Selby, Sorrentino's next prose work, *Splendide-Hôtel*, was an antidote to what he saw as this general neglect of prose. Written in late 1970 and early 1971, the book was accepted for publication by James Laughlin at New Directions, despite his sense that it was not commercially viable. The overall structure of the work is provided by the alphabet, and Sorrentino assembles fragments that tell no story and make no cumulative point. The title is taken from Arthur Rimbaud's poem "Les Illuminations," and frequent allusions substantiate the sense that in part *Splendide-Hôtel* was written in homage to the poet and his work.

Sorrentino aims in *Splendide-Hôtel* to preserve the creative tradition in which he detects "a slender but absolute continuity between the work of the damned Frenchman [Rimbaud] and the patronized American" William Carlos Williams, who was eight years old when Rimbaud died. These literary artists are touchstones for this series of exquisite exercises in style, which conserves the value of the artist in an age devoted to being entertained. The parts of the book constitute a celebration of language and of creativity and are written in the faith that art is the last bastion of genuine life, rather than some pallid imitation. Sor-

(all drenched in deshabille)   (i.e., the professional pauper);
Georgia, ladies of the evening, the Limehouse blues, lovin' Sam, the Sheik of
(am what he am);   (than whom which)
Alabam', the South Sea moon, Nellie Kelly, being on the Alamo, Rose of the Rio
(who ate the moldy casserole);
Grande, stumbling, being 'way down yonder in New Orleans, Annabelle, Barney Google,
("all the news from shit to hint");   (the nose-flute king);
the bugle call rag, Charleston, dizzy fingers, raggedy Ann, that old gang of his,
(cf. "Anomie in Cincinnati");
being all alone by the telephone, the day that Sally went away, the Indian love
(vide further adventures by Venus Furze);
call, someone who could make him feel glad just to be sad, memory lane, nobody's
(or "Framed!");
sweetheart, a prisoner's song, Rose Marie, sugar cake, a photograph to tell his
and ¶ He like to fainted from ennui when entertaining the thoughts of
troubles to, the Bam, Bam, Bamy shore, Cecilia, gypsy eyes blazing, Rose with the
(partial as he was to opera stockings);   (read: "mountings")
turned-down hose, drinking songs, the hills of home, jalousie, a cottage small by
(where a pall of smoke did plash);   (courtesy Texas-Pacific RR);
a waterfall, when lights were low, the song of the vagabonds, Sunny, that ukulele
(E.R.A.);
lady, Valencia, baby face, the birth of the blues, hard-luck stories that they
(with determined mien)
handed him, desert songs, horses, climbing the highest mountain, stars peek-a-
(vide "Honky myths in Western Architecture")
booing down, little white houses, when nighttime came stealing, the moonlight on
(fondly floodlights flotsam foul);   (played a trick on him);   (k)   (k)
the Ganges, muddy water, his little nest of heavenly blue, playing and dancing
(day left);   (greetings from Lake Valentine, N.J.)
gypsies, the Riff song, when day was done, a broken heart, among his souvenirs,
(and other novelty acts);
Bill, crazy words and crazy tunes, a dancing tambourine, a funny face, looking
(peep?)
over, a four-leaf clover, Mississippi mud, his blue heaven, when his heart stood
(vide Farm Desertion in 1918-19);   and ¶ His head was a calabash of dreariness about
still, Paree, the rangers' song, Rio Rita, Sam, the old accordion man, going along
(known to all as the lewd lineman);   (and kasha for two);
singing a song, the varsity drag, Miss Annabelle Lee, his land and their land,
(and fog in the brain);   (a windowpane)
x pain in his tum-tum, crazy rhythm, women crazy for him, rain, and darkness too,
(and his pornographic prong);   (the "sweetheart of Racine");
a ding-dong daddy, a red, red rose, Jeannine, the Manhattan serenade, one kiss,
(those WAC-y women)
shortnin' bread, stout-hearted men, sweethearts, on parade, a rainbow round his
(and the egg in his beer);
shoulder, the sail on his dreamboat, those tears in his eyes, deep night, a talking
(cf. Venereal Vagrants);
picture of her, vagabond lovers, magic spells that were everywhere, moaning low,
(whispered in crepuscular confessional);
his sin, the one rose that was left in his heart, pagan love songs, the lonely hours,
(that go "jingle-jingle");
stardust, wedding bells, that thing called love, a man who ain't got a friend, a
plus ¶ How his rheumy eyes snapped vengefully when he heard tales of
bench in the park, Betty Co-Ed, biding his time, any Russian play, a cheerful little

Page from an early draft for Mulligan Stew *(courtesy of Gilbert Sorrentino)*

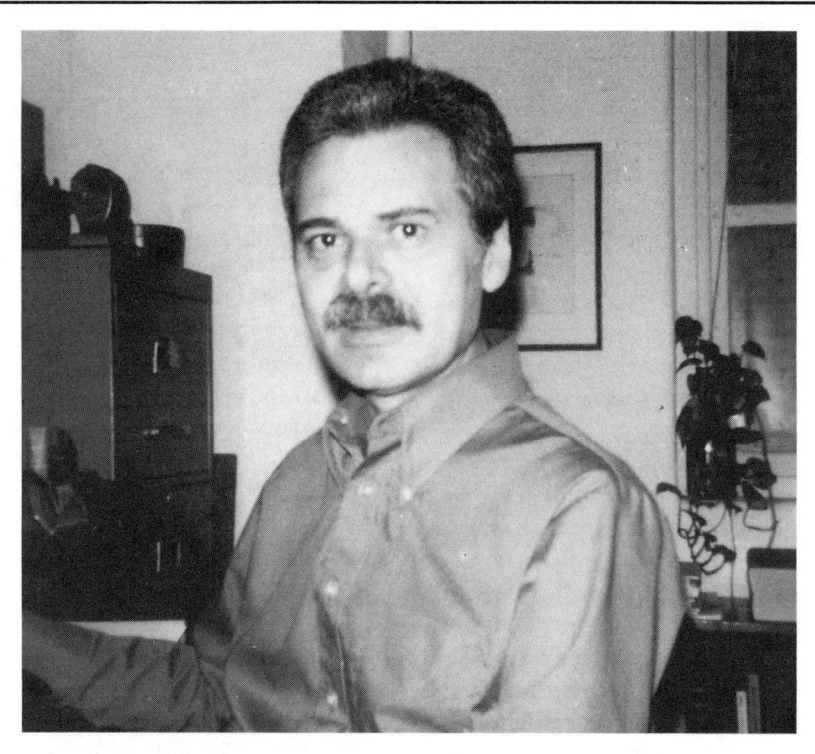

Sorrentino at the time of Mulligan Stew *(photograph by Victoria Sorrentino)*

rentino includes a verse from a poem by Thomas Nashe, first published in 1600, for as he told O'Brien, it exemplifies the worth of literary art:

> To realize that was written so many centuries ago and that it has survived as something utterly beautiful, a construction of language as thrilling as long as English survives: I don't think that there's anything more interesting for a man to do than to make language work that way, to make a perfect beauty out of all the rubbish in the world and in his own mind.

In *Splendide-Hôtel* Sorrentino attempts to realize his own instance of changeless beauty.

After teaching at Sarah Lawrence College (1971–1972), Sorrentino received his first Guggenheim Fellowship in 1973 (he was awarded a second in 1987). In 1974 he won a Samuel S. Fels Award in fiction for a short story titled "Catechism" and received a Creative Artists Public Service grant (1974–1975). That same year saw the publication of *Flawless Play Restored: The Masque of Fungo,* a satire in the manner of Ben Jonson that on its title page declared itself "part of a novel-in-progress presented in play form, but not intended for the stage." Martin welcomed its caustic satire with enthusiasm, observing in a 21 April 1973 letter to Sorrentino, "It will reduce every author I don't like to whimpering fury. It will enrich and edify all the authors I like."

In 1975 Sorrentino completed the novel, initially titled "Synthetic Ink," in which the play was the centerpiece. Sections of the book appeared in various magazines beginning in 1973, but the nearly 450-page work was rejected by many publishing houses before being accepted by Grove Press, whose owner, Barney Rosset, disliked the original title. Rosset agreed to Sorrentino's substitute title, *Mulligan Stew,* with its punning allusion to James Joyce's Buck Mulligan, and the novel was published in May 1979. Despite its ostensible lack of commercial appeal, the book sold relatively well. A novel of comic exuberance, which defiantly rejects the conventions of realistic fiction, it prompted reviews that invoked François Rabelais and Laurence Sterne and puts Sorrentino in the line of such writers as the Gustave Flaubert of *Bouvard et Pécuchet* (1881), Joyce, and Flann O'Brien, author of *At Swim-Two-Birds* (1939). Sorrentino dedicated his novel to the memory of Irish novelist O'Brien, who is also the source for an epigraph that prepares the reader for a book considered as a "personal musical instrument," upon which the author will play his own tunes for his private satisfaction.

The epigraph from O'Brien is balanced by a postscript attributed to Emile Fion, a fictional character from French novelist Robert Pinget's *Mahu* (1952). While the postscript ostensibly refers to the

Impressionist painter Paul Cézanne, it may be read as a confirmation of Sorrentino's approach to writing:

> he desired a synthesis that would allow him to *decorate* nature with the forms and colors that existed nowhere except in his own secret thought. Thus, his late painting nowhere shows forth nature's splendors, but instead, is a failure precipitated by his surrender to the pleasures of the imagination.

Such ironic self-deprecation scarcely conceals the enormous assurance with which Sorrentino has pursued his aesthetic goals.

A culmination of literary modernism, *Mulligan Stew* is prefaced by a series of letters and a reader's report suggesting the difficulty of getting such a novel into print; the novel is thus self-parodic, as well as parodic of other writing. One of the letters warns that what follows wallows "in the mortal sin of bookishness," and the novel is indeed composed ostentatiously of fictional documents – more letters; extracts from journals, scrapbooks, and notebooks; interviews; reviews; poems; as well as *The Masque of Fungo*.

Sorrentino told John O'Brien that "Every one of my books is an attempt to solve another fictional problem that I set myself. And one of the ways I solve the problem is by inventing another voice or another group of voices." Sorrentino lifts characters from other novels to populate *Mulligan Stew*, drawing Ned Beaumont from Dashiell Hammett's *The Glass Key* (1931) and Antony Lamont from *At Swim-Two-Birds*. Martin Halpin finds himself "plucked out of the wry, the amused footnote in which I have resided faceless, for all these years, in the work of that gentlemanly Irishman, Mr. Joyce," and transplanted into a novel being written by Lamont, within the work of Sorrentino. *Mulligan Stew* traces the decline of Lamont into bitterness and paranoia, the squandering of his creative energies in his struggle to write. But the power of the novel is its creative energy on the level of verbal play; it supplies a diagnosis while providing an antidote, however diluted by Sorrentino's pessimism concerning the state of American cultural life.

While *Mulligan Stew* went the rounds of the publishers, Sorrentino continued to write and win awards. In 1975 he received a grant from the Ariadne Foundation as well as the first of three National Endowment for the Arts Awards (1975–1976, 1978–1979, and 1983–1984). In July 1976 he completed *Crystal Vision* (1981) a novel begun early the previous year, composed largely of dialogue. It was preceded into print by *Aberration of Starlight* (1980), a novel told from four different points of view that construct four distinct realities from the events of thirty-six hours at a New Jersey boardinghouse. In a 16 May 1980 letter written to John O'Brien, Sorrentino compared the novel to "an old photograph album, i.e. what is happening *outside* the edges of the photos? I also like it because it is, though set in summer 1939, devoid of the nostalgic."

The focus of *Aberration of Starlight* is a fractured family group: ten-year-old Billy Recco; his divorced mother, Marie; her father; and a salesman out to seduce Marie. As in *Steelwork*, Sorrentino is concerned with qualities of ignorance, waste, and greed. Again mood prevails over involvement with character. This approach is in accord with Sorrentino's perception registered in "The Various Isolated: William Carlos Williams' Prose," an essay he wrote in 1972 and collected in *Something Said*: "American life is not tragic, it is dull; its losses are almost silent, inexpressible, obscure." No melodrama is to be found in the novel, nor sentimentality; instead, Sorrentino, through his meticulously controlled selection of materials, reveals stark existential facts as perceived through a distorting cloud of emotions, vague desires, and prejudices. He portrays mundane failures of human love and intelligence and characters whose lack of insight or care leaves them participants in their own degradation.

While some of the fragments that compose the world of the novel seem naturalistic in their detail, Sorrentino uses other techniques to focus on the writing and preclude the reader's empathic involvement with the characters. There are question-and-answer sequences, reminiscent of Joyce's use of catechism, and a dialogue between Marie and a widow is supplemented by absurd footnotes more appropriate to the world of *Mulligan Stew*. Sorrentino deliberately disrupts his reader, but as Jerome Klinkowitz notes in *Literary Disruptions* (1980), "the irony, and success of Sorrentino's method is that in the process of his anti-illusionistic, self-consciously artistic writing, brilliantly conceived persons, places, and things are brought before the reader's eyes." His characters or, as Mottram calls them, "characterological presentations," are not allowed to escape the page.

Sorrentino's achievement in *Aberration of Starlight* is matched by that of *Crystal Vision*, which is composed almost entirely of fictional conversations. Although it is the lightest in tone of his novels, it was still rejected by the editors of commercial houses before it was published by North Point Press. In 1981 Sorrentino won the John Dos Passos Prize for Literature and was the subject for the first

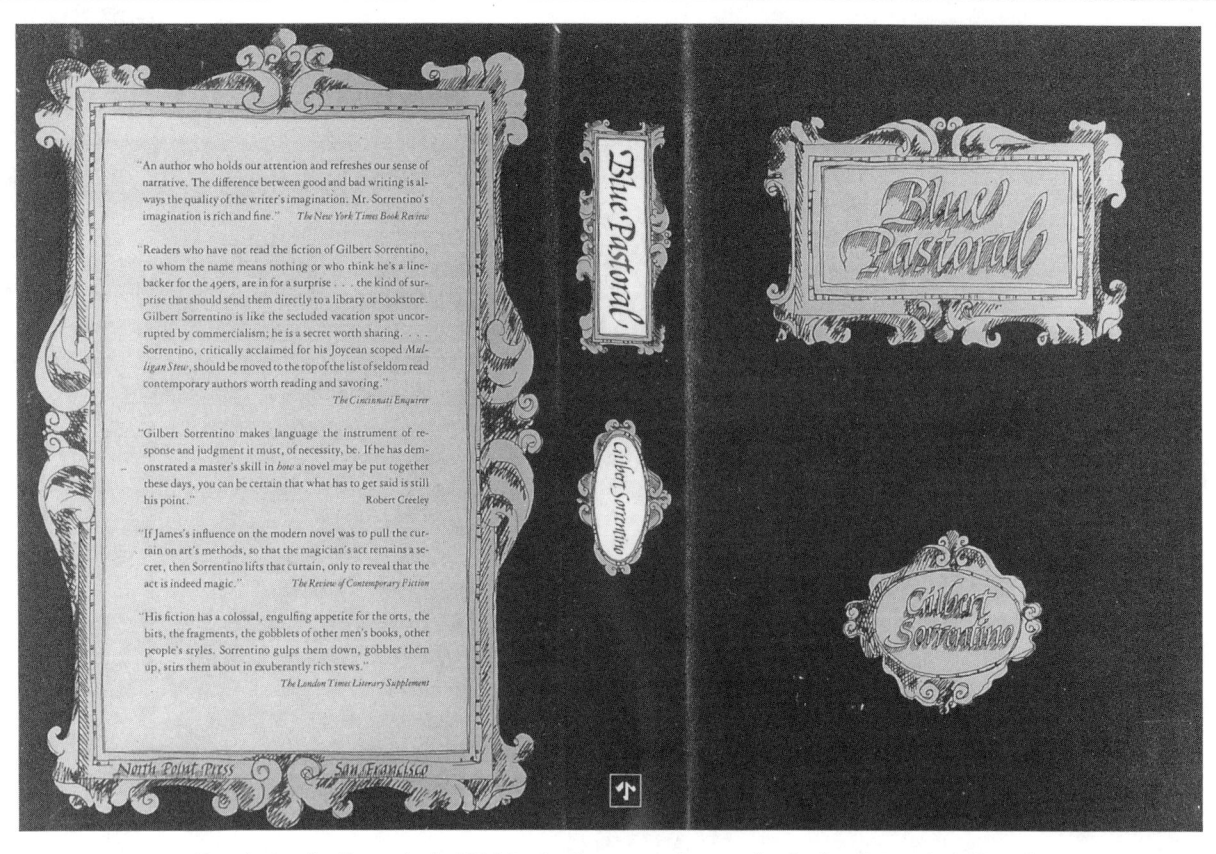

Dust jacket for Sorrentino's 1983 book, about a man's quest for the "perfect musical phrase"

issue of the *Review of Contemporary Fiction*. *Crystal Vision* transforms street-corner speech into rich verbal art. No conventional story is told; rather, the seventy-eight chapters organized in a sequence suggested by the cards of a Tarot deck consist of anecdotes, dreams, fantasies, memories, and exercises in composition, including letters and a playlet.

While *Crystal Vision* is infused with the spirit of Joyce and Flann O'Brien, its germ can be traced to Sorrentino's interest in William Carlos Williams. In "The Various Isolated: William Carlos Williams' Prose" Sorrentino quotes from *A Novelette and Other Prose (1921–1931)* (1932), where Williams speaks of conversation as "pure design," arguing that "to be conversation, it must have only the effect of itself, not on him to whom it has a special meaning but as a dog or a store window." Stylization of dialogue, not transmission of information, is Sorrentino's preoccupation in *Crystal Vision*.

The time and the place are the same as for *Steelwork*, and characters recur, but in *Crystal Vision* characterization is distilled to voice alone. The brutality evident in the earlier novel is submerged beneath a brilliant linguistic fabric, with loss and impotence being occasional piquant departures from the prevailing good humor. The novel's final chapter, titled "Red White and Blue," particularly conveys the sense that there is "something lost, something to hell and gone," specifically "the *American* aspects of the loss of innocence and youth." Sorrentino's answer to this loss, as ever, is the crystalline artifact, "unsullied by time." In *Imaginative Qualities of Actual Things* the artistic decline of the writer Guy Lewis sees "all his finest prose wasted in oral stories." In *Crystal Vision* oral stories are raised to the level of art and resist the ravages of time.

Sorrentino taught in New York City at the New School for Social Research from 1976 to 1979, when he became the Edwin S. Quain Professor of Literature at the University of Scranton, Pennsylvania. In 1978 he started work on the novel that became *Blue Pastoral* (1983), arguably his finest comic achievement to date. As *Crystal Vision* may be paired with *Steelwork*, so might *Blue Pastoral* be compared to *The Sky Changes*. Here another couple travel across America: "Blue" Serge Gavotte, in search of the "perfect musical phrase," and his wife, Helene. On 14 August 1979, still early in the novel's composition, Sorrentino wrote to John O'Brien that he was "inventing a syntax so that not even the language

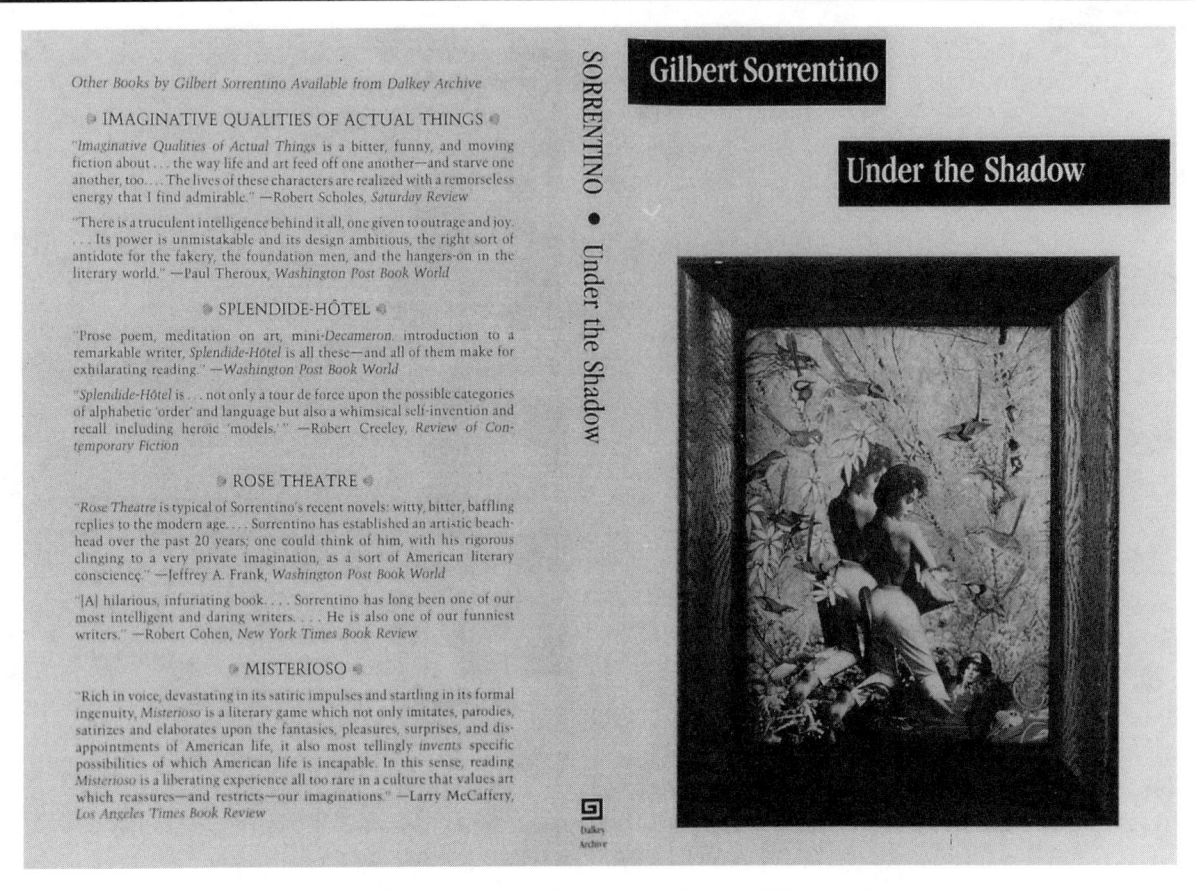

Dust jacket for Sorrentino's 1991 book, a collection of fifty-nine vignettes

has reference to 'reality.'" The completed novel is a remarkable feat of literary mimicry, as Sorrentino switches voices with startling disregard for continuity and stylistic coherence. The dominant voice is an imitation of English Renaissance prose peppered with Brooklyn colloquialisms, an incongruous mix that sits yet more incongruously with the tale it relates. Sorrentino along the way introduces parodically stereotypical ethnic voices and relentlessly pillories the academic establishment.

After Sorrentino took up his current position as professor of English at Stanford University in 1982, he gathered the materials for *Something Said,* a selection of his essays, reviews, and critical articles stretching back to the 1960s, mainly on writing and writers. Among the writers treated are Jack Spicer, Louis Zukofsky, Edward Dahlberg, Paul Bowles, Italo Calvino, Raymond Queneau, and, of course, Williams. In an essay from 1983, "Genetic Coding," Sorrentino reveals his own artistic tendencies: "an obsessive concern with formal structure, a dislike of the replication of experience, a love of digression and embroidery, a great pleasure in false or ambiguous information, a desire to invent problems that only the invention of new forms can solve, and a joy in making mountains out of molehills."

In 1985, the year his sustained achievement was acknowledged with an American Academy and Institute of Arts and Letters Award for literature, Sorrentino published *Odd Number,* which with *Rose Theatre* (1987) and *Misterioso* (1989) forms a trilogy that stands as his most uncompromising work. He began writing *Odd Number* in December 1981 and commented in an 8 January 1982 letter to O'Brien that it was "the most complicated piece of fiction ever devised by mankind." Its working title was *Triad,* but in 1984 Sorrentino renamed the novel, deriving its new title from *At Swim-Two-Birds:* "Evil is even, truth is an odd number and death is a full stop."

Sorrentino conceived the idea for *Rose Theatre* and its place as the second of a trilogy of works well before he completed *Odd Number.* He alluded to his tentative plans in a 15 January 1983 letter to O'Brien: "I have a feeling that a novel might be made of names only. I know one can be made of lists, and some day I'll write one. Maybe the next one, already in my head, based on an inventory made by Philip Henslowe of the Rose Theatre's props in 1598 in London, when he moved the company to a new location" (the fifteen chapters of the novel are named after the props on this list). Sorrentino began real work on the book in October 1984 with, as he confided in a 12 November 1985 letter to O'Brien, the aim of forging a new literary language, "a kind of demotic, scattered, haphazard, 'style-less' language that falls in and out of cliché, a kind of useless language." With the book all but finished, he wrote to O'Brien on 12 November 1986 that he had come to experience writing as "an endless questioning of endless choices, none of which ever seem 'right.'"

For the jacket of *Rose Theatre,* Sorrentino wrote that "*Odd Number* investigated the ways in which 'facts' assert themselves through the various encodings of experience contained in the answers to a rigidly circumscribed set of questions; i.e., the answers, whether colored by prejudice, opinion, distortion both conscious and unconscious, or presented as objective retorts based upon absolute data, reveal themselves as wholly incapable of telling anything that might be construed as the truth. As the book progresses, all is contradicted, refuted, thrown into turmoil." *Rose Theatre* sets out to correct the errors of its predecessor, but this novel "in its desire to stabilize and clarify, adds new and unsettling material to that which we already possess."

Misterioso takes its title from a song by jazz pianist and composer Thelonious Monk, whom Sorrentino considers one of the great modern artists. On 29 July 1983, four years before he started writing it, he wrote to O'Brien that he envisaged "a book that is a series of lists and catalogues – no narrative, no characters, no author, and no place or time or action, no nothing but those words that 'tend towards maximum entropy.'" While the actual novel is not quite as chaotic as Sorrentino anticipated, it is a singularly opaque recapitulation of figures and events from the first two books of the trilogy. A cast of angels and demons add to the enigmatic quality of *Misterioso,* whose structure is based on the alphabet.

Sorrentino's next book, *Under the Shadow* (1991), is an elegant assemblage of fifty-nine enigmatic fragments. Each vignette has a simple noun for its title, so the contents page reads as a heterogeneous list, starting with "Memorial" and concluding with "Things." Its coherence is that of a collage rather than of a narrative, but cross-references between the vignettes create a shadowy, intense yet blurred impression of events. Looking back on the writing of *Splendide-Hôtel* in "The Act of Creation and Its Artifact," a 1981 essay included in *Something Said,* Sorrentino remarked that "it is well-nigh impossible to give a coherent account of how one composes." But while there is always improvisational inventiveness in his work, Sorrentino in his later fiction has clearly relied upon underlying structures and patterning, so that elements recur as a consequence of preliminary compositional decisions rather than in accordance with the dictates of storyline or of verisimilitude, which are alien to this fictional world.

In 1981 Sorrentino reviewed *Exercises in Style,* Barbara Wright's translation of Raymond Queneau's stunning set of variations on a banal theme. His conclusion neatly sums up the position from which Sorrentino has written all his fiction, but which appears most immediately pertinent to the works beginning with *Blue Pastoral,* continuing through the trilogy, and finishing with *Under the Shadow:* "What it posits, in a great bravura performance, is the joyous heresy that will not go away, despite the recrudescence of such aesthetic nonsense as Moral Responsibility, Great Themes, and Vast Issues as the business of fiction, and that heresy simply states: form determines content."

With *Red the Fiend* (1995) Sorrentino returned to the quasi-naturalistic mode of *Steelwork.* Worthy to stand beside *A Portrait of the Artist as a Young Man,* the novel presents scenes from an Irish American Roman Catholic boyhood. Sorrentino creates a subtle voice to render Red's perceptions of and responses to an environment that is all too often incomprehensible, hostile, and menacing. In *Red the Fiend* Sorrentino is ostensibly closer to conventional narrative than in any of his previous novels as he traces Red's painful and hilarious passage from childhood into adolescence. Yet his concern, as before, is not storytelling but preserving the texture of experience in prose.

Red the Fiend has a power of evocation that should ensure it a substantial readership. It harks back to the considerable achievement of Sorrentino's early fiction; yet it is similar to, rather than a departure from, his ostentatiously nonmimetic novels. The continuity is established by the quality of Sorrentino's prose, for his singular dedication to the art of writing has produced one of the most important and accomplished bodies of work by any living writer.

BRITTANY, CLARA, MOTHER'S DEATH

At the very moment that my mother died, Clara and I were in bed together in the Hotel Brittany. She and I had met by accident on Vanderbilt Avenue and had come downtown together in a cab. Clara, in her astoundingly ramshackle and reckless way, lied to me that she was going to meet an old girlfriend from Bennington, and I contributed my own lie. We wound up drinking in a bar off Sheridan Square and I was soon taking liberties, as the creaking phrase has it, with her, Clara and I had already been intimate—another prizewinning euphemism—with each other, on and off, off and on, for some two years, but we had decided to break our adultery off. It would be a small pleasure for me to be able to say that we were concerned about Ben's feelings, but in truth we were somewhat worried that a full-blown affair might impinge upon our freedom to have affairs with others. We had spent, as I recall, some hours thrashing this out. We were serious indeed about our prospective lusts.

The afternoon had turned into a windy, bitter night, and a thin, powder-dry snow lashed the streets every once in a while in a stinging drizzle. We walked through this weather a few blocks to the Brittany, a faded and somewhat decrepit old hotel that still retained a semblance of old downtown glamour in the appointments of its raffish bar and taproom, a locale that still featured a weekend pianist, some gifted hack with a name like Tommy Jazzino or Chip Mellodius. I always liked the rooms in the Brittany, mostly because of the really large closets, a strange thing, I grant you, to care about, since I never once registered at the desk with anything even remotely like luggage. The desk clerk nodded at us as I signed and paid; he probably thought he knew us from the night before or the week before. God knows, the desperately sex-driven all have the same weirdly lost yet hopeful look, the same imploring face that whines

Page from a draft for a short story (courtesy of Gilbert Sorrentino)

Interviews:

David Ossman, "Gilbert Sorrentino," in *The Sullen Art: Interviews with Modern American Poets* (New York: Corinth Books, 1963), pp. 46-55;

John O'Brien, "Imaginative Qualities of Gilbert Sorrentino: An Interview," *Grosseteste Review*, 6, no. 1-4 (1973): 69-84;

Barry Alpert, "Gilbert Sorrentino – An Interview," *Vort*, 6 (Fall 1974): 3-30;

Randy Sue Coburn, "Sorrentino's Stew Starts to Bubble," *Washington Star*, 21 June 1979, C5, C10;

David W. McCullough, "Eye on Books," *Book of the Month Club News*, Fall 1979, p. 12; reprinted as "Gilbert Sorrentino" in McCullough's *People, Books & Book People* (New York: Harmony Books, 1981), pp. 165-166;

O'Brien, "An Interview with Gilbert Sorrentino," *Review of Contemporary Fiction*, 1 (Spring 1981): 5-27;

Dennis Barone, "An Interview with Gilbert Sorrentino," *Partisan Review*, 48, no. 2 (1981): 236-246;

Charles Trueheart, "PW interviews Gilbert Sorrentino," *Publishers Weekly*, 223 (27 May 1983): 70-71;

Lynn Gray, "Interview: Gilbert Sorrentino," *Fiction Monthly* (December 1984): 3, 10;

Jean W. Ross, "Interview with Sorrentino," *Contemporary Authors*, New Revision Series, 14 (Detroit: Gale Research, 1985), pp. 454-456;

George Myers Jr., "Starting Where Joyce Ended," *Columbus Dispatch*, 6 December 1987, C9;

S. E. Gontarski, "Working at Grove: An Interview with Gilbert Sorrentino," *Review of Contemporary Fiction*, 10 (Fall 1990): 97-110.

Bibliography:

William McPheron, *Gilbert Sorrentino: A Descriptive Bibliography* (Elmwood Park, Ill.: Dalkey Archive Press, 1991).

References:

William Bronk, "The Person of Fiction, the Fiction of Person," *Sulfur*, 4 (1983): 168-172;

Harold Brown, "Self-Reference in Logic and *Mulligan Stew*," *Diogenes*, 118 (Summer 1982): 121-142;

Robert L. Caserio, "Gilbert Sorrentino's Prose Fiction," *Vort*, 6 (Fall 1974): 63-69;

Stephen Emerson, "Imaginative Qualities of Actual Things," *Vort*, 6 (Fall 1974): 85-89;

David Hayman, "Surface Disturbances/Grave Disorders," *TriQuarterly*, 52 (Fall 1981): 182-196;

Jerome Klinkowitz, "The Extra-Literary in Contemporary American Fiction," in *Contemporary American Fiction*, edited by Malcolm Bradbury and Sigmund Ro (London: Edward Arnold, 1987), pp. 19-37;

Klinkowitz, *The Life of Fiction* (Urbana: University of Illinois Press, 1977), pp. 7-15;

Klinkowitz, *Literary Disruptions: The Making of a Post-Contemporary Literature*, second edition (Urbana: University of Illinois Press, 1980), pp. 154-167, 188-194;

Louis Mackey, "Representation and Reflection: Philosophy and Literature in Gilbert Sorrentino's *Crystal Vision*," *Contemporary Literature*, 28 (Summer 1987): 206-222;

Eric Mottram, "Psychic Dismembering and Staying Sane: The Fiction of Gilbert Sorrentino," *Reality Studios*, 3 (April-September 1981): 41-52;

John O'Brien, "Gilbert Sorrentino: Some Various Looks," *Vort*, 6 (Fall 1974): 79-85;

Review of Contemporary Fiction, special issue on Sorrentino, 1 (Spring 1981);

Michael Stephens, "Gilbert Sorrentino," in his *The Dramaturgy of Style: Voice in Short Fiction* (Carbondale: Southern Illinois University Press, 1986), pp. 85-101.

Papers:

Gilbert Sorrentino's papers are being collected at the University of Delaware.

Jean Stafford
(1 July 1915 - 26 March 1979)

Jeanette W. Mann
California State University, Northridge

See also the Stafford entry in *DLB 2: American Novelists Since World War II* [first series].

BOOKS: *Boston Adventure* (New York: Harcourt, Brace, 1944; London: Faber & Faber, 1946);
The Mountain Lion (New York: Harcourt, Brace, 1947; London: Faber & Faber, 1948);
The Catherine Wheel (New York: Harcourt, Brace, 1952; London: Eyre & Spottiswoode, 1952);
Children Are Bored on Sunday (New York: Harcourt, Brace, 1953; London: Gollancz, 1954);
The Interior Castle (New York: Harcourt, Brace, 1953);
New Short Novels, by Stafford, Elizabeth Etnier, Shelby Foote, and Clyde Miller (New York: Ballantine, 1954);
Stories, by Stafford, John Cheever, Daniel Fuchs, and William Maxwell (New York: Farrar, Straus & Cudahy, 1956); republished as *A Book of Stories* (London: Gollancz, 1957);
Elephi, The Cat With a High I.Q. (New York: Farrar, Straus & Cudahy, 1962);
The Lion and the Carpenter and Other Tales from The Arabian Nights (New York: Macmillan, 1962; London: Macmillan, 1963);
Bad Characters (New York: Farrar, Straus, 1964; London: Chatto & Windus, 1965);
A Mother in History (New York: Farrar, Straus & Giroux, 1966; London: Chatto & Windus, 1966);
Selected Stories of Jean Stafford (New York: NAL, 1966);
The Collected Stories of Jean Stafford (New York: Farrar, Straus & Giroux, 1969; London: Chatto & Windus, 1970).

SELECTED PERIODICAL PUBLICATIONS – UNCOLLECTED:
FICTION
"An Influx of Poets," *New Yorker,* 54 (6 November 1978): 43-60;

Jean Stafford (courtesy of the Lilly Library, Indiana University)

"Woden's Day," *Shenandoah,* 30 (Autumn 1979): 5-26.
NONFICTION
"The Psychological Novel," *Kenyon Review,* 10 (Spring 1948): 214-227;
"Letter from Germany," *New Yorker,* 25 (3 December 1949): 69-81;
"Truth and the Novelist," *Harper's Bazaar,* 85 (August 1951): 139, 187-189;
"Souvenirs of Survival: The Thirties Revisited," *Mademoiselle,* 50 (February 1960): 90-91, 174-176;
"Truth in Fiction," *Library Journal,* 91 (1 October 1966): 4557-4565;

"The Plight of the American Language," *Saturday Review World*, 1 (4 December 1973): 14–18.

Jean Wilson Stafford, a brilliant practitioner of the craft of fiction, has few equals among the post–World War II generation of novelists and short-story writers who worked within the literary modes and conventions of the realistic tradition. Early in her career, in a lecture on "The Psychological Novel" delivered at Bard College in 1947, she defined the role of the novelist as that of telling the truth: "the problem is how to tell the story so persuasively and vividly that our readers are taken in and made to believe that the tale is true, that these events have happened and could happen again and do happen everywhere all the time." Accepting as given that the writer can "know that our perceptions are accurate and that only one set of conclusions can be drawn from them," she saw the writer's problem as one of technique: "how to communicate the findings perceptively and conclusively." In a period of literary innovation Stafford's fiction remained firmly rooted within the formal structure of the traditional, realistic novel of Gustave Flaubert and Henry James and the post-Joycean short story. In a period of social upheaval she presented the survival of inflexible, inexorable cultural modes of experience that restrict, confine, and destroy the individual. The critical response to Stafford's fiction has also been within the conventions of the realistic tradition; the standard critical readings of her work are historical and biographical. Her contribution to American letters is in the truths she has told — about the lives of women and about the West — and in the sureness of the telling.

Jean Stafford was born on 1 July 1915 in rural Covina, California, the fourth and youngest child of John Richard and Ethel McKillop Stafford. Her father, a classics major in college, was a writer of western stories within the tradition of frontier adventure and humor. At the age of twenty-five he inherited a fortune substantial enough to enable him to retire to the family farm in London, Missouri; marry; and devote his time to writing fiction. In 1910, after eleven years of writing, he had published some short stories and one novel, *When Cattle Kingdom Fell*. The publication of this novel marked the high point of his literary career. In 1911 he moved with his wife and children to California.

As a young child Stafford lived a life of solid, middle-class comfort. When she was five, her father sold the walnut farm in Covina and moved to San Diego to be nearer the stock market. In less than a year he had lost his entire fortune and moved the family to Colorado. Although the family had financial difficulties (reduced to surviving on legacies and allowances from their families, income generated by Ethel Stafford, who took in college students as boarders, and the earnings of the Stafford children), Stafford's father devoted his time to writing western fiction and economic treatises on the iniquities of the stock market.

Jean Stafford (front left) with her sisters, Marjorie and Mary Lee, and her brother, Dick

Jean Stafford attended the University of Colorado on a scholarship. Majoring in English literature, in 1936 she graduated cum laude, the only student in her class to be awarded both a B.A. and an M.A. Upon receipt of a fellowship from the German government, she traveled to Europe to study philology at the University of Heidelberg. In the summer of 1937 she met Robert Lowell, an aspiring poet and member of the prominent New England Lowell family, at the Boulder Writers' Conference. They were married on 2 April 1940; after six years of a stormy marriage, they separated and were divorced in 1948. From 1950 to 1953 Stafford was married to Oliver Jensen, an editor at *Life,* and she was later

261

married to writer and *New Yorker* columnist A. J. Liebling from 1959 until his death just before Christmas in 1963. Stafford spent the last fifteen years of her life in relative seclusion at her home in the Springs, near East Hampton on eastern Long Island. She died in 1979 of complications following a stroke and left her estate to her housekeeper. She had no children.

When Stafford's first novel, *Boston Adventure,* was published in 1944, she was an unknown writer with only a few published short stories. Except for one year teaching at Stephens College in Columbia, Missouri (1936-1937), she had supported herself and Lowell through secretarial work. The novel became a best-seller and made Stafford famous overnight. Seven months after publication it was in a fifth printing; forty thousand hardcover copies were sold, and another three hundred thousand copies were sold through book clubs and overseas editions. For the first time since she was six Stafford experienced financial security.

When *Boston Adventure* begins, Sonia Marburg, the central character, is living in poverty in Chichester, Massachusetts, with her father, Hermann, a well-educated German shoemaker; her mother, Shura, a beautiful Russian who works as a chambermaid at the Hotel Barstow; and her younger brother, Ivan, an epileptic. Sonia works summers at the Hotel Barstow and dreams of being adopted by a wealthy hotel guest, the aging Miss Pride, and entering the world of the rich and wellborn Bostonians. Instead Sonia's father deserts the family; her brother dies; and her mother is committed to a state mental hospital. Miss Pride rescues Sonia and takes her across the bridge from Chichester to Pickney Street in Boston to share her home and work for her as her secretary.

In the second half of the novel Sonia is introduced to the world of the Boston aristocracy. She falls in love with a society doctor, Philip McAllister, but he marries Hopestill Mather, Miss Pride's beautiful niece. Forced by her pregnancy into a loveless marriage, Hopestill takes her own life. When Sonia learns that her mother's condition is improving and that she may be released from the hospital, she agrees to serve Miss Pride for life as her secretary-companion if Miss Pride will pay for the permanent confinement of her mother in a private hospital.

All the figures of Stafford's imagination – her major themes, character types, method, and style – are represented fully in *Boston Adventure*. The novel is the story of a young girl's adventure – her journey toward selfhood and her integration into society. The central conflict is between Sonia's mother and Miss Pride for the possession of Sonia's youth, her sexuality, and her innermost being. Loose and disjointed, the novel is divided into two distinct parts: "Hotel Barstow," the resort where Shura and Sonia work in the poor fishing village of Chichester; and "Pickney Street," the street where Miss Pride lives across the bay in Boston. These parts function either as the disparate terms of a single metaphor or as the opposing poles that pull the novel apart. Sonia must function as the synthesizing force and the bridge between these two worlds. As Ann Hulbert has noted, Stafford uses a doppelgänger relationship between Sonia and Hopestill Mather, Miss Pride's young niece, as one means of bridging the two worlds. Stafford creates "two black sheep, one the insider [Hope] and one the outsider [Sonia]." Stafford thus has "found a way to have both drama and detachment in her story's plot and her protagonist's psyche." Stafford uses this device often in her fiction. Sonia can maintain her distance and independence as a detached observer while Hope is destroyed by her rebellion against a brutal and sterile social order. Sonia is barred from the exploration of her innermost self (symbolized in a vision of a red room) by the presence of Miss Pride's intruding eyes. Only after Hope's death does Sonia understand that she is both bereft of her inner psyche and trapped in the arid decadence of Boston society. For Sonia there can be no escape either through madness, like her mother, or death, like Hope.

The critical response to *Boston Adventure* was mixed but generally favorable. Acclaimed as one of the best first novels of the decade, it was also found to be overwritten and derivative. The novel, however, was included on most of the critics' lists of the best books of 1944, and Stafford received a *Mademoiselle* magazine Merit Award as one of the "10 Outstanding Women of the Year." Although reprinted almost a dozen times, *Boston Adventure* has been almost forgotten and has received little critical attention. This neglect has been attributed to a failure in Stafford's vision, a too-narrow limiting of scope, an imitative style, a general critical neglect of realistic portrayals of women's experience, an incompatibility with the popular imagination, and a lack of distance from autobiographical material. *Boston Adventure* has been read as a novel of manners, flawed by Stafford's superficial understanding of the society she portrays; as a Proustian melodramatic rendering of a dreamlike childhood in contrast to a vivid, satirical portrayal of contemporary society; as a Jamesian portrait of an innocent young woman's initiation into a decaying and corrupt social order; as a female Bildungsroman; and as a thinly disguised, disjointed autobiographical account of her own journey from Boulder, Colorado, to the drawing room of her Lowell in-laws.

Although Stafford's fiction is not unassimilated autobiography as critics sometimes assume, two autobiographical incidents that haunt Stafford's fiction are central to *Boston Adventure:* the suicide of her college friend Lucy McKee and Stafford's severe and disfiguring injuries resulting from an automobile accident. During her junior year at the University of Colorado, Stafford became friends with Lucy McKee and her husband, Andrew Cooke, wealthy and sophisticated law students. She moved into their home and became deeply involved in their dissolute life, which included sexual experimentation and heavy consumption of alcohol. In November Lucy, returning from a visit to her physician, shot herself in the head in the presence of Stafford and Andrew. The reason for her suicide remains unclear. Ten years later Stafford wrote, "I am almost ready to write about it [Lucy's suicide], although I have written about nothing else ever." In *Boston Adventure* Stafford based Hopestill on Lucy McKee and gave the name Lucy to Hopestill's aunt, Miss Pride. Furthermore, in each of Stafford's three novels the denouement involves the violent death of a woman or girl. Some critics believe that Stafford's relationship with Lucy is the source of one of the major conflicts that dominates both her life and her fiction. Her biographers agree that the physical and psychological ill health, including alcoholism, that blighted Stafford's life and eventually made it impossible for her to write fiction began while she was part of the group dominated by Lucy McKee.

The serious injuries that Stafford received in 1938 while riding in a car driven by Lowell are also central to an understanding of her fiction. As he and Stafford were returning from a date, Lowell took a wrong turn and drove his parents' car into a wall in Cambridge. He was not hurt, but Stafford's nose was smashed into many pieces; her skull and jaw were fractured; and her face was lacerated. Several extremely painful operations were required to reconstruct her face. A beautiful young woman who had modeled for art classes while in college, Stafford was now permanently disfigured. The themes of disfigurement and physical deformity are prominent in Stafford's fiction, as is the theme of physical threat to an inner consciousness. Although these

Peter Taylor, Jean Stafford, and Robert Lowell in New Orleans, 1941

themes are most fully developed in the short story "The Interior Castle," in *Boston Adventure* Sonia twice experiences a deep sense of peace and psychic wholeness embodied in her vision of a red room. This mystical sense of self, of a wonderfully perfect pearl, is first threatened by the mad eyes of her mother and then by the flat, omniscient eyes of Miss Pride. Thus, the red room, emblem of Sonia's psyche, her "loaded, seamless ball," functions as the battleground for the conflict that dominates the novel.

Stafford's growing reputation is evident in her receiving both a National Institute of Arts and Letters grant and a Guggenheim Fellowship in the spring of 1945. That same year she also taught a course in short-story writing at Queens College in New York City. With money from the sale of *Boston Adventure* she bought a house in the village of Damariscotta Mills, Maine. There she wrote her second novel, *The Mountain Lion* (1947), as her marriage to Lowell came apart. In November 1946 Stafford agreed to be hospitalized at the Payne Whitney Clinic for psychiatric treatment; she was there two weeks short of a year. During this time her mother died, and *The Mountain Lion* was published. The novel was dedicated to Lowell and her brother, Dick, who

Dust jacket for Stafford's first book, a best-seller that some critics have called one of the best first novels of the 1940s (courtesy of the Lilly Library, Indiana University)

had been killed in a jeep accident while on active duty in France in 1944.

Much of Stafford's own childhood experience is incorporated in *The Mountain Lion,* both through the dual California and Colorado settings and through the character of Molly Fawcett, a lonely child who spends her time reading and writing poems and stories that nobody understands. Stafford herself had begun writing at the age of six; one of Molly's poems was actually composed by Stafford as a child. Her narrative method, although more consciously symbolic, is that of the earlier novel.

The Mountain Lion is the story of Molly and her brother, Ralph, sickly and ugly children who live in California with their widowed mother and two older sisters, Leah and Rachel. Unsociable, Molly and Ralph rebel against the eastern values of their mother, their sisters, and their Grandfather Bonney, a conventional, middle-class manufacturer of buttons and an avid admirer of Alfred, Lord Tennyson. Instead, they identify with the western values of their Grandfather Kenyon, a crude, wealthy, almost illiterate owner of cattle ranches and a friend of Jesse James. After Grandfather Kenyon collapses and dies during his annual visit, the children spend summers with their Uncle Claude at his Colorado ranch.

When Mrs. Fawcett decides to take her two older daughters on a journey around the world, Ralph and Molly are sent to spend the year with their Uncle Claude. While traveling to Colorado by train, Ralph effectively destroys his and his sister's childhood when he asks her to tell him all the dirty words she knows. Clinging to her innocence as a talisman against sexuality, Molly adds her brother's name to her list of the unforgivable people, a list that includes Grandfather Bonney, her mother, and her sisters.

Only Ralph accepts Uncle Claude as the mentor who initiates him into the world of Grandfather Kenyon, Colorado, and the West. He enters into the life of the ranch, rides, and hunts for the mountain lion, Goldilocks. Molly stays at home and writes. Her only possible mentor at the ranch, the housekeeper's daughter, Winifred, betrays her by becoming a fresher version of her sisters. Unable to accept her own sexuality or the brutal fecundity of ranch life, Molly can only survive by withdrawing further into the extremely limited world of her imagination. This world is peopled only by parts of bodies posing as men and by her father and Grandfather Kenyon – the only ones she can forgive because they are dead. The novel concludes when Ralph mistakes Molly for the mountain lion and shoots and kills her.

In *The Mountain Lion* Stafford also uses dual cultures to present a psychic quest and an initiation into society. In this novel, however, the two cultures are fully integrated within the characters' experience through the two grandfathers. Indeed, like *Boston Adventure, The Mountain Lion* is structured around a carefully constructed doubling. This time it is Molly, the observer, who is destroyed by brutal social and natural forces. Blinded in her refusal to sacrifice any part of her inner self, even for Ralph, she is alienated from both worlds and can only retain her innocence and psychic identity through death. Ralph, on the other hand, actively embarks on a conventional initiation – the journey toward manhood and his proper place in both worlds. If he is successful in his quest to kill the beautiful feline Goldilocks, not only will he have triumphed over Uncle Claude (the representative of Grandfather Kenyon, who also seeks Goldilocks as a trophy), but he will also have earned a place in the world of Grandfather Bonney. When Ralph kills Molly, he destroys not only her inner psychic self but also his own. Many critics believe that Ralph can enter manhood only by destroying Molly, the symbol of his feminine self.

Although generally recognized as Stafford's finest work, *The Mountain Lion* was not a best-seller. The initial printing was cut from thirty thousand to ten thousand; there were no paperback or book-club editions. Yet *The Mountain Lion* has received more critical attention than any of Stafford's other novels. Most of this attention has come from western and feminist critics. Western critics have read *The Mountain Lion* as a brilliant, realistic portrayal of the modern West; feminist critics read the novel as a female Bildungsroman, or a realistic portrait of the young girl in the West. Other critics have read the novel as a portrait of the artist, who happens to be a young woman; as an ironic debunking of the myths of the West and of the hunt; or as an autobiographical accounting of Stafford's childhood in California and Colorado and of her relationship with her brother.

The modest sales of *The Mountain Lion,* combined with heavy medical expenses and the dissolution of her marriage, created serious financial problems for Stafford. Late in 1947 *The New Yorker* bought "Children Are Bored on Sunday," the first of her short stories to appear in that magazine. In spring 1948 Stafford received a National Press Club Award, and her Guggenheim Fellowship was renewed. During the next decade she published twenty-one additional stories in *The New Yorker* and supported herself from the sale of her stories, journalistic pieces, and an advance from Harcourt, Brace for her novel "In the Snowfall," which she never completed.

The hundreds of pages of various drafts of "In the Snowfall" that exist among Stafford's papers reveal it to be a highly autobiographical novel. Returning to her student days at the University of Colorado, Stafford narrates the stories of the life and the events leading up to the suicide of her friend Lucy McKee and of her own efforts to establish her independence from her family, particularly her father. Whether because of insufficient emotional distance from her subject matter, a structural conflict between two equally ambitious themes, or – as Stafford indicated in the essay "Truth and the Novelist" – her hatred of her material and the characters, Stafford abandoned work on the novel after three years and began *The Catherine Wheel* (1952). Although she returned to "In the Snowfall" many times, she never completed the novel; one episode appeared as "The Tea Time of Stouthearted Ladies" in the *Kenyon Review* in 1964; in 1968 another episode was published as "The Philosophy Lesson" in *The New Yorker.*

Although her most brilliant in concept and her finest in execution, Stafford's third novel, *The Catherine Wheel,* is also her most neglected. It is the story of Katherine Congreve, a wealthy, aristocratic Bostonian who lives in a state of physical and spiritual suspension. Time stopped for her twenty years before the novel begins when, on her seventeenth birthday, she saw that the man she loved, John Shipley, loved her cousin Maeve. The action of the novel is limited to one summer at Congreve House, Katherine's summer home in the New England town of Hawthorne. The Shipley children – twelve-year-old Andrew and his older twin sisters, Honor and Harriet – are spending the summer with their cousin Katherine while their parents are away on a cruise. Set in a perpetual summer, virtually outside time, the incidents that are narrated – Andrew's trip into Hawthorne, his wanderings through the empty house on a rainy afternoon, and the endless tea parties – are less immediate than the three major incidents that have occurred before the action of the novel begins – Katherine's vision of John and Maeve's love, Andrew's loss of his only friend, Victor Smithwick, and John's discovery of Katherine. Absorbed in her love for the middle-aged, bored

Dust jacket for the novel in which Stafford drew on her childhood experiences in California and Colorado (courtesy of the Lilly Library, Indiana University)

dabbler that John has become, Katherine is oblivious to the distress and despair Andrew experiences because his friend Victor is devoting all his time and attention to Victor's older brother, Charles. The summer concludes with Katherine's traditional garden party; during the fireworks display her old-fashioned clothing catches fire as she attempts to save Charles Smithwick from the fire. She dies after exacting a promise from Andrew to destroy her secret diary.

In this novel Stafford's method is much closer to the romance of Nathaniel Hawthorne than to the realistic novel. In her first two novels she used a conventional structure in which significant dramatic action occurs in the foreground and is the product of common social patterns. In *The Catherine Wheel* she used a closed symbol system, the Catherine wheel, and concentrated on the consequences of an act rather than on the act itself. Katherine is the most fully developed of all Stafford's characters who make the conscious decision to sacrifice their psychic identity and freedom to a cultural role. At seventeen, when Katherine sees that John loves Maeve, she refuses to taste the knowledge of defeat but rather chooses to withdraw from life. Fully conscious of the consequence of her decision, Katherine even orders her own tombstone, on which she is depicted lying under a fig tree crowned by a marble Catherine wheel. Living in a state of spiritual death symbolized by her white hair, she creates a life of static perfection for John and Maeve's children and her friends, the Ancients, in the perpetual summer of Congreve House. Since Katherine refuses to acknowledge any time but time past, her relationship with each character is rigidly fixed and patterned.

The dominant symbol of the novel, the Catherine wheel, functions not only as the physical embodiment of the action of the novel but also as the controlling structure – the circle. The action of the novel begins on "The First Day of Summer" and ends "On the Final Night of Summer." Katherine's life replicates the same pattern: her spiritual death occurs at a garden party, when she sees by the light of the Catherine wheel that John loves Maeve; her physical death occurs as flames engulf the same dress she wore twenty years earlier, and she becomes a Katherine wheel. Furthermore, the consequences of Katherine's withdrawal from life through her guilt over her love for John reinforces the controlling symbol of the novel by creating another cycle of guilt in Andrew. Having sacrificed her own spirit by denying its reality, she violates the boy's spirit by misinterpreting Andrew's fear that she had heard his inner voice, which cries for Charles's death, as evidence that the boy knows of her love for his father. Even in death she interprets his expression of love as a statement of her guilt. Stafford clearly condemns Katherine's sacrifice through her portrayal of Katherine's self-immolation. When she asks the boy to destroy her secret diary, the only remnant of her inner self that she could not force into her given role, he obeys. In doing so he not only destroys the sacred symbol of the martyrdom of Saint Catherine of Alexandria, the patron saint of knowledge, but also sets in motion the Catherine wheel of guilt that will bind him as it had bound Katherine and his father.

The Catherine Wheel sold quite well; twelve thousand copies were sold in the first three months, and it reached the bottom of *The New York Times* best-seller list. The reviews, however, were mixed. Some reviewers wrote that Stafford's brilliant narrative technique and style distracted from what they should have revealed; others found the novel manipulative and lifeless. Stafford herself wrote several self-deprecatory letters about the novel to friends who were writers, warning them that *The Catherine Wheel* was not very good and asking not to be judged by it. The critical neglect of the novel has been attributed to the subject matter; the novel is out of touch not only with the fiction of the 1950s but also with Stafford's own work. Both Katherine and Andrew have been read as autobiographical characters: Katherine as Stafford the mature woman and Andrew as Stafford the child.

Stafford was thirty-seven when *The Catherine Wheel* was published. Although she continued writing for twenty-seven years, she never published another novel. In a manner uncannily reminiscent of her father, she worked intermittently for years on a novel called "The Parliament of Women," which she was never able to complete. After Stafford had become incapacitated by a stroke in 1976, her longtime editor and friend Robert Giroux was able to extract two highly autobiographical stories from the manuscript. One story, "An Influx of Poets," published in *The New Yorker* in 1978, is a brilliant comic portrayal of her marriage to Lowell; the other, "Woden's Day," published in *Shenandoah* in 1979, after Stafford's death, is a disjointed portrait of her father, John Stafford.

In her frequently anthologized short stories Stafford works within the traditional forms of Anton Chekhov and Henry James. Some critics believe that this form is more compatible to her than is that of the novel. In each story she creates a moment of experience, through the use of realistic settings, characters, and dialogue, so as to present, often through the device of dramatic irony, the sudden illumination or understanding, the symbolic crisis, or the unresolved glimpse into the heart of the situation. She relies heavily on the use of the symbolic object and often uses it to reflect changes and development within the characters. In her short stories she introduced no new character types or themes, although she deepened and enriched those of the novels.

Stafford's first published short story, "And Lots of Solid Color," appeared in *American Prefaces* in 1939. Between 1944 and 1957 she published regularly in many leading periodicals. In 1953 she published a collection of ten short stories, *Children Are Bored on Sunday,* all of which had originally appeared in *Harper's Bazaar,* the *Partisan Review,* or *The New Yorker. A Winter's Tale,* a novella, was published in 1954 in *New Short Novels* along with works by Elizabeth Etnier, Shelby Foote, and Clyde Miller. In 1955 Stafford received the O. Henry Memorial

Dust jacket for Stafford's last completed novel, published more than twenty-five years before her death

Award for best short story of the year for "In the Zoo," which was originally published in *The New Yorker. Stories,* which comprises five stories by Stafford (all of which had been published in *The New Yorker*) and stories by John Cheever, Daniel Fuchs, and William Maxwell, was published in 1956. Almost a decade later, in 1964, she published *Bad Characters,* a collection of nine short stories and the novella *A Winter's Tale.* Eight of the stories had been published originally in *The New Yorker;* the other had appeared in the *Sewanee Review. Selected Stories of Jean Stafford,* published in 1966, comprises sixteen previously published short stories (fourteen in *The New Yorker*). For *The Collected Stories of Jean Stafford* (1969) – thirty short stories, all written at least a decade earlier – Stafford was awarded the Pulitzer Prize for fiction in 1970.

In 1959 Stafford married the journalist A. J. Liebling. During the four and a half years of their marriage she published little fiction – only one new

A. J. Liebling and Jean Stafford at their home on eastern Long Island, 1961 (photograph by Therese Mitchell)

short story, "The Ordeal of Conrad Pardee," in the *Ladies' Home Journal,* and two children's books, *Elephi, The Cat With a High I.Q.* (1962) and *The Lion and the Carpenter and Other Tales from The Arabian Nights* (1962), a volume in a series of fairy tales retold by contemporary writers. Although *Elephi,* a charming story about Stafford and Liebling's cat, received generally favorable reviews, it sold fewer than three thousand copies.

After Liebling's death in 1963, Stafford supported herself by writing nonfiction, primarily book reviews. In 1964 she accepted a position regularly writing reviews for *Vogue.* She also published reviews in *The New York Review of Books* and the *Washington Post Book World. A Mother in History* (1966), based on Stafford's interviews with Lee Harvey Oswald's mother, is Stafford's only nonfiction book and probably her best-known work. The reviews were generally hostile; many reviewers found Stafford's injection of herself into the book offensive; others criticized her superciliousness and her snobbery. In 1969, after publication of *The Collected Stories,* Stafford once again became well known. She received both an Ingram-Merrill Foundation Grant and a Chapelbrook grant. From 1970 to 1975 she wrote an annual roundup of children's books, "Christmas Books for Children," for *The New Yorker.*

There is much speculation among critics and Stafford's biographers about the reason she stopped writing fiction in the mid 1950s. Some believe that her need for money led her to nonfiction, which paid better than fiction; others, that serious health problems made it impossible for her to continue to write fiction. Stafford herself revealed an awareness of the limitations of traditional realistic fiction and a reluctance to go beyond the dominant literary forms. Maureen Ryan has suggested that Stafford may have chosen to write nonfiction because the New Journalism of the 1960s was more compatible with her mastery of the techniques of realistic fiction than those of experimental fiction.

Stafford's major literary contribution is as an interpreter of human experience within a conventional social system in the period immediately preceding and following World War II through the conventions, modes, and forms of the realistic tradition. Her reputation rests on the stylistic brilliance and the psychological sureness of her short fiction. Her influence cannot be measured at this time because of general critical neglect of her work, particularly of the novels, and because, as noted by Joyce

Carol Oates, "she worked within the dominant fiction mode of her time ... the Jamesian-Chekhovian-Joycean model in which most 'literary' writers wrote during those years" at a time when both fiction and critical theory was undergoing great changes.

Letters:

"Some Letters to Peter and Eleanor Taylor," *Shenandoah*, 30 (Autumn 1979): 27-55.

Interviews:

Harvey Breit, "Talk with Jean Stafford," *New York Times Book Review*, 20 January 1952, p. 18; republished in his *The Writer Observed* (New York: World, 1956), pp. 223-225;

John K. Hutchens, "On an Author," *New York Herald Tribune Book Review*, 24 May 1953, p. 2;

Wilfrid Sheed, "Writer as Something Else," *New York Times Book Review*, 4 March 1973, p. 2;

Alden Whitman, "Jean Stafford and Her Secretary 'Harvey' Reigning in Hamptons," *New York Times*, 26 August 1973, p. 104.

Bibliography:

Wanda Avila, *Jean Stafford: A Comprehensive Bibliography* (New York: Garland, 1983).

Biographies:

David Roberts, *Jean Stafford: A Biography* (Boston: Little, Brown, 1988);

Charlotte Margolis Goodman, *Jean Stafford: The Savage Heart* (Austin: University of Texas Press, 1990);

Ann Hulbert, *The Interior Castle: The Art and Life of Jean Stafford* (New York: Knopf, 1992).

References:

Louis Auchincloss, "Jean Stafford," in his *Pioneers and Caretakers: A Study of Nine American Women Novelists* (Minneapolis: University of Minnesota Press, 1965), pp. 152-160;

Bruce Bawer, "Jean Stafford's Triumph," *New Criterion*, 7 (November 1988): 61-72;

Stuart L. Burns, "Counterpoint in Jean Stafford's *The Mountain Lion*," *Critique*, 9 (Spring 1967): 20-32;

Richard A. Condon, "Stafford's 'The Interior Castle,'" *Explicator*, 15 (October 1956): 6;

Mary V. Davidson, "'Defying the Stars and Challenging the Moon': The Early Correspondence of Evelyn Scott and Jean Stafford," *Southern Quarterly*, 28 (Summer 1990): 25-34;

Stacey D'Erasmo, "The Lion in Winter: Jean Stafford's Heart of Darkness," *Village Voice Literary Supplement*, 106 (June 1992): 31-32;

Chester E. Eisinger, *Fiction of the Forties* (Chicago: University of Chicago Press, 1963), pp. 294-307;

Nancy Flagg, "People to Stay," *Shenandoah*, 30 (Autumn 1979): 65-76;

Blanche H. Gelfant, "Reconsideration: *The Mountain Lion* by Jean Stafford," *New Republic*, 172 (10 May 1975): 22-25;

Gelfant, "Revolutionary Turnings: *The Mountain Lion* Reread," *Massachusetts Review*, 20 (Spring 1979): 117-125;

Charlotte Goodman, "The Lost Brother, The Twin: Women Novelists and the Male-Female Double *Bildungsroman*," *Novel*, 17 (Fall 1983): 28-43;

Melody Graulich, "Jean Stafford's Western Childhood: Huck Finn Joins the Campfire Girls," *Denver Quarterly*, 18 (Spring 1983): 39-55;

Ihab Hassan, "The Character of Post-War Fiction in America," *English Journal*, 51 (January 1962): 1-8;

Hassan, "The Idea of Adolescence in American Fiction," *American Quarterly*, 10 (Fall 1958): 312-324;

Hassan, "Jean Stafford: The Expense of Style and the Scope of Sensibility," *Western Review*, 19 (Spring 1955): 185-203;

Hassan, *Radical Innocence: Studies in the Contemporary American Novel* (Princeton, N.J.: Princeton University Press, 1961), pp. 70-72, 100;

Sidney L. Jenson, "The Noble Wicked West of Jean Stafford," *Western American Literature*, 7 (Winter 1973): 261-270;

William G. Leary, "Checkmate: Jean Stafford's 'A Slight Maneuver,'" *Western American Literature*, 21 (August 1986): 99-109;

Leary, "Grafting onto Her Roots: Jean Stafford, 'Woden's Day,'" *Western American Literature*, 23 (August 1988): 129-139;

Leary, "Jean Stafford, Katherine White, and the *New Yorker*," *Sewanee Review*, 93 (Fall 1985): 584-596;

Leary, "Jean Stafford: The Wound and the Bow," *Sewanee Review*, 98 (Summer 1990): 333-349;

Leary, "Jean Stafford's 'The Philosophy Lesson,'" *Southwest Review*, 72 (Summer 1987): 389-403;

Leary, "Native Daughter: Jean Stafford's California," *Western American Literature*, 21 (November 1986): 195-205;

Leary, "Pictures at an Exhibition: Jean Stafford's 'Children Are Bored on Sunday,'" *Kenyon Review*, 9 (Spring 1987): 1-8;

Leary, "Through Caverns Measureless to Man: Jean Stafford's 'The Interior Castle,'" *Shenandoah*, 34 (Winter 1983): 79-95;

Jeanette W. Mann, "Toward New Archetypal Forms: *Boston Adventure*," *Studies in the Novel*, 8 (Fall 1976): 291-303;

Mann, "Toward New Archetypal Forms: Jean Stafford's *The Catherine Wheel*," *Critique*, 17 (December 1975): 77-92;

Mary Davidson McConahay, "'Heidelberry Braids' and Yankee *Politesse*: Jean Stafford and Robert Lowell Reconsidered," *Virginia Quarterly Review*, 62 (Spring 1986): 213-236;

Howard Moss, "Jean: Some Fragments," *Shenandoah*, 30 (Fall 1979): 77-84;

Joyce Carol Oates, "*The Interior Castle*: The Art of Jean Stafford's Short Fiction," *Shenandoah*, 30 (Fall 1979): 61-64;

David Roberts, "Jean & Joe: The Stafford-Liebling Marriage," *American Scholar*, 57 (Summer 1988): 373-391;

Maureen Ryan, "Green Visors and Ivory Towers: Jean Stafford and the New Journalism," *Kenyon Review*, 16 (Fall 1994): 104-119;

Ryan, *Innocence and Estrangement in the Fiction of Jean Stafford* (Baton Rouge: Louisiana State University Press, 1987);

Wilfrid Sheed, "Miss Jean Stafford," *Shenandoah*, 30 (Fall 1979): 92-99;

Carol Steinhagen, "Stalking the Feline Female: The Significance of Hunting in *The Cub of the Panther* and *The Mountain Lion*," in *Women and Violence in Literature: An Essay Collection*, edited by Katherine Anne Ackley (New York: Garland, 1990), pp. 207-220;

Philip Stevick, "Scheherazade Runs Out of Plots, Goes on Talking; The King, Puzzled, Listens: An Essay on New Fiction," *Tri-quarterly*, 26 (Winter 1973): 332-362;

Dorothea Straus, "Jean Stafford," *Shenandoah*, 30 (Autumn 1979): 85-91;

Peter Taylor, "A Commemorative Tribute to Jean Stafford," *Shenandoah*, 30 (Autumn 1979): 56-60;

Olga W. Vickery, "Jean Stafford and the Ironic Vision," *South Atlantic Quarterly*, 61 (Autumn 1962): 484-491;

Vickery, "The Novels of Jean Stafford," *Critique*, 5 (Spring-Summer 1962): 14-26;

Mary Ellen Williams Walsh, *Jean Stafford* (Boston: Twayne, 1985);

Walsh, "The Young Girl in the West: Disenchantment in Jean Stafford's Short Fiction," in *Women and Western American Literature*, edited by Helen Winter Stauffer and Susan J. Rosowski (Troy, N.Y.: Whitston, 1982), pp. 230-243;

Barbara White, "Initiation, the West, and the Hunt in Jean Stafford's *The Mountain Lion*," *Essays in Literature*, 9 (Fall 1982): 194-210;

Mary Ann Wilson, "In Another Country: Jean Stafford's Literary Apprenticeship in Baton Rouge," *Southern Review*, 29 (Winter 1993): 58-66;

Wilson, *Jean Stafford: A Study of the Short Fiction* (New York: Twayne, 1995);

W. Tasker Witham, *The Adolescent in the American Novel: 1920-1960* (New York: Ungar, 1964);

James Wolcott, "Blowing Smoke into the Zeitgeist," *Harper's*, 266 (June 1983): 57-59.

Papers:

Most of Stafford's papers are located in the Jean Stafford Collection of the Norlin Library at the University of Colorado in Boulder. Forty-seven letters from Stafford to Lowell following their separation in August 1946 are in the Houghton Library, Harvard University.

Ronald Sukenick

(14 July 1932 -)

Julian Cowley
University of Luton

See also the Sukenick entry in *DLB Yearbook: 1981*.

BOOKS: *Wallace Stevens: Musing the Obscure* (New York: New York University Press, 1967; London: University of London Press, 1969);
UP (New York: Dial, 1968);
The Death of the Novel and Other Stories (New York: Dial, 1969);
Out (Chicago: Swallow Press, 1973);
98.6 (New York: Fiction Collective, 1975);
Long Talking Bad Conditions Blues (New York: Fiction Collective, 1979);
In Form: Digressions on the Act of Fiction (Carbondale & Edwardsville: Southern Illinois University Press, 1985);
The Endless Short Story (New York: Fiction Collective, 1986);
Blown Away (Los Angeles: Sun & Moon Press, 1986);
Down and In: Life in the Underground (New York: Beech Tree Books/Morrow, 1987);
Doggy Bag (Normal, Ill.: FC2/Black Ice Books, 1994).

OTHER: "Statement," in *Statements: New Fiction from the Fiction Collective,* edited by Jonathan Baumbach (New York: Braziller, 1975), pp. 7–8.

SELECTED PERIODICAL PUBLICATIONS:
"The Flood," *Fiction International,* 22 (1992): 327–334;
"50,010,008," *TO* (1993): 77–86;
"From: Mosaic Man," *Fiction,* 11, no. 3 (1993): 162–172;
"The Wondering Jew and the Black Widow Murders, or the Return of the Planet of the Apes," *Southern Plains Review* (Fall 1993): 23–34.

For more than a quarter of a century, Ronald Sukenick has been prominent among writers of innovative fiction in America. In addition to producing his own novels and collections of short stories, he has acted as theorist, publisher, and catalyst for new writing. His fiction is notable for its improvisatory energy and its focus on the processes of writing and reading, which take precedence over the conventional concerns of characterization and plot. Against the flow of those processes, he often counterpoints bold structural arrangements, which make his books visually striking and distinctive. Far from being innovative for the sake of innovation, Sukenick aims through his art to intensify and expand his readers' experience of their own lives. Underpinning his approach is the view stated in his

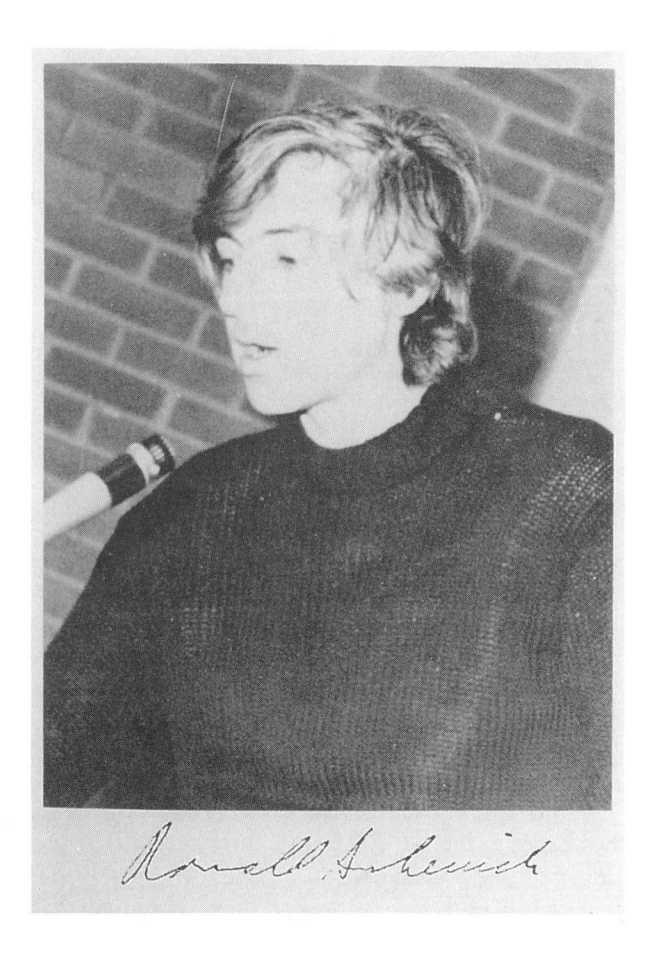

Dust jacket for Sukenick's first novel, in which the character Ron Sukenick is engaged in writing a novel titled Up

1974 essay "Twelve Digressions Toward a Study of Composition," collected in *In Form: Digressions on the Act of Fiction* (1985): "the form of the traditional novel is a metaphor for a society that no longer exists."

Sukenick was born in Brooklyn, New York, the son of a dentist, Louis Sukenick, and his wife, Ceceile Frey Sukenick. He was an undergraduate at Cornell University, where he established the campus literary magazine, *The Cornell Writer,* with other students including David Behrens, later a Pulitzer Prize–winning journalist, and Martin Washburn, who became a painter. Sukenick was the magazine's fiction editor, and the first issue, in November 1953, opened with "Indian Love Call," his first published work. Looking back on his student days in *Down and In: Life in the Underground* (1987), Sukenick sees the story as "aggressively sophomoric," its concern as the "suppression of teenage lust in the deenergized fifties." Despite the clumsiness and immaturity of the piece, Sukenick recognizes value in "a kind of antiliterary energy threatening to explode out of the wellmade literary frame of the story," which, he adds, "is badly made." Resistance to the demands of literary decorum would persist into his accomplished later work.

Sukenick received a B.A. degree from Cornell in 1955 and proceeded to Brandeis University, which was "funneling the first large influx of Jewish intellectuals, with and without academic degrees, into the American university system." Drawn by that aspect of the institution, Sukenick also found it "an exceptional Europhile enclave within American culture." It appeared to be "a short cut to the underground of intellectual resistance that seems the best alternative to an oppressive middle-class." Soon disillusioned, he received an M.A. in 1957 and a Ph.D. in 1962. During this time he wrote "The Permanent Crisis," which he regards as his "first real story." It subsequently became the initial story in his first collection, *The Death of the Novel and Other Stories* (1969). Sukenick wrote the story as a single long sentence, a feat he says was inspired in part by his intensive study under Irving Howe of William Faulkner's work. He was an instructor at Brandeis (1956–1961) and at Hofstra University (1961–1962). In 1961 Sukenick married the writer Lynn Luria; they were divorced in 1984.

Between 1962 and 1966 Sukenick toured Europe, wrote, and taught in various schools. He was assistant professor of English at City College of the City University of New York (1966-1967). Sukenick revised his doctoral dissertation for publication as *Wallace Stevens: Musing the Obscure* (1967), a series of close readings of Stevens's poems. Denis Donoghue commented in the *New York Review of Books* that "Mr. Sukenick's readings are remarkably acute, so that even to disagree with them is exhilarating." The relevance of Stevens to Sukenick's creative work is most evident in their shared concern for relationships of order and chaos, change and stasis, and imagination and reality.

Sukenick's first novel, *UP* (1968), was published through the efforts of literary agent Lynn Nesbit. He has recorded in *Down and In* the surprise he felt at her enthusiastic reception of the book: "This wasn't supposed to happen. High-powered literary agents were not supposed to like my book. I was supposed to struggle for years to get it published. I was supposed to encounter nothing but hostile indifference from the literary establishment. Sooner or later the book was supposed to be discovered by a prestigious underground press, like Allan Swallow or New Directions. It was supposed to be ignored by the media as too, quote, experimental." *UP* is a ground-clearing work, establishing through parody the kind of novel Sukenick refused to write while signaling the way forward through its amalgam of autobiographical materials and invention. Set in New York's Lower East Side, it makes no pretense to objective realism but instead registers the author's participation in a way of living that closes the distinction between art and life.

UP is a compendium of metafictional techniques and digressive strategies, adopted to the end of exploring not what is known but ways of knowing. From the start of his writing career, Sukenick's aim has been "to plunge through literature into the world," as he put it in his 1976 essay "Thirteen Digressions" (*In Form*). He notes in that essay that *UP* is "quite contrary to the doctrine of self-expression," even though it was fed by events from his own life. As a character in *UP*, Ronald Sukenick worries about how his time should be divided to meet the requirements of teaching and the demands made by writing a novel. The character anticipates reviews his book will receive and throws a party where real friends and fictional characters mingle. In his life outside the novel, Sukenick continued his teaching career as an assistant professor of English and writing at Sarah Lawrence College (1968-1969) and writer-in-residence at Cornell (1969-1970).

The reality of the novel is the record of a writer writing; as with an Abstract Expressionist painting, the space of the book is a field of action, rather than the scene for linear unfolding of a coherent and continuous story. Eschewing both the illusions of realism and the hermeticism of modernism, Sukenick, with the artifice of Laurence Sterne and the energy of Henry Miller, affirms in *UP* the continuity of art and experience. Miller has remained an important example for Sukenick of the writer as improviser, refusing to subordinate the act of writing to a priori ideas. Jack Kerouac and Frank O'Hara furnished him with further models for this approach to composition. The sociopolitical ambition of Sukenick's work is made explicit in *Down and In*, where he declares that "in the hands of an artist familiar with the ways of the imagination, the breakdown of conventional limits for the imagination places art in the service of the actual, to the enrichment of both."

In 1969 Sukenick collected six short stories as *The Death of the Novel and Other Stories*. He has continued to write in what he regards as outmoded generic categories – "the novel" and "the story" – but his approach is ironic, as he continually demystifies the process of creating fiction. In the title story he writes: "We improvise our art as we improvise our lives. No hysterical impositions of meaning." Sukenick believes that received forms, in life as in literature, distort the reality of experience. The work of the artist, in his view, is to intuit contemporary conditions and grant them appropriate expression, but he sees the unquestioning acceptance of the formal imperatives of a previous age as not merely conservative but actively irresponsible.

In each story Sukenick aims to create a singular form, an intention apparent in his use of devices such as side-by-side conversations, marginal comments, and minimal punctuation. In fiction of this kind, as Sukenick notes in "Thirteen Digressions," "the placement of print on the page becomes an expressive resource," complicating the process by which meaning is derived. The most impressive story among the six is "The Birds," which has been widely anthologized to illustrate possibilities for unconventional composition. It is an arresting combination of collage and improvisational techniques, which takes as its model Simone Rodia's construction Watts Towers in Los Angeles: "Built entirely without design precedent or orderly planning, created bit by bit on sheer impulse, a natural artist's instinct and the fantasy of the moment." "The Birds" juxtaposes documentary fragments, statistics, representations of birdsongs, excerpts from a letter about

Ronald Sukenick (photograph by Lynn Sukenick)

French student uprisings, and even a midterm examination on the story itself. The collage technique allows ample space for divergent readings as well as for "a more and more spacious syntax" – one of the goals for contemporary writing that Sukenick identifies in "Thirteen Digressions."

In his 1984 essay "Nine Digressions on Narrative Authority" (*In Form*) Sukenick recalls his experiments with a tape recorder: "In *The Death of the Novel and Other Stories,* I attempted, with intentional naivete, a new realism by taking imprints of 'reality' with a tape recorder." The two resulting stories, "Momentum" and "Roast Beef: A Slice of Life," are diverting, but their limitations are evident. As Sukenick himself noted in his 1977 essay "Fiction in the Seventies" (*In Form*), "composition by tape recorder can be suggestive and energizing. But composition and finished artifact are two different things. Fiction, finally, involves print on a page, and that is not an incidental convenience of production and distribution, but an essential of the medium."

Sukenick was writer-in-residence at the University of California, Irvine, from 1970 to 1972, during which time he worked on his second novel,

Out (1973). In this novel that might be said to be *about* a conspiracy that carries its protean characters from New York to California, Sukenick again emphasizes improvisational inventiveness, while his syntax and light punctuation create the impression of energy and rapidity: "speeding along on the breaking crest of the present toward god knows what destination after the first word everything follows nothing follows the world is pure invention from one minute to the next." Characters change names and identities, sometimes even within a single sentence. Adding to the mania is a countdown structure, with the number of lines on each page being gradually reduced as the work progresses from section nine to section zero, so that the reader physically turns the pages noticeably faster as the book nears its conclusion.

Out challenges the dominance of analytical intelligence; in its place it offers synthesis, attained through intuitive and extrarational means. In the ending a character named "R" drifts out to sea while communicating telepathically with his teacher, Sailor. This is an image of liberation, but that freedom is achieved only at the cost of isolation from any social context, and is, finally, unacceptable to a writer of commitment such as Sukenick. At this "zero point" where all the narrative threads have disintegrated and language has drifted into silence, the novel culminates in a series of blank pages, "the void where everything is called into question," as Sukenick asserts in "Twelve Digressions." The silence of the ending is deeply ambivalent, signifying an escape from social controls that also carries the risk of being lost. A film version of *Out* was released in 1982, produced and directed by Eli Hollander, with a cast that included Peter Coyote, Danny Glover, and Olan Shepard (at that time Sam Shepard's wife). Sukenick wrote the screenplay and spent time on the set, but Hollander made considerable modifications to the story, most notably to the ending.

In 1975 Sukenick was one of a group of writers who, dissatisfied with the requirements and emphases of commercial publishing houses, established the Fiction Collective (subsequently Fiction Collective Two), of which he has since been a director. This affiliation has a distinguished record of fostering innovative fiction from diverse writers, including Raymond Federman, Clarence Major, Russell Banks, and Ursule Molinaro. Sukenick's *98.6* (1975) was among its first, and remains one of the most significant, publications.

The novel is divided into three sections, titled "Frankenstein," "Children of Frankenstein," and

Dust jacket for Sukenick's 1986 satire about the making of a pornographic movie titled Blown Away

"Palestine." The first section concludes with a nameless character, floating in coastal waters, being driven home on a river current to face a culture that has turned monstrous. The momentum of *Out* is reversed, and the technique of "Frankenstein" reflects this. A collage of fragments from newspaper reports and other fictional and nonfictional accounts – indexes of the degeneracy Sukenick saw in contemporary life – creates an oppressive, claustrophobic sense of violence and banality. As Sukenick remarked to Larry McCaffery, "I diagnosed the culture as lapsing into sado-masochism and suggested this was a kind of sickness." "The Children of Frankenstein" presents an account of an attempt to create an alternative community, with "Ron Sukenick" among its members, trying to write a novel out of the experience. "Palestine," the concluding section, contains a vision of Israel as a fantastic land ruled by the Mosaic Law, "a way of dealing with parts in the absence of wholes." It offers an ideal solution to the Frankenstein reality of "life energy in the absence of creative forms turning against itself." The artist's role is once again the provision of forms to promote positive action and to dispel "negative hallucination," alternatively diagnosed, in "Thirteen Digressions," as "those cheap or outlived fictions which separate us from our world."

Sukenick became a professor of English at the University of Colorado at Boulder in 1975. He served as the director of creative writing from 1975 to 1977, a period in which he also was chairman of the board of directors of the Coordinating Council of Literary Magazines (CCLM). In 1977 he established the *American Book Review* to address what he perceived as the neglect by established literary journals of alternative writing, especially that which ostentatiously took risks in its strategies and aspirations. He remains publisher of the *Review*. In 1981 Sukenick held the Butler Chair at the State University of New York, Buffalo, but then returned to Colorado. From 1986 to 1994 he was director of the University of Colorado English department publications center.

Long Talking Bad Conditions Blues, published by the Fiction Collective in 1979, is a single 114-page sentence without conventional punctuation. The novel addresses the "new conditions," the accelerated technological and cultural changes to which human beings must adapt. But Sukenick does not engage in large speculation, opting instead to register specific responses and possibilities. A prerequisite for appropriate adaptation, he asserts, is the capacity to resist "City Hall's official version of life compiled by some bored clerk or statistician roughly on the basis of crude figures highly modi-

Pop.

You know what I hate? People who wear trade marks on their clothes. As if to say you are what you buy. But hey, do it yourself. Make up your own mark. So make a statement. Write yourself in to the book of life.

It's happening. I see signs everywhere. They are signs that say, "Hey, I'm me. Pay attention." And the reason is is that nobody is.

It's true I'm sensitive to style. Especially in clothes. Even for a woman, I mean. But this is not a fad. This is a movement. A movement about persons. But it's not exclusive. It includes second persons and third persons as well as first persons.

I saw a t-shirt the other day that said, "I'm On Hold." It was on an older woman, maybe pushing sixty, which gave it a kind of twist. Then I saw one on a young woman that said "Handle With Care." That was over her breasts, which were big and bouncey. On her back it said, "This Side Up." She was with a big, strong guy whose chest said, "Agile."

In the state where I live residents worried about too many people moving in started using bumper stickers that said "Native." Soon bumper stickers appeared that said "Alien,"

Pages from an early draft for "50,010,008," a story published in Doggy Bag *(1994; courtesy of Ronald Sukenick)* others that said "Naive." Another series began when religious types started sticking "I Found It" on their bumpers. A sticker immediately appeared saying "I Lost It," and another saying "Keep It." In California where things often get started people have long since used their license plates to declare identity rather than acquiesce in anonymity. "I 1 BB ME." "4Q." "I M A QT." "U R 2 MUCH." "Y W8." "OVER 8." "E Z."

Grafitti is in a different kind of writing, writing beyond language. And it countries. It's spread to France where they call it "le tagging." What's it all about? Maybe people willing to be the blank page. Maybe people want a clean slate. To write their own the first of which is "I exist." Or maybe, like animals, they need to mark a territory, tagging it with a signature.

But there are a lot of people who don't exist. Living, breathing people, some of whom have just slipped between the cracks and there are more and more of those, but also plenty of people who go to work every day, who have bank accounts, relatives, social networks, boyfriends or girlfriends, some of them even raise children, belong to the P.T.A. It's not they aren't alive, it's that they don't exist. They don't count. Ask them.

Even so, I'm beginning to find traces of them. More and more evidence that they're crawling out from under whatever. Rocks, old newspapers, tupperware, corporate desks. And this fied by political necessity and mostly conditioned by remnants of Victorian novels floating through his underdeveloped imagination like surprising things at the bottom of yesterday's chicken soup."

A year after publishing *In Form: Digressions on the Act of Fiction* – which includes among its theoretical discussions a distillation of Sukenick's interviews between 1970 and 1982 titled "Cross Examination" as well as essays on Stevens and Carlos Castenada – Sukenick brought out *The Endless Short Story* (1986). Simone Rodia, a hero in "The Birds," is once again a touchstone for creative integrity and ingenuity in "What's Watts," the opening fiction in *The Endless Short Story*. In the course of the book Sukenick introduces the notion of "wordbombs," words and phrases configured in unfamiliar ways, that can "explode into meaning." He disrupts conventional reading habits not only through the calculated distortion of words such as *love, sex, violence,* and *salvation* but also through unconventional typography. The story "Boxes," for example, is told in small, square blocks of print that checker the page. Another piece, "Duck Tape," mimics a conversation played back on a tape recorder, exploring the relationships of speech, immediacy, and truth; it also constitutes an ironic commentary on his stories from *The Death of the Novel* "Momentum" and "Roast Beef: A Slice of Life."

In "Dong Wang" the title character, whose name is ribald yet respectfully parodic of Castenada's Don Juan, has had trouble reading: "Maybe the trouble was that he wanted to read but he didn't want to read in straight lines, he wanted to read two or three lines alternately, simultaneously, in his own order not the order that was already there in the straight lines." He may well be Sukenick's ideal reader. Equally, he reflects the author's own position: "It takes years to find a style and once you find it you go on to something else or else you're lost. Finding your style is like being back from a trip, it's just the beginning of another trip." The emphasis, as always with Sukenick, is on technique as a means to pass beyond the formulaic and the preconceived, to break away from cliché. This preoccupation underlies his admiration for writers as diverse as Raymond Roussel and William Burroughs.

Blown Away (1986) has the most conventional appearance of all of Sukenick's fictions. A fabulous satire on Hollywood, the novel is also a meditation upon the role of the artist in adjusting human intelligence to the dynamics of cultural change. Sukenick parodies the epistemological assumptions of traditional fiction: "I am the omniscient narrator. But while most tellers tell a tale already set, I tell tales that haven't happened yet." The satire works against novelists who cling to anachronistic conventions and also against writers of screenplays, who perpetuate well-made stories in the electronic media. In "Fiction in the Seventies" Sukenick argues that "what we call realism saps our experience of its immediacy and authority, a process tremendously augmented by the electronic media and probably one reason for their great success."

The villain is Victor Plotz, "stillborn son of a bad English novelist," who is also "a hack screenwriter" incapable of telling fortunes. Reading the future, or rather writing the future, is the province of the sorcerer, and Sukenick combats the consolidators of the trite and premeditated with a team of characters including Castenada, Rodia, Henry Miller, and Anaïs Nin. In his 1973 essay "Castenada: Upward and Juanward" (*In Form*), Sukenick writes: "The sorcerer, the artist sees beyond any particular form fiction may take to the fictive power itself, and in the absence of powerful fictions in our lives, maybe it's time for all of us to become sorcerers." The erotic work of Miller and Nin is implicitly contrasted to the debased sexuality of the pornographic film, titled *Blown Away,* that is being made. The imaginative energy of these writers is played against the stark data of the newspaper account and the historical record. In "Nine Digressions on Narrative Authority" Sukenick speculates: "Journalism and history are oriented toward the present and the past. It may be that the claim of fiction, incorporating as it does our attempt to reconcile our hopes with our fate, is on the future."

Down and In: Life in the Underground is a cultural history of Greenwich Village that received the American Book Award from the Before Columbus Foundation in 1988. Nearly twenty years after venturing *up* and almost fifteen years after heading *out* in his fiction, Sukenick moves *down* and *in* to immerse himself in the lives of artists, eccentrics, celebrities, and criminals who have inhabited this singular area of New York City since the end of World War II. Sukenick refers to it as the product of research in "the science of comparative experience," indicating that its raw materials were interviews with such luminaries of the Bohemian scene as Gregory Corso, Ted Joans, Robert Creeley, and Jackson MacLow as well as the author's own recollections of youthful experiences. Sukenick's skills as a collagist stand him in good stead as he weaves fragments of report and recollection into a vivid and highly informative evocation of a place and its people. The book contains reminiscence from his student days, including an account of a meeting with Vladimir Nabokov at Cornell University in 1954.

Since 1989 as the editor of *Black Ice* magazine, Sukenick has helped to launch Black Ice Books, signaling his continued dedication to voices alternative to the cultural mainstream. Black Ice specializes in energetic, often controversial fiction, and particularly promotes what McCaffery has termed the *Avant-Pop,* writing that exploits and simultaneously subverts the forms and modes of popular culture, such as thrillers, science fiction, and even pornography. Through such writing, those who espouse radical programs for literary and cultural renewal aim to attract a more general readership than that captured by innovative writing in the past.

In 1994 Black Ice published Sukenick's *Doggy Bag,* which declares itself as a collection of *hyperfictions,* a term that seems to be no more than a parodic marketing ploy. Henry James is invoked on its opening page, and the book is Sukenick's contribution to what James called the "international theme." Sukenick characteristically blends personal experience with bold invention as his American in Europe makes cross-cultural observations and evaluations. First-person accounts are juxtaposed with tales in which Roland Sycamore, the latest in a line of mutations acting as print surrogates for Sukenick, becomes a European operative for the Guardian Angels Mind Liberation Unit. Under the code name Rico, Sycamore searches for an antidote to "the white voodoo mind control plague." Always ready to pun, Sukenick notes: "Rico's cover is as a novelist, but everything he writes is really in the service of the intelligence. Everything he writes is an intelligence report."

Doggy Bag, as usual in Sukenick's fiction, has a pronounced sociopolitical dimension. As he remarked in *Down and In,* "In the hands of a skilled social critic an analysis of the part imagination plays in what we call reality helps demystify our experience." The main aim of *Doggy Bag* is to analyze a polarized cultural situation in which mass media implement behavioral programming in the guise of entertainment, while the European tradition of high culture constitutes no real alternative for those who would live fully in contemporary conditions. Sukenick provocatively signals his rejection of Old World cultural values: "When high culture is invoked I always think of Beethoven as interpreted by the Auschwitz Philharmonic."

Ronald Sukenick (photograph by Julia Frey)

Sukenick's means of resisting these powerful cultural forces, both high and low, is the formal inventiveness and creative energy of his writing.

In 1982, in an interview with Jerzy Kutnik included in *In Form,* Sukenick remarked, "I grew up with an idea of writing as a form of resistance to the establishment and culture at large." He has sustained that oppositional stance into maturity and through a career that distinguishes him as an important writer of innovative fiction. Among his awards are Fulbright scholar in 1958 and 1984, a Guggenheim Fellowship in 1977, and National Endowment for the Arts Fellowships in 1980 and 1989. In 1985 he was granted the CCLM Award for Editorial Excellence and the Western Book Award for publishing. His work has also been recognized at Colorado University, where he has received faculty fellowships in 1982 and 1990 and in 1993 won a BFA Award for Excellence in Research, Scholarly, and Creative Work. In March 1992 Sukenick married Julia Frey, author of *Toulouse-Lautrec: A Life* (1994). His new novel, "Mosaic Man," is currently awaiting publication.

Interviews:

Joe David Bellamy, ed., "The Tape Recorder Records," *Falcon,* no. 2/3 (April 1971): 5-25;

James Nagel, "Imagination as Perception," *Chicago Review,* 23 (Winter 1972): 59-72; reprinted in *The New Fiction: Interviews with Innovative American Writers,* edited by Joe David Bellamy (Urbana: University of Illinois Press, 1974), pp. 55-74;

Nagel, "A Conversation in Boston," in his *American Fiction* (Boston: Northeastern University Press, 1977), pp. 175-202;

Bruce Kawin, "Interview with Ronald Sukenick," *Arts at Santa Cruz,* 1, no. 1 (1981);

Charlotte M. Meyer, "Interview with Ronald Sukenick," *Contemporary Literature,* 23 (Spring 1982): 129-144;

Larry McCaffery, "Interview with Ronald Sukenick," in *Anything Can Happen,* edited by Tom LeClair and Larry McCaffery (Urbana: University of Illinois Press, 1983), pp. 279-297;

Zolton Abady-Nagy, "A Talk with Ronald Sukenick," *Hungarian Studies in English,* 16 (1983): 5-22;

David Seed, "Interview with Ronald Sukenick," *Over Here* (University of Nottingham) (Summer 1990): 1-7.

References:

Timothy Dow Adams, "Obscuring the Muse: The Mock-Autobiographies of Ronald Sukenick," *Critique,* 20, no. 1 (1978): 27-39;

Alan Cheuse, "Way Out West: The Exploratory Fiction of 'Ronald Sukenick,'" in *Essays on California Writers,* edited by Charles L. Crow (Bowling Green, Ohio: Bowling Green State University Press, 1979), pp. 115-121;

Marcel Cornis-Pope, "Narrative Innovation and Cultural Rewriting: The Pynchon-Morrison-Sukenick Connection," in *Narrative and Culture,* edited by Janice Carlisle and Daniel R. Schwarz (Athens: University of Georgia Press, 1994), pp. 216-237;

Julian Cowley, "Ronald Sukenick's New Departures from the Terminal of Language," *Critique,* 28 (Winter 1987): 87-99;

Denis Donoghue, "Fabulous Salad," review of *Wallace Stevens: Musing the Obscure, New York Review of Books* (1 February 1968): 23-26;

Ihab Hassan, "Reading Out," *Fiction International,* 1 (Fall 1973): 108-109;

Alfred Hornung, "Absent Presence: The Fictions of Raymond Federman and Ronald Sukenick," *Indian Journal of American Studies,* 14 (1984): 17-31;

Jerome Klinkowitz, "Getting Real: Making It (Up) with Ronald Sukenick," *Chicago Review,* 23 (Winter 1972): 73-82;

Klinkowitz, *The Life of Fiction* (Urbana: University of Illinois Press, 1977), pp. 18-30;

Klinkowitz, "Ronald Sukenick and Raymond Federman," in his *Literary Disruptions: The Making of a Post-Contemporary American Fiction* (Urbana: University of Illinois Press, 1975; second edition, 1980), pp. 119-153, 228-230;

Jerzy Kutnik, *Fiction as Performance: The Fiction of Ronald Sukenick and Raymond Federman* (Carbondale & Edwardsville: Southern Illinois University Press, 1986);

Brian McHale, *Postmodernist Fiction* (New York: Methuen, 1987);

Daniel Noel, "Tales of Fictive Power: Dreaming and Imagination in Ronald Sukenick's Postmodern Fictions," *Boundary,* 2 (Fall 1976): 117-135;

Richard Pearce, *The Novel in Motion* (Columbus: Ohio State University Press, 1983), pp. 123-130;

Manfred Pütz, *The Story of Identity: American Fiction of the Sixties* (Stuttgart: Mezler, 1979), pp. 176-193;

Charles Russell, *Poets, Prophets and Revolutionaries: The Literary Avant Garde from Rimbaud Through Postmodernism* (Oxford: Oxford University Press, 1985), pp. 249-267.

Amy Tan

(19 February 1952 -)

Pin-chia Feng
National Chiao-Tung University, Taiwan

BOOKS: *The Joy Luck Club* (New York: Putnam, 1989; London: Heinemann, 1989);
The Kitchen God's Wife (New York: Putnam, 1991; London: Collins, 1991);
The Moon Lady (New York: Macmillan, 1992; London: Hamilton, 1992);
The Chinese Siamese Cat (New York: Macmillan, 1994; London: Hamilton, 1994);
The Hundred Secret Senses (New York: Putnam, 1995; London: Flamingo, 1996).

MOTION PICTURE: *The Joy Luck Club,* screenplay by Tan and Ronald Bass, Hollywood Pictures, 1993.

Amy Tan, 1993 (AP/Wide World)

On the publication of her first novel, *The Joy Luck Club* (1989), Amy Tan became an instant star in the publishing world; and her second novel, *The Kitchen God's Wife* (1991), was a triumph as well. Tan's skillful renditions of mother-daughter relationships reach the hearts of millions of readers. Moreover, her work – which comes more than a dozen years after Maxine Hong Kingston's *The Woman Warrior* (1976) – has helped to create a renaissance of Chinese American writing. Tan's books also include two children's books and a third novel, *The Hundred Secret Senses* (1995).

Amy Tan's roots are in a sorrowful family history and painful personal traumas. Her father, John Tan, immigrated to the United States in 1947. He worked as an engineer and served as a Baptist minister. Amy's mother, Daisy, came to the United States in 1949, leaving behind three daughters from a previous marriage. When Amy was born in Oakland, California, her parents chose the Chinese name En-Mai, meaning Blessing of America. But the blessing seemed inadequate when Amy's elder brother, Peter, died of brain cancer in 1967 and only months later John Tan died of the same disease. After consulting a Chinese geomancer, Daisy Tan decided to move to Europe with fifteen-year-old Amy and her younger brother, John, to cleanse the evil influence of their "diseased house" in Santa Clara. They went first to the Netherlands and finally found affordable housing in a hundred-year-old chalet set amid fourteenth-century houses in Montreux, Switzerland. Tan finished high school at the College Monte Rosa Internationale in Montreux, an outsider among the children of ambassadors, tycoons, and princes and still burdened by her losses and her anger. Because being good had not saved her father and brother, she decided to turn bad. She made friends with drug-dealing hippies and was arrested at sixteen. The nadir of her Montreux year came when she nearly eloped to Australia with a mental patient who claimed he was a German army deserter.

When the Tans returned to the United States, Amy Tan enrolled at Linfield College in Oregon, majoring first in premed and later in English. After meeting Lou DiMattei on a blind date, eighteen-year-old Amy transferred to San Jose State University, where DiMattei was a law student, and put herself through college with the help of a scholarship and income from a job in a pizza parlor. She earned a B.A. in 1973 and married DiMattei in 1974, the same year she completed a master's degree in English and linguistics and enrolled in a doctoral program at the University of California, Berkeley. She quit in 1976, when the murder of her best friend brought back her sense of loss and anger. From 1976 to 1981 she worked as a language-development specialist for disabled children. She edited a medical journal in 1981–1983, and from 1983 to 1987 she was a technical writer specializing in corporate business proposals. Tan and her husband, a tax attorney, live in San Francisco and New York City.

Tan's work as a technical writer turned her into a workaholic who spent ninety hours a week at her job. In her late thirties, after an unsuccessful attempt at a cure through psychological counseling, Tan decided to cure herself by taking jazz piano lessons and joining the Squaw Valley Community of Writers, a weekly group, where she wrote her first fiction. At first she tried to write from a non-Chinese perspective because she thought that Chinese people could not get their work published in the United States. Later she realized that writing about the events of her own life could be therapeutic. In 1987 G. P. Putnam bought her short story "Rules of the Game" and the outline of a novel. Within four months she finished the rest of the stories, which turned into *The Joy Luck Club*. The book made *The New York Times* best-seller list in spring 1989 and stayed on the list for nine months. It also won the 1989 Bay Area Book Reviewer Award for Best Fiction and the Best Book for Young Adults Award from the American Library Association.

Tan refuses to be pegged a mother-daughter expert, but both *The Joy Luck Club* and *The Kitchen God's Wife* center around the love and antagonism between Chinese immigrant mothers and their American daughters. In real life Tan and her mother experienced similar emotional turmoil. Daisy Tan had high expectations for her daughter. Amy Tan recalls that as a child she was expected to grow up to be a neurosurgeon by profession with the "hobby" of concert pianist. She also remembers her mother's disappointment when she changed her undergraduate major from premed to English. Like Waverly Jong in *The Joy Luck Club,* who always felt inadequate in the face of her mother, Amy Tan was pressured by Daisy Tan's standards. When *The Joy Luck Club* was fourth on *The New York Times* best-seller list, for instance, Daisy remarked that Amy should have aimed for first, explaining that Amy was so talented she deserved to be the best.

At first Tan thought of *The Joy Luck Club* as a collection of stories rather than a novel, but the arrangement of these stories created a formal wholeness. Tan carefully structured them into antiphonal exchanges among four pairs of mothers and daughters: Suyuan and Jing-mei "June" Woo, An-mei and Rose Hsu, Lindo and Waverly Jong, and Ying-ying and Lena St. Clair. Maternal voices can be heard in the four vignettes preceding the four main segments and in six of the sixteen stories. The first two segments, "Feathers from a Thousand Li Away" and "The Twenty-six Malignant Gates," cover the mothers' pasts in China and the daughters' childhoods in the United States. The third section, "American Translation," tells the stories of the adult daughters' struggles to resolve mother-daughter conflicts. The mothers again tell their stories in the final segment, "Queen Mother from the Western Skies," and achieve a kind of reconciliation with their daughters. Suyuan, the founder of the Joy Luck Club and the mother who passed away, has no narrative voice in the novel. Instead, June opens the novel by retelling her mother's stories, as well as replacing her in the mothers' mah-jongg game. Thus the daughters' stories are cradled by the two segments of maternal voices, with June's narrative providing a frame for all the others. This formal orchestration embodies the major theme of the novel: the continuation of the matriarchal line. An-mei Hsu visualizes this matrilineage when she observes the link among three generations of women in her family: "All of us are like stairs, one step after another, going up and down, but all going the same way." This apparently fatalistic statement reveals a sense of generational interconnectedness that brings eventual reconciliation and mother-daughter bonding. A complex ensemble of stories told by mothers and daughters, the novel, as Marina Heung argues, is an innovative variation of the traditional mother-daughter plot, which focuses on the daughter's perspective.

Tan acknowledges her own matrilineage by dedicating her first novel to her mother and mater-

Dust jacket for Tan's first book, interconnected stories about Chinese immigrant mothers and their Chinese American daughters

nal grandmother. *The Joy Luck Club* pays special homage to her grandmother, who before her suicide at thirty-nine was the number-three concubine to a wealthy man, much like An-mei Hsu's mother in the novel. This allusion to the grandmother hints at the theme of the female's triumph in the face of victimization. An-mei's mother represents all women who have been persecuted by rigid Chinese traditions. After her family has driven her away for her alleged violation of the rule of chastity, she is forced to serve a rapist as one of his concubines. Yet she returns as a dutiful daughter and sacrifices her own flesh to cook a soup for her dying mother. Instead of continuing as a silent victim of patriarchy, she deploys her spiteful suicide to teach An-mei the power of language, thereby transforming her victimization into victory. An-mei in turn passes on this story of empowerment to her own daughter, Rose, who finds the voice and selfhood buried in her marriage. Both An-mei and Rose, therefore, benefit from the grandmother's suffering and strength. By dedicating her novel to her own grandmother Tan suggests that, like An-mei and Rose, she owes part of her power of language to the inspiration of her grandmother.

Yet Tan wrote *The Joy Luck Club* mainly for Daisy, fulfilling a vow she made when her mother was hospitalized and nearly died of a heart attack in 1986, an event that forced Tan to face the possibility of losing her mother. In her dedication Tan writes, "You asked me once what I would remember. This, and much more," an effort to reassure her mother that she and her stories will not be forgotten. The Joy Luck Club mothers also fear oblivion and discontinuity of familial lineage. June detects it in her Joy Luck "aunties" when she claims not to have known Suyuan well enough to describe the dead mother to her half sisters:

> They are frightened. In me, they see their own daughters, just as ignorant, just as unmindful of all the truths and hopes they have brought to America. They see daughters who grow impatient when their mothers talk in Chinese, who think they are stupid when they explain things in fractured English. They see that joy and luck do not mean the same to their daughters, that to these closed American-born minds "joy luck" is not a word, it does not exist. They see daughters who will

Tan at the time of The Joy Luck Club *(photograph © 1989 Robert Foothorap)*

bear grandchildren born without any connecting hope passed from generation to generation.

In short, the immigrant mothers are afraid that the younger generations will lose their Chinese heritage and thereby forfeit their faith in joy and luck.

The true spirit of the Joy Luck Club is a hope against hopelessness and a battle to create one's own space. Suyuan describes the joy luck spirit when she tells June, "It is not that we have no heart or eyes for pain. We were all afraid. We all had our miseries. But to despair was to wish back for something already lost. Or to prolong what was already unbearable.... What was worse, we asked among ourselves, to sit and wait for our own deaths with proper somber faces? Or to choose our own happiness?" The women of the club choose to withstand physical hardship with their carnivalesque spirit. Both the Kweilin and San Francisco versions of the Joy Luck Club are more than social gatherings of women; they are support networks. Whereas in China the hope of joy holds back the fear of the war, in San Francisco it helps the immigrant women to survive the equally terrifying experiences of cultural transplantation. To the American daughters, however, the mah-jongg–playing Joy Luck Club seems to be, as June remarks, "a shameful Chinese custom, like the secret gathering of the Ku Klux Klan or the tom-tom dances of TV Indians preparing for wars." This association of her mother's invention with racist practices and stereotyping indicates June's misunderstanding and mistrust of her Chinese heritage. Only after her mother's death and a trip to China does June come to realize the significance of joy and luck.

Like June, Tan herself used to distrust joy and luck. In fact, for most of her life she felt "jinxed" because of all her tragic losses. She also felt dissatisfied with her Asian looks and with her mother's lack of "progress" in the New World. Like June, Tan had to make a trip to China to recognize the Chineseness inside her fully. In 1987, when she and her husband accompanied Daisy Tan on a visit to China, she experienced a magical moment of "homecoming": "It was just as my mother said: As soon as my feet touched China, I became Chinese." At the same time Tan realized how American she really was. No matter how she attempted to blend in, she always stood out among the Chinese. She emerged from the trip better equipped than before to cope with her double heritage and hybrid identity.

This double heritage is evident in Tan's insertion of Mandarin words – such as *hulihudu* for confusion – in the American English prose. Tan admits that she can read and speak little Chinese. Yet her fine ear for the nuances of languages and her sensitivity as a linguist enable her to capture the spirit of Chinese phrases most of the time. Tan says that her mother speaks English as if it is a direct translation from Chinese, and her language has more imagery than English. Tan has also spent much time studying the rhythm of Chinese American speech. Her efforts are apparent in language of the immigrant mothers in *The Joy Luck Club*. An-mei Hsu, for instance, refers to Rose's psychiatrist as "psycheatrick." In this case the effect of this creolized English is more than comic; it also carries a certain weight of truth. Heung identifies the mothers' "border" language as representing Tan's effort to reclaim language "as an instrument of intersubjectivity and dialogue, and as a medium of transmission from mothers to daughters." Instead of being "fractured English," the mothers' language becomes a location of cultural and generational communication. In a 1989 interview with Julie Lew, Tan explained her effort to "speak" to her mother: "I wanted her to know what I thought about China and what I thought about growing up in this country. And I wanted those words to almost fall off the page so that she could just see the story, that the language would be simple enough, almost like a little curtain that would fall away." She says the greatest compliment she has received for *The Joy Luck Club* came from Daisy Tan, who remarked how easy it was to read, a remark that serves as a confirmation of her success in integrating her imagined "maternal tongue" with perfect American English.

The ending of *The Joy Luck Club* – June's reunion with her Chinese sisters Chwun Yu (Spring Rain) and Chwun Hwa (Spring Flower) – also shows Tan's effort to integrate her Chinese and American heritages. On her 1987 visit to China, Tan met her three half sisters for the first time. June's reunion with her two Chinese sisters apparently draws on the emotional intensity of Tan's experience. The names of June and her sisters allude to the regenerative powers associated with the seasons of spring and summer. During the reunion scene in the 1993 movie version of the novel, for which Tan helped to write the screenplay, June momentarily sees the face of her mother in one of her sisters, highlighting the symbolic resurrection of the lost mother after the unification of her Chinese and American parts. With this hopeful note Tan demonstrates the double meaning of Suyuan, the mother's name. The reunion of her daughters fulfills her "Long-Cherished Wish," and her "Long-held Grudge," the abandonment of her twin daughters, is finally resolved.

Tan's second novel, *The Kitchen God's Wife,* also focuses on generational conflicts and reconciliation, as well as female victimization and triumph. Instead of four pairs of mothers and daughters, however, Tan concentrates on one mother and daughter, Winnie Louie and Pearl, with Pearl's present-day narrative providing a frame for her mother's storytelling. Yet the novel is more than a traditional framed narrative. It appears to be dialogic, with two alternating narrative voices and hints toward the possibility of communication. It opens with Tan's familiar theme of mother-daughter conflict. At first Pearl appears reluctant to travel to Chinatown in San Francisco to visit her family, especially her mother, whom she calls "a Chinese version of Freud, or worse." As her first-person narrative unfolds, the reader learns that Pearl, who is suffering from multiple sclerosis and could soon become paralyzed, feels guilty for not telling her mother her secret. When she visits her mother, Winnie Louie unexpectedly reveals her other identity as Jaing Weili in China. In what appears to be a storytelling marathon, Winnie discloses a series of surprises about her past. She was the daughter of a Shanghai tycoon and his number-two wife, who resisted the fate of concubinage and disappeared when Weili was six. To avoid family disgrace Weili was sent to live with her uncle's family on an island, and at eighteen she married a scheming brute who abused her physically and mentally. After suffering the loss of her three children during the Sino-Japanese War, she fell in love with a Chinese American soldier and tried to elope with him, but she was tried for "stealing" her husband's son and property and imprisoned for two years. She escaped China on the last flight from Shanghai before the Communist takeover and started her American life. The most shocking secret of the mother's past, however, is revealed as an afterthought. She tells Pearl that she is most likely the daughter of Winnie's sadistic first husband, Wen Fu, who raped Winnie just before her escape from China. After her mother's confession, Pearl finally feels free to talk about her medical condition. This talk around the kitchen table, a traditional place for female communion, becomes a ritual of secret sharing that bridges generations. Like *The Joy Luck Club, The Kitchen God's Wife* ends on a clear reconciliatory note: Winnie invents a new goddess, Lady Sorrowfree, who will grant Pearl a life of "happiness winning over bitterness, no regrets in the world."

The Kitchen God's Wife is the fictionalized life story of Daisy Tan. After the success of her first novel, Tan felt pressured by the fear that her second book would not be as good, or as well received, as her first. At first she tried to write something completely different from *The Joy Luck Club,* but after several false starts she again turned to her mother for inspiration. Having often complained that she had to tell every acquaintance that she was not the model for the mother in *The Joy Luck Club,* Daisy Tan wanted her true story told. In 1989, when she learned that her first husband had died, the past broke free and Daisy started telling her story. Her daughter videotaped her mother's storytelling and transformed it into a novel. Thus *The Kitchen God's Wife* is virtually a collaboration by Daisy and Amy. "My mother wanted me to write this book about her," Tan told Patti Doten in 1991. "She not only wanted to give me her story but I think she was looking for a way to release the pain and the anger over 'that bad man.'" Although many details are changed, the plot of *The Kitchen God's Wife* closely corresponds to the outlines of Daisy's life in China from before the Sino-Japanese War until she immigrated to the United States: "Every-

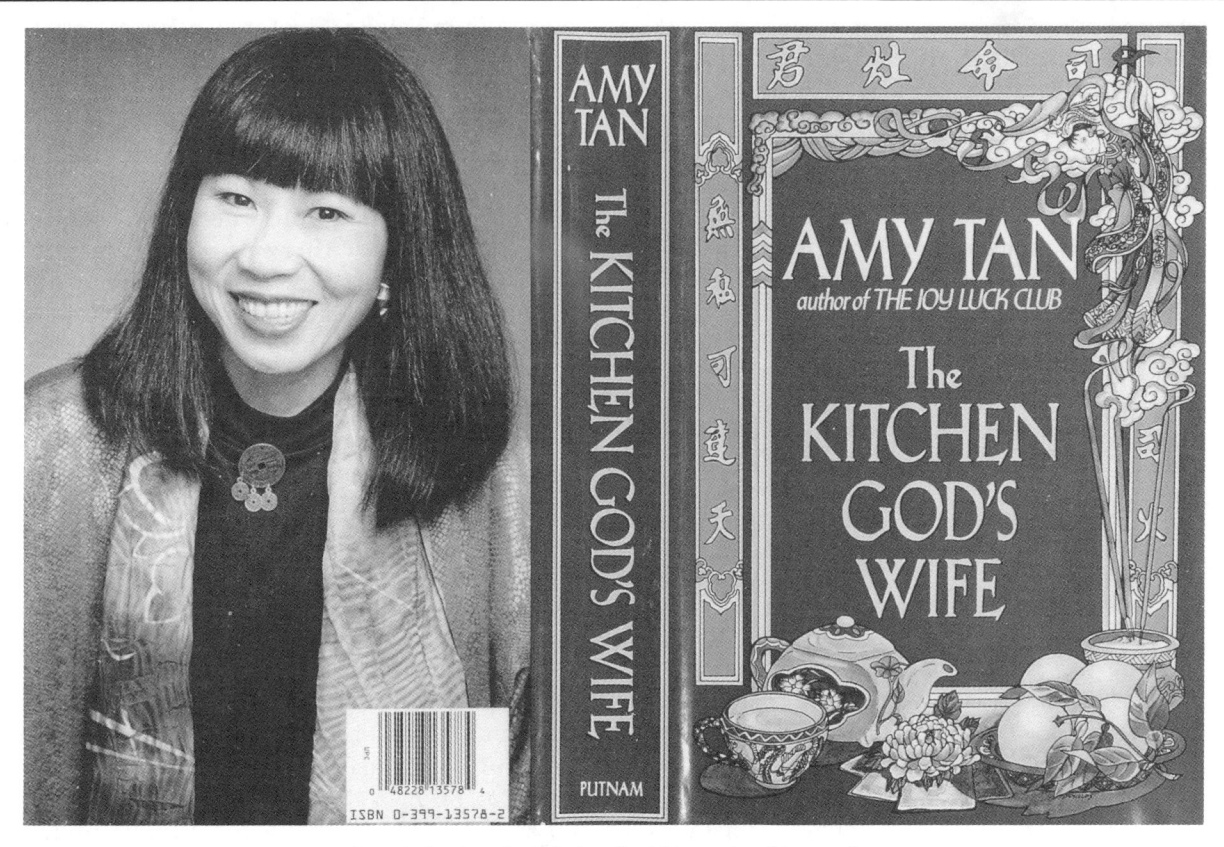

Dust jacket for Tan's fictionalized biography of her mother

thing from her horrible marriage to her children dying, to being in jail, to escaping right before the revolution in 1949." With her writing, moreover, Tan tried to uncover the reasons behind her mother's extraordinary endurance during a terrible first marriage that lasted twelve years, and she came to understand the oppressive patriarchal myths under which Chinese women have been governed for thousands of years, myths that had taught Daisy to suffer silently. The spirit of the 1989 student demonstrations in Tiananmen Square, Beijing, also finds its way into Tan's writing, as she attempts to capture the spirit of the students' resistance and to comprehend "what it is like to live a life of repression and to understand the fear that one has, and what you have to do to rise above that fear."

The Kitchen God's Wife is not only a fictionalized biography but also an effort to rewrite mythology. Like Kingston, Amy Tan deliberately revises Chinese mythology, as in her creation of the new goddess Lady Sorrowfree. In telling the story of the Kitchen God, Tan exposes the poignant irony in the old myth: a wife abuser was apotheosized as a household deity and the guardian of kitchens, the space traditionally assigned to women. She also reveals the internalization of patriarchal values by traditional Chinese women, who have been educated to worship male oppressors such as the Kitchen God, whose story is a mythological parallel to that of Winnie's abusive first husband, who lives to an old age and dies with honor. Tan regards the Kitchen God's story as a perfect metaphor for unquestioned governing myths, or the master plot, as Toni Morrison would term it. As Winnie says in the novel: "I was like that wife of Kitchen God. Nobody worshipped her either. He got all the excuses. He got all the credit. She was forgotten." Winnie's denial of the Kitchen God and her creation of a new goddess embody Tan's textual "revenge" for oppressed Chinese women. *Sorrowfree* is also a translation of the name of Winnie's stillborn daughter, Mochou, whose spirit Winnie symbolically resurrects in her reconciliation with Pearl. The final message of the novel, therefore, is one of forgiveness and hope, which leads to a "sorrowfree" life.

Besides replacing a patriarchal god with a female deity, Tan also supplants the patriarchal family structure with the circle of sisterhood. The most significant example of sisterhood is the commune of runaway wives, "an underground hiding place, filled with women and children." The ma-

Dust jacket for Tan's novel about a Eurasian American woman who travels to China with her American husband and her Chinese half sister

tron of this house once colluded in forcing her daughter to suffer a dead-end marriage in silence and was "awakened" only after her daughter committed suicide – which, according to Tan, is the only way for a Chinese wife to free herself from such bondage. The commune provides an alternative for a suffering wife, and although it eventually dissolves, the novel clearly carries a message that sisterly support is a sanctuary against oppression and victimization.

This celebration of sisterhood is also revisionist because female friendship goes against the Confucian patriarchal master plot. Winnie confesses that she used to blame Wen Fu's mother for her misery, "And perhaps this was wrong of me, to blame another woman for my own miseries. But that was how I was raised – never to criticize men or the society they ruled, or Confucius, that awful man who made that society. I could blame only other women who were more fearful than I." Winnie's statement is a testimony of how internalization of patriarchal rules turns woman against woman. In *The Kitchen God's Wife,* however, women often support each other.

For example, Aunt Du serves as a mother figure who partially compensates for Weili's loss of her mother. The friendship between Winnie and Helen, although interlaced with competition and tension, is sustaining and nourishing. Helen even initiates the process of communication between Winnie and Pearl. Only with the aid of her community of women can Winnie finally break away from her physical and mental imprisonment.

Tan's renditions of her mother's stories have been faulted as unauthentic and as stereotypical redactions of the "Orient" for the benefit of mainstream readers. As with Kingston's works, the details of China and Chinese culture in Tan's books are often under critical scrutiny. Sau-ling Wong explains what she terms "the Amy Tan phenomenon," the enormous appeal and blockbuster success of Tan's fiction, by arguing that Tan's complex interplay of self-orientalizing and counterorientalist possibilities enables her to acquire a large readership. Yet, Wong charges, while "The nonintellectual consumer of Orientalism can find much in *The Joy Luck Club* and *The Kitchen God's Wife* to satisfy her curiosity about China and Chinatown; at the same time, subversions of naive voyeurism can be detected by the reader attuned to questions of cultural production." There is justice in Wong's critique. Nevertheless, Tan's ongoing feminist revisionist project has real significance.

In her best-selling third novel, *The Hundred Secret Senses,* Tan's portrayal of China is at its most questionable. Tan continues to concentrate on the conflicts and final reconciliation between mother and daughter figures as she again delves into Chinese history to contextualize her portrayal of Chinese American experiences. Her story is set in rural southeastern China during the nineteenth-century Taiping Rebellion and in the twentieth century in contemporary San Francisco. The war-torn, or Communist-ruled, Chinese village is juxtaposed with the postmodern metropolis of San Francisco. In a new twist Tan gives her American protagonist, Olivia, a Chinese half sister, Kwan, as the representative of Chinese culture and values. At six Olivia met the eighteen-year-old Kwan, then recently arrived from Communist China. At thirty-six Olivia and her estranged husband, Simon, are accompanied by Kwan on a trip to China. This venture is intended to save their marriage, but in a development unplanned by them, it settles business from another life. Instead of the revisionist mythmaking in her first two novels, Tan takes a step toward "Chinese superstitions" to embrace the concept of reincarnation. The result, if sensational, is also unbelievable and disappointing.

Tan's indulgence in implausible mysticism makes *The Hundred Secret Senses* unconvincing, and the many reincarnations in the novel appear whimsical and melodramatic. For example, it strains the reader's imagination to believe that the American yuppie couple Olivia and Simon are reincarnations of a nineteenth-century American woman, Miss Banner, and a Eurasian interpreter, Yiban, a pair of unfortunate lovers slaughtered by war-hysterical Manchu soldiers, and that Kwan was Miss Banner's maid and confidant, Nunumu, in her previous life. The body-snatcher story – in which Kwan has switched bodies with her drowned playmate in order to come back to keep her promise to Miss Banner – also lacks credibility. The sense of predestination that successfully set the mood of Tan's previous works overwhelms the plot in *The Hundred Secret Senses.*

Moreover, Tan becomes trapped in her schematic of binary opposition between Chinese and Chinese American values. As a Eurasian, Olivia is a racial and cultural hybrid. Yet Tan fails to develop the identity problems faced by such a character. Instead Tan repeats the familiar theme of American-born "daughter" entangled in a love-hate-guilt relationship with a mother figure. Kwan, who conveniently takes over the maternal role because of Olivia's irresponsible Caucasian mother, comes from a younger generation of Chinese women than the Joy Luck mothers and Winnie Louie; yet she appears little different from the older women. Whereas in her previous fiction Tan successfully created the sense of mother/daughter interconnectedness, in *The Hundred Secret Senses* her concept of reincarnation, which borders on mysticism, weakens the empathetic power of her mother-daughter plot.

Perhaps because of her own homecoming experience, Tan often uses China as a place to settle unresolved personal crises originating in the United States. In *The Hundred Secret Senses,* however, the American couple goes to China to do research for an essay on Chinese village cuisine to be written by Simon with photographs by Olivia. This project seems to objectify China as a site of Western tourist and anthropological interest, and Nunumu/Kwan's extreme devotion to Miss Banner/Olivia puts the former in a position of servitude to the latter – again suggesting a kind of unbalanced power relationship between the two cultures.

In both *The Joy Luck Club* and *The Kitchen God's Wife* Tan captures the culturally specific experiences of Chinese American women, having learned much from her mother about the lives of women who grew up in pre-Communist China. For Tan, growing up with a Chinese mother means constantly hearing three basic rules. As she told Susan Kepner in 1989: "First, if it's too easy, it's not worth pursuing. Second, you have to try harder, no matter what other people might have to do in the same situation – that's your lot in life. And if you're a woman, you're supposed to suffer in silence." She is willing to live by the first two dicta but refuses to accept the third decree. Speaking out against misogyny in traditional Chinese culture, Tan's novels have earned her riches and fame. For Tan, her most significant theme is mother-daughter communion. As she told Donn Fry in 1991, "My books have amounted to taking her stories – a gift to me – and giving them back to her. To me, it was the ultimate thing I ever could have done for myself and my mother." In her own way Tan has succeeded in speaking for and with her mother.

Though her third novel is not as artistically successful as her first two, Tan has great potential to create new works of literary merit.

Interviews:

Susan Kepner, "Imagine This: The Amazing Adventure of Amy Tan," *San Francisco Examiner Focus,* May 1989, pp. 58–60, 161–162;

Julie Lew, "How Stories Written for Mother Became Amy Tan's Best Seller," *New York Times,* 4 July 1989, p. 23;

Mervyn Rothstein, "A New Novel by Amy Tan, Who's Still Trying to Adapt to Success," *New York Times,* 11 June 1991, pp. 13–14;

Patti Doten, "Sharing Her Mother's Secrets," *Boston Globe,* 21 June 1991, p. 63;

D. C. Denison, "Amy Tan," *Boston Sunday Globe,* 28 June 1991, p. 8;

Donn Fry, "The Joy and Luck of Amy Tan," *Seattle Times,* 7 July 1991;

Don Stanley, "Amy Tan Is Having Fun," *Sacramento Bee,* 14 July 1991;

Mark Morrison, "Joy, Luck – and a Movie Deal," *USA Weekend,* 10–12 September 1993, pp. 4–6.

References:

Marina Heung, "Daughter-Text/Mother-Text: Matrilineage in Amy Tan's *Joy Luck Club*," *Feminist Studies,* 19 (Fall 1993): 597–616;

Amy Ling, *Between Worlds: Women Writers of Chinese Ancestry* (New York: Pergamon, 1990);

Malini Johar Schueller, "Theorizing Ethnicity and Subjectivity: Maxine Hong Kingston's *Tripmaster Monkey* and Amy Tan's *The Joy Luck Club*," *Genders,* 15 (Winter 1992): 72–85;

Walter Shear, "Generational Differences and the Diaspora in *The Joy Luck Club*," *Critique,* 34 (Spring 1993): 193–199;

Sau-ling Cynthia Wong, *Reading Asian American Literatures: From Necessity to Extravagance* (Princeton, N.J.: Princeton University Press, 1993);

Wong, "'Sugar Sisterhood': Situating the Amy Tan Phenomenon," in *The Ethnic Canon: Histories, Institutions, and Interventions,* edited by David Palumbo-Liu (Minneapolis & London: University of Minnesota Press, 1995), pp. 174–210.

Rudolph Wurlitzer
(1937 -)

Julian Cowley
University of Luton

BOOKS: *Nog* (New York: Random House, 1969); republished as *The Octopus* (London: Weidenfeld & Nicolson, 1969);

Flats (New York: Dutton, 1970; London: Gollancz, 1971);

Two-Lane Blacktop, by Wurlitzer and Will Cory (New York: Award Books, 1971);

Quake (New York: Dutton, 1972; London: Picador, 1974);

Pat Garrett and Billy the Kid (New York: Signet, 1973);

Slow Fade (New York: Knopf, 1984; London: Picador, 1985);

Walker (New York: Harper & Row, 1987);

Hard Travel to Sacred Places (Boston: Shambhala, 1994).

MOTION PICTURES: *Two-Lane Blacktop,* screenplay by Wurlitzer and Will Cory, Universal, 1971;

Glen and Randa, screenplay by Wurlitzer, Lorenzo Mans, and Jim McBride, UMC Pictures, 1971;

Pat Garrett and Billy the Kid, screenplay by Wurlitzer, M-G-M, 1973;

Walker, screenplay by Wurlitzer, Recorded Picture Company/Walker Films, 1987;

Candy Mountain, written by Wurlitzer, directed by Wurlitzer and Robert Frank, Oasis/Xanadu, 1988;

Voyager, screenplay by Wurlitzer, Palace, 1991;

Wind, screenplay by Wurlitzer and Mac Gudgeon, American Zoetrope/Filmlink International, 1992;

Little Buddah, screenplay by Wurlitzer, Recorded Picture Company, 1994.

OTHER: "For Philip Glass," in *Anti-Illusion: Procedures/Materials,* edited by Marcia Tucker and James Monte (New York: Whitney Museum of Modern Art, 1969), p. 14;

Introduction to *Robert Frank* (New York: Aperture Books, 1976), p. 6.

SELECTED PERIODICAL PUBLICATIONS –
UNCOLLECTED: "The Boiler Room," *Atlantic Monthly,* 217 (March 1966): 127–132, 134–139;

"Riding Through – After Reading the First Pages of Louis L'Amour," *For Now,* 10 (1970): 3–5.

Rudolph Wurlitzer is a writer best known for his work in cinema, although he attracted attention from reviewers and critics at the end of the 1960s with two boldly unconventional novels. His most impressive work has appeared subsequently and has been largely neglected, possibly because of his reputation following from those uncompromising early novels. In his fiction and in that work for film that is most distinctly his own, his persistent concern has been with space and its promise of freedom. He writes of dreams of individual liberation and the inevitability of disillusionment. In this respect he is archetypally an American writer, committed to exploring extreme conditions and the margins of culture.

Wurlitzer was born in Cincinnati, a member of the famous musical family. In the following year his parents, Rembert and Anna Lee Little Wurlitzer, moved to New York City, where he attended grade school before pursuing his education at Milton Academy, near Boston; at Columbia University, where he took courses in English and American literature; and at the University of Aix-en-Provence, where he read French authors mainly on his own.

After service in the U.S. Army (1959–1960), Wurlitzer returned to Columbia and then spent much of a decade wandering through Europe, Turkey, and India, working at odd jobs. In New York in the 1960s, he frequented jazz clubs, heard influential musicians such as Thelonious Monk and John Coltrane, and became a close friend of composer Philip Glass. He also made friends among visual artists, notably Richard Serra, and in the late 1960s made a documentary on Claes Oldenburg for National Educational Television. Wurlitzer's adult life has been spent traveling, and he has rarely settled in one place for more than a few months before resuming a nomadic lifestyle. He established two bases – an apartment in New York and a home in Nova Scotia – from which to pursue his wandering and follow the requirements of his work in film, to Hollywood as well as to locations in Europe and Latin America.

Nog (1969), Wurlitzer's first novel, stands as an extreme expression of the disorientation that characterized the end of the 1960s. On its appearance many reviewers found it striking but obscure; reading it was an uncomfortable experience. Richard Poirier considered it a "brilliant" book, an "accomplishment of some historic consequence." In *The Performing Self* (1971) Poirier described *Nog* as an attempt to render "states of being in which separate identities can barely be located and, when they are, seem merely accidental. Identities fuse and separate without intention and without feeling, as if persons had the consistency of air, with no one able to find himself in himself, in anyone else or, with any certainty, even in space." Clearly there are radical departures here from familiar conceptions of plot and characterization, but for Poirier *Nog* performed the important service of articulating experiences of contemporary life, felt particularly by the young, and usually relegated to silence and marginality.

Wurlitzer in an interview acknowledged that *Nog* was not a novel for readers "interested in knowing what they already know"; it was exploratory rather than confirmatory and deliberately failed to supply "the kind of information that most people want when they read a book." Further frustration of expectations arises from his determination "to try to break habits of time that one takes for granted." By rendering memory arbitrary, he aimed to grant his narrative "a kind of autonomous immediacy." The confusion is exacerbated by Wurlitzer's adoption of a first-person narrator who is fallible, to say the least. He thus creates a narrative of "pure movement" through a deceptive, even hallucinatory environment. Fellow novelist Ronald Sukenick comments on the difficulty of Wurlitzer's novel in his essay "The New Tradition in Fiction":

> Rudolph Wurlitzer is a writer whose work gets very close to the quality that I have in mind when I speak of opacity. His novels have the interesting effect of passing through your mind the way ice cream passes over your tongue – you get the taste and that's it. The experience exists in and for itself. It is opaque the way that abstract painting is opaque in that it cannot be explained as representing some other kind of experience. You cannot look through it to reality – it is the reality in question and if you don't see it you don't see anything at all.

Wurlitzer asserts that *Nog* is really about "a West Coast state of mind," endorsing the customary distinction between America's East Coast as historical and looking toward Europe and the West Coast, where a significant number of people, especially in the 1960s, were "living outside of cultural definition." The novel was a representation of this "weird frontier," where a nomadic way of life was by no means extraordinary. Having attained the status of underground classic, *Nog* in retrospect does appear to belong distinctly to its period, when concern for cultural innovation produced not only alternative lifestyles but also a host of literary experiments, the abandonment of well-established conventions for characterization and plot in favor of the exploration of technical and formal possibilities. It reflects a time when personal liberation was widely identified with deliberate strategies of risk taking and disorientation, the precarious freedoms of nonattachment. Nonetheless, its thrust into the present conforms to an archetypal American trope, and in subsequent fictions Wurlitzer has demonstrated his ability to play virtuosic variations on the theme of how to escape the determinism of precedent and received authority.

If *Nog* can be said to have a story, it is focused upon the narrator and his relationship to a cherished possession – an octopus (for publication in the United Kingdom, the book was renamed *The Octopus*). A sweeping geographical movement can be traced from the West to the East Coast, from a small coastal town in California south of San Francisco, to the desert badlands of the Southwest, to Los Angeles and through the Panama Canal, and finally to New York. But more essentially the novel is an account of a man on a journey through fluid space, without beginning or end. Wurlitzer has noted parallels between his first novel and Philip Glass's early compositions with their concern for process, their insistent repetition and focus upon the ongoing present.

Wurlitzer's relationship with Glass and his wife, JoAnne Akalaitis, began a new stage in 1969, when he bought a property in Nova Scotia with the

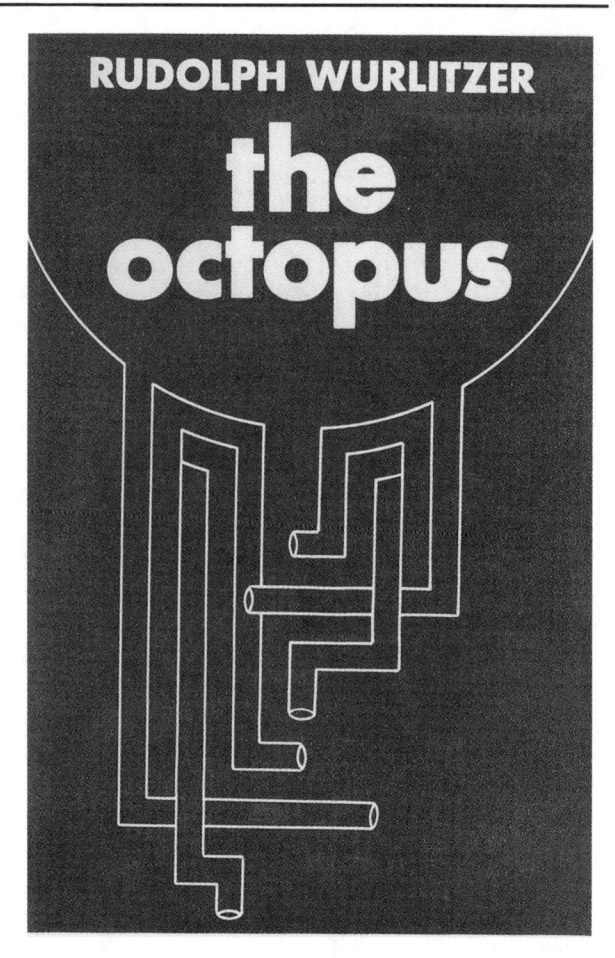

Dust jackets for the American edition and the retitled British edition of Wurlitzer's first novel, in which he consciously tried to frustrate his reader's expectations (courtesy of the Lilly Library, Indiana University)

couple. In his book *Opera on the Beach* (1988) Glass recalls how he and his wife sought out a summer home near the town of Mabou Mines. Imitating travel-agent prose, Glass describes it as "an abandoned summer camp on a cliff overlooking the sea, containing a sprawling main lodge, a handful of log shacks buried in an expanse of pine forest, and a vast and bleakly beautiful stretch of beach. Satisfyingly remote."

Wurlitzer's residence in Nova Scotia also led to his friendship with Swiss-born photographer and filmmaker Robert Frank, who moved to Mabou from New York in the same year. Frank, whose book *The Americans* (1958) is a classic of photography, proved inspirational for Wurlitzer in his refusal to compromise or to conform. After the success of his book, Frank shunned the limelight and invested his time and energy in making singular, quite uncommercial films. These included *Pull My Daisy*, his 1959 collaboration with Alfred Leslie, which featured members of the Beat generation and was written and narrated by Jack Kerouac. Wurlitzer would later collaborate with Frank.

Wurlitzer shared Glass and Akalaitis's interest in Samuel Beckett's work. Akalaitis's theater company, which took the name Mabou Mines, had staged Beckett's *Play* in New York City in 1965 with music by Glass and continued their dedication to the Irish playwright through a series of productions, including *Company* in 1984. The sense of a life invented from moment to moment, with memory depicted as arbitrary, produces in *Nog* occasional echoes of Beckett's work. During the late 1960s Wurlitzer wrote two plays on Beckettian themes, *Double Dribble* and *The Waiting Hexagram*. Neither has been published.

Comparisons between Beckett and Wurlitzer were frequent in reviews of Wurlitzer's second novel, *Flats* (1970), though they tended to be invidious as the reception of the book was generally unfavorable. The Beckettian overtones are evident in the narrator's lament from the concluding pages of the novel:

I no longer know who Mobile is. I am not attached to his crawling form. That is his problem: where he goes, where he doesn't go. I would gladly give him up. Perhaps I have given him up. There is no comfort in prodding dying forms. Let them go. Gravity will take care of them. Gravity will press them into oblivion. I want to say the same words over and over. I want just the sound. I want to fill up what space I am with one note. I want to follow the note beyond my own conclusion. I want a sound that is not involved with beginning or ending. I want to release my own attention to let in the light. There is light. I no longer know how to notice or present an explanation of myself. Mobile is gone. No one will take his place. I want to say the same words over and over. We are no longer involved in strategies of going somewhere together. I don't have to say that again. Let Mobile crawl on. As he wishes. The journey is already over or it never happened. Let Mobile crawl on.

Representative of the novel's general tone and style, this passage encapsulates its overall concern with impotence, loss, and decline toward immobility. A series of characters appear, named after particular places in the United States; yet as in Beckett's work, they are less characters than protean forms that drift through the narrating consciousness without specific location. The potential for freedom attained through letting go is here displaced by bleak recognition of impermanence and instability. Somewhat mannered and derivative, *Flats* seems the least satisfactory of Wurlitzer's books despite his evident skills.

In a 27 June 1988 letter to David Seed quoted in Seed's *Rudolph Wurlitzer, American Novelist and Screenwriter* (1992), Wurlitzer remarked that he turned to writing screenplays initially "for relief and therapy as my prose was so much on the edge of being solipsistic, as well as introverted. I needed, or so I thought then, to be more out in the world, even if it meant being battered by a relentlessly profane market place." He contributed to the script of Jim McBride's *Glen and Randa* (1971), a post-Holocaust film in which two travelers set out west in search of a metropolis but find only a hole in the ground. His third novel, *Quake* (1972), was published between the production of two significant movies for which Wurlitzer wrote the screenplays, Monte Hellman's *Two-Lane Blacktop* (1971) and Sam Peckinpah's *Pat Garrett and Billy the Kid* (1973).

The entire screenplay for *Two-Lane Blacktop*, which Wurlitzer developed from preliminary work by Will Cory, was presented in the April 1971 *Esquire* as the "first movie worth reading" and subsequently published as a paperback book. In the movie, though, the dialogue is pared to a minimum; the emphasis is placed on action, as four characters travel across America in two cars. The Mechanic and the Driver (played by the musicians Dennis Wilson and James Taylor) are largely taciturn, engaged, as Philip French remarks, in an attempt "to pare down their lives to reach an individual inner core that's free from corruption." They are joined by the Girl, whose presence intensifies the rivalry displayed by the garrulous driver of a Pontiac GTO (Warren Oates). A race ensues, to a destination picked at random, and never reached. Greg Ford comments that the film's "prevailing atmosphere suggests that these nomads are traveling to nowhere, driving to oblivion." The movie ends with a drag race, and as the Driver accelerates, the film itself slows down and then starts to burn up. Wurlitzer played a cameo role as the driver of a Plymouth Road Runner and also made a brief appearance in *Pat Garrett and Billy the Kid*.

Wurlitzer wrote the script for *Pat Garrett and Billy the Kid* with Hellman's direction in mind, but major studios shied away from this uncommercial combination. Peckinpah's involvement ensured backing for the project, but he reworked Wurlitzer's screenplay, and further changes were imposed by M-G-M. Seed observes that "Wurlitzer's decision to publish his screenplay was a gesture of protest against the Hollywood machine." Wurlitzer made no attempt to conceal his distaste for the imperatives and prejudices of commercial filmmaking. In his introduction to the published screenplay, he outlines the serious intent that marks the script as the work of the author of *Nog* and *Flats,* asserting that he "became consumed with philosophical questions about the phenomenology of western space, of establishing a continuity outside of cultural time, and of trying to work the dialectics of interior and exterior space. In other words: of experiencing the present outside of language; of being alone without historical direction."

Quake is Wurlitzer's imagination of disaster, an apocalyptic novel, one among many written in America in the late 1960s and early 1970s, which depicts social disintegration in the wake of an earthquake that hits Los Angeles. His work writing for movies may have led to the greater overt formal coherence of this novel over its predecessors. In *Hard Travel to Sacred Places* (1994) Wurlitzer identifies "the first axiom of the screenwriter, which is to sublimate language to image." The elusive figures and shifting contours of *Nog* and *Flats* are here superseded by the clear definition of an ostensibly stable reality, plunged into chaos by a catastrophe. Despite its first-person narration, the focus of *Quake* is on the external world, with sexual degeneracy and mass violence the indices of a parallel collapse of interior worlds. At the end of the novel Wurlitzer has arrived at the kind of devastated landscape that had been the point of departure in *Flats*.

Wurlitzer collaborated with Frank in 1975 to produce *Keep Busy,* a short, improvised film about life on an island off Cape Breton whose only contact with the outside world is through a lighthouse keeper's radio. There is an evident parallel between Cape Breton and the isolated Slab Island Wurlitzer would write about in *Slow Fade* (1984). In 1981 Wurlitzer and Frank made *Energy and How to Get It,* a "mutated documentary" blending fiction and factual information derived from Wurlitzer's reading about Robert Golka, who tried to achieve nuclear fusion through experiments with massive electrical charges conducted in the Utah desert. William S. Burroughs was among members of the cast.

The radical challenge to convention posed by his first two novels and the disturbing nature of his third may in part explain the neglect shown *Slow Fade,* to date Wurlitzer's major novelistic achievement, which deserves recognition as a major work of American literature. Janet Wiehe, in an August 1984 review for the *Library Journal,* noted that the novel is a "darkly comic satire of the movie business, where reality is manipulated and all relationships are 'deals.'" Wurlitzer's involvement with the movies had continued in the years leading up to his novel. In 1978 he contributed to the script for *Coming Home* (1978), directed by his friend Hal Ashby. He then produced a screenplay from Frank Herbert's *Dune* (1965), but the treatment did not win the author's approval and was rejected. In 1982 he acted in Robert Downey's film *America* (1986). During 1984 he spent several months working with Michelangelo Antonioni on *Two Telegrams,* which was never produced.

Neil Karlen, writing in the 13 August 1984 *Newsweek,* compared *Slow Fade* to Nathanael West's novel *Day of the Locust* (1939), a comparison that might also extend to *Quake*. Karlen finds "greed, lust and revenge" the only motives for action in the novel. The book's reviews were accurate to a point but do scant justice to a work that pursues crucial American themes to the point of exhaustion, in a narrative constructed with considerable craft and technical resourcefulness. The betrayal of ideals and spiritual values by material reality and the exigencies of history is treated in *Slow Fade* in a way that emphatically precludes the capacity for hope, on cultural rather than merely individual terms. Wurlitzer's literary aspirations in his earlier books are here contained within recognizably conventional form; characterization is subtle, drawing on American archetypes without lapsing into cliché. Virtually all Wurlitzer has written has been about traveling, about being on the road. In *Slow Fade* the long open road of American mythology finally runs out.

A main character in the novel is Wesley Hardin, a veteran filmmaker based to some extent, as Wurlitzer has acknowledged, upon Peckinpah. Hardin is a frontiersman of the cinema, a maverick pioneer like Howard Hawks and John Ford. His son, Walker Hardin, has traveled to India in search of his sister, Clementine. Searching for enlightenment and spiritual rejuvenation, Walker finds only death and physical corruption. On his return to America, Walker is commissioned by his father to translate his experiences into a screenplay. He does so during the course of a car journey across the country from Santa Fe to New York City. The journey holds no promise of liberation; the urge to keep in motion no longer guarantees even the temporary consolations described by Kerouac in *On the Road* (1957). In the narrative reconstruction Walker becomes a character named Jim. This device allows for critical distance and also indicates the fictive aspects of memory, a major theme of Wurlitzer's first two novels.

A suggestive combination of talking cure and strong emotion recollected in the relative tranquillity of a burnt-out condition, Walker's articulation of his experiences is transcribed from tape recordings, the draft being distinguished in the text through use of italics. The transcription is made by A. D. Ballou, an opportunistic hustler, scrambling to survive by making deals among pop musicians and movie people. Ballou's involvement with a punk-rock band at the start of the novel suggests the anachronism of the hippie trail to the East, a point made explicit in his attack on Walker: "What went down over there that you lost it so bad? You must have booked yourself into some kind of religious act. The street is where it's at now and how to get off it. Dash for cash." The displacement of naive hope by cynicism and despair sets the tone for what follows, as the father and son become focal points for a devastating portrayal of the loss of creative energy and opportunity. The project to turn bleak historic data into film, to dematerialize the unpalatable truth, as the western movie has transformed the grim history of western settlement, is destined to fail; that alchemical action is not an option in the world of Wurlitzer's fiction.

Dust jacket for Wurlitzer's 1972 book, in which an earthquake plunges Los Angeles in chaos (courtesy of the Lilly Library, Indiana University)

At the end of *Slow Fade,* Wes Hardin flies north to Slab Island, his desolate childhood home off the Canadian coast that evokes the tough, frontier life of his own father. But his search for authentic values ends in unequivocal failure, as the island's degenerating inhabitants clamor for satellite television to anesthetize them to the pain of their existence and to draw them finally from their remoteness into the heart of the United States. Hardin's physical and psychic disintegration has reached a point where there is no alternative but to endure his own slow fade toward death.

Noting Wurlitzer's "abiding preoccupation with form," Seed summarizes the nature of the novels in *Rudolph Wurlitzer, American Novelist and Screenwriter:*

> *Nog* erodes its own narrative propositions as soon as they are made; narrating turns in on itself towards stasis in *Flats;* and *Quake* depicts a breakdown of cultural forms. *Slow Fade* repeatedly identifies itself as a road novel but denies the coherence of a single perceiving consciousness or narrative voice. Wurlitzer renders the text itself as mobile by alternating the methods of screenplay and quasi-realistic narration. By exploring this alternation at length *Slow Fade* expansively departs from the minimalist methods of Wurlitzer's first three novels.

Following the publication of *Slow Fade,* Wurlitzer returned to film work, collaborating uneasily with British director Alex Cox on *Walker* (1987). Cox's film tells the story of Tennessee-born William Walker, who invaded Nicaragua with a band of adventurers and ruled the country from 1855 to 1857. It was shot entirely in Nicaragua, and Cox sought to make a political point relevant to that country. Wurlitzer articulated his reservations about the project in *Walker,* a book published to tie in with the movie. The book comprises quotations from the script; extracts from the diary of Ed Harris, who played the title role; biographical material on Walker; and a lengthy dialogue between Wurlitzer and Cox. Wurlitzer complains of "the invasion of a film company coming down here and strip mining images and ripping them off and carrying them back as loot and booty to show on the screens of an affluent and decadent society."

Candy Mountain (1987), a film for which Wurlitzer wrote the screenplay and that he codirected with Frank, tells the story of a young musician, Julius (played by Kevin J. O'Connor) who goes in search of Elmore Silk (Harris Yulin), a legendary guitar maker who had voluntarily disappeared twenty years before. It is in one sense a quite personal film, dealing with the relationship between Wurlitzer and Frank and their orientation toward both New York City and Nova Scotia. Wurlitzer has described it as "an odyssey, a journey from the center of one culture (American) to the margins of another (Canadian)." This is the movement of *Slow Fade* and more generally the dynamic that his work typically assumes, from the hub to the periphery, where things always threaten to fall apart and where the loss of one's sense of self proves a prerequisite for the possibility of more profound and, invariably, more disturbing kinds of self-discovery.

Wurlitzer's *Hard Travel to Sacred Places* is a harrowing account of the author's journey through Southeast Asia with his photographer wife, Lynn Davis, six months after the death of her twenty-one-year-old son in a car crash. The book is spiritual autobiography as much as travel writing. As the couple moves through Thailand, Burma, and Cambodia, struggling to come to terms with their loss, there are curious echoes of the world Wurlitzer created in *Nog* a quarter century before. That book of the West Coast reverberates into this documentary account of the Far East, as Wurlitzer confides his need to escape "the old encrusted and habitual patterns of personality" and "to push toward the margins of my 'aloneness,' to give in to alienation, exhaustion, and grief."

Wurlitzer again brings to the fore the nature of memory and the possibility of freeing oneself from its determinant presence. But here he discloses a profound personal need to inhabit the margins of culture delineated in his fiction. Before *Quake* he recognized the need to engage with the world to resist Beckettian solipsism, but in this book he asserts, "I am attached to the willful isolation of writing novels as much as to the raw, deluded 'business' of making films." He clarifies the attraction of "writing an occasional script," which enabled him to avoid teaching fiction in the academic context of creative writing classes. Wurlitzer defiantly asserts that he does not know what fiction is: "Nor do I want to. I prefer to keep the jeopardy of that process to myself."

At times in *Hard Travel to Sacred Places* Wurlitzer is drawn by force of contrast to idealize simple lifestyles in opposition to the turmoil of Asia's westernized urban centers. In rural Thailand he notes "a life of constant movement and change, seemingly removed from modern alienation and the ordinary horrors of dysfunctional family life"; but with characteristic resistance to the illusory fictions that insulate human beings from harsh realities, he adds, "who knows what really goes on." His work invariably modulates from dreams of freedom to recognition of the state of entrapment; the emphasis always falls, finally, on the latter, but the relationship of desire to disillusionment provides the essential dynamic of his narratives: "I am attached to escape, to the illusions of 'the road' as well as to the barest 'no exit' cul-de-sac."

Hard Travel to Sacred Places clearly shows how Buddhist teachings increasingly have sustained Wurlitzer amid the tensions of hope and despair; the account of his travels is peppered with Buddhist citations that act as a resolute counterpoint to his sense of his own instability and the instability he encounters in everyday reality. Wurlitzer describes himself here as having been a student of dharma for twenty-five years, in India and Nepal as well as America. Despite his long-held interest Wurlitzer was tormented by his lack of knowledge of Buddhism during his work on the script for Bernardo Bertolucci's film *Little Buddah* (1994). The year spent on that project ended in "a bad case of burnout and self-recrimination."

Wurlitzer's involvement with Bertolucci and other movie projects indicates his ongoing interest in the processes of filmmaking, despite his uneasiness with its many compromises and frustrations. *Hard Travel to Sacred Places* demonstrates unequivocally that, for Wurlitzer, writing is a highly personal quest, leading to explorations of the self that are difficult and may be painful. In those books, notably *Slow Fade,* where he fuses this quest with archetypal concerns of American culture, he has produced work that deserves to be read far more widely than has been the case.

Interview:

"Interview with Rudolph Wurlitzer," *Rutgers Anthologist,* 41, no. 1 (1969-1970): 34-41; excerpted in *Cutting Edges: Young American Fiction for the '70s,* edited by Jack Hicks (New York: Holt, Rinehart & Winston, 1973), pp. 551-552.

References:

Jan Aghed, "Pat Garrett and Billy the Kid," *Sight and Sound* (Spring 1970): 64-69;

Douglass Bolling, "Rudolph Wurlitzer's *Nog* and *Flats*," *Critique,* 14, no. 3 (1973): 5-15;

Bolling, "The Waking Nightmare: American Society in Rudolph Wurlitzer's *Quake*," *Critique,* 16, no. 3 (1975): 70-80;

Greg Ford, "Two-Lane Blacktop," *Film Quarterly,* 25 (Winter 1971-1972): 54;

Philip Glass, *Opera on the Beach* (London: Faber & Faber, 1988), p. 8;

Richard Poirier, *The Performing Self: Compositions and Decompositions in the Languages of Contemporary Life* (London: Chatto & Windus, 1971), p. 26;

Manfred Pütz, "Alternative Fictions," *Fiction International,* no. 2/3 (1974): 134-139;

David Seed, "Rudolph Wurlitzer," in *Post-war Literature in English,* edited by Hans Bertens (Groningen: Wolters-Noordhoff, 1991), part 12, pp. 1-11;

Seed, *Rudolph Wurlitzer, American Novelist and Screenwriter* (Lewiston, N.Y.: Edward Mellen Press, 1992);

Ronald Sukenick, "The New Tradition in Fiction," in *Surfiction: Fiction Now and Tomorrow,* edited by Raymond Federman, second edition (Chicago: Swallow Press, 1981), pp. 35-45.

Books for Further Reading

This list is a selection of general studies relating to the contemporary novel. Fuller bibliographies can be found in Lewis Leary, *Articles on American Literature, 1950–1967* (Durham, N.C.: Duke University Press, 1970); the annual MLA International Bibliography; and *American Literary Scholarship: An Annual* (Durham, N.C.: Duke University Press, 1965–   ).

Aldridge, John W. *Classics and Contemporaries.* Columbia: University of Missouri Press, 1992.

Aldridge. *The Devil in the Fire: Retrospective Essays on American Literature and Culture, 1951–1971.* New York: Harper's Magazine Press, 1972.

Aldridge. *In Search of Heresy: American Literature in an Age of Conformity.* New York: McGraw-Hill, 1956.

Aldridge. *Talents and Technicians: Literary Chic and the New Assembly-Line Fiction.* New York: Scribners, 1992.

Aldridge. *Time to Murder and Create: The Contemporary Novel in Crisis.* New York: McKay, 1966.

Allen, Mary. *The Necessary Blankness: Women in Major American Fiction of the Sixties.* Urbana: University of Illinois Press, 1976.

Alter, Robert. *After the Tradition: Essays on Modern Jewish Writing.* New York: Dutton, 1969.

Auchincloss, Louis. *Pioneers & Caretakers: A Study of 9 American Women Novelists.* Minneapolis: University of Minnesota Press, 1965.

Bachelard, Gaston. *The Poetics of Space,* translated by Maria Jolas. New York: Orion, 1964.

Baker, Houston A. *Blues, Ideology, and Afro-American Literature: A Vernacular Theory.* Chicago: University of Chicago Press, 1984.

Baker, ed. *Three American Literatures: Essays in Chicano, Native American, and Asian-American Literature for Teachers of American Literature.* New York: Modern Language Association of America, 1982.

Balakian, Nona, and Charles Simmons, eds. *The Creative Present: Notes on Contemporary American Fiction.* Garden City, N.Y.: Doubleday, 1963.

Baumbach, Jonathan. *The Landscape of Nightmare: Studies in the Contemporary American Novel.* New York: New York University Press, 1965.

Bell, Bernard W. *The Afro-American Novel and Its Tradition.* Amherst: University of Massachusetts Press, 1987.

Bellamy, Joe David. *The New Fiction: Interviews with Innovative American Writers.* Urbana: University of Illinois Press, 1974.

Bercovitch, Sacvan, ed. *Reconstructing American Literary History.* Cambridge, Mass.: Harvard University Press, 1986.

Berman, Ronald. *America in the Sixties: An Intellectual History.* New York: Free Press, 1968.

Bigsby, C. W. E., ed. *The Black American Writer*. DeLand, Fla.: Everett/Edwards, 1969.

Blotner, Joseph. *The Modern American Political Novel, 1900–1960*. Austin: University of Texas Press, 1966.

Boelhower, William. *Through a Glass Darkly: Ethnic Semiosis in American Literature*. New York: Oxford University Press, 1987.

Bone, Robert A. *The Negro Novel in America*, revised edition. New Haven: Yale University Press, 1965.

Bradbury, John M. *Renaissance in the South: A Critical History of the Literature, 1920–1960*. Chapel Hill: University of North Carolina Press, 1963.

Bradbury, Malcolm. *The Modern American Novel*, revised edition. Oxford & New York: Oxford University Press, 1992.

Bredahl, A. Carl, Jr. *New Ground: Western American Narrative and the Literary Canon*. Chapel Hill: University of North Carolina Press, 1989.

Bryant, Jerry H. *The Open Decision: The Contemporary American Novel and Its Intellectual Background*. New York: Free Press, 1970.

Byerman, Keith E. *Fingering the Jagged Grain: Tradition and Form in Recent Black Fiction*. Athens: University of Georgia Press, 1985.

Campbell, Jane. *Mythic Black Fiction: The Transformation of History*. Knoxville: University of Tennessee Press, 1986.

Carr, John, ed. *Kite-Flying and Other Irrational Acts: Conversations with Twelve Southern Writers*. Baton Rouge: Louisiana State University Press, 1972.

Chametzky, Jules. *Our Decentralized Literature: Cultural Mediations in Selected Jewish and Southern Writers*. Amherst: University of Massachusetts Press, 1986.

Christian, Barbara. *Black Women Novelists: The Development of a Tradition, 1892–1976*. Westport, Conn.: Greenwood Press, 1980.

Civello, Paul. *American Literary Naturalism and Its Twentieth-Century Transformations: Frank Norris, Ernest Hemingway, Don DeLillo*. Athens: University of Georgia Press, 1994.

Conversations with Writers, 2 volumes. Detroit: Bruccoli Clark/Gale Research, 1977, 1978.

Cook, Bruce. *The Beat Generation*. New York: Scribners, 1971.

Cook, M. G., ed. *Modern Black Novelists: A Collection of Critical Essays*. Englewood Cliffs, N. J.: Prentice-Hall, 1971.

Core, George, ed. *Southern Fiction Today: Renascence and Beyond*. Athens: University of Georgia Press, 1969.

Cowan, Louise. *The Fugitive Group: A Literary History*. Baton Rouge: Louisiana State University Press, 1959.

Cowley, Malcolm. *The Literary Situation*. New York: Viking, 1954.

Cunliffe, Marcus, ed. *American Literature Since 1900*, revised edition. London: Penguin, 1993.

Darby, William. *Necessary American Fictions: Popular Literature of the 1950s.* Bowling Green, Ohio: Bowling Green University Popular Press, 1987.

Dekker, George. *The American Historical Romance.* Cambridge: Cambridge University Press, 1987.

Drake, Robert, ed. *The Writer and His Tradition.* Knoxville: University of Tennessee, 1969.

Eco, Umberto. *Travels in Hyperreality: Essays,* translated by William Weaver. San Diego: Harcourt Brace Jovanovich, 1983.

Eisinger, Chester E. *Fiction of the Forties.* Chicago: University of Chicago Press, 1963.

Elliott, Emory, ed. *The Columbia History of the American Novel.* New York: Columbia University Press, 1991.

Elliott, ed. *The Columbia Literary History of the United States.* New York: Columbia University Press, 1988.

Etulain, Richard W., and Michael T. Marsden, eds. *The Popular Western: Essays toward a Definition.* Bowling Green, Ohio: Bowling Green State University Popular Press, 1974.

Federman, Raymond, ed. *Surfiction: Fiction Now and Tomorrow.* Chicago: Swallow Press, 1975.

Feldman, Gene, and Max Gartenberg, eds. *The Beat Generation and the Angry Young Men.* New York: Citadel, 1958.

Folsom, James K. *The American Western Novel.* New Haven: College & University Press, 1966.

Fox, Robert Elliott. *Conscientious Sorcerers: The Black Postmodernist Fiction of LeRoi Jones/Amiri Baraka, Ishmael Reed, and Samuel R. Delany.* New York: Greenwood Press, 1987.

French, Warren, ed. *The Fifties: Fiction, Poetry, Drama.* De Land, Fla.: Everett/Edwards, 1970.

Friedman, Melvin J., and John B. Vickery, eds. *The Shaken Realist: Essays in Modern Literature in Honor of Frederick J. Hoffman.* Baton Rouge: Louisiana State University Press, 1970.

Fuller, Edmund. *Man in Modern Fiction: Some Minority Opinions on Contemporary American Writing.* New York: Random House, 1958.

Gado, Frank, ed. *First Person: Conversations on Writers and Writing.* Schenectady, N.Y.: Union College Press, 1973.

Galloway, David D. *The Absurd Hero in American Fiction: Updike, Styron, Bellow, Salinger,* second revised edition. Austin: University of Texas Press, 1981.

Gass, William H. *Fiction and the Figures of Life.* New York: Knopf, 1970.

Gass. *On Being Blue: A Philosophical Inquiry.* Boston: Godine, 1976.

Gates, Henry Louis, Jr. *The Signifying Monkey: A Theory of Afro-American Literary Criticism.* New York: Oxford University Press, 1988.

Gayle, Addison, Jr. *The Way of the New World: The Black Novel in America.* Garden City, N.Y.: Anchor/Doubleday, 1975.

Gayle, ed. *Black Expression: Essays by and about Black Americans in the Creative Arts*. New York: Weybright & Talley, 1969.

Geismar, Maxwell. *American Moderns: From Rebellion to Conformity*. New York: Hill & Wang, 1958.

Gerstenberger, Donna, and George Hendrick. *The American Novel, 1789–1959: A Checklist of Twentieth Century Criticism*. Chicago: Swallow Press, 1970.

Giles, James R. *The Naturalistic Inner-City Novel in America: Encounters With the Fat Man*. Columbia: University of South Carolina Press, 1995.

Gilman, Richard. *The Confusion of Realms*. New York: Random House, 1969.

Glicksberg, Charles I. *The Sexual Revolution in Modern American Literature*. The Hague: Nijhoff, 1971.

Gold, Herbert, ed. *First Person Singular: Essays for the Sixties*. New York: Dial, 1963.

González Echevarría, Roberto. *The Voice of the Masters: Writing and Authority in Modern Latin American Literature*. Austin: University of Texas Press, 1985.

Gossett, Louise Y. *Violence in Recent Southern Fiction*. Durham, N.C.: Duke University Press, 1965.

Green, Martin. *Re-appraisals: Some Commonsense Readings in American Literature*. London: Hugh Evelyn, 1963.

Greiner, Donald J. *Women Enter the Wilderness: Male Bonding and the American Novel of the 1980s*. Columbia: University of South Carolina Press, 1991.

Greiner. *Women Without Men: Female Bonding and the American Novel of the 1980s*. Columbia: University of South Carolina Press, 1993.

Gruen, John. *The Party's Over Now: Reminiscences of the Fifties*. New York: Viking, 1972.

Guttmann, Allen. *The Jewish Writer in America: Assimilation and the Crisis of Identity*. New York: Oxford University Press, 1971.

Hamilton, Cynthia S. *Western and Hard-Boiled Detective Fiction in America: From High Noon to Midnight*. Iowa City: University of Iowa Press, 1987.

Handy, William J. *Modern Fiction: A Formalist Approach*. Carbondale: Southern Illinois University Press, 1971.

Harap, Louis. *In the Mainstream: The Jewish Presence in Twentieth-Century American Literature, 1950s–1980s*. New York: Greenwood Press, 1987.

Hardwick, Elizabeth. *A View of My Own: Essays in Literature and Society*. New York: Farrar, Straus & Cudahy, 1962.

Harper, Howard M., Jr. *Desperate Faith: A Study of Bellow, Salinger, Mailer, Baldwin, and Updike*. Chapel Hill: University of North Carolina Press, 1967.

Harris, Charles B. *Contemporary American Novelists of the Absurd*. New Haven: College & University Press, 1971.

Haslam, Gerald W., ed. *Western Writing*. Albuquerque: University of New Mexico Press, 1974.

Hassan, Ihab. *Contemporary American Literature, 1945–1972: An Introduction*. New York: Ungar, 1973.

Hassan. *The Postmodern Turn: Essays in Postmodernist Theory and Culture.* Columbus: Ohio State University Press, 1987.

Hassan. *Radical Innocence: Studies in the Contemporary American Novel.* Princeton: Princeton University Press, 1961.

Hassan. *The Right Promethean Fire: Imagination, Science, and Cultural Change.* Urbana: University of Illinois Press, 1979.

Hauck, Richard Boyd. *A Cheerful Nihilism: Confidence and "The Absurd" in American Humorous Fiction.* Bloomington: Indiana University Press, 1971.

Hicks, Granville, ed. *The Living Novel: A Symposium.* New York: Macmillan, 1957.

Hicks, Jack. *In the Singer's Temple: Prose Fictions of Barthelme, Gaines, Brautigan, Piercy, Kesey, and Kosinski.* Chapel Hill: University of North Carolina Press, 1981.

Hilfer, Tony. *American Fiction Since 1940.* London & New York: Longman, 1992.

Hill, Herbert, ed. *Anger and Beyond: The Negro Writer in the United States.* New York: Harper & Row, 1966.

Hobson, Fred. *Tell about the South: The Southern Rage to Explain.* Baton Rouge: Louisiana State University Press, 1983.

Hoffman, Daniel, ed. *Harvard Guide to Contemporary American Writing.* Cambridge, Mass.: Belknap Press of Harvard University Press, 1979.

Hoffman, Frederick J. *The Art of Southern Fiction: A Study of Some Modern Novelists.* Carbondale: Southern Illinois University Press, 1967.

Hurm, Gerd. *Fragmented Urban Images: The American City in Modern Fiction from Stephen Crane to Thomas Pynchon.* Frankfurt am Main & New York: Peter Lang, 1991.

Jackson, Blyden. *The History of Afro-American Literature,* 1 volume to date. Baton Rouge: Louisiana State University Press, 1989- .

Johnson, Charles R. *Being and Race: Black Writing Since 1970.* Bloomington: Indiana University Press, 1988.

Jones, Peter G. *War and the Novelist: Appraising the American War Novel.* Columbia: University of Missouri Press, 1976.

Karl, Frederick Robert. *American Fictions, 1940–1980: A Comprehensive History and Critical Evaluation.* New York: Harper & Row, 1983.

Kazin, Alfred. *Bright Book of Life: American Novelists and Storytellers from Hemingway to Mailer.* Boston & Toronto: Atlantic/Little, Brown, 1973.

Kazin. *Contemporaries: Essays.* Boston: Little, Brown, 1962.

Kennard, Jean E. *Number and Nightmare: Forms of Fantasy in Contemporary Fiction.* Hamden, Conn.: Archon, 1975.

Kim, Elaine H. *Asian American Literature: An Introduction to the Writings and Their Social Contexts.* Philadelphia: Temple University Press, 1982.

Klein, Marcus. *After Alienation: American Novels in Mid-century*. Cleveland & New York: World, 1964.

Klein, ed. *The American Novel Since World War II*. Greenwich, Conn.: Fawcett, 1969.

Klinkowitz, Jerome. *The Life of Fiction*. Urbana: University of Illinois Press, 1977.

Klinkowitz. *Literary Disruptions: The Making of a Post-contemporary American Fiction*. Urbana: University of Illinois Press, 1975.

Klinkowitz. *The New American Novel of Manners: The Fiction of Richard Yates, Dan Wakefield, Thomas McGuane*. Athens: University of Georgia Press, 1986.

Klotman, Phyllis Rauch. *Another Man Gone: The Black Runner in Contemporary Afro-American Literature*. Port Washington, N.Y.: Kennikat Press, 1977.

Kort, Wesley A. *Shriven Selves: Religious Problems in Recent American Fiction*. Philadelphia: Fortress, 1972.

Kostelanetz, Richard. *The End of Intelligent Writing: Literary Politics in America*. New York: Sheed & Ward, 1974.

Kostelanetz. *Master Minds: Portraits of Contemporary American Artists and Intellectuals*. New York: Macmillan, 1969.

Kostelanetz, ed. *The New American Arts*. New York: Horizon, 1965.

Kostelanetz, ed. *On Contemporary Literature: An Anthology of Critical Essays on the Major Movements and Writers of Contemporary Literature*. New York: Avon, 1964.

Kostelanetz, ed. *The Young American Writers: Fiction, Poetry, Drama, and Criticism*. New York: Funk & Wagnalls, 1967.

Kremer, S. Lillian. *Witness Through the Imagination: Jewish American Holocaust Literature*. Detroit: Wayne State University Press, 1989.

Krim, Seymour. *Shake It for the World, Smartass*. New York: Dial, 1970.

Lebowitz, Naomi. *Humanism and the Absurd in the Modern Novel*. Evanston, Ill.: Northwestern University Press, 1971.

Lehan, Richard. *A Dangerous Crossing: French Literary Existentialism and the Modern American Novel*. Carbondale: Southern Illinois University Press, 1973.

Ling, Amy. *Between Worlds: Women Writers of Chinese Ancestry*. New York: Pergamon Press, 1990.

Lipton, Lawrence. *The Holy Barbarians*. New York: Messner, 1959.

Litz, A. Walton, ed. *Modern American Fiction: Essays in Criticism*. New York: Oxford University Press, 1963.

Lord, William J., Jr. *How Authors Make a Living: An Analysis of Free Lance Writers' Incomes, 1953–1957*. New York: Scarecrow Press, 1962.

Ludwig, Jack. *Recent American Novelists*. Minneapolis: University of Minnesota Press, 1962.

Lupack, Barbara Tepa. *Insanity as Redemption in Contemporary American Fiction: Inmates Running the Asylum*. Gainesville: University Press of Florida, 1995.

Lutwack, Leonard. *Heroic Fiction: The Epic Tradition and American Novels of the Twentieth Century*. Carbondale: Southern Illinois University Press, 1971.

Madden, Charles F., ed. *Talks with Authors*. Carbondale: Southern Illinois University Press, 1968.

Madden, David, ed. *American Dreams, American Nightmares*. Carbondale: Southern Illinois University Press, 1970.

Madden, ed. *Rediscoveries: Informal Essays in Which Well-Known Novelists Rediscover Neglected Works of Fiction by One of Their Favorite Authors*. New York: Crown, 1971.

Malin, Irving. *New American Gothic*. Carbondale: Southern Illinois University Press, 1962.

Margolies, Edward. *Native Sons: A Critical Study of Twentieth-Century Negro American Authors*. Philadelphia & New York: Lippincott, 1968.

May, John R. *Toward a New Earth: Apocalypse in the American Novel*. Notre Dame, Ind.: University of Notre Dame Press, 1972.

McHale, Brian. *Postmodernist Fiction*. New York & London: Methuen, 1987.

Milton, John R. *The Novel of the American West*. Lincoln: University of Nebraska Press, 1980.

Moore, Harry T., ed. *Contemporary American Novelists*. Carbondale: Southern Illinois University Press, 1964.

Myers, Carol Fairbanks. *Women in Literature: Criticism of the Seventies*. Metuchen, N.J.: Scarecrow Press, 1976.

Newman, Charles. *The Post-modern Aura: The Act of Fiction in an Age of Inflation*. Evanston, Ill.: Northwestern University Press, 1985.

Newquist, Roy. *Counterpoint*. Chicago: Rand, McNally, 1964.

Nin, Anaïs. *The Novel of the Future*. New York: Macmillan, 1968.

O'Brien, John, ed. *Interviews with Black Writers*. New York: Liveright, 1973.

Olderman, Raymond M. *Beyond the Waste Land: A Study of the American Novel in the Nineteen-Sixties*. New Haven: Yale University Press, 1972.

Olster, Stacey Michele. *Reminiscence and Re-creation in Contemporary American Fiction*. Cambridge: Cambridge University Press, 1989.

Panichas, George A., ed. *The Politics of Twentieth-Century Novelists*. New York: Hawthorn Books, 1971.

Parkinson, Thomas, ed. *A Casebook on The Beat*. New York: Crowell, 1961.

Pearce, Richard. *Stages of the Clown: Perspectives on Modern Fiction from Dostoyevsky to Beckett*. Carbondale: Southern Illinois University Press, 1970.

Peden, William. *The American Short Story: Front Line in the National Defense of Literature*. Boston: Houghton Mifflin, 1964. Revised and enlarged as *The American Short Story: Continuity and Change, 1940-1975*. Boston: Houghton Mifflin, 1975.

Pinsker, Sanford. *The Schlemiel as Metaphor: Studies in the Yiddish and American Jewish Novel.* Carbondale: Southern Illinois University Press, 1971.

Podhoretz, Norman. *Doings and Undoings: The Fifties and After in American Writing.* New York: Farrar, Straus, 1964.

Rocard, Marcienne. *The Children of the Sun: Mexican-Americans in the Literature of the United States,* translated by Edward G. Brown Jr. Tucson: University of Arizona Press, 1989.

Rosenblatt, Roger. *Black Fiction.* Cambridge, Mass.: Harvard University Press, 1974.

Rubin, Louis D., Jr. *The Faraway Country: Writers in the Modern South.* Seattle: University of Washington Press, 1963.

Rubin, ed. *The American South: Portrait of a Culture.* Baton Rouge: Louisiana State University Press, 1979.

Rubin and Robert D. Jacobs, eds. *South: Modern Southern Literature in Its Cultural Setting.* Garden City, N.Y.: Doubleday, 1961.

Rubin and others, eds. *The History of Southern Literature.* Baton Rouge: Louisiana State University Press, 1985.

Ruland, Richard, and Malcolm Bradbury. *From Puritanism to Postmodernism: A History of American Literature.* New York: Viking, 1991.

Ruoff, A. LaVonne Brown, and Jerry W. Ward Jr., eds. *Redefining American Literary History.* New York: Modern Language Association of America, 1990.

Scholes, Robert. *The Fabulators.* New York: Oxford University Press, 1967.

Scholes and Robert Kellogg. *The Nature of Narrative.* London & New York: Oxford University Press, 1966.

Schraufnagel, Noel. *From Apology to Protest: The Black American Novel.* De Land, Fla.: Everett/Edwards, 1973.

Schulz, Max F. *Black Humor Fiction of the Sixties: A Pluralistic Definition of Man and His World.* Athens: Ohio University Press, 1973.

Schulz. *Radical Sophistication: Studies in Contemporary Jewish-American Novelists.* Athens: Ohio University Press, 1969.

Scott, Nathan A., Jr. *Three American Moralists: Mailer, Bellow, Trilling.* Notre Dame, Ind.: University of Notre Dame Press, 1973.

Sherzer, Joel, and Anthony Woodbury, eds. *Native American Discourse: Poetics and Rhetoric.* New York: Cambridge University Press, 1987.

Simonson, Harold P. *Beyond the Frontier: Writers, Western Regionalism and a Sense of Place.* Fort Worth: Texas Christian University Press, 1989.

Smith, Valerie. *Self-Discovery and Authority in Afro-American Narrative.* Cambridge, Mass.: Harvard University Press, 1987.

Sollors, Werner. *Beyond Ethnicity: Consent and Descent in American Culture.* New York: Oxford University Press, 1986.

Spiller, Robert, ed. *A Time of Harvest: American Literature, 1910–1960.* New York: Hill & Wang, 1962.

Stark, John. *The Literature of Exhaustion: Borges, Nabokov, and Barth.* Durham, N.C.: Duke University Press, 1974.

Stepto, Robert. *From Behind the Veil: A Study of Afro-American Narrative.* Urbana: University of Illinois Press, 1979.

Stuckey, William J. *The Pulitzer Prize Novels: A Critical Backward Look.* Norman: University of Oklahoma Press, 1966.

Sutherland, William O. S., ed. *Six Contemporary Novels: Six Introductory Essays in Modern Fiction.* Austin: University of Texas Department of English, 1962.

Tanner, Tony. *City of Words: American Fiction, 1950–1970.* New York: Harper & Row, 1971.

Tanner. *The Reign of Wonder: Naivety and Reality in American Literature.* Cambridge: Cambridge University Press, 1965.

Tate, Claudia. *Black Women Writers at Work.* New York: Continuum, 1983.

Taylor, J. Golden, and Thomas J. Lyon, eds. *A Literary History of the American West.* Fort Worth: Texas Christian University Press, 1987.

Tilton, John W. *Cosmic Satire in the Contemporary Novel.* Lewisburg, Pa.: Bucknell University Press, 1977.

Turner, Darwin T. *Afro-American Writers.* New York: Appleton-Century-Crofts, 1970.

Tuttleton, James W. *The Novel of Manners in America.* Chapel Hill: University of North Carolina Press, 1972.

Tytell, John. *Naked Angels: The Lives and Literature of the Beat Generation.* New York: McGraw-Hill, 1976.

Waldmeir, Joseph J., ed. *Recent American Fiction: Some Critical Views.* Boston: Houghton Mifflin, 1963.

Watkins, Floyd C. *The Death of Art: Black and White in the Recent Southern Novel.* Athens: University of Georgia Press, 1970.

Watson, Carole McAlphine. *Prologue: The Novels of Black American Women, 1891–1965.* New York: Greenwood Press, 1985.

Weber, Ronald, ed. *America in Change: Reflections on the 60's and 70's.* Notre Dame, Ind.: University of Notre Dame Press, 1972.

West, James L. W. *American Authors and the Literary Marketplace Since 1900.* Philadelphia: University of Pennsylvania Press, 1988.

Westbrook, Max, ed. *The Modern American Novel: Essays in Criticism.* New York: Random House, 1966.

Whitlow, Roger. *Black American Literature: A Critical History.* Chicago: Nelson Hall, 1973.

Wiget, Andrew. *Native American Literature.* Boston: Twayne, 1985.

Wiget, ed. *Critical Essays on Native American Literature.* Boston: G. K. Hall, 1985.

Wilde, Alan. *Middle Grounds: Studies in Contemporary American Fiction.* Philadelphia: University of Pennsylvania Press, 1987.

Williams, John A., and Charles F. Harris, eds. *Amistad I: Writings of Black History and Culture.* New York: Knopf, 1970.

Williams and Harris, eds. *Amistad II.* New York: Knopf, 1971.

Writers at Work: The Paris Review *Interviews,* series 1-9. New York: Viking, 1958-1992.

Contributors

Paul Civello	*University of Minnesota*
Julian Cowley	*University of Luton*
William Dowie	*Southeastern Louisiana University*
Bernard Duyfhuizen	*University of Wisconsin – Eau Claire*
David H. Everson	*University of Illinois at Springfield*
Judith L. Everson	*University of Illinois at Springfield*
Pin-chia Feng	*National Chiao-Tung University, Taiwan*
Douglas Fowler	*Florida State University*
Warren French	*University of Wales, Swansea*
John D. Kalb	*Salisbury State University*
John M. Krafft	*Miami University – Hamilton*
S. Lillian Kremer	*Kansas State University*
Leon Lewis	*Appalachian State University*
Vashti Crutcher Lewis	*Northern Illinois University*
Jeanette W. Mann	*California State University, Northridge*
William Nelles	*University of Massachusetts – Dartmouth*
Joe Nordgren	*Lamar University*
Mark Royden Winchell	*Clemson University*

Cumulative Index

Dictionary of Literary Biography, Volumes 1-173
Dictionary of Literary Biography Yearbook, 1980-1995
Dictionary of Literary Biography Documentary Series, Volumes 1-14

Cumulative Index

DLB before number: *Dictionary of Literary Biography,* Volumes 1-173
Y before number: *Dictionary of Literary Biography Yearbook,* 1980-1995
DS before number: *Dictionary of Literary Biography Documentary Series,* Volumes 1-14

A

Abbey Press DLB-49

The Abbey Theatre and Irish Drama,
  1900-1945 .... DLB-10

Abbot, Willis J. 1863-1934 .... DLB-29

Abbott, Jacob 1803-1879 .... DLB-1

Abbott, Lee K. 1947- DLB-130

Abbott, Lyman 1835-1922 .... DLB-79

Abbott, Robert S. 1868-1940 ....DLB-29, 91

Abelard, Peter circa 1079-1142 .....DLB-115

Abelard-Schuman DLB-46

Abell, Arunah S. 1806-1888 .... DLB-43

Abercrombie, Lascelles 1881-1938 ...DLB-19

Aberdeen University Press
  Limited DLB-106

Abish, Walter 1931- DLB-130

Ablesimov, Aleksandr Onisimovich
  1742-1783 .... DLB-150

Abraham à Sancta Clara
  1644-1709 .... DLB-168

Abrahams, Peter 1919- DLB-117

Abrams, M. H. 1912- DLB-67

Abrogans circa 790-800 .... DLB-148

Abschatz, Hans Aßmann von
  1646-1699 .... DLB-168

Abse, Dannie 1923- DLB-27

Academy Chicago Publishers DLB-46

Accrocca, Elio Filippo 1923- DLB-128

Ace Books DLB-46

Achebe, Chinua 1930- DLB-117

Achtenberg, Herbert 1938- DLB-124

Ackerman, Diane 1948- DLB-120

Ackroyd, Peter 1949- DLB-155

Acorn, Milton 1923-1986 .... DLB-53

Acosta, Oscar Zeta 1935?- DLB-82

Actors Theatre of Louisville DLB-7

Adair, James 1709?-1783? DLB-30

Adam, Graeme Mercer 1839-1912 ... DLB-99

Adame, Leonard 1947- DLB-82

Adamic, Louis 1898-1951 .... DLB-9

Adams, Alice 1926- Y-86

Adams, Brooks 1848-1927 .... DLB-47

Adams, Charles Francis, Jr.
  1835-1915 .... DLB-47

Adams, Douglas 1952- Y-83

Adams, Franklin P. 1881-1960 ..... DLB-29

Adams, Henry 1838-1918 .... DLB-12, 47

Adams, Herbert Baxter 1850-1901 ... DLB-47

Adams, J. S. and C.
  [publishing house] DLB-49

Adams, James Truslow 1878-1949 ... DLB-17

Adams, John 1735-1826 .... DLB-31

Adams, John Quincy 1767-1848 ..... DLB-37

Adams, Léonie 1899-1988 .... DLB-48

Adams, Levi 1802-1832 .... DLB-99

Adams, Samuel 1722-1803 .... DLB-31, 43

Adams, Thomas
  1582 or 1583-1652 .... DLB-151

Adams, William Taylor 1822-1897 .. DLB-42

Adamson, Sir John 1867-1950 ..... DLB-98

Adcock, Arthur St. John
  1864-1930 .... DLB-135

Adcock, Betty 1938- DLB-105

Adcock, Betty, Certain Gifts DLB-105

Adcock, Fleur 1934- DLB-40

Addison, Joseph 1672-1719 .... DLB-101

Ade, George 1866-1944 .... DLB-11, 25

Adeler, Max (see Clark, Charles Heber)

Adonias Filho 1915-1990 .... DLB-145

Advance Publishing Company DLB-49

AE 1867-1935 .... DLB-19

Ælfric circa 955-circa 1010 .... DLB-146

Aesthetic Poetry (1873), by
  Walter Pater DLB-35

After Dinner Opera Company Y-92

Afro-American Literary Critics:
  An Introduction DLB-33

Agassiz, Jean Louis Rodolphe
  1807-1873 .... DLB-1

Agee, James 1909-1955 .... DLB-2, 26, 152

The Agee Legacy: A Conference at
  the University of Tennessee
  at Knoxville Y-89

Aguilera Malta, Demetrio
  1909-1981 .... DLB-145

Ai 1947- DLB-120

Aichinger, Ilse 1921- DLB-85

Aidoo, Ama Ata 1942- DLB-117

Aiken, Conrad 1889-1973 ....DLB-9, 45, 102

Aiken, Joan 1924- DLB-161

Aikin, Lucy 1781-1864 ....DLB-144, 163

Ainsworth, William Harrison
  1805-1882 .... DLB-21

Aitken, George A. 1860-1917 ...... DLB-149

Aitken, Robert [publishing house] ... DLB-49

Akenside, Mark 1721-1770 .... DLB-109

Akins, Zoë 1886-1958 .... DLB-26

Alabaster, William 1568-1640 ..... DLB-132

Alain-Fournier 1886-1914 .... DLB-65

Alarcón, Francisco X. 1954- DLB-122

Alba, Nanina 1915-1968 .... DLB-41

Albee, Edward 1928- DLB-7

Albert the Great circa 1200-1280 ... DLB-115

Alberti, Rafael 1902- DLB-108

Albertinus, Aegidius
  circa 1560-1620 .... DLB-164

Alcott, Amos Bronson 1799-1888 ..... DLB-1

Alcott, Louisa May
  1832-1888 .... DLB-1, 42, 79; DS-14

Alcott, William Andrus 1798-1859 .... DLB-1

Alcuin circa 732-804 .... DLB-148

Alden, Henry Mills 1836-1919 ..... DLB-79

Alden, Isabella 1841-1930 .... DLB-42

Alden, John B. [publishing house] DLB-49

Cumulative Index

Alden, Beardsley and Company DLB-49

Aldington, Richard
1892-1962 .... DLB-20, 36, 100, 149

Aldis, Dorothy 1896-1966 .... DLB-22

Aldiss, Brian W. 1925- DLB-14

Aldrich, Thomas Bailey
1836-1907 .... DLB-42, 71, 74, 79

Alegría, Ciro 1909-1967 .... DLB-113

Alegría, Claribel 1924- DLB-145

Aleixandre, Vicente 1898-1984 .... DLB-108

Aleramo, Sibilla 1876-1960 .... DLB-114

Alexander, Charles 1868-1923 ..... DLB-91

Alexander, Charles Wesley
[publishing house] DLB-49

Alexander, James 1691-1756 .... DLB-24

Alexander, Lloyd 1924- DLB-52

Alexander, Sir William, Earl of Stirling
1577?-1640 .... DLB-121

Alexis, Willibald 1798-1871 .... DLB-133

Alfred, King 849-899 .... DLB-146

Alger, Horatio, Jr. 1832-1899 .... DLB-42

Algonquin Books of Chapel Hill DLB-46

Algren, Nelson
1909-1981 .... DLB-9; Y-81, 82

Allan, Andrew 1907-1974 .... DLB-88

Allan, Ted 1916- DLB-68

Allbeury, Ted 1917- DLB-87

Alldritt, Keith 1935- DLB-14

Allen, Ethan 1738-1789 .... DLB-31

Allen, Frederick Lewis 1890-1954 .. DLB-137

Allen, Gay Wilson
1903-1995 .... DLB-103; Y-95

Allen, George 1808-1876 .... DLB-59

Allen, George [publishing house] ... DLB-106

Allen, George, and Unwin
Limited DLB-112

Allen, Grant 1848-1899 .... DLB-70, 92

Allen, Henry W. 1912- Y-85

Allen, Hervey 1889-1949 .... DLB-9, 45

Allen, James 1739-1808 .... DLB-31

Allen, James Lane 1849-1925 .... DLB-71

Allen, Jay Presson 1922- DLB-26

Allen, John, and Company DLB-49

Allen, Samuel W. 1917- DLB-41

Allen, Woody 1935- DLB-44

Allende, Isabel 1942- DLB-145

Alline, Henry 1748-1784 .... DLB-99

Allingham, Margery 1904-1966 ...... DLB-77

Allingham, William 1824-1889 ...... DLB-35

Allison, W. L. [publishing house] DLB-49

The *Alliterative Morte Arthure* and
the *Stanzaic Morte Arthur*
circa 1350-1400 .... DLB-146

Allott, Kenneth 1912-1973 .... DLB-20

Allston, Washington 1779-1843 ...... DLB-1

Almon, John [publishing house] DLB-154

Alonzo, Dámaso 1898-1990 .... DLB-108

Alsop, George 1636-post 1673 .... DLB-24

Alsop, Richard 1761-1815 .... DLB-37

Altemus, Henry, and Company DLB-49

Altenberg, Peter 1885-1919 .... DLB-81

Altolaguirre, Manuel 1905-1959 .... DLB-108

Aluko, T. M. 1918- DLB-117

Alurista 1947- DLB-82

Alvarez, A. 1929- DLB-14, 40

Amadi, Elechi 1934- DLB-117

Amado, Jorge 1912- DLB-113

Ambler, Eric 1909- DLB-77

*America: or, a Poem on the Settlement of the
British Colonies* (1780?), by Timothy
Dwight DLB-37

American Conservatory Theatre DLB-7

American Fiction and the 1930s DLB-9

American Humor: A Historical Survey
East and Northeast
South and Southwest
Midwest
West DLB-11

The American Library in Paris Y-93

American News Company DLB-49

The American Poets' Corner: The First
Three Years (1983-1986) Y-86

American Proletarian Culture:
The 1930s DS-11

American Publishing Company DLB-49

American Stationers' Company DLB-49

American Sunday-School Union DLB-49

American Temperance Union DLB-49

American Tract Society DLB-49

The American Writers Congress
(9-12 October 1981) Y-81

The American Writers Congress: A Report
on Continuing Business Y-81

Ames, Fisher 1758-1808 .... DLB-37

Ames, Mary Clemmer 1831-1884 .... DLB-23

Amini, Johari M. 1935- DLB-41

Amis, Kingsley 1922-
.... DLB-15, 27, 100, 139

Amis, Martin 1949- DLB-14

Ammons, A. R. 1926- DLB-5, 165

Amory, Thomas 1691?-1788 .... DLB-39

Anaya, Rudolfo A. 1937- DLB-82

Ancrene Riwle circa 1200-1225 .... DLB-146

Andersch, Alfred 1914-1980 .... DLB-69

Anderson, Margaret 1886-1973 ... DLB-4, 91

Anderson, Maxwell 1888-1959 .... DLB-7

Anderson, Patrick 1915-1979 .... DLB-68

Anderson, Paul Y. 1893-1938 .... DLB-29

Anderson, Poul 1926- DLB-8

Anderson, Robert 1750-1830 .... DLB-142

Anderson, Robert 1917- DLB-7

Anderson, Sherwood
1876-1941 .... DLB-4, 9, 86; DS-1

Andreae, Johann Valentin
1586-1654 .... DLB-164

Andreas-Salomé, Lou 1861-1937 .... DLB-66

Andres, Stefan 1906-1970 .... DLB-69

Andreu, Blanca 1959- DLB-134

Andrewes, Lancelot
1555-1626 .... DLB-151, 172

Andrews, Charles M. 1863-1943 ..... DLB-17

Andrews, Miles Peter ?-1814 .... DLB-89

Andrian, Leopold von 1875-1951 .... DLB-81

Andrić, Ivo 1892-1975 .... DLB-147

Andrieux, Louis (see Aragon, Louis)

Andrus, Silas, and Son DLB-49

Angell, James Burrill 1829-1916 ...... DLB-64

Angell, Roger 1920- DLB-171

Angelou, Maya 1928- DLB-38

Anger, Jane flourished 1589 .... DLB-136

Angers, Félicité (see Conan, Laure)

Anglo-Norman Literature in the Development
of Middle English Literature DLB-146

The Anglo-Saxon Chronicle
circa 890-1154 .... DLB-146

The "Angry Young Men" DLB-15

Angus and Robertson (UK)
Limited DLB-112

Anhalt, Edward 1914- DLB-26

Anners, Henry F. [publishing house] ...DLB-49

Annolied between 1077 and 1081 .... DLB-148

Anselm of Canterbury 1033-1109 ... DLB-115

Anstey, F. 1856-1934 .... DLB-141

Anthony, Michael 1932- DLB-125

Anthony, Piers 1934- DLB-8

Anthony Burgess's *99 Novels*:
An Opinion Poll Y-84

Antin, David 1932- DLB-169

Antin, Mary 1881-1949 ....Y-84

Anton Ulrich, Duke of Brunswick-Lüneburg
1633-1714 ....DLB-168

Antschel, Paul (see Celan, Paul)

Anyidoho, Kofi 1947- DLB-157

Anzaldúa, Gloria 1942- DLB-122

Anzengruber, Ludwig 1839-1889 ...DLB-129

Apodaca, Rudy S. 1939- DLB-82

Apple, Max 1941- DLB-130

Appleton, D., and Company DLB-49

Appleton-Century-Crofts DLB-46

Applewhite, James 1935- DLB-105

Apple-wood Books DLB-46

Aquin, Hubert 1929-1977 ....DLB-53

Aquinas, Thomas 1224 or
1225-1274 ....DLB-115

Aragon, Louis 1897-1982 ....DLB-72

Arbor House Publishing
Company DLB-46

Arbuthnot, John 1667-1735 ....DLB-101

Arcadia House DLB-46

Arce, Julio G. (see Ulica, Jorge)

Archer, William 1856-1924 ....DLB-10

The Archpoet circa 1130?-? DLB-148

Archpriest Avvakum (Petrovich)
1620?-1682 ....DLB-150

Arden, John 1930- DLB-13

Arden of Faversham DLB-62

Ardis Publishers Y-89

Ardizzone, Edward 1900-1979 .....DLB-160

Arellano, Juan Estevan 1947- DLB-122

The Arena Publishing Company DLB-49

Arena Stage DLB-7

Arenas, Reinaldo 1943-1990 ......DLB-145

Arensberg, Ann 1937- Y-82

Arguedas, José María 1911-1969 ....DLB-113

Argueta, Manilio 1936- DLB-145

Arias, Ron 1941- DLB-82

Arland, Marcel 1899-1986 ....DLB-72

Arlen, Michael 1895-1956 ..DLB-36, 77, 162

Armah, Ayi Kwei 1939- DLB-117

Der arme Hartmann
?-after 1150 ....DLB-148

Armed Services Editions DLB-46

Armstrong, Richard 1903- DLB-160

Arndt, Ernst Moritz 1769-1860 .....DLB-90

Arnim, Achim von 1781-1831 ......DLB-90

Arnim, Bettina von 1785-1859 ......DLB-90

Arno Press DLB-46

Arnold, Edwin 1832-1904 ....DLB-35

Arnold, Matthew 1822-1888 .....DLB-32, 57

Arnold, Thomas 1795-1842 ....DLB-55

Arnold, Edward
[publishing house] DLB-112

Arnow, Harriette Simpson
1908-1986 ....DLB-6

Arp, Bill (see Smith, Charles Henry)

Arreola, Juan José 1918- DLB-113

Arrowsmith, J. W.
[publishing house] DLB-106

Arthur, Timothy Shay
1809-1885 ....DLB-3, 42, 79; DS-13

The Arthurian Tradition and Its European
Context DLB-138

Artmann, H. C. 1921- DLB-85

Arvin, Newton 1900-1963 ....DLB-103

As I See It, by Carolyn Cassady DLB-16

Asch, Nathan 1902-1964 ....DLB-4, 28

Ash, John 1948- DLB-40

Ashbery, John 1927- DLB-5, 165; Y-81

Ashendene Press DLB-112

Asher, Sandy 1942- Y-83

Ashton, Winifred (see Dane, Clemence)

Asimov, Isaac 1920-1992 ....DLB-8; Y-92

Askew, Anne circa 1521-1546 ......DLB-136

Asselin, Olivar 1874-1937 ....DLB-92

Asturias, Miguel Angel
1899-1974 ....DLB-113

Atheneum Publishers DLB-46

Atherton, Gertrude 1857-1948 ....DLB-9, 78

Athlone Press DLB-112

Atkins, Josiah circa 1755-1781 .....DLB-31

Atkins, Russell 1926- DLB-41

The Atlantic Monthly Press DLB-46

Attaway, William 1911-1986 ....DLB-76

Atwood, Margaret 1939- DLB-53

Aubert, Alvin 1930- DLB-41

Aubert de Gaspé, Phillipe-Ignace-François
1814-1841 ....DLB-99

Aubert de Gaspé, Phillipe-Joseph
1786-1871 ....DLB-99

Aubin, Napoléon 1812-1890 ....DLB-99

Aubin, Penelope 1685-circa 1731 ....DLB-39

Aubrey-Fletcher, Henry Lancelot
(see Wade, Henry)

Auchincloss, Louis 1917- DLB-2; Y-80

Auden, W. H. 1907-1973 ....DLB-10, 20

Audio Art in America: A Personal
Memoir Y-85

Auerbach, Berthold 1812-1882 .....DLB-133

Auernheimer, Raoul 1876-1948 .....DLB-81

Augustine 354-430 ....DLB-115

Austen, Jane 1775-1817 ....DLB-116

Austin, Alfred 1835-1913 ....DLB-35

Austin, Mary 1868-1934 ....DLB-9, 78

Austin, William 1778-1841 ....DLB-74

Author-Printers, 1476–1599 ....DLB-167

The Author's Apology for His Book
(1684), by John Bunyan DLB-39

An Author's Response, by
Ronald Sukenick Y-82

Authors and Newspapers
Association DLB-46

Authors' Publishing Company DLB-49

Avalon Books DLB-46

Avancini, Nicolaus 1611-1686 ......DLB-164

Avendaño, Fausto 1941- DLB-82

Averroës 1126-1198 ....DLB-115

Avery, Gillian 1926- DLB-161

Avicenna 980-1037 ....DLB-115

Avison, Margaret 1918- DLB-53

Avon Books DLB-46

Awdry, Wilbert Vere 1911- DLB-160

Awoonor, Kofi 1935- DLB-117

Ayckbourn, Alan 1939- DLB-13

Aymé, Marcel 1902-1967 ....DLB-72

Aytoun, Sir Robert 1570-1638 .....DLB-121

Aytoun, William Edmondstoune
1813-1865 ....DLB-32, 159

B

B. V. (see Thomson, James)

Babbitt, Irving 1865-1933 ....DLB-63

Cumulative Index

Babbitt, Natalie 1932- DLB-52

Babcock, John [publishing house] ... DLB-49

Baca, Jimmy Santiago 1952- DLB-122

Bache, Benjamin Franklin 1769-1798 .... DLB-43

Bachmann, Ingeborg 1926-1973 ..... DLB-85

Bacon, Delia 1811-1859 .... DLB-1

Bacon, Francis 1561-1626 .... DLB-151

Bacon, Roger circa 1214/1220-1292 .... DLB-115

Bacon, Sir Nicholas circa 1510-1579 .... DLB-132

Bacon, Thomas circa 1700-1768 .... DLB-31

Badger, Richard G., and Company DLB-49

Bage, Robert 1728-1801 .... DLB-39

Bagehot, Walter 1826-1877 .... DLB-55

Bagley, Desmond 1923-1983 .... DLB-87

Bagnold, Enid 1889-1981 ..... DLB-13, 160

Bagryana, Elisaveta 1893-1991 ..... DLB-147

Bahr, Hermann 1863-1934 ..... DLB-81, 118

Bailey, Alfred Goldsworthy 1905- DLB-68

Bailey, Francis [publishing house] ... DLB-49

Bailey, H. C. 1878-1961 .... DLB-77

Bailey, Jacob 1731-1808 .... DLB-99

Bailey, Paul 1937- DLB-14

Bailey, Philip James 1816-1902 ..... DLB-32

Baillargeon, Pierre 1916-1967 .... DLB-88

Baillie, Hugh 1890-1966 .... DLB-29

Baillie, Joanna 1762-1851 .... DLB-93

Bailyn, Bernard 1922- DLB-17

Bainbridge, Beryl 1933- DLB-14

Baird, Irene 1901-1981 .... DLB-68

Baker, Augustine 1575-1641 .... DLB-151

Baker, Carlos 1909-1987 .... DLB-103

Baker, David 1954- DLB-120

Baker, Herschel C. 1914-1990 ..... DLB-111

Baker, Houston A., Jr. 1943- DLB-67

Baker, Samuel White 1821-1893 .... DLB-166

Baker, Walter H., Company ("Baker's Plays") DLB-49

The Baker and Taylor Company DLB-49

Balaban, John 1943- DLB-120

Bald, Wambly 1902- DLB-4

Balde, Jacob 1604-1668 .... DLB-164

Balderston, John 1889-1954 .... DLB-26

Baldwin, James 1924-1987 .... DLB-2, 7, 33; Y-87

Baldwin, Joseph Glover 1815-1864 .... DLB-3, 11

Baldwin, Richard and Anne [publishing house] DLB-170

Baldwin, William circa 1515-1563 .... DLB-132

Bale, John 1495-1563 .... DLB-132

Balestrini, Nanni 1935- DLB-128

Ballantine Books DLB-46

Ballantyne, R. M. 1825-1894 .... DLB-163

Ballard, J. G. 1930- DLB-14

Ballerini, Luigi 1940- DLB-128

Ballou, Maturin Murray 1820-1895 .... DLB-79

Ballou, Robert O. [publishing house] DLB-46

Balzac, Honoré de 1799-1855 ...... DLB-119

Bambara, Toni Cade 1939- DLB-38

Bancroft, A. L., and Company DLB-49

Bancroft, George 1800-1891 .... DLB-1, 30, 59

Bancroft, Hubert Howe 1832-1918 .... DLB-47, 140

Bangs, John Kendrick 1862-1922 .... DLB-11, 79

Banim, John 1798-1842 ...DLB-116, 158, 159

Banim, Michael 1796-1874 ....DLB-158, 159

Banks, John circa 1653-1706 .... DLB-80

Banks, Russell 1940- DLB-130

Bannerman, Helen 1862-1946 ...... DLB-141

Bantam Books DLB-46

Banville, John 1945- DLB-14

Baraka, Amiri 1934- DLB-5, 7, 16, 38; DS-8

Barbauld, Anna Laetitia 1743-1825 ...... DLB-107, 109, 142, 158

Barbeau, Marius 1883-1969 .... DLB-92

Barber, John Warner 1798-1885 ..... DLB-30

Bàrberi Squarotti, Giorgio 1929- DLB-128

Barbey d'Aurevilly, Jules-Amédée 1808-1889 .... DLB-119

Barbour, John circa 1316-1395 ..... DLB-146

Barbour, Ralph Henry 1870-1944 .... DLB-22

Barbusse, Henri 1873-1935 .... DLB-65

Barclay, Alexander circa 1475-1552 .... DLB-132

Barclay, E. E., and Company DLB-49

Bardeen, C. W. [publishing house] DLB-49

Barham, Richard Harris 1788-1845 .... DLB-159

Baring, Maurice 1874-1945 .... DLB-34

Baring-Gould, Sabine 1834-1924 ....DLB-156

Barker, A. L. 1918- DLB-14, 139

Barker, George 1913-1991 ....DLB-20

Barker, Harley Granville 1877-1946 .... DLB-10

Barker, Howard 1946- DLB-13

Barker, James Nelson 1784-1858 ..... DLB-37

Barker, Jane 1652-1727 .... DLB-39, 131

Barker, Lady Mary Anne 1831-1911 .... DLB-166

Barker, William circa 1520-after 1576 .... DLB-132

Barker, Arthur, Limited DLB-112

Barkov, Ivan Semenovich 1732-1768 .... DLB-150

Barks, Coleman 1937- DLB-5

Barlach, Ernst 1870-1938 ...... DLB-56, 118

Barlow, Joel 1754-1812 ....DLB-37

Barnard, John 1681-1770 ....DLB-24

Barne, Kitty (Mary Catherine Barne) 1883-1957 .... DLB-160

Barnes, Barnabe 1571-1609 ....DLB-132

Barnes, Djuna 1892-1982 ...... DLB-4, 9, 45

Barnes, Julian 1946- Y-93

Barnes, Margaret Ayer 1886-1967 .....DLB-9

Barnes, Peter 1931- DLB-13

Barnes, William 1801-1886 ....DLB-32

Barnes, A. S., and Company DLB-49

Barnes and Noble Books DLB-46

Barnet, Miguel 1940- DLB-145

Barney, Natalie 1876-1972 ....DLB-4

Barnfield, Richard 1574-1627 ....DLB-172

Baron, Richard W., Publishing Company DLB-46

Barr, Robert 1850-1912 .... DLB-70, 92

Barral, Carlos 1928-1989 ....DLB-134

Barrax, Gerald William 1933- DLB-41, 120

Barrès, Maurice 1862-1923 ....DLB-123

Barrett, Eaton Stannard 1786-1820 ...DLB-116

Barrie, J. M. 1860-1937 ....DLB-10, 141, 156

Barrie and Jenkins ...DLB-112

Barrio, Raymond 1921- ...DLB-82

Barrios, Gregg 1945- ...DLB-122

Barry, Philip 1896-1949 ...DLB-7

Barry, Robertine (see Françoise)

Barse and Hopkins ...DLB-46

Barstow, Stan 1928- ...DLB-14, 139

Barth, John 1930- ...DLB-2

Barthelme, Donald 1931-1989 ...DLB-2; Y-80, 89

Barthelme, Frederick 1943- ...Y-85

Bartholomew, Frank 1898-1985 ...DLB-127

Bartlett, John 1820-1905 ...DLB-1

Bartol, Cyrus Augustus 1813-1900 ...DLB-1

Barton, Bernard 1784-1849 ...DLB-96

Barton, Thomas Pennant 1803-1869 ...DLB-140

Bartram, John 1699-1777 ...DLB-31

Bartram, William 1739-1823 ...DLB-37

Basic Books ...DLB-46

Basille, Theodore (see Becon, Thomas)

Bass, T. J. 1932- ...Y-81

Bassani, Giorgio 1916- ...DLB-128

Basse, William circa 1583-1653 ...DLB-121

Bassett, John Spencer 1867-1928 ...DLB-17

Bassler, Thomas Joseph (see Bass, T. J.)

Bate, Walter Jackson 1918- ...DLB-67, 103

Bateman, Christopher [publishing house] ...DLB-170

Bateman, Stephen circa 1510-1584 ...DLB-136

Bates, H. E. 1905-1974 ...DLB-162

Bates, Katharine Lee 1859-1929 ...DLB-71

Batsford, B. T. [publishing house] ...DLB-106

Battiscombe, Georgina 1905- ...DLB-155

The Battle of Maldon circa 1000 ...DLB-146

Bauer, Bruno 1809-1882 ...DLB-133

Bauer, Wolfgang 1941- ...DLB-124

Baum, L. Frank 1856-1919 ...DLB-22

Baum, Vicki 1888-1960 ...DLB-85

Baumbach, Jonathan 1933- ...Y-80

Bausch, Richard 1945- ...DLB-130

Bawden, Nina 1925- ...DLB-14, 161

Bax, Clifford 1886-1962 ...DLB-10, 100

Baxter, Charles 1947- ...DLB-130

Bayer, Eleanor (see Perry, Eleanor)

Bayer, Konrad 1932-1964 ...DLB-85

Baynes, Pauline 1922- ...DLB-160

Bazin, Hervé 1911- ...DLB-83

Beach, Sylvia 1887-1962 ...DLB-4

Beacon Press ...DLB-49

Beadle and Adams ...DLB-49

Beagle, Peter S. 1939- ...Y-80

Beal, M. F. 1937- ...Y-81

Beale, Howard K. 1899-1959 ...DLB-17

Beard, Charles A. 1874-1948 ...DLB-17

A Beat Chronology: The First Twenty-five Years, 1944-1969 ...DLB-16

Beattie, Ann 1947- ...Y-82

Beattie, James 1735-1803 ...DLB-109

Beauchemin, Nérée 1850-1931 ...DLB-92

Beauchemin, Yves 1941- ...DLB-60

Beaugrand, Honoré 1848-1906 ...DLB-99

Beaulieu, Victor-Lévy 1945- ...DLB-53

Beaumont, Francis circa 1584-1616 and Fletcher, John 1579-1625 ...DLB-58

Beaumont, Sir John 1583?-1627 ...DLB-121

Beaumont, Joseph 1616–1699 ...DLB-126

Beauvoir, Simone de 1908-1986 ...DLB-72; Y-86

Becher, Ulrich 1910- ...DLB-69

Becker, Carl 1873-1945 ...DLB-17

Becker, Jurek 1937- ...DLB-75

Becker, Jurgen 1932- ...DLB-75

Beckett, Samuel 1906-1989 ...DLB-13, 15; Y-90

Beckford, William 1760-1844 ...DLB-39

Beckham, Barry 1944- ...DLB-33

Becon, Thomas circa 1512-1567 ...DLB-136

Beddoes, Thomas 1760-1808 ...DLB-158

Beddoes, Thomas Lovell 1803-1849 ...DLB-96

Bede circa 673-735 ...DLB-146

Beecher, Catharine Esther 1800-1878 ...DLB-1

Beecher, Henry Ward 1813-1887 ...DLB-3, 43

Beer, George L. 1872-1920 ...DLB-47

Beer, Johann 1655-1700 ...DLB-168

Beer, Patricia 1919- ...DLB-40

Beerbohm, Max 1872-1956 ...DLB-34, 100

Beer-Hofmann, Richard 1866-1945 ...DLB-81

Beers, Henry A. 1847-1926 ...DLB-71

Beeton, S. O. [publishing house] ...DLB-106

Bégon, Elisabeth 1696-1755 ...DLB-99

Behan, Brendan 1923-1964 ...DLB-13

Behn, Aphra 1640?-1689 ...DLB-39, 80, 131

Behn, Harry 1898-1973 ...DLB-61

Behrman, S. N. 1893-1973 ...DLB-7, 44

Belaney, Archibald Stansfeld (see Grey Owl)

Belasco, David 1853-1931 ...DLB-7

Belford, Clarke and Company ...DLB-49

Belitt, Ben 1911- ...DLB-5

Belknap, Jeremy 1744-1798 ...DLB-30, 37

Bell, Clive 1881-1964 ...DS-10

Bell, James Madison 1826-1902 ...DLB-50

Bell, Marvin 1937- ...DLB-5

Bell, Millicent 1919- ...DLB-111

Bell, Quentin 1910- ...DLB-155

Bell, Vanessa 1879-1961 ...DS-10

Bell, George, and Sons ...DLB-106

Bell, Robert [publishing house] ...DLB-49

Bellamy, Edward 1850-1898 ...DLB-12

Bellamy, John [publishing house] ...DLB-170

Bellamy, Joseph 1719-1790 ...DLB-31

Bellezza, Dario 1944- ...DLB-128

La Belle Assemblée 1806-1837 ...DLB-110

Belloc, Hilaire 1870-1953 ...DLB-19, 100, 141

Bellow, Saul 1915- ...DLB-2, 28; Y-82; DS-3

Belmont Productions ...DLB-46

Bemelmans, Ludwig 1898-1962 ...DLB-22

Bemis, Samuel Flagg 1891-1973 ...DLB-17

Bemrose, William [publishing house] ...DLB-106

Benchley, Robert 1889-1945 ...DLB-11

Benedetti, Mario 1920- ...DLB-113

Benedictus, David 1938- ...DLB-14

Benedikt, Michael 1935- ...DLB-5

Benét, Stephen Vincent 1898-1943 ...DLB-4, 48, 102

Benét, William Rose 1886-1950 ...DLB-45

Benford, Gregory 1941- ...Y-82

Benjamin, Park 1809-1864 .... DLB-3, 59, 73

Benlowes, Edward 1602-1676 ...... DLB-126

Benn, Gottfried 1886-1956 .... DLB-56

Benn Brothers Limited DLB-106

Bennett, Arnold
  1867-1931 .... DLB-10, 34, 98, 135

Bennett, Charles 1899- DLB-44

Bennett, Gwendolyn 1902- DLB-51

Bennett, Hal 1930- DLB-33

Bennett, James Gordon 1795-1872 ... DLB-43

Bennett, James Gordon, Jr.
  1841-1918 .... DLB-23

Bennett, John 1865-1956 .... DLB-42

Bennett, Louise 1919- DLB-117

Benoit, Jacques 1941- DLB-60

Benson, A. C. 1862-1925 .... DLB-98

Benson, E. F. 1867-1940 ...... DLB-135, 153

Benson, Jackson J. 1930- DLB-111

Benson, Robert Hugh 1871-1914 ... DLB-153

Benson, Stella 1892-1933 ...... DLB-36, 162

Bentham, Jeremy 1748-1832 ... DLB-107, 158

Bentley, E. C. 1875-1956 .... DLB-70

Bentley, Richard
  [publishing house] DLB-106

Benton, Robert 1932- and Newman,
  David 1937- DLB-44

Benziger Brothers DLB-49

Beowulf circa 900-1000
  or 790-825 .... DLB-146

Beresford, Anne 1929- DLB-40

Beresford, John Davys
  1873-1947 .... DLB-162

Beresford-Howe, Constance
  1922- DLB-88

Berford, R. G., Company DLB-49

Berg, Stephen 1934- DLB-5

Bergengruen, Werner 1892-1964 .... DLB-56

Berger, John 1926- DLB-14

Berger, Meyer 1898-1959 .... DLB-29

Berger, Thomas 1924- DLB-2; Y-80

Berkeley, Anthony 1893-1971 ...... DLB-77

Berkeley, George 1685-1753 .... DLB-31, 101

The Berkley Publishing
  Corporation DLB-46

Berlin, Lucia 1936- DLB-130

Bernal, Vicente J. 1888-1915 ...... DLB-82

Bernanos, Georges 1888-1948 ...... DLB-72

Bernard, Harry 1898-1979 .... DLB-92

Bernard, John 1756-1828 .... DLB-37

Bernard of Chartres
  circa 1060-1124? DLB-115

Bernhard, Thomas
  1931-1989 ....DLB-85, 124

Bernstein, Charles 1950- DLB-169

Berriault, Gina 1926- DLB-130

Berrigan, Daniel 1921- DLB-5

Berrigan, Ted 1934-1983 .... DLB-5, 169

Berry, Wendell 1934- DLB-5, 6

Berryman, John 1914-1972 .... DLB-48

Bersianik, Louky 1930- DLB-60

Berthelet, Thomas
  [publishing house] DLB-170

Bertolucci, Attilio 1911- DLB-128

Berton, Pierre 1920- DLB-68

Besant, Sir Walter 1836-1901 ..... DLB-135

Bessette, Gerard 1920- DLB-53

Bessie, Alvah 1904-1985 .... DLB-26

Bester, Alfred 1913-1987 .... DLB-8

The Bestseller Lists: An Assessment Y-84

Betjeman, John 1906-1984 ..... DLB-20; Y-84

Betocchi, Carlo 1899-1986 .... DLB-128

Bettarini, Mariella 1942- DLB-128

Betts, Doris 1932- Y-82

Beveridge, Albert J. 1862-1927 ...... DLB-17

Beverley, Robert
  circa 1673-1722 .... DLB-24, 30

Beyle, Marie-Henri (see Stendhal)

Bianco, Margery Williams
  1881-1944 .... DLB-160

Bibaud, Adèle 1854-1941 .... DLB-92

Bibaud, Michel 1782-1857 .... DLB-99

Bibliographical and Textual Scholarship
  Since World War II Y-89

The Bicentennial of James Fenimore
  Cooper: An International
  Celebration Y-89

Bichsel, Peter 1935- DLB-75

Bickerstaff, Isaac John
  1733-circa 1808 .... DLB-89

Biddle, Drexel [publishing house] DLB-49

Bidermann, Jacob
  1577 or 1578-1639 .... DLB-164

Bidwell, Walter Hilliard
  1798-1881 .... DLB-79

Bienek, Horst 1930- DLB-75

Bierbaum, Otto Julius 1865-1910 .....DLB-66

Bierce, Ambrose
  1842-1914? DLB-11, 12, 23, 71, 74

Bigelow, William F. 1879-1966 ......DLB-91

Biggle, Lloyd, Jr. 1923- DLB-8

Biglow, Hosea (see Lowell, James Russell)

Bigongiari, Piero 1914- DLB-128

Billinger, Richard 1890-1965 ....DLB-124

Billings, John Shaw 1898-1975 ......DLB-137

Billings, Josh (see Shaw, Henry Wheeler)

Binding, Rudolf G. 1867-1938 ....DLB-66

Bingham, Caleb 1757-1817 ....DLB-42

Bingham, George Barry
  1906-1988 ....DLB-127

Bingley, William
  [publishing house] DLB-154

Binyon, Laurence 1869-1943 ....DLB-19

Biographia Brittanica DLB-142

Biographical Documents I Y-84

Biographical Documents II Y-85

Bioren, John [publishing house] DLB-49

Bioy Casares, Adolfo 1914- DLB-113

Bird, Isabella Lucy 1831-1904 ......DLB-166

Bird, William 1888-1963 ....DLB-4

Birken, Sigmund von 1626-1681 ....DLB-164

Birney, Earle 1904- DLB-88

Birrell, Augustine 1850-1933 ....DLB-98

Bisher, Furman 1918- DLB-171

Bishop, Elizabeth 1911-1979 ..... DLB-5, 169

Bishop, John Peale 1892-1944 .. DLB-4, 9, 45

Bismarck, Otto von 1815-1898 ......DLB-129

Bisset, Robert 1759-1805 ....DLB-142

Bissett, Bill 1939- DLB-53

Bitzius, Albert (see Gotthelf, Jeremias)

Black, David (D. M.) 1941- DLB-40

Black, Winifred 1863-1936 ....DLB-25

Black, Walter J.
  [publishing house] DLB-46

The Black Aesthetic: Background DS-8

The Black Arts Movement, by
  Larry Neal DLB-38

Black Theaters and Theater Organizations in
  America, 1961-1982:
  A Research List DLB-38

Black Theatre: A Forum
  [excerpts] DLB-38

Blackamore, Arthur 1679-? DLB-24, 39

Blackburn, Alexander L. 1929- Y-85

Blackburn, Paul 1926-1971 ....DLB-16; Y-81

Blackburn, Thomas 1916-1977 ......DLB-27

Blackmore, R. D. 1825-1900 ....DLB-18

Blackmore, Sir Richard
 1654-1729 ....DLB-131

Blackmur, R. P. 1904-1965 ....DLB-63

Blackwell, Basil, Publisher DLB-106

Blackwood, Algernon Henry
 1869-1951 ....DLB-153, 156

Blackwood, Caroline 1931- DLB-14

Blackwood, William, and
 Sons, Ltd. DLB-154

Blackwood's Edinburgh Magazine
 1817-1980 ....DLB-110

Blair, Eric Arthur (see Orwell, George)

Blair, Francis Preston 1791-1876 .....DLB-43

Blair, James circa 1655-1743 ....DLB-24

Blair, John Durburrow 1759-1823 ....DLB-37

Blais, Marie-Claire 1939- DLB-53

Blaise, Clark 1940- DLB-53

Blake, Nicholas 1904-1972 ....DLB-77
 (see Day Lewis, C.)

Blake, William
 1757-1827 .... DLB-93, 154, 163

The Blakiston Company DLB-49

Blanchot, Maurice 1907- DLB-72

Blanckenburg, Christian Friedrich von
 1744-1796 ....DLB-94

Blaser, Robin 1925- DLB-165

Bledsoe, Albert Taylor
 1809-1877 ....DLB-3, 79

Blelock and Company DLB-49

Blennerhassett, Margaret Agnew
 1773-1842 ....DLB-99

Bles, Geoffrey
 [publishing house] DLB-112

Blessington, Marguerite, Countess of
 1789-1849 ....DLB-166

The Blickling Homilies
 circa 971 ....DLB-146

Blish, James 1921-1975 ....DLB-8

Bliss, E., and E. White
 [publishing house] DLB-49

Bliven, Bruce 1889-1977 ....DLB-137

Bloch, Robert 1917-1994 ....DLB-44

Block, Rudolph (see Lessing, Bruno)

Blondal, Patricia 1926-1959 ....DLB-88

Bloom, Harold 1930- DLB-67

Bloomer, Amelia 1818-1894 .... DLB-79

Bloomfield, Robert 1766-1823 ...... DLB-93

Bloomsbury Group DS-10

Blotner, Joseph 1923- DLB-111

Bloy, Léon 1846-1917 .... DLB-123

Blume, Judy 1938- DLB-52

Blunck, Hans Friedrich 1888-1961 ... DLB-66

Blunden, Edmund
 1896-1974 .... DLB-20, 100, 155

Blunt, Wilfrid Scawen 1840-1922 .... DLB-19

Bly, Nellie (see Cochrane, Elizabeth)

Bly, Robert 1926- DLB-5

Blyton, Enid 1897-1968 .... DLB-160

Boaden, James 1762-1839 .... DLB-89

Boas, Frederick S. 1862-1957 ..... DLB-149

The Bobbs-Merrill Archive at the
 Lilly Library, Indiana University ... Y-90

The Bobbs-Merrill Company DLB-46

Bobrov, Semen Sergeevich
 1763?-1810 .... DLB-150

Bobrowski, Johannes 1917-1965 ..... DLB-75

Bodenheim, Maxwell 1892-1954 .. DLB-9, 45

Bodenstedt, Friedrich von
 1819-1892 .... DLB-129

Bodini, Vittorio 1914-1970 .... DLB-128

Bodkin, M. McDonnell
 1850-1933 .... DLB-70

Bodley Head DLB-112

Bodmer, Johann Jakob 1698-1783 ... DLB-97

Bodmershof, Imma von 1895-1982 .. DLB-85

Bodsworth, Fred 1918- DLB-68

Boehm, Sydney 1908- DLB-44

Boer, Charles 1939- DLB-5

Boethius circa 480-circa 524 .... DLB-115

Boethius of Dacia circa 1240-? DLB-115

Bogan, Louise 1897-1970 ...... DLB-45, 169

Bogarde, Dirk 1921- DLB-14

Bogdanovich, Ippolit Fedorovich
 circa 1743-1803 .... DLB-150

Bogue, David [publishing house] ... DLB-106

Böhme, Jakob 1575-1624 .... DLB-164

Bohn, H. G. [publishing house] DLB-106

Bohse, August 1661-1742 .... DLB-168

Boie, Heinrich Christian
 1744-1806 .... DLB-94

Bok, Edward W. 1863-1930 .... DLB-91

Boland, Eavan 1944- DLB-40

Bolingbroke, Henry St. John, Viscount
 1678-1751 ....DLB-101

Böll, Heinrich 1917-1985 ......Y-85, DLB-69

Bolling, Robert 1738-1775 ....DLB-31

Bolotov, Andrei Timofeevich
 1738-1833 ....DLB-150

Bolt, Carol 1941- DLB-60

Bolt, Robert 1924- DLB-13

Bolton, Herbert E. 1870-1953 ....DLB-17

Bonaventura DLB-90

Bonaventure circa 1217-1274 .....DLB-115

Bond, Edward 1934- DLB-13

Bond, Michael 1926- DLB-161

Boni, Albert and Charles
 [publishing house] DLB-46

Boni and Liveright DLB-46

Robert Bonner's Sons DLB-49

Bontemps, Arna 1902-1973 ......DLB-48, 51

The Book League of America DLB-46

Book Reviewing in America: I Y-87

Book Reviewing in America: II Y-88

Book Reviewing in America: III Y-89

Book Reviewing in America: IV Y-90

Book Reviewing in America: V Y-91

Book Reviewing in America: VI Y-92

Book Reviewing in America: VII Y-93

Book Reviewing in America: VIII Y-94

Book Reviewing in America and the
 Literary Scene Y-95

Book Supply Company DLB-49

The Book Trade History Group Y-93

The Booker Prize
 Address by Anthony Thwaite,
 Chairman of the Booker Prize Judges
 Comments from Former Booker
 Prize Winners Y-86

Boorde, Andrew circa 1490-1549 ...DLB-136

Boorstin, Daniel J. 1914- DLB-17

Booth, Mary L. 1831-1889 ....DLB-79

Booth, Philip 1925- Y-82

Booth, Wayne C. 1921- DLB-67

Borchardt, Rudolf 1877-1945 ....DLB-66

Borchert, Wolfgang
 1921-1947 ....DLB-69, 124

Borel, Pétrus 1809-1859 ....DLB-119

Borges, Jorge Luis
 1899-1986 ....DLB-113; Y-86

Börne, Ludwig 1786-1837 ....DLB-90

Cumulative Index

Borrow, George
  1803-1881 ....DLB-21, 55, 166

Bosch, Juan 1909- DLB-145

Bosco, Henri 1888-1976 ....DLB-72

Bosco, Monique 1927- DLB-53

Boston, Lucy M. 1892-1990 ....DLB-161

Boswell, James 1740-1795 .....DLB-104, 142

Botev, Khristo 1847-1876 ....DLB-147

Botta, Anne C. Lynch 1815-1891 ......DLB-3

Bottomley, Gordon 1874-1948 ......DLB-10

Bottoms, David 1949- DLB-120; Y-83

Bottrall, Ronald 1906- DLB-20

Boucher, Anthony 1911-1968 ....DLB-8

Boucher, Jonathan 1738-1804 ....DLB-31

Boucher de Boucherville, George
  1814-1894 .... DLB-99

Boudreau, Daniel (see Coste, Donat)

Bourassa, Napoléon 1827-1916 .....DLB-99

Bourget, Paul 1852-1935 ....DLB-123

Bourinot, John George 1837-1902 ...DLB-99

Bourjaily, Vance 1922- DLB-2, 143

Bourne, Edward Gaylord
  1860-1908 .... DLB-47

Bourne, Randolph 1886-1918 ....DLB-63

Bousoño, Carlos 1923- DLB-108

Bousquet, Joë 1897-1950 ....DLB-72

Bova, Ben 1932- Y-81

Bovard, Oliver K. 1872-1945 ....DLB-25

Bove, Emmanuel 1898-1945 ....DLB-72

Bowen, Elizabeth 1899-1973 ....DLB-15, 162

Bowen, Francis 1811-1890 .... DLB-1, 59

Bowen, John 1924- DLB-13

Bowen, Marjorie 1886-1952 ....DLB-153

Bowen-Merrill Company DLB-49

Bowering, George 1935- DLB-53

Bowers, Claude G. 1878-1958 ......DLB-17

Bowers, Edgar 1924- DLB-5

Bowers, Fredson Thayer
  1905-1991 .... DLB-140; Y-91

Bowles, Paul 1910- DLB-5, 6

Bowles, Samuel III 1826-1878 ......DLB-43

Bowles, William Lisles 1762-1850 ... DLB-93

Bowman, Louise Morey
  1882-1944 .... DLB-68

Boyd, James 1888-1944 ....DLB-9

Boyd, John 1919- DLB-8

Boyd, Thomas 1898-1935 ....DLB-9

Boyesen, Hjalmar Hjorth
  1848-1895 .... DLB-12, 71; DS-13

Boyle, Kay
  1902-1992 .... DLB-4, 9, 48, 86; Y-93

Boyle, Roger, Earl of Orrery
  1621-1679 .... DLB-80

Boyle, T. Coraghessan 1948- Y-86

Brackenbury, Alison 1953- DLB-40

Brackenridge, Hugh Henry
  1748-1816 ....DLB-11, 37

Brackett, Charles 1892-1969 ....DLB-26

Brackett, Leigh 1915-1978 ....DLB-8, 26

Bradburn, John
  [publishing house] DLB-49

Bradbury, Malcolm 1932- DLB-14

Bradbury, Ray 1920- DLB-2, 8

Bradbury and Evans DLB-106

Braddon, Mary Elizabeth
  1835-1915 ....DLB-18, 70, 156

Bradford, Andrew 1686-1742 ....DLB-43, 73

Bradford, Gamaliel 1863-1932 ......DLB-17

Bradford, John 1749-1830 ....DLB-43

Bradford, Roark 1896-1948 ....DLB-86

Bradford, William 1590-1657 ....DLB-24, 30

Bradford, William III
  1719-1791 ....DLB-43, 73

Bradlaugh, Charles 1833-1891 ......DLB-57

Bradley, David 1950- DLB-33

Bradley, Marion Zimmer 1930- DLB-8

Bradley, William Aspenwall
  1878-1939 .... DLB-4

Bradley, Ira, and Company DLB-49

Bradley, J. W., and Company DLB-49

Bradstreet, Anne
  1612 or 1613-1672 .... DLB-24

Bradwardine, Thomas circa
  1295-1349 .... DLB-115

Brady, Frank 1924-1986 ....DLB-111

Brady, Frederic A.
  [publishing house] DLB-49

Bragg, Melvyn 1939- DLB-14

Brainard, Charles H.
  [publishing house] DLB-49

Braine, John 1922-1986 ....DLB-15; Y-86

Braithwait, Richard 1588-1673 .....DLB-151

Braithwaite, William Stanley
  1878-1962 ....DLB-50, 54

Braker, Ulrich 1735-1798 ....DLB-94

Bramah, Ernest 1868-1942 ....DLB-70

Branagan, Thomas 1774-1843 ....DLB-37

Branch, William Blackwell
  1927- DLB-76

Branden Press DLB-46

Brassey, Lady Annie (Allnutt)
  1839-1887 ....DLB-166

Brathwaite, Edward Kamau
  1930- DLB-125

Brault, Jacques 1933- DLB-53

Braun, Volker 1939- DLB-75

Brautigan, Richard
  1935-1984 .... DLB-2, 5; Y-80, 84

Braxton, Joanne M. 1950- DLB-41

Bray, Anne Eliza 1790-1883 ....DLB-116

Bray, Thomas 1656-1730 ....DLB-24

Braziller, George
  [publishing house] DLB-46

The Bread Loaf Writers'
  Conference 1983 .... Y-84

The Break-Up of the Novel (1922),
  by John Middleton Murry DLB-36

Breasted, James Henry 1865-1935 ....DLB-47

Brecht, Bertolt 1898-1956 ...... DLB-56, 124

Bredel, Willi 1901-1964 ....DLB-56

Breitinger, Johann Jakob
  1701-1776 ....DLB-97

Bremser, Bonnie 1939- DLB-16

Bremser, Ray 1934- DLB-16

Brentano, Bernard von
  1901-1964 ....DLB-56

Brentano, Clemens 1778-1842 ....DLB-90

Brentano's DLB-49

Brenton, Howard 1942- DLB-13

Breton, André 1896-1966 ....DLB-65

Breton, Nicholas
  circa 1555-circa 1626 ....DLB-136

The Breton Lays
  1300-early fifteenth century DLB-146

Brewer, Warren and Putnam DLB-46

Brewster, Elizabeth 1922- DLB-60

Bridgers, Sue Ellen 1942- DLB-52

Bridges, Robert 1844-1930 ...... DLB-19, 98

Bridie, James 1888-1951 ....DLB-10

Briggs, Charles Frederick
  1804-1877 ....DLB-3

Brighouse, Harold 1882-1958 ....DLB-10

Bright, Mary Chavelita Dunne
  (see Egerton, George)

Brimmer, B. J., Company DLB-46

Brines, Francisco 1932- DLB-134

Brinley, George, Jr. 1817-1875 .....DLB-140

Brinnin, John Malcolm 1916- DLB-48

Brisbane, Albert 1809-1890 ....DLB-3

Brisbane, Arthur 1864-1936 ....DLB-25

British Academy DLB-112

The British Library and the Regular
  Readers' Group Y-91

The British Critic 1793-1843 ....DLB-110

*The British Review and London
  Critical Journal* 1811-1825 ....DLB-110

Brito, Aristeo 1942- DLB-122

Broadway Publishing Company DLB-46

Broch, Hermann 1886-1951 .....DLB-85, 124

Brochu, André 1942- DLB-53

Brock, Edwin 1927- DLB-40

Brockes, Barthold Heinrich
  1680-1747 ....DLB-168

Brod, Max 1884-1968 ....DLB-81

Brodber, Erna 1940- DLB-157

Brodhead, John R. 1814-1873 ....DLB-30

Brodkey, Harold 1930- DLB-130

Broeg, Bob 1918- DLB-171

Brome, Richard circa 1590-1652 .....DLB-58

Brome, Vincent 1910- DLB-155

Bromfield, Louis 1896-1956 .... DLB-4, 9, 86

Broner, E. M. 1930- DLB-28

Bronk, William 1918- DLB-165

Bronnen, Arnolt 1895-1959 ....DLB-124

Brontë, Anne 1820-1849 ....DLB-21

Brontë, Charlotte 1816-1855 ....DLB-21, 159

Brontë, Emily 1818-1848 ....DLB-21, 32

Brooke, Frances 1724-1789 ......DLB-39, 99

Brooke, Henry 1703?-1783 ....DLB-39

Brooke, L. Leslie 1862-1940 ....DLB-141

Brooke, Rupert 1887-1915 ....DLB-19

Brooker, Bertram 1888-1955 ....DLB-88

Brooke-Rose, Christine 1926- DLB-14

Brookner, Anita 1928- Y-87

Brooks, Charles Timothy
  1813-1883 ....DLB-1

Brooks, Cleanth 1906-1994 ....DLB-63; Y-94

Brooks, Gwendolyn
  1917- DLB-5, 76, 165

Brooks, Jeremy 1926- DLB-14

Brooks, Mel 1926- DLB-26

Brooks, Noah 1830-1903 ..... DLB-42; DS-13

Brooks, Richard 1912-1992 .... DLB-44

Brooks, Van Wyck
  1886-1963 .... DLB-45, 63, 103

Brophy, Brigid 1929- DLB-14

Brossard, Chandler 1922-1993 ...... DLB-16

Brossard, Nicole 1943- DLB-53

Broster, Dorothy Kathleen
  1877-1950 .... DLB-160

Brother Antoninus (see Everson, William)

Brougham and Vaux, Henry Peter
  Brougham, Baron
  1778-1868 .... DLB-110, 158

Brougham, John 1810-1880 .... DLB-11

Broughton, James 1913- DLB-5

Broughton, Rhoda 1840-1920 .... DLB-18

Broun, Heywood 1888-1939 .... DLB-29, 171

Brown, Alice 1856-1948 .... DLB-78

Brown, Bob 1886-1959 .... DLB-4, 45

Brown, Cecil 1943- DLB-33

Brown, Charles Brockden
  1771-1810 .... DLB-37, 59, 73

Brown, Christy 1932-1981 .... DLB-14

Brown, Dee 1908- Y-80

Brown, Frank London 1927-1962 ... DLB-76

Brown, Fredric 1906-1972 .... DLB-8

Brown, George Mackay
  1921- DLB-14, 27, 139

Brown, Harry 1917-1986 .... DLB-26

Brown, Marcia 1918- DLB-61

Brown, Margaret Wise
  1910-1952 .... DLB-22

Brown, Morna Doris (see Ferrars, Elizabeth)

Brown, Oliver Madox
  1855-1874 .... DLB-21

Brown, Sterling
  1901-1989 .... DLB-48, 51, 63

Brown, T. E. 1830-1897 .... DLB-35

Brown, William Hill 1765-1793 ..... DLB-37

Brown, William Wells
  1814-1884 .... DLB-3, 50

Browne, Charles Farrar
  1834-1867 .... DLB-11

Browne, Francis Fisher
  1843-1913 .... DLB-79

Browne, Michael Dennis
  1940- DLB-40

Browne, Sir Thomas 1605-1682 .... DLB-151

Browne, William, of Tavistock
  1590-1645 .... DLB-121

Browne, Wynyard 1911-1964 .... DLB-13

Browne and Nolan DLB-106

Brownell, W. C. 1851-1928 ....DLB-71

Browning, Elizabeth Barrett
  1806-1861 .... DLB-32

Browning, Robert
  1812-1889 ....DLB-32, 163

Brownjohn, Allan 1931- DLB-40

Brownson, Orestes Augustus
  1803-1876 ....DLB-1, 59, 73

Bruccoli, Matthew J. 1931- DLB-103

Bruce, Charles 1906-1971 ....DLB-68

Bruce, Leo 1903-1979 ....DLB-77

Bruce, Philip Alexander
  1856-1933 .... DLB-47

Bruce Humphries
  [publishing house] DLB-46

Bruce-Novoa, Juan 1944- DLB-82

Bruckman, Clyde 1894-1955 ....DLB-26

Bruckner, Ferdinand 1891-1958 ....DLB-118

Brundage, John Herbert (see Herbert, John)

Brutus, Dennis 1924- DLB-117

Bryant, Arthur 1899-1985 ....DLB-149

Bryant, William Cullen
  1794-1878 ....DLB-3, 43, 59

Bryce Echenique, Alfredo
  1939- DLB-145

Bryce, James 1838-1922 ....DLB-166

Brydges, Sir Samuel Egerton
  1762-1837 .... DLB-107

Bryskett, Lodowick 1546?-1612 ....DLB-167

Buchan, John 1875-1940 ... DLB-34, 70, 156

Buchanan, George 1506-1582 ......DLB-132

Buchanan, Robert 1841-1901 ....DLB-18, 35

Buchman, Sidney 1902-1975 ....DLB-26

Buchner, Augustus 1591-1661 ......DLB-164

Büchner, Georg 1813-1837 ....DLB-133

Bucholtz, Andreas Heinrich
  1607-1671 .... DLB-168

Buck, Pearl S. 1892-1973 ....DLB-9, 102

Bucke, Charles 1781-1846 ....DLB-110

Bucke, Richard Maurice
  1837-1902 .... DLB-99

Buckingham, Joseph Tinker 1779-1861 and
  Buckingham, Edwin
  1810-1833 .... DLB-73

Buckler, Ernest 1908-1984 ....DLB-68

Buckley, William F., Jr. 1925- DLB-137; Y-80

Buckminster, Joseph Stevens 1784-1812 .... DLB-37

Buckner, Robert 1906- DLB-26

Budd, Thomas ?-1698 .... DLB-24

Budrys, A. J. 1931- DLB-8

Buechner, Frederick 1926- Y-80

Buell, John 1927- DLB-53

Buffum, Job [publishing house] DLB-49

Bugnet, Georges 1879-1981 .... DLB-92

Buies, Arthur 1840-1901 .... DLB-99

Building the New British Library at St Pancras Y-94

Bukowski, Charles 1920-1994 .... DLB-5, 130, 169

Bulger, Bozeman 1877-1932 .... DLB-171

Bullein, William between 1520 and 1530-1576 ... DLB-167

Bullins, Ed 1935- DLB-7, 38

Bulwer-Lytton, Edward (also Edward Bulwer) 1803-1873 .... DLB-21

Bumpus, Jerry 1937- Y-81

Bunce and Brother DLB-49

Bunner, H. C. 1855-1896 .... DLB-78, 79

Bunting, Basil 1900-1985 .... DLB-20

Bunyan, John 1628-1688 .... DLB-39

Burch, Robert 1925- DLB-52

Burciaga, José Antonio 1940- DLB-82

Bürger, Gottfried August 1747-1794 .... DLB-94

Burgess, Anthony 1917-1993 .... DLB-14

Burgess, Gelett 1866-1951 .... DLB-11

Burgess, John W. 1844-1931 .... DLB-47

Burgess, Thornton W. 1874-1965 .... DLB-22

Burgess, Stringer and Company DLB-49

Burick, Si 1909-1986 .... DLB-171

Burk, John Daly circa 1772-1808 .... DLB-37

Burke, Edmund 1729?-1797 .... DLB-104

Burke, Kenneth 1897-1993 ...... DLB-45, 63

Burlingame, Edward Livermore 1848-1922 .... DLB-79

Burnet, Gilbert 1643-1715 .... DLB-101

Burnett, Frances Hodgson 1849-1924 .... DLB-42, 141; DS-13, 14

Burnett, W. R. 1899-1982 .... DLB-9

Burnett, Whit 1899-1973 and Martha Foley 1897-1977 .... DLB-137

Burney, Fanny 1752-1840 .... DLB-39

Burns, Alan 1929- DLB-14

Burns, John Horne 1916-1953 .... Y-85

Burns, Robert 1759-1796 .... DLB-109

Burns and Oates DLB-106

Burnshaw, Stanley 1906- DLB-48

Burr, C. Chauncey 1815?-1883 ...... DLB-79

Burroughs, Edgar Rice 1875-1950 .... DLB-8

Burroughs, John 1837-1921 .... DLB-64

Burroughs, Margaret T. G. 1917- DLB-41

Burroughs, William S., Jr. 1947-1981 .... DLB-16

Burroughs, William Seward 1914- DLB-2, 8, 16, 152; Y-81

Burroway, Janet 1936- DLB-6

Burt, Maxwell S. 1882-1954 .... DLB-86

Burt, A. L., and Company DLB-49

Burton, Hester 1913- DLB-161

Burton, Isabel Arundell 1831-1896 .... DLB-166

Burton, Miles (see Rhode, John)

Burton, Richard Francis 1821-1890 .... DLB-55, 166

Burton, Robert 1577-1640 .... DLB-151

Burton, Virginia Lee 1909-1968 ..... DLB-22

Burton, William Evans 1804-1860 .... DLB-73

Burwell, Adam Hood 1790-1849 ..... DLB-99

Bury, Lady Charlotte 1775-1861 .... DLB-116

Busch, Frederick 1941- DLB-6

Busch, Niven 1903-1991 .... DLB-44

Bushnell, Horace 1802-1876 .... DS-13

Bussieres, Arthur de 1877-1913 ..... DLB-92

Butler, Juan 1942-1981 .... DLB-53

Butler, Octavia E. 1947- DLB-33

Butler, Robert Owen 1945- DLB-173

Butler, Samuel 1613-1680 ..... DLB-101, 126

Butler, Samuel 1835-1902 .... DLB-18, 57

Butler, William Francis 1838-1910 .... DLB-166

Butler, E. H., and Company DLB-49

Butor, Michel 1926- DLB-83

Butter, Nathaniel [publishing house] DLB-170

Butterworth, Hezekiah 1839-1905 ....DLB-42

Buttitta, Ignazio 1899- DLB-114

Byars, Betsy 1928- DLB-52

Byatt, A. S. 1936- DLB-14

Byles, Mather 1707-1788 .... DLB-24

Bynneman, Henry [publishing house] DLB-170

Bynner, Witter 1881-1968 .... DLB-54

Byrd, William circa 1543-1623 ...... DLB-172

Byrd, William II 1674-1744 .... DLB-24, 140

Byrne, John Keyes (see Leonard, Hugh)

Byron, George Gordon, Lord 1788-1824 .... DLB-96, 110

C

Caballero Bonald, José Manuel 1926- DLB-108

Cabañero, Eladio 1930- DLB-134

Cabell, James Branch 1879-1958 .... DLB-9, 78

Cabeza de Baca, Manuel 1853-1915 .... DLB-122

Cabeza de Baca Gilbert, Fabiola 1898- DLB-122

Cable, George Washington 1844-1925 .... DLB-12, 74; DS-13

Cabrera, Lydia 1900-1991 .... DLB-145

Cabrera Infante, Guillermo 1929- DLB-113

Cadell [publishing house] DLB-154

Cady, Edwin H. 1917- DLB-103

Caedmon flourished 658-680 .... DLB-146

Caedmon School circa 660-899 ..... DLB-146

Cahan, Abraham 1860-1951 .... DLB-9, 25, 28

Cain, George 1943- DLB-33

Caldecott, Randolph 1846-1886 ..... DLB-163

Calder, John (Publishers), Limited DLB-112

Caldwell, Ben 1937- DLB-38

Caldwell, Erskine 1903-1987 ..... DLB-9, 86

Caldwell, H. M., Company DLB-49

Calhoun, John C. 1782-1850 .... DLB-3

Calisher, Hortense 1911- DLB-2

A Call to Letters and an Invitation to the Electric Chair, by Siegfried Mandel DLB-75

Callaghan, Morley 1903-1990 .... DLB-68

Callaloo Y-87

Calmer, Edgar 1907- DLB-4

Calverley, C. S. 1831-1884 ....DLB-35

Calvert, George Henry
    1803-1889 ....DLB-1, 64

Cambridge Press DLB-49

Cambridge Songs (Carmina Cantabrigensia)
    circa 1050 ....DLB-148

Cambridge University Press DLB-170

Camden, William 1551-1623 ....DLB-172

Camden House: An Interview with
    James Hardin Y-92

Cameron, Eleanor 1912- DLB-52

Cameron, George Frederick
    1854-1885 ....DLB-99

Cameron, Lucy Lyttelton
    1781-1858 ....DLB-163

Cameron, William Bleasdell
    1862-1951 ....DLB-99

Camm, John 1718-1778 ....DLB-31

Campana, Dino 1885-1932 ....DLB-114

Campbell, Gabrielle Margaret Vere
    (see Shearing, Joseph, and Bowen, Marjorie)

Campbell, James Dykes
    1838-1895 ....DLB-144

Campbell, James Edwin
    1867-1896 ....DLB-50

Campbell, John 1653-1728 ....DLB-43

Campbell, John W., Jr.
    1910-1971 ....DLB-8

Campbell, Roy 1901-1957 ....DLB-20

Campbell, Thomas
    1777-1844 ....DLB-93, 144

Campbell, William Wilfred
    1858-1918 ....DLB-92

Campion, Edmund 1539-1581 ......DLB-167

Campion, Thomas
    1567-1620 ....DLB-58, 172

Camus, Albert 1913-1960 ....DLB-72

Canby, Henry Seidel 1878-1961 .....DLB-91

Candelaria, Cordelia 1943- DLB-82

Candelaria, Nash 1928- DLB-82

Candour in English Fiction (1890),
    by Thomas Hardy DLB-18

Canetti, Elias 1905-1994 ....DLB-85, 124

Canham, Erwin Dain
    1904-1982 ....DLB-127

Canitz, Friedrich Rudolph Ludwig von
    1654-1699 ....DLB-168

Cankar, Ivan 1876-1918 ....DLB-147

Cannan, Gilbert 1884-1955 ....DLB-10

Cannell, Kathleen 1891-1974 .... DLB-4

Cannell, Skipwith 1887-1957 .... DLB-45

Canning, George 1770-1827 .... DLB-158

Cannon, Jimmy 1910-1973 .... DLB-171

Cantwell, Robert 1908-1978 .... DLB-9

Cape, Jonathan, and Harrison Smith
    [publishing house] DLB-46

Cape, Jonathan, Limited DLB-112

Capen, Joseph 1658-1725 .... DLB-24

Capes, Bernard 1854-1918 .... DLB-156

Capote, Truman
    1924-1984 .... DLB-2; Y-80, 84

Caproni, Giorgio 1912-1990 .... DLB-128

Cardarelli, Vincenzo 1887-1959 .... DLB-114

Cárdenas, Reyes 1948- DLB-122

Cardinal, Marie 1929- DLB-83

Carew, Jan 1920- DLB-157

Carew, Thomas
    1594 or 1595-1640 .... DLB-126

Carey, Henry
    circa 1687-1689-1743 .... DLB-84

Carey, Mathew 1760-1839 ...... DLB-37, 73

Carey and Hart DLB-49

Carey, M., and Company DLB-49

Carlell, Lodowick 1602-1675 .... DLB-58

Carleton, William 1794-1869 ...... DLB-159

Carleton, G. W.
    [publishing house] DLB-49

Carlile, Richard 1790-1843 .... DLB-110, 158

Carlyle, Jane Welsh 1801-1866 ..... DLB-55

Carlyle, Thomas 1795-1881 .... DLB-55, 144

Carman, Bliss 1861-1929 .... DLB-92

Carmina Burana circa 1230 .... DLB-138

Carnero, Guillermo 1947- DLB-108

Carossa, Hans 1878-1956 .... DLB-66

Carpenter, Humphrey 1946- DLB-155

Carpenter, Stephen Cullen
    ?-1820? DLB-73

Carpentier, Alejo 1904-1980 .... DLB-113

Carrier, Roch 1937- DLB-53

Carrillo, Adolfo 1855-1926 .... DLB-122

Carroll, Gladys Hasty 1904- DLB-9

Carroll, John 1735-1815 .... DLB-37

Carroll, John 1809-1884 .... DLB-99

Carroll, Lewis 1832-1898 ..... DLB-18, 163

Carroll, Paul 1927- DLB-16

Carroll, Paul Vincent 1900-1968 ..... DLB-10

Carroll and Graf Publishers DLB-46

Carruth, Hayden 1921- DLB-5, 165

Carryl, Charles E. 1841-1920 .... DLB-42

Carswell, Catherine 1879-1946 ...... DLB-36

Carter, Angela 1940-1992 .... DLB-14

Carter, Elizabeth 1717-1806 .... DLB-109

Carter, Henry (see Leslie, Frank)

Carter, Hodding, Jr. 1907-1972 ..... DLB-127

Carter, Landon 1710-1778 .... DLB-31

Carter, Lin 1930- Y-81

Carter, Martin 1927- DLB-117

Carter and Hendee DLB-49

Carter, Robert, and Brothers DLB-49

Cartwright, John 1740-1824 .... DLB-158

Cartwright, William circa
    1611-1643 ....DLB-126

Caruthers, William Alexander
    1802-1846 ....DLB-3

Carver, Jonathan 1710-1780 ....DLB-31

Carver, Raymond
    1938-1988 .... DLB-130; Y-84, 88

Cary, Joyce 1888-1957 ....DLB-15, 100

Cary, Patrick 1623?-1657 ....DLB-131

Casey, Juanita 1925- DLB-14

Casey, Michael 1947- DLB-5

Cassady, Carolyn 1923- DLB-16

Cassady, Neal 1926-1968 ....DLB-16

Cassell and Company DLB-106

Cassell Publishing Company DLB-49

Cassill, R. V. 1919- DLB-6

Cassity, Turner 1929- DLB-105

The Castle of Perseverance
    circa 1400-1425 ....DLB-146

Castellano, Olivia 1944- DLB-122

Castellanos, Rosario 1925-1974 ....DLB-113

Castillo, Ana 1953- DLB-122

Castlemon, Harry (see Fosdick, Charles Austin)

Caswall, Edward 1814-1878 ....DLB-32

Catacalos, Rosemary 1944- DLB-122

Cather, Willa
    1873-1947 .... DLB-9, 54, 78; DS-1

Catherine II (Ekaterina Alekseevna), "The
    Great," Empress of Russia
    1729-1796 ....DLB-150

Catherwood, Mary Hartwell
    1847-1902 ....DLB-78

Catledge, Turner 1901-1983 .... DLB-127

Cattafi, Bartolo 1922-1979 .... DLB-128

Catton, Bruce 1899-1978 .... DLB-17

Causley, Charles 1917- DLB-27

Caute, David 1936- DLB-14

Cavendish, Duchess of Newcastle,
 Margaret Lucas 1623-1673 .... DLB-131

Cawein, Madison 1865-1914 .... DLB-54

The Caxton Printers, Limited DLB-46

Caxton, William
 [publishing house] DLB-170

Cayrol, Jean 1911- DLB-83

Cecil, Lord David 1902-1986 ...... DLB-155

Celan, Paul 1920-1970 .... DLB-69

Celaya, Gabriel 1911-1991 .... DLB-108

Céline, Louis-Ferdinand
 1894-1961 .... DLB-72

The Celtic Background to Medieval English
 Literature DLB-146

Center for Bibliographical Studies and
 Research at the University of
 California, Riverside Y-91

The Center for the Book in the Library
 of Congress Y-93

Center for the Book Research Y-84

Centlivre, Susanna 1669?-1723 ..... DLB-84

The Century Company DLB-49

Cernuda, Luis 1902-1963 .... DLB-134

Cervantes, Lorna Dee 1954- DLB-82

Chacel, Rosa 1898- DLB-134

Chacón, Eusebio 1869-1948 ...... DLB-82

Chacón, Felipe Maximiliano
 1873-? DLB-82

Chadwyck-Healey's Full-Text Literary Databases: Editing Commercial Databases of
 Primary Literary Texts Y-95

Challans, Eileen Mary (see Renault, Mary)

Chalmers, George 1742-1825 .... DLB-30

Chaloner, Sir Thomas
 1520-1565 .... DLB-167

Chamberlain, Samuel S.
 1851-1916 .... DLB-25

Chamberland, Paul 1939- DLB-60

Chamberlin, William Henry
 1897-1969 .... DLB-29

Chambers, Charles Haddon
 1860-1921 .... DLB-10

Chambers, W. and R.
 [publishing house] DLB-106

Chamisso, Albert von
 1781-1838 .... DLB-90

Champfleury 1821-1889 .... DLB-119

Chandler, Harry 1864-1944 .... DLB-29

Chandler, Norman 1899-1973 ..... DLB-127

Chandler, Otis 1927- DLB-127

Chandler, Raymond 1888-1959 .... DS-6

Channing, Edward 1856-1931 ...... DLB-17

Channing, Edward Tyrrell
 1790-1856 .... DLB-1, 59

Channing, William Ellery
 1780-1842 .... DLB-1, 59

Channing, William Ellery, II
 1817-1901 .... DLB-1

Channing, William Henry
 1810-1884 .... DLB-1, 59

Chaplin, Charlie 1889-1977 .... DLB-44

Chapman, George
 1559 or 1560 - 1634 .... DLB-62, 121

Chapman, John DLB-106

Chapman, William 1850-1917 .... DLB-99

Chapman and Hall DLB-106

Chappell, Fred 1936- DLB-6, 105

Chappell, Fred, A Detail
 in a Poem DLB-105

Charbonneau, Jean 1875-1960 ...... DLB-92

Charbonneau, Robert 1911-1967 .... DLB-68

Charles, Gerda 1914- DLB-14

Charles, William
 [publishing house] DLB-49

The Charles Wood Affair:
 A Playwright Revived Y-83

Charlotte Forten: Pages from
 her Diary DLB-50

Charteris, Leslie 1907-1993 .... DLB-77

Charyn, Jerome 1937- Y-83

Chase, Borden 1900-1971 .... DLB-26

Chase, Edna Woolman
 1877-1957 .... DLB-91

Chase-Riboud, Barbara 1936- DLB-33

Chateaubriand, François-René de
 1768-1848 .... DLB-119

Chatterton, Thomas 1752-1770 .... DLB-109

Chatto and Windus DLB-106

Chaucer, Geoffrey 1340?-1400 ..... DLB-146

Chauncy, Charles 1705-1787 .... DLB-24

Chauveau, Pierre-Joseph-Olivier
 1820-1890 .... DLB-99

Chávez, Denise 1948- DLB-122

Chávez, Fray Angélico 1910- DLB-82

Chayefsky, Paddy
 1923-1981 .... DLB-7, 44; Y-81

Cheever, Ezekiel 1615-1708 .... DLB-24

Cheever, George Barrell
 1807-1890 .... DLB-59

Cheever, John
 1912-1982 .... DLB-2, 102; Y-80, 82

Cheever, Susan 1943- Y-82

Cheke, Sir John 1514-1557 .... DLB-132

Chelsea House DLB-46

Cheney, Ednah Dow (Littlehale)
 1824-1904 .... DLB-1

Cheney, Harriet Vaughn
 1796-1889 .... DLB-99

Cherry, Kelly 1940 .... Y-83

Cherryh, C. J. 1942- Y-80

Chesnutt, Charles Waddell
 1858-1932 .... DLB-12, 50, 78

Chester, Alfred 1928-1971 .... DLB-130

Chester, George Randolph
 1869-1924 .... DLB-78

The Chester Plays circa 1505-1532;
 revisions until 1575 .... DLB-146

Chesterfield, Philip Dormer Stanhope,
 Fourth Earl of 1694-1773 ...... DLB-104

Chesterton, G. K.
 1874-1936 .... DLB-10, 19, 34, 70, 98, 149

Chettle, Henry
 circa 1560-circa 1607 .... DLB-136

Chew, Ada Nield 1870-1945 ...... DLB-135

Cheyney, Edward P. 1861-1947 ..... DLB-47

Chicano History DLB-82

Chicano Language DLB-82

Child, Francis James
 1825-1896 .... DLB-1, 64

Child, Lydia Maria
 1802-1880 .... DLB-1, 74

Child, Philip 1898-1978 .... DLB-68

Childers, Erskine 1870-1922 .... DLB-70

Children's Book Awards
 and Prizes DLB-61

Children's Illustrators,
 1800-1880 .... DLB-163

Childress, Alice 1920-1994 .... DLB-7, 38

Childs, George W. 1829-1894 .... DLB-23

Chilton Book Company DLB-46

Chinweizu 1943- DLB-157

Chitham, Edward 1932- DLB-155

Chittenden, Hiram Martin 1858-1917 ...... DLB-47
Chivers, Thomas Holley 1809-1858 ...... DLB-3
Chopin, Kate 1850-1904 ...... DLB-12, 78
Chopin, Rene 1885-1953 ...... DLB-92
Choquette, Adrienne 1915-1973 ...... DLB-68
Choquette, Robert 1905- DLB-68
The Christian Publishing Company DLB-49
Christie, Agatha 1890-1976 ...... DLB-13, 77
Christus und die Samariterin circa 950 ...... DLB-148
Chulkov, Mikhail Dmitrievich 1743?-1792 ...... DLB-150
Church, Benjamin 1734-1778 ...... DLB-31
Church, Francis Pharcellus 1839-1906 ...... DLB-79
Church, William Conant 1836-1917 ...... DLB-79
Churchill, Caryl 1938- DLB-13
Churchill, Charles 1731-1764 ...... DLB-109
Churchill, Sir Winston 1874-1965 ...... DLB-100
Churchyard, Thomas 1520?-1604 ...... DLB-132
Churton, E., and Company DLB-106
Chute, Marchette 1909-1994 ...... DLB-103
Ciardi, John 1916-1986 ...... DLB-5; Y-86
Cibber, Colley 1671-1757 ...... DLB-84
Cima, Annalisa 1941- DLB-128
Cirese, Eugenio 1884-1955 ...... DLB-114
Cisneros, Sandra 1954- DLB-122, 152
City Lights Books DLB-46
Cixous, Hélène 1937- DLB-83
Clampitt, Amy 1920-1994 ...... DLB-105
Clapper, Raymond 1892-1944 ...... DLB-29
Clare, John 1793-1864 ...... DLB-55, 96
Clarendon, Edward Hyde, Earl of 1609-1674 ...... DLB-101
Clark, Alfred Alexander Gordon (see Hare, Cyril)
Clark, Ann Nolan 1896- DLB-52
Clark, Catherine Anthony 1892-1977 ...... DLB-68
Clark, Charles Heber 1841-1915 ...... DLB-11
Clark, Davis Wasgatt 1812-1871 ...... DLB-79
Clark, Eleanor 1913- DLB-6

Clark, J. P. 1935- DLB-117
Clark, Lewis Gaylord 1808-1873 ...... DLB-3, 64, 73
Clark, Walter Van Tilburg 1909-1971 ...... DLB-9
Clark, C. M., Publishing Company DLB-46
Clarke, Austin 1896-1974 ...... DLB-10, 20
Clarke, Austin C. 1934- DLB-53, 125
Clarke, Gillian 1937- DLB-40
Clarke, James Freeman 1810-1888 ...... DLB-1, 59
Clarke, Pauline 1921- DLB-161
Clarke, Rebecca Sophia 1833-1906 ...... DLB-42
Clarke, Robert, and Company DLB-49
Clarkson, Thomas 1760-1846 ...... DLB-158
Claudius, Matthias 1740-1815 ...... DLB-97
Clausen, Andy 1943- DLB-16
Claxton, Remsen and Haffelfinger DLB-49
Clay, Cassius Marcellus 1810-1903 ...... DLB-43
Cleary, Beverly 1916- DLB-52
Cleaver, Vera 1919- and Cleaver, Bill 1920-1981 ...... DLB-52
Cleland, John 1710-1789 ...... DLB-39
Clemens, Samuel Langhorne 1835-1910 ...... DLB-11, 12, 23, 64, 74
Clement, Hal 1922- DLB-8
Clemo, Jack 1916- DLB-27
Cleveland, John 1613-1658 ...... DLB-126
Cliff, Michelle 1946- DLB-157
Clifford, Lady Anne 1590-1676 ...... DLB-151
Clifford, James L. 1901-1978 ...... DLB-103
Clifford, Lucy 1853?-1929 ...... DLB-135, 141
Clifton, Lucille 1936- DLB-5, 41
Clode, Edward J. [publishing house] DLB-46
Clough, Arthur Hugh 1819-1861 ...... DLB-32
Cloutier, Cécile 1930- DLB-60
Clutton-Brock, Arthur 1868-1924 ...... DLB-98
Coates, Robert M. 1897-1973 ...... DLB-4, 9, 102
Coatsworth, Elizabeth 1893- DLB-22
Cobb, Charles E., Jr. 1943- DLB-41
Cobb, Frank I. 1869-1923 ...... DLB-25

Cobb, Irvin S. 1876-1944 ...... DLB-11, 25, 86
Cobbett, William 1763-1835 ...... DLB-43, 107
Cobbledick, Gordon 1898-1969 ...... DLB-171
Cochran, Thomas C. 1902- DLB-17
Cochrane, Elizabeth 1867-1922 ...... DLB-25
Cockerill, John A. 1845-1896 ...... DLB-23
Cocteau, Jean 1889-1963 ...... DLB-65
Coderre, Emile (see Jean Narrache)
Coffee, Lenore J. 1900?-1984 ...... DLB-44
Coffin, Robert P. Tristram 1892-1955 ...... DLB-45
Cogswell, Fred 1917- DLB-60
Cogswell, Mason Fitch 1761-1830 ...... DLB-37
Cohen, Arthur A. 1928-1986 ...... DLB-28
Cohen, Leonard 1934- DLB-53
Cohen, Matt 1942- DLB-53
Colden, Cadwallader 1688-1776 ...... DLB-24, 30
Cole, Barry 1936- DLB-14
Cole, George Watson 1850-1939 ...... DLB-140
Colegate, Isabel 1931- DLB-14
Coleman, Emily Holmes 1899-1974 ...... DLB-4
Coleman, Wanda 1946- DLB-130
Coleridge, Hartley 1796-1849 ...... DLB-96
Coleridge, Mary 1861-1907 ...... DLB-19, 98
Coleridge, Samuel Taylor 1772-1834 ...... DLB-93, 107
Colet, John 1467-1519 ...... DLB-132
Colette 1873-1954 ...... DLB-65
Colette, Sidonie Gabrielle (see Colette)
Colinas, Antonio 1946- DLB-134
Collier, John 1901-1980 ...... DLB-77
Collier, Mary 1690-1762 ...... DLB-95
Collier, Robert J. 1876-1918 ...... DLB-91
Collier, P. F. [publishing house] DLB-49
Collin and Small DLB-49
Collingwood, W. G. 1854-1932 ...... DLB-149
Collins, An floruit circa 1653 ...... DLB-131
Collins, Merle 1950- DLB-157
Collins, Mortimer 1827-1876 ...... DLB-21, 35
Collins, Wilkie 1824-1889 ...... DLB-18, 70, 159
Collins, William 1721-1759 ...... DLB-109

Collins, William, Sons and Company ... DLB-154

Collins, Isaac [publishing house] ... DLB-49

Collyer, Mary 1716?-1763? ... DLB-39

Colman, Benjamin 1673-1747 ... DLB-24

Colman, George, the Elder 1732-1794 ... DLB-89

Colman, George, the Younger 1762-1836 ... DLB-89

Colman, S. [publishing house] ... DLB-49

Colombo, John Robert 1936- ... DLB-53

Colquhoun, Patrick 1745-1820 ... DLB-158

Colter, Cyrus 1910- ... DLB-33

Colum, Padraic 1881-1972 ... DLB-19

Colvin, Sir Sidney 1845-1927 ... DLB-149

Colwin, Laurie 1944-1992 ... Y-80

Comden, Betty 1919- and Green, Adolph 1918- ... DLB-44

Comi, Girolamo 1890-1968 ... DLB-114

The Comic Tradition Continued [in the British Novel] ... DLB-15

Commager, Henry Steele 1902- ... DLB-17

The Commercialization of the Image of Revolt, by Kenneth Rexroth ... DLB-16

Community and Commentators: Black Theatre and Its Critics ... DLB-38

Compton-Burnett, Ivy 1884?-1969 ... DLB-36

Conan, Laure 1845-1924 ... DLB-99

Conde, Carmen 1901- ... DLB-108

Conference on Modern Biography ... Y-85

Congreve, William 1670-1729 ... DLB-39, 84

Conkey, W. B., Company ... DLB-49

Connell, Evan S., Jr. 1924- ... DLB-2; Y-81

Connelly, Marc 1890-1980 ... DLB-7; Y-80

Connolly, Cyril 1903-1974 ... DLB-98

Connolly, James B. 1868-1957 ... DLB-78

Connor, Ralph 1860-1937 ... DLB-92

Connor, Tony 1930- ... DLB-40

Conquest, Robert 1917- ... DLB-27

Conrad, Joseph 1857-1924 ... DLB-10, 34, 98, 156

Conrad, John, and Company ... DLB-49

Conroy, Jack 1899-1990 ... Y-81

Conroy, Pat 1945- ... DLB-6

The Consolidation of Opinion: Critical Responses to the Modernists ... DLB-36

Constable, Henry 1562-1613 ... DLB-136

Constable and Company Limited ... DLB-112

Constable, Archibald, and Company ... DLB-154

Constant, Benjamin 1767-1830 ... DLB-119

Constant de Rebecque, Henri-Benjamin de (see Constant, Benjamin)

Constantine, David 1944- ... DLB-40

Constantin-Weyer, Maurice 1881-1964 ... DLB-92

Contempo Caravan: Kites in a Windstorm ... Y-85

A Contemporary Flourescence of Chicano Literature ... Y-84

The Continental Publishing Company ... DLB-49

A Conversation with Chaim Potok ... Y-84

Conversations with Editors ... Y-95

Conversations with Publishers I: An Interview with Patrick O'Connor ... Y-84

Conversations with Publishers II: An Interview with Charles Scribner III ... Y-94

Conversations with Publishers III: An Interview with Donald Lamm ... Y-95

Conversations with Rare Book Dealers I: An Interview with Glenn Horowitz ... Y-90

Conversations with Rare Book Dealers II: An Interview with Ralph Sipper ... Y-94

The Conversion of an Unpolitical Man, by W. H. Bruford ... DLB-66

Conway, Moncure Daniel 1832-1907 ... DLB-1

Cook, Ebenezer circa 1667-circa 1732 ... DLB-24

Cook, Edward Tyas 1857-1919 ... DLB-149

Cook, Michael 1933- ... DLB-53

Cook, David C., Publishing Company ... DLB-49

Cooke, George Willis 1848-1923 ... DLB-71

Cooke, Increase, and Company ... DLB-49

Cooke, John Esten 1830-1886 ... DLB-3

Cooke, Philip Pendleton 1816-1850 ... DLB-3, 59

Cooke, Rose Terry 1827-1892 ... DLB-12, 74

Coolbrith, Ina 1841-1928 ... DLB-54

Cooley, Peter 1940- ... DLB-105

Cooley, Peter, Into the Mirror ... DLB-105

Coolidge, Susan (see Woolsey, Sarah Chauncy)

Coolidge, George [publishing house] ... DLB-49

Cooper, Giles 1918-1966 ... DLB-13

Cooper, James Fenimore 1789-1851 ... DLB-3

Cooper, Kent 1880-1965 ... DLB-29

Cooper, Susan 1935- ... DLB-161

Cooper, William [publishing house] ... DLB-170

Coote, J. [publishing house] ... DLB-154

Coover, Robert 1932- ... DLB-2; Y-81

Copeland and Day ... DLB-49

Copland, Robert 1470?-1548 ... DLB-136

Coppard, A. E. 1878-1957 ... DLB-162

Coppel, Alfred 1921- ... Y-83

Coppola, Francis Ford 1939- ... DLB-44

Corazzini, Sergio 1886-1907 ... DLB-114

Corbett, Richard 1582-1635 ... DLB-121

Corcoran, Barbara 1911- ... DLB-52

Corelli, Marie 1855-1924 ... DLB-34, 156

Corle, Edwin 1906-1956 ... Y-85

Corman, Cid 1924- ... DLB-5

Cormier, Robert 1925- ... DLB-52

Corn, Alfred 1943- ... DLB-120; Y-80

Cornish, Sam 1935- ... DLB-41

Cornish, William circa 1465-circa 1524 ... DLB-132

Cornwall, Barry (see Procter, Bryan Waller)

Cornwallis, Sir William, the Younger circa 1579-1614 ... DLB-151

Cornwell, David John Moore (see le Carré, John)

Corpi, Lucha 1945- ... DLB-82

Corrington, John William 1932- ... DLB-6

Corrothers, James D. 1869-1917 ... DLB-50

Corso, Gregory 1930- ... DLB-5, 16

Cortázar, Julio 1914-1984 ... DLB-113

Cortez, Jayne 1936- ... DLB-41

Corvinus, Gottlieb Siegmund 1677-1746 ... DLB-168

Corvo, Baron (see Rolfe, Frederick William)

Cory, Annie Sophie (see Cross, Victoria)

Cory, William Johnson 1823-1892 ... DLB-35

Coryate, Thomas 1577?-1617 ... DLB-151, 172

Cosin, John 1595-1672 ... DLB-151

Cosmopolitan Book Corporation ... DLB-46

Costain, Thomas B. 1885-1965 ....DLB-9

Coste, Donat 1912-1957 ....DLB-88

Costello, Louisa Stuart 1799-1870 ..DLB-166

Cota-Cárdenas, Margarita
  1941- DLB-122

Cotter, Joseph Seamon, Sr.
  1861-1949 ....DLB-50

Cotter, Joseph Seamon, Jr.
  1895-1919 ....DLB-50

Cottle, Joseph [publishing house] ...DLB-154

Cotton, Charles 1630-1687 ....DLB-131

Cotton, John 1584-1652 ....DLB-24

Coulter, John 1888-1980 ....DLB-68

Cournos, John 1881-1966 ....DLB-54

Cousins, Margaret 1905- DLB-137

Cousins, Norman 1915-1990 ....DLB-137

Coventry, Francis 1725-1754 ....DLB-39

Coverdale, Miles
  1487 or 1488-1569 ....DLB-167

Coverly, N. [publishing house] DLB-49

Covici-Friede DLB-46

Coward, Noel 1899-1973 ....DLB-10

Coward, McCann and
  Geoghegan DLB-46

Cowles, Gardner 1861-1946 ....DLB-29

Cowles, Gardner ("Mike"), Jr.
  1903-1985 ....DLB-127, 137

Cowley, Abraham
  1618-1667 ....DLB-131, 151

Cowley, Hannah 1743-1809 ....DLB-89

Cowley, Malcolm
  1898-1989 .... DLB-4, 48; Y-81, 89

Cowper, William
  1731-1800 ....DLB-104, 109

Cox, A. B. (see Berkeley, Anthony)

Cox, James McMahon
  1903-1974 ....DLB-127

Cox, James Middleton
  1870-1957 ....DLB-127

Cox, Palmer 1840-1924 ....DLB-42

Coxe, Louis 1918-1993 ....DLB-5

Coxe, Tench 1755-1824 ....DLB-37

Cozzens, James Gould
  1903-1978 .... DLB-9; Y-84; DS-2

Crabbe, George 1754-1832 ....DLB-93

Crackanthorpe, Hubert
  1870-1896 ....DLB-135

Craddock, Charles Egbert
  (see Murfree, Mary N.)

Cradock, Thomas 1718-1770 .... DLB-31

Craig, Daniel H. 1811-1895 .... DLB-43

Craik, Dinah Maria
  1826-1887 .... DLB-35, 136

Cranch, Christopher Pearse
  1813-1892 .... DLB-1, 42

Crane, Hart 1899-1932 .... DLB-4, 48

Crane, R. S. 1886-1967 .... DLB-63

Crane, Stephen 1871-1900 ...DLB-12, 54, 78

Crane, Walter 1845-1915 .... DLB-163

Cranmer, Thomas 1489-1556 ...... DLB-132

Crapsey, Adelaide 1878-1914 .... DLB-54

Crashaw, Richard
  1612 or 1613-1649 .... DLB-126

Craven, Avery 1885-1980 .... DLB-17

Crawford, Charles
  1752-circa 1815 .... DLB-31

Crawford, F. Marion 1854-1909 .... DLB-71

Crawford, Isabel Valancy
  1850-1887 .... DLB-92

Crawley, Alan 1887-1975 .... DLB-68

Crayon, Geoffrey (see Irving, Washington)

Creamer, Robert W. 1922- DLB-171

Creasey, John 1908-1973 .... DLB-77

Creative Age Press DLB-46

Creech, William
  [publishing house] DLB-154

Creede, Thomas
  [publishing house] DLB-170

Creel, George 1876-1953 .... DLB-25

Creeley, Robert 1926- DLB-5, 16, 169

Creelman, James 1859-1915 .... DLB-23

Cregan, David 1931- DLB-13

Creighton, Donald Grant
  1902-1979 .... DLB-88

Cremazie, Octave 1827-1879 .... DLB-99

Crémer, Victoriano 1909?- DLB-108

Crescas, Hasdai
  circa 1340-1412? DLB-115

Crespo, Angel 1926- DLB-134

Cresset Press DLB-112

Cresswell, Helen 1934- DLB-161

Crèvecoeur, Michel Guillaume Jean de
  1735-1813 .... DLB-37

Crews, Harry 1935- DLB-6, 143

Crichton, Michael 1942- Y-81

A Crisis of Culture: The Changing Role
  of Religion in the New Republic
  .... DLB-37

Crispin, Edmund 1921-1978 ....DLB-87

Cristofer, Michael 1946- DLB-7

"The Critic as Artist" (1891), by
  Oscar Wilde DLB-57

"Criticism In Relation To Novels" (1863),
  by G. H. Lewes DLB-21

Crnjanski, Miloš 1893-1977 ....DLB-147

Crockett, David (Davy)
  1786-1836 ....DLB-3, 11

Croft-Cooke, Rupert (see Bruce, Leo)

Crofts, Freeman Wills
  1879-1957 ....DLB-77

Croker, John Wilson
  1780-1857 ....DLB-110

Croly, George 1780-1860 ....DLB-159

Croly, Herbert 1869-1930 ....DLB-91

Croly, Jane Cunningham
  1829-1901 ....DLB-23

Crompton, Richmal 1890-1969 .....DLB-160

Crosby, Caresse 1892-1970 ....DLB-48

Crosby, Caresse 1892-1970 and Crosby,
  Harry 1898-1929 ....DLB-4

Crosby, Harry 1898-1929 ....DLB-48

Cross, Gillian 1945- DLB-161

Cross, Victoria 1868-1952 ....DLB-135

Crossley-Holland, Kevin
  1941- DLB-40, 161

Crothers, Rachel 1878-1958 ....DLB-7

Crowell, Thomas Y., Company DLB-49

Crowley, John 1942- Y-82

Crowley, Mart 1935- DLB-7

Crown Publishers DLB-46

Crowne, John 1641-1712 ....DLB-80

Crowninshield, Edward Augustus
  1817-1859 ....DLB-140

Crowninshield, Frank 1872-1947 ....DLB-91

Croy, Homer 1883-1965 ....DLB-4

Crumley, James 1939- Y-84

Cruz, Victor Hernández 1949- DLB-41

Csokor, Franz Theodor
  1885-1969 ....DLB-81

Cuala Press DLB-112

Cullen, Countee 1903-1946 ....DLB-4, 48, 51

Culler, Jonathan D. 1944- DLB-67

The Cult of Biography
  Excerpts from the Second Folio Debate:
  "Biographies are generally a disease of
  English Literature" – Germaine Greer,
  Victoria Glendinning, Auberon Waugh,
  and Richard Holmes Y-86

Cumulative Index

Cumberland, Richard 1732-1811 .... DLB-89

Cummings, E. E. 1894-1962 ...... DLB-4, 48

Cummings, Ray 1887-1957 ....DLB-8

Cummings and Hilliard DLB-49

Cummins, Maria Susanna
  1827-1866 .... DLB-42

Cundall, Joseph
  [publishing house] DLB-106

Cuney, Waring 1906-1976 .... DLB-51

Cuney-Hare, Maude 1874-1936 ..... DLB-52

Cunningham, Allan
  1784-1842 .... DLB-116, 144

Cunningham, J. V. 1911- DLB-5

Cunningham, Peter F.
  [publishing house] DLB-49

Cunquiero, Alvaro 1911-1981 ..... DLB-134

Cuomo, George 1929- Y-80

Cupples and Leon DLB-46

Cupples, Upham and Company DLB-49

Cuppy, Will 1884-1949 .... DLB-11

Curll, Edmund
  [publishing house] DLB-154

Currie, James 1756-1805 .... DLB-142

Currie, Mary Montgomerie Lamb Singleton,
  Lady Currie (see Fane, Violet)

Cursor Mundi circa 1300 .... DLB-146

Curti, Merle E. 1897- DLB-17

Curtis, Anthony 1926- DLB-155

Curtis, Cyrus H. K. 1850-1933 .... DLB-91

Curtis, George William
  1824-1892 .... DLB-1, 43

Curzon, Robert 1810-1873 .... DLB-166

Curzon, Sarah Anne 1833-1898 ..... DLB-99

Cynewulf circa 770-840 .... DLB-146

Czepko, Daniel 1605-1660 .... DLB-164

D

D. M. Thomas: The Plagiarism
  Controversy Y-82

Dabit, Eugène 1898-1936 .... DLB-65

Daborne, Robert circa 1580-1628 ... DLB-58

Dacey, Philip 1939- DLB-105

Dacey, Philip, Eyes Across Centuries:
  Contemporary Poetry and "That
  Vision Thing" DLB-105

Dach, Simon 1605-1659 .... DLB-164

Daggett, Rollin M. 1831-1901 ..... DLB-79

D'Aguiar, Fred 1960- DLB-157

Dahl, Roald 1916-1990 .... DLB-139

Dahlberg, Edward 1900-1977 .... DLB-48

Dahn, Felix 1834-1912 .... DLB-129

Dale, Peter 1938- DLB-40

Daley, Arthur 1904-1974 .... DLB-171

Dall, Caroline Wells (Healey)
  1822-1912 .... DLB-1

Dallas, E. S. 1828-1879 .... DLB-55

The Dallas Theater Center DLB-7

D'Alton, Louis 1900-1951 .... DLB-10

Daly, T. A. 1871-1948 .... DLB-11

Damon, S. Foster 1893-1971 .... DLB-45

Damrell, William S.
  [publishing house] DLB-49

Dana, Charles A. 1819-1897 ...... DLB-3, 23

Dana, Richard Henry, Jr
  1815-1882 .... DLB-1

Dandridge, Ray Garfield DLB-51

Dane, Clemence 1887-1965 .... DLB-10

Danforth, John 1660-1730 .... DLB-24

Danforth, Samuel, I 1626-1674 ..... DLB-24

Danforth, Samuel, II 1666-1727 ..... DLB-24

Dangerous Years: London Theater,
  1939-1945 .... DLB-10

Daniel, John M. 1825-1865 .... DLB-43

Daniel, Samuel
  1562 or 1563-1619 .... DLB-62

Daniel Press DLB-106

Daniells, Roy 1902-1979 .... DLB-68

Daniels, Jim 1956- DLB-120

Daniels, Jonathan 1902-1981 ...... DLB-127

Daniels, Josephus 1862-1948 ...... DLB-29

Dannay, Frederic 1905-1982 and
  Manfred B. Lee 1905-1971 ..... DLB-137

Danner, Margaret Esse 1915- DLB-41

Danter, John [publishing house] DLB-170

Dantin, Louis 1865-1945 .... DLB-92

Danzig, Allison 1898-1987 .... DLB-171

D'Arcy, Ella circa 1857-1937 ..... DLB-135

Darley, George 1795-1846 .... DLB-96

Darwin, Charles 1809-1882 ..... DLB-57, 166

Darwin, Erasmus 1731-1802 .... DLB-93

Daryush, Elizabeth 1887-1977 ..... DLB-20

Dashkova, Ekaterina Romanovna
  (née Vorontsova) 1743-1810 .... DLB-150

Dashwood, Edmée Elizabeth Monica
  de la Pasture (see Delafield, E. M.)

Daudet, Alphonse 1840-1897 .... DLB-123

d'Aulaire, Edgar Parin 1898- and
  d'Aulaire, Ingri 1904- DLB-22

Davenant, Sir William
  1606-1668 .... DLB-58, 126

Davenport, Guy 1927- DLB-130

Davenport, Robert ?-? DLB-58

Daves, Delmer 1904-1977 .... DLB-26

Davey, Frank 1940- DLB-53

Davidson, Avram 1923-1993 .... DLB-8

Davidson, Donald 1893-1968 .... DLB-45

Davidson, John 1857-1909 .... DLB-19

Davidson, Lionel 1922- DLB-14

Davie, Donald 1922- DLB-27

Davie, Elspeth 1919- DLB-139

Davies, Sir John 1569-1626 .... DLB-172

Davies, John, of Hereford
  1565?-1618 .... DLB-121

Davies, Rhys 1901-1978 .... DLB-139

Davies, Robertson 1913- DLB-68

Davies, Samuel 1723-1761 .... DLB-31

Davies, Thomas 1712?-1785 ... DLB-142, 154

Davies, W. H. 1871-1940 .... DLB-19

Davies, Peter, Limited DLB-112

Daviot, Gordon 1896?-1952 .... DLB-10
  (see also Tey, Josephine)

Davis, Charles A. 1795-1867 ...... DLB-11

Davis, Clyde Brion 1894-1962 ...... DLB-9

Davis, Dick 1945- DLB-40

Davis, Frank Marshall 1905-? DLB-51

Davis, H. L. 1894-1960 .... DLB-9

Davis, John 1774-1854 .... DLB-37

Davis, Lydia 1947- DLB-130

Davis, Margaret Thomson 1926- ...DLB-14

Davis, Ossie 1917- DLB-7, 38

Davis, Paxton 1925-1994 .... Y-94

Davis, Rebecca Harding
  1831-1910 .... DLB-74

Davis, Richard Harding
  1864-1916 ..... DLB-12, 23, 78, 79; DS-13

Davis, Samuel Cole 1764-1809 ...... DLB-37

Davison, Peter 1928- DLB-5

Davys, Mary 1674-1732 .... DLB-39

DAW Books DLB-46

Dawson, Ernest 1882-1947 .... DLB-140

Dawson, Fielding 1930- DLB-130

326

Dawson, William 1704-1752 ....DLB-31

Day, Angel flourished 1586 ....DLB-167

Day, Benjamin Henry 1810-1889 ....DLB-43

Day, Clarence 1874-1935 ....DLB-11

Day, Dorothy 1897-1980 ....DLB-29

Day, Frank Parker 1881-1950 ....DLB-92

Day, John circa 1574-circa 1640 .....DLB-62

Day, John [publishing house] DLB-170

Day Lewis, C. 1904-1972 ....DLB-15, 20
(see also Blake, Nicholas)

Day, Thomas 1748-1789 ....DLB-39

Day, The John, Company DLB-46

Day, Mahlon [publishing house] DLB-49

Deacon, William Arthur
1890-1977 ....DLB-68

Deal, Borden 1922-1985 ....DLB-6

de Angeli, Marguerite 1889-1987 ....DLB-22

De Angelis, Milo 1951- DLB-128

De Bow, James Dunwoody Brownson
1820-1867 ....DLB-3, 79

de Bruyn, Günter 1926- DLB-75

de Camp, L. Sprague 1907- DLB-8

The Decay of Lying (1889),
by Oscar Wilde [excerpt] DLB-18

Dedication, *Ferdinand Count Fathom* (1753),
by Tobias Smollett DLB-39

Dedication, *The History of Pompey the Little*
(1751), by Francis Coventry DLB-39

Dedication, *Lasselia* (1723), by Eliza
Haywood [excerpt] DLB-39

Dedication, *The Wanderer* (1814),
by Fanny Burney DLB-39

Dee, John 1527-1609 ....DLB-136

Deeping, George Warwick
1877-1950 ....DLB 153

Defense of *Amelia* (1752), by
Henry Fielding DLB-39

Defoe, Daniel 1660-1731 ... DLB-39, 95, 101

de Fontaine, Felix Gregory
1834-1896 ....DLB-43

De Forest, John William
1826-1906 ....DLB-12

DeFrees, Madeline 1919- DLB-105

DeFrees, Madeline, The Poet's Kaleidoscope:
The Element of Surprise in the Making
of the Poem DLB-105

de Graff, Robert 1895-1981 ....Y-81

de Graft, Joe 1924-1978 ....DLB-117

De Heinrico circa 980? DLB-148

Deighton, Len 1929- DLB-87

DeJong, Meindert 1906-1991 ....DLB-52

Dekker, Thomas
circa 1572-1632 .... DLB-62, 172

Delacorte, Jr., George T.
1894-1991 ....DLB-91

Delafield, E. M. 1890-1943 ....DLB-34

Delahaye, Guy 1888-1969 ....DLB-92

de la Mare, Walter
1873-1956 ....DLB-19, 153, 162

Deland, Margaret 1857-1945 ....DLB-78

Delaney, Shelagh 1939- DLB-13

Delany, Martin Robinson
1812-1885 ....DLB-50

Delany, Samuel R. 1942- DLB-8, 33

de la Roche, Mazo 1879-1961 ....DLB-68

Delbanco, Nicholas 1942- DLB-6

De León, Nephtal 1945- DLB-82

Delgado, Abelardo Barrientos
1931- DLB-82

De Libero, Libero 1906-1981 ......DLB-114

DeLillo, Don 1936- DLB-6, 173

de Lisser H. G. 1878-1944 ....DLB-117

Dell, Floyd 1887-1969 ....DLB-9

Dell Publishing Company DLB-46

delle Grazie, Marie Eugene
1864-1931 ....DLB-81

Deloney, Thomas died 1600 ....DLB-167

del Rey, Lester 1915-1993 ....DLB-8

Del Vecchio, John M. 1947- DS-9

de Man, Paul 1919-1983 ....DLB-67

Demby, William 1922- DLB-33

Deming, Philander 1829-1915 ......DLB-74

Demorest, William Jennings
1822-1895 ....DLB-79

De Morgan, William 1839-1917 ....DLB-153

Denham, Henry
[publishing house] DLB-170

Denham, Sir John
1615-1669 ....DLB-58, 126

Denison, Merrill 1893-1975 ....DLB-92

Denison, T. S., and Company DLB-49

Dennie, Joseph
1768-1812 ....DLB-37, 43, 59, 73

Dennis, John 1658-1734 ....DLB-101

Dennis, Nigel 1912-1989 ....DLB-13, 15

Dent, Tom 1932- DLB-38

Dent, J. M., and Sons DLB-112

Denton, Daniel circa 1626-1703 .....DLB-24

DePaola, Tomie 1934- DLB-61

De Quincey, Thomas
1785-1859 ....DLB-110, 144

Derby, George Horatio
1823-1861 ....DLB-11

Derby, J. C., and Company DLB-49

Derby and Miller DLB-49

Derleth, August 1909-1971 ....DLB-9

The Derrydale Press DLB-46

Derzhavin, Gavriil Romanovich
1743-1816 ....DLB-150

Desaulniers, Gonsalve
1863-1934 ....DLB-92

Desbiens, Jean-Paul 1927- DLB-53

des Forêts, Louis-Rene 1918- DLB-83

DesRochers, Alfred 1901-1978 ......DLB-68

Desrosiers, Léo-Paul 1896-1967 .....DLB-68

Destouches, Louis-Ferdinand
(see Céline, Louis-Ferdinand)

De Tabley, Lord 1835-1895 ....DLB-35

Deutsch, Babette 1895-1982 ....DLB-45

Deutsch, André, Limited DLB-112

Deveaux, Alexis 1948- DLB-38

The Development of the Author's Copyright
in Britain DLB-154

The Development of Lighting in the Staging
of Drama, 1900-1945 ....DLB-10

de Vere, Aubrey 1814-1902 ....DLB-35

Devereux, second Earl of Essex, Robert
1565-1601 ....DLB-136

The Devin-Adair Company DLB-46

De Voto, Bernard 1897-1955 ....DLB-9

De Vries, Peter 1910-1993 ......DLB-6; Y-82

Dewdney, Christopher 1951- DLB-60

Dewdney, Selwyn 1909-1979 ....DLB-68

DeWitt, Robert M., Publisher DLB-49

DeWolfe, Fiske and Company DLB-49

Dexter, Colin 1930- DLB-87

de Young, M. H. 1849-1925 ....DLB-25

Dhlomo, H. I. E. 1903-1956 ....DLB-157

Dhuoda circa 803-after 843 ....DLB-148

The Dial Press DLB-46

Diamond, I. A. L. 1920-1988 ......DLB-26

Di Cicco, Pier Giorgio 1949- DLB-60

Dick, Philip K. 1928-1982 ....DLB-8

Dick and Fitzgerald DLB-49

Cumulative Index

Dickens, Charles
1812-1870 ...... DLB-21, 55, 70, 159, 166

Dickinson, Peter 1927- DLB-161

Dickey, James
1923- DLB-5; Y-82, 93; DS-7

Dickey, William 1928-1994 .... DLB-5

Dickinson, Emily 1830-1886 .... DLB-1

Dickinson, John 1732-1808 .... DLB-31

Dickinson, Jonathan 1688-1747 ..... DLB-24

Dickinson, Patric 1914- DLB-27

Dickinson, Peter 1927- DLB-87

Dicks, John [publishing house] DLB-106

Dickson, Gordon R. 1923- DLB-8

Dictionary of Literary Biography Yearbook Awards Y-92, 93

The Dictionary of National Biography DLB-144

Didion, Joan 1934- ... DLB-2, 173; Y-81, 86

Di Donato, Pietro 1911- DLB-9

Diego, Gerardo 1896-1987 .... DLB-134

Digges, Thomas circa 1546-1595 ... DLB-136

Dillard, Annie 1945- Y-80

Dillard, R. H. W. 1937- DLB-5

Dillingham, Charles T., Company DLB-49

The Dillingham, G. W., Company DLB-49

Dilly, Edward and Charles [publishing house] DLB-154

Dilthey, Wilhelm 1833-1911 .... DLB-129

Dingelstedt, Franz von 1814-1881 .... DLB-133

Dintenfass, Mark 1941- Y-84

Diogenes, Jr. (see Brougham, John)

DiPrima, Diane 1934- DLB-5, 16

Disch, Thomas M. 1940- DLB-8

Disney, Walt 1901-1966 .... DLB-22

Disraeli, Benjamin 1804-1881 .... DLB-21, 55

D'Israeli, Isaac 1766-1848 .... DLB-107

Ditzen, Rudolf (see Fallada, Hans)

Dix, Dorothea Lynde 1802-1887 ..... DLB-1

Dix, Dorothy (see Gilmer, Elizabeth Meriwether)

Dix, Edwards and Company DLB-49

Dixon, Paige (see Corcoran, Barbara)

Dixon, Richard Watson
1833-1900 .... DLB-19

Dixon, Stephen 1936- DLB-130

Dmitriev, Ivan Ivanovich
1760-1837 .... DLB-150

Dobell, Sydney 1824-1874 .... DLB-32

Döblin, Alfred 1878-1957 .... DLB-66

Dobson, Austin
1840-1921 .... DLB-35, 144

Doctorow, E. L.
1931- DLB-2, 28, 173; Y-80

Documents on Sixteenth-Century Literature DLB-167, 172

Dodd, William E. 1869-1940 .... DLB-17

Dodd, Anne [publishing house] DLB-154

Dodd, Mead and Company DLB-49

Doderer, Heimito von 1896-1968 .... DLB-85

Dodge, Mary Mapes
1831?-1905 .... DLB-42, 79; DS-13

Dodge, B. W., and Company DLB-46

Dodge Publishing Company DLB-49

Dodgson, Charles Lutwidge (see Carroll, Lewis)

Dodsley, Robert 1703-1764 .... DLB-95

Dodsley, R. [publishing house] DLB-154

Dodson, Owen 1914-1983 .... DLB-76

Doesticks, Q. K. Philander, P. B. (see Thomson, Mortimer)

Doheny, Carrie Estelle
1875-1958 .... DLB-140

Domínguez, Sylvia Maida
1935- DLB-122

Donahoe, Patrick [publishing house] DLB-49

Donald, David H. 1920- DLB-17

Donaldson, Scott 1928- DLB-111

Donleavy, J. P. 1926- DLB-6, 173

Donnadieu, Marguerite (see Duras, Marguerite)

Donne, John 1572-1631 .... DLB-121, 151

Donnelley, R. R., and Sons Company DLB-49

Donnelly, Ignatius 1831-1901 .... DLB-12

Donohue and Henneberry DLB-49

Donoso, José 1924- DLB-113

Doolady, M. [publishing house] DLB-49

Dooley, Ebon (see Ebon)

Doolittle, Hilda 1886-1961 .... DLB-4, 45

Doplicher, Fabio 1938- DLB-128

Dor, Milo 1923- DLB-85

Doran, George H., Company DLB-46

Dorgelès, Roland 1886-1973 .... DLB-65

Dorn, Edward 1929- DLB-5

Dorr, Rheta Childe 1866-1948 ...... DLB-25

Dorset and Middlesex, Charles Sackville, Lord Buckhurst,
Earl of 1643-1706 .... DLB-131

Dorst, Tankred 1925- DLB-75, 124

Dos Passos, John
1896-1970 .... DLB-4, 9; DS-1

Doubleday and Company DLB-49

Dougall, Lily 1858-1923 .... DLB-92

Doughty, Charles M.
1843-1926 .... DLB-19, 57

Douglas, Gavin 1476-1522 .... DLB-132

Douglas, Keith 1920-1944 .... DLB-27

Douglas, Norman 1868-1952 .... DLB-34

Douglass, Frederick
1817?-1895 .... DLB-1, 43, 50, 79

Douglass, William circa
1691-1752 .... DLB-24

Dourado, Autran 1926- DLB-145

Dove, Rita 1952- DLB-120

Dover Publications DLB-46

Doves Press DLB-112

Dowden, Edward 1843-1913 ... DLB-35, 149

Dowell, Coleman 1925-1985 .... DLB-130

Dowland, John 1563-1626 .... DLB-172

Downes, Gwladys 1915- DLB-88

Downing, J., Major (see Davis, Charles A.)

Downing, Major Jack (see Smith, Seba)

Dowriche, Anne
before 1560-after 1613 .... DLB-172

Dowson, Ernest 1867-1900 ..... DLB-19, 135

Doxey, William [publishing house] DLB-49

Doyle, Sir Arthur Conan
1859-1930 .... DLB-18, 70, 156

Doyle, Kirby 1932- DLB-16

Drabble, Margaret 1939- DLB-14, 155

Drach, Albert 1902- DLB-85

The Dramatic Publishing Company DLB-49

Dramatists Play Service DLB-46

Drant, Thomas
early 1540s?-1578 .... DLB-167

Draper, John W. 1811-1882 .... DLB-30

Draper, Lyman C. 1815-1891 .... DLB-30

Drayton, Michael 1563-1631 .... DLB-121

Dreiser, Theodore
1871-1945 ..... DLB-9, 12, 102, 137; DS-1

Drewitz, Ingeborg 1923-1986 ....DLB-75

Drieu La Rochelle, Pierre
  1893-1945 ....DLB-72

Drinkwater, John 1882-1937
  .... DLB-10, 19, 149

Droste-Hülshoff, Annette von
  1797-1848 ....DLB-133

The Drue Heinz Literature Prize
  Excerpt from "Excerpts from a Report
  of the Commission," in David
  Bosworth's *The Death of Descartes*
  An Interview with David
  Bosworth Y-82

Drummond, William Henry
  1854-1907 ....DLB-92

Drummond, William, of Hawthornden
  1585-1649 ....DLB-121

Dryden, Charles 1860?-1931 ....DLB-171

Dryden, John 1631-1700 .. DLB-80, 101, 131

Držić, Marin circa 1508-1567 ....DLB-147

Duane, William 1760-1835 ....DLB-43

Dubé, Marcel 1930- DLB-53

Dubé, Rodolphe (see Hertel, François)

Dubie, Norman 1945- DLB-120

Du Bois, W. E. B.
  1868-1963 .... DLB-47, 50, 91

Du Bois, William Pène 1916- DLB-61

Dubus, Andre 1936- DLB-130

Ducharme, Réjean 1941- DLB-60

Dučić, Jovan 1871-1943 ....DLB-147

Duck, Stephen 1705?-1756 ....DLB-95

Duckworth, Gerald, and
  Company Limited DLB-112

Dudek, Louis 1918- DLB-88

Duell, Sloan and Pearce DLB-46

Duff Gordon, Lucie 1821-1869 .....DLB-166

Duffield and Green DLB-46

Duffy, Maureen 1933- DLB-14

Dugan, Alan 1923- DLB-5

Dugard, William
  [publishing house] DLB-170

Dugas, Marcel 1883-1947 ....DLB-92

Dugdale, William
  [publishing house] DLB-106

Duhamel, Georges 1884-1966 ....DLB-65

Dujardin, Edouard 1861-1949 ......DLB-123

Dukes, Ashley 1885-1959 ....DLB-10

Du Maurier, George 1834-1896 .....DLB-153

Dumas, Alexandre, *père*
  1802-1870 ....DLB-119

Dumas, Henry 1934-1968 .... DLB-41

Dunbar, Paul Laurence
  1872-1906 ....DLB-50, 54, 78

Dunbar, William
  circa 1460-circa 1522 ...... DLB-132, 146

Duncan, Norman 1871-1916 ....DLB-92

Duncan, Quince 1940- DLB-145

Duncan, Robert 1919-1988 .... DLB-5, 16

Duncan, Ronald 1914-1982 .... DLB-13

Duncan, Sara Jeannette
  1861-1922 .... DLB-92

Dunigan, Edward, and Brother DLB-49

Dunlap, John 1747-1812 .... DLB-43

Dunlap, William
  1766-1839 .... DLB-30, 37, 59

Dunn, Douglas 1942- DLB-40

Dunn, Stephen 1939- DLB-105

Dunn, Stephen, The Good,
  The Not So Good DLB-105

Dunne, Finley Peter
  1867-1936 .... DLB-11, 23

Dunne, John Gregory 1932- Y-80

Dunne, Philip 1908-1992 .... DLB-26

Dunning, Ralph Cheever
  1878-1930 .... DLB-4

Dunning, William A. 1857-1922 .... DLB-17

Duns Scotus, John
  circa 1266-1308 .... DLB-115

Dunsany, Lord (Edward John Moreton
  Drax Plunkett, Baron Dunsany)
  1878-1957 ....DLB-10, 77, 153, 156

Dunton, John [publishing house] ... DLB-170

Dupin, Amantine-Aurore-Lucile (see Sand,
  George)

Durand, Lucile (see Bersianik, Louky)

Duranty, Walter 1884-1957 .... DLB-29

Duras, Marguerite 1914- DLB-83

Durfey, Thomas 1653-1723 .... DLB-80

Durrell, Lawrence
  1912-1990 ....DLB-15, 27; Y-90

Durrell, William
  [publishing house] DLB-49

Dürrenmatt, Friedrich
  1921 1990 .... DLB-69, 124

Dutton, E. P., and Company DLB-49

Duvoisin, Roger 1904-1980 .... DLB-61

Duyckinck, Evert Augustus
  1816-1878 .... DLB-3, 64

Duyckinck, George L. 1823-1863 ..... DLB-3

Duyckinck and Company DLB-49

Dwight, John Sullivan 1813-1893 ..... DLB-1

Dwight, Timothy 1752-1817 ....DLB-37

Dybek, Stuart 1942- DLB-130

Dyer, Charles 1928- DLB-13

Dyer, George 1755-1841 ....DLB-93

Dyer, John 1699-1757 ....DLB-95

Dyer, Sir Edward 1543-1607 ....DLB-136

Dylan, Bob 1941- DLB-16

E

Eager, Edward 1911-1964 ....DLB-22

Eames, Wilberforce 1855-1937 .....DLB-140

Earle, James H., and Company DLB-49

Earle, John 1600 or 1601-1665 .....DLB-151

Early American Book Illustration,
  by Sinclair Hamilton DLB-49

Eastlake, William 1917- DLB-6

Eastman, Carol ?- DLB-44

Eastman, Max 1883-1969 ....DLB-91

Eaton, Daniel Isaac 1753-1814 .....DLB-158

Eberhart, Richard 1904- DLB-48

Ebner, Jeannie 1918- DLB-85

Ebner-Eschenbach, Marie von
  1830-1916 ....DLB-81

Ebon 1942- DLB-41

Ecbasis Captivi circa 1045 ....DLB-148

Ecco Press DLB-46

Eckhart, Meister
  circa 1260-circa 1328 ....DLB-115

The Eclectic Review 1805-1868 ....DLB-110

Edel, Leon 1907- DLB-103

Edes, Benjamin 1732-1803 ....DLB-43

Edgar, David 1948- DLB-13

Edgeworth, Maria
  1768-1849 ....DLB-116, 159, 163

The Edinburgh Review 1802-1929 .....DLB-110

Edinburgh University Press DLB-112

The Editor Publishing Company DLB-49

Editorial Statements DLB-137

Edmonds, Randolph 1900- DLB-51

Edmonds, Walter D. 1903- DLB-9

Edschmid, Kasimir 1890-1966 ......DLB-56

Edwards, Jonathan 1703-1758 ....DLB-24

Edwards, Jonathan, Jr. 1745-1801 ....DLB-37

Edwards, Junius 1929- DLB-33

Cumulative Index

Edwards, Richard 1524-1566 .... DLB-62

Edwards, James
    [publishing house] DLB-154

Effinger, George Alec 1947- DLB-8

Egerton, George 1859-1945 .... DLB-135

Eggleston, Edward 1837-1902 ...... DLB-12

Eggleston, Wilfred 1901-1986 ...... DLB-92

Ehrenstein, Albert 1886-1950 .... DLB-81

Ehrhart, W. D. 1948- DS-9

Eich, Günter 1907-1972 .... DLB-69, 124

Eichendorff, Joseph Freiherr von
    1788-1857 .... DLB-90

1873 Publishers' Catalogues DLB-49

Eighteenth-Century Aesthetic
    Theories DLB-31

Eighteenth-Century Philosophical
    Background DLB-31

Eigner, Larry 1927- DLB-5

Eikon Basilike 1649 .... DLB-151

Eilhart von Oberge
    circa 1140-circa 1195 .... DLB-148

Einhard circa 770-840 .... DLB-148

Eisenreich, Herbert 1925-1986 ...... DLB-85

Eisner, Kurt 1867-1919 .... DLB-66

Eklund, Gordon 1945- Y-83

Ekwensi, Cyprian 1921- DLB-117

Eld, George
    [publishing house] DLB-170

Elder, Lonne III 1931- DLB-7, 38, 44

Elder, Paul, and Company DLB-49

Elements of Rhetoric (1828; revised, 1846),
    by Richard Whately [excerpt] ... DLB-57

Elie, Robert 1915-1973 .... DLB-88

Elin Pelin 1877-1949 .... DLB-147

Eliot, George 1819-1880 ..... DLB-21, 35, 55

Eliot, John 1604-1690 .... DLB-24

Eliot, T. S. 1888-1965 ..... DLB-7, 10, 45, 63

Eliot's Court Press DLB-170

Elizabeth I 1533-1603 .... DLB-136

Elizondo, Salvador 1932- DLB-145

Elizondo, Sergio 1930- DLB-82

Elkin, Stanley 1930- DLB-2, 28; Y-80

Elles, Dora Amy (see Wentworth, Patricia)

Ellet, Elizabeth F. 1818?-1877 ...... DLB-30

Elliot, Ebenezer 1781-1849 .... DLB-96

Elliot, Frances Minto (Dickinson)
    1820-1898 .... DLB-166

Elliott, George 1923- DLB-68

Elliott, Janice 1931- DLB-14

Elliott, William 1788-1863 .... DLB-3

Elliott, Thomes and Talbot DLB-49

Ellis, Edward S. 1840-1916 .... DLB-42

Ellis, Frederick Staridge
    [publishing house] DLB-106

The George H. Ellis Company DLB-49

Ellison, Harlan 1934- DLB-8

Ellison, Ralph Waldo
    1914-1994 .... DLB-2, 76; Y-94

Ellmann, Richard
    1918-1987 .... DLB-103; Y-87

The Elmer Holmes Bobst Awards in Arts
    and Letters Y-87

Elyot, Thomas 1490?-1546 .... DLB-136

Emanuel, James Andrew 1921- DLB-41

Emecheta, Buchi 1944- DLB-117

The Emergence of Black Women
    Writers DS-8

Emerson, Ralph Waldo
    1803-1882 .... DLB-1, 59, 73

Emerson, William 1769-1811 .... DLB-37

Emin, Fedor Aleksandrovich
    circa 1735-1770 .... DLB-150

Empson, William 1906-1984 .... DLB-20

The End of English Stage Censorship,
    1945-1968 .... DLB-13

Ende, Michael 1929- DLB-75

Engel, Marian 1933-1985 .... DLB-53

Engels, Friedrich 1820-1895 .... DLB-129

Engle, Paul 1908- DLB-48

English Composition and Rhetoric (1866),
    by Alexander Bain [excerpt] DLB-57

The English Language:
    410 to 1500 .... DLB-146

The English Renaissance of Art (1908),
    by Oscar Wilde DLB-35

Enright, D. J. 1920- DLB-27

Enright, Elizabeth 1909-1968 .... DLB-22

L'Envoi (1882), by Oscar Wilde DLB-35

Epps, Bernard 1936- DLB-53

Epstein, Julius 1909- and
    Epstein, Philip 1909-1952 ...... DLB-26

Equiano, Olaudah
    circa 1745-1797 .... DLB-37, 50

Eragny Press DLB-112

Erasmus, Desiderius 1467-1536 .... DLB-136

Erba, Luciano 1922- DLB-128

Erdrich, Louise 1954- DLB-152

Erichsen-Brown, Gwethalyn Graham
    (see Graham, Gwethalyn)

Eriugena, John Scottus
    circa 810-877 .... DLB-115

Ernest Hemingway's Toronto Journalism
    Revisited: With Three Previously
    Unrecorded Stories Y-92

Ernst, Paul 1866-1933 .... DLB-66, 118

Erskine, Albert 1911-1993 .... Y-93

Erskine, John 1879-1951 .... DLB-9, 102

Ervine, St. John Greer 1883-1971 ....DLB-10

Eschenburg, Johann Joachim
    1743-1820 .... DLB-97

Escoto, Julio 1944- DLB-145

Eshleman, Clayton 1935- DLB-5

Espriu, Salvador 1913-1985 .... DLB-134

Ess Ess Publishing Company DLB-49

Essay on Chatterton (1842), by
    Robert Browning DLB-32

Essex House Press DLB-112

Estes, Eleanor 1906-1988 .... DLB-22

Estes and Lauriat DLB-49

Etherege, George 1636-circa 1692 ....DLB-80

Ethridge, Mark, Sr. 1896-1981 ...... DLB-127

Ets, Marie Hall 1893- DLB-22

Etter, David 1928- DLB-105

Ettner, Johann Christoph
    1654-1724 .... DLB-168

Eudora Welty: Eye of the Storyteller ... Y-87

Eugene O'Neill Memorial Theater
    Center DLB-7

Eugene O'Neill's Letters: A Review Y-88

Eupolemius
    flourished circa 1095 .... DLB-148

Evans, Caradoc 1878-1945 .... DLB-162

Evans, Donald 1884-1921 .... DLB-54

Evans, George Henry 1805-1856 .....DLB-43

Evans, Hubert 1892-1986 .... DLB-92

Evans, Mari 1923- DLB-41

Evans, Mary Ann (see Eliot, George)

Evans, Nathaniel 1742-1767 .... DLB-31

Evans, Sebastian 1830-1909 .... DLB-35

Evans, M., and Company DLB-46

Everett, Alexander Hill
    790-1847 .... DLB-59

Everett, Edward 1794-1865 ...... DLB-1, 59

Everson, R. G. 1903- DLB-88

Everson, William 1912-1994 ......DLB-5, 16

Every Man His Own Poet; or, The
  Inspired Singer's Recipe Book (1877),
  by W. H. Mallock DLB-35

Ewart, Gavin 1916- DLB-40

Ewing, Juliana Horatia
  1841-1885 ....DLB-21, 163

The Examiner 1808-1881 ....DLB-110

Exley, Frederick
  1929-1992 ....DLB-143; Y-81

Experiment in the Novel (1929),
  by John D. Beresford DLB-36

Eyre and Spottiswoode DLB-106

Ezzo ?-after 1065 ....DLB-148

F

"F. Scott Fitzgerald: St. Paul's Native Son
  and Distinguished American Writer":
  University of Minnesota Conference,
  29-31 October 1982 ....Y-82

Faber, Frederick William
  1814-1863 ....DLB-32

Faber and Faber Limited DLB-112

Faccio, Rena (see Aleramo, Sibilla)

Fagundo, Ana María 1938- DLB-134

Fair, Ronald L. 1932- DLB-33

Fairfax, Beatrice (see Manning, Marie)

Fairlie, Gerard 1899-1983 ....DLB-77

Fallada, Hans 1893-1947 ....DLB-56

Fancher, Betsy 1928- Y-83

Fane, Violet 1843-1905 ....DLB-35

Fanfrolico Press DLB-112

Fanning, Katherine 1927 ....DLB-127

Fanshawe, Sir Richard
  1608-1666 ....DLB-126

Fantasy Press Publishers DLB-46

Fante, John 1909-1983 ....DLB-130; Y-83

Al-Farabi circa 870-950 ....DLB-115

Farah, Nuruddin 1945- DLB-125

Farber, Norma 1909-1984 ....DLB-61

Farigoule, Louis (see Romains, Jules)

Farjeon, Eleanor 1881-1965 ....DLB-160

Farley, Walter 1920-1989 ....DLB-22

Farmer, Penelope 1939- DLB-161

Farmer, Philip José 1918- DLB-8

Farquhar, George circa 1677-1707 ...DLB-84

Farquharson, Martha (see Finley, Martha)

Farrar, Frederic William
  1831-1903 ....DLB-163

Farrar and Rinehart DLB-46

Farrar, Straus and Giroux DLB-46

Farrell, James T.
  1904-1979 ....DLB-4, 9, 86; DS-2

Farrell, J. G. 1935-1979 ....DLB-14

Fast, Howard 1914- DLB-9

Faulkner, William 1897-1962
  .... DLB-9, 11, 44, 102; DS-2; Y-86

Faulkner, George
  [publishing house] DLB-154

Fauset, Jessie Redmon 1882-1961 ... DLB-51

Faust, Irvin 1924- DLB-2, 28; Y-80

Fawcett Books DLB-46

Fearing, Kenneth 1902-1961 ....DLB-9

Federal Writers' Project DLB-46

Federman, Raymond 1928- Y-80

Feiffer, Jules 1929- DLB-7, 44

Feinberg, Charles E. 1899-1988 ....Y-88

Feind, Barthold 1678-1721 ....DLB-168

Feinstein, Elaine 1930- DLB-14, 40

Feldman, Irving 1928- DLB-169

Felipe, Léon 1884-1968 ....DLB-108

Fell, Frederick, Publishers DLB-46

Felltham, Owen 1602?-1668 ... DLB-126, 151

Fels, Ludwig 1946- DLB-75

Felton, Cornelius Conway
  1807-1862 .... DLB-1

Fennario, David 1947- DLB-60

Fenno, John 1751-1798 ....DLB-43

Fenno, R. F., and Company DLB-49

Fenton, Geoffrey 1539?-1608 ......DLB-136

Fenton, James 1949- DLB-40

Ferber, Edna 1885-1968 ......DLB-9, 28, 86

Ferdinand, Vallery III (see Salaam, Kalamu ya)

Ferguson, Sir Samuel 1810-1886 .... DLB-32

Ferguson, William Scott
  1875-1954 ....DLB-47

Fergusson, Robert 1750-1774 ......DLB-109

Ferland, Albert 1872-1943 ....DLB-92

Ferlinghetti, Lawrence 1919- DLB-5, 16

Fern, Fanny (see Parton, Sara Payson Willis)

Ferrars, Elizabeth 1907- DLB-87

Ferré, Rosario 1942- DLB-145

Ferret, E., and Company DLB-49

Ferrier, Susan 1782-1854 ....DLB-116

Ferrini, Vincent 1913- DLB-48

Ferron, Jacques 1921-1985 ....DLB-60

Ferron, Madeleine 1922- DLB-53

Fetridge and Company DLB-49

Feuchtersleben, Ernst Freiherr von
  1806-1849 ....DLB-133

Feuchtwanger, Lion 1884-1958 ......DLB-66

Feuerbach, Ludwig 1804-1872 .....DLB-133

Fichte, Johann Gottlieb
  1762-1814 ....DLB-90

Ficke, Arthur Davison 1883-1945 ....DLB-54

Fiction Best-Sellers, 1910-1945 ....DLB-9

Fiction into Film, 1928-1975: A List of Movies
  Based on the Works of Authors in
  British Novelists, 1930-1959 ....DLB-15

Fiedler, Leslie A. 1917- DLB-28, 67

Field, Edward 1924- DLB-105

Field, Edward, The Poetry File DLB-105

Field, Eugene
  1850-1895 ...... DLB-23, 42, 140; DS-13

Field, John 1545?-1588 ....DLB-167

Field, Marshall, III 1893-1956 ......DLB-127

Field, Marshall, IV 1916-1965 ......DLB-127

Field, Marshall, V 1941- DLB-127

Field, Nathan 1587-1619 or 1620 ....DLB-58

Field, Rachel 1894-1942 ....DLB-9, 22

A Field Guide to Recent Schools of American
  Poetry Y-86

Fielding, Henry
  1707-1754 .... DLB-39, 84, 101

Fielding, Sarah 1710-1768 ....DLB-39

Fields, James Thomas 1817-1881 ..... DLB-1

Fields, Julia 1938- DLB-41

Fields, W. C. 1880-1946 ....DLB-44

Fields, Osgood and Company DLB-49

Fifty Penguin Years Y-85

Figes, Eva 1932- DLB-14

Figuera, Angela 1902-1984 ....DLB-108

Filmer, Sir Robert 1586-1653 ....DLB-151

Filson, John circa 1753-1788 ....DLB-37

Finch, Anne, Countess of Winchilsea
  1661-1720 ....DLB-95

Finch, Robert 1900- DLB-88

Findley, Timothy 1930- DLB-53

Finlay, Ian Hamilton 1925- DLB-40

Finley, Martha 1828-1909 ....DLB-42

331

Finn, Elizabeth Anne (McCaul)
1825-1921 .... DLB-166

Finney, Jack 1911- DLB-8

Finney, Walter Braden (see Finney, Jack)

Firbank, Ronald 1886-1926 .... DLB-36

Firmin, Giles 1615-1697 .... DLB-24

First Edition Library/Collectors'
Reprints, Inc. Y-91

First International F. Scott Fitzgerald
Conference Y-92

First Strauss "Livings" Awarded to Cynthia
Ozick and Raymond Carver
An Interview with Cynthia Ozick
An Interview with Raymond
Carver Y-83

Fischer, Karoline Auguste Fernandine
1764-1842 .... DLB-94

Fish, Stanley 1938- DLB-67

Fishacre, Richard 1205-1248 ...... DLB-115

Fisher, Clay (see Allen, Henry W.)

Fisher, Dorothy Canfield
1879-1958 .... DLB-9, 102

Fisher, Leonard Everett 1924- DLB-61

Fisher, Roy 1930- DLB-40

Fisher, Rudolph 1897-1934 ..... DLB-51, 102

Fisher, Sydney George 1856-1927 ... DLB-47

Fisher, Vardis 1895-1968 .... DLB-9

Fiske, John 1608-1677 .... DLB-24

Fiske, John 1842-1901 .... DLB-47, 64

Fitch, Thomas circa 1700-1774 ..... DLB-31

Fitch, William Clyde 1865-1909 ..... DLB-7

FitzGerald, Edward 1809-1883 ...... DLB-32

Fitzgerald, F. Scott
1896-1940 ...... DLB-4, 9, 86; Y-81; DS-1

Fitzgerald, Penelope 1916- DLB-14

Fitzgerald, Robert 1910-1985 .... Y-80

Fitzgerald, Thomas 1819-1891 ..... DLB-23

Fitzgerald, Zelda Sayre 1900-1948 ...... Y-84

Fitzhugh, Louise 1928-1974 .... DLB-52

Fitzhugh, William
circa 1651-1701 .... DLB-24

Flanagan, Thomas 1923- Y-80

Flanner, Hildegarde 1899-1987 ..... DLB-48

Flanner, Janet 1892-1978 ....DLB-4

Flaubert, Gustave 1821-1880 ...... DLB-119

Flavin, Martin 1883-1967 ....DLB-9

Fleck, Konrad (flourished circa 1220)
.... DLB-138

Flecker, James Elroy 1884-1915 .. DLB-10, 19

Fleeson, Doris 1901-1970 .... DLB-29

Fleißer, Marieluise 1901-1974 ...DLB-56, 124

Fleming, Ian 1908-1964 .... DLB-87

Fleming, Paul 1609-1640 .... DLB-164

The Fleshly School of Poetry and Other
Phenomena of the Day (1872), by Robert
Buchanan DLB-35

The Fleshly School of Poetry: Mr. D. G.
Rossetti (1871), by Thomas Maitland
(Robert Buchanan) DLB-35

Fletcher, Giles, the Elder
1546-1611 .... DLB-136

Fletcher, Giles, the Younger
1585 or 1586-1623 .... DLB-121

Fletcher, J. S. 1863-1935 .... DLB-70

Fletcher, John (see Beaumont, Francis)

Fletcher, John Gould 1886-1950 ...DLB-4, 45

Fletcher, Phineas 1582-1650 .... DLB-121

Flieg, Helmut (see Heym, Stefan)

Flint, F. S. 1885-1960 .... DLB-19

Flint, Timothy 1780-1840 .... DLB-734

Florio, John 1553?-1625 .... DLB-172

Foix, J. V. 1893-1987 .... DLB-134

Foley, Martha (see Burnett, Whit, and
Martha Foley)

Folger, Henry Clay 1857-1930 ..... DLB-140

Folio Society DLB-112

Follen, Eliza Lee (Cabot) 1787-1860 ... DLB-1

Follett, Ken 1949- Y-81, DLB-87

Follett Publishing Company DLB-46

Folsom, John West
[publishing house] DLB-49

Fontane, Theodor 1819-1898 ...... DLB-129

Fonvisin, Denis Ivanovich
1744 or 1745-1792 .... DLB-150

Foote, Horton 1916- DLB-26

Foote, Samuel 1721-1777 .... DLB-89

Foote, Shelby 1916- DLB-2, 17

Forbes, Calvin 1945- DLB-41

Forbes, Ester 1891-1967 .... DLB-22

Forbes and Company DLB-49

Force, Peter 1790-1868 .... DLB-30

Forché, Carolyn 1950- DLB-5

Ford, Charles Henri 1913- DLB-4, 48

Ford, Corey 1902-1969 .... DLB-11

Ford, Ford Madox
1873-1939 ....DLB-34, 98, 162

Ford, Jesse Hill 1928- DLB-6

Ford, John 1586-? DLB-58

Ford, R. A. D. 1915- DLB-88

Ford, Worthington C. 1858-1941 ....DLB-47

Ford, J. B., and Company DLB-49

Fords, Howard, and Hulbert DLB-49

Foreman, Carl 1914-1984 ....DLB-26

Forester, Frank (see Herbert, Henry William)

Fornés, María Irene 1930- DLB-7

Forrest, Leon 1937- DLB-33

Forster, E. M.
1879-1970 ....DLB-34, 98, 162; DS-10

Forster, Georg 1754-1794 ....DLB-94

Forster, John 1812-1876 ....DLB-144

Forster, Margaret 1938- DLB-155

Forsyth, Frederick 1938- DLB-87

Forten, Charlotte L. 1837-1914 ......DLB-50

Fortini, Franco 1917- DLB-128

Fortune, T. Thomas 1856-1928 ......DLB-23

Fosdick, Charles Austin
1842-1915 ....DLB-42

Foster, Genevieve 1893-1979 ....DLB-61

Foster, Hannah Webster
1758-1840 ....DLB-37

Foster, John 1648-1681 ....DLB-24

Foster, Michael 1904-1956 ....DLB-9

Foulis, Robert and Andrew / R. and A.
[publishing house] DLB-154

Fouqué, Caroline de la Motte
1774-1831 ....DLB-90

Fouqué, Friedrich de la Motte
1777-1843 ....DLB-90

Four Essays on the Beat Generation,
by John Clellon Holmes DLB-16

Four Seas Company DLB-46

Four Winds Press DLB-46

Fournier, Henri Alban (see Alain-Fournier)

Fowler and Wells Company DLB-49

Fowles, John 1926- DLB-14, 139

Fox, John, Jr. 1862 or
1863-1919 .... DLB-9; DS-13

Fox, Paula 1923- DLB-52

Fox, Richard Kyle 1846-1922 ....DLB-79

Fox, William Price 1926- DLB-2; Y-81

Fox, Richard K.
[publishing house] DLB-49

Foxe, John 1517-1587 ....DLB-132

Fraenkel, Michael 1896-1957 ....DLB-4

France, Anatole 1844-1924 ....DLB-123
France, Richard 1938- DLB-7
Francis, Convers 1795-1863 ....DLB-1
Francis, Dick 1920- DLB-87
Francis, Jeffrey, Lord 1773-1850 ....DLB-107
Francis, C. S. [publishing house] DLB-49
François 1863-1910 ....DLB-92
François, Louise von 1817-1893 ....DLB-129
Francke, Kuno 1855-1930 ....DLB-71
Frank, Bruno 1887-1945 ....DLB-118
Frank, Leonhard 1882-1961 .....DLB-56, 118
Frank, Melvin (see Panama, Norman)
Frank, Waldo 1889-1967 ....DLB-9, 63
Franken, Rose 1895?-1988 ....Y-84
Franklin, Benjamin
  1706-1790 .... DLB-24, 43, 73
Franklin, James 1697-1735 ....DLB-43
Franklin Library DLB-46
Frantz, Ralph Jules 1902-1979 ....DLB-4
Franzos, Karl Emil 1848-1904 ......DLB-129
Fraser, G. S. 1915-1980 ....DLB-27
Fraser, Kathleen 1935- DLB-169
Frattini, Alberto 1922- DLB-128
Frau Ava ?-1127 ....DLB-148
Frayn, Michael 1933- DLB-13, 14
Frederic, Harold
  1856-1898 .... DLB-12, 23; DS-13
Freeling, Nicolas 1927- DLB-87
Freeman, Douglas Southall
  1886-1953 ....DLB-17
Freeman, Legh Richmond
  1842-1915 ....DLB-23
Freeman, Mary E. Wilkins
  1852-1930 ....DLB-12, 78
Freeman, R. Austin 1862-1943 ......DLB-70
Freidank circa 1170-circa 1233 .....DLB-138
Freiligrath, Ferdinand 1810-1876 ...DLB-133
French, Alice 1850-1934 ..... DLB-74; DS-13
French, David 1939- DLB-53
French, James [publishing house] DLB-49
French, Samuel [publishing house] ...DLB-49
Samuel French, Limited DLB-106
Freneau, Philip 1752-1832 ....DLB-37, 43
Freni, Melo 1934- DLB-128
Freytag, Gustav 1816-1895 ....DLB-129
Fried, Erich 1921-1988 ....DLB-85

Friedman, Bruce Jay 1930- DLB-2, 28
Friedrich von Hausen
  circa 1171-1190 ....DLB-138
Friel, Brian 1929- DLB-13
Friend, Krebs 1895?-1967? DLB-4
Fries, Fritz Rudolf 1935- DLB-75
Fringe and Alternative Theater
  in Great Britain DLB-13
Frisch, Max 1911-1991 ....DLB-69, 124
Frischmuth, Barbara 1941- DLB-85
Fritz, Jean 1915- DLB-52
Fromentin, Eugene 1820-1876 .....DLB-123
From *The Gay Science*, by
  E. S. Dallas DLB-21
Frost, A. B. 1851-1928 ....DS-13
Frost, Robert 1874-1963 ...... DLB-54; DS-7
Frothingham, Octavius Brooks
  1822-1895 ....DLB-1
Froude, James Anthony
  1818-1894 ....DLB-18, 57, 144
Fry, Christopher 1907- DLB-13
Fry, Roger 1866-1934 ....DS-10
Frye, Northrop 1912-1991 ......DLB-67, 68
Fuchs, Daniel
  1909-1993 ....DLB-9, 26, 28; Y-93
Fuentes, Carlos 1928- DLB-113
Fuertes, Gloria 1918- DLB-108
The Fugitives and the Agrarians:
  The First Exhibition Y-85
Fulbecke, William 1560-1603? DLB-172
Fuller, Charles H., Jr. 1939- DLB-38
Fuller, Henry Blake 1857-1929 .....DLB-12
Fuller, John 1937- DLB-40
Fuller, Roy 1912-1991 ....DLB-15, 20
Fuller, Samuel 1912- DLB-26
Fuller, Sarah Margaret, Marchesa
  D'Ossoli 1810-1850 ....DLB-1, 59, 73
Fuller, Thomas 1608-1661 ....DLB-151
Fullerton, Hugh 1873-1945 ....DLB-171
Fulton, Len 1934- Y-86
Fulton, Robin 1937- DLB-40
Furbank, P. N. 1920- DLB-155
Furman, Laura 1945- Y-86
Furness, Horace Howard
  1833-1912 ....DLB-64
Furness, William Henry 1802-1896 ... DLB-1
Furthman, Jules 1888-1966 ....DLB-26

The Future of the Novel (1899), by
  Henry James DLB-18
Fyleman, Rose 1877-1957 ....DLB-160

G

The G. Ross Roy Scottish Poetry
  Collection at the University of
  South Carolina Y-89
Gaddis, William 1922- DLB-2
Gág, Wanda 1893-1946 ....DLB-22
Gagnon, Madeleine 1938- DLB-60
Gaine, Hugh 1726-1807 ....DLB-43
Gaine, Hugh [publishing house] DLB-49
Gaines, Ernest J.
  1933- DLB-2, 33, 152; Y-80
Gaiser, Gerd 1908-1976 ....DLB-69
Galarza, Ernesto 1905-1984 ....DLB-122
Galaxy Science Fiction Novels DLB-46
Gale, Zona 1874-1938 ....DLB-9, 78
Gall, Louise von 1815-1855 ....DLB-133
Gallagher, Tess 1943- DLB-120
Gallagher, Wes 1911- DLB-127
Gallagher, William Davis
  1808-1894 ....DLB-73
Gallant, Mavis 1922- DLB-53
Gallico, Paul 1897-1976 ....DLB-9, 171
Galsworthy, John
  1867-1933 .... DLB-10, 34, 98, 162
Galt, John 1779-1839 ....DLB-99, 116
Galton, Sir Francis 1822-1911 ......DLB-166
Galvin, Brendan 1938- DLB-5
Gambit DLB-46
Gamboa, Reymundo 1948- DLB-122
Gammer Gurton's Needle DLB-62
Gannett, Frank E. 1876-1957 ....DLB-29
Gaos, Vicente 1919-1980 ....DLB-134
García, Lionel G. 1935- DLB-82
García Lorca, Federico
  1898-1936 ....DLB-108
García Márquez, Gabriel
  1928- DLB-113
Gardam, Jane 1928- DLB-14, 161
Garden, Alexander
  circa 1685-1756 ....DLB-31
Gardiner, Margaret Power Farmer (see
  Blessington, Marguerite, Countess of)
Gardner, John 1933-1982 ....DLB-2; Y-82

Cumulative Index

Garfield, Leon 1921- DLB-161

Garis, Howard R. 1873-1962 .... DLB-22

Garland, Hamlin
    1860-1940 .... DLB-12, 71, 78

Garneau, Francis-Xavier
    1809-1866 .... DLB-99

Garneau, Hector de Saint-Denys
    1912-1943 .... DLB-88

Garneau, Michel 1939- DLB-53

Garner, Alan 1934- DLB-161

Garner, Hugh 1913-1979 .... DLB-68

Garnett, David 1892-1981 .... DLB-34

Garnett, Eve 1900-1991 .... DLB-160

Garraty, John A. 1920- DLB-17

Garrett, George
    1929- DLB-2, 5, 130, 152; Y-83

Garrick, David 1717-1779 .... DLB-84

Garrison, William Lloyd
    1805-1879 .... DLB-1, 43

Garro, Elena 1920- DLB-145

Garth, Samuel 1661-1719 .... DLB-95

Garve, Andrew 1908- DLB-87

Gary, Romain 1914-1980 .... DLB-83

Gascoigne, George 1539?-1577 .... DLB-136

Gascoyne, David 1916- DLB-20

Gaskell, Elizabeth Cleghorn
    1810-1865 .... DLB-21, 144, 159

Gaspey, Thomas 1788-1871 .... DLB-116

Gass, William Howard 1924- DLB-2

Gates, Doris 1901- DLB-22

Gates, Henry Louis, Jr. 1950- DLB-67

Gates, Lewis E. 1860-1924 .... DLB-71

Gatto, Alfonso 1909-1976 .... DLB-114

Gautier, Théophile 1811-1872 ..... DLB-119

Gauvreau, Claude 1925-1971 .... DLB-88

The *Gawain*-Poet
    flourished circa 1350-1400 ..... DLB-146

Gay, Ebenezer 1696-1787 .... DLB-24

Gay, John 1685-1732 .... DLB-84, 95

The Gay Science (1866), by E. S. Dallas
    [excerpt] DLB-21

Gayarré, Charles E. A. 1805-1895 ... DLB-30

Gaylord, Edward King
    1873-1974 .... DLB-127

Gaylord, Edward Lewis 1919- ... DLB-127

Gaylord, Charles
    [publishing house] DLB-49

Geddes, Gary 1940- DLB-60

Geddes, Virgil 1897- DLB-4

Gedeon (Georgii Andreevich Krinovsky)
    circa 1730-1763 .... DLB-150

Geibel, Emanuel 1815-1884 .... DLB-129

Geis, Bernard, Associates DLB-46

Geisel, Theodor Seuss
    1904-1991 .... DLB-61; Y-91

Gelb, Arthur 1924- DLB-103

Gelb, Barbara 1926- DLB-103

Gelber, Jack 1932- DLB-7

Gelinas, Gratien 1909- DLB-88

Gellert, Christian Füerchtegott
    1715-1769 .... DLB-97

Gellhorn, Martha 1908- Y-82

Gems, Pam 1925- DLB-13

A General Idea of the College of Mirania (1753),
    by William Smith [excerpts] DLB-31

Genet, Jean 1910-1986 .... DLB-72; Y-86

Genevoix, Maurice 1890-1980 .... DLB-65

Genovese, Eugene D. 1930- DLB-17

Gent, Peter 1942- Y-82

Geoffrey of Monmouth
    circa 1100-1155 .... DLB-146

George, Henry 1839-1897 .... DLB-23

George, Jean Craighead 1919- DLB-52

Georgslied 896? DLB-148

Gerhardie, William 1895-1977 ...... DLB-36

Gerhardt, Paul 1607-1676 .... DLB-164

Gérin, Winifred 1901-1981 .... DLB-155

Gérin-Lajoie, Antoine 1824-1882 .... DLB-99

German Drama 800-1280 .... DLB-138

German Drama from Naturalism
    to Fascism: 1889-1933 .... DLB-118

German Literature and Culture from
    Charlemagne to the Early Courtly
    Period DLB-148

German Radio Play, The DLB-124

German Transformation from the Baroque
    to the Enlightenment, The DLB-97

The Germanic Epic and Old English Heroic
    Poetry: *Widseth, Waldere,* and *The
    Fight at Finnsburg* DLB-146

Germanophilism, by Hans Kohn DLB-66

Gernsback, Hugo 1884-1967 ..... DLB-8, 137

Gerould, Katharine Fullerton
    1879-1944 .... DLB-78

Gerrish, Samuel [publishing house] .. DLB-49

Gerrold, David 1944- DLB-8

Gersonides 1288-1344 .... DLB-115

Gerstäcker, Friedrich 1816-1872 ....DLB-129

Gerstenberg, Heinrich Wilhelm von
    1737-1823 ....DLB-97

Gervinus, Georg Gottfried
    1805-1871 ....DLB-133

Geßner, Salomon 1730-1788 ....DLB-97

Geston, Mark S. 1946- DLB-8

Al-Ghazali 1058-1111 ....DLB-115

Gibbon, Edward 1737-1794 ....DLB-104

Gibbon, John Murray 1875-1952 .....DLB-92

Gibbon, Lewis Grassic (see Mitchell,
    James Leslie)

Gibbons, Floyd 1887-1939 ....DLB-25

Gibbons, Reginald 1947- DLB-120

Gibbons, William ?-? DLB-73

Gibson, Charles Dana 1867-1944 ..... DS-13

Gibson, Charles Dana 1867-1944 ..... DS-13

Gibson, Graeme 1934- DLB-53

Gibson, Margaret 1944- DLB-120

Gibson, Wilfrid 1878-1962 ....DLB-19

Gibson, William 1914- DLB-7

Gide, André 1869-1951 ....DLB-65

Giguère, Diane 1937- DLB-53

Giguère, Roland 1929- DLB-60

Gil de Biedma, Jaime 1929-1990 ....DLB-108

Gil-Albert, Juan 1906- DLB-134

Gilbert, Anthony 1899-1973 ....DLB-77

Gilbert, Michael 1912- DLB-87

Gilbert, Sandra M. 1936- DLB-120

Gilbert, Sir Humphrey
    1537-1583 ....DLB-136

Gilchrist, Alexander
    1828-1861 ....DLB-144

Gilchrist, Ellen 1935- DLB-130

Gilder, Jeannette L. 1849-1916 ....DLB-79

Gilder, Richard Watson
    1844-1909 .... DLB-64, 79

Gildersleeve, Basil 1831-1924 ....DLB-71

Giles, Henry 1809-1882 ....DLB-64

Giles of Rome circa 1243-1316 .....DLB-115

Gilfillan, George 1813-1878 ....DLB-144

Gill, Eric 1882-1940 ....DLB-98

Gill, William F., Company DLB-49

Gillespie, A. Lincoln, Jr.
    1895-1950 ....DLB-4

Gilliam, Florence ?-? DLB-4

Gilliatt, Penelope 1932-1993 ....DLB-14

Gillott, Jacky 1939-1980 .... DLB-14
Gilman, Caroline H. 1794-1888 ... DLB-3, 73
Gilman, W. and J.
    [publishing house] DLB-49
Gilmer, Elizabeth Meriwether
    1861-1951 .... DLB-29
Gilmer, Francis Walker
    1790-1826 .... DLB-37
Gilroy, Frank D. 1925- DLB-7
Gimferrer, Pere (Pedro) 1945- DLB-134
Gingrich, Arnold 1903-1976 .... DLB-137
Ginsberg, Allen 1926- DLB-5, 16, 169
Ginzkey, Franz Karl 1871-1963 ...... DLB-81
Gioia, Dana 1950- DLB-120
Giono, Jean 1895-1970 .... DLB-72
Giotti, Virgilio 1885-1957 .... DLB-114
Giovanni, Nikki 1943- DLB-5, 41
Gipson, Lawrence Henry
    1880-1971 .... DLB-17
Girard, Rodolphe 1879-1956 .... DLB-92
Giraudoux, Jean 1882-1944 .... DLB-65
Gissing, George 1857-1903 ..... DLB-18, 135
Giudici, Giovanni 1924- DLB-128
Giuliani, Alfredo 1924- DLB-128
Gladstone, William Ewart
    1809-1898 .... DLB-57
Glaeser, Ernst 1902-1963 .... DLB-69
Glanville, Brian 1931- DLB-15, 139
Glapthorne, Henry 1610-1643? DLB-58
Glasgow, Ellen 1873-1945 ...... DLB-9, 12
Glaspell, Susan 1876-1948 ..... DLB-7, 9, 78
Glass, Montague 1877-1934 .... DLB-11
Glassco, John 1909-1981 .... DLB-68
Glauser, Friedrich 1896-1938 .... DLB-56
F. Gleason's Publishing Hall DLB-49
Gleim, Johann Wilhelm Ludwig
    1719-1803 .... DLB-97
Glendinning, Victoria 1937- DLB-155
Glover, Richard 1712-1785 .... DLB-95
Glück, Louise 1943- DLB-5
Glyn, Elinor 1864-1943 .... DLB-153
Gobineau, Joseph-Arthur de
    1816-1882 .... DLB-123
Godbout, Jacques 1933- DLB-53
Goddard, Morrill 1865-1937 .... DLB-25
Goddard, William 1740-1817 .... DLB-43
Godden, Rumer 1907- DLB-161

Godey, Louis A. 1804-1878 .... DLB-73
Godey and McMichael DLB-49
Godfrey, Dave 1938- DLB-60
Godfrey, Thomas 1736-1763 .... DLB-31
Godine, David R., Publisher DLB-46
Godkin, E. L. 1831-1902 .... DLB-79
Godolphin, Sidney 1610-1643 ..... DLB-126
Godwin, Gail 1937- DLB-6
Godwin, Mary Jane Clairmont
    1766-1841 .... DLB-163
Godwin, Parke 1816-1904 .... DLB-3, 64
Godwin, William
    1756-1836 ... DLB-39, 104, 142, 158, 163
Godwin, M. J., and Company DLB-154
Goering, Reinhard 1887-1936 ...... DLB-118
Goes, Albrecht 1908- DLB-69
Goethe, Johann Wolfgang von
    1749-1832 .... DLB-94
Goetz, Curt 1888-1960 .... DLB-124
Goffe, Thomas circa 1592-1629 ..... DLB-58
Goffstein, M. B. 1940- DLB-61
Gogarty, Oliver St. John
    1878-1957 .... DLB-15, 19
Goines, Donald 1937-1974 .... DLB-33
Gold, Herbert 1924- DLB-2; Y-81
Gold, Michael 1893-1967 .... DLB-9, 28
Goldbarth, Albert 1948- DLB-120
Goldberg, Dick 1947- DLB-7
Golden Cockerel Press DLB-112
Golding, Arthur 1536-1606 .... DLB-136
Golding, William 1911-1993 .... DLB-15, 100
Goldman, William 1931- DLB-44
Goldsmith, Oliver
    1730?-1774 ... DLB-39, 89, 104, 109, 142
Goldsmith, Oliver 1794-1861 ...... DLB-99
Goldsmith Publishing Company DLB-46
Gollancz, Victor, Limited DLB-112
Gómez-Quiñones, Juan 1942- DLB-122
Gomme, Laurence James
    [publishing house] DLB-46
Goncourt, Edmond de 1822-1896 .. DLB-123
Goncourt, Jules de 1830-1870 ...... DLB-123
Gonzales, Rodolfo "Corky"
    1928- DLB-122
González, Angel 1925- DLB-108
Gonzalez, Genaro 1949- DLB-122
Gonzalez, Ray 1952- DLB-122

González de Mireles, Jovita
    1899-1983 .... DLB-122
González-T., César A. 1931- DLB-82
Goodbye, Gutenberg? A Lecture at
    the New York Public Library,
    18 April 1995 .... Y-95
Goodison, Lorna 1947- DLB-157
Goodman, Paul 1911-1972 .... DLB-130
The Goodman Theatre DLB-7
Goodrich, Frances 1891-1984 and
    Hackett, Albert 1900- DLB-26
Goodrich, Samuel Griswold
    1793-1860 .... DLB-1, 42, 73
Goodrich, S. G. [publishing house] ... DLB-49
Goodspeed, C. E., and Company DLB-49
Goodwin, Stephen 1943- Y-82
Googe, Barnabe 1540-1594 .... DLB-132
Gookin, Daniel 1612-1687 .... DLB-24
Gordon, Caroline
    1895-1981 .... DLB-4, 9, 102; Y-81
Gordon, Giles 1940- DLB-14, 139
Gordon, Lyndall 1941- DLB-155
Gordon, Mary 1949- DLB-6; Y-81
Gordone, Charles 1925- DLB-7
Gore, Catherine 1800-1861 .... DLB-116
Gorey, Edward 1925- DLB-61
Görres, Joseph 1776-1848 .... DLB-90
Gosse, Edmund 1849-1928 ..... DLB-57, 144
Gosson, Stephen 1554-1624 .... DLB-172
Gotlieb, Phyllis 1926- DLB-88
Gottfried von Straßburg
    died before 1230 .... DLB-138
Gotthelf, Jeremias 1797-1854 ...... DLB-133
Gottschalk circa 804/808-869 ...... DLB-148
Gottsched, Johann Christoph
    1700-1766 .... DLB-97
Götz, Johann Nikolaus
    1721-1781 .... DLB-97
Gould, Wallace 1882-1940 .... DLB-54
Govoni, Corrado 1884-1965 .... DLB-114
Gower, John circa 1330-1408 ...... DLB-146
Goyen, William 1915-1983 ..... DLB-2; Y-83
Goytisolo, José Augustín 1928- ... DLB-134
Gozzano, Guido 1883-1916 .... DLB-114
Grabbe, Christian Dietrich
    1801-1836 .... DLB-133
Gracq, Julien 1910- DLB-83
Grady, Henry W. 1850-1889 .... DLB-23

Graf, Oskar Maria 1894-1967 ...... DLB-56

Graf Rudolf between circa 1170
    and circa 1185 .... DLB-148

Grafton, Richard
    [publishing house] DLB-170

Graham, George Rex 1813-1894 .... DLB-73

Graham, Gwethalyn 1913-1965 ..... DLB-88

Graham, Jorie 1951- DLB-120

Graham, Katharine 1917- DLB-127

Graham, Lorenz 1902-1989 .... DLB-76

Graham, Philip 1915-1963 .... DLB-127

Graham, R. B. Cunninghame
    1852-1936 .... DLB-98, 135

Graham, Shirley 1896-1977 .... DLB-76

Graham, W. S. 1918- DLB-20

Graham, William H.
    [publishing house] DLB-49

Graham, Winston 1910- DLB-77

Grahame, Kenneth
    1859-1932 .... DLB-34, 141

Grainger, Martin Allerdale
    1874-1941 .... DLB-92

Gramatky, Hardie 1907-1979 .... DLB-22

Grand, Sarah 1854-1943 .... DLB-135

Grandbois, Alain 1900-1975 .... DLB-92

Grange, John circa 1556-? DLB-136

Granich, Irwin (see Gold, Michael)

Grant, Duncan 1885-1978 .... DS-10

Grant, George 1918-1988 .... DLB-88

Grant, George Monro 1835-1902 .... DLB-99

Grant, Harry J. 1881-1963 .... DLB-29

Grant, James Edward 1905-1966 .... DLB-26

Grass, Günter 1927- DLB-75, 124

Grasty, Charles H. 1863-1924 ..... DLB-25

Grau, Shirley Ann 1929- DLB-2

Graves, John 1920- Y-83

Graves, Richard 1715-1804 .... DLB-39

Graves, Robert
    1895-1985 .... DLB-20, 100; Y-85

Gray, Asa 1810-1888 .... DLB-1

Gray, David 1838-1861 .... DLB-32

Gray, Simon 1936- DLB-13

Gray, Thomas 1716-1771 .... DLB-109

Grayson, William J. 1788-1863 ... DLB-3, 64

The Great Bibliographers Series Y-93

The Great War and the Theater, 1914-1918
    [Great Britain] DLB-10

Greeley, Horace 1811-1872 .... DLB-3, 43

Green, Adolph (see Comden, Betty)

Green, Duff 1791-1875 .... DLB-43

Green, Gerald 1922- DLB-28

Green, Henry 1905-1973 .... DLB-15

Green, Jonas 1712-1767 .... DLB-31

Green, Joseph 1706-1780 .... DLB-31

Green, Julien 1900- DLB-4, 72

Green, Paul 1894-1981 .... DLB-7, 9; Y-81

Green, T. and S.
    [publishing house] DLB-49

Green, Timothy
    [publishing house] DLB-49

Greenaway, Kate 1846-1901 .... DLB-141

Greenberg: Publisher DLB-46

Green Tiger Press DLB-46

Greene, Asa 1789-1838 .... DLB-11

Greene, Benjamin H.
    [publishing house] DLB-49

Greene, Graham 1904-1991
    .... DLB-13, 15, 77, 100, 162; Y-85, Y-91

Greene, Robert 1558-1592 ...... DLB-62, 167

Greenhow, Robert 1800-1854 .... DLB-30

Greenough, Horatio 1805-1852 .... DLB-1

Greenwell, Dora 1821-1882 .... DLB-35

Greenwillow Books DLB-46

Greenwood, Grace (see Lippincott, Sara Jane
    Clarke)

Greenwood, Walter 1903-1974 ...... DLB-10

Greer, Ben 1948- DLB-6

Greflinger, Georg 1620?-1677 ..... DLB-164

Greg, W. R. 1809-1881 .... DLB-55

Gregg Press DLB-46

Gregory, Isabella Augusta
    Persse, Lady 1852-1932 .... DLB-10

Gregory, Horace 1898-1982 .... DLB-48

Gregory of Rimini
    circa 1300-1358 .... DLB-115

Gregynog Press DLB-112

Greiffenberg, Catharina Regina von
    1633-1694 .... DLB-168

Grenfell, Wilfred Thomason
    1865-1940 .... DLB-92

Greve, Felix Paul (see Grove, Frederick Philip)

Greville, Fulke, First Lord Brooke
    1554-1628 .... DLB-62, 172

Grey, Lady Jane 1537-1554 .... DLB-132

Grey Owl 1888-1938 .... DLB-92

Grey, Zane 1872-1939 .... DLB-9

Grey Walls Press DLB-112

Grier, Eldon 1917- DLB-88

Grieve, C. M. (see MacDiarmid, Hugh)

Griffin, Bartholomew
    flourished 1596 .... DLB-172

Griffin, Gerald 1803-1840 .... DLB-159

Griffith, Elizabeth 1727?-1793 ... DLB-39, 89

Griffiths, Trevor 1935- DLB-13

Griffiths, Ralph
    [publishing house] DLB-154

Griggs, S. C., and Company DLB-49

Griggs, Sutton Elbert 1872-1930 ..... DLB-50

Grignon, Claude-Henri 1894-1976 ... DLB-68

Grigson, Geoffrey 1905- DLB-27

Grillparzer, Franz 1791-1872 ..... DLB-133

Grimald, Nicholas
    circa 1519-circa 1562 .... DLB-136

Grimké, Angelina Weld
    1880-1958 .... DLB-50, 54

Grimm, Hans 1875-1959 .... DLB-66

Grimm, Jacob 1785-1863 .... DLB-90

Grimm, Wilhelm 1786-1859 .... DLB-90

Grimmelshausen, Johann Jacob Christoffel von
    1621 or 1622-1676 .... DLB-168

Grindal, Edmund
    1519 or 1520-1583 .... DLB-132

Griswold, Rufus Wilmot
    1815-1857 .... DLB-3, 59

Gross, Milt 1895-1953 .... DLB-11

Grosset and Dunlap DLB-49

Grossman Publishers DLB-46

Grosseteste, Robert
    circa 1160-1253 .... DLB-115

Grosvenor, Gilbert H. 1875-1966 ... DLB-91

Groth, Klaus 1819-1899 .... DLB-129

Groulx, Lionel 1878-1967 .... DLB-68

Grove, Frederick Philip 1879-1949 ... DLB-92

Grove Press DLB-46

Grubb, Davis 1919-1980 .... DLB-6

Gruelle, Johnny 1880-1938 .... DLB-22

Grymeston, Elizabeth
    before 1563-before 1604 .... DLB-136

Gryphius, Andreas 1616-1664 ..... DLB-164

Gryphius, Christian 1649-1706 .... DLB-168

Guare, John 1938- DLB-7

Guerra, Tonino 1920- DLB-128

Guest, Barbara 1920- DLB-5

Guèvremont, Germaine
  1893-1968 ....DLB-68

Guidacci, Margherita 1921-1992 ....DLB-128

Guide to the Archives of Publishers, Journals,
  and Literary Agents in North American
  Libraries Y-93

Guillén, Jorge 1893-1984 ....DLB-108

Guilloux, Louis 1899-1980 ....DLB-72

Guilpin, Everard
  circa 1572-after 1608? DLB-136

Guiney, Louise Imogen 1861-1920 ...DLB-54

Guiterman, Arthur 1871-1943 ....DLB-11

Günderrode, Caroline von
  1780-1806 ....DLB-90

Gundulić, Ivan 1589-1638 ....DLB-147

Gunn, Bill 1934-1989 ....DLB-38

Gunn, James E. 1923- DLB-8

Gunn, Neil M. 1891-1973 ....DLB-15

Gunn, Thom 1929- DLB-27

Gunnars, Kristjana 1948- DLB-60

Günther, Johann Christian
  1695-1723 ....DLB-168

Gurik, Robert 1932- DLB-60

Gustafson, Ralph 1909- DLB-88

Gütersloh, Albert Paris 1887-1973 ...DLB-81

Guthrie, A. B., Jr. 1901- DLB-6

Guthrie, Ramon 1896-1973 ....DLB-4

The Guthrie Theater DLB-7

Gutzkow, Karl 1811-1878 ....DLB-133

Guy, Ray 1939- DLB-60

Guy, Rosa 1925- DLB-33

Guyot, Arnold 1807-1884 ....DS-13

Gwynne, Erskine 1898-1948 ....DLB-4

Gyles, John 1680-1755 ....DLB-99

Gysin, Brion 1916- DLB-16

H

H. D. (see Doolittle, Hilda)

Habington, William 1605-1654 .....DLB-126

Hacker, Marilyn 1942- DLB-120

Hackett, Albert (see Goodrich, Frances)

Hacks, Peter 1928- DLB-124

Hadas, Rachel 1948- DLB-120

Hadden, Briton 1898-1929 ....DLB-91

Hagedorn, Friedrich von
  1708-1754 ....DLB-168

Hagelstange, Rudolf 1912-1984 .....DLB-69

Haggard, H. Rider 1856-1925 ... DLB-70, 156

Haggard, William 1907-1993 ....Y-93

Hahn-Hahn, Ida Gräfin von
  1805-1880 ....DLB-133

Haig-Brown, Roderick 1908-1976 ...DLB-88

Haight, Gordon S. 1901-1985 ......DLB-103

Hailey, Arthur 1920- DLB-88; Y-82

Haines, John 1924- DLB-5

Hake, Edward
  flourished 1566-1604 ....DLB-136

Hake, Thomas Gordon 1809-1895 ...DLB-32

Hakluyt, Richard 1552?-1616 ......DLB-136

Halbe, Max 1865-1944 ....DLB-118

Haldane, J. B. S. 1892-1964 ....DLB-160

Haldeman, Joe 1943- DLB-8

Haldeman-Julius Company DLB-46

Hale, E. J., and Son DLB-49

Hale, Edward Everett
  1822-1909 .... DLB-1, 42, 74

Hale, Kathleen 1898- DLB-160

Hale, Leo Thomas (see Ebon)

Hale, Lucretia Peabody
  1820-1900 .... DLB-42

Hale, Nancy 1908-1988 .... DLB-86; Y-80, 88

Hale, Sarah Josepha (Buell)
  1788-1879 .... DLB-1, 42, 73

Hales, John 1584-1656 ....DLB-151

Haley, Alex 1921-1992 ....DLB-38

Haliburton, Thomas Chandler
  1796-1865 .... DLB-11, 99

Hall, Anna Maria 1800-1881 ......DLB-159

Hall, Donald 1928- DLB-5

Hall, Edward 1497-1547 ....DLB-132

Hall, James 1793-1868 .... DLB-73, 74

Hall, Joseph 1574-1656 .... DLB-121, 151

Hall, Samuel [publishing house] DLB-49

Hallam, Arthur Henry 1811-1833 ...DLB-32

Halleck, Fitz-Greene 1790-1867 ......DLB-3

Haller, Albrecht von 1708-1777 ....DLB-168

Hallmann, Johann Christian
  1640-1704 or 1716? DLB-168

Hallmark Editions DLB-46

Halper, Albert 1904-1984 .... DLB-9

Halperin, John William 1941- DLB-111

Halstead, Murat 1829-1908 .... DLB-23

Hamann, Johann Georg 1730-1788 .. DLB-97

Hamburger, Michael 1924- DLB-27

Hamilton, Alexander 1712-1756 .....DLB-31

Hamilton, Alexander 1755?-1804 ....DLB-37

Hamilton, Cicely 1872-1952 ....DLB-10

Hamilton, Edmond 1904-1977 ....DLB-8

Hamilton, Elizabeth 1758-1816 .. DLB-116, 158

Hamilton, Gail (see Corcoran, Barbara)

Hamilton, Ian 1938- DLB-40, 155

Hamilton, Patrick 1904-1962 ....DLB-10

Hamilton, Virginia 1936- DLB-33, 52

Hamilton, Hamish, Limited DLB-112

Hammett, Dashiell 1894-1961 .... DS-6

Dashiell Hammett:
  An Appeal in *TAC* Y-91

Hammon, Jupiter 1711-died between
  1790 and 1806 ....DLB-31, 50

Hammond, John ?-1663 ....DLB-24

Hamner, Earl 1923- DLB-6

Hampton, Christopher 1946- DLB-13

Handel-Mazzetti, Enrica von
  1871-1955 ....DLB-81

Handke, Peter 1942- DLB-85, 124

Handlin, Oscar 1915- DLB-17

Hankin, St. John 1869-1909 ....DLB-10

Hanley, Clifford 1922- DLB-14

Hannah, Barry 1942- DLB-6

Hannay, James 1827-1873 ....DLB-21

Hansberry, Lorraine 1930-1965 ...DLB-7, 38

Hapgood, Norman 1868-1937 ....DLB-91

Happel, Eberhard Werner
  1647-1690 ....DLB-168

Harcourt Brace Jovanovich DLB-46

Hardenberg, Friedrich von (see Novalis)

Harding, Walter 1917- DLB-111

Hardwick, Elizabeth 1916- DLB-6

Hardy, Thomas 1840-1928 ... DLB-18, 19, 135

Hare, Cyril 1900-1958 ....DLB-77

Hare, David 1947- DLB-13

Hargrove, Marion 1919- DLB-11

Häring, Georg Wilhelm Heinrich (see Alexis,
  Willibald)

Harington, Donald 1935- DLB-152

Harington, Sir John 1560-1612 .....DLB-136

Harjo, Joy 1951- DLB-120

Harlow, Robert 1923- DLB-60

Cumulative Index

Harman, Thomas flourished 1566-1573 .... DLB-136

Harness, Charles L. 1915- DLB-8

Harnett, Cynthia 1893-1981 .... DLB-161

Harper, Fletcher 1806-1877 .... DLB-79

Harper, Frances Ellen Watkins 1825-1911 .... DLB-50

Harper, Michael S. 1938- DLB-41

Harper and Brothers DLB-49

Harraden, Beatrice 1864-1943 ..... DLB-153

Harrap, George G., and Company Limited DLB-112

Harriot, Thomas 1560-1621 .... DLB-136

Harris, Benjamin ?-circa 1720 ... DLB-42, 43

Harris, Christie 1907- DLB-88

Harris, Frank 1856-1931 .... DLB-156

Harris, George Washington 1814-1869 .... DLB-3, 11

Harris, Joel Chandler 1848-1908 .... DLB-11, 23, 42, 78, 91

Harris, Mark 1922- DLB-2; Y-80

Harris, Wilson 1921- DLB-117

Harrison, Charles Yale 1898-1954 .... DLB-68

Harrison, Frederic 1831-1923 .... DLB-57

Harrison, Harry 1925- DLB-8

Harrison, Jim 1937- Y-82

Harrison, Mary St. Leger Kingsley (see Malet, Lucas)

Harrison, Paul Carter 1936- DLB-38

Harrison, Susan Frances 1859-1935 .... DLB-99

Harrison, Tony 1937- DLB-40

Harrison, William 1535-1593 ...... DLB-136

Harrison, James P., Company DLB-49

Harrisse, Henry 1829-1910 .... DLB-47

Harsdörffer, Georg Philipp 1607-1658 .... DLB-164

Harsent, David 1942- DLB-40

Hart, Albert Bushnell 1854-1943 .... DLB-17

Hart, Julia Catherine 1796-1867 .... DLB-99

The Lorenz Hart Centenary Y-95

Hart, Moss 1904-1961 .... DLB-7

Hart, Oliver 1723-1795 .... DLB-31

Hart-Davis, Rupert, Limited DLB-112

Harte, Bret 1836-1902 .... DLB-12, 64, 74, 79

Harte, Edward Holmead 1922- ... DLB-127

Harte, Houston Harriman 1927- ... DLB-127

Hartlaub, Felix 1913-1945 .... DLB-56

Hartlebon, Otto Erich 1864-1905 .... DLB-118

Hartley, L. P. 1895-1972 .... DLB-15, 139

Hartley, Marsden 1877-1943 .... DLB-54

Hartling, Peter 1933- DLB-75

Hartman, Geoffrey H. 1929- DLB-67

Hartmann, Sadakichi 1867-1944 ..... DLB-54

Hartmann von Aue circa 1160-circa 1205 .... DLB-138

Harvey, Gabriel 1550?-1631 .... DLB-167

Harvey, Jean-Charles 1891-1967 ..... DLB-88

Harvill Press Limited DLB-112

Harwood, Lee 1939- DLB-40

Harwood, Ronald 1934- DLB-13

Haskins, Charles Homer 1870-1937 .... DLB-47

Hass, Robert 1941- DLB-105

The Hatch-Billops Collection DLB-76

Hathaway, William 1944- DLB-120

Hauff, Wilhelm 1802-1827 .... DLB-90

A Haughty and Proud Generation (1922), by Ford Madox Hueffer DLB-36

Haugwitz, August Adolph von 1647-1706 .... DLB-168

Hauptmann, Carl 1858-1921 .... DLB-66, 118

Hauptmann, Gerhart 1862-1946 .... DLB-66, 118

Hauser, Marianne 1910- Y-83

Hawes, Stephen 1475?-before 1529 .... DLB-132

Hawker, Robert Stephen 1803-1875 .... DLB-32

Hawkes, John 1925- DLB-2, 7; Y-80

Hawkesworth, John 1720-1773 ..... DLB-142

Hawkins, Sir Anthony Hope (see Hope, Anthony)

Hawkins, Sir John 1719-1789 .... DLB-104, 142

Hawkins, Walter Everette 1883-? DLB-50

Hawthorne, Nathaniel 1804-1864 .... DLB-1, 74

Hay, John 1838-1905 .... DLB-12, 47

Hayden, Robert 1913-1980 ...... DLB-5, 76

Haydon, Benjamin Robert 1786-1846 .... DLB-110

Hayes, John Michael 1919- DLB-26

Hayley, William 1745-1820 .... DLB-93, 142

Haym, Rudolf 1821-1901 .... DLB-129

Hayman, Robert 1575-1629 .... DLB-99

Hayman, Ronald 1932- DLB-155

Hayne, Paul Hamilton 1830-1886 .... DLB-3, 64, 79

Hays, Mary 1760-1843 .... DLB-142, 158

Haywood, Eliza 1693?-1756 .... DLB-39

Hazard, Willis P. [publishing house] ... DLB-49

Hazlitt, William 1778-1830 .... DLB-110, 158

Hazzard, Shirley 1931- Y-82

Head, Bessie 1937-1986 .... DLB-117

Headley, Joel T. 1813-1897 .. DLB-30; DS-13

Heaney, Seamus 1939- DLB-40

Heard, Nathan C. 1936- DLB-33

Hearn, Lafcadio 1850-1904 ..... DLB-12, 78

Hearne, John 1926- DLB-117

Hearne, Samuel 1745-1792 .... DLB-99

Hearst, William Randolph 1863-1951 .... DLB-25

Hearst, William Randolph, Jr 1908-1993 .... DLB-127

Heath, Catherine 1924- DLB-14

Heath, Roy A. K. 1926- DLB-117

Heath-Stubbs, John 1918- DLB-27

Heavysege, Charles 1816-1876 ..... DLB-99

Hebbel, Friedrich 1813-1863 .... DLB-129

Hebel, Johann Peter 1760-1826 ..... DLB-90

Hébert, Anne 1916- DLB-68

Hébert, Jacques 1923- DLB-53

Hecht, Anthony 1923- DLB-5, 169

Hecht, Ben 1894-1964 .... DLB-7, 9, 25, 26, 28, 86

Hecker, Isaac Thomas 1819-1888 ..... DLB-1

Hedge, Frederic Henry 1805-1890 .... DLB-1, 59

Hefner, Hugh M. 1926- DLB-137

Hegel, Georg Wilhelm Friedrich 1770-1831 .... DLB-90

Heidish, Marcy 1947- Y-82

Heißenbüttel 1921- DLB-75

Hein, Christoph 1944- DLB-124

Heine, Heinrich 1797-1856 .... DLB-90

Heinemann, Larry 1944- DS-9

Heinemann, William, Limited DLB-112

Heinlein, Robert A. 1907-1988 .... DLB-8

Heinrich Julius of Brunswick
    1564-1613 ....DLB-164

Heinrich von dem Türlîn
    flourished circa 1230 ....DLB-138

Heinrich von Melk
    flourished after 1160 ....DLB-148

Heinrich von Veldeke
    circa 1145-circa 1190 ....DLB-138

Heinrich, Willi 1920- DLB-75

Heiskell, John 1872-1972 ....DLB-127

Heinse, Wilhelm 1746-1803 ....DLB-94

Heinz, W. C. 1915- DLB-171

Hejinian, Lyn 1941- DLB-165

Heliand circa 850 ....DLB-148

Heller, Joseph 1923- DLB-2, 28; Y-80

Heller, Michael 1937- DLB-165

Hellman, Lillian 1906-1984 .....DLB-7; Y-84

Hellwig, Johann 1609-1674 ....DLB-164

Helprin, Mark 1947- Y-85

Helwig, David 1938- DLB-60

Hemans, Felicia 1793-1835 ....DLB-96

Hemingway, Ernest 1899-1961
    ....DLB-4, 9, 102; Y-81, 87; DS-1

Hemingway: Twenty-Five Years
    Later Y-85

Hémon, Louis 1880-1913 ....DLB-92

Hemphill, Paul 1936- Y-87

Hénault, Gilles 1920- DLB-88

Henchman, Daniel 1689-1761 ....DLB-24

Henderson, Alice Corbin
    1881-1949 ....DLB-54

Henderson, Archibald
    1877-1963 ....DLB-103

Henderson, David 1942- DLB-41

Henderson, George Wylie
    1904- DLB-51

Henderson, Zenna 1917-1983 ....DLB-8

Henisch, Peter 1943- DLB-85

Henley, Beth 1952- Y-86

Henley, William Ernest
    1849-1903 ....DLB-19

Henniker, Florence 1855-1923 ......DLB-135

Henry, Alexander 1739-1824 ....DLB-99

Henry, Buck 1930- DLB-26

Henry VIII of England
    1491-1547 ....DLB-132

Henry, Marguerite 1902- DLB-22

Henry, O. (see Porter, William Sydney)

Henry of Ghent
    circa 1217-1229 - 1293 ....DLB-115

Henry, Robert Selph 1889-1970 .....DLB-17

Henry, Will (see Allen, Henry W.)

Henryson, Robert
    1420s or 1430s-circa 1505 .....DLB-146

Henschke, Alfred (see Klabund)

Hensley, Sophie Almon 1866-1946 .. DLB-99

Henty, G. A. 1832?-1902 ....DLB-18, 141

Hentz, Caroline Lee 1800-1856 ...... DLB-3

Herbert, Alan Patrick 1890-1971 .... DLB-10

Herbert, Edward, Lord, of Cherbury
    1582-1648 ....DLB-121, 151

Herbert, Frank 1920-1986 ....DLB-8

Herbert, George 1593-1633 ....DLB-126

Herbert, Henry William
    1807-1858 ....DLB-3, 73

Herbert, John 1926- DLB-53

Herbert, Mary Sidney, Countess of Pembroke
    (see Sidney, Mary)

Herbst, Josephine 1892-1969 ....DLB-9

Herburger, Gunter 1932- DLB-75, 124

Hercules, Frank E. M. 1917- DLB-33

Herder, Johann Gottfried
    1744-1803 ....DLB-97

Herder, B., Book Company DLB-49

Herford, Charles Harold
    1853-1931 ....DLB-149

Hergesheimer, Joseph
    1880-1954 ....DLB-9, 102

Heritage Press DLB-46

Hermann the Lame 1013-1054 .....DLB-148

Hermes, Johann Timotheus
    1738-1821 ....DLB-97

Hermlin, Stephan 1915- DLB-69

Hernández, Alfonso C. 1938- DLB-122

Hernández, Inés 1947- DLB-122

Hernández, Miguel 1910-1942 .....DLB-134

Hernton, Calvin C. 1932- DLB-38

"The Hero as Man of Letters: Johnson,
    Rousseau, Burns" (1841), by Thomas
    Carlyle [excerpt] DLB-57

The Hero as Poet. Dante; Shakspeare (1841),
    by Thomas Carlyle DLB-32

Heron, Robert 1764-1807 ....DLB-142

Herrera, Juan Felipe 1948- DLB-122

Herrick, Robert 1591-1674 ....DLB-126

Herrick, Robert 1868-1938 .... DLB-9, 12, 78

Herrick, William 1915- Y-83

Herrick, E. R., and Company DLB-49

Herrmann, John 1900-1959 ....DLB-4

Hersey, John 1914-1993 ....DLB-6

Hertel, François 1905-1985 ....DLB-68

Hervé-Bazin, Jean Pierre Marie (see Bazin,
    Hervé)

Hervey, John, Lord 1696-1743 .....DLB-101

Herwig, Georg 1817-1875 ....DLB-133

Herzog, Emile Salomon Wilhelm (see Maurois,
    André)

Hesse, Hermann 1877-1962 ....DLB-66

Hewat, Alexander
    circa 1743-circa 1824 ....DLB-30

Hewitt, John 1907- DLB-27

Hewlett, Maurice 1861-1923 ....DLB-34, 156

Heyen, William 1940- DLB-5

Heyer, Georgette 1902-1974 ....DLB-77

Heym, Stefan 1913- DLB-69

Heyse, Paul 1830-1914 ....DLB-129

Heytesbury, William
    circa 1310-1372 or 1373 ....DLB-115

Heyward, Dorothy 1890-1961 ....DLB-7

Heyward, DuBose
    1885-1940 ....DLB-7, 9, 45

Heywood, John 1497?-1580? DLB-136

Heywood, Thomas
    1573 or 1574-1641 ....DLB-62

Hibbs, Ben 1901-1975 ....DLB-137

Hichens, Robert S. 1864-1950 ......DLB-153

Hickman, William Albert
    1877-1957 ....DLB-92

Hidalgo, José Luis 1919-1947 ......DLB-108

Hiebert, Paul 1892-1987 ....DLB-68

Hierro, José 1922- DLB-108

Higgins, Aidan 1927- DLB-14

Higgins, Colin 1941-1988 ....DLB-26

Higgins, George V. 1939- DLB-2; Y-81

Higginson, Thomas Wentworth
    1823-1911 ....DLB-1, 64

Highwater, Jamake 1942?- ...DLB-52; Y-85

Hijuelos, Oscar 1951- DLB-145

Hildegard von Bingen
    1098-1179 ....DLB-148

Das Hildesbrandslied circa 820 ....DLB-148

Hildesheimer, Wolfgang
    1916-1991 ....DLB-69, 124

Hildreth, Richard
    1807-1865 ....DLB-1, 30, 59

Cumulative Index

Hill, Aaron 1685-1750 .... DLB-84

Hill, Geoffrey 1932- DLB-40

Hill, "Sir" John 1714?-1775 .... DLB-39

Hill, Leslie 1880-1960 .... DLB-51

Hill, Susan 1942- DLB-14, 139

Hill, Walter 1942- DLB-44

Hill and Wang DLB-46

Hill, George M., Company DLB-49

Hill, Lawrence, and Company, Publishers DLB-46

Hillberry, Conrad 1928- DLB-120

Hilliard, Gray and Company DLB-49

Hills, Lee 1906- DLB-127

Hillyer, Robert 1895-1961 .... DLB-54

Hilton, James 1900-1954 .... DLB-34, 77

Hilton, Walter died 1396 .... DLB-146

Hilton and Company DLB-49

Himes, Chester 1909-1984 .... DLB-2, 76, 143

Hindmarsh, Joseph [publishing house] DLB-170

Hine, Daryl 1936- DLB-60

Hingley, Ronald 1920- DLB-155

Hinojosa-Smith, Rolando 1929- DLB-82

Hippel, Theodor Gottlieb von 1741-1796 .... DLB-97

Hirsch, E. D., Jr. 1928- DLB-67

Hirsch, Edward 1950- DLB-120

The History of the Adventures of Joseph Andrews (1742), by Henry Fielding [excerpt] DLB-39

Hoagland, Edward 1932- DLB-6

Hoagland, Everett H., III 1942- ... DLB-41

Hoban, Russell 1925- DLB-52

Hobbes, Thomas 1588-1679 .... DLB-151

Hobby, Oveta 1905- DLB-127

Hobby, William 1878-1964 .... DLB-127

Hobsbaum, Philip 1932- DLB-40

Hobson, Laura Z. 1900- DLB-28

Hoby, Thomas 1530-1566 .... DLB-132

Hoccleve, Thomas circa 1368-circa 1437 .... DLB-146

Hochhuth, Rolf 1931- DLB-124

Hochman, Sandra 1936- DLB-5

Hodder and Stoughton, Limited ... DLB-106

Hodgins, Jack 1938- DLB-60

Hodgman, Helen 1945- DLB-14

Hodgskin, Thomas 1787-1869 ..... DLB-158

Hodgson, Ralph 1871-1962 .... DLB-19

Hodgson, William Hope 1877-1918 ....DLB-70, 153, 156

Hoffenstein, Samuel 1890-1947 ...... DLB-11

Hoffman, Charles Fenno 1806-1884 .... DLB-3

Hoffman, Daniel 1923- DLB-5

Hoffmann, E. T. A. 1776-1822 ...... DLB-90

Hoffmanswaldau, Christian Hoffman von 1616-1679 .... DLB-168

Hofmann, Michael 1957- DLB-40

Hofmannsthal, Hugo von 1874-1929 ....DLB-81, 118

Hofstadter, Richard 1916-1970 ...... DLB-17

Hogan, Desmond 1950- DLB-14

Hogan and Thompson DLB-49

Hogarth Press DLB-112

Hogg, James 1770-1835 ....DLB-93, 116, 159

Hohberg, Wolfgang Helmhard Freiherr von 1612-1688 .... DLB-168

Hohl, Ludwig 1904-1980 .... DLB-56

Holbrook, David 1923- DLB-14, 40

Holcroft, Thomas 1745-1809 ....DLB-39, 89, 158

Holden, Jonathan 1941- DLB-105

Holden, Jonathan, Contemporary Verse Story-telling DLB-105

Holden, Molly 1927-1981 .... DLB-40

Hölderlin, Friedrich 1770-1843 ...... DLB-90

Holiday House DLB-46

Holinshed, Raphael died 1580 ..... DLB-167

Holland, J. G. 1819-1881 ....DS-13

Holland, Norman N. 1927- DLB-67

Hollander, John 1929- DLB-5

Holley, Marietta 1836-1926 .... DLB-11

Hollingsworth, Margaret 1940- DLB-60

Hollo, Anselm 1934- DLB-40

Holloway, Emory 1885-1977 .... DLB-103

Holloway, John 1920- DLB-27

Holloway House Publishing Company DLB-46

Holme, Constance 1880-1955 ...... DLB-34

Holmes, Abraham S. 1821?-1908 .... DLB-99

Holmes, John Clellon 1926-1988 .... DLB-16

Holmes, Oliver Wendell 1809-1894 ....DLB-1

Holmes, Richard 1945- DLB-155

Holroyd, Michael 1935- DLB-155

Holst, Hermann E. von 1841-1904 ....DLB-47

Holt, John 1721-1784 ....DLB-43

Holt, Henry, and Company DLB-49

Holt, Rinehart and Winston DLB-46

Holthusen, Hans Egon 1913- DLB-69

Hölty, Ludwig Christoph Heinrich 1748-1776 ....DLB-94

Holz, Arno 1863-1929 ....DLB-118

Home, Henry, Lord Kames (see Kames, Henry Home, Lord)

Home, John 1722-1808 ....DLB-84

Home, William Douglas 1912- DLB-13

Home Publishing Company DLB-49

Homes, Geoffrey (see Mainwaring, Daniel)

Honan, Park 1928- DLB-111

Hone, William 1780-1842 ..... DLB-110, 158

Hongo, Garrett Kaoru 1951- DLB-120

Honig, Edwin 1919- DLB-5

Hood, Hugh 1928- DLB-53

Hood, Thomas 1799-1845 ....DLB-96

Hook, Theodore 1788-1841 ....DLB-116

Hooker, Jeremy 1941- DLB-40

Hooker, Richard 1554-1600 ....DLB-132

Hooker, Thomas 1586-1647 ....DLB-24

Hooper, Johnson Jones 1815-1862 .... DLB-3, 11

Hope, Anthony 1863-1933 .... DLB-153, 156

Hopkins, Gerard Manley 1844-1889 .... DLB-35, 57

Hopkins, John (see Sternhold, Thomas)

Hopkins, Lemuel 1750-1801 ....DLB-37

Hopkins, Pauline Elizabeth 1859-1930 ....DLB-50

Hopkins, Samuel 1721-1803 ....DLB-31

Hopkins, John H., and Son DLB-46

Hopkinson, Francis 1737-1791 ....DLB-31

Horgan, Paul 1903- DLB-102; Y-85

Horizon Press DLB-46

Horne, Frank 1899-1974 ....DLB-51

Horne, Richard Henry (Hengist) 1802 or 1803-1884 ....DLB-32

Hornung, E. W. 1866-1921 ....DLB-70

Horovitz, Israel 1939- DLB-7

Horton, George Moses
1797?-1883? DLB-50

Horváth, Ödön von
1901-1938 ....DLB-85, 124

Horwood, Harold 1923- DLB-60

Hosford, E. and E.
[publishing house] DLB-49

Hoskyns, John 1566-1638 ....DLB-121

Hotchkiss and Company DLB-49

Hough, Emerson 1857-1923 ....DLB-9

Houghton Mifflin Company DLB-49

Houghton, Stanley 1881-1913 ....DLB-10

Household, Geoffrey 1900-1988 .....DLB-87

Housman, A. E. 1859-1936 ....DLB-19

Housman, Laurence 1865-1959 ......DLB-10

Houwald, Ernst von 1778-1845 ......DLB-90

Hovey, Richard 1864-1900 ....DLB-54

Howard, Donald R. 1927-1987 .....DLB-111

Howard, Maureen 1930- Y-83

Howard, Richard 1929- DLB-5

Howard, Roy W. 1883-1964 ....DLB-29

Howard, Sidney 1891-1939 ....DLB-7, 26

Howe, E. W. 1853-1937 ....DLB-12, 25

Howe, Henry 1816-1893 ....DLB-30

Howe, Irving 1920-1993 ....DLB-67

Howe, Joseph 1804-1873 ....DLB-99

Howe, Julia Ward 1819-1910 ....DLB-1

Howe, Percival Presland
1886-1944 ....DLB-149

Howe, Susan 1937- DLB-120

Howell, Clark, Sr. 1863-1936 ....DLB-25

Howell, Evan P. 1839-1905 ....DLB-23

Howell, James 1594?-1666 ....DLB-151

Howell, Warren Richardson
1912-1984 ....DLB-140

Howell, Soskin and Company DLB-46

Howells, William Dean
1837-1920 ....DLB-12, 64, 74, 79

Howitt, William 1792-1879 and
Howitt, Mary 1799-1888 ....DLB-110

Hoyem, Andrew 1935- DLB-5

Hoyers, Anna Ovena 1584-1655 ....DLB-164

Hoyos, Angela de 1940- DLB-82

Hoyt, Palmer 1897-1979 ....DLB-127

Hoyt, Henry [publishing house] DLB-49

Hrabanus Maurus 776?-856 ....DLB-148

Hrotsvit of Gandersheim
circa 935-circa 1000 ....DLB-148

Hubbard, Elbert 1856-1915 ....DLB-91

Hubbard, Kin 1868-1930 ....DLB-11

Hubbard, William circa 1621-1704 ..DLB-24

Huber, Therese 1764-1829 ....DLB-90

Huch, Friedrich 1873-1913 ....DLB-66

Huch, Ricarda 1864-1947 ....DLB-66

Huck at 100: How Old Is
Huckleberry Finn? Y-85

Huddle, David 1942- DLB-130

Hudgins, Andrew 1951- DLB-120

Hudson, Henry Norman
1814-1886 ....DLB-64

Hudson, W. H. 1841-1922 .....DLB-98, 153

Hudson and Goodwin DLB-49

Huebsch, B. W.
[publishing house] DLB-46

Hughes, David 1930- DLB-14

Hughes, John 1677-1720 ....DLB-84

Hughes, Langston
1902-1967 ....DLB-4, 7, 48, 51, 86

Hughes, Richard 1900-1976 ....DLB-15, 161

Hughes, Ted 1930- DLB-40, 161

Hughes, Thomas 1822-1896 ....DLB-18, 163

Hugo, Richard 1923-1982 ....DLB-5

Hugo, Victor 1802-1885 ....DLB-119

Hugo Awards and Nebula Awards ...DLB-8

Hull, Richard 1896-1973 ....DLB-77

Hulme, T. E. 1883-1917 ....DLB-19

Humboldt, Alexander von
1769-1859 ....DLB-90

Humboldt, Wilhelm von
1767-1835 ....DLB-90

Hume, David 1711-1776 ....DLB-104

Hume, Fergus 1859-1932 ....DLB-70

Hummer, T. R. 1950- DLB-120

Humorous Book Illustration DLB-11

Humphrey, William 1924- DLB-6

Humphreys, David 1752-1818 ....DLB-37

Humphreys, Emyr 1919- DLB-15

Huncke, Herbert 1915- DLB-16

Huneker, James Gibbons
1857-1921 ....DLB-71

Hunold, Christian Friedrich
1681-1721 ....DLB-168

Hunt, Irene 1907- DLB-52

Hunt, Leigh 1784-1859 ....DLB-96, 110, 144

Hunt, Violet 1862-1942 ....DLB-162

Hunt, William Gibbes 1791-1833 ....DLB-73

Hunter, Evan 1926- Y-82

Hunter, Jim 1939- DLB-14

Hunter, Kristin 1931- DLB-33

Hunter, Mollie 1922- DLB-161

Hunter, N. C. 1908-1971 ....DLB-10

Hunter-Duvar, John 1821-1899 ......DLB-99

Huntington, Henry E.
1850-1927 ....DLB-140

Hurd and Houghton DLB-49

Hurst, Fannie 1889-1968 ....DLB-86

Hurst and Blackett DLB-106

Hurst and Company DLB-49

Hurston, Zora Neale
1901?-1960 ....DLB-51, 86

Husson, Jules-François-Félix (see Champfleury)

Huston, John 1906-1987 ....DLB-26

Hutcheson, Francis 1694-1746 ......DLB-31

Hutchinson, Thomas
1711-1780 ....DLB-30, 31

Hutchinson and Company
(Publishers) Limited DLB-112

Hutton, Richard Holt 1826-1897 ....DLB-57

Huxley, Aldous
1894-1963 ....DLB-36, 100, 162

Huxley, Elspeth Josceline 1907- DLB-77

Huxley, T. H. 1825-1895 ....DLB-57

Huyghue, Douglas Smith
1816-1891 ....DLB-99

Huysmans, Joris-Karl 1848-1907 ....DLB-123

Hyman, Trina Schart 1939- DLB-61

I

Iavorsky, Stefan 1658-1722 ....DLB-150

Ibn Bajja circa 1077-1138 ....DLB-115

Ibn Gabirol, Solomon
circa 1021-circa 1058 ....DLB-115

The Iconography of Science-Fiction
Art DLB-8

Iffland, August Wilhelm
1759-1814 ....DLB-94

Ignatow, David 1914- DLB-5

Ike, Chukwuemeka 1931- DLB-157

Iles, Francis (see Berkeley, Anthony)

The Illustration of Early German
 Literary Manuscripts,
 circa 1150-circa 1300 .... DLB-148

Imbs, Bravig 1904-1946 .... DLB-4

Imbuga, Francis D. 1947- DLB-157

Immermann, Karl 1796-1840 ...... DLB-133

Inchbald, Elizabeth 1753-1821 ... DLB-39, 89

Inge, William 1913-1973 .... DLB-7

Ingelow, Jean 1820-1897 .... DLB-35, 163

Ingersoll, Ralph 1900-1985 .... DLB-127

The Ingersoll Prizes Y-84

Ingoldsby, Thomas (see Barham, Richard
 Harris)

Ingraham, Joseph Holt 1809-1860 ..... DLB-3

Inman, John 1805-1850 .... DLB-73

Innerhofer, Franz 1944- DLB-85

Innis, Harold Adams 1894-1952 .... DLB-88

Innis, Mary Quayle 1899-1972 ...... DLB-88

International Publishers Company .. DLB-46

An Interview with David Rabe Y-91

An Interview with George Greenfield,
 Literary Agent Y-91

An Interview with James Ellroy Y-91

An Interview with Peter S. Prescott Y-86

An Interview with Russell Hoban Y-90

An Interview with Tom Jenks Y-86

Introduction to Paul Laurence Dunbar,
 Lyrics of Lowly Life (1896),
 by William Dean Howells DLB-50

Introductory Essay: Letters of Percy Bysshe
 Shelley (1852), by Robert
 Browning DLB-32

Introductory Letters from the Second Edition
 of Pamela (1741), by Samuel
 Richardson DLB-39

Irving, John 1942- DLB-6; Y-82

Irving, Washington
 1783-1859 ..... DLB-3, 11, 30, 59, 73, 74

Irwin, Grace 1907- DLB-68

Irwin, Will 1873-1948 .... DLB-25

Isherwood, Christopher
 1904-1986 .... DLB-15; Y-86

The Island Trees Case: A Symposium on
 School Library Censorship
 An Interview with Judith Krug
 An Interview with Phyllis Schlafly
 An Interview with Edward B. Jenkinson
 An Interview with Lamarr Mooneyham
 An Interview with Harriet
 Bernstein Y-82

Islas, Arturo 1938-1991 .... DLB-122

Ivers, M. J., and Company DLB-49

Iyayi, Festus 1947- DLB-157

J

Jackmon, Marvin E. (see Marvin X)

Jacks, L. P. 1860-1955 .... DLB-135

Jackson, Angela 1951- DLB-41

Jackson, Helen Hunt
 1830-1885 .... DLB-42, 47

Jackson, Holbrook 1874-1948 .... DLB-98

Jackson, Laura Riding 1901-1991 .... DLB-48

Jackson, Shirley 1919-1965 .... DLB-6

Jacob, Piers Anthony Dillingham (see Anthony,
 Piers)

Jacobi, Friedrich Heinrich
 1743-1819 .... DLB-94

Jacobi, Johann Georg 1740-1841 ..... DLB-97

Jacobs, Joseph 1854-1916 .... DLB-141

Jacobs, W. W. 1863-1943 .... DLB-135

Jacobs, George W., and Company ... DLB-49

Jacobson, Dan 1929- DLB-14

Jaggard, William
 [publishing house] DLB-170

Jahier, Piero 1884-1966 .... DLB-114

Jahnn, Hans Henny
 1894-1959 .... DLB-56, 124

Jakes, John 1932- Y-83

James, C. L. R. 1901-1989 .... DLB-125

James, George P. R. 1801-1860 ..... DLB-116

James, Henry
 1843-1916 .... DLB-12, 71, 74; DS-13

James, John circa 1633-1729 .... DLB-24

The James Jones Society Y-92

James, M. R. 1862-1936 .... DLB-156

James, P. D. 1920- DLB-87

James Joyce Centenary: Dublin, 1982 ... Y-82

James Joyce Conference Y-85

James VI of Scotland, I of England
 1566-1625 .... DLB-151, 172

James, U. P. [publishing house] DLB-49

Jameson, Anna 1794-1860 ...... DLB-99, 166

Jameson, Fredric 1934- DLB-67

Jameson, J. Franklin 1859-1937 ...... DLB-17

Jameson, Storm 1891-1986 .... DLB-36

Janés, Clara 1940- DLB-134

Jaramillo, Cleofas M. 1878-1956 .... DLB-122

Jarman, Mark 1952- DLB-120

Jarrell, Randall 1914-1965 ...... DLB-48, 52

Jarrold and Sons DLB-106

Jasmin, Claude 1930- DLB-60

Jay, John 1745-1829 .... DLB-31

Jefferies, Richard 1848-1887 .... DLB-98, 141

Jeffers, Lance 1919-1985 .... DLB-41

Jeffers, Robinson 1887-1962 .... DLB-45

Jefferson, Thomas 1743-1826 .... DLB-31

Jelinek, Elfriede 1946- DLB-85

Jellicoe, Ann 1927- DLB-13

Jenkins, Elizabeth 1905- DLB-155

Jenkins, Robin 1912- DLB-14

Jenkins, William Fitzgerald (see Leinster,
 Murray)

Jenkins, Herbert, Limited DLB-112

Jennings, Elizabeth 1926- DLB-27

Jens, Walter 1923- DLB-69

Jensen, Merrill 1905-1980 .... DLB-17

Jephson, Robert 1736-1803 .... DLB-89

Jerome, Jerome K.
 1859-1927 .... DLB-10, 34, 135

Jerome, Judson 1927-1991 .... DLB-105

Jerome, Judson, Reflections: After a
 Tornado DLB-105

Jerrold, Douglas 1803-1857 ... DLB-158, 159

Jesse, F. Tennyson 1888-1958 .... DLB-77

Jewett, Sarah Orne 1849-1909 ... DLB-12, 74

Jewett, John P., and Company DLB-49

The Jewish Publication Society DLB-49

Jewitt, John Rodgers 1783-1821 ...... DLB-99

Jewsbury, Geraldine 1812-1880 ...... DLB-21

Jhabvala, Ruth Prawer 1927- DLB-139

Jiménez, Juan Ramón 1881-1958 ....DLB-134

Joans, Ted 1928- DLB-16, 41

John, Eugenie (see Marlitt, E.)

John of Dumbleton
 circa 1310-circa 1349 .... DLB-115

John Edward Bruce: Three
 Documents DLB-50

John O'Hara's Pottsville Journalism Y-88

John Steinbeck Research Center Y-85

John Webster: The Melbourne
 Manuscript Y-86

Johns, Captain W. E. 1893-1968 ....DLB-160

Johnson, B. S. 1933-1973 .... DLB-14, 40

Johnson, Charles 1679-1748 .... DLB-84

Johnson, Charles R. 1948- DLB-33
Johnson, Charles S. 1893-1956 ...DLB-51, 91
Johnson, Denis 1949- DLB-120
Johnson, Diane 1934- Y-80
Johnson, Edgar 1901- DLB-103
Johnson, Edward 1598-1672 ....DLB-24
Johnson, Fenton 1888-1958 ......DLB-45, 50
Johnson, Georgia Douglas
  1886-1966 ....DLB-51
Johnson, Gerald W. 1890-1980 ......DLB-29
Johnson, Helene 1907- DLB-51
Johnson, James Weldon
  1871-1938 ....DLB-51
Johnson, John H. 1918- DLB-137
Johnson, Linton Kwesi 1952- DLB-157
Johnson, Lionel 1867-1902 ....DLB-19
Johnson, Nunnally 1897-1977 ....DLB-26
Johnson, Owen 1878-1952 ....Y-87
Johnson, Pamela Hansford
  1912- DLB-15
Johnson, Pauline 1861-1913 ....DLB-92
Johnson, Ronald 1935- DLB-169
Johnson, Samuel 1696-1772 ....DLB-24
Johnson, Samuel
  1709-1784 .... DLB-39, 95, 104, 142
Johnson, Samuel 1822-1882 ....DLB-1
Johnson, Uwe 1934-1984 ....DLB-75
Johnson, Benjamin
  [publishing house] DLB-49
Johnson, Benjamin, Jacob, and
  Robert [publishing house] DLB-49
Johnson, Jacob, and Company DLB-49
Johnson, Joseph [publishing house] ...DLB-154
Johnston, Annie Fellows 1863-1931 ..DLB-42
Johnston, Basil H. 1929- DLB-60
Johnston, Denis 1901-1984 ....DLB-10
Johnston, George 1913- DLB-88
Johnston, Jennifer 1930- DLB-14
Johnston, Mary 1870-1936 ....DLB-9
Johnston, Richard Malcolm
  1822-1898 ....DLB-74
Johnstone, Charles 1719?-1800? DLB-39
Johst, Hanns 1890-1978 ....DLB-124
Jolas, Eugene 1894-1952 ....DLB-4, 45
Jones, Alice C. 1853-1933 ....DLB-92
Jones, Charles C., Jr. 1831-1893 ....DLB-30
Jones, D. G. 1929- DLB-53

Jones, David 1895-1974 .... DLB-20, 100
Jones, Diana Wynne 1934- DLB-161
Jones, Ebenezer 1820-1860 .... DLB-32
Jones, Ernest 1819-1868 .... DLB-32
Jones, Gayl 1949- DLB-33
Jones, Glyn 1905- DLB-15
Jones, Gwyn 1907- DLB-15, 139
Jones, Henry Arthur 1851-1929 ..... DLB-10
Jones, Hugh circa 1692-1760 .... DLB-24
Jones, James 1921-1977 .... DLB-2, 143
Jones, Jenkin Lloyd 1911- DLB-127
Jones, LeRoi (see Baraka, Amiri)
Jones, Lewis 1897-1939 .... DLB-15
Jones, Madison 1925- DLB-152
Jones, Major Joseph (see Thompson, William
  Tappan)
Jones, Preston 1936-1979 .... DLB-7
Jones, Rodney 1950- DLB-120
Jones, Sir William 1746-1794 ..... DLB-109
Jones, William Alfred 1817-1900 .... DLB-59
Jones's Publishing House DLB-49
Jong, Erica 1942- DLB-2, 5, 28, 152
Jonke, Gert F. 1946- DLB-85
Jonson, Ben 1572?-1637 .... DLB-62, 121
Jordan, June 1936- DLB-38
Joseph, Jenny 1932- DLB-40
Joseph, Michael, Limited DLB-112
Josephson, Matthew 1899-1978 ...... DLB-4
Josiah Allen's Wife (see Holley, Marietta)
Josipovici, Gabriel 1940- DLB-14
Josselyn, John ?-1675 .... DLB-24
Joudry, Patricia 1921- DLB-88
Jovine, Giuseppe 1922- DLB-128
Joyaux, Philippe (see Sollers, Philippe)
Joyce, Adrien (see Eastman, Carol)
Joyce, James
  1882-1941 ....DLB-10, 19, 36, 162
Judd, Sylvester 1813-1853 .... DLB-1
Judd, Orange, Publishing
  Company DLB-49
Judith circa 930 .... DLB-146
Julian of Norwich
  1342-circa 1420 .... DLB-1146
Julian Symons at Eighty Y-92
June, Jennie (see Croly, Jane Cunningham)

Jung, Franz 1888-1963 ....DLB-118
Jünger, Ernst 1895- DLB-56
Der jüngere Titurel circa 1275 ....DLB-138
Jung-Stilling, Johann Heinrich
  1740-1817 ....DLB-94
Justice, Donald 1925- Y-83
The Juvenile Library (see Godwin, M. J., and
  Company)

K

Kacew, Romain (see Gary, Romain)
Kafka, Franz 1883-1924 ....DLB-81
Kahn, Roger 1927 ....DLB-171
Kaiser, Georg 1878-1945 ....DLB-124
Kaiserchronik circca 1147 ....DLB-148
Kalechofsky, Roberta 1931- DLB-28
Kaler, James Otis 1848-1912 ....DLB-12
Kames, Henry Home, Lord
  1696-1782 ....DLB-31, 104
Kandel, Lenore 1932- DLB-16
Kanin, Garson 1912- DLB-7
Kant, Hermann 1926- DLB-75
Kant, Immanuel 1724-1804 ....DLB-94
Kantemir, Antiokh Dmitrievich
  1708-1744 ....DLB-150
Kantor, Mackinlay 1904-1977 ....DLB-9, 102
Kaplan, Fred 1937- DLB-111
Kaplan, Johanna 1942- DLB-28
Kaplan, Justin 1925- DLB-111
Kapnist, Vasilii Vasilevich
  1758?-1823 ....DLB-150
Karadžić, Vuk Stefanović
  1787-1864 ....DLB-147
Karamzin, Nikolai Mikhailovich
  1766-1826 ....DLB-150
Karsch, Anna Louisa 1722-1791 .....DLB-97
Kasack, Hermann 1896-1966 ....DLB-69
Kaschnitz, Marie Luise 1901-1974 ...DLB-69
Kaštelan, Jure 1919-1990 ....DLB-147
Kästner, Erich 1899-1974 ....DLB-56
Kattan, Naim 1928- DLB-53
Katz, Steve 1935- Y-83
Kauffman, Janet 1945- Y-86
Kauffmann, Samuel 1898-1971 .....DLB-127
Kaufman, Bob 1925- DLB-16, 41
Kaufman, George S. 1889-1961 ....DLB-7
Kavanagh, P. J. 1931- DLB-40

Kavanagh, Patrick 1904-1967 .... DLB-15, 20	Kennelly, Brendan 1936- DLB-40	King, Francis 1923- DLB-15, 139
Kaye-Smith, Sheila 1887-1956 ...... DLB-36	Kenner, Hugh 1923- DLB-67	King, Grace 1852-1932 .... DLB-12, 78
Kazin, Alfred 1915- DLB-67	Kennerley, Mitchell [publishing house] DLB-46	King, Henry 1592-1669 .... DLB-126
Keane, John B. 1928- DLB-13	Kent, Frank R. 1877-1958 .... DLB-29	King, Stephen 1947- DLB-143; Y-80
Keary, Annie 1825-1879 .... DLB-163	Kenyon, Jane 1947- DLB-120	King, Woodie, Jr. 1937- DLB-38
Keating, H. R. F. 1926- DLB-87	Keough, Hugh Edmund 1864-1912 . DLB-171	King, Solomon [publishing house] DLB-49
Keats, Ezra Jack 1916-1983 .... DLB-61	Keppler and Schwartzmann DLB-49	Kinglake, Alexander William 1809-1891 .... DLB-55, 166
Keats, John 1795-1821 .... DLB-96, 110	Kerner, Justinus 1776-1862 .... DLB-90	
Keble, John 1792-1866 .... DLB-32, 55	Kerouac, Jack 1922-1969 ... DLB-2, 16; DS-3	Kingsley, Charles 1819-1875 .... DLB-21, 32, 163
Keeble, John 1944- Y-83	The Jack Kerouac Revival Y-95	
Keeffe, Barrie 1945- DLB-13	Kerouac, Jan 1952- DLB-16	Kingsley, Henry 1830-1876 .... DLB-21
Keeley, James 1867-1934 .... DLB-25	Kerr, Orpheus C. (see Newell, Robert Henry)	Kingsley, Sidney 1906- DLB-7
W. B. Keen, Cooke and Company DLB-49	Kerr, Charles H., and Company DLB-49	Kingsmill, Hugh 1889-1949 .... DLB-149
	Kesey, Ken 1935- DLB-2, 16	Kingston, Maxine Hong 1940- DLB-173; Y-80
Keillor, Garrison 1942- Y-87	Kessel, Joseph 1898-1979 .... DLB-72	
Keith, Marian 1874?-1961 .... DLB-92	Kessel, Martin 1901- DLB-56	Kingston, William Henry Giles 1814-1880 .... DLB-163
Keller, Gary D. 1943- DLB-82	Kesten, Hermann 1900- DLB-56	
Keller, Gottfried 1819-1890 .... DLB-129	Keun, Irmgard 1905-1982 .... DLB-69	Kinnell, Galway 1927- DLB-5; Y-87
Kelley, Edith Summers 1884-1956 ..... DLB-9	Key and Biddle DLB-49	Kinsella, Thomas 1928- DLB-27
Kelley, William Melvin 1937- DLB-33	Keynes, John Maynard 1883-1946 ..... DS-10	Kipling, Rudyard 1865-1936 .... DLB-19, 34, 141, 156
Kellogg, Ansel Nash 1832-1886 ..... DLB-23	Keyserling, Eduard von 1855-1918 .. DLB-66	
Kellogg, Steven 1941- DLB-61	Khan, Ismith 1925- DLB-125	Kipphardt, Heinar 1922-1982 .... DLB-124
Kelly, George 1887-1974 .... DLB-7	Khemnitser, Ivan Ivanovich 1745-1784 .... DLB-150	Kirby, William 1817-1906 .... DLB-99
Kelly, Hugh 1739-1777 .... DLB-89		Kircher, Athanasius 1602-1680 ..... DLB-164
Kelly, Robert 1935- DLB-5, 130, 165	Kheraskov, Mikhail Matveevich 1733-1807 .... DLB-150	Kirk, John Foster 1824-1904 .... DLB-79
Kelly, Piet and Company DLB-49	Khvostov, Dmitrii Ivanovich 1757-1835 .... DLB-150	Kirkconnell, Watson 1895-1977 ...... DLB-68
Kelmscott Press DLB-112		Kirkland, Caroline M. 1801-1864 .... DLB-3, 73, 74; DS-13
Kemble, Fanny 1809-1893 .... DLB-32	Kidd, Adam 1802?-1831 .... DLB-99	
Kemelman, Harry 1908- DLB-28	Kidd, William [publishing house] DLB-106	Kirkland, Joseph 1830-1893 .... DLB-12
Kempe, Margery circa 1373-1438 .... DLB-146		Kirkman, Francis [publishing house] DLB-170
	Kiely, Benedict 1919- DLB-15	
Kempner, Friederike 1836-1904 .... DLB-129	Kieran, John 1892-1981 .... DLB-171	Kirkpatrick, Clayton 1915- DLB-127
Kempowski, Walter 1929- DLB-75	Kiggins and Kellogg DLB-49	Kirkup, James 1918- DLB-27
Kendall, Claude [publishing company] DLB-46	Kiley, Jed 1889-1962 .... DLB-4	Kirouac, Conrad (see Marie-Victorin, Frère)
	Kilgore, Bernard 1908-1967 .... DLB-127	Kirsch, Sarah 1935- DLB-75
Kendell, George 1809-1867 .... DLB-43	Killens, John Oliver 1916- DLB-33	Kirst, Hans Hellmut 1914-1989 ..... DLB-69
Kenedy, P. J., and Sons DLB-49	Killigrew, Anne 1660-1685 .... DLB-131	Kitcat, Mabel Greenhow 1859-1922 .... DLB-135
Kennedy, Adrienne 1931- DLB-38	Killigrew, Thomas 1612-1683 .... DLB-58	
Kennedy, John Pendleton 1795-1870 .... DLB-3	Kilmer, Joyce 1886-1918 .... DLB-45	Kitchin, C. H. B. 1895-1967 .... DLB-77
Kennedy, Leo 1907- DLB-88	Kilwardby, Robert circa 1215-1279 .... DLB-115	Kizer, Carolyn 1925- DLB-5, 169
Kennedy, Margaret 1896-1967 ...... DLB-36		Klabund 1890-1928 .... DLB-66
Kennedy, Patrick 1801-1873 .... DLB-159	Kincaid, Jamaica 1949- DLB-157	Klaj, Johann 1616-1656 .... DLB-164
Kennedy, Richard S. 1920- DLB-111	King, Clarence 1842-1901 .... DLB-12	Klappert, Peter 1942- DLB-5
Kennedy, William 1928- ... DLB-143; Y-85	King, Florence 1936 .... Y-85	Klass, Philip (see Tenn, William)
Kennedy, X. J. 1929- DLB-5		Klein, A. M. 1909-1972 .... DLB-68
		Kleist, Ewald von 1715-1759 .... DLB-97
		Kleist, Heinrich von 1777-1811 ..... DLB-90

Klinger, Friedrich Maximilian 1752-1831 .... DLB-94

Klopstock, Friedrich Gottlieb 1724-1803 .... DLB-97

Klopstock, Meta 1728-1758 .... DLB-97

Kluge, Alexander 1932- DLB-75

Knapp, Joseph Palmer 1864-1951 .... DLB-91

Knapp, Samuel Lorenzo 1783-1838 .... DLB-59

Knapton, J. J. and P. [publishing house] DLB-154

Kniazhnin, Iakov Borisovich 1740-1791 .... DLB-150

Knickerbocker, Diedrich (see Irving, Washington)

Knigge, Adolph Franz Friedrich Ludwig, Freiherr von 1752-1796 .... DLB-94

Knight, Damon 1922- DLB-8

Knight, Etheridge 1931-1992 .... DLB-41

Knight, John S. 1894-1981 .... DLB-29

Knight, Sarah Kemble 1666-1727 .... DLB-24

Knight, Charles, and Company DLB-106

Knister, Raymond 1899-1932 .... DLB-68

Knoblock, Edward 1874-1945 .... DLB-10

Knopf, Alfred A. 1892-1984 .... Y-84

Knopf, Alfred A. [publishing house] DLB-46

Knorr von Rosenroth, Christian 1636-1689 .... DLB-168

Knowles, John 1926- DLB-6

Knox, Frank 1874-1944 .... DLB-29

Knox, John circa 1514-1572 .... DLB-132

Knox, John Armoy 1850-1906 .... DLB-23

Knox, Ronald Arbuthnott 1888-1957 .... DLB-77

Kober, Arthur 1900-1975 .... DLB-11

Kocbek, Edvard 1904-1981 .... DLB-147

Koch, Howard 1902- DLB-26

Koch, Kenneth 1925- DLB-5

Koenigsberg, Moses 1879-1945 ...... DLB-25

Koeppen, Wolfgang 1906- DLB-69

Koertge, Ronald 1940- DLB-105

Koestler, Arthur 1905-1983 .... Y-83

Kokoschka, Oskar 1886-1980 ...... DLB-124

Kolb, Annette 1870-1967 .... DLB-66

Kolbenheyer, Erwin Guido 1878-1962 .... DLB-66, 124

Kolleritsch, Alfred 1931- DLB-85

Kolodny, Annette 1941- DLB-67

Komarov, Matvei circa 1730-1812 .... DLB-150

Komroff, Manuel 1890-1974 .... DLB-4

Komunyakaa, Yusef 1947- DLB-120

Konigsburg, E. L. 1930- DLB-52

Konrad von Würzburg circa 1230-1287 .... DLB-138

Konstantinov, Aleko 1863-1897 .... DLB-147

Kooser, Ted 1939- DLB-105

Kopit, Arthur 1937- DLB-7

Kops, Bernard 1926?- DLB-13

Kornbluth, C. M. 1923-1958 .... DLB-8

Körner, Theodor 1791-1813 .... DLB-90

Kornfeld, Paul 1889-1942 .... DLB-118

Kosinski, Jerzy 1933-1991 ...... DLB-2; Y-82

Kosovel, Srečko 1904-1926 .... DLB-147

Kostrov, Ermil Ivanovich 1755-1796 .... DLB-150

Kotzebue, August von 1761-1819 .... DLB-94

Kotzwinkle, William 1938- DLB-173

Kovačić, Ante 1854-1889 .... DLB-147

Kraf, Elaine 1946- Y-81

Kranjčević, Silvije Strahimir 1865-1908 .... DLB-147

Krasna, Norman 1909-1984 .... DLB-26

Kraus, Karl 1874-1936 .... DLB-118

Krauss, Ruth 1911-1993 .... DLB-52

Kreisel, Henry 1922- DLB-88

Kreuder, Ernst 1903-1972 .... DLB-69

Kreymborg, Alfred 1883-1966 .... DLB-4, 54

Krieger, Murray 1923- DLB-67

Krim, Seymour 1922-1989 .... DLB-16

Krleža, Miroslav 1893-1981 ...... DLB-147

Krock, Arthur 1886-1974 .... DLB-29

Kroetsch, Robert 1927- DLB-53

Krutch, Joseph Wood 1893-1970 .... DLB-63

Krylov, Ivan Andreevich 1769-1844 .... DLB-150

Kubin, Alfred 1877-1959 .... DLB-81

Kubrick, Stanley 1928- DLB-26

Kudrun circa 1230-1240 .... DLB-138

Kuffstein, Hans Ludwig von 1582-1656 .... DLB-164

Kuhlmann, Quirinus 1651-1689 .... DLB-168

Kuhnau, Johann 1660-1722 .... DLB-168

Kumin, Maxine 1925- DLB-5

Kunene, Mazisi 1930- DLB-117

Kunitz, Stanley 1905- DLB-48

Kunjufu, Johari M. (see Amini, Johari M.)

Kunnert, Gunter 1929- DLB-75

Kunze, Reiner 1933- DLB-75

Kupferberg, Tuli 1923- DLB-16

Kürnberger, Ferdinand 1821-1879 .... DLB-129

Kurz, Isolde 1853-1944 .... DLB-66

Kusenberg, Kurt 1904-1983 .... DLB-69

Kuttner, Henry 1915-1958 .... DLB-8

Kyd, Thomas 1558-1594 .... DLB-62

Kyffin, Maurice circa 1560?-1598 .... DLB-136

Kyger, Joanne 1934- DLB-16

Kyne, Peter B. 1880-1957 .... DLB-78

L

L. E. L. (see Landon, Letitia Elizabeth)

Laberge, Albert 1871-1960 .... DLB-68

Laberge, Marie 1950- DLB-60

Lacombe, Patrice (see Trullier-Lacombe, Joseph Patrice)

Lacretelle, Jacques de 1888-1985 ..... DLB-65

Lacy, Sam 1903- DLB-171

Ladd, Joseph Brown 1764-1786 ...... DLB-37

La Farge, Oliver 1901-1963 .... DLB-9

Lafferty, R. A. 1914- DLB-8

La Guma, Alex 1925-1985 .... DLB-117

Lahaise, Guillaume (see Delahaye, Guy)

Lahontan, Louis-Armand de Lom d'Arce, Baron de 1666-1715? DLB-99

Laing, Kojo 1946- DLB-157

Laird, Carobeth 1895- Y-82

Laird and Lee DLB-49

Lalonde, Michèle 1937- DLB-60

Lamantia, Philip 1927- DLB-16

Lamb, Charles 1775-1834 .... DLB-93, 107, 163

Lamb, Lady Caroline 1785-1828 .... DLB-116

Lamb, Mary 1764-1874 .... DLB-163

Lambert, Betty 1933-1983 .... DLB-60

Lamming, George 1927- DLB-125

L'Amour, Louis 1908?- Y-80

Lampman, Archibald 1861-1899 ..... DLB-92

Cumulative Index

Lamson, Wolffe and Company DLB-49

Lancer Books DLB-46

Landesman, Jay 1919- and
  Landesman, Fran 1927- DLB-16

Landon, Letitia Elizabeth 1802-1838 . DLB-96

Landor, Walter Savage
  1775-1864 .... DLB-93, 107

Landry, Napoléon-P. 1884-1956 .... DLB-92

Lane, Charles 1800-1870 .... DLB-1

Lane, Laurence W. 1890-1967 ...... DLB-91

Lane, M. Travis 1934- DLB-60

Lane, Patrick 1939- DLB-53

Lane, Pinkie Gordon 1923- DLB-41

Lane, John, Company DLB-49

Laney, Al 1896-1988 .... DLB-4, 171

Lang, Andrew 1844-1912 ...... DLB-98, 141

Langevin, André 1927- DLB-60

Langgässer, Elisabeth 1899-1950 .... DLB-69

Langhorne, John 1735-1779 .... DLB-109

Langland, William
  circa 1330-circa 1400 .... DLB-146

Langton, Anna 1804-1893 .... DLB-99

Lanham, Edwin 1904-1979 .... DLB-4

Lanier, Sidney 1842-1881 .... DLB-64; DS-13

Lanyer, Aemilia 1569-1645 .... DLB-121

Lapointe, Gatien 1931-1983 ...... DLB-88

Lapointe, Paul-Marie 1929- DLB-88

Lardner, John 1912-1960 .... DLB-171

Lardner, Ring
  1885-1933 .... DLB-11, 25, 86, 171

Lardner, Ring, Jr. 1915- DLB-26

Lardner 100: Ring Lardner
  Centennial Symposium Y-85

Larkin, Philip 1922-1985 .... DLB-27

La Roche, Sophie von 1730-1807 .... DLB-94

La Rocque, Gilbert 1943-1984 ..... DLB-60

Laroque de Roquebrune, Robert (see Roquebrune, Robert de)

Larrick, Nancy 1910- DLB-61

Larsen, Nella 1893-1964 .... DLB-51

Lasker-Schüler, Else
  1869-1945 .... DLB-66, 124

Lasnier, Rina 1915- DLB-88

Lassalle, Ferdinand 1825-1864 .... DLB-129

Lathrop, Dorothy P. 1891-1980 ..... DLB-22

Lathrop, George Parsons
  1851-1898 .... DLB-71

Lathrop, John, Jr. 1772-1820 .... DLB-37

Latimer, Hugh 1492?-1555 .... DLB-136

Latimore, Jewel Christine McLawler
  (see Amini, Johari M.)

Latymer, William 1498-1583 .... DLB-132

Laube, Heinrich 1806-1884 .... DLB-133

Laughlin, James 1914- DLB-48

Laumer, Keith 1925- DLB-8

Lauremberg, Johann 1590-1658 .... DLB-164

Laurence, Margaret 1926-1987 ...... DLB-53

Laurentius von Schnüffis
  1633-1702 .... DLB-168

Laurents, Arthur 1918- DLB-26

Laurie, Annie (see Black, Winifred)

Laut, Agnes Christiana 1871-1936 ... DLB-92

Lavater, Johann Kaspar 1741-1801 ... DLB-97

Lavin, Mary 1912- DLB-15

Lawes, Henry 1596-1662 .... DLB-126

Lawless, Anthony (see MacDonald, Philip)

Lawrence, D. H.
  1885-1930 ...... DLB-10, 19, 36, 98, 162

Lawrence, David 1888-1973 .... DLB-29

Lawrence, Seymour 1926-1994 .... Y-94

Lawson, John ?-1711 .... DLB-24

Lawson, Robert 1892-1957 .... DLB-22

Lawson, Victor F. 1850-1925 .... DLB-25

Layard, Sir Austen Henry
  1817-1894 .... DLB-166

Layton, Irving 1912- DLB-88

LaZamon flourished circa 1200 ..... DLB-146

Lazarević, Laza K. 1851-1890 ...... DLB-147

Lea, Henry Charles 1825-1909 ..... DLB-47

Lea, Sydney 1942- DLB-120

Lea, Tom 1907- DLB-6

Leacock, John 1729-1802 .... DLB-31

Leacock, Stephen 1869-1944 .... DLB-92

Lead, Jane Ward 1623-1704 ..... DLB-131

Leadenhall Press DLB-106

Leapor, Mary 1722-1746 .... DLB-109

Lear, Edward 1812-1888 ...DLB-32, 163, 166

Leary, Timothy 1920-1996 .... DLB-16

Leary, W. A., and Company DLB-49

Léautaud, Paul 1872-1956 .... DLB-65

Leavitt, David 1961- DLB-130

Leavitt and Allen DLB-49

le Carré, John 1931- DLB-87

Lécavelé, Roland (see Dorgeles, Roland)

Lechlitner, Ruth 1901- DLB-48

Leclerc, Félix 1914- DLB-60

Le Clézio, J. M. G. 1940- DLB-83

Lectures on Rhetoric and Belles Lettres (1783),
  by Hugh Blair [excerpts] DLB-31

Leder, Rudolf (see Hermlin, Stephan)

Lederer, Charles 1910-1976 .... DLB-26

Ledwidge, Francis 1887-1917 .... DLB-20

Lee, Dennis 1939- DLB-53

Lee, Don L. (see Madhubuti, Haki R.)

Lee, George W. 1894-1976 .... DLB-51

Lee, Harper 1926- DLB-6

Lee, Harriet (1757-1851) and
  Lee, Sophia (1750-1824) DLB-39

Lee, Laurie 1914- DLB-27

Lee, Li-Young 1957- DLB-165

Lee, Manfred B. (see Dannay, Frederic, and
  Manfred B. Lee)

Lee, Nathaniel circa 1645 - 1692 ..... DLB-80

Lee, Sir Sidney 1859-1926 .... DLB-149

Lee, Sir Sidney, "Principles of Biography," in
  Elizabethan and Other Essays DLB-149

Lee, Vernon 1856-1935 .... DLB-57, 153, 156

Lee and Shepard DLB-49

Le Fanu, Joseph Sheridan
  1814-1873 .... DLB-21, 70, 159

Leffland, Ella 1931- Y-84

le Fort, Gertrud von 1876-1971 ..... DLB-66

Le Gallienne, Richard 1866-1947 ..... DLB-4

Legaré, Hugh Swinton
  1797-1843 .... DLB-3, 59, 73

Legaré, James M. 1823-1859 .... DLB-3

The Legends of the Saints and a Medieval
  Christian Worldview DLB-148

Léger, Antoine-J. 1880-1950 .... DLB-88

Le Guin, Ursula K. 1929- DLB-8, 52

Lehman, Ernest 1920- DLB-44

Lehmann, John 1907- DLB-27, 100

Lehmann, Rosamond 1901-1990 ..... DLB-15

Lehmann, Wilhelm 1882-1968 .... DLB-56

Lehmann, John, Limited DLB-112

Leiber, Fritz 1910-1992 .... DLB-8

Leibniz, Gottfried Wilhelm
  1646-1716 .... DLB-168

Leicester University Press DLB-112

Leinster, Murray 1896-1975 . . . . DLB-8	Letter from Japan Y-94	Lighthall, William Douw 1857-1954 . . . . DLB-92
Leisewitz, Johann Anton 1752-1806 . . . . DLB-94	Letter to [Samuel] Richardson on *Clarissa* (1748), by Henry Fielding DLB-39	Lilar, Françoise (see Mallet-Joris, Françoise)
Leitch, Maurice 1933- DLB-14	Lever, Charles 1806-1872 . . . . DLB-21	Lillo, George 1691-1739 . . . . DLB-84
Leithauser, Brad 1943- DLB-120	Leverson, Ada 1862-1933 . . . . DLB-153	Lilly, J. K., Jr. 1893-1966 . . . . DLB-140
Leland, Charles G. 1824-1903 . . . . . . DLB-11	Levertov, Denise 1923- DLB-5, 165	Lilly, Wait and Company DLB-49
Leland, John 1503?-1552 . . . . DLB-136	Levi, Peter 1931- DLB-40	Lily, William circa 1468-1522 . . . . . . DLB-132
Lemay, Pamphile 1837-1918 . . . . DLB-99	Levien, Sonya 1888-1960 . . . . DLB-44	Limited Editions Club DLB-46
Lemelin, Roger 1919- DLB-88	Levin, Meyer 1905-1981 . . . . DLB-9, 28; Y-81	Lincoln and Edmands DLB-49
Lemon, Mark 1809-1870 . . . . DLB-163	Levine, Norman 1923- DLB-88	Lindsay, Jack 1900- Y-84
Le Moine, James MacPherson 1825-1912 . . . . DLB-99	Levine, Philip 1928- DLB-5	Lindsay, Sir David circa 1485-1555 . . . . DLB-132
Le Moyne, Jean 1913- DLB-88	Levis, Larry 1946- DLB-120	Lindsay, Vachel 1879-1931 . . . . DLB-54
L'Engle, Madeleine 1918- DLB-52	Levy, Amy 1861-1889 . . . . DLB-156	Linebarger, Paul Myron Anthony (see Smith, Cordwainer)
Lennart, Isobel 1915-1971 . . . . DLB-44	Levy, Benn Wolfe 1900-1973 . . . . DLB-13; Y-81	Link, Arthur S. 1920- DLB-17
Lennox, Charlotte 1729 or 1730-1804 . . . . DLB-39	Lewald, Fanny 1811-1889 . . . . DLB-129	Linn, John Blair 1777-1804 . . . . DLB-37
Lenox, James 1800-1880 . . . . DLB-140	Lewes, George Henry 1817-1878 . . . . DLB-55, 144	Lins, Osman 1924-1978 . . . . DLB-145
Lenski, Lois 1893-1974 . . . . DLB-22	Lewis, Alfred H. 1857-1914 . . . . DLB-25	Linton, Eliza Lynn 1822-1898 . . . . . . DLB-18
Lenz, Hermann 1913- DLB-69	Lewis, Alun 1915-1944 . . . . DLB-20, 162	Linton, William James 1812-1897 . . . . DLB-32
Lenz, J. M. R. 1751-1792 . . . . DLB-94	Lewis, C. Day (see Day Lewis, C.)	Lintot, Barnaby Bernard [publishing house] DLB-170
Lenz, Siegfried 1926- DLB-75	Lewis, C. S. 1898-1963 . . . . DLB-15, 100, 160	Lion Books DLB-46
Leonard, Elmore 1925- DLB-173	Lewis, Charles B. 1842-1924 . . . . DLB-11	Lionni, Leo 1910- DLB-61
Leonard, Hugh 1926- DLB-13	Lewis, Henry Clay 1825-1850 . . . . DLB-3	Lippincott, Sara Jane Clarke 1823-1904 . . . . DLB-43
Leonard, William Ellery 1876-1944 . . . . DLB-54	Lewis, Janet 1899- Y-87	Lippincott, J. B., Company DLB-49
Leonowens, Anna 1834-1914 . . . . DLB-99, 166	Lewis, Matthew Gregory 1775-1818 . . . . DLB-39, 158	Lippmann, Walter 1889-1974 . . . . . . DLB-29
LePan, Douglas 1914- DLB-88	Lewis, R. W. B. 1917- DLB-111	Lipton, Lawrence 1898-1975 . . . . DLB-16
Leprohon, Rosanna Eleanor 1829-1879 . . . . DLB-99	Lewis, Richard circa 1700-1734 . . . . . DLB-24	Liscow, Christian Ludwig 1701-1760 . . . . DLB-97
Le Queux, William 1864-1927 . . . . . . DLB-70	Lewis, Sinclair 1885-1951 . . . . DLB-9, 102; DS-1	Lish, Gordon 1934- DLB-130
Lerner, Max 1902-1992 . . . . DLB-29	Lewis, Wilmarth Sheldon 1895-1979 . . . . DLB-140	Lispector, Clarice 1925-1977 . . . . DLB-113
Lernet-Holenia, Alexander 1897-1976 . . . . DLB-85	Lewis, Wyndham 1882-1957 . . . . DLB-15	*The Literary Chronicle and Weekly Review* 1819-1828 . . . . DLB-110
Le Rossignol, James 1866-1969 . . . . . . DLB-92	Lewisohn, Ludwig 1882-1955 . . . . DLB-4, 9, 28, 102	Literary Documents: William Faulkner and the People-to-People Program Y-86
Lescarbot, Marc circa 1570-1642 . . . . . DLB-99	Lezama Lima, José 1910-1976 . . . . . DLB-113	
LeSeur, William Dawson 1840-1917 . . . . DLB-92	The Library of America DLB-46	Literary Documents II: *Library Journal* Statements and Questionnaires from First Novelists Y-87
LeSieg, Theo. (see Geisel, Theodor Seuss)	The Licensing Act of 1737 . . . . DLB-84	
Leslie, Frank 1821-1880 . . . . DLB-43, 79	Lichfield, Leonard I [publishing house] DLB-170	Literary Effects of World War II [British novel] DLB-15
Leslie, Frank, Publishing House DLB-49	Lichtenberg, Georg Christoph 1742-1799 . . . . DLB-94	Literary Prizes [British] DLB-15
Lesperance, John 1835?-1891 . . . . DLB-99	Lieb, Fred 1888-1980 . . . . DLB-171	Literary Research Archives: The Humanities Research Center, University of Texas Y-82
Lessing, Bruno 1870-1940 . . . . DLB-28	Liebling, A. J. 1904-1963 . . . . . . DLB-4, 171	
Lessing, Doris 1919- . . . DLB-15, 139; Y-85	Lieutenant Murray (see Ballou, Maturin Murray)	Literary Research Archives II: Berg Collection of English and American Literature of the New York Public Library Y-83
Lessing, Gotthold Ephraim 1729-1781 . . . . DLB-97		
Lettau, Reinhard 1929- DLB-75		

347

Literary Research Archives III:
  The Lilly Library Y-84

Literary Research Archives IV:
  The John Carter Brown Library Y-85

Literary Research Archives V:
  Kent State Special Collections Y-86

Literary Research Archives VI: The Modern
  Literary Manuscripts Collection in the
  Special Collections of the Washington
  University Libraries Y-87

Literary Research Archives VII:
  The University of Virginia
  Libraries Y-91

Literary Research Archives VIII:
  The Henry E. Huntington
  Library Y-92

"Literary Style" (1857), by William
  Forsyth [excerpt] DLB-57

Literatura Chicanesca: The View From
  Without DLB-82

Literature at Nurse, or Circulating Morals (1885),
  by George Moore DLB-18

Littell, Eliakim 1797-1870 .... DLB-79

Littell, Robert S. 1831-1896 .... DLB-79

Little, Brown and Company DLB-49

Littlewood, Joan 1914- DLB-13

Lively, Penelope 1933- DLB-14, 161

Liverpool University Press DLB-112

The Lives of the Poets DLB-142

Livesay, Dorothy 1909- DLB-68

Livesay, Florence Randal
  1874-1953 .... DLB-92

Livings, Henry 1929- DLB-13

Livingston, Anne Howe
  1763-1841 .... DLB-37

Livingston, Myra Cohn 1926- DLB-61

Livingston, William 1723-1790 ..... DLB-31

Livingstone, David 1813-1873 ..... DLB-166

Liyong, Taban lo (see Taban lo Liyong)

Lizárraga, Sylvia S. 1925- DLB-82

Llewellyn, Richard 1906-1983 ..... DLB-15

Lloyd, Edward
  [publishing house] DLB-106

Lobel, Arnold 1933- DLB-61

Lochridge, Betsy Hopkins (see Fancher, Betsy)

Locke, David Ross 1833-1888 ... DLB-11, 23

Locke, John 1632-1704 .... DLB-31, 101

Locke, Richard Adams 1800-1871 ... DLB-43

Locker-Lampson, Frederick
  1821-1895 .... DLB-35

Lockhart, John Gibson
  1794-1854 .... DLB-110, 116 144

Lockridge, Ross, Jr.
  1914-1948 .... DLB-143; Y-80

Locrine and *Selimus* DLB-62

Lodge, David 1935- DLB-14

Lodge, George Cabot 1873-1909 .... DLB-54

Lodge, Henry Cabot 1850-1924 ..... DLB-47

Lodge, Thomas 1558-1625 .... DLB-172

Loeb, Harold 1891-1974 .... DLB-4

Loeb, William 1905-1981 .... DLB-127

Lofting, Hugh 1886-1947 .... DLB-160

Logan, James 1674-1751 .... DLB-24, 140

Logan, John 1923- DLB-5

Logan, William 1950- DLB-120

Logau, Friedrich von 1605-1655 .... DLB-164

Logue, Christopher 1926- DLB-27

Lohenstein, Daniel Casper von
  1635-1683 .... DLB-168

Lomonosov, Mikhail Vasil'evich
  1711-1765 .... DLB-150

London, Jack 1876-1916 ...... DLB-8, 12, 78

The London Magazine 1820-1829 ..... DLB-110

Long, Haniel 1888-1956 .... DLB-45

Long, Ray 1878-1935 .... DLB-137

Long, H., and Brother DLB-49

Longfellow, Henry Wadsworth
  1807-1882 .... DLB-1, 59

Longfellow, Samuel 1819-1892 .... DLB-1

Longford, Elizabeth 1906- DLB-155

Longley, Michael 1939- DLB-40

Longman, T. [publishing house] DLB-154

Longmans, Green and Company DLB-49

Longmore, George 1793?-1867 ...... DLB-99

Longstreet, Augustus Baldwin
  1790-1870 .... DLB-3, 11, 74

Longworth, D. [publishing house] ... DLB-49

Lonsdale, Frederick 1881-1954 ...... DLB-10

A Look at the Contemporary Black Theatre
  Movement DLB-38

Loos, Anita 1893-1981 ..... DLB-11, 26; Y-81

Lopate, Phillip 1943- Y-80

López, Diana (see Isabella, Ríos)

Loranger, Jean-Aubert 1896-1942 .... DLB-92

Lorca, Federico García 1898-1936 .. DLB-108

Lord, John Keast 1818-1872 .... DLB-99

The Lord Chamberlain's Office and Stage
  Censorship in England DLB-10

Lorde, Audre 1934-1992 .... DLB-41

Lorimer, George Horace
  1867-1939 .... DLB-91

Loring, A. K. [publishing house] DLB-49

Loring and Mussey DLB-46

Lossing, Benson J. 1813-1891 .... DLB-30

Lothar, Ernst 1890-1974 .... DLB-81

Lothrop, Harriet M. 1844-1924 ...... DLB-42

Lothrop, D., and Company DLB-49

Loti, Pierre 1850-1923 .... DLB-123

Lott, Emeline ?-? DLB-166

The Lounger, no. 20 (1785), by Henry
  Mackenzie DLB-39

Lounsbury, Thomas R. 1838-1915 ...DLB-71

Louÿs, Pierre 1870-1925 .... DLB-123

Lovelace, Earl 1935- DLB-125

Lovelace, Richard 1618-1657 .... DLB-131

Lovell, Coryell and Company DLB-49

Lovell, John W., Company DLB-49

Lover, Samuel 1797-1868 .... DLB-159

Lovesey, Peter 1936- DLB-87

Lovingood, Sut (see Harris,
  George Washington)

Low, Samuel 1765-? DLB-37

Lowell, Amy 1874-1925 .... DLB-54, 140

Lowell, James Russell
  1819-1891 .... DLB-1, 11, 64, 79

Lowell, Robert 1917-1977 .... DLB-5, 169

Lowenfels, Walter 1897-1976 .... DLB-4

Lowndes, Marie Belloc 1868-1947 ....DLB-70

Lownes, Humphrey
  [publishing house] DLB-170

Lowry, Lois 1937- DLB-52

Lowry, Malcolm 1909-1957 .... DLB-15

Lowther, Pat 1935-1975 .... DLB-53

Loy, Mina 1882-1966 .... DLB-4, 54

Lozeau, Albert 1878-1924 .... DLB-92

Lubbock, Percy 1879-1965 .... DLB-149

Lucas, E. V. 1868-1938 .... DLB-98, 149, 153

Lucas, Fielding, Jr.
  [publishing house] DLB-49

Luce, Henry R. 1898-1967 .... DLB-91

Luce, John W., and Company DLB-46

Lucie-Smith, Edward 1933- DLB-40

Lucini, Gian Pietro 1867-1914 ......DLB-114

348

Ludlum, Robert 1927- Y-82

Ludus de Antichristo circa 1160 ....DLB-148

Ludvigson, Susan 1942- DLB-120

Ludwig, Jack 1922- DLB-60

Ludwig, Otto 1813-1865 ....DLB-129

Ludwigslied 881 or 882 ....DLB-148

Luera, Yolanda 1953- DLB-122

Luft, Lya 1938- DLB-145

Luke, Peter 1919- DLB-13

Lupton, F. M., Company DLB-49

Lupus of Ferrières
circa 805-circa 862 ....DLB-148

Lurie, Alison 1926- DLB-2

Luzi, Mario 1914- DLB-128

L'vov, Nikolai Aleksandrovich
1751-1803 ....DLB-150

Lyall, Gavin 1932- DLB-87

Lydgate, John circa 1370-1450 .....DLB-146

Lyly, John circa 1554-1606 .....DLB-62, 167

Lynch, Patricia 1898-1972 ....DLB-160

Lynch, Richard
flourished 1596-1601 ....DLB-172

Lynd, Robert 1879-1949 ....DLB-98

Lyon, Matthew 1749-1822 ....DLB-43

Lytle, Andrew 1902-1995 ....DLB-6; Y-95

Lytton, Edward (see Bulwer-Lytton, Edward)

Lytton, Edward Robert Bulwer
1831-1891 ....DLB-32

M

Maass, Joachim 1901-1972 ....DLB-69

Mabie, Hamilton Wright
1845-1916 ....DLB-71

Mac A'Ghobhainn, Iain (see Smith, Iain Crichton)

MacArthur, Charles
1895-1956 .... DLB-7, 25, 44

Macaulay, Catherine 1731-1791 ....DLB-104

Macaulay, David 1945- DLB-61

Macaulay, Rose 1881-1958 ....DLB-36

Macaulay, Thomas Babington
1800-1859 ....DLB-32, 55

Macaulay Company DLB-46

MacBeth, George 1932- DLB-40

Macbeth, Madge 1880-1965 ....DLB-92

MacCaig, Norman 1910- DLB-27

MacDiarmid, Hugh 1892-1978 ....DLB-20

MacDonald, Cynthia 1928- DLB-105

MacDonald, George
1824-1905 .... DLB-18, 163

MacDonald, John D.
1916-1986 .... DLB-8; Y-86

MacDonald, Philip 1899?-1980 ..... DLB-77

Macdonald, Ross (see Millar, Kenneth)

MacDonald, Wilson 1880-1967 ..... DLB-92

Macdonald and Company
(Publishers) DLB-112

MacEwen, Gwendolyn 1941- DLB-53

Macfadden, Bernarr
1868-1955 .... DLB-25, 91

MacGregor, John 1825-1892 .... DLB-166

MacGregor, Mary Esther (see Keith, Marian)

Machado, Antonio 1875-1939 ..... DLB-108

Machado, Manuel 1874-1947 ...... DLB-108

Machar, Agnes Maule 1837-1927 .... DLB-92

Machen, Arthur Llewelyn Jones
1863-1947 .... DLB-36, 156

MacInnes, Colin 1914-1976 .... DLB-14

MacInnes, Helen 1907-1985 .... DLB-87

Mack, Maynard 1909- DLB-111

Mackall, Leonard L. 1879-1937 .... DLB-140

MacKaye, Percy 1875-1956 .... DLB-54

Macken, Walter 1915-1967 .... DLB-13

Mackenzie, Alexander 1763-1820 .... DLB-99

Mackenzie, Compton
1883-1972 .... DLB-34, 100

Mackenzie, Henry 1745-1831 .... DLB-39

Mackey, Nathaniel 1947- DLB-169

Mackey, William Wellington
1937- DLB-38

Mackintosh, Elizabeth (see Tey, Josephine)

Mackintosh, Sir James
1765-1832 .... DLB-158

Maclaren, Ian (see Watson, John)

Macklin, Charles 1699-1797 .... DLB-89

MacLean, Katherine Anne 1925- ... DLB-8

MacLeish, Archibald
1892-1982 ....DLB-4, 7, 45; Y-82

MacLennan, Hugh 1907-1990 ...... DLB-68

Macleod, Fiona (see Sharp, William)

MacLeod, Alistair 1936- DLB-60

Macleod, Norman 1906-1985 .... DLB-4

Macmillan and Company DLB-106

The Macmillan Company DLB-49

Macmillan's English Men of Letters,
First Series (1878-1892) DLB-144

MacNamara, Brinsley 1890-1963 ....DLB-10

MacNeice, Louis 1907-1963 ......DLB-10, 20

MacPhail, Andrew 1864-1938 ....DLB-92

Macpherson, James 1736-1796 .....DLB-109

Macpherson, Jay 1931- DLB-53

Macpherson, Jeanie 1884-1946 ......DLB-44

Macrae Smith Company DLB-46

Macrone, John
[publishing house] DLB-106

MacShane, Frank 1927- DLB-111

Macy-Masius DLB-46

Madden, David 1933- DLB-6

Maddow, Ben 1909-1992 ....DLB-44

Maddux, Rachel 1912-1983 ....Y-93

Madgett, Naomi Long 1923- DLB-76

Madhubuti, Haki R.
1942- DLB-5, 41; DS-8

Madison, James 1751-1836 ....DLB-37

Maginn, William 1794-1842 ...DLB-110, 159

Mahan, Alfred Thayer 1840-1914 ....DLB-47

Maheux-Forcier, Louise 1929- DLB-60

Mahin, John Lee 1902-1984 ....DLB-44

Mahon, Derek 1941- DLB-40

Maikov, Vasilii Ivanovich
1728-1778 ....DLB-150

Mailer, Norman
1923- DLB-2, 16, 28; Y-80, 83; DS-3

Maillet, Adrienne 1885-1963 ....DLB-68

Maimonides, Moses 1138-1204 .....DLB-115

Maillet, Antonine 1929- DLB-60

Maillu, David G. 1939- DLB-157

Main Selections of the Book-of-the-Month
Club, 1926-1945 ....DLB-9

Main Trends in Twentieth-Century Book
Clubs DLB-46

Mainwaring, Daniel 1902-1977 ......DLB-44

Mair, Charles 1838-1927 ....DLB-99

Mais, Roger 1905-1955 ....DLB-125

Major, Andre 1942- DLB-60

Major, Clarence 1936- DLB-33

Major, Kevin 1949- DLB-60

Major Books DLB-46

Makemie, Francis circa 1658-1708 ...DLB-24

The Making of a People, by
J. M. Ritchie DLB-66

Maksimović, Desanka 1898-1993 ... DLB-147

Malamud, Bernard 1914-1986 ...... DLB-2, 28, 152; Y-80, 86

Malet, Lucas 1852-1931 .... DLB-153

Malleson, Lucy Beatrice (see Gilbert, Anthony)

Mallet-Joris, Françoise 1930- DLB-83

Mallock, W. H. 1849-1923 ...... DLB-18, 57

Malone, Dumas 1892-1986 .... DLB-17

Malone, Edmond 1741-1812 .... DLB-142

Malory, Sir Thomas circa 1400-1410 - 1471 .... DLB-146

Malraux, André 1901-1976 .... DLB-72

Malthus, Thomas Robert 1766-1834 .... DLB-107, 158

Maltz, Albert 1908-1985 .... DLB-102

Malzberg, Barry N. 1939- DLB-8

Mamet, David 1947- DLB-7

Manaka, Matsemela 1956- DLB-157

Manchester University Press DLB-112

Mandel, Eli 1922- DLB-53

Mandeville, Bernard 1670-1733 .... DLB-101

Mandeville, Sir John mid fourteenth century DLB-146

Mandiargues, André Pieyre de 1909- DLB-83

Manfred, Frederick 1912-1994 .... DLB-6

Mangan, Sherry 1904-1961 .... DLB-4

Mankiewicz, Herman 1897-1953 .... DLB-26

Mankiewicz, Joseph L. 1909-1993 ... DLB-44

Mankowitz, Wolf 1924- DLB-15

Manley, Delarivière 1672?-1724 .... DLB-39, 80

Mann, Abby 1927- DLB-44

Mann, Heinrich 1871-1950 ..... DLB-66, 118

Mann, Horace 1796-1859 .... DLB-1

Mann, Klaus 1906-1949 .... DLB-56

Mann, Thomas 1875-1955 .... DLB-66

Mann, William D'Alton 1839-1920 .... DLB-137

Manning, Marie 1873?-1945 .... DLB-29

Manning and Loring DLB-49

Mannyng, Robert flourished 1303-1338 .... DLB-146

Mano, D. Keith 1942- DLB-6

Manor Books DLB-46

Mansfield, Katherine 1888-1923 ... DLB-162

Mapanje, Jack 1944- DLB-157

March, William 1893-1954 .... DLB-9, 86

Marchand, Leslie A. 1900- DLB-103

Marchant, Bessie 1862-1941 ..... DLB-160

Marchessault, Jovette 1938- DLB-60

Marcus, Frank 1928- DLB-13

Marden, Orison Swett 1850-1924 .... DLB-137

Marechera, Dambudzo 1952-1987 .... DLB-157

Marek, Richard, Books DLB-46

Mares, E. A. 1938- DLB-122

Mariani, Paul 1940- DLB-111

Marie-Victorin, Frère 1885-1944 ..... DLB-92

Marin, Biagio 1891-1985 .... DLB-128

Marincović, Ranko 1913- DLB-147

Marinetti, Filippo Tommaso 1876-1944 .... DLB-114

Marion, Frances 1886-1973 .... DLB-44

Marius, Richard C. 1933- Y-85

The Mark Taper Forum DLB-7

Mark Twain on Perpetual Copyright Y-92

Markfield, Wallace 1926- DLB-2, 28

Markham, Edwin 1852-1940 .... DLB-54

Markle, Fletcher 1921-1991 .... DLB-68; Y-91

Marlatt, Daphne 1942- DLB-60

Marlitt, E. 1825-1887 .... DLB-129

Marlowe, Christopher 1564-1593 .... DLB-62

Marlyn, John 1912- DLB-88

Marmion, Shakerley 1603-1639 ..... DLB-58

Der Marner before 1230-circa 1287 .... DLB-138

The *Marprelate* Tracts 1588-1589 .... DLB-132

Marquand, John P. 1893-1960 ... DLB-9, 102

Marqués, René 1919-1979 .... DLB-113

Marquis, Don 1878-1937 .... DLB-11, 25

Marriott, Anne 1913- DLB-68

Marryat, Frederick 1792-1848 ... DLB-21, 163

Marsh, George Perkins 1801-1882 .... DLB-1, 64

Marsh, James 1794-1842 .... DLB-1, 59

Marsh, Capen, Lyon and Webb DLB-49

Marsh, Ngaio 1899-1982 .... DLB-77

Marshall, Edison 1894-1967 .... DLB-102

Marshall, Edward 1932- DLB-16

Marshall, Emma 1828-1899 .... DLB-163

Marshall, James 1942-1992 .... DLB-61

Marshall, Joyce 1913- DLB-88

Marshall, Paule 1929- DLB-33, 157

Marshall, Tom 1938- DLB-60

Marsilius of Padua circa 1275-circa 1342 .... DLB-115

Marson, Una 1905-1965 .... DLB-157

Marston, John 1576-1634 ...... DLB-58, 172

Marston, Philip Bourke 1850-1887 ... DLB-35

Martens, Kurt 1870-1945 .... DLB-66

Martien, William S. [publishing house] DLB-49

Martin, Abe (see Hubbard, Kin)

Martin, Charles 1942- DLB-120

Martin, Claire 1914- DLB-60

Martin, Jay 1935- DLB-111

Martin, Johann (see Laurentius von Schnüffis)

Martin, Violet Florence (see Ross, Martin)

Martin du Gard, Roger 1881-1958 ...DLB-65

Martineau, Harriet 1802-1876 ..... DLB-21, 55, 159, 163, 166

Martínez, Eliud 1935- DLB-122

Martínez, Max 1943- DLB-82

Martyn, Edward 1859-1923 .... DLB-10

Marvell, Andrew 1621-1678 .... DLB-131

Marvin X 1944- DLB-38

Marx, Karl 1818-1883 .... DLB-129

Marzials, Theo 1850-1920 .... DLB-35

Masefield, John 1878-1967 .... DLB-10, 19, 153, 160

Mason, A. E. W. 1865-1948 .... DLB-70

Mason, Bobbie Ann 1940- DLB-173; Y-87

Mason, William 1725-1797 .... DLB-142

Mason Brothers DLB-49

Massey, Gerald 1828-1907 .... DLB-32

Massinger, Philip 1583-1640 .... DLB-58

Masson, David 1822-1907 .... DLB-144

Masters, Edgar Lee 1868-1950 .... DLB-54

Mather, Cotton 1663-1728 .... DLB-24, 30, 140

Mather, Increase 1639-1723 .... DLB-24

Mather, Richard 1596-1669 .... DLB-24

Matheson, Richard 1926- DLB-8, 44

Matheus, John F. 1887- DLB-51

Mathews, Cornelius 1817?-1889 .... DLB-3, 64

Mathews, Elkin
[publishing house] DLB-112

Mathias, Roland 1915- DLB-27

Mathis, June 1892-1927 ....DLB-44

Mathis, Sharon Bell 1937- DLB-33

Matoš, Antun Gustav 1873-1914 ....DLB-147

The Matter of England
1240-1400 ....DLB-146

The Matter of Rome
early twelfth to late fifteenth
century DLB-146

Matthews, Brander
1852-1929 ....DLB-71, 78; DS-13

Matthews, Jack 1925- DLB-6

Matthews, William 1942- DLB-5

Matthiessen, F. O. 1902-1950 ....DLB-63

Matthiessen, Peter 1927- DLB-6, 173

Maugham, W. Somerset
1874-1965 .....DLB-10, 36, 77, 100, 162

Maupassant, Guy de 1850-1893 ....DLB-123

Mauriac, Claude 1914- DLB-83

Mauriac, François 1885-1970 ....DLB-65

Maurice, Frederick Denison
1805-1872 ....DLB-55

Maurois, André 1885-1967 ....DLB-65

Maury, James 1718-1769 ....DLB-31

Mavor, Elizabeth 1927- DLB-14

Mavor, Osborne Henry (see Bridie, James)

Maxwell, H. [publishing house] DLB-49

Maxwell, John [publishing house] ...DLB-106

Maxwell, William 1908- Y-80

May, Elaine 1932- DLB-44

May, Karl 1842-1912 ....DLB-129

May, Thomas 1595 or 1596-1650 ....DLB-58

Mayer, Bernadette 1945- DLB-165

Mayer, Mercer 1943- DLB-61

Mayer, O. B. 1818-1891 ....DLB-3

Mayes, Herbert R. 1900-1987 ......DLB-137

Mayes, Wendell 1919-1992 ....DLB-26

Mayfield, Julian 1928-1984 ....DLB-33; Y-84

Mayhew, Henry 1812-1887 ......DLB-18, 55

Mayhew, Jonathan 1720-1766 ......DLB-31

Mayne, Jasper 1604-1672 ....DLB-126

Mayne, Seymour 1944- DLB-60

Mayor, Flora Macdonald
1872-1932 ....DLB-36

Mayrocker, Friederike 1924- DLB-85

Mazrui, Ali A. 1933- DLB-125

Mažuranić, Ivan 1814-1890 ....DLB-147

Mazursky, Paul 1930- DLB-44

McAlmon, Robert 1896-1956 ..... DLB-4, 45

McArthur, Peter 1866-1924 .... DLB-92

McBride, Robert M., and
Company DLB-46

McCaffrey, Anne 1926- DLB-8

McCarthy, Cormac 1933- DLB-6, 143

McCarthy, Mary 1912-1989 .... DLB-2; Y-81

McCay, Winsor 1871-1934 .... DLB-22

McClane, Albert Jules 1922-1991 ... DLB-171

McClatchy, C. K. 1858-1936 .... DLB-25

McClellan, George Marion
1860-1934 .... DLB-50

McCloskey, Robert 1914- DLB-22

McClung, Nellie Letitia 1873-1951 .. DLB-92

McClure, Joanna 1930- DLB-16

McClure, Michael 1932- DLB-16

McClure, Phillips and Company DLB-46

McClure, S. S. 1857-1949 .... DLB-91

McClurg, A. C., and Company DLB-49

McCluskey, John A., Jr. 1944- DLB-33

McCollum, Michael A. 1946 .... Y-87

McConnell, William C. 1917- DLB-88

McCord, David 1897- DLB-61

McCorkle, Jill 1958- Y-87

McCorkle, Samuel Eusebius
1746-1811 .... DLB-37

McCormick, Anne O'Hare
1880-1954 .... DLB-29

McCormick, Robert R. 1880-1955 ... DLB-29

McCourt, Edward 1907-1972 .... DLB-88

McCoy, Horace 1897-1955 .... DLB-9

McCrae, John 1872-1918 .... DLB-92

McCullagh, Joseph B. 1842-1896 .... DLB-23

McCullers, Carson
1917-1967 .... DLB-2, 7, 173

McCulloch, Thomas 1776-1843 ..... DLB-99

McDonald, Forrest 1927- DLB-17

McDonald, Walter
1934- DLB-105, DS-9

McDonald, Walter, Getting Started:
Accepting the Regions You Own—
or Which Own You DLB-105

McDougall, Colin 1917-1984 .... DLB-68

McDowell, Obolensky DLB-46

McEwan, Ian 1948- DLB-14

McFadden, David 1940- DLB-60

McFall, Frances Elizabeth Clarke
(see Grand, Sarah)

McFarlane, Leslie 1902-1977 ....DLB-88

McFee, William 1881-1966 ....DLB-153

McGahern, John 1934- DLB-14

McGee, Thomas D'Arcy
1825-1868 ....DLB-99

McGeehan, W. O. 1879-1933 ...DLB-25, 171

McGill, Ralph 1898-1969 ....DLB-29

McGinley, Phyllis 1905-1978 .....DLB-11, 48

McGirt, James E. 1874-1930 ....DLB-50

McGlashan and Gill DLB-106

McGough, Roger 1937- DLB-40

McGraw-Hill DLB-46

McGuane, Thomas 1939- DLB-2; Y-80

McGuckian, Medbh 1950- DLB-40

McGuffey, William Holmes
1800-1873 ....DLB-42

McIlvanney, William 1936- DLB-14

McIlwraith, Jean Newton
1859-1938 ....DLB-92

McIntyre, James 1827-1906 ....DLB-99

McIntyre, O. O. 1884-1938 ....DLB-25

McKay, Claude
1889-1948 ....DLB-4, 45, 51, 117

The David McKay Company DLB-49

McKean, William V. 1820-1903 .....DLB-23

McKinley, Robin 1952- DLB-52

McLachlan, Alexander 1818-1896 ...DLB-99

McLaren, Floris Clark 1904-1978 ....DLB-68

McLaverty, Michael 1907- DLB-15

McLean, John R. 1848-1916 ....DLB-23

McLean, William L. 1852-1931 ......DLB-25

McLennan, William 1856-1904 .....DLB-92

McLoughlin Brothers DLB-49

McLuhan, Marshall 1911-1980 ......DLB-88

McMaster, John Bach 1852-1932 ....DLB-47

McMurtry, Larry
1936- DLB-2, 143; Y-80, 87

McNally, Terrence 1939- DLB-7

McNeil, Florence 1937- DLB-60

McNeile, Herman Cyril
1888-1937 ....DLB-77

McPherson, James Alan 1943- DLB-38

McPherson, Sandra 1943- Y-86

351

Cumulative Index

McWhirter, George 1939- DLB-60

McWilliams, Carey 1905-1980 ..... DLB-137

Mead, L. T. 1844-1914 .... DLB-141

Mead, Matthew 1924- DLB-40

Mead, Taylor ?- DLB-16

Meany, Tom 1903-1964 .... DLB-171

Mechthild von Magdeburg
circa 1207-circa 1282 .... DLB-138

Medill, Joseph 1823-1899 .... DLB-43

Medoff, Mark 1940- DLB-7

Meek, Alexander Beaufort
1814-1865 ....DLB-3

Meeke, Mary ?-1816? DLB-116

Meinke, Peter 1932- DLB-5

Mejia Vallejo, Manuel 1923- DLB-113

Melançon, Robert 1947- DLB-60

Mell, Max 1882-1971 .... DLB-81, 124

Mellow, James R. 1926- DLB-111

Meltzer, David 1937- DLB-16

Meltzer, Milton 1915- DLB-61

Melville, Elizabeth, Lady Culross
circa 1585-1640 .... DLB-172

Melville, Herman 1819-1891 ..... DLB-3, 74

Memoirs of Life and Literature (1920),
by W. H. Mallock [excerpt] DLB-57

Menantes (see Hunold, Christian Friedrich)

Mencke, Johann Burckhard
1674-1732 .... DLB-168

Mencken, H. L.
1880-1956 .... DLB-11, 29, 63, 137

Mencken and Nietzsche: An Unpublished
Excerpt from H. L. Mencken's *My Life
as Author and Editor* Y-93

Mendelssohn, Moses 1729-1786 ..... DLB-97

Méndez M., Miguel 1930- DLB-82

Mercer, Cecil William (see Yates, Dornford)

Mercer, David 1928-1980 .... DLB-13

Mercer, John 1704-1768 .... DLB-31

Meredith, George
1828-1909 .... DLB-18, 35, 57, 159

Meredith, Louisa Anne
1812-1895 .... DLB-166

Meredith, Owen (see Lytton, Edward Robert Bulwer)

Meredith, William 1919- DLB-5

Mergerle, Johann Ulrich
(see Abraham ä Sancta Clara)

Mérimée, Prosper 1803-1870 ...... DLB-119

Merivale, John Herman
1779-1844 .... DLB-96

Meriwether, Louise 1923- DLB-33

Merlin Press DLB-112

Merriam, Eve 1916-1992? DLB-61

The Merriam Company DLB-49

Merrill, James
1926-1995 .... DLB-5, 165; Y-85

Merrill and Baker DLB-49

The Mershon Company DLB-49

Merton, Thomas 1915-1968 ...DLB-48; Y-81

Merwin, W. S. 1927- DLB-5, 169

Messner, Julian [publishing house] ... DLB-46

Metcalf, J. [publishing house] DLB-49

Metcalf, John 1938- DLB-60

The Methodist Book Concern DLB-49

Methuen and Company DLB-112

Mew, Charlotte 1869-1928 .....DLB-19, 135

Mewshaw, Michael 1943- Y-80

Meyer, Conrad Ferdinand
1825-1898 .... DLB-129

Meyer, E. Y. 1946- DLB-75

Meyer, Eugene 1875-1959 .... DLB-29

Meyer, Michael 1921- DLB-155

Meyers, Jeffrey 1939- DLB-111

Meynell, Alice
1847-1922 .... DLB-19, 98

Meynell, Viola 1885-1956 .... DLB-153

Meyrink, Gustav 1868-1932 .... DLB-81

Michaels, Leonard 1933- DLB-130

Micheaux, Oscar 1884-1951 .... DLB-50

Michel of Northgate, Dan
circa 1265-circa 1340 .... DLB-146

Micheline, Jack 1929- DLB-16

Michener, James A. 1907?- DLB-6

Micklejohn, George
circa 1717-1818 .... DLB-31

Middle English Literature:
An Introduction DLB-146

The Middle English Lyric DLB-146

Middle Hill Press DLB-106

Middleton, Christopher 1926- DLB-40

Middleton, Richard 1882-1911 ..... DLB-156

Middleton, Stanley 1919- DLB-14

Middleton, Thomas 1580-1627 ...... DLB-58

Miegel, Agnes 1879-1964 .... DLB-56

Miles, Josephine 1911-1985 .... DLB-48

Milius, John 1944- DLB-44

Mill, James 1773-1836 .... DLB-107, 158

Mill, John Stuart 1806-1873 ....DLB-55

Millar, Kenneth
1915-1983 .... DLB-2; Y-83; DS-6

Millar, Andrew
[publishing house] DLB-154

Millay, Edna St. Vincent
1892-1950 ....DLB-45

Miller, Arthur 1915- DLB-7

Miller, Caroline 1903-1992 ....DLB-9

Miller, Eugene Ethelbert 1950- DLB-41

Miller, Heather Ross 1939- DLB-120

Miller, Henry 1891-1980 ..... DLB-4, 9; Y-80

Miller, J. Hillis 1928- DLB-67

Miller, James [publishing house] DLB-49

Miller, Jason 1939- DLB-7

Miller, May 1899- DLB-41

Miller, Paul 1906-1991 ....DLB-127

Miller, Perry 1905-1963 .... DLB-17, 63

Miller, Sue 1943- DLB-143

Miller, Walter M., Jr. 1923- DLB-8

Miller, Webb 1892-1940 ....DLB-29

Millhauser, Steven 1943- DLB-2

Millican, Arthenia J. Bates
1920- DLB-38

Mills and Boon DLB-112

Milman, Henry Hart 1796-1868 .....DLB-96

Milne, A. A.
1882-1956 .... DLB-10, 77, 100, 160

Milner, Ron 1938- DLB-38

Milner, William
[publishing house] DLB-106

Milnes, Richard Monckton (Lord Houghton)
1809-1885 ....DLB-32

Milton, John 1608-1674 ...... DLB-131, 151

The Minerva Press DLB-154

Minnesang circa 1150-1280 ....DLB-138

Minns, Susan 1839-1938 ....DLB-140

Minor Illustrators, 1880-1914 ....DLB-141

Minor Poets of the Earlier Seventeenth
Century DLB-121

Minton, Balch and Company DLB-46

Mirbeau, Octave 1848-1917 ....DLB-123

Mirk, John died after 1414? DLB-146

Miron, Gaston 1928- DLB-60

A Mirror for Magistrates DLB-167

Mitchel, Jonathan 1624-1668 ....DLB-24	Monsarrat, Nicholas 1910-1979 .....DLB-15	Morales, Rafael 1919- DLB-108
Mitchell, Adrian 1932- DLB-40	Montagu, Lady Mary Wortley 1689-1762 ....DLB-95, 101	Morality Plays: *Mankind* circa 1450-1500 and *Everyman* circa 1500 ....DLB-146
Mitchell, Donald Grant 1822-1908 ....DLB-1; DS-13	Montague, John 1929- DLB-40	More, Hannah 1745-1833 ......DLB-107, 109, 116, 158
Mitchell, Gladys 1901-1983 ....DLB-77	Montale, Eugenio 1896-1981 .....DLB-114	More, Henry 1614-1687 ....DLB-126
Mitchell, James Leslie 1901-1935 ....DLB-15	Monterroso, Augusto 1921- DLB-145	More, Sir Thomas 1477 or 1478-1535 ....DLB-136
Mitchell, John (see Slater, Patrick)	Montgomerie, Alexander circa 1550?-1598 ....DLB-167	Moreno, Dorinda 1939- DLB-122
Mitchell, John Ames 1845-1918 ......DLB-79	Montgomery, James 1771-1854 ....DLB-93, 158	Morency, Pierre 1942- DLB-60
Mitchell, Julian 1935- DLB-14	Montgomery, John 1919- DLB-16	Moretti, Marino 1885-1979 ....DLB-114
Mitchell, Ken 1940- DLB-60	Montgomery, Lucy Maud 1874-1942 ....DLB-92; DS-14	Morgan, Berry 1919- DLB-6
Mitchell, Langdon 1862-1935 ....DLB-7	Montgomery, Marion 1925- DLB-6	Morgan, Charles 1894-1958 ....DLB-34, 100
Mitchell, Loften 1919- DLB-38	Montgomery, Robert Bruce (see Crispin, Edmund)	Morgan, Edmund S. 1916- DLB-17
Mitchell, Margaret 1900-1949 ....DLB-9	Montherlant, Henry de 1896-1972 ...DLB-72	Morgan, Edwin 1920- DLB-27
Mitchell, W. O. 1914- DLB-88	*The Monthly Review* 1749-1844 ......DLB-110	Morgan, John Pierpont 1837-1913 ....DLB-140
Mitchison, Naomi Margaret (Haldane) 1897- DLB-160	Montigny, Louvigny de 1876-1955 ..DLB-92	Morgan, John Pierpont, Jr. 1867-1943 ....DLB-140
Mitford, Mary Russell 1787-1855 ....DLB-110, 116	Montoya, José 1932- DLB-122	Morgan, Robert 1944- DLB-120
Mittelholzer, Edgar 1909-1965 .....DLB-117	Moodie, John Wedderburn Dunbar 1797-1869 ....DLB-99	Morgan, Sydney Owenson, Lady 1776?-1859 ....DLB-116, 158
Mitterer, Erika 1906- DLB-85	Moodie, Susanna 1803-1885 ....DLB-99	Morgner, Irmtraud 1933- DLB-75
Mitterer, Felix 1948- DLB-124	Moody, Joshua circa 1633-1697 .....DLB-24	Morhof, Daniel Georg 1639-1691 ....DLB-164
Mitternacht, Johann Sebastian 1613-1679 ....DLB-168	Moody, William Vaughn 1869-1910 ....DLB-7, 54	Morier, James Justinian 1782 or 1783?-1849 ....DLB-116
Mizener, Arthur 1907-1988 ....DLB-103	Moorcock, Michael 1939- DLB-14	Mörike, Eduard 1804-1875 ....DLB-133
Modern Age Books DLB-46	Moore, Catherine L. 1911- DLB-8	Morin, Paul 1889-1963 ....DLB-92
"Modern English Prose" (1876), by George Saintsbury DLB-57	Moore, Clement Clarke 1779-1863 ..DLB-42	Morison, Richard 1514?-1556 ......DLB-136
The Modern Language Association of America Celebrates Its Centennial Y-84	Moore, Dora Mavor 1888-1979 .....DLB-92	Morison, Samuel Eliot 1887-1976 ....DLB-17
The Modern Library DLB-46	Moore, George 1852-1933 ....DLB-10, 18, 57, 135	Moritz, Karl Philipp 1756-1793 ......DLB-94
"Modern Novelists – Great and Small" (1855), by Margaret Oliphant DLB-21	Moore, Marianne 1887-1972 ....DLB-45; DS-7	*Moriz von Craûn* circa 1220-1230 ....DLB-138
"Modern Style" (1857), by Cockburn Thomson [excerpt] DLB-57	Moore, Mavor 1919- DLB-88	Morley, Christopher 1890-1957 ......DLB-9
The Modernists (1932), by Joseph Warren Beach DLB-36	Moore, Richard 1927- DLB-105	Morley, John 1838-1923 ....DLB-57, 144
Modiano, Patrick 1945- DLB-83	Moore, Richard, The No Self, the Little Self, and the Poets DLB-105	Morris, George Pope 1802-1864 .....DLB-73
Moffat, Yard and Company DLB-46	Moore, T. Sturge 1870-1944 ....DLB-19	Morris, Lewis 1833-1907 ....DLB-35
Moffet, Thomas 1553-1604 ....DLB-136	Moore, Thomas 1779-1852 .....DLB-96, 144	Morris, Richard B. 1904-1989 ....DLB-17
Mohr, Nicholasa 1938- DLB-145	Moore, Ward 1903-1978 .... DLB-8	Morris, William 1834-1896 ....DLB-18, 35, 57, 156
Moix, Ana María 1947- DLB-134	Moore, Wilstach, Keys and Company DLB-49	Morris, Willie 1934- Y-80
Molesworth, Louisa 1839-1921 .....DLB-135	The Moorland-Spingarn Research Center DLB-76	Morris, Wright 1910- DLB-2; Y-81
Möllhausen, Balduin 1825-1905 ....DLB-129	Moorman, Mary C. 1905-1994 .....DLB-155	Morrison, Arthur 1863-1945 ....DLB-70, 135
Momaday, N. Scott 1934- DLB-143	Moraga, Cherríe 1952- DLB-82	Morrison, Charles Clayton 1874-1966 ....DLB-91
Monkhouse, Allan 1858-1936 ....DLB-10	Morales, Alejandro 1944- DLB-82	Morrison, Toni 1931- DLB-6, 33, 143; Y-81
Monro, Harold 1879-1932 ....DLB-19	Morales, Mario Roberto 1947- DLB-145	Morrow, William, and Company DLB-46
Monroe, Harriet 1860-1936 ......DLB-54, 91		

Cumulative Index

Morse, James Herbert 1841-1923 .... DLB-71

Morse, Jedidiah 1761-1826 .... DLB-37

Morse, John T., Jr. 1840-1937 ...... DLB-47

Mortimer, Favell Lee 1802-1878 ... DLB-163

Mortimer, John 1923- DLB-13

Morton, Carlos 1942- DLB-122

Morton, John P., and Company DLB-49

Morton, Nathaniel 1613-1685 ...... DLB-24

Morton, Sarah Wentworth
   1759-1846 .... DLB-37

Morton, Thomas
   circa 1579-circa 1647 .... DLB-24

Moscherosch, Johann Michael
   1601-1669 .... DLB-164

Moseley, Humphrey
   [publishing house] DLB-170

Möser, Justus 1720-1794 .... DLB-97

Mosley, Nicholas 1923- DLB-14

Moss, Arthur 1889-1969 .... DLB-4

Moss, Howard 1922-1987 .... DLB-5

Moss, Thylias 1954- DLB-120

The Most Powerful Book Review in America
   [*New York Times Book Review*] Y-82

Motion, Andrew 1952- DLB-40

Motley, John Lothrop
   1814-1877 .... DLB-1, 30, 59

Motley, Willard 1909-1965 ..... DLB-76, 143

Motte, Benjamin Jr.
   [publishing house] DLB-154

Motteux, Peter Anthony
   1663-1718 .... DLB-80

Mottram, R. H. 1883-1971 .... DLB-36

Mouré, Erin 1955- DLB-60

Movies from Books, 1920-1974 .... DLB-9

Mowat, Farley 1921- DLB-68

Mowbray, A. R., and Company,
   Limited DLB-106

Mowrer, Edgar Ansel 1892-1977 .... DLB-29

Mowrer, Paul Scott 1887-1971 ...... DLB-29

Moxon, Edward
   [publishing house] DLB-106

Moxon, Joseph
   [publishing house] DLB-170

Mphahlele, Es'kia (Ezekiel)
   1919- DLB-125

Mtshali, Oswald Mbuyiseni
   1940- DLB-125

Mucedorus DLB-62

Mudford, William 1782-1848 ...... DLB-159

Mueller, Lisel 1924- DLB-105

Muhajir, El (see Marvin X)

Muhajir, Nazzam Al Fitnah (see Marvin X)

Mühlbach, Luise 1814-1873 .... DLB-133

Muir, Edwin 1887-1959 ....DLB-20, 100

Muir, Helen 1937- DLB-14

Mukherjee, Bharati 1940- DLB-60

Mulcaster, Richard
   1531 or 1532-1611 .... DLB-167

Muldoon, Paul 1951- DLB-40

Müller, Friedrich (see Müller, Maler)

Müller, Heiner 1929- DLB-124

Müller, Maler 1749-1825 .... DLB-94

Müller, Wilhelm 1794-1827 .... DLB-90

Mumford, Lewis 1895-1990 .... DLB-63

Munby, Arthur Joseph 1828-1910 ... DLB-35

Munday, Anthony 1560-1633 ...DLB-62, 172

Mundt, Clara (see Mühlbach, Luise)

Mundt, Theodore 1808-1861 ...... DLB-133

Munford, Robert circa 1737-1783 .... DLB-31

Mungoshi, Charles 1947- DLB-157

Munonye, John 1929- DLB-117

Munro, Alice 1931- DLB-53

Munro, H. H. 1870-1916 ....DLB-34, 162

Munro, Neil 1864-1930 .... DLB-156

Munro, George
   [publishing house] DLB-49

Munro, Norman L.
   [publishing house] DLB-49

Munroe, James, and Company DLB-49

Munroe, Kirk 1850-1930 .... DLB-42

Munroe and Francis DLB-49

Munsell, Joel [publishing house] DLB-49

Munsey, Frank A. 1854-1925 ....DLB-25, 91

Munsey, Frank A., and
   Company DLB-49

Murav'ev, Mikhail Nikitich
   1757-1807 .... DLB-150

Murdoch, Iris 1919- DLB-14

Murdoch, Rupert 1931- DLB-127

Murfree, Mary N. 1850-1922 ....DLB-12, 74

Murger, Henry 1822-1861 .... DLB-119

Murger, Louis-Henri (see Murger, Henry)

Muro, Amado 1915-1971 .... DLB-82

Murphy, Arthur 1727-1805 .....DLB-89, 142

Murphy, Beatrice M. 1908- DLB-76

Murphy, Emily 1868-1933 .... DLB-99

Murphy, John H., III 1916- DLB-127

Murphy, John, and Company DLB-49

Murphy, Richard 1927-1993 .... DLB-40

Murray, Albert L. 1916- DLB-38

Murray, Gilbert 1866-1957 .... DLB-10

Murray, Judith Sargent 1751-1820 ...DLB-37

Murray, Pauli 1910-1985 .... DLB-41

Murray, John [publishing house] DLB-154

Murry, John Middleton
   1889-1957 .... DLB-149

Musäus, Johann Karl August
   1735-1787 .... DLB-97

Muschg, Adolf 1934- DLB-75

The Music of *Minnesang* DLB-138

Musil, Robert 1880-1942 ...... DLB-81, 124

Muspilli circa 790-circa 850 .... DLB-148

Mussey, Benjamin B., and
   Company DLB-49

Mwangi, Meja 1948- DLB-125

Myers, Gustavus 1872-1942 .... DLB-47

Myers, L. H. 1881-1944 .... DLB-15

Myers, Walter Dean 1937- DLB-33

N

Nabbes, Thomas circa 1605-1641 ....DLB-58

Nabl, Franz 1883-1974 .... DLB-81

Nabokov, Vladimir
   1899-1977 ...... DLB-2; Y-80, Y-91; DS-3

Nabokov Festival at Cornell Y-83

The Vladimir Nabokov Archive
   in the Berg Collection Y-91

Nafis and Cornish DLB-49

Naipaul, Shiva 1945-1985 .... DLB-157; Y-85

Naipaul, V. S. 1932- DLB-125; Y-85

Nancrede, Joseph
   [publishing house] DLB-49

Naranjo, Carmen 1930- DLB-145

Narrache, Jean 1893-1970 .... DLB-92

Nasby, Petroleum Vesuvius (see Locke, David Ross)

Nash, Ogden 1902-1971 .... DLB-11

Nash, Eveleigh
   [publishing house] DLB-112

Nashe, Thomas 1567-1601? DLB-167

Nast, Conde 1873-1942 .... DLB-91

Nastasijević, Momčilo 1894-1938 ...DLB-147

Nathan, George Jean 1882-1958 ....DLB-137

Nathan, Robert 1894-1985 ....DLB-9

The National Jewish Book Awards Y-85

The National Theatre and the Royal Shakespeare Company: The National Companies DLB-13

Naughton, Bill 1910- DLB-13

Naylor, Gloria 1950- DLB-173

Nazor, Vladimir 1876-1949 ....DLB-147

Ndebele, Njabulo 1948- DLB-157

Neagoe, Peter 1881-1960 ....DLB-4

Neal, John 1793-1876 ....DLB-1, 59

Neal, Joseph C. 1807-1847 ....DLB-11

Neal, Larry 1937-1981 ....DLB-38

The Neale Publishing Company DLB-49

Neely, F. Tennyson [publishing house] DLB-49

Negri, Ada 1870-1945 ....DLB-114

"The Negro as a Writer," by G. M. McClellan DLB-50

"Negro Poets and Their Poetry," by Wallace Thurman DLB-50

Neidhart von Reuental circa 1185-circa 1240 ....DLB-138

Neihardt, John G. 1881-1973 .....DLB-9, 54

Neledinsky-Meletsky, Iurii Aleksandrovich 1752-1828 ....DLB-150

Nelligan, Emile 1879-1941 ....DLB-92

Nelson, Alice Moore Dunbar 1875-1935 ....DLB-50

Nelson, Thomas, and Sons [U.S.] DLB-49

Nelson, Thomas, and Sons [U.K.] ...DLB-106

Nelson, William 1908-1978 ....DLB-103

Nelson, William Rockhill 1841-1915 ....DLB-23

Nemerov, Howard 1920-1991 .. DLB-5, 6; Y-83

Nesbit, E. 1858-1924 ....DLB-141, 153

Ness, Evaline 1911-1986 ....DLB-61

Nestroy, Johann 1801-1862 ....DLB-133

Neukirch, Benjamin 1655-1729 .....DLB-168

Neugeboren, Jay 1938- DLB-28

Neumann, Alfred 1895-1952 ....DLB-56

Neumark, Georg 1621-1681 ....DLB-164

Neumeister, Erdmann 1671-1756 ...DLB-168

Nevins, Allan 1890-1971 ....DLB-17

Nevinson, Henry Woodd 1856-1941 ....DLB-135

The New American Library DLB-46

New Approaches to Biography: Challenges from Critical Theory, USC Conference on Literary Studies, 1990 .... Y-90

New Directions Publishing Corporation DLB-46

A New Edition of *Huck Finn* Y-85

New Forces at Work in the American Theatre: 1915-1925 .... DLB-7

New Literary Periodicals: A Report for 1987 .... Y-87

New Literary Periodicals: A Report for 1988 .... Y-88

New Literary Periodicals: A Report for 1989 .... Y-89

New Literary Periodicals: A Report for 1990 .... Y-90

New Literary Periodicals: A Report for 1991 .... Y-91

New Literary Periodicals: A Report for 1992 .... Y-92

New Literary Periodicals: A Report for 1993 .... Y-93

The New Monthly Magazine 1814-1884 .... DLB-110

The New *Ulysses* Y-84

The New Variorum Shakespeare Y-85

A New Voice: The Center for the Book's First Five Years Y-83

The New Wave [Science Fiction] DLB-8

New York City Bookshops in the 1930s and 1940s: The Recollections of Walter Goldwater Y-93

Newbery, John [publishing house] DLB-154

Newbolt, Henry 1862-1938 .... DLB-19

Newbound, Bernard Slade (see Slade, Bernard)

Newby, P. H. 1918- DLB-15

Newby, Thomas Cautley [publishing house] DLB-106

Newcomb, Charles King 1820-1894 ... DLB-1

Newell, Peter 1862-1924 .... DLB-42

Newell, Robert Henry 1836-1901 .... DLB-11

Newhouse, Samuel I. 1895-1979 ... DLB-127

Newman, Cecil Earl 1903-1976 .... DLB-127

Newman, David (see Benton, Robert)

Newman, Frances 1883-1928 .... Y-80

Newman, John Henry 1801-1890 ....DLB-18, 32, 55

Newman, Mark [publishing house] .. DLB-49

Newnes, George, Limited DLB-112

Newsome, Effie Lee 1885-1979 ......DLB-76

Newspaper Syndication of American Humor DLB-11

Newton, A. Edward 1864-1940 .....DLB-140

Ngugi wa Thiong'o 1938- DLB-125

The *Nibelungenlied* and the *Klage* circa 1200 ....DLB-138

Nichol, B. P. 1944- DLB-53

Nicholas of Cusa 1401-1464 ....DLB-115

Nichols, Dudley 1895-1960 ....DLB-26

Nichols, Grace 1950- DLB-157

Nichols, John 1940- Y-82

Nichols, Mary Sargeant (Neal) Gove 1810-1884 ....DLB-1

Nichols, Peter 1927- DLB-13

Nichols, Roy F. 1896-1973 ....DLB-17

Nichols, Ruth 1948- DLB-60

Nicholson, Norman 1914- DLB-27

Nicholson, William 1872-1949 .....DLB-141

Ní Chuilleanáin, Eiléan 1942- DLB-40

Nicol, Eric 1919- DLB-68

Nicolai, Friedrich 1733-1811 ....DLB-97

Nicolay, John G. 1832-1901 and Hay, John 1838-1905 ....DLB-47

Nicolson, Harold 1886-1968 ...DLB-100, 149

Nicolson, Nigel 1917- DLB-155

Niebuhr, Reinhold 1892-1971 ....DLB-17

Niedecker, Lorine 1903-1970 ....DLB-48

Nieman, Lucius W. 1857-1935 .....DLB-25

Nietzsche, Friedrich 1844-1900 .....DLB-129

Niggli, Josefina 1910- Y-80

Nightingale, Florence 1820-1910 ....DLB-166

Nikolev, Nikolai Petrovich 1758-1815 ....DLB-150

Niles, Hezekiah 1777-1839 ....DLB-43

Nims, John Frederick 1913- DLB-5

Nin, Anaïs 1903-1977 ....DLB-2, 4, 152

1985: The Year of the Mystery: A Symposium Y-85

Nissenson, Hugh 1933- DLB-28

Niven, Frederick John 1878-1944 ....DLB-92

Niven, Larry 1938- DLB-8

Nizan, Paul 1905-1940 ....DLB-72

Njegoš, Petar II Petrović 1813-1851 ....DLB-147

Nkosi, Lewis 1936- DLB-157

Nobel Peace Prize
The 1986 Nobel Peace Prize
  Nobel Lecture 1986: Hope, Despair and Memory
  Tributes from Abraham Bernstein, Norman Lamm, and John R. Silber Y-86

The Nobel Prize and Literary Politics ... Y-86

Nobel Prize in Literature
The 1982 Nobel Prize in Literature
  Announcement by the Swedish Academy of the Nobel Prize Nobel Lecture 1982: The Solitude of Latin America Excerpt from *One Hundred Years of Solitude* The Magical World of Macondo A Tribute to Gabriel García Márquez Y-82

The 1983 Nobel Prize in Literature
  Announcement by the Swedish Academy Nobel Lecture 1983 The Stature of William Golding Y-83

The 1984 Nobel Prize in Literature
  Announcement by the Swedish Academy Jaroslav Seifert Through the Eyes of the English-Speaking Reader Three Poems by Jaroslav Seifert Y-84

The 1985 Nobel Prize in Literature
  Announcement by the Swedish Academy Nobel Lecture 1985 .... Y-85

The 1986 Nobel Prize in Literature
  Nobel Lecture 1986: This Past Must Address Its Present Y-86

The 1987 Nobel Prize in Literature
  Nobel Lecture 1987 .... Y-87

The 1988 Nobel Prize in Literature
  Nobel Lecture 1988 .... Y-88

The 1989 Nobel Prize in Literature
  Nobel Lecture 1989 .... Y-89

The 1990 Nobel Prize in Literature
  Nobel Lecture 1990 .... Y-90

The 1991 Nobel Prize in Literature
  Nobel Lecture 1991 .... Y-91

The 1992 Nobel Prize in Literature
  Nobel Lecture 1992 .... Y-92

The 1993 Nobel Prize in Literature
  Nobel Lecture 1993 .... Y-93

The 1994 Nobel Prize in Literature
  Nobel Lecture 1994 .... Y-94

The 1995 Nobel Prize in Literature
  Nobel Lecture 1995 .... Y-95

Nodier, Charles 1780-1844 .... DLB-119
Noel, Roden 1834-1894 .... DLB-35
Nolan, William F. 1928- DLB-8
Noland, C. F. M. 1810?-1858 .... DLB-11
Nonesuch Press DLB-112
Noonday Press DLB-46
Noone, John 1936- DLB-14
Nora, Eugenio de 1923- DLB-134

Nordhoff, Charles 1887-1947 .... DLB-9
Norman, Charles 1904- DLB-111
Norman, Marsha 1947- Y-84
Norris, Charles G. 1881-1945 .... DLB-9
Norris, Frank 1870-1902 .... DLB-12
Norris, Leslie 1921- DLB-27
Norse, Harold 1916- DLB-16
North Point Press DLB-46
Nortje, Arthur 1942-1970 .... DLB-125
Norton, Alice Mary (see Norton, Andre)
Norton, Andre 1912- DLB-8, 52
Norton, Andrews 1786-1853 .... DLB-1
Norton, Caroline 1808-1877 .... DLB-21, 159
Norton, Charles Eliot 1827-1908 ..DLB-1, 64
Norton, John 1606-1663 .... DLB-24
Norton, Mary 1903-1992 .... DLB-160
Norton, Thomas (see Sackville, Thomas)
Norton, W. W., and Company DLB-46
Norwood, Robert 1874-1932 .... DLB-92
Nossack, Hans Erich 1901-1977 ..... DLB-69
Notker Balbulus circa 840-912 ..... DLB-148
Notker III of Saint Gall circa 950-1022 .... DLB-148
Notker von Zweifalten ?-1095 ...... DLB-148
A Note on Technique (1926), by Elizabeth A. Drew [excerpts] DLB-36
Nourse, Alan E. 1928- DLB-8
Novak, Vjenceslav 1859-1905 ...... DLB-147
Novalis 1772-1801 .... DLB-90
Novaro, Mario 1868-1944 .... DLB-114
Novás Calvo, Lino 1903-1983 ...... DLB-145
"The Novel in [Robert Browning's] 'The Ring and the Book'" (1912), by Henry James DLB-32
The Novel of Impressionism, by Jethro Bithell DLB-66
Novel-Reading: *The Works of Charles Dickens, The Works of W. Makepeace Thackeray* (1879), by Anthony Trollope DLB-21
The Novels of Dorothy Richardson (1918), by May Sinclair DLB-36
Novels with a Purpose (1864), by Justin M'Carthy DLB-21
Noventa, Giacomo 1898-1960 ...... DLB-114
Novikov, Nikolai Ivanovich 1744-1818 .... DLB-150
Nowlan, Alden 1933-1983 .... DLB-53
Noyes, Alfred 1880-1958 .... DLB-20

Noyes, Crosby S. 1825-1908 .... DLB-23
Noyes, Nicholas 1647-1717 .... DLB-24
Noyes, Theodore W. 1858-1946 ..... DLB-29
N-Town Plays circa 1468 to early sixteenth century DLB-146
Nugent, Frank 1908-1965 .... DLB-44
Nugent, Richard Bruce 1906- DLB-151
Nusic, Branislav 1864-1938 .... DLB-147
Nutt, David [publishing house] DLB-106
Nwapa, Flora 1931- DLB-125
Nye, Edgar Wilson (Bill) 1850-1896 .... DLB-11, 23
Nye, Naomi Shihab 1952- DLB-120
Nye, Robert 1939- DLB-14

O

Oakes, Urian circa 1631-1681 .... DLB-24
Oates, Joyce Carol 1938- DLB-2, 5, 130; Y-81
Ober, William 1920-1993 .... Y-93
Oberholtzer, Ellis Paxson 1868-1936 .... DLB-47
Obradović, Dositej 1740?-1811 ..... DLB-147
O'Brien, Edna 1932- DLB-14
O'Brien, Fitz-James 1828-1862 .... DLB-74
O'Brien, Kate 1897-1974 .... DLB-15
O'Brien, Tim 1946- DLB-152; Y-80; DS-9
O'Casey, Sean 1880-1964 .... DLB-10
Ochs, Adolph S. 1858-1935 .... DLB-25
Ochs-Oakes, George Washington 1861-1931 .... DLB-137
O'Connor, Flannery 1925-1964 ...... DLB-2, 152; Y-80; DS-12
O'Connor, Frank 1903-1966 .... DLB-162
Octopus Publishing Group DLB-112
Odell, Jonathan 1737-1818 ...... DLB-31, 99
O'Dell, Scott 1903-1989 .... DLB-52
Odets, Clifford 1906-1963 .... DLB-7, 26
Odhams Press Limited DLB-112
O'Donnell, Peter 1920- DLB-87
O'Donovan, Michael (see O'Connor, Frank)
O'Faolain, Julia 1932- DLB-14
O'Faolain, Sean 1900- DLB-15, 162
Off Broadway and Off-Off Broadway ..DLB-7

Off-Loop Theatres DLB-7

Offord, Carl Ruthven 1910- DLB-76

O'Flaherty, Liam
1896-1984 .... DLB-36, 162; Y-84

Ogilvie, J. S., and Company DLB-49

Ogot, Grace 1930- DLB-125

O'Grady, Desmond 1935- DLB-40

Ogunyemi, Wale 1939- DLB-157

O'Hagan, Howard 1902-1982 ....DLB-68

O'Hara, Frank 1926-1966 ....DLB-5, 16

O'Hara, John 1905-1970 .... DLB-9, 86; DS-2

Okara, Gabriel 1921- DLB-125

O'Keeffe, John 1747-1833 ....DLB-89

Okes, Nicholas
[publishing house] DLB-170

Okigbo, Christopher 1930-1967 ....DLB-125

Okot p'Bitek 1931-1982 ....DLB-125

Okpewho, Isidore 1941- DLB-157

Okri, Ben 1959- DLB-157

Olaudah Equiano and Unfinished Journeys:
The Slave-Narrative Tradition and
Twentieth-Century Continuities, by
Paul Edwards and Pauline T.
Wangman DLB-117

Old English Literature:
An Introduction DLB-146

Old English Riddles
eighth to tenth centuries DLB-146

Old Franklin Publishing House DLB-49

Old German Genesis and *Old German Exodus*
circa 1050-circa 1130 ....DLB-148

Old High German Charms and
Blessings DLB-148

The *Old High German Isidor*
circa 790-800 ....DLB-148

Older, Fremont 1856-1935 ....DLB-25

Oldham, John 1653-1683 ....DLB-131

Olds, Sharon 1942- DLB-120

Olearius, Adam 1599-1671 ....DLB-164

Oliphant, Laurence
1829?-1888 ....DLB-18, 166

Oliphant, Margaret 1828-1897 ......DLB-18

Oliver, Chad 1928- DLB-8

Oliver, Mary 1935- DLB-5

Ollier, Claude 1922- DLB-83

Olsen, Tillie 1913?- DLB-28; Y-80

Olson, Charles 1910-1970 ....DLB-5, 16

Olson, Elder 1909- DLB-48, 63

Omotoso, Kole 1943- DLB-125

"On Art in Fiction "(1838),
by Edward Bulwer DLB-21

On Learning to Write Y-88

On Some of the Characteristics of Modern
Poetry and On the Lyrical Poems of
Alfred Tennyson (1831), by Arthur
Henry Hallam DLB-32

"On Style in English Prose" (1898), by
Frederic Harrison DLB-57

"On Style in Literature: Its Technical
Elements" (1885), by Robert Louis
Stevenson DLB-57

"On the Writing of Essays" (1862),
by Alexander Smith DLB-57

Ondaatje, Michael 1943- DLB-60

O'Neill, Eugene 1888-1953 .... DLB-7

Onetti, Juan Carlos 1909-1994 ..... DLB-113

Onions, George Oliver
1872-1961 .... DLB-153

Onofri, Arturo 1885-1928 .... DLB-114

Opie, Amelia 1769-1853 ..... DLB-116, 159

Opitz, Martin 1597-1639 .... DLB-164

Oppen, George 1908-1984 ...... DLB-5, 165

Oppenheim, E. Phillips 1866-1946 ... DLB-70

Oppenheim, James 1882-1932 .... DLB-28

Oppenheimer, Joel 1930- DLB-5

Optic, Oliver (see Adams, William Taylor)

Orczy, Emma, Baroness
1865-1947 .... DLB-70

Origo, Iris 1902-1988 .... DLB-155

Orlovitz, Gil 1918-1973 .... DLB-2, 5

Orlovsky, Peter 1933- DLB-16

Ormond, John 1923- DLB-27

Ornitz, Samuel 1890-1957 .... DLB-28, 44

Ortiz, Simon 1941- DLB-120

Ortnit and *Wolfdietrich*
circa 1225-1250 .... DLB-138

Orton, Joe 1933-1967 .... DLB-13

Orwell, George 1903-1950 ...... DLB-15, 98

The Orwell Year Y-84

Ory, Carlos Edmundo de 1923- .. DLB-134

Osbey, Brenda Marie 1957- DLB-120

Osbon, B. S. 1827-1912 .... DLB-43

Osborne, John 1929-1994 .... DLB-13

Osgood, Herbert L. 1855-1918 ...... DLB-47

Osgood, James R., and
Company DLB-49

Osgood, McIlvaine and
Company DLB-112

O'Shaughnessy, Arthur
1844-1881 ....DLB-35

O'Shea, Patrick
[publishing house] DLB-49

Osipov, Nikolai Petrovich
1751-1799 ....DLB-150

Osofisan, Femi 1946- DLB-125

Ostenso, Martha 1900-1963 ....DLB-92

Ostriker, Alicia 1937- DLB-120

Osundare, Niyi 1947- DLB-157

Oswald, Eleazer 1755-1795 ....DLB-43

Otero, Blas de 1916-1979 ....DLB-134

Otero, Miguel Antonio
1859-1944 ....DLB-82

Otero Silva, Miguel 1908-1985 .....DLB-145

Otfried von Weißenburg
circa 800-circa 875? DLB-148

Otis, James (see Kaler, James Otis)

Otis, James, Jr. 1725-1783 ....DLB-31

Otis, Broaders and Company DLB-49

Ottaway, James 1911- DLB-127

Ottendorfer, Oswald 1826-1900 .....DLB-23

Otto-Peters, Louise 1819-1895 .....DLB-129

Otway, Thomas 1652-1685 ....DLB-80

Ouellette, Fernand 1930- DLB-60

Ouida 1839-1908 ....DLB-18, 156

Outing Publishing Company DLB-46

Outlaw Days, by Joyce Johnson DLB-16

Overbury, Sir Thomas
circa 1581-1613 ....DLB-151

The Overlook Press DLB-46

Overview of U.S. Book Publishing,
1910-1945 ....DLB-9

Owen, Guy 1925- DLB-5

Owen, John 1564-1622 ....DLB-121

Owen, John [publishing house] DLB-49

Owen, Robert 1771-1858 ......DLB-107, 158

Owen, Wilfred 1893-1918 ....DLB-20

Owen, Peter, Limited DLB-112

The *Owl and the Nightingale*
circa 1189-1199 ....DLB-146

Owsley, Frank L. 1890-1956 ....DLB-17

Oxford, Seventeenth Earl of, Edward de Vere
1550-1604 ....DLB-172

Ozerov, Vladislav Aleksandrovich
1769-1816 ....DLB-150

Ozick, Cynthia 1928- DLB-28, 152; Y-82

357

Cumulative Index

P

Pace, Richard 1482?-1536 .... DLB-167

Pacey, Desmond 1917-1975 .... DLB-88

Pack, Robert 1929- DLB-5

Packaging Papa: *The Garden of Eden* Y-86

Padell Publishing Company DLB-46

Padgett, Ron 1942- DLB-5

Padilla, Ernesto Chávez 1944- ... DLB-122

Page, L. C., and Company DLB-49

Page, P. K. 1916- DLB-68

Page, Thomas Nelson
1853-1922 .... DLB-12, 78; DS-13

Page, Walter Hines 1855-1918 ... DLB-71, 91

Paget, Francis Edward
1806-1882 .... DLB-163

Paget, Violet (see Lee, Vernon)

Pagliarani, Elio 1927- DLB-128

Pain, Barry 1864-1928 .... DLB-135

Pain, Philip ?-circa 1666 .... DLB-24

Paine, Robert Treat, Jr. 1773-1811 .. DLB-37

Paine, Thomas
1737-1809 .... DLB-31, 43, 73, 158

Painter, George D. 1914- DLB-155

Painter, William 1540?-1594 ...... DLB-136

Palazzeschi, Aldo 1885-1974 .... DLB-114

Paley, Grace 1922- DLB-28

Palfrey, John Gorham
1796-1881 .... DLB-1, 30

Palgrave, Francis Turner
1824-1897 .... DLB-35

Palmer, Joe H. 1904-1952 .... DLB-171

Palmer, Michael 1943- DLB-169

Paltock, Robert 1697-1767 .... DLB-39

Pan Books Limited DLB-112

Panamaa, Norman 1914- and
Frank, Melvin 1913-1988 .... DLB-26

Pancake, Breece D'J 1952-1979 .... DLB-130

Panero, Leopoldo 1909-1962 ..... DLB-108

Pangborn, Edgar 1909-1976 .... DLB-8

"Panic Among the Philistines": A Postscript,
An Interview with Bryan Griffin Y-81

Panneton, Philippe (see Ringuet)

Panshin, Alexei 1940- DLB-8

Pansy (see Alden, Isabella)

Pantheon Books DLB-46

Paperback Library DLB-46

Paperback Science Fiction DLB-8

Paquet, Alfons 1881-1944 .... DLB-66

Paradis, Suzanne 1936- DLB-53

Pareja Diezcanseco, Alfredo
1908-1993 .... DLB-145

Pardoe, Julia 1804-1862 .... DLB-166

Parents' Magazine Press DLB-46

Parisian Theater, Fall 1984: Toward
A New Baroque Y-85

Parizeau, Alice 1930- DLB-60

Parke, John 1754-1789 .... DLB-31

Parker, Dorothy
1893-1967 .... DLB-11, 45, 86

Parker, Gilbert 1860-1932 .... DLB-99

Parker, James 1714-1770 .... DLB-43

Parker, Theodore 1810-1860 .... DLB-1

Parker, William Riley 1906-1968 ... DLB-103

Parker, J. H. [publishing house] DLB-106

Parker, John [publishing house] DLB-106

Parkman, Francis, Jr.
1823-1893 .... DLB-1, 30

Parks, Gordon 1912- DLB-33

Parks, William 1698-1750 .... DLB-43

Parks, William [publishing house] ... DLB-49

Parley, Peter (see Goodrich, Samuel Griswold)

Parnell, Thomas 1679-1718 .... DLB-95

Parr, Catherine 1513?-1548 .... DLB-136

Parrington, Vernon L.
1871-1929 .... DLB-17, 63

Parronchi, Alessandro 1914- DLB-128

Partridge, S. W., and Company DLB-106

Parton, James 1822-1891 .... DLB-30

Parton, Sara Payson Willis
1811-1872 .... DLB-43, 74

Pasolini, Pier Paolo 1922- DLB-128

Pastan, Linda 1932- DLB-5

Paston, George 1860-1936 .... DLB-149

The *Paston Letters* 1422-1509 ..... DLB-146

Pastorius, Francis Daniel
1651-circa 1720 .... DLB-24

Patchen, Kenneth 1911-1972 ..... DLB-16, 48

Pater, Walter 1839-1894 .... DLB-57, 156

Paterson, Katherine 1932- DLB-52

Patmore, Coventry 1823-1896 ... DLB-35, 98

Paton, Joseph Noel 1821-1901 ...... DLB-35

Paton Walsh, Jill 1937- DLB-161

Patrick, Edwin Hill ("Ted")
1901-1964 .... DLB-137

Patrick, John 1906- DLB-7

Pattee, Fred Lewis 1863-1950 .... DLB-71

Pattern and Paradigm: History as
Design, by Judith Ryan DLB-75

Patterson, Alicia 1906-1963 .... DLB-127

Patterson, Eleanor Medill
1881-1948 .... DLB-29

Patterson, Eugene 1923- DLB-127

Patterson, Joseph Medill
1879-1946 .... DLB-29

Pattillo, Henry 1726-1801 .... DLB-37

Paul, Elliot 1891-1958 .... DLB-4

Paul, Jean (see Richter, Johann Paul Friedrich)

Paul, Kegan, Trench, Trubner and Company
Limited DLB-106

Paul, Peter, Book Company DLB-49

Paul, Stanley, and Company
Limited DLB-112

Paulding, James Kirke
1778-1860 .... DLB-3, 59, 74

Paulin, Tom 1949- DLB-40

Pauper, Peter, Press DLB-46

Pavese, Cesare 1908-1950 .... DLB-128

Paxton, John 1911-1985 .... DLB-44

Payn, James 1830-1898 .... DLB-18

Payne, John 1842-1916 .... DLB-35

Payne, John Howard 1791-1852 .... DLB-37

Payson and Clarke DLB-46

Peabody, Elizabeth Palmer
1804-1894 .... DLB-1

Peabody, Elizabeth Palmer
[publishing house] DLB-49

Peabody, Oliver William Bourn
1799-1848 .... DLB-59

Peace, Roger 1899-1968 .... DLB-127

Peacham, Henry 1578-1644? DLB-151

Peacham, Henry, the Elder
1547-1634 .... DLB-172

Peachtree Publishers, Limited DLB-46

Peacock, Molly 1947- DLB-120

Peacock, Thomas Love
1785-1866 .... DLB-96, 116

Pead, Deuel ?-1727 .... DLB-24

Peake, Mervyn 1911-1968 ..... DLB-15, 160

Pear Tree Press DLB-112

Pearce, Philippa 1920- DLB-161

Pearson, H. B. [publishing house] DLB-49

Pearson, Hesketh 1887-1964 ....DLB-149

Peck, George W. 1840-1916 ......DLB-23, 42

Peck, H. C., and Theo. Bliss
[publishing house] DLB-49

Peck, Harry Thurston
1856-1914 ....DLB-71, 91

Peele, George 1556-1596 ....DLB-62, 167

Pegler, Westbrook 1894-1969 ......DLB-171

Pellegrini and Cudahy DLB-46

Pelletier, Aimé (see Vac, Bertrand)

Pemberton, Sir Max 1863-1950 ......DLB-70

Penguin Books [U.S.] DLB-46

Penguin Books [U.K.] DLB-112

Penn Publishing Company DLB-49

Penn, William 1644-1718 ....DLB-24

Penna, Sandro 1906-1977 ....DLB-114

Penner, Jonathan 1940- Y-83

Pennington, Lee 1939- Y-82

Pepys, Samuel 1633-1703 ....DLB-101

Percy, Thomas 1729-1811 ....DLB-104

Percy, Walker 1916-1990 ... DLB-2; Y-80, 90

Percy, William 1575-1648 ....DLB-172

Perec, Georges 1936-1982 ....DLB-83

Perelman, S. J. 1904-1979 ....DLB-11, 44

Perez, Raymundo "Tigre"
1946- DLB-122

Peri Rossi, Cristina 1941- DLB-145

Periodicals of the Beat Generation ...DLB-16

Perkins, Eugene 1932- DLB-41

Perkoff, Stuart Z. 1930-1974 ....DLB-16

Perley, Moses Henry 1804-1862 .....DLB-99

Permabooks DLB-46

Perrin, Alice 1867-1934 ....DLB-156

Perry, Bliss 1860-1954 ....DLB-71

Perry, Eleanor 1915-1981 ....DLB-44

Perry, Sampson 1747-1823 ....DLB-158

"Personal Style" (1890), by John Addington
Symonds DLB-57

Perutz, Leo 1882-1957 ....DLB-81

Pesetsky, Bette 1932- DLB-130

Pestalozzi, Johann Heinrich
1746-1827 ....DLB-94

Peter, Laurence J. 1919-1990 ....DLB-53

Peter of Spain circa 1205-1277 .....DLB-115

Peterkin, Julia 1880-1961 ....DLB-9

Peters, Lenrie 1932- DLB-117

Peters, Robert 1924- DLB-105

Peters, Robert, Foreword to
Ludwig of Bavaria DLB-105

Petersham, Maud 1889-1971 and
Petersham, Miska 1888-1960 .... DLB-22

Peterson, Charles Jacobs
1819-1887 .... DLB-79

Peterson, Len 1917- DLB-88

Peterson, Louis 1922- DLB-76

Peterson, T. B., and Brothers DLB-49

Petitclair, Pierre 1813-1860 .... DLB-99

Petrov, Gavriil 1730-1801 .... DLB-150

Petrov, Vasilii Petrovich
1736-1799 .... DLB-150

Petrović, Rastko 1898-1949 ...... DLB-147

Petruslied circa 854? DLB-148

Petry, Ann 1908- DLB-76

Pettie, George circa 1548-1589 ..... DLB-136

Peyton, K. M. 1929- DLB-161

Pfaffe Konrad
flourished circa 1172 .... DLB-148

Pfaffe Lamprecht
flourished circa 1150 .... DLB-148

Pforzheimer, Carl H. 1879-1957 ... DLB-140

Phaer, Thomas 1510?-1560 .... DLB-167

Phaidon Press Limited DLB-112

Pharr, Robert Deane 1916-1992 ..... DLB-33

Phelps, Elizabeth Stuart
1844-1911 .... DLB-74

Philander von der Linde
(see Mencke, Johann Burckhard)

Philip, Marlene Nourbese
1947- DLB-157

Philippe, Charles-Louis
1874-1909 .... DLB-65

Philips, John 1676-1708 .... DLB-95

Philips, Katherine 1632-1664 ...... DLB-131

Phillips, Caryl 1958- DLB-157

Phillips, David Graham
1867-1911 .... DLB-9, 12

Phillips, Jayne Anne 1952- Y-80

Phillips, Robert 1938- DLB-105

Phillips, Robert, Finding, Losing,
Reclaiming: A Note on My
Poems DLB-105

Phillips, Stephen 1864-1915 .... DLB-10

Phillips, Ulrich B. 1877-1934 .... DLB-17

Phillips, Willard 1784-1873 .... DLB-59

Phillips, William 1907- DLB-137

Phillips, Sampson and Company DLB-49

Phillpotts, Eden
1862-1960 .... DLB-10, 70, 135, 153

Philosophical Library DLB-46

"The Philosophy of Style" (1852), by
Herbert Spencer DLB-57

Phinney, Elihu [publishing house] ...DLB-49

Phoenix, John (see Derby, George Horatio)

PHYLON (Fourth Quarter, 1950),
The Negro in Literature:
The Current Scene DLB-76

Physiologus
circa 1070-circa 1150 ....DLB-148

Piccolo, Lucio 1903-1969 ....DLB-114

Pickard, Tom 1946- DLB-40

Pickering, William
[publishing house] DLB-106

Pickthall, Marjorie 1883-1922 ....DLB-92

Pictorial Printing Company DLB-49

Piel, Gerard 1915- DLB-137

Piercy, Marge 1936- DLB-120

Pierro, Albino 1916- DLB-128

Pignotti, Lamberto 1926- DLB-128

Pike, Albert 1809-1891 ....DLB-74

Pilon, Jean-Guy 1930- DLB-60

Pinckney, Josephine 1895-1957 ....DLB-6

Pindar, Peter (see Wolcot, John)

Pinero, Arthur Wing 1855-1934 .....DLB-10

Pinget, Robert 1919- DLB-83

Pinnacle Books DLB-46

Piñon, Nélida 1935- DLB-145

Pinsky, Robert 1940- Y-82

Pinter, Harold 1930- DLB-13

Piontek, Heinz 1925- DLB-75

Piozzi, Hester Lynch [Thrale]
1741-1821 ....DLB-104, 142

Piper, H. Beam 1904-1964 ....DLB-8

Piper, Watty DLB-22

Pisar, Samuel 1929- Y-83

Pitkin, Timothy 1766-1847 ....DLB-30

The Pitt Poetry Series: Poetry Publishing
Today Y-85

Pitter, Ruth 1897- DLB-20

Pix, Mary 1666-1709 ....DLB-80

Plaatje, Sol T. 1876-1932 ....DLB-125

The Place of Realism in Fiction (1895), by
George Gissing DLB-18

Cumulative Index

Plante, David 1940- Y-83

Platen, August von 1796-1835 ...... DLB-90

Plath, Sylvia 1932-1963 .... DLB-5, 6, 152

Platon 1737-1812 .... DLB-150

Platt and Munk Company DLB-46

Playboy Press DLB-46

Playford, John
  [publishing house] DLB-170

Plays, Playwrights, and Playgoers ... DLB-84

Playwrights and Professors, by
  Tom Stoppard DLB-13

Playwrights on the Theater DLB-80

Der Pleier flourished circa 1250 .... DLB-138

Plenzdorf, Ulrich 1934- DLB-75

Plessen, Elizabeth 1944- DLB-75

Plievier, Theodor 1892-1955 .... DLB-69

Plomer, William 1903-1973 .... DLB-20, 162

Plumly, Stanley 1939- DLB-5

Plumpp, Sterling D. 1940- DLB-41

Plunkett, James 1920- DLB-14

Plymell, Charles 1935- DLB-16

Pocket Books DLB-46

Poe, Edgar Allan
  1809-1849 .... DLB-3, 59, 73, 74

Poe, James 1921-1980 .... DLB-44

The Poet Laureate of the United States
  Statements from Former Consultants
  in Poetry Y-86

Pohl, Frederik 1919- DLB-8

Poirier, Louis (see Gracq, Julien)

Polanyi, Michael 1891-1976 .... DLB-100

Pole, Reginald 1500-1558 .... DLB-132

Poliakoff, Stephen 1952- DLB-13

Polidori, John William
  1795-1821 .... DLB-116

Polite, Carlene Hatcher 1932- DLB-33

Pollard, Edward A. 1832-1872 ..... DLB-30

Pollard, Percival 1869-1911 .... DLB-71

Pollard and Moss DLB-49

Pollock, Sharon 1936- DLB-60

Polonsky, Abraham 1910- DLB-26

Polotsky, Simeon 1629-1680 ...... DLB-150

Ponce, Mary Helen 1938- DLB-122

Ponce-Montoya, Juanita 1949- ... DLB-122

Ponet, John 1516?-1556 .... DLB-132

Poniatowski, Elena 1933- DLB-113

Ponsonby, William
  [publishing house] DLB-170

Pony Stories DLB-160

Poole, Ernest 1880-1950 .... DLB-9

Poole, Sophia 1804-1891 .... DLB-166

Poore, Benjamin Perley
  1820-1887 .... DLB-23

Pope, Abbie Hanscom
  1858-1894 .... DLB-140

Pope, Alexander 1688-1744 ..... DLB-95, 101

Popov, Mikhail Ivanovich
  1742-circa 1790 .... DLB-150

Popular Library DLB-46

Porlock, Martin (see MacDonald, Philip)

Porpoise Press DLB-112

Porta, Antonio 1935-1989 .... DLB-128

Porter, Anna Maria
  1780-1832 .... DLB-116, 159

Porter, Eleanor H. 1868-1920 .... DLB-9

Porter, Gene Stratton (see Stratton-Porter, Gene)

Porter, Henry ?-? DLB-62

Porter, Jane 1776-1850 .... DLB-116, 159

Porter, Katherine Anne
  1890-1980 ... DLB-4, 9, 102; Y-80; DS-12

Porter, Peter 1929- DLB-40

Porter, William Sydney
  1862-1910 .... DLB-12, 78, 79

Porter, William T. 1809-1858 ..... DLB-3, 43

Porter and Coates DLB-49

Portis, Charles 1933- DLB-6

Postans, Marianne
  circa 1810-1865 .... DLB-166

Postl, Carl (see Sealsfield, Carl)

Poston, Ted 1906-1974 .... DLB-51

Postscript to [the Third Edition of] Clarissa
  (1751), by Samuel Richardson ... DLB-39

Potok, Chaim 1929- DLB-28, 152; Y-84

Potter, Beatrix 1866-1943 .... DLB-141

Potter, David M. 1910-1971 .... DLB-17

Potter, John E., and Company DLB-49

Pottle, Frederick A.
  1897-1987 .... DLB-103; Y-87

Poulin, Jacques 1937- DLB-60

Pound, Ezra 1885-1972 ..... DLB-4, 45, 63

Povich, Shirley 1905- DLB-171

Powell, Anthony 1905- DLB-15

Powers, J. F. 1917- DLB-130

Pownall, David 1938- DLB-14

Powys, John Cowper 1872-1963 ..... DLB-15

Powys, Llewelyn 1884-1939 .... DLB-98

Powys, T. F. 1875-1953 .... DLB-36, 162

Poynter, Nelson 1903-1978 .... DLB-127

The Practice of Biography: An Interview
  with Stanley Weintraub Y-82

The Practice of Biography II: An Interview
  with B. L. Reid Y-83

The Practice of Biography III: An Interview
  with Humphrey Carpenter Y-84

The Practice of Biography IV: An Interview
  with William Manchester Y-85

The Practice of Biography V: An Interview
  with Justin Kaplan Y-86

The Practice of Biography VI: An Interview
  with David Herbert Donald Y-87

The Practice of Biography VII: An Interview
  with John Caldwell Guilds Y-92

The Practice of Biography VIII: An Interview
  with Joan Mellen Y-94

The Practice of Biography IX: An Interview
  with Michael Reynolds Y-95

Prados, Emilio 1899-1962 .... DLB-134

Praed, Winthrop Mackworth
  1802-1839 .... DLB-96

Praeger Publishers DLB-46

Praetorius, Johannes 1630-1680 .... DLB-168

Pratt, E. J. 1882-1964 .... DLB-92

Pratt, Samuel Jackson 1749-1814 ..... DLB-39

Preface to Alwyn (1780), by
  Thomas Holcroft DLB-39

Preface to Colonel Jack (1722), by
  Daniel Defoe DLB-39

Preface to Evelina (1778), by
  Fanny Burney DLB-39

Preface to Ferdinand Count Fathom (1753), by
  Tobias Smollett DLB-39

Preface to Incognita (1692), by
  William Congreve DLB-39

Preface to Joseph Andrews (1742), by
  Henry Fielding DLB-39

Preface to Moll Flanders (1722), by
  Daniel Defoe DLB-39

Preface to Poems (1853), by
  Matthew Arnold DLB-32

Preface to Robinson Crusoe (1719), by
  Daniel Defoe DLB-39

Preface to Roderick Random (1748), by
  Tobias Smollett DLB-39

Preface to Roxana (1724), by
  Daniel Defoe DLB-39

Preface to St. Leon (1799), by
  William Godwin DLB-39

DLB 173   Cumulative Index

Preface to Sarah Fielding's *Familiar Letters* (1747), by Henry Fielding [excerpt] DLB-39

Preface to Sarah Fielding's *The Adventures of David Simple* (1744), by Henry Fielding DLB-39

Preface to *The Cry* (1754), by Sarah Fielding DLB-39

Preface to *The Delicate Distress* (1769), by Elizabeth Griffin DLB-39

Preface to *The Disguis'd Prince* (1733), by Eliza Haywood [excerpt] DLB-39

Preface to *The Farther Adventures of Robinson Crusoe* (1719), by Daniel Defoe ...DLB-39

Preface to the First Edition of *Pamela* (1740), by Samuel Richardson DLB-39

Preface to the First Edition of *The Castle of Otranto* (1764), by Horace Walpole DLB-39

Preface to *The History of Romances* (1715), by Pierre Daniel Huet [excerpts] DLB-39

Preface to *The Life of Charlotta du Pont* (1723), by Penelope Aubin DLB-39

Preface to *The Old English Baron* (1778), by Clara Reeve DLB-39

Preface to the Second Edition of *The Castle of Otranto* (1765), by Horace Walpole DLB-39

Preface to *The Secret History, of Queen Zarah, and the Zarazians* (1705), by Delariviere Manley DLB-39

Preface to the Third Edition of *Clarissa* (1751), by Samuel Richardson [excerpt] DLB-39

Preface to *The Works of Mrs. Davys* (1725), by Mary Davys DLB-39

Preface to Volume 1 of *Clarissa* (1747), by Samuel Richardson DLB-39

Preface to Volume 3 of *Clarissa* (1748), by Samuel Richardson DLB-39

Préfontaine, Yves 1937- DLB-53

Prelutsky, Jack 1940- DLB-61

Premisses, by Michael Hamburger ...DLB-66

Prentice, George D. 1802-1870 ......DLB-43

Prentice-Hall DLB-46

Prescott, William Hickling 1796-1859 .... DLB-1, 30, 59

The Present State of the English Novel (1892), by George Saintsbury DLB-18

Prešeren, Francè 1800-1849 ....DLB-147

Preston, Thomas 1537-1598 ....DLB-62

Price, Reynolds 1933- DLB-2

Price, Richard 1723-1791 ....DLB-158

Price, Richard 1949- Y-81

Priest, Christopher 1943- DLB-14

Priestley, J. B. 1894-1984 .... DLB-10, 34, 77, 100, 139; Y-84

Primary Bibliography: A Retrospective Y-95

Prime, Benjamin Young 1733-1791 .. DLB-31

Primrose, Diana floruit circa 1630 ....DLB-126

Prince, F. T. 1912- DLB-20

Prince, Thomas 1687-1758 ..... DLB-24, 140

The Principles of Success in Literature (1865), by George Henry Lewes [excerpt] .. DLB-57

Printz, Wolfgang Casper 1641-1717 ....DLB-168

Prior, Matthew 1664-1721 ....DLB-95

Pritchard, William H. 1932- DLB-111

Pritchett, V. S. 1900- DLB-15, 139

Procter, Adelaide Anne 1825-1864 ...DLB-32

Procter, Bryan Waller 1787-1874 ....DLB-96, 144

The Profession of Authorship: Scribblers for Bread Y-89

The Progress of Romance (1785), by Clara Reeve [excerpt] DLB-39

Prokopovich, Feofan 1681?-1736 ... DLB-150

Prokosch, Frederic 1906-1989 ...... DLB-48

The Proletarian Novel DLB-9

Propper, Dan 1937- DLB-16

The Prospect of Peace (1778), by Joel Barlow DLB-37

Proud, Robert 1728-1813 ....DLB-30

Proust, Marcel 1871-1922 ....DLB-65

Prynne, J. H. 1936- DLB-40

Przybyszewski, Stanislaw 1868-1927 ....DLB-66

Pseudo-Dionysius the Areopagite floruit circa 500 ....DLB-115

The Public Lending Right in America Statement by Sen. Charles McC. Mathias, Jr. PLR and the Meaning of Literary Property Statements on PLR by American Writers Y-83

The Public Lending Right in the United Kingdom Public Lending Right: The First Year in the United Kingdom Y-83

The Publication of English Renaissance Plays DLB-62

Publications and Social Movements [Transcendentalism] DLB-1

Publishers and Agents: The Columbia Connection Y-87

A Publisher's Archives: G. P. Putnam ...Y-92

Publishing Fiction at LSU Press Y-87

Pückler-Muskau, Hermann von 1785-1871 ....DLB-133

Pufendorf, Samuel von 1632-1694 ....DLB-168

Pugh, Edwin William 1874-1930 ...DLB-135

Pugin, A. Welby 1812-1852 ....DLB-55

Puig, Manuel 1932-1990 ....DLB-113

Pulitzer, Joseph 1847-1911 ....DLB-23

Pulitzer, Joseph, Jr. 1885-1955 ....DLB-29

Pulitzer Prizes for the Novel, 1917-1945 ....DLB-9

Pulliam, Eugene 1889-1975 ....DLB-127

Purchas, Samuel 1577?-1626 ....DLB-151

Purdy, Al 1918- DLB-88

Purdy, James 1923- DLB-2

Purdy, Ken W. 1913-1972 ....DLB-137

Pusey, Edward Bouverie 1800-1882 ....DLB-55

Putnam, George Palmer 1814-1872 ....DLB-3, 79

Putnam, Samuel 1892-1950 ....DLB-4

G. P. Putnam's Sons [U.S.] DLB-49

G. P. Putnam's Sons [U.K.] DLB-106

Puzo, Mario 1920- DLB-6

Pyle, Ernie 1900-1945 ....DLB-29

Pyle, Howard 1853-1911 .... DLB-42; DS-13

Pym, Barbara 1913-1980 ....DLB-14; Y-87

Pynchon, Thomas 1937- DLB-2, 173

Pyramid Books DLB-46

Pyrnelle, Louise-Clarke 1850-1907 ...DLB-42

Q

Quad, M. (see Lewis, Charles B.)

Quarles, Francis 1592-1644 ....DLB-126

The Quarterly Review 1809-1967 ....DLB-110

Quasimodo, Salvatore 1901-1968 ...DLB-114

Queen, Ellery (see Dannay, Frederic, and Manfred B. Lee)

The Queen City Publishing House ...DLB-49

Queneau, Raymond 1903-1976 ......DLB-72

Quennell, Sir Peter 1905-1993 ......DLB-155

Quesnel, Joseph 1746-1809 ....DLB-99

The Question of American Copyright
  in the Nineteenth Century
    Headnote
    Preface, by George Haven Putnam
    The Evolution of Copyright, by Brander
      Matthews
    Summary of Copyright Legislation in
      the United States, by R. R. Bowker
    Analysis of the Provisions of the
      Copyright Law of 1891, by
      George Haven Putnam
    The Contest for International Copyright,
      by George Haven Putnam
    Cheap Books and Good Books,
      by Brander Matthews DLB-49

Quiller-Couch, Sir Arthur Thomas
  1863-1944 .... DLB-135, 153

Quin, Ann 1936-1973 .... DLB-14

Quincy, Samuel, of Georgia ?-? DLB-31

Quincy, Samuel, of Massachusetts
  1734-1789 .... DLB-31

Quinn, Anthony 1915- DLB-122

Quintana, Leroy V. 1944- DLB-82

Quintana, Miguel de 1671-1748
  A Forerunner of Chicano
  Literature DLB-122

Quist, Harlin, Books DLB-46

Quoirez, Françoise (see Sagan, Franççise)

R

Raabe, Wilhelm 1831-1910 .... DLB-129

Rabe, David 1940- DLB-7

Raboni, Giovanni 1932- DLB-128

Rachilde 1860-1953 .... DLB-123

Racin, Kočo 1908-1943 .... DLB-147

Rackham, Arthur 1867-1939 ..... DLB-141

Radcliffe, Ann 1764-1823 .... DLB-39

Raddall, Thomas 1903- DLB-68

Radiguet, Raymond 1903-1923 ..... DLB-65

Radishchev, Aleksandr Nikolaevich
  1749-1802 .... DLB-150

Radványi, Netty Reiling (see Seghers, Anna)

Rahv, Philip 1908-1973 .... DLB-137

Raimund, Ferdinand Jakob
  1790-1836 .... DLB-90

Raine, Craig 1944- DLB-40

Raine, Kathleen 1908- DLB-20

Rainolde, Richard
  circa 1530-1606 .... DLB-136

Rakić, Milan 1876-1938 .... DLB-147

Ralegh, Sir Walter 1554?-1618 ..... DLB-172

Ralph, Julian 1853-1903 .... DLB-23

Ralph Waldo Emerson in 1982 .... Y-82

Ramat, Silvio 1939- DLB-128

Rambler, no. 4 (1750), by Samuel Johnson
  [excerpt] DLB-39

Ramée, Marie Louise de la (see Ouida)

Ramírez, Sergío 1942- DLB-145

Ramke, Bin 1947- DLB-120

Ramler, Karl Wilhelm 1725-1798 .... DLB-97

Ramon Ribeyro, Julio 1929- DLB-145

Ramous, Mario 1924- DLB-128

Rampersad, Arnold 1941- DLB-111

Ramsay, Allan 1684 or 1685-1758 ... DLB-95

Ramsay, David 1749-1815 .... DLB-30

Ranck, Katherine Quintana
  1942- DLB-122

Rand, Avery and Company DLB-49

Rand McNally and Company DLB-49

Randall, David Anton
  1905-1975 .... DLB-140

Randall, Dudley 1914- DLB-41

Randall, Henry S. 1811-1876 .... DLB-30

Randall, James G. 1881-1953 .... DLB-17

The Randall Jarrell Symposium: A Small
  Collection of Randall Jarrells
  Excerpts From Papers Delivered at
  the Randall Jarrell
  Symposium Y-86

Randolph, A. Philip 1889-1979 ...... DLB-91

Randolph, Anson D. F.
  [publishing house] DLB-49

Randolph, Thomas 1605-1635 ..DLB-58, 126

Random House DLB-46

Ranlet, Henry [publishing house] DLB-49

Ransom, John Crowe
  1888-1974 ....DLB-45, 63

Ransome, Arthur 1884-1967 .... DLB-160

Raphael, Frederic 1931- DLB-14

Raphaelson, Samson 1896-1983 ..... DLB-44

Raskin, Ellen 1928-1984 .... DLB-52

Rastell, John 1475?-1536 .....DLB-136, 170

Rattigan, Terence 1911-1977 .... DLB-13

Rawlings, Marjorie Kinnan
  1896-1953 ....DLB-9, 22, 102

Raworth, Tom 1938- DLB-40

Ray, David 1932- DLB-5

Ray, Gordon Norton
  1915-1986 ....DLB-103, 140

Ray, Henrietta Cordelia
  1849-1916 ....DLB-50

Raymond, Henry J. 1820-1869 ... DLB-43, 79

Raymond Chandler Centenary Tributes
  from Michael Avallone, James Elroy, Joe
  Gores,
  and William F. Nolan Y-88

Reach, Angus 1821-1856............DLB-70

Read, Herbert 1893-1968 ...... DLB-20, 149

Read, Herbert, "The Practice of Biography," in
  *The English Sense of Humour and Other
  Essays* DLB-149

Read, Opie 1852-1939 ....DLB-23

Read, Piers Paul 1941- DLB-14

Reade, Charles 1814-1884 ....DLB-21

Reader's Digest Condensed
  Books DLB-46

Reading, Peter 1946- DLB-40

Reaney, James 1926- DLB-68

Rèbora, Clemente 1885-1957 ....DLB-114

Rechy, John 1934- DLB-122; Y-82

The Recovery of Literature: Criticism in the
  1990s: A Symposium Y-91

Redding, J. Saunders
  1906-1988 .... DLB-63, 76

Redfield, J. S. [publishing house] DLB-49

Redgrove, Peter 1932- DLB-40

Redmon, Anne 1943- Y-86

Redmond, Eugene B. 1937- DLB-41

Redpath, James [publishing house] ...DLB-49

Reed, Henry 1808-1854 ....DLB-59

Reed, Henry 1914- DLB-27

Reed, Ishmael
  1938- DLB-2, 5, 33, 169; DS-8

Reed, Sampson 1800-1880 ....DLB-1

Reed, Talbot Baines 1852-1893 .....DLB-141

Reedy, William Marion 1862-1920 ...DLB-91

Reese, Lizette Woodworth
  1856-1935 ....DLB-54

Reese, Thomas 1742-1796 ....DLB-37

Reeve, Clara 1729-1807 ....DLB-39

Reeves, James 1909-1978 ....DLB-161

Reeves, John 1926- DLB-88

Regnery, Henry, Company DLB-46

Rehberg, Hans 1901-1963 ....DLB-124

Rehfisch, Hans José 1891-1960 .....DLB-124

Reid, Alastair 1926- DLB-27

Reid, B. L. 1918-1990 ....DLB-111

Reid, Christopher 1949- DLB-40	Reznikoff, Charles 1894-1976 .... DLB-28, 45	Riis, Jacob 1849-1914 .... DLB-23
Reid, Forrest 1875-1947 .... DLB-153	"Rhetoric" (1828; revised, 1859), by Thomas de Quincey [excerpt] ... DLB-57	Riker, John C. [publishing house] DLB-49
Reid, Helen Rogers 1882-1970 ...... DLB-29		Riley, John 1938-1978 .... DLB-40
Reid, James ?-? DLB-31	Rhett, Robert Barnwell 1800-1876 ... DLB-43	Rilke, Rainer Maria 1875-1926 ...... DLB-81
Reid, Mayne 1818-1883 .... DLB-21, 163	Rhode, John 1884-1964 .... DLB-77	Rinehart and Company DLB-46
Reid, Thomas 1710-1796 .... DLB-31	Rhodes, James Ford 1848-1927 ..... DLB-47	Ringuet 1895-1960 .... DLB-68
Reid, V. S. (Vic) 1913-1987 .... DLB-125	Rhys, Jean 1890-1979 ..... DLB-36, 117, 162	Ringwood, Gwen Pharis 1910-1984 .... DLB-88
Reid, Whitelaw 1837-1912 .... DLB-23	Ricardo, David 1772-1823 .... DLB-107, 158	
Reilly and Lee Publishing Company DLB-46	Ricardou, Jean 1932- DLB-83	Rinser, Luise 1911- DLB-69
	Rice, Elmer 1892-1967 .... DLB-4, 7	Ríos, Alberto 1952- DLB-122
Reimann, Brigitte 1933-1973 .... DLB-75	Rice, Grantland 1880-1954 ..... DLB-29, 171	Ríos, Isabella 1948- DLB-82
Reinmar der Alte circa 1165-circa 1205 .... DLB-138	Rich, Adrienne 1929- DLB-5, 67	Ripley, Arthur 1895-1961 .... DLB-44
	Richards, David Adams 1950- DLB-53	Ripley, George 1802-1880 ..... DLB-1, 64, 73
Reinmar von Zweter circa 1200-circa 1250 .... DLB-138	Richards, George circa 1760-1814 ... DLB-37	The Rising Glory of America: Three Poems DLB-37
Reisch, Walter 1903-1983 .... DLB-44	Richards, I. A. 1893-1979 .... DLB-27	
Remarque, Erich Maria 1898-1970 ... DLB-56	Richards, Laura E. 1850-1943 ..... DLB-42	The Rising Glory of America: Written in 1771 (1786), by Hugh Henry Brackenridge and Philip Freneau DLB-37
"Re-meeting of Old Friends": The Jack Kerouac Conference Y-82	Richards, William Carey 1818-1892 .... DLB-73	
	Richards, Grant [publishing house] DLB-112	Riskin, Robert 1897-1955 .... DLB-26
Remington, Frederic 1861-1909 ...... DLB-12		Risse, Heinz 1898- DLB-69
Renaud, Jacques 1943- DLB-60	Richardson, Charles F. 1851-1913 ... DLB-71	Rist, Johann 1607-1667 .... DLB-164
Renault, Mary 1905-1983 .... Y-83	Richardson, Dorothy M. 1873-1957 .... DLB-36	Ritchie, Anna Mowatt 1819-1870 ..... DLB-3
Rendell, Ruth 1930- DLB-87		Ritchie, Anne Thackeray 1837-1919 .... DLB-18
Representative Men and Women: A Historical Perspective on the British Novel, 1930-1960 .... DLB-15	Richardson, Jack 1935- DLB-7	
	Richardson, John 1796-1852 .... DLB-99	Ritchie, Thomas 1778-1854 .... DLB-43
	Richardson, Samuel 1689-1761 .... DLB-39, 154	Rites of Passage [on William Saroyan] Y-83
(Re-)Publishing Orwell Y-86		
Rettenbacher, Simon 1634-1706 .... DLB-168	Richardson, Willis 1889-1977 .... DLB-51	The Ritz Paris Hemingway Award Y-85
Reuter, Christian 1665-after 1712 ... DLB-168	Riche, Barnabe 1542-1617 .... DLB-136	Rivard, Adjutor 1868-1945 .... DLB-92
Reuter, Fritz 1810-1874 .... DLB-129	Richler, Mordecai 1931- DLB-53	Rive, Richard 1931-1989 .... DLB-125
Reuter, Gabriele 1859-1941 .... DLB-66	Richter, Conrad 1890-1968 .... DLB-9	Rivera, Marina 1942- DLB-122
Revell, Fleming H., Company DLB-49	Richter, Hans Werner 1908- DLB-69	Rivera, Tomás 1935-1984 .... DLB-82
Reventlow, Franziska Gräfin zu 1871-1918 .... DLB-66	Richter, Johann Paul Friedrich 1763-1825 .... DLB-94	Rivers, Conrad Kent 1933-1968 ..... DLB-41
		Riverside Press DLB-49
Review of Reviews Office DLB-112	Rickerby, Joseph [publishing house] DLB-106	Rivington, James circa 1724-1802 .... DLB-43
Review of [Samuel Richardson's] Clarissa (1748), by Henry Fielding DLB-39		Rivington, Charles [publishing house] DLB-154
	Rickword, Edgell 1898-1982 .... DLB-20	
The Revolt (1937), by Mary Colum [excerpts] DLB-36	Riddell, Charlotte 1832-1906 ...... DLB-156	Rivkin, Allen 1903-1990 .... DLB-26
	Riddell, John (see Ford, Corey)	Roa Bastos, Augusto 1917- DLB-113
Rexroth, Kenneth 1905-1982 .... DLB-16, 48, 165; Y-82	Ridge, Lola 1873-1941 .... DLB-54	Robbe-Grillet, Alain 1922- DLB-83
	Ridge, William Pett 1859-1930 ..... DLB-135	Robbins, Tom 1936- Y-80
Rey, H. A. 1898-1977 .... DLB-22	Riding, Laura (see Jackson, Laura Riding)	Roberts, Charles G. D. 1860-1943 ... DLB-92
Reynal and Hitchcock DLB-46	Ridler, Anne 1912- DLB-27	Roberts, Dorothy 1906-1993 .... DLB-88
Reynolds, G. W. M. 1814-1879 ..... DLB-21	Ridruego, Dionisio 1912-1975 ..... DLB-108	Roberts, Elizabeth Madox 1881-1941 .... DLB-9, 54, 102
Reynolds, John Hamilton 1794-1852 .... DLB-96	Riel, Louis 1844-1885 .... DLB-99	
Reynolds, Mack 1917- DLB-8	Riemer, Johannes 1648-1714 ...... DLB-168	Roberts, Kenneth 1885-1957 .... DLB-9
Reynolds, Sir Joshua 1723-1792 .... DLB-104	Riffaterre, Michael 1924- DLB-67	Roberts, William 1767-1849 .... DLB-142

Roberts Brothers DLB-49	Romero, Leo 1950- DLB-122	Routledge, George, and Sons DLB-106
Roberts, James [publishing house] .. DLB-154	Romero, Lin 1947- DLB-122	Roversi, Roberto 1923- DLB-128
Robertson, A. M., and Company DLB-49	Romero, Orlando 1945- DLB-82	Rowe, Elizabeth Singer 1674-1737 .... DLB-39, 95
Robertson, William 1721-1793 ..... DLB-104	Rook, Clarence 1863-1915 .... DLB-135	
Robinson, Casey 1903-1979 .... DLB-44	Roosevelt, Theodore 1858-1919 ..... DLB-47	Rowe, Nicholas 1674-1718 .... DLB-84
Robinson, Edwin Arlington 1869-1935 .... DLB-54	Root, Waverley 1903-1982 .... DLB-4	Rowlands, Samuel circa 1570-1630 .... DLB-121
	Root, William Pitt 1941- DLB-120	
Robinson, Henry Crabb 1775-1867 .... DLB-107	Roquebrune, Robert de 1889-1978 ... DLB-68	Rowlandson, Mary circa 1635-circa 1678 .... DLB-24
Robinson, James Harvey 1863-1936 .... DLB-47	Rosa, João Guimarāres 1908-1967 .... DLB-113	Rowley, William circa 1585-1626 .... DLB-58
	Rosales, Luis 1910-1992 .... DLB-134	Rowse, A. L. 1903- DLB-155
Robinson, Lennox 1886-1958 .... DLB-10	Roscoe, William 1753-1831 .... DLB-163	Rowson, Susanna Haswell circa 1762-1824 .... DLB-37
Robinson, Mabel Louise 1874-1962 .... DLB-22	Rose, Reginald 1920- DLB-26	
	Rosegger, Peter 1843-1918 .... DLB-129	Roy, Camille 1870-1943 .... DLB-92
Robinson, Mary 1758-1800 .... DLB-158	Rosei, Peter 1946- DLB-85	Roy, Gabrielle 1909-1983 .... DLB-68
Robinson, Richard circa 1545-1607 .... DLB-167	Rosen, Norma 1925- DLB-28	Roy, Jules 1907- DLB-83
	Rosenbach, A. S. W. 1876-1952 .... DLB-140	The Royal Court Theatre and the English Stage Company DLB-13
Robinson, Therese 1797-1870 .... DLB-59, 133	Rosenberg, Isaac 1890-1918 .... DLB-20	
	Rosenfeld, Isaac 1918-1956 .... DLB-28	The Royal Court Theatre and the New Drama DLB-10
Robison, Mary 1949- DLB-130	Rosenthal, M. L. 1917- DLB-5	
Roblès, Emmanuel 1914- DLB-83	Ross, Alexander 1591-1654 .... DLB-151	The Royal Shakespeare Company at the Swan Y-88
Roccatagliata Ceccardi, Ceccardo 1871-1919 .... DLB-114	Ross, Harold 1892-1951 .... DLB-137	
	Ross, Leonard Q. (see Rosten, Leo)	Royall, Anne 1769-1854 .... DLB-43
Rochester, John Wilmot, Earl of 1647-1680 .... DLB-131	Ross, Martin 1862-1915 .... DLB-135	The Roycroft Printing Shop DLB-49
	Ross, Sinclair 1908- DLB-88	Royster, Vermont 1914- DLB-127
Rock, Howard 1911-1976 .... DLB-127	Ross, W. W. E. 1894-1966 .... DLB-88	Royston, Richard [publishing house] DLB-170
Rodgers, Carolyn M. 1945- DLB-41	Rosselli, Amelia 1930- DLB-128	
Rodgers, W. R. 1909-1969 .... DLB-20	Rossen, Robert 1908-1966 .... DLB-26	Ruark, Gibbons 1941- DLB-120
Rodríguez, Claudio 1934- DLB-134	Rossetti, Christina Georgina 1830-1894 ....DLB-35, 163	Ruban, Vasilii Grigorevich 1742-1795 .... DLB-150
Rodriguez, Richard 1944- DLB-82		
Rodríguez Julia, Edgardo 1946- DLB-145	Rossetti, Dante Gabriel 1828-1882 ... DLB-35	Rubens, Bernice 1928- DLB-14
	Rossner, Judith 1935- DLB-6	Rudd and Carleton DLB-49
Roethke, Theodore 1908-1963 ....DLB-5	Rosten, Leo 1908- DLB-11	Rudkin, David 1936- DLB-13
Rogers, Pattiann 1940- DLB-105	Rostenberg, Leona 1908- DLB-140	Rudolf von Ems circa 1200-circa 1254 .... DLB-138
Rogers, Samuel 1763-1855 .... DLB-93	Rostovsky, Dimitrii 1651-1709 ..... DLB-150	
Rogers, Will 1879-1935 .... DLB-11	Bertram Rota and His Bookshop Y-91	Ruffin, Josephine St. Pierre 1842-1924 .... DLB-79
Rohmer, Sax 1883-1959 .... DLB-70	Roth, Gerhard 1942- DLB-85, 124	
Roiphe, Anne 1935- Y-80	Roth, Henry 1906?- DLB-28	Ruganda, John 1941- DLB-157
Rojas, Arnold R. 1896-1988 .... DLB-82	Roth, Joseph 1894-1939 .... DLB-85	Ruggles, Henry Joseph 1813-1906 .... DLB-64
Rolfe, Frederick William 1860-1913 .... DLB-34, 156	Roth, Philip 1933- DLB-2, 28, 173; Y-82	Rukeyser, Muriel 1913-1980 .... DLB-48
	Rothenberg, Jerome 1931- DLB-5	Rule, Jane 1931- DLB-60
Rolland, Romain 1866-1944 .... DLB-65	Rotimi, Ola 1938- DLB-125	Rulfo, Juan 1918-1986 .... DLB-113
Rolle, Richard circa 1290-1300 - 1340 .... DLB-146	Routhier, Adolphe-Basile 1839-1920 .... DLB-99	Rumaker, Michael 1932- DLB-16
		Rumens, Carol 1944- DLB-40
Rolvaag, O. E. 1876-1931 ....DLB-9	Routier, Simone 1901-1987 .... DLB-88	Runyon, Damon 1880-1946 . DLB-11, 86, 171
Romains, Jules 1885-1972 .... DLB-65		*Ruodlieb* circa 1050-1075 .... DLB-148
Roman, A., and Company DLB-49		Rush, Benjamin 1746-1813 .... DLB-37
Romano, Octavio 1923- DLB-122		Rusk, Ralph L. 1888-1962 .... DLB-103

Ruskin, John 1819-1900 ....DLB-55, 163

Russ, Joanna 1937- DLB-8

Russell, B. B., and Company DLB-49

Russell, Benjamin 1761-1845 ....DLB-43

Russell, Bertrand 1872-1970 ....DLB-100

Russell, Charles Edward
 1860-1941 ....DLB-25

Russell, George William (see AE)

Russell, R. H., and Son DLB-49

Rutherford, Mark 1831-1913 ....DLB-18

Ryan, Michael 1946- Y-82

Ryan, Oscar 1904- DLB-68

Ryga, George 1932- DLB-60

Rymer, Thomas 1643?-1713 ....DLB-101

Ryskind, Morrie 1895-1985 ....DLB-26

Rzhevsky, Aleksei Andreevich
 1737-1804 ....DLB-150

S

The Saalfield Publishing
 Company DLB-46

Saba, Umberto 1883-1957 ....DLB-114

Sábato, Ernesto 1911- DLB-145

Saberhagen, Fred 1930- DLB-8

Sacer, Gottfried Wilhelm
 1635-1699 ....DLB-168

Sackler, Howard 1929-1982 ....DLB-7

Sackville, Thomas 1536-1608 ......DLB-132

Sackville, Thomas 1536-1608
 and Norton, Thomas
 1532-1584 ....DLB-62

Sackville-West, V. 1892-1962 ....DLB-34

Sadlier, D. and J., and Company DLB-49

Sadlier, Mary Anne 1820-1903 ......DLB-99

Sadoff, Ira 1945- DLB-120

Saenz, Jaime 1921-1986 ....DLB-145

Saffin, John circa 1626-1710 ....DLB-24

Sagan, Françoise 1935- DLB-83

Sage, Robert 1899-1962 ....DLB-4

Sagel, Jim 1947- DLB-82

Sagendorph, Robb Hansell
 1900-1970 ....DLB-137

Sahagún, Carlos 1938- DLB-108

Sahkomaapii, Piitai (see Highwater, Jamake)

Sahl, Hans 1902- DLB-69

Said, Edward W. 1935- DLB-67

Saiko, George 1892-1962 ....DLB-85

St. Dominic's Press DLB-112

Saint-Exupéry, Antoine de
 1900-1944 ....DLB-72

St. Johns, Adela Rogers 1894-1988 .. DLB-29

St. Martin's Press DLB-46

St. Omer, Garth 1931- DLB-117

Saint Pierre, Michel de 1916-1987 ... DLB-83

Saintsbury, George
 1845-1933 .... DLB-57, 149

Saki (see Munro, H. H.)

Salaam, Kalamu ya 1947- DLB-38

Salas, Floyd 1931- DLB-82

Sálaz-Marquez, Rubén 1935- DLB-122

Salemson, Harold J. 1910-1988 ...... DLB-4

Salinas, Luis Omar 1937- DLB-82

Salinas, Pedro 1891-1951 .... DLB-134

Salinger, J. D. 1919- DLB-2, 102, 173

Salkey, Andrew 1928- DLB-125

Salt, Waldo 1914- DLB-44

Salter, James 1925- DLB-130

Salter, Mary Jo 1954- DLB-120

Salustri, Carlo Alberto (see Trilussa)

Salverson, Laura Goodman
 1890-1970 .... DLB-92

Sampson, Richard Henry (see Hull, Richard)

Samuels, Ernest 1903- DLB-111

Sanborn, Franklin Benjamin
 1831-1917 .... DLB-1

Sánchez, Luis Rafael 1936- DLB-145

Sánchez, Philomeno "Phil"
 1917- DLB-122

Sánchez, Ricardo 1941- DLB-82

Sanchez, Sonia 1934- DLB-41; DS-8

Sand, George 1804-1876 .... DLB-119

Sandburg, Carl 1878-1967 ...... DLB-17, 54

Sanders, Ed 1939- DLB-16

Sandoz, Mari 1896-1966 .... DLB-9

Sandwell, B. K. 1876-1954 .... DLB-92

Sandy, Stephen 1934- DLB-165

Sandys, George 1578-1644 ..... DLB-24, 121

Sangster, Charles 1822-1893 .... DLB-99

Sanguineti, Edoardo 1930- DLB-128

Sansom, William 1912-1976 .... DLB-139

Santayana, George
 1863-1952 ....DLB-54, 71; DS-13

Santiago, Danny 1911-1988 ....DLB-122

Santmyer, Helen Hooven 1895-1986 ....Y-84

Sapir, Edward 1884-1939 ....DLB-92

Sapper (see McNeile, Herman Cyril)

Sarduy, Severo 1937- DLB-113

Sargent, Pamela 1948- DLB-8

Saro-Wiwa, Ken 1941- DLB-157

Saroyan, William
 1908-1981 .... DLB-7, 9, 86; Y-81

Sarraute, Nathalie 1900- DLB-83

Sarrazin, Albertine 1937-1967 ......DLB-83

Sarton, May 1912- DLB-48; Y-81

Sartre, Jean-Paul 1905-1980 ....DLB-72

Sassoon, Siegfried 1886-1967 ....DLB-20

Saturday Review Press DLB-46

Saunders, James 1925- DLB-13

Saunders, John Monk 1897-1940 ....DLB-26

Saunders, Margaret Marshall
 1861-1947 ....DLB-92

Saunders and Otley DLB-106

Savage, James 1784-1873 ....DLB-30

Savage, Marmion W. 1803?-1872 ....DLB-21

Savage, Richard 1697?-1743 ....DLB-95

Savard, Félix-Antoine 1896-1982 ....DLB-68

Saville, (Leonard) Malcolm
 1901-1982 ....DLB-160

Sawyer, Ruth 1880-1970 ....DLB-22

Sayers, Dorothy L.
 1893-1957 .... DLB-10, 36, 77, 100

Sayles, John Thomas 1950- DLB-44

Sbarbaro, Camillo 1888-1967 ......DLB-114

Scannell, Vernon 1922- DLB-27

Scarry, Richard 1919-1994 ....DLB-61

Schaeffer, Albrecht 1885-1950 ......DLB-66

Schaeffer, Susan Fromberg 1941- ...DLB-28

Schaff, Philip 1819-1893 .... DS-13

Schaper, Edzard 1908-1984 ....DLB-69

Scharf, J. Thomas 1843-1898 ....DLB-47

Scheffel, Joseph Viktor von
 1826-1886 ....DLB-129

Scheffler, Johann 1624-1677 ....DLB-164

Schelling, Friedrich Wilhelm Joseph von
 1775-1854 ....DLB-90

Scherer, Wilhelm 1841-1886 ....DLB-129

Schickele, René 1883-1940 ....DLB-66

Schiff, Dorothy 1903-1989 ....DLB-127

Cumulative Index

Schiller, Friedrich 1759-1805 .... DLB-94

Schirmer, David 1623-1687 .... DLB-164

Schlaf, Johannes 1862-1941 .... DLB-118

Schlegel, August Wilhelm
1767-1845 .... DLB-94

Schlegel, Dorothea 1763-1839 ...... DLB-90

Schlegel, Friedrich 1772-1829 .... DLB-90

Schleiermacher, Friedrich
1768-1834 .... DLB-90

Schlesinger, Arthur M., Jr. 1917- .. DLB-17

Schlumberger, Jean 1877-1968 ...... DLB-65

Schmid, Eduard Hermann Wilhelm (see Edschmid, Kasimir)

Schmidt, Arno 1914-1979 .... DLB-69

Schmidt, Johann Kaspar (see Stirner, Max)

Schmidt, Michael 1947- DLB-40

Schmidtbonn, Wilhelm August
1876-1952 .... DLB-118

Schmitz, James H. 1911- DLB-8

Schnabel, Johann Gottfried
1692-1760 .... DLB-168

Schnackenberg, Gjertrud 1953- ... DLB-120

Schnitzler, Arthur 1862-1931 ... DLB-81, 118

Schnurre, Wolfdietrich 1920- DLB-69

Schocken Books DLB-46

Schönbeck, Virgilio (see Giotti, Virgilio)

School Stories, 1914-1960 .... DLB-160

Schönherr, Karl 1867-1943 .... DLB-118

Scholartis Press DLB-112

The Schomburg Center for Research
in Black Culture DLB-76

Schopenhauer, Arthur 1788-1860 ... DLB-90

Schopenhauer, Johanna 1766-1838 .. DLB-90

Schorer, Mark 1908-1977 .... DLB-103

Schottelius, Justus Georg
1612-1676 .... DLB-164

Schouler, James 1839-1920 .... DLB-47

Schrader, Paul 1946- DLB-44

Schreiner, Olive 1855-1920 ..... DLB-18, 156

Schroeder, Andreas 1946- DLB-53

Schubart, Christian Friedrich Daniel
1739-1791 .... DLB-97

Schubert, Gotthilf Heinrich
1780-1860 .... DLB-90

Schücking, Levin 1814-1883 ...... DLB-133

Schulberg, Budd
1914- DLB-6, 26, 28; Y-81

Schulte, F. J., and Company DLB-49

Schulze, Hans (see Praetorius, Johannes)

Schupp, Johann Balthasar
1610-1661 .... DLB-164

Schurz, Carl 1829-1906 .... DLB-23

Schuyler, George S. 1895-1977 ...DLB-29, 51

Schuyler, James 1923-1991 ......DLB-5, 169

Schwartz, Delmore 1913-1966 ....DLB-28, 48

Schwartz, Jonathan 1938- Y-82

Schwarz, Sibylle 1621-1638 .... DLB-164

Schwerner, Armand 1927- DLB-165

Schwob, Marcel 1867-1905 .... DLB-123

Science Fantasy DLB-8

Science-Fiction Fandom and
Conventions DLB-8

Science-Fiction Fanzines: The Time
Binders DLB-8

Science-Fiction Films DLB-8

Science Fiction Writers of America and the
Nebula Awards DLB-8

Scot, Reginald circa 1538-1599 ..... DLB-136

Scotellaro, Rocco 1923-1953 .... DLB-128

Scott, Dennis 1939-1991 .... DLB-125

Scott, Dixon 1881-1915 .... DLB-98

Scott, Duncan Campbell
1862-1947 .... DLB-92

Scott, Evelyn 1893-1963 ....DLB-9, 48

Scott, F. R. 1899-1985 .... DLB-88

Scott, Frederick George
1861-1944 .... DLB-92

Scott, Geoffrey 1884-1929 .... DLB-149

Scott, Harvey W. 1838-1910 .... DLB-23

Scott, Paul 1920-1978 .... DLB-14

Scott, Sarah 1723-1795 .... DLB-39

Scott, Tom 1918- DLB-27

Scott, Sir Walter
1771-1832 ... DLB-93, 107, 116, 144, 159

Scott, William Bell 1811-1890 .... DLB-32

Scott, Walter, Publishing
Company Limited DLB-112

Scott, William R.
[publishing house] DLB-46

Scott-Heron, Gil 1949- DLB-41

Scribner, Charles, Jr. 1921-1995 ....Y-95

Charles Scribner's Sons DLB-49; DS-13

Scripps, E. W. 1854-1926 .... DLB-25

Scudder, Horace Elisha
1838-1902 ....DLB-42, 71

Scudder, Vida Dutton 1861-1954 .... DLB-71

Scupham, Peter 1933- DLB-40

Seabrook, William 1886-1945 .... DLB-4

Seabury, Samuel 1729-1796 .... DLB-31

Seacole, Mary Jane Grant
1805-1881 .... DLB-166

The Seafarer circa 970 ....DLB-146

Sealsfield, Charles 1793-1864 ...... DLB-133

Sears, Edward I. 1819?-1876 ....DLB-79

Sears Publishing Company DLB-46

Seaton, George 1911-1979 .... DLB-44

Seaton, William Winston
1785-1866 .... DLB-43

Secker, Martin, and Warburg
Limited DLB-112

Secker, Martin [publishing house] ...DLB-112

Second-Generation Minor Poets of the
Seventeenth Century DLB-126

Sedgwick, Arthur George
1844-1915 .... DLB-64

Sedgwick, Catharine Maria
1789-1867 .... DLB-1, 74

Sedgwick, Ellery 1872-1930 ....DLB-91

Sedley, Sir Charles 1639-1701 ...... DLB-131

Seeger, Alan 1888-1916 ....DLB-45

Seers, Eugene (see Dantin, Louis)

Segal, Erich 1937- Y-86

Seghers, Anna 1900-1983 ....DLB-69

Seid, Ruth (see Sinclair, Jo)

Seidel, Frederick Lewis 1936- Y-84

Seidel, Ina 1885-1974 ....DLB-56

Seigenthaler, John 1927- DLB-127

Seizin Press DLB-112

Séjour, Victor 1817-1874 ....DLB-50

Séjour Marcou et Ferrand, Juan Victor (see Séjour, Victor)

Selby, Hubert, Jr. 1928- DLB-2

Selden, George 1929-1989 ....DLB-52

Selected English-Language Little Magazines
and Newspapers [France,
1920-1939] DLB-4

Selected Humorous Magazines
(1820-1950) DLB-11

Selected Science-Fiction Magazines and
Anthologies DLB-8

Self, Edwin F. 1920- DLB-137

Seligman, Edwin R. A. 1861-1939 ....DLB-47

Seltzer, Chester E. (see Muro, Amado)

Seltzer, Thomas
[publishing house] DLB-46

366

Selvon, Sam 1923-1994 ....DLB-125

Senancour, Etienne de 1770-1846 ...DLB-119

Sendak, Maurice 1928- DLB-61

Senécal, Eva 1905- DLB-92

Sengstacke, John 1912- DLB-127

Senior, Olive 1941- DLB-157

Šenoa, August 1838-1881 ....DLB-147

"Sensation Novels" (1863), by
   H. L. Manse DLB-21

Sepamla, Sipho 1932- DLB-157

Seredy, Kate 1899-1975 ....DLB-22

Sereni, Vittorio 1913-1983 ....DLB-128

Seres, William
   [publishing house] DLB-170

Serling, Rod 1924-1975 ....DLB-26

Serote, Mongane Wally 1944- ...DLB-125

Serraillier, Ian 1912-1994 ....DLB-161

Serrano, Nina 1934- DLB-122

Service, Robert 1874-1958 ....DLB-92

Seth, Vikram 1952- DLB-120

Seton, Ernest Thompson
   1860-1942 .... DLB-92; DS-13

Settle, Mary Lee 1918- DLB-6

Seume, Johann Gottfried
   1763-1810 ....DLB-94

Seuss, Dr. (see Geisel, Theodor Seuss)

The Seventy-fifth Anniversary of the Armistice:
   The Wilfred Owen Centenary and the
   Great War Exhibit at the University of
   Virginia Y-93

Sewall, Joseph 1688-1769 ....DLB-24

Sewall, Richard B. 1908- DLB-111

Sewell, Anna 1820-1878 ....DLB-163

Sewell, Samuel 1652-1730 ....DLB-24

Sex, Class, Politics, and Religion [in the
   British Novel, 1930-1959] DLB-15

Sexton, Anne 1928-1974 ....DLB-5, 169

Seymour-Smith, Martin 1928- DLB-155

Shaara, Michael 1929-1988 ....Y-83

Shadwell, Thomas 1641?-1692 .....DLB-80

Shaffer, Anthony 1926- DLB-13

Shaffer, Peter 1926- DLB-13

Shaftesbury, Anthony Ashley Cooper,
   Third Earl of 1671-1713 ....DLB-101

Shairp, Mordaunt 1887-1939 ....DLB-10

Shakespeare, William
   1564-1616 ....DLB-62, 172

The Shakespeare Globe Trust Y-93

Shakespeare Head Press DLB-112

Shakhovskoi, Aleksandr Aleksandrovich
   1777-1846 ....DLB-150

Shange, Ntozake 1948- DLB-38

Shapiro, Karl 1913- DLB-48

Sharon Publications DLB-46

Sharp, Margery 1905-1991 ....DLB-161

Sharp, William 1855-1905 ....DLB-156

Sharpe, Tom 1928 ....DLB-14

Shaw, Albert 1857-1947 ....DLB-91

Shaw, Bernard 1856-1950 ....DLB-10, 57

Shaw, Henry Wheeler 1818-1885 ...DLB-11

Shaw, Joseph T. 1874-1952 ....DLB-137

Shaw, Irwin 1913-1984 ....DLB-6, 102; Y-84

Shaw, Robert 1927-1978 ....DLB-13, 14

Shaw, Robert B. 1947- DLB-120

Shawn, William 1907-1992 ....DLB-137

Shay, Frank [publishing house] DLB-46

Shea, John Gilmary 1824-1892 ......DLB-30

Sheaffer, Louis 1912-1993 ....DLB-103

Shearing, Joseph 1886-1952 ....DLB-70

Shebbeare, John 1709-1788 ....DLB-39

Sheckley, Robert 1928- DLB-8

Shedd, William G. T. 1820-1894 ....DLB-64

Sheed, Wilfred 1930- DLB-6

Sheed and Ward [U.S.] DLB-46

Sheed and Ward Limited [U.K.] ...DLB-112

Sheldon, Alice B. (see Tiptree, James, Jr.)

Sheldon, Edward 1886-1946 ....DLB-7

Sheldon and Company DLB-49

Shelley, Mary Wollstonecraft
   1797-1851 ....DLB-110, 116, 159

Shelley, Percy Bysshe
   1792-1822 ....DLB-96, 110, 158

Shelnutt, Eve 1941- DLB-130

Shenstone, William 1714-1763 ......DLB-95

Shepard, Ernest Howard
   1879-1976 ....DLB-160

Shepard, Sam 1943- DLB-7

Shepard, Thomas I,
   1604 or 1605-1649 ....DLB-24

Shepard, Thomas II, 1635-1677 .....DLB-24

Shepard, Clark and Brown DLB-49

Shepherd, Luke
   flourished 1547-1554 ....DLB-136

Sherburne, Edward 1616-1702 .....DLB-131

Sheridan, Frances 1724-1766 .....DLB-39, 84

Sheridan, Richard Brinsley
   1751-1816 ....DLB-89

Sherman, Francis 1871-1926 ....DLB-92

Sherriff, R. C. 1896-1975 ....DLB-10

Sherry, Norman 1935- DLB-155

Sherwood, Mary Martha
   1775-1851 ....DLB-163

Sherwood, Robert 1896-1955 .....DLB-7, 26

Shiel, M. P. 1865-1947 ....DLB-153

Shiels, George 1886-1949 ....DLB-10

Shillaber, B.[enjamin] P.[enhallow]
   1814-1890 ....DLB-1, 11

Shine, Ted 1931- DLB-38

Ship, Reuben 1915-1975 ....DLB-88

Shirer, William L. 1904-1993 ....DLB-4

Shirinsky-Shikhmatov, Sergii Aleksandrovich
   1783-1837 ....DLB-150

Shirley, James 1596-1666 ....DLB-58

Shishkov, Aleksandr Semenovich
   1753-1841 ....DLB-150

Shockley, Ann Allen 1927- DLB-33

Short, Peter
   [publishing house] DLB-170

Shorthouse, Joseph Henry
   1834-1903 ....DLB-18

Showalter, Elaine 1941- DLB-67

Shulevitz, Uri 1935- DLB-61

Shulman, Max 1919-1988 ....DLB-11

Shute, Henry A. 1856-1943 ....DLB-9

Shuttle, Penelope 1947- DLB-14, 40

Sibbes, Richard 1577-1635 ....DLB-151

Sidgwick and Jackson Limited DLB-112

Sidney, Margaret (see Lothrop, Harriet M.)

Sidney, Mary 1561-1621 ....DLB-167

Sidney, Sir Philip 1554-1586 ....DLB-167

Sidney's Press DLB-49

Siegfried Loraine Sassoon: A Centenary Essay
   Tributes from Vivien F. Clarke and
   Michael Thorpe Y-86

Sierra, Rubén 1946- DLB-122

Sierra Club Books DLB-49

Siger of Brabant
   circa 1240-circa 1284 ....DLB-115

Sigourney, Lydia Howard (Huntley)
   1791-1865 ....DLB-1, 42, 73

Silkin, Jon 1930- DLB-27

Silko, Leslie Marmon 1948- DLB-143

Silliman, Ron 1946- DLB-169

Silliphant, Stirling 1918- DLB-26

Sillitoe, Alan 1928- DLB-14, 139

Silman, Roberta 1934- DLB-28

Silva, Beverly 1930- DLB-122

Silverberg, Robert 1935- DLB-8

Silverman, Kenneth 1936- DLB-111

Simak, Clifford D. 1904-1988 .... DLB-8

Simcoe, Elizabeth 1762-1850 .... DLB-99

Simcox, George Augustus
 1841-1905 .... DLB-35

Sime, Jessie Georgina 1868-1958 .... DLB-92

Simenon, Georges
 1903-1989 .... DLB-72; Y-89

Simic, Charles 1938- DLB-105

Simic, Charles,
 Images and "Images" DLB-105

Simmel, Johannes Mario 1924- DLB-69

Simmes, Valentine
 [publishing house] DLB-170

Simmons, Ernest J. 1903-1972 ..... DLB-103

Simmons, Herbert Alfred 1930- ... DLB-33

Simmons, James 1933- DLB-40

Simms, William Gilmore
 1806-1870 .... DLB-3, 30, 59, 73

Simms and M'Intyre DLB-106

Simon, Claude 1913- DLB-83

Simon, Neil 1927- DLB-7

Simon and Schuster DLB-46

Simons, Katherine Drayton Mayrant
 1890-1969 .... Y-83

Simpkin and Marshall
 [publishing house] DLB-154

Simpson, Helen 1897-1940 .... DLB-77

Simpson, Louis 1923- DLB-5

Simpson, N. F. 1919- DLB-13

Sims, George 1923- DLB-87

Sims, George Robert
 1847-1922 .... DLB-35, 70, 135

Sinán, Rogelio 1904- DLB-145

Sinclair, Andrew 1935- DLB-14

Sinclair, Bertrand William
 1881-1972 .... DLB-92

Sinclair, Catherine
 1800-1864 .... DLB-163

Sinclair, Jo 1913- DLB-28

Sinclair Lewis Centennial
 Conference Y-85

Sinclair, Lister 1921- DLB-88

Sinclair, May 1863-1946 .... DLB-36, 135

Sinclair, Upton 1878-1968 .... DLB-9

Sinclair, Upton [publishing house] ... DLB-46

Singer, Isaac Bashevis
 1904-1991 .... DLB-6, 28, 52; Y-91

Singmaster, Elsie 1879-1958 .... DLB-9

Sinisgalli, Leonardo 1908-1981 ..... DLB-114

Siodmak, Curt 1902- DLB-44

Sissman, L. E. 1928-1976 .... DLB-5

Sisson, C. H. 1914- DLB-27

Sitwell, Edith 1887-1964 .... DLB-20

Sitwell, Osbert 1892-1969 .... DLB-100

Skármeta, Antonio 1940- DLB-145

Skeffington, William
 [publishing house] DLB-106

Skelton, John 1463-1529 .... DLB-136

Skelton, Robin 1925- DLB-27, 53

Skinner, Constance Lindsay
 1877-1939 .... DLB-92

Skinner, John Stuart 1788-1851 ...... DLB-73

Skipsey, Joseph 1832-1903 .... DLB-35

Slade, Bernard 1930- DLB-53

Slater, Patrick 1880-1951 .... DLB-68

Slaveykov, Pencho 1866-1912 ...... DLB-147

Slavitt, David 1935- DLB-5, 6

Sleigh, Burrows Willcocks Arthur
 1821-1869 .... DLB-99

A Slender Thread of Hope: The Kennedy
 Center Black Theatre Project DLB-38

Slesinger, Tess 1905-1945 .... DLB-102

Slick, Sam (see Haliburton, Thomas Chandler)

Sloane, William, Associates DLB-46

Small, Maynard and Company DLB-49

Small Presses in Great Britain and Ireland,
 1960-1985 .... DLB-40

Small Presses I: Jargon Society Y-84

Small Presses II: The Spirit That Moves Us
 Press Y-85

Small Presses III: Pushcart Press Y-87

Smart, Christopher 1722-1771 ..... DLB-109

Smart, David A. 1892-1957 .... DLB-137

Smart, Elizabeth 1913-1986 .... DLB-88

Smellie, William
 [publishing house] DLB-154

Smiles, Samuel 1812-1904 .... DLB-55

Smith, A. J. M. 1902-1980 .... DLB-88

Smith, Adam 1723-1790 .... DLB-104

Smith, Alexander 1829-1867 .... DLB-32, 55

Smith, Betty 1896-1972 .... Y-82

Smith, Carol Sturm 1938- Y-81

Smith, Charles Henry 1826-1903 .... DLB-11

Smith, Charlotte 1749-1806 .... DLB-39, 109

Smith, Chet 1899-1973 .... DLB-171

Smith, Cordwainer 1913-1966 .... DLB-8

Smith, Dave 1942- DLB-5

Smith, Dodie 1896- DLB-10

Smith, Doris Buchanan 1934- DLB-52

Smith, E. E. 1890-1965 .... DLB-8

Smith, Elihu Hubbard 1771-1798 .... DLB-37

Smith, Elizabeth Oakes (Prince)
 1806-1893 .... DLB-1

Smith, F. Hopkinson 1838-1915 .... DS-13

Smith, George D. 1870-1920 ...... DLB-140

Smith, George O. 1911-1981 .... DLB-8

Smith, Goldwin 1823-1910 .... DLB-99

Smith, H. Allen 1907-1976 ...... DLB-11, 29

Smith, Hazel Brannon 1914- DLB-127

Smith, Henry
 circa 1560-circa 1591 .... DLB-136

Smith, Horatio (Horace)
 1779-1849 .... DLB-116

Smith, Horatio (Horace) 1779-1849 and
 James Smith 1775-1839 .... DLB-96

Smith, Iain Crichton
 1928- DLB-40, 139

Smith, J. Allen 1860-1924 .... DLB-47

Smith, John 1580-1631 .... DLB-24, 30

Smith, Josiah 1704-1781 .... DLB-24

Smith, Ken 1938- DLB-40

Smith, Lee 1944- DLB-143; Y-83

Smith, Logan Pearsall 1865-1946 .... DLB-98

Smith, Mark 1935- Y-82

Smith, Michael 1698-circa 1771 ..... DLB-31

Smith, Red 1905-1982 .... DLB-29, 171

Smith, Roswell 1829-1892 .... DLB-79

Smith, Samuel Harrison
 1772-1845 .... DLB-43

Smith, Samuel Stanhope
 1751-1819 .... DLB-37

Smith, Sarah (see Stretton, Hesba)

Smith, Seba 1792-1868 .... DLB-1, 11

Smith, Sir Thomas 1513-1577 ..... DLB-132

Smith, Stevie 1902-1971 .... DLB-20

Smith, Sydney 1771-1845 ....DLB-107

Smith, Sydney Goodsir 1915-1975 ...DLB-27

Smith, Wendell 1914-1972 ....DLB-171

Smith, William
  flourished 1595-1597 ....DLB-136

Smith, William 1727-1803 ....DLB-31

Smith, William 1728-1793 ....DLB-30

Smith, William Gardner
  1927-1974 ....DLB-76

Smith, William Henry
  1808-1872 ....DLB-159

Smith, William Jay 1918- DLB-5

Smith, Elder and Company DLB-154

Smith, Harrison, and Robert Haas
  [publishing house] DLB-46

Smith, J. Stilman, and Company DLB-49

Smith, W. B., and Company DLB-49

Smith, W. H., and Son DLB-106

Smithers, Leonard
  [publishing house] DLB-112

Smollett, Tobias 1721-1771 .....DLB-39, 104

Snellings, Rolland (see Touré, Askia Muhammad)

Snodgrass, W. D. 1926- DLB-5

Snow, C. P. 1905-1980 ....DLB-15, 77

Snyder, Gary 1930- DLB-5, 16, 165

Sobiloff, Hy 1912-1970 ....DLB-48

The Society for Textual Scholarship and
  TEXT Y-87

The Society for the History of Authorship,
  Reading and Publishing Y-92

Soffici, Ardengo 1879-1964 ....DLB-114

Sofola, 'Zulu 1938- DLB-157

Solano, Solita 1888-1975 ....DLB-4

Sollers, Philippe 1936- DLB-83

Solmi, Sergio 1899-1981 ....DLB-114

Solomon, Carl 1928- DLB-16

Solway, David 1941- DLB-53

Solzhenitsyn and America Y-85

Somerville, Edith Œnone
  1858-1949 ....DLB-135

Song, Cathy 1955- DLB-169

Sontag, Susan 1933- DLB-2, 67

Sorge, Reinhard Johannes
  1892-1916 ....DLB-118

Sorrentino, Gilbert
  1929- DLB-5, 173; Y-80

Sotheby, William 1757-1833 ....DLB-93

Soto, Gary 1952- DLB-82

Sources for the Study of Tudor and Stuart
  Drama DLB-62

Souster, Raymond 1921- DLB-88

The *South English Legendary*
  circa thirteenth-fifteenth
  centuries DLB-146

Southerland, Ellease 1943- DLB-33

Southern Illinois University Press Y-95

Southern, Terry 1924- DLB-2

Southern Writers Between the
  Wars DLB-9

Southerne, Thomas 1659-1746 ...... DLB-80

Southey, Caroline Anne Bowles
  1786-1854 .... DLB-116

Southey, Robert
  1774-1843 ....DLB-93, 107, 142

Southwell, Robert 1561?-1595 ..... DLB-167

Sowande, Bode 1948- DLB-157

Sowle, Tace
  [publishing house] DLB-170

Soyfer, Jura 1912-1939 .... DLB-124

Soyinka, Wole 1934- ... DLB-125; Y-86, 87

Spacks, Barry 1931- DLB-105

Spalding, Frances 1950- DLB-155

Spark, Muriel 1918- DLB-15, 139

Sparke, Michael
  [publishing house] DLB-170

Sparks, Jared 1789-1866 .... DLB-1, 30

Sparshott, Francis 1926- DLB-60

Späth, Gerold 1939- DLB-75

Spatola, Adriano 1941-1988 .... DLB-128

Spaziani, Maria Luisa 1924- DLB-128

The Spectator 1828- DLB-110

Spedding, James 1808-1881 .... DLB-144

Spee von Langenfeld, Friedrich
  1591-1635 .... DLB-164

Speght, Rachel 1597-after 1630 .... DLB-126

Speke, John Hanning 1827-1864 .... DLB-166

Spellman, A. B. 1935- DLB-41

Spence, Thomas 1750-1814 .... DLB-158

Spencer, Anne 1882-1975 .... DLB-51, 54

Spencer, Elizabeth 1921- DLB-6

Spencer, Herbert 1820-1903 .... DLB-57

Spencer, Scott 1945- Y-86

Spender, J. A. 1862-1942 .... DLB-98

Spender, Stephen 1909- DLB-20

Spener, Philipp Jakob 1635-1705 ....DLB-164

Spenser, Edmund circa 1552-1599 ..DLB-167

Sperr, Martin 1944- DLB-124

Spicer, Jack 1925-1965 ....DLB-5, 16

Spielberg, Peter 1929- Y-81

Spielhagen, Friedrich 1829-1911 ....DLB-129

"*Spielmannsepen*"
  (circa 1152-circa 1500) DLB-148

Spier, Peter 1927- DLB-61

Spinrad, Norman 1940- DLB-8

Spires, Elizabeth 1952- DLB-120

Spitteler, Carl 1845-1924 ....DLB-129

Spivak, Lawrence E. 1900- DLB-137

Spofford, Harriet Prescott
  1835-1921 ....DLB-74

Squibob (see Derby, George Horatio)

Stacpoole, H. de Vere
  1863-1951 ....DLB-153

Staël, Germaine de 1766-1817 ......DLB-119

Staël-Holstein, Anne-Louise Germaine de
  (see Staël, Germaine de)

Stafford, Jean 1915-1979 ....DLB-2, 173

Stafford, William 1914- DLB-5

Stage Censorship: "The Rejected Statement"
  (1911), by Bernard Shaw
  [excerpts] DLB-10

Stallings, Laurence 1894-1968 .....DLB-7, 44

Stallworthy, Jon 1935- DLB-40

Stampp, Kenneth M. 1912- DLB-17

Stanford, Ann 1916- DLB-5

Stanković, Borisav ("Bora")
  1876-1927 ....DLB-147

Stanley, Henry M. 1841-1904 .... DS-13

Stanley, Thomas 1625-1678 ....DLB-131

Stannard, Martin 1947- DLB-155

Stansby, William
  [publishing house] DLB-170

Stanton, Elizabeth Cady 1815-1902 ..DLB-79

Stanton, Frank L. 1857-1927 ....DLB-25

Stanton, Maura 1946- DLB-120

Stapledon, Olaf 1886-1950 ....DLB-15

Star Spangled Banner Office DLB-49

Starkey, Thomas circa 1499-1538 ...DLB-132

Starkweather, David 1935- DLB-7

Statements on the Art of Poetry DLB-54

Stationers' Company of
  London, The DLB-170

Cumulative Index

Stead, Robert J. C. 1880-1959 ...... DLB-92

Steadman, Mark 1930- DLB-6

The Stealthy School of Criticism (1871), by
Dante Gabriel Rossetti DLB-35

Stearns, Harold E. 1891-1943 .... DLB-4

Stedman, Edmund Clarence
1833-1908 .... DLB-64

Steegmuller, Francis 1906-1994 .... DLB-111

Steel, Flora Annie
1847-1929 .... DLB-153, 156

Steele, Max 1922- Y-80

Steele, Richard 1672-1729 ...... DLB-84, 101

Steele, Timothy 1948- DLB-120

Steele, Wilbur Daniel 1886-1970 .... DLB-86

Steere, Richard circa 1643-1721 ..... DLB-24

Stegner, Wallace 1909-1993 .... DLB-9; Y-93

Stehr, Hermann 1864-1940 .... DLB-66

Steig, William 1907- DLB-61

Stieler, Caspar 1632-1707 .... DLB-164

Stein, Gertrude 1874-1946 .... DLB-4, 54, 86

Stein, Leo 1872-1947 ....DLB-4

Stein and Day Publishers DLB-46

Steinbeck, John 1902-1968 ... DLB-7, 9; DS-2

Steiner, George 1929- DLB-67

Stendhal 1783-1842 .... DLB-119

Stephen Crane: A Revaluation Virginia
Tech Conference, 1989 .... Y-89

Stephen, Leslie 1832-1904 ...... DLB-57, 144

Stephens, Alexander H. 1812-1883 .. DLB-47

Stephens, Ann 1810-1886 .... DLB-3, 73

Stephens, Charles Asbury
1844?-1931 .... DLB-42

Stephens, James
1882?-1950 .... DLB-19, 153, 162

Sterling, George 1869-1926 .... DLB-54

Sterling, James 1701-1763 .... DLB-24

Sterling, John 1806-1844 .... DLB-116

Stern, Gerald 1925- DLB-105

Stern, Madeleine B. 1912- ... DLB-111, 140

Stern, Gerald, Living in Ruin DLB-105

Stern, Richard 1928- Y-87

Stern, Stewart 1922- DLB-26

Sterne, Laurence 1713-1768 .... DLB-39

Sternheim, Carl 1878-1942 .... DLB-56, 118

Sternhold, Thomas ?-1549 and
John Hopkins ?-1570 .... DLB-132

Stevens, Henry 1819-1886 .... DLB-140

Stevens, Wallace 1879-1955 .... DLB-54

Stevenson, Anne 1933- DLB-40

Stevenson, Lionel 1902-1973 ...... DLB-155

Stevenson, Robert Louis
1850-1894 ... DLB-18, 57, 141, 156; DS-13

Stewart, Donald Ogden
1894-1980 ....DLB-4, 11, 26

Stewart, Dugald 1753-1828 .... DLB-31

Stewart, George, Jr. 1848-1906 ...... DLB-99

Stewart, George R. 1895-1980 .... DLB-8

Stewart and Kidd Company DLB-46

Stewart, Randall 1896-1964 .... DLB-103

Stickney, Trumbull 1874-1904 .... DLB-54

Stifter, Adalbert 1805-1868 .... DLB-133

Stiles, Ezra 1727-1795 .... DLB-31

Still, James 1906- DLB-9

Stirner, Max 1806-1856 .... DLB-129

Stith, William 1707-1755 .... DLB-31

Stock, Elliot [publishing house] DLB-106

Stockton, Frank R.
1834-1902 .... DLB-42, 74; DS-13

Stoddard, Ashbel
[publishing house] DLB-49

Stoddard, Richard Henry
1825-1903 .... DLB-3, 64; DS-13

Stoddard, Solomon 1643-1729 ...... DLB-24

Stoker, Bram 1847-1912 .... DLB-36, 70

Stokes, Frederick A., Company DLB-49

Stokes, Thomas L. 1898-1958 .... DLB-29

Stokesbury, Leon 1945- DLB-120

Stolberg, Christian Graf zu
1748-1821 .... DLB-94

Stolberg, Friedrich Leopold Graf zu
1750-1819 .... DLB-94

Stone, Herbert S., and Company DLB-49

Stone, Lucy 1818-1893 .... DLB-79

Stone, Melville 1848-1929 .... DLB-25

Stone, Robert 1937- DLB-152

Stone, Ruth 1915- DLB-105

Stone, Samuel 1602-1663 .... DLB-24

Stone and Kimball DLB-49

Stoppard, Tom 1937- DLB-13; Y-85

Storey, Anthony 1928- DLB-14

Storey, David 1933- DLB-13, 14

Storm, Theodor 1817-1888 .... DLB-129

Story, Thomas circa 1670-1742 ..... DLB-31

Story, William Wetmore 1819-1895 ... DLB-1

Storytelling: A Contemporary
Renaissance Y-84

Stoughton, William 1631-1701 ....DLB-24

Stow, John 1525-1605 .... DLB-132

Stowe, Harriet Beecher
1811-1896 .... DLB-1, 12, 42, 74

Stowe, Leland 1899- DLB-29

Stoyanov, Dimitŭr Ivanov (see Elin Pelin)

Strachey, Lytton
1880-1932 .... DLB-149; DS-10

Strachey, Lytton, Preface to *Eminent
Victorians* DLB-149

Strahan and Company DLB-106

Strahan, William
[publishing house] DLB-154

Strand, Mark 1934- DLB-5

The Strasbourg Oaths 842 ....DLB-148

Stratemeyer, Edward 1862-1930 .....DLB-42

Stratton and Barnard DLB-49

Stratton-Porter, Gene 1863-1924 ...... DS-14

Straub, Peter 1943- Y-84

Strauß, Botho 1944- DLB-124

Strauß, David Friedrich
1808-1874 ....DLB-133

The Strawberry Hill Press DLB-154

Streatfeild, Noel 1895-1986 ....DLB-160

Street, Cecil John Charles (see Rhode, John)

Street, G. S. 1867-1936 ....DLB-135

Street and Smith DLB-49

Streeter, Edward 1891-1976 ....DLB-11

Streeter, Thomas Winthrop
1883-1965 ....DLB-140

Stretton, Hesba 1832-1911 ....DLB-163

Stribling, T. S. 1881-1965 ....DLB-9

Der Stricker circa 1190-circa 1250 ...DLB-138

Strickland, Samuel 1804-1867 ....DLB-99

Stringer and Townsend DLB-49

Stringer, Arthur 1874-1950 ....DLB-92

Strittmatter, Erwin 1912- DLB-69

Strode, William 1630-1645 ....DLB-126

Strother, David Hunter 1816-1888 ....DLB-3

Strouse, Jean 1945- DLB-111

Stuart, Dabney 1937- DLB-105

Stuart, Dabney, Knots into Webs: Some Autobiographical Sources DLB-105

Stuart, Jesse
1906-1984 .... DLB-9, 48, 102; Y-84

Stuart, Lyle [publishing house] DLB-46

Stubbs, Harry Clement (see Clement, Hal)

Stubenberg, Johann Wilhelm von
    1619-1663 ....DLB-164

Studio DLB-112

The Study of Poetry (1880), by
    Matthew Arnold DLB-35

Sturgeon, Theodore
    1918-1985 ....DLB-8; Y-85

Sturges, Preston 1898-1959 ....DLB-26

"Style" (1840; revised, 1859), by
    Thomas de Quincey [excerpt] DLB-57

"Style" (1888), by Walter Pater DLB-57

Style (1897), by Walter Raleigh
    [excerpt] DLB-57

"Style" (1877), by T. H. Wright
    [excerpt] DLB-57

"Le Style c'est l'homme" (1892), by
    W. H. Mallock DLB-57

Styron, William 1925- ... DLB-2, 143; Y-80

Suárez, Mario 1925- DLB-82

Such, Peter 1939- DLB-60

Suckling, Sir John 1609-1641? ...DLB-58, 126

Suckow, Ruth 1892-1960 ....DLB-9, 102

Sudermann, Hermann 1857-1928 ...DLB-118

Sue, Eugène 1804-1857 ....DLB-119

Sue, Marie-Joseph (see Sue, Eugène)

Suggs, Simon (see Hooper, Johnson Jones)

Sukenick, Ronald 1932- DLB-173; Y-81

Suknaski, Andrew 1942- DLB-53

Sullivan, Alan 1868-1947 ....DLB-92

Sullivan, C. Gardner 1886-1965 .....DLB-26

Sullivan, Frank 1892-1976 ....DLB-11

Sulte, Benjamin 1841-1923 ....DLB-99

Sulzberger, Arthur Hays
    1891-1968 ....DLB-127

Sulzberger, Arthur Ochs 1926- DLB-127

Sulzer, Johann Georg 1720-1779 .....DLB-97

Sumarokov, Aleksandr Petrovich
    1717-1777 ....DLB-150

Summers, Hollis 1916- DLB-6

Sumner, Henry A.
    [publishing house] DLB-49

Surtees, Robert Smith 1803-1864 ....DLB-21

A Survey of Poetry Anthologies,
    1879-1960 ....DLB-54

Surveys of the Year's Biographies

A Transit of Poets and Others: American
    Biography in 1982 ....Y-82

The Year in Literary Biography ... Y-83–Y-95

Survey of the Year's Book Publishing

The Year in Book Publishing Y-86

Survey of the Year's Children's Books

The Year in Children's Books Y-92–Y-95

Surveys of the Year's Drama

The Year in Drama
    .... Y-82–Y-85, Y-87–Y-95

The Year in London Theatre Y-92

Surveys of the Year's Fiction

The Year's Work in Fiction:
    A Survey Y-82

The Year in Fiction: A Biased View Y-83

The Year in
    Fiction Y-84–Y-86, Y-89, Y-94, Y-95

The Year in the
    Novel Y-87, Y-88, Y-90–Y-93

The Year in Short Stories Y-87

The Year in the
    Short Story Y-88, Y-90–Y-93

Survey of the Year's Literary Theory

The Year in Literary Theory Y-92–Y-93

Surveys of the Year's Poetry

The Year's Work in American
    Poetry Y-82

The Year in Poetry ...Y-83–Y-92, Y-94, Y-95

Sutherland, Efua Theodora
    1924- DLB-117

Sutherland, John 1919-1956 .... DLB-68

Sutro, Alfred 1863-1933 .... DLB-10

Swados, Harvey 1920-1972 .... DLB-2

Swain, Charles 1801-1874 .... DLB-32

Swallow Press DLB-46

Swan Sonnenschein Limited DLB-106

Swanberg, W. A. 1907- DLB-103

Swenson, May 1919-1989 .... DLB-5

Swerling, Jo 1897- DLB-44

Swift, Jonathan
    1667-1745 ....DLB-39, 95, 101

Swinburne, A. C. 1837-1909 ..... DLB-35, 57

Swineshead, Richard floruit
    circa 1350 .... DLB-115

Swinnerton, Frank 1884-1982 .... DLB-34

Swisshelm, Jane Grey 1815-1884 .... DLB-43

Swope, Herbert Bayard 1882-1958 .. DLB-25

Swords, T. and J., and Company DLB-49

Swords, Thomas 1763-1843 and
    Swords, James ?-1844 .... DLB-73

Sylvester, Josuah
    1562 or 1563 - 1618 ....DLB-121

Symonds, Emily Morse (see Paston, George)

Symonds, John Addington
    1840-1893 ....DLB-57, 144

Symons, A. J. A. 1900-1941 .... DLB-149

Symons, Arthur
    1865-1945 .... DLB-19, 57, 149

Symons, Julian
    1912-1994 .... DLB-87, 155; Y-92

Symons, Scott 1933- DLB-53

A Symposium on *The Columbia History of
    the Novel* Y-92

Synge, John Millington
    1871-1909 ....DLB-10, 19

Synge Summer School: J. M. Synge and the
    Irish Theater, Rathdrum, County Wiclow,
    Ireland Y-93

Syrett, Netta 1865-1943 ....DLB-135

T

Taban lo Liyong 1939?- DLB-125

Taché, Joseph-Charles 1820-1894 ....DLB-99

Tafolla, Carmen 1951- DLB-82

Taggard, Genevieve 1894-1948 ......DLB-45

Tagger, Theodor (see Bruckner, Ferdinand)

Tait, J. Selwin, and Sons DLB-49

Tait's Edinburgh Magazine
    1832-1861 ....DLB-110

The Takarazaka Revue Company Y-91

Talander (see Bohse, August)

Tallent, Elizabeth 1954- DLB-130

Talvj 1797-1870 ....DLB-59, 133

Tan, Amy 1952- DLB-173

Taradash, Daniel 1913- DLB-44

Tarbell, Ida M. 1857-1944 ....DLB-47

Tardivel, Jules-Paul 1851-1905 ......DLB-99

Targan, Barry 1932- DLB-130

Tarkington, Booth 1869-1946 ....DLB-9, 102

Tashlin, Frank 1913-1972 ....DLB-44

Tate, Allen 1899-1979 ....DLB-4, 45, 63

Tate, James 1943- DLB-5, 169

Tate, Nahum circa 1652-1715 ....DLB-80

Tatian circa 830 ....DLB-148

Tavčar, Ivan 1851-1923 ....DLB-147

Taylor, Ann 1782-1866 ....DLB-163

Taylor, Bayard 1825-1878 .... DLB-3

Cumulative Index

Taylor, Bert Leston 1866-1921 ..... DLB-25

Taylor, Charles H. 1846-1921 ...... DLB-25

Taylor, Edward circa 1642-1729 .... DLB-24

Taylor, Elizabeth 1912-1975 .... DLB-139

Taylor, Henry 1942- DLB-5

Taylor, Sir Henry 1800-1886 .... DLB-32

Taylor, Jane 1783-1824 .... DLB-163

Taylor, Jeremy circa 1613-1667 .... DLB-151

Taylor, John 1577 or 1578 - 1653 .... DLB-121

Taylor, Mildred D. ?- DLB-52

Taylor, Peter 1917-1994 .... Y-81, Y-94

Taylor, William, and Company DLB-49

Taylor-Made Shakespeare? Or Is "Shall I Die?" the Long-Lost Text of Bottom's Dream? Y-85

Teasdale, Sara 1884-1933 .... DLB-45

The Tea-Table (1725), by Eliza Haywood [excerpt] DLB-39

Telles, Lygia Fagundes 1924- DLB-113

Temple, Sir William 1628-1699 .... DLB-101

Tenn, William 1919- DLB-8

Tennant, Emma 1937- DLB-14

Tenney, Tabitha Gilman 1762-1837 .... DLB-37

Tennyson, Alfred 1809-1892 .... DLB-32

Tennyson, Frederick 1807-1898 ..... DLB-32

Terhune, Albert Payson 1872-1942 ....DLB-9

Terhune, Mary Virginia 1830-1922 .... DS-13

Terry, Megan 1932- DLB-7

Terson, Peter 1932- DLB-13

Tesich, Steve 1943- Y-83

Tessa, Delio 1886-1939 .... DLB-114

Testori, Giovanni 1923-1993 ...... DLB-128

Tey, Josephine 1896?-1952 .... DLB-77

Thacher, James 1754-1844 .... DLB-37

Thackeray, William Makepeace 1811-1863 .... DLB-21, 55, 159, 163

Thames and Hudson Limited DLB-112

Thanet, Octave (see French, Alice)

The Theater in Shakespeare's Time DLB-62

The Theatre Guild DLB-7

Thegan and the Astronomer flourished circa 850 .... DLB-148

Thelwall, John 1764-1834 ..... DLB-93, 158

Theodulf circa 760-circa 821 ..... DLB-148

Theriault, Yves 1915-1983 .... DLB-88

Thério, Adrien 1925- DLB-53

Theroux, Paul 1941- DLB-2

Thibaudeau, Colleen 1925- DLB-88

Thielen, Benedict 1903-1965 .... DLB-102

Thiong'o Ngugi wa (see Ngugi wa Thiong'o)

Third-Generation Minor Poets of the Seventeenth Century DLB-131

Thoma, Ludwig 1867-1921 .... DLB-66

Thoma, Richard 1902- DLB-4

Thomas, Audrey 1935- DLB-60

Thomas, D. M. 1935- DLB-40

Thomas, Dylan 1914-1953 .... DLB-13, 20, 139

Thomas, Edward 1878-1917 .... DLB-19, 98, 156

Thomas, Gwyn 1913-1981 .... DLB-15

Thomas, Isaiah 1750-1831 .... DLB-43, 73

Thomas, Isaiah [publishing house] ... DLB-49

Thomas, Johann 1624-1679 .... DLB-168

Thomas, John 1900-1932 .... DLB-4

Thomas, Joyce Carol 1938- DLB-33

Thomas, Lorenzo 1944- DLB-41

Thomas, R. S. 1915- DLB-27

Thomasîn von Zerclære circa 1186-circa 1259 .... DLB-138

Thomasius, Christian 1655-1728 ... DLB-168

Thompson, David 1770-1857 .... DLB-99

Thompson, Dorothy 1893-1961 ..... DLB-29

Thompson, Francis 1859-1907 ..... DLB-19

Thompson, George Selden (see Selden, George)

Thompson, John 1938-1976 .... DLB-60

Thompson, John R. 1823-1873 .... DLB-3, 73

Thompson, Lawrance 1906-1973 ... DLB-103

Thompson, Maurice 1844-1901 .... DLB-71, 74

Thompson, Ruth Plumly 1891-1976 .... DLB-22

Thompson, Thomas Phillips 1843-1933 .... DLB-99

Thompson, William 1775-1833 .... DLB-158

Thompson, William Tappan 1812-1882 .... DLB-3, 11

Thomson, Edward William 1849-1924 .... DLB-92

Thomson, James 1700-1748 .... DLB-95

Thomson, James 1834-1882 ..... DLB-35

DLB 173

Thomson, Mortimer 1831-1875 ......DLB-11

Thoreau, Henry David 1817-1862 .....DLB-1

Thorpe, Thomas Bangs 1815-1878 .... DLB-3, 11

Thoughts on Poetry and Its Varieties (1833), by John Stuart Mill DLB-32

Thrale, Hester Lynch (see Piozzi, Hester Lynch [Thrale])

Thümmel, Moritz August von 1738-1817 .... DLB-97

Thurber, James 1894-1961 .... DLB-4, 11, 22, 102

Thurman, Wallace 1902-1934 .... DLB-51

Thwaite, Anthony 1930- DLB-40

Thwaites, Reuben Gold 1853-1913 .... DLB-47

Ticknor, George 1791-1871 .... DLB-1, 59, 140

Ticknor and Fields DLB-49

Ticknor and Fields (revived) DLB-46

Tieck, Ludwig 1773-1853 .... DLB-90

Tietjens, Eunice 1884-1944 .... DLB-54

Tilney, Edmund circa 1536-1610 .... DLB-136

Tilt, Charles [publishing house] DLB-106

Tilton, J. E., and Company DLB-49

Time and Western Man (1927), by Wyndham Lewis [excerpts] DLB-36

Time-Life Books DLB-46

Times Books DLB-46

Timothy, Peter circa 1725-1782 ......DLB-43

Timrod, Henry 1828-1867 .... DLB-3

Tinker, Chauncey Brewster 1876-1963 ....DLB-140

Tinsley Brothers DLB-106

Tiptree, James, Jr. 1915-1987 ....DLB-8

Titus, Edward William 1870-1952 ....DLB-4

Tlali, Miriam 1933- DLB-157

Todd, Barbara Euphan 1890-1976 ....DLB-160

Tofte, Robert 1561 or 1562-1619 or 1620 .....DLB-172

Toklas, Alice B. 1877-1967 ....DLB-4

Tolkien, J. R. R. 1892-1973 .... DLB-15, 160

Toller, Ernst 1893-1939 ....DLB-124

Tollet, Elizabeth 1694-1754 ....DLB-95

Tolson, Melvin B. 1898-1966 .... DLB-48, 76

Tom Jones (1749), by Henry Fielding [excerpt] DLB-39

Tomalin, Claire 1933- DLB-155

372

Tomlinson, Charles 1927- DLB-40	Trediakovsky, Vasilii Kirillovich 1703-1769 .... DLB-150	Tucker, St. George 1752-1827 .... DLB-37
Tomlinson, H. M. 1873-1958 ...DLB-36, 100	Treece, Henry 1911-1966 .... DLB-160	Tuckerman, Henry Theodore 1813-1871 .... DLB-64
Tompkins, Abel [publishing house] ..DLB-49	Trejo, Ernesto 1950- DLB-122	Tunis, John R. 1889-1975 ......DLB-22, 171
Tompson, Benjamin 1642-1714 ......DLB-24	Trelawny, Edward John 1792-1881 .... DLB-110, 116, 144	Tunstall, Cuthbert 1474-1559 ..... DLB-132
Tonks, Rosemary 1932- DLB-14	Tremain, Rose 1943- DLB-14	Tuohy, Frank 1925- DLB-14, 139
Tonna, Charlotte Elizabeth 1790-1846 ....DLB-163	Tremblay, Michel 1942- DLB-60	Tupper, Martin F. 1810-1889 .... DLB-32
Tonson, Jacob the Elder [publishing house] DLB-170	Trends in Twentieth-Century Mass Market Publishing DLB-46	Turbyfill, Mark 1896- DLB-45
Toole, John Kennedy 1937-1969 ....Y-81	Trent, William P. 1862-1939 .... DLB-47	Turco, Lewis 1934- Y-84
Toomer, Jean 1894-1967 ....DLB-45, 51	Trescot, William Henry 1822-1898 .... DLB-30	Turnbull, Andrew 1921-1970 ...... DLB-103
Tor Books DLB-46	Trevelyan, Sir George Otto 1838-1928 .... DLB-144	Turnbull, Gael 1928- DLB-40
Torberg, Friedrich 1908-1979 ....DLB-85	Trevisa, John circa 1342-circa 1402 .... DLB-146	Turner, Arlin 1909-1980 .... DLB-103
Torrence, Ridgely 1874-1950 ....DLB-54	Trevor, William 1928- DLB-14, 139	Turner, Charles (Tennyson) 1808-1879 .... DLB-32
Torres-Metzger, Joseph V. 1933- DLB-122	*Trierer Floyris* circa 1170-1180 ...... DLB-138	Turner, Frederick 1943- DLB-40
Toth, Susan Allen 1940- Y-86	Trilling, Lionel 1905-1975 ...... DLB-28, 63	Turner, Frederick Jackson 1861-1932 .... DLB-17
Tottell, Richard [publishing house] DLB-170	Trilussa 1871-1950 .... DLB-114	Turner, Joseph Addison 1826-1868 .... DLB-79
Tough-Guy Literature DLB-9	Trimmer, Sarah 1741-1810 .... DLB-158	Turpin, Waters Edward 1910-1968 .... DLB-51
Touré, Askia Muhammad 1938- ...DLB-41	Triolet, Elsa 1896-1970 .... DLB-72	Turrini, Peter 1944- DLB-124
Tourgée, Albion W. 1838-1905 ......DLB-79	Tripp, John 1927- DLB-40	Tutuola, Amos 1920- DLB-125
Tourneur, Cyril circa 1580-1626 .....DLB-58	Trocchi, Alexander 1925- DLB-15	Twain, Mark (see Clemens, Samuel Langhorne)
Tournier, Michel 1924- DLB-83	Trollope, Anthony 1815-1882 ....DLB-21, 57, 159	The 'Twenties and Berlin, by Alex Natan DLB-66
Tousey, Frank [publishing house] DLB-49	Trollope, Frances 1779-1863 ... DLB-21, 166	Tyler, Anne 1941- DLB-6, 143; Y-82
Tower Publications DLB-46	Troop, Elizabeth 1931- DLB-14	Tyler, Moses Coit 1835-1900 ....DLB-47, 64
Towne, Benjamin circa 1740-1793 ...DLB-43	Trotter, Catharine 1679-1749 .... DLB-84	Tyler, Royall 1757-1826 .... DLB-37
Towne, Robert 1936- DLB-44	Trotti, Lamar 1898-1952 .... DLB-44	Tylor, Edward Burnett 1832-1917 ...DLB-57
The Townely Plays fifteenth and sixteenth centuries....................DLB-146	Trottier, Pierre 1925- DLB-60	Tynan, Katharine 1861-1931 .... DLB-153
Townshend, Aurelian by 1583 - circa 1651 ....DLB-121	Troupe, Quincy Thomas, Jr. 1943- DLB-41	Tyndale, William circa 1494-1536 .... DLB-132
Tracy, Honor 1913- DLB-15	Trow, John F., and Company DLB-49	
Traherne, Thomas 1637?-1674 .....DLB-131	Truillier-Lacombe, Joseph-Patrice 1807-1863 .... DLB-99	# U
Traill, Catharine Parr 1802-1899 ....DLB-99	Trumbo, Dalton 1905-1976 .... DLB-26	Udall, Nicholas 1504-1556 .... DLB-62
Train, Arthur 1875-1945 ....DLB-86	Trumbull, Benjamin 1735-1820 ..... DLB-30	Uhland, Ludwig 1787-1862 ....DLB-90
The Transatlantic Publishing Company DLB-49	Trumbull, John 1750-1831 .... DLB-31	Uhse, Bodo 1904-1963 .... DLB-69
Transcendentalists, American DS-5	Tscherning, Andreas 1611-1659 .... DLB-164	Ujević, Augustin ("Tin") 1891-1955 .... DLB-147
Translators of the Twelfth Century: Literary Issues Raised and Impact Created DLB-115	T. S. Eliot Centennial Y-88	Ulenhart, Niclas flourished circa 1600 .... DLB-164
Travel Writing, 1837-1875 ....DLB-166	Tucholsky, Kurt 1890-1935 .... DLB-56	Ulibarrí, Sabine R. 1919- DLB-82
Traven, B. 1882? or 1890?-1969? DLB-9, 56	Tucker, Charlotte Maria 1821-1893 .... DLB-163	Ulica, Jorge 1870-1926 .... DLB-82
Travers, Ben 1886-1980 ....DLB-10	Tucker, George 1775-1861 ..... DLB-3, 30	Ulizio, B. George 1889-1969 .... DLB-140
Travers, P. L. (Pamela Lyndon) 1899- DLB-160	Tucker, Nathaniel Beverley 1784-1851 .... DLB-3	Ulrich von Liechtenstein circa 1200-circa 1275 .... DLB-138

Cumulative Index

Ulrich von Zatzikhoven before 1194-after 1214 .... DLB-138

Unamuno, Miguel de 1864-1936 ... DLB-108

Under the Microscope (1872), by A. C. Swinburne DLB-35

Unger, Friederike Helene 1741-1813 .... DLB-94

Ungaretti, Giuseppe 1888-1970 .... DLB-114

United States Book Company DLB-49

Universal Publishing and Distributing Corporation DLB-46

The University of Iowa Writers' Workshop Golden Jubilee Y-86

The University of South Carolina Press Y-94

University of Wales Press DLB-112

"The Unknown Public" (1858), by Wilkie Collins [excerpt] DLB-57

Unruh, Fritz von 1885-1970 .... DLB-56, 118

Unspeakable Practices II: The Festival of Vanguard Narrative at Brown University Y-93

Unwin, T. Fisher [publishing house] DLB-106

Upchurch, Boyd B. (see Boyd, John)

Updike, John 1932- ... DLB-2, 5, 143; Y-80, 82; DS-3

Upton, Bertha 1849-1912 .... DLB-141

Upton, Charles 1948- DLB-16

Upton, Florence K. 1873-1922 ..... DLB-141

Upward, Allen 1863-1926 .... DLB-36

Urista, Alberto Baltazar (see Alurista)

Urzidil, Johannes 1896-1976 .... DLB-85

Urquhart, Fred 1912- DLB-139

The Uses of Facsimile Y-90

Usk, Thomas died 1388 .... DLB-146

Uslar Pietri, Arturo 1906- DLB-113

Ustinov, Peter 1921- DLB-13

Uttley, Alison 1884-1976 .... DLB-160

Uz, Johann Peter 1720-1796 .... DLB-97

V

Vac, Bertrand 1914- DLB-88

Vail, Laurence 1891-1968 ....DLB-4

Vailland, Roger 1907-1965 .... DLB-83

Vajda, Ernest 1887-1954 .... DLB-44

Valdés, Gina 1943- DLB-122

Valdez, Luis Miguel 1940- DLB-122

Valduga, Patrizia 1953- DLB-128

Valente, José Angel 1929- DLB-108

Valenzuela, Luisa 1938- DLB-113

Valeri, Diego 1887-1976 .... DLB-128

Valgardson, W. D. 1939- DLB-60

Valle, Víctor Manuel 1950- DLB-122

Valle-Inclán, Ramón del 1866-1936 .... DLB-134

Vallejo, Armando 1949- DLB-122

Vallès, Jules 1832-1885 .... DLB-123

Vallette, Marguerite Eymery (see Rachilde)

Valverde, José María 1926- DLB-108

Van Allsburg, Chris 1949- DLB-61

Van Anda, Carr 1864-1945 .... DLB-25

Van Doren, Mark 1894-1972 .... DLB-45

van Druten, John 1901-1957 .... DLB-10

Van Duyn, Mona 1921- DLB-5

Van Dyke, Henry 1852-1933 .... DLB-71; DS-13

Van Dyke, Henry 1928- DLB-33

van Itallie, Jean-Claude 1936- DLB-7

Van Loan, Charles E. 1876-1919 ... DLB-171

Van Rensselaer, Mariana Griswold 1851-1934 .... DLB-47

Van Rensselaer, Mrs. Schuyler (see Van Rensselaer, Mariana Griswold)

Van Vechten, Carl 1880-1964 ...... DLB-4, 9

van Vogt, A. E. 1912- DLB-8

Vanbrugh, Sir John 1664-1726 ...... DLB-80

Vance, Jack 1916?- DLB-8

Vane, Sutton 1888-1963 .... DLB-10

Vanguard Press DLB-46

Vann, Robert L. 1879-1940 .... DLB-29

Vargas, Llosa, Mario 1936- DLB-145

Varley, John 1947- Y-81

Varnhagen von Ense, Karl August 1785-1858 .... DLB-90

Varnhagen von Ense, Rahel 1771-1833 .... DLB-90

Vásquez Montalbán, Manuel 1939- DLB-134

Vassa, Gustavus (see Equiano, Olaudah)

Vassalli, Sebastiano 1941- DLB-128

Vaughan, Henry 1621-1695 .... DLB-131

Vaughan, Thomas 1621-1666 ..... DLB-131

Vaux, Thomas, Lord 1509-1556 ... DLB-132

Vazov, Ivan 1850-1921 .... DLB-147

Vega, Janine Pommy 1942- DLB-16

Veiller, Anthony 1903-1965 ....DLB-44

Velásquez-Trevino, Gloria 1949- DLB-122

Veloz Maggiolo, Marcio 1936- DLB-145

Venegas, Daniel ?-? DLB-82

Vergil, Polydore circa 1470-1555 ....DLB-132

Veríssimo, Erico 1905-1975 .... DLB-145

Verne, Jules 1828-1905 .... DLB-123

Verplanck, Gulian C. 1786-1870 .....DLB-59

Very, Jones 1813-1880 .... DLB-1

Vian, Boris 1920-1959 .... DLB-72

Vickers, Roy 1888?-1965 .... DLB-77

Victoria 1819-1901 .... DLB-55

Victoria Press DLB-106

Vidal, Gore 1925- DLB-6, 152

Viebig, Clara 1860-1952 .... DLB-66

Viereck, George Sylvester 1884-1962 .... DLB-54

Viereck, Peter 1916- DLB-5

Viets, Roger 1738-1811 .... DLB-99

Viewpoint: Politics and Performance, by David Edgar DLB-13

Vigil-Piñon, Evangelina 1949- DLB-122

Vigneault, Gilles 1928- DLB-60

Vigny, Alfred de 1797-1863 .... DLB-119

Vigolo, Giorgio 1894-1983 .... DLB-114

The Viking Press DLB-46

Villanueva, Alma Luz 1944- DLB-122

Villanueva, Tino 1941- DLB-82

Villard, Henry 1835-1900 .... DLB-23

Villard, Oswald Garrison 1872-1949 .... DLB-25, 91

Villarreal, José Antonio 1924- DLB-82

Villegas de Magnón, Leonor 1876-1955 .... DLB-122

Villemaire, Yolande 1949- DLB-60

Villena, Luis Antonio de 1951- DLB-134

Villiers de l'Isle-Adam, Jean-Marie Mathias Philippe-Auguste, Comte de 1838-1889 .... DLB-123

Villiers, George, Second Duke of Buckingham 1628-1687 .... DLB-80

Vine Press DLB-112

Viorst, Judith ?- DLB-52

Vipont, Elfrida (Elfrida Vipont Foulds, Charles Vipont) 1902-1992 ..... DLB-160

Viramontes, Helena María 1954- DLB-122

Vischer, Friedrich Theodor 1807-1887 .....DLB-133

Vivanco, Luis Felipe 1907-1975 ....DLB-108

Viviani, Cesare 1947- DLB-128

Vizetelly and Company DLB-106

Voaden, Herman 1903- DLB-88

Voigt, Ellen Bryant 1943- DLB-120

Vojnović, Ivo 1857-1929 .....DLB-147

Volkoff, Vladimir 1932- DLB-83

Volland, P. F., Company DLB-46

von der Grün, Max 1926- DLB-75

Vonnegut, Kurt 1922- DLB-2, 8, 152; Y-80; DS-3

Voranc, Prežihov 1893-1950 .....DLB-147

Voß, Johann Heinrich 1751-1826 ....DLB-90

Vroman, Mary Elizabeth circa 1924-1967 .....DLB-33

W

Wace, Robert ("Maistre") circa 1100-circa 1175 .....DLB-146

Wackenroder, Wilhelm Heinrich 1773-1798 .....DLB-90

Wackernagel, Wilhelm 1806-1869 .....DLB-133

Waddington, Miriam 1917- DLB-68

Wade, Henry 1887-1969 .....DLB-77

Wagenknecht, Edward 1900- DLB-103

Wagner, Heinrich Leopold 1747-1779 .....DLB-94

Wagner, Henry R. 1862-1957 .....DLB-140

Wagner, Richard 1813-1883 .....DLB-129

Wagoner, David 1926- DLB-5

Wah, Fred 1939- DLB-60

Waiblinger, Wilhelm 1804-1830 .....DLB-90

Wain, John 1925-1994 .....DLB-15, 27, 139, 155

Wainwright, Jeffrey 1944- DLB-40

Waite, Peirce and Company DLB-49

Wakoski, Diane 1937- DLB-5

Walahfrid Strabo circa 808-849 .....DLB-148

Walck, Henry Z. DLB-46

Walcott, Derek 1930- DLB-117; Y-81, 92

Waldegrave, Robert [publishing house] DLB-170

Waldman, Anne 1945- DLB-16

Waldrop, Rosmarie 1935- DLB-169

Walker, Alice 1944- DLB-6, 33, 143

Walker, George F. 1947- DLB-60

Walker, Joseph A. 1935- DLB-38

Walker, Margaret 1915- DLB-76, 152

Walker, Ted 1934- DLB-40

Walker and Company DLB-49

Walker, Evans and Cogswell Company DLB-49

Walker, John Brisben 1847-1931 ....DLB-79

Wallace, Dewitt 1889-1981 and Lila Acheson Wallace 1889-1984 .....DLB-137

Wallace, Edgar 1875-1932 .....DLB-70

Wallace, Lila Acheson (see Wallace, Dewitt, and Lila Acheson Wallace)

Wallant, Edward Lewis 1926-1962 .....DLB-2, 28, 143

Waller, Edmund 1606-1687 .....DLB-126

Walpole, Horace 1717-1797 ....DLB-39, 104

Walpole, Hugh 1884-1941 .....DLB-34

Walrond, Eric 1898-1966 .....DLB-51

Walser, Martin 1927- DLB-75, 124

Walser, Robert 1878-1956 .....DLB-66

Walsh, Ernest 1895-1926 .....DLB-4, 45

Walsh, Robert 1784-1859 .....DLB-59

Waltharius circa 825 .....DLB-148

Walters, Henry 1848-1931 .....DLB-140

Walther von der Vogelweide circa 1170-circa 1230 .....DLB-138

Walton, Izaak 1593-1683 .....DLB-151

Wambaugh, Joseph 1937- DLB-6; Y-83

Waniek, Marilyn Nelson 1946- ...DLB-120

Warburton, William 1698-1779 ....DLB-104

Ward, Aileen 1919- DLB-111

Ward, Artemus (see Browne, Charles Farrar)

Ward, Arthur Henry Sarsfield (see Rohmer, Sax)

Ward, Douglas Turner 1930- ...DLB-7, 38

Ward, Lynd 1905-1985 .....DLB-22

Ward, Lock and Company DLB-106

Ward, Mrs. Humphry 1851-1920 ...DLB-18

Ward, Nathaniel circa 1578-1652 ....DLB-24

Ward, Theodore 1902-1983 .....DLB-76

Wardle, Ralph 1909-1988 .....DLB-103

Ware, William 1797-1852 .....DLB-1

Warne, Frederick, and Company [U.S.] DLB-49

Warne, Frederick, and Company [U.K.] DLB-106

Warner, Charles Dudley 1829-1900 .....DLB-64

Warner, Rex 1905- DLB-15

Warner, Susan Bogert 1819-1885 .....DLB-3, 42

Warner, Sylvia Townsend 1893-1978 .....DLB-34, 139

Warner, William 1558-1609 .....DLB-172

Warner Books DLB-46

Warr, Bertram 1917-1943 .....DLB-88

Warren, John Byrne Leicester (see De Tabley, Lord)

Warren, Lella 1899-1982 .....Y-83

Warren, Mercy Otis 1728-1814 .....DLB-31

Warren, Robert Penn 1905-1989 .....DLB-2, 48, 152; Y-80, 89

Die Wartburgkrieg circa 1230-circa 1280 .....DLB-138

Warton, Joseph 1722-1800 .....DLB-104, 109

Warton, Thomas 1728-1790 ...DLB-104, 109

Washington, George 1732-1799 .....DLB-31

Wassermann, Jakob 1873-1934 .....DLB-66

Wasson, David Atwood 1823-1887 ...DLB-1

Waterhouse, Keith 1929- DLB-13, 15

Waterman, Andrew 1940- DLB-40

Waters, Frank 1902- Y-86

Waters, Michael 1949- DLB-120

Watkins, Tobias 1780-1855 .....DLB-73

Watkins, Vernon 1906-1967 .....DLB-20

Watmough, David 1926- DLB-53

Watson, James Wreford (see Wreford, James)

Watson, John 1850-1907 .....DLB-156

Watson, Sheila 1909- DLB-60

Watson, Thomas 1545?-1592 .....DLB-132

Watson, Wilfred 1911- DLB-60

Watt, W. J., and Company DLB-46

Watterson, Henry 1840-1921 .....DLB-25

Watts, Alan 1915-1973 .....DLB-16

Watts, Franklin [publishing house] ...DLB-46

Watts, Isaac 1674-1748 .....DLB-95

Waugh, Auberon 1939- DLB-14

Waugh, Evelyn 1903-1966 .....DLB-15, 162

Way and Williams DLB-49

375

Wayman, Tom 1945- DLB-53

Weatherly, Tom 1942- DLB-41

Weaver, Gordon 1937- DLB-130

Weaver, Robert 1921- DLB-88

Webb, Frank J. ?-? DLB-50

Webb, James Watson 1802-1884 .... DLB-43

Webb, Mary 1881-1927 .... DLB-34

Webb, Phyllis 1927- DLB-53

Webb, Walter Prescott 1888-1963 ... DLB-17

Webbe, William ?-1591 .... DLB-132

Webster, Augusta 1837-1894 ...... DLB-35

Webster, Charles L., and Company DLB-49

Webster, John 1579 or 1580-1634? DLB-58

Webster, Noah 1758-1843 ....DLB-1, 37, 42, 43, 73

Weckherlin, Georg Rodolf 1584-1653 .... DLB-164

Wedekind, Frank 1864-1918 ...... DLB-118

Weeks, Edward Augustus, Jr. 1898-1989 .... DLB-137

Weems, Mason Locke 1759-1825 .... DLB-30, 37, 42

Weerth, Georg 1822-1856 .... DLB-129

Weidenfeld and Nicolson DLB-112

Weidman, Jerome 1913- DLB-28

Weigl, Bruce 1949- DLB-120

Weinbaum, Stanley Grauman 1902-1935 ....DLB-8

Weintraub, Stanley 1929- DLB-111

Weise, Christian 1642-1708 .... DLB-168

Weisenborn, Gunther 1902-1969 .... DLB-69, 124

Weiß, Ernst 1882-1940 .... DLB-81

Weiss, John 1818-1879 ....DLB-1

Weiss, Peter 1916-1982 .... DLB-69, 124

Weiss, Theodore 1916- DLB-5

Weisse, Christian Felix 1726-1804 ... DLB-97

Weitling, Wilhelm 1808-1871 ..... DLB-129

Welch, Lew 1926-1971? DLB-16

Weldon, Fay 1931- DLB-14

Wellek, René 1903- DLB-63

Wells, Carolyn 1862-1942 .... DLB-11

Wells, Charles Jeremiah circa 1800-1879 .... DLB-32

Wells, Gabriel 1862-1946 .... DLB-140

Wells, H. G. 1866-1946 .....DLB-34, 70, 156

Wells, Robert 1947- DLB-40

Wells-Barnett, Ida B. 1862-1931 ..... DLB-23

Welty, Eudora 1909- DLB-2, 102, 143; Y-87; DS-12

Wendell, Barrett 1855-1921 .... DLB-71

Wentworth, Patricia 1878-1961 ..... DLB-77

Werder, Diederich von dem 1584-1657 .... DLB-164

Werfel, Franz 1890-1945 ....DLB-81, 124

The Werner Company DLB-49

Werner, Zacharias 1768-1823 ...... DLB-94

Wersba, Barbara 1932- DLB-52

Wescott, Glenway 1901- DLB-4, 9, 102

Wesker, Arnold 1932- DLB-13

Wesley, Charles 1707-1788 .... DLB-95

Wesley, John 1703-1791 .... DLB-104

Wesley, Richard 1945- DLB-38

Wessels, A., and Company DLB-46

Wessobrunner Gebet circa 787-815 .... DLB-148

West, Anthony 1914-1988 .... DLB-15

West, Dorothy 1907- DLB-76

West, Jessamyn 1902-1984 ..... DLB-6; Y-84

West, Mae 1892-1980 .... DLB-44

West, Nathanael 1903-1940 .....DLB-4, 9, 28

West, Paul 1930- DLB-14

West, Rebecca 1892-1983 ..... DLB-36; Y-83

West and Johnson DLB-49

Western Publishing Company DLB-46

The Westminster Review 1824-1914 ... DLB-110

Weston, Elizabeth Jane circa 1582-1612 .... DLB-172

Wetherald, Agnes Ethelwyn 1857-1940 .... DLB-99

Wetherell, Elizabeth (see Warner, Susan Bogert)

Wetzel, Friedrich Gottlob 1779-1819 .... DLB-90

Weyman, Stanley J. 1855-1928 ....DLB-141, 156

Wezel, Johann Karl 1747-1819 ...... DLB-94

Whalen, Philip 1923- DLB-16

Whalley, George 1915-1983 .... DLB-88

Wharton, Edith 1862-1937 ...... DLB-4, 9, 12, 78; DS-13

Wharton, William 1920s?- Y-80

Whately, Mary Louisa 1824-1889 ....DLB-166

What's Really Wrong With Bestseller Lists Y-84

Wheatley, Dennis Yates 1897-1977 ....DLB-77

Wheatley, Phillis circa 1754-1784 .... DLB-31, 50

Wheeler, Anna Doyle 1785-1848? DLB-158

Wheeler, Charles Stearns 1816-1843 ....DLB-1

Wheeler, Monroe 1900-1988 ....DLB-4

Wheelock, John Hall 1886-1978 .....DLB-45

Wheelwright, John circa 1592-1679 ....DLB-24

Wheelwright, J. B. 1897-1940 ....DLB-45

Whetstone, Colonel Pete (see Noland, C. F. M.)

Whetstone, George 1550-1587 ......DLB-136

Whicher, Stephen E. 1915-1961 .....DLB-111

Whipple, Edwin Percy 1819-1886 .... DLB-1, 64

Whitaker, Alexander 1585-1617 .....DLB-24

Whitaker, Daniel K. 1801-1881 ......DLB-73

Whitcher, Frances Miriam 1814-1852 ....DLB-11

White, Andrew 1579-1656 ....DLB-24

White, Andrew Dickson 1832-1918 ....DLB-47

White, E. B. 1899-1985 .... DLB-11, 22

White, Edgar B. 1947- DLB-38

White, Ethel Lina 1887-1944 ....DLB-77

White, Henry Kirke 1785-1806 ......DLB-96

White, Horace 1834-1916 ....DLB-23

White, Phyllis Dorothy James (see James, P. D.)

White, Richard Grant 1821-1885 ....DLB-64

White, T. H. 1906-1964 ....DLB-160

White, Walter 1893-1955 ....DLB-51

White, William, and Company DLB-49

White, William Allen 1868-1944 .... DLB-9, 25

White, William Anthony Parker (see Boucher, Anthony)

White, William Hale (see Rutherford, Mark)

Whitechurch, Victor L. 1868-1933 ....DLB-70

Whitehead, Alfred North 1861-1947 ....DLB-100

Whitehead, James 1936- Y-81

Whitehead, William
1715-1785 ....DLB-84, 109

Whitfield, James Monroe
1822-1871 ....DLB-50

Whitgift, John circa 1533-1604 .....DLB-132

Whiting, John 1917-1963 ....DLB-13

Whiting, Samuel 1597-1679 ....DLB-24

Whitlock, Brand 1869-1934 ....DLB-12

Whitman, Albert, and Company DLB-46

Whitman, Albery Allson
1851-1901 ....DLB-50

Whitman, Alden 1913-1990 ....Y-91

Whitman, Sarah Helen (Power)
1803-1878 ....DLB-1

Whitman, Walt 1819-1892 ....DLB-3, 64

Whitman Publishing Company DLB-46

Whitney, Geoffrey
1548 or 1552?-1601 ....DLB-136

Whitney, Isabella
flourished 1566-1573 ....DLB-136

Whitney, John Hay 1904-1982 .....DLB-127

Whittemore, Reed 1919- DLB-5

Whittier, John Greenleaf 1807-1892 ...DLB-1

Whittlesey House DLB-46

Who Runs American Literature? Y-94

Wideman, John Edgar 1941- ...DLB-33, 143

Widener, Harry Elkins 1885-1912 ...DLB-140

Wiebe, Rudy 1934- DLB-60

Wiechert, Ernst 1887-1950 ....DLB-56

Wied, Martina 1882-1957 ....DLB-85

Wieland, Christoph Martin
1733-1813 ....DLB-97

Wienbarg, Ludolf 1802-1872 ....DLB-133

Wieners, John 1934- DLB-16

Wier, Ester 1910- DLB-52

Wiesel, Elie 1928- DLB-83; Y-87

Wiggin, Kate Douglas 1856-1923 ....DLB-42

Wigglesworth, Michael 1631-1705 ...DLB-24

Wilberforce, William 1759-1833 ....DLB-158

Wilbrandt, Adolf 1837-1911 ....DLB-129

Wilbur, Richard 1921- DLB-5, 169

Wild, Peter 1940- DLB-5

Wilde, Oscar
1854-1900 ....DLB-10, 19, 34, 57, 141, 156

Wilde, Richard Henry
1789-1847 ....DLB-3, 59

Wilde, W. A., Company DLB-49

Wilder, Billy 1906- DLB-26

Wilder, Laura Ingalls 1867-1957 ....DLB-22

Wilder, Thornton 1897-1975 ....DLB-4, 7, 9

Wildgans, Anton 1881-1932 ....DLB-118

Wiley, Bell Irvin 1906-1980 ....DLB-17

Wiley, John, and Sons DLB-49

Wilhelm, Kate 1928- DLB-8

Wilkes, George 1817-1885 ....DLB-79

Wilkinson, Anne 1910-1961 ....DLB-88

Wilkinson, Sylvia 1940- Y-86

Wilkinson, William Cleaver
1833-1920 ....DLB-71

Willard, Barbara 1909-1994 ....DLB-161

Willard, L. [publishing house] DLB-49

Willard, Nancy 1936- DLB-5, 52

Willard, Samuel 1640-1707 ....DLB-24

William of Auvergne 1190-1249 ...DLB-115

William of Conches
circa 1090-circa 1154 ....DLB-115

William of Ockham
circa 1285-1347 ....DLB-115

William of Sherwood
1200/1205 - 1266/1271 ....DLB-115

The William Chavrat American Fiction
Collection at the Ohio State University
Libraries Y-92

Williams, A., and Company DLB-49

Williams, Ben Ames 1889-1953 ....DLB-102

Williams, C. K. 1936- DLB-5

Williams, Chancellor 1905- DLB-76

Williams, Charles
1886-1945 ....DLB-100, 153

Williams, Denis 1923- DLB-117

Williams, Emlyn 1905- DLB-10, 77

Williams, Garth 1912- DLB-22

Williams, George Washington
1849-1891 ....DLB-47

Williams, Heathcote 1941- DLB-13

Williams, Helen Maria
1761-1827 ....DLB-158

Williams, Hugo 1942- DLB-40

Williams, Isaac 1802-1865 ....DLB-32

Williams, Joan 1928- DLB-6

Williams, John A. 1925- DLB-2, 33

Williams, John E. 1922-1994 ....DLB-6

Williams, Jonathan 1929- DLB-5

Williams, Miller 1930- DLB-105

Williams, Raymond 1921- DLB-14

Williams, Roger circa 1603-1683 ....DLB-24

Williams, Samm-Art 1946- DLB-38

Williams, Sherley Anne 1944- DLB-41

Williams, T. Harry 1909-1979 ......DLB-17

Williams, Tennessee
1911-1983 ....DLB-7; Y-83; DS-4

Williams, Ursula Moray 1911- ...DLB-160

Williams, Valentine 1883-1946 ......DLB-77

Williams, William Appleman
1921- DLB-17

Williams, William Carlos
1883-1963 ....DLB-4, 16, 54, 86

Williams, Wirt 1921- DLB-6

Williams Brothers DLB-49

Williamson, Jack 1908- DLB-8

Willingham, Calder Baynard, Jr.
1922- DLB-2, 44

Williram of Ebersberg
circa 1020-1085 ....DLB-148

Willis, Nathaniel Parker
1806-1867 .....DLB-3, 59, 73, 74; DS-13

Willkomm, Ernst 1810-1886 ....DLB-133

Wilmer, Clive 1945- DLB-40

Wilson, A. N. 1950- DLB-14, 155

Wilson, Angus
1913-1991 ....DLB-15, 139, 155

Wilson, Arthur 1595-1652 ....DLB-58

Wilson, Augusta Jane Evans
1835-1909 ....DLB-42

Wilson, Colin 1931- DLB-14

Wilson, Edmund 1895-1972 ....DLB-63

Wilson, Ethel 1888-1980 ....DLB-68

Wilson, Harriet E. Adams
1828?-1863? DLB-50

Wilson, Harry Leon 1867-1939 ....DLB-9

Wilson, John 1588-1667 ....DLB-24

Wilson, John 1785-1854 ....DLB-110

Wilson, Lanford 1937- DLB-7

Wilson, Margaret 1882-1973 ....DLB-9

Wilson, Michael 1914-1978 ....DLB-44

Wilson, Mona 1872-1954 ....DLB-149

Wilson, Thomas
1523 or 1524-1581 ....DLB-132

Wilson, Woodrow 1856-1924 ....DLB-47

Wilson, Effingham
[publishing house] DLB-154

Cumulative Index

Wimsatt, William K., Jr.
1907-1975 . . . . DLB-63

Winchell, Walter 1897-1972 . . . . DLB-29

Winchester, J. [publishing house] DLB-49

Winckelmann, Johann Joachim
1717-1768 . . . . DLB-97

Winckler, Paul 1630-1686 . . . . DLB-164

Wind, Herbert Warren 1916- DLB-171

Windet, John [publishing house] . . . DLB-170

Windham, Donald 1920- DLB-6

Wingate, Allan [publishing house] . . DLB-112

Winnifrith, Tom 1938- DLB-155

Winsloe, Christa 1888-1944 . . . . DLB-124

Winsor, Justin 1831-1897 . . . . DLB-47

John C. Winston Company DLB-49

Winters, Yvor 1900-1968 . . . . DLB-48

Winthrop, John 1588-1649 . . . . . DLB-24, 30

Winthrop, John, Jr. 1606-1676 . . . . . . DLB-24

Wirt, William 1772-1834 . . . . DLB-37

Wise, John 1652-1725 . . . . DLB-24

Wiseman, Adele 1928- DLB-88

Wishart and Company DLB-112

Wisner, George 1812-1849 . . . . DLB-43

Wister, Owen 1860-1938 . . . . DLB-9, 78

Wither, George 1588-1667 . . . . DLB-121

Witherspoon, John 1723-1794 . . . . . . DLB-31

Withrow, William Henry 1839-1908 . . . DLB-99

Wittig, Monique 1935- DLB-83

Wodehouse, P. G.
1881-1975 . . . . DLB-34, 162

Wohmann, Gabriele 1932- DLB-75

Woiwode, Larry 1941- DLB-6

Wolcot, John 1738-1819 . . . . DLB-109

Wolcott, Roger 1679-1767 . . . . DLB-24

Wolf, Christa 1929- DLB-75

Wolf, Friedrich 1888-1953 . . . . DLB-124

Wolfe, Gene 1931- DLB-8

Wolfe, John [publishing house] DLB-170

Wolfe, Reyner (Reginald)
[publishing house] DLB-170

Wolfe, Thomas
1900-1938 . . . . . . DLB-9, 102; Y-85; DS-2

Wolfe, Tom 1931- DLB-152

Wolff, Helen 1906-1994 . . . . Y-94

Wolff, Tobias 1945- DLB-130

Wolfram von Eschenbach
circa 1170-after 1220 . . . . DLB-138

Wolfram von Eschenbach's *Parzival*:
Prologue and Book 3 . . . . DLB-138

Wollstonecraft, Mary
1759-1797 . . . . DLB-39, 104, 158

Wondratschek, Wolf 1943- DLB-75

Wood, Benjamin 1820-1900 . . . . DLB-23

Wood, Charles 1932- DLB-13

Wood, Mrs. Henry 1814-1887 . . . . . . DLB-18

Wood, Joanna E. 1867-1927 . . . . DLB-92

Wood, Samuel [publishing house] . . . DLB-49

Wood, William ?-? DLB-24

Woodberry, George Edward
1855-1930 . . . . DLB-71, 103

Woodbridge, Benjamin 1622-1684 . . . DLB-24

Woodcock, George 1912- DLB-88

Woodhull, Victoria C. 1838-1927 . . . DLB-79

Woodmason, Charles circa 1720-? . . . DLB-31

Woodress, Jr., James Leslie
1916- DLB-111

Woodson, Carter G. 1875-1950 . . . . . DLB-17

Woodward, C. Vann 1908- DLB-17

Woodward, Stanley 1895-1965 . . . . DLB-171

Wooler, Thomas
1785 or 1786-1853 . . . . DLB-158

Woolf, David (see Maddow, Ben)

Woolf, Leonard 1880-1969 . . . DLB-100; DS-10

Woolf, Virginia
1882-1941 . . . . . DLB-36, 100, 162; DS-10

Woolf, Virginia, "The New Biography," *New York Herald Tribune*, 30 October 1927
. . . . DLB-149

Woollcott, Alexander 1887-1943 . . . . DLB-29

Woolman, John 1720-1772 . . . . DLB-31

Woolner, Thomas 1825-1892 . . . . . . DLB-35

Woolsey, Sarah Chauncy
1835-1905 . . . . DLB-42

Woolson, Constance Fenimore
1840-1894 . . . . DLB-12, 74

Worcester, Joseph Emerson
1784-1865 . . . . DLB-1

Worde, Wynkyn de
[publishing house] DLB-170

Wordsworth, Christopher
1807-1885 . . . . DLB-166

Wordsworth, Dorothy
1771-1855 . . . . DLB-107

Wordsworth, Elizabeth
1840-1932 . . . . DLB-98

Wordsworth, William
1770-1850 . . . . DLB-93, 107

The Works of the Rev. John Witherspoon
(1800-1801) [excerpts] DLB-31

A World Chronology of Important Science
Fiction Works (1818-1979) DLB-8

World Publishing Company DLB-46

World War II Writers Symposium at the
University of South Carolina,
12–14 April 1995 . . . . Y-95

Worthington, R., and Company DLB-49

Wotton, Sir Henry 1568-1639 . . . . . DLB-121

Wouk, Herman 1915- Y-82

Wreford, James 1915- DLB-88

Wren, Percival Christopher
1885-1941 . . . . DLB-153

Wrenn, John Henry 1841-1911 . . . . DLB-140

Wright, C. D. 1949- DLB-120

Wright, Charles 1935- DLB-165; Y-82

Wright, Charles Stevenson 1932- . . . DLB-33

Wright, Frances 1795-1852 . . . . DLB-73

Wright, Harold Bell 1872-1944 . . . . . . DLB-9

Wright, James 1927-1980 . . . . . . DLB-5, 169

Wright, Jay 1935- DLB-41

Wright, Louis B. 1899-1984 . . . . DLB-17

Wright, Richard
1908-1960 . . . . DLB-76, 102; DS-2

Wright, Richard B. 1937- DLB-53

Wright, Sarah Elizabeth 1928- DLB-33

Writers and Politics: 1871-1918,
by Ronald Gray DLB-66

Writers and their Copyright Holders:
the WATCH Project Y-94

Writers' Forum Y-85

Writing for the Theatre, by
Harold Pinter DLB-13

Wroth, Lady Mary 1587-1653 . . . . . DLB-121

Wurlitzer, Rudolph 1937- DLB-173

Wyatt, Sir Thomas
circa 1503-1542 . . . . DLB-132

Wycherley, William 1641-1715 . . . . . DLB-80

Wyclif, John
circa 1335-31 December 1384 . . . DLB-146

Wylie, Elinor 1885-1928 . . . . DLB-9, 45

Wylie, Philip 1902-1971 . . . . DLB-9

Wyllie, John Cook 1908-1968 . . . . . DLB-140

Y

Yates, Dornford 1885-1960 . . . . . DLB-77, 153

Yates, J. Michael 1938- DLB-60

Yates, Richard 1926-1992 ... DLB-2; Y-81, 92

Yavorov, Peyo 1878-1914 .... DLB-147

Yearsley, Ann 1753-1806 .... DLB-109

Yeats, William Butler 1865-1939 .... DLB-10, 19, 98, 156

Yep, Laurence 1948- DLB-52

Yerby, Frank 1916-1991 .... DLB-76

Yezierska, Anzia 1885-1970 .... DLB-28

Yolen, Jane 1939- DLB-52

Yonge, Charlotte Mary 1823-1901 .... DLB-18, 163

The York Cycle circa 1376-circa 1569 .... DLB-146

A Yorkshire Tragedy DLB-58

Yoseloff, Thomas [publishing house] DLB-46

Young, Al 1939- DLB-33

Young, Arthur 1741-1820 .... DLB-158

Young, Dick 1917 or 1918 - 1987 ...DLB-171

Young, Edward 1683-1765 .... DLB-95

Young, Stark 1881-1963 ....DLB-9, 102

Young, Waldeman 1880-1938 .... DLB-26

Young, William [publishing house] .. DLB-49

Yourcenar, Marguerite 1903-1987 .... DLB-72; Y-88

"You've Never Had It So Good," Gusted by "Winds of Change": British Fiction in the 1950s, 1960s, and After DLB-14

Yovkov, Yordan 1880-1937 .... DLB-147

Z

Zachariä, Friedrich Wilhelm 1726-1777 .... DLB-97

Zamora, Bernice 1938- DLB-82

Zand, Herbert 1923-1970 .... DLB-85

Zangwill, Israel 1864-1926 ..... DLB-10, 135

Zanzotto, Andrea 1921- DLB-128

Zapata Olivella, Manuel 1920- ... DLB-113

Zebra Books DLB-46

Zebrowski, George 1945- DLB-8

Zech, Paul 1881-1946 .... DLB-56

Zepheria DLB-172

Zeidner, Lisa 1955- DLB-120

Zelazny, Roger 1937-1995 .... DLB-8

Zenger, John Peter 1697-1746 ... DLB-24, 43

Zesen, Philipp von 1619-1689 ...... DLB-164

Zieber, G. B., and Company DLB-49

Zieroth, Dale 1946- DLB-60

Zigler und Kliphausen, Heinrich Anshelm von 1663-1697 .... DLB-168

Zimmer, Paul 1934- DLB-5

Zingref, Julius Wilhelm 1591-1635 .... DLB-164

Zindel, Paul 1936- DLB-7, 52

Zinzendorf, Nikolaus Ludwig von 1700-1760 .... DLB-168

Zola, Emile 1840-1902 .... DLB-123

Zolotow, Charlotte 1915- DLB-52

Zschokke, Heinrich 1771-1848 ...... DLB-94

Zubly, John Joachim 1724-1781 ..... DLB-31

Zu-Bolton II, Ahmos 1936- DLB-41

Zuckmayer, Carl 1896-1977 ....DLB-56, 124

Zukofsky, Louis 1904-1978 ......DLB-5, 165

Župančič, Oton 1878-1949 .... DLB-147

zur Mühlen, Hermynia 1883-1951 ...DLB-56

Zweig, Arnold 1887-1968 .... DLB-66

Zweig, Stefan 1881-1942 ....DLB-81, 118

ISBN 0-8103-9936-9